# WHAT HAPPENED WHEN

# WHAT
# *happened when*

A NOTED RESEARCHER'S ALMANAC OF YESTERDAYS

by STANFORD M. MIRKIN

IVES WASHBURN, INC.

New York

WHAT HAPPENED WHEN

TO MY

MOTHER AND FATHER

WHOSE REGULAR SACRIFICES

HAVE PROVIDED ME WITH THE

LEISURE TO READ

# Foreword

The inspiration for this book came from a President of the United States. I like to recall the incident which started me compiling the tens of thousands of dates and facts and figures that ended up in a modern-day almanac. It was in 1938 when President Franklin D. Roosevelt, in making his preparations for a fireside chat, wanted a detailed chronology of the rise of the National Socialist party in Germany. I was a member of the program staff of the Columbia Broadcasting System and a member of our Washington bureau appealed to me for help. Apparently, the chronology I put together for the White House was helpful and some weeks later I learned that the President had suggested to our Washington correspondent that "Mr. Mirkin should really prepare an up-to-date dictionary of dates. But be sure to tell him," the President added, "to include human-interest events as well as the sober dates of history."

Nineteen years later, my first book appeared, entitled originally *"When Did It Happen?"* And now here is a new updated, retitled version. It should be noted that this almanac is not intended for a specialized readership but, hopefully, for a cross-section of readers that will include political scientists, journalists, broadcasters, students, teachers, writers, etc. No attempt has been made to provide complete research about a given event. Furthermore, it is immediately obvious that thousands of events are missing from these pages. The selection of material for an almanac is often arbitrary and always personal, reflecting the individual interests of the author. Quite deliberately, I have placed greatest stress on the major events of the 19th and 20th centuries. In addition, as President Roosevelt suggested, I have gone to some length to include, not only the solemn and sober deeds of history, but many of the human-interest incidents of other years.

STANFORD M. MIRKIN

Ossining, New York
June 15, 1965

# JANUARY

## JANUARY 1

### New Year's Day

**1863**   Lincoln frees the slaves: President Lincoln signs the Emancipation Proclamation, approved by his Cabinet on September 22, 1862. The proclamation states: "I, Abraham Lincoln, President of the United States of America, do proclaim that on the first day of January, 1863, all persons held as slaves within any State, or designated part of a State, the people whereof shall then be in rebellion against the United States, shall then be, thenceforth and forever, free; and the executive Government of the United States, including the military authorities thereof, will recognize and maintain the freedom of such persons, and will do no act, or acts, to repress such persons, or any of them, in any efforts they may make for their actual freedom...."

**1863**   The Homestead Act of the United States goes into effect, the first "Homesteader" being Daniel Freeman, a soldier in the Northern army, who stakes out a claim to a tract of land near Beatrice, Nebraska.

**1900**   William J. Witt and Anna Wassilove become the first American couple to be married in the 20th century as they repeat their marriage vows before the Reverend Rufus Johnson in Liederkranz Hall, Jersey City, New Jersey. The time: one minute after midnight.

**1902**   The first Rose Bowl football match takes place at Pasadena, California, as the University of Michigan defeats Stanford, 49–0. (The football classic did not become a regular New Year's Day event, however, until 1916.)

**1923**   Aimée Semple McPherson, once described as "Christendom's most flamboyant evangelist," opens the doors of her Angelus Temple in Los Angeles. As trumpets blare, the controversial Mrs. McPherson unveils an electrically illuminated rotating cross, so large that it can be seen 50 miles away. (Before her death in 1944, Aimée had baptized 40,000 persons in the Temple.)

1

**1925**     Notre Dame's celebrated "Four Horsemen" play together for the last time as their team defeats Stanford, 27–10, at the Rose Bowl in Pasadena. ("The most famous backfield combination of all time" consisted of Harry Stuhldreher, Don Miller, James Crowley, and Elmer Layden.)

**1925**     John McCormack, noted Irish tenor, and Lucrezia Bori, Metropolitan Opera diva, make their radio singing debuts over Station WEAF, New York. (This was an historic broadcast because it encouraged other famous artists, most of whom had heretofore frowned on broadcasting, to accept radio engagements.)

**1931**     Adolf Hitler opens the "Brown House" in Munich, Germany, to serve as a headquarters for followers of his National Socialist movement.

**1938**     Fans of "swing music" jam Times Square, New York, to greet Benny Goodman, "The King of Swing," as he starts an engagement at the Paramount Theatre. (Long lines of people, mostly teen-age boys and girls, formed outside the theatre at 5 o'clock in the morning. By 7:30, the theatre management put in a riot call to the Police Department. A quarter of an hour later, there were 3,634 people seated inside and at least 1,800 more crowding the foyers and staircases. When the famous concert started, a fourth of those present danced in the aisles.)

**1959**     The Cuban revolution led by Fidel Castro triumphs as dictator Fulgencio Batista flees from his homeland.

## JANUARY 2

**1788**     By a unanimous vote, Georgia ratifies the Constitution and is admitted into the Union.

**1828**     James Gordon Bennett becomes the first Washington correspondent of importance as he starts a series of articles for *The New York Enquirer,* all of them sent exclusively to that paper from the nation's capital.

**1890**     The first woman ever to be employed in the Executive Offices of a U.S. President reports for work. She is Miss Alice B. Sanger of Indianapolis, recently appointed by President Benjamin Harrison to be a White House stenographer at a salary of $1,400 a year.

**1900**     Secretary of State John Hay describes in detail his successful negotiations with other governments for an "Open Door" policy in China. Under this policy, all major governments have agreed that each other's trade rights will be respected in China without providing special advantages for any one government.

**1921**     Religious services are broadcast over the radio for the first time when Station KDKA, Pittsburgh, Pennsylvania, transmits the regular Sunday service of the city's Calvary Episcopal Church.

**1935** Newspaper reporters and radio commentators gather at Flemington, New Jersey, to "cover" the beginning of the trial of Bruno Richard Hauptmann, charged with kidnapping and murdering the baby son of Colonel Charles A. Lindbergh. (*See April 3.*)

**1942** "Manila, Cavite lost; MacArthur fights on, holding Corregidor and nearby mainland." This message is radioed to Washington, as the Japanese invaders capture Manila in the Philippines, 26 days after the start of World War II.

**1960** Senator John F. Kennedy of Massachusetts announces his candidacy for the 1960 Democratic Presidential nomination. Kennedy tells a press conference that he would reject a Vice Presidential nomination "under any circumstances."

**1965** University of Alabama quarterback Joe Namath signs a $400,000 contract with the New York Jets, thus becoming the richest rookie in professional football history. The contract signed by Namath, 21-year-old son of a Beaver Falls, Pennsylvania, steelworker, provides a $100,000 annual salary for the next 3 years, $100,-000 in bonuses, and a $5,000 guaranteed annual pension at the end of his career.

# JANUARY 3

**1777** George Washington scores one of his most brilliant military triumphs as his hungry and tattered soldiers defeat three British regiments at the Battle of Princeton, New Jersey.

**1866** Edwin Booth, in retirement from the stage since the assassination of President Lincoln by his brother, John Wilkes Booth, makes a comeback in New York where he opens in *Hamlet.* The celebrated actor receives a tremendous ovation from the audience, a sure sign that the public does not associate him with his younger brother's crime.

**1882** Asked if he has anything to declare, Oscar Wilde, docking in New York on his first visit to America, shocks the customs inspector by replying coolly, "Nothing but my genius."

**1905** In the current issue of the *Ladies' Home Journal,* a housewife tells "How I Plan a Week's Work Without a Servant": "Monday—rise at 5 a.m. and go to the kitchen and put on a large apron, sweeping cap, and gloves. Remove ashes from the range and make fire. Rub range with strong soapsuds. While teakettle is boiling, begin soaking a boilerful of clothes...."

**1935** Ninety percent of the people living in the Saar vote for a reunion with Germany. The area has been detached from Germany since the Treaty of Versailles went into effect after World War I.

**1938** The "March of Dimes" campaign to fight polio is organized, an outgrowth of President Franklin D. Roosevelt's Warm Springs Foundation.

**1947**    As the first session of the Eightieth Congress gets under way, the first business before the U.S. Senate is to institute proceedings to prevent Senator Theodore Bilbo (D., Miss.) from taking his seat. (Senator Bilbo, an ardent racist charged with conduct unbecoming a U.S. Senator, was never able to take his seat at this session. A lengthy illness, and finally death, removed him from the Washington scene.)

**1959**    By the stroke of a pen, President Dwight D. Eisenhower signs a proclamation admitting Alaska into the Union as the 49th state. A few minutes later, the President signs an Executive Order setting a new design of 49 stars for the official flag of the United States.

**1961**    The United States severs diplomatic relations with Cuba. In a White House statement, President Eisenhower says: "There is a limit to what the United States in self-respect can endure. That limit has now been reached." (The rupture in United States–Cuban relations, after a year of increasing antagonism, was precipitated by Premier Fidel Castro's demand the day before that the United States reduce its Havana Embassy staff to 11 employees within 48 hours.)

**1964**    At a press conference held outside his home near Phoenix, Arizona, Senator Barry M. Goldwater, the conservative Republican Senator from Arizona, tells why he will seek the 1964 Republican Presidential nomination: "... I decided to do this ... because I have not heard from any announced Republican candidate a declaration of conscience or of political position that could possibly offer to the American people a clear choice in the next Presidential election. ... I once was asked what kind of Republican I was. I replied that I was not a 'me-too' Republican. That still holds. I will not change my beliefs to win votes. I will offer a choice, not an echo. ..."

## JANUARY 4

**1642**    Birthday of Sir Isaac Newton, one of the world's great scientists, discoverer of the law of gravity. ("Nature and nature's laws lay hid in night: God said Let Newton be! and all was light." —Alexander Pope.)

**1896**    Utah, the 45th state, is admitted into the Union.

**1924**    Word comes to the French Line in New York that the usual 9-day camel-back journey across the Sahara Desert, between southern Tunisia and southern Algeria, has been reduced to 3 days of comfortable travel by automobile.

**1928**    One of the earliest "variety hours" in radio broadcasting is produced over the National Broadcasting Company when the "Dodge Victory Hour," sponsored by the Dodge Automobile Company, presents Will Rogers, Paul Whiteman and his band, Al Jolson, and Fred and Dorothy Stone. (The program was considered

4

very expensive, the talent fees, telephone wires, and station time coming to a total of $67,600.)

**1933**    Angered by increasing farm foreclosures, farmers in Iowa threaten to lynch any insurance company representatives or officials of the law who institute foreclosure proceedings for the duration of the Depression.

**1941**    Charles Chaplin, who has been awarded the New York Film Critics' Award for his 1940 performance in *The Great Dictator,* says he will not accept the award because he seeks "only to please the public." Mr. Chaplin says that if he were to accept the award it would recognize the fact "that actors are competing with each other."

**1948**    Burma becomes an independent republic.

**1965**    As the Eighty-ninth Congress gets under way, 169 senior representatives move into their new House Office Building in Washington. Never before has a governmental building caused so much controversy. Named in honor of Sam Rayburn, the longtime Speaker of the House, it was built at a cost of $122 million, making it the most expensive public structure in history. According to *The New York Times:* "... Critics say it.... cost more than the Pyramids at Giza, the Hanging Gardens of Babylon, and the Colossus of Rhodes. Each of those monuments has it admirers, but almost nobody loves the Rayburn Building—except those who want to work there...."

## JANUARY 5

**1895**    Captain Alfred Dreyfus, already convicted by a French court-martial on charges of transmitting military intelligence to Germany, is summoned before an army garrison in Paris and subjected to degradation. The commanding general tells Dreyfus: "Alfred Dreyfus, you are unworthy to bear arms. In the name of the French people we degrade you!" A warrant officer then strips the prisoner of his badge and buttons, and, drawing the officer's saber from its scabbard, breaks it across his knee. Dreyfus, standing erect, shouts out in a loud voice: "Soldiers! An innocent man is being degraded! Soldiers! An innocent is dishonored! Long live France! Long live the Army!" (*See December 22 and January 13.*)

**1905**    All over America people are humming and whistling "Meet Me in St. Louis, Louis," written by the song-writing team of Andrew Sterling and Kerry Mills to commemorate the St. Louis Exposition which opened nine months ago.

**1914**    James Couzens, general manager of the Ford Motor Company, announces that the company will more than double its current wage scale and thus inaugurate a basic $5 daily minimum wage. Further, the work day will be reduced from 9 to 8 hours. The Ford management claims that this new policy will initiate "the greatest revolution in the matter of rewards for its workers ever known in the industrial world." (It seems strange today that this progressive step in labor relations should have aroused so much hostile comment. *The Wall Street Journal,* for example, was moved to say that to double the minimum wage was "to apply Biblical or spiritual principles where they do not belong.") (*See January 14.*)

**1919**    Theodore Roosevelt's last public words are read aloud at a great mass meeting held by the American Defense Society at the New York Hippodrome: "There must be no sagging back in the fight for Americanism merely because the war is over. There can be no divided allegiance here. We have room for but one flag.... We have room for but one language.... We have room for but one soul loyalty, and that is loyalty to the American people...." (*See January 6.*)

**1925**    For the first time in the history of the United States, a woman is sworn in as the governor of a state. She is Mrs. Nellie Tayloe Ross, inducted into office on this date by Chief Justice C. N. Potter of the Wyoming Supreme Court, after being elected governor of that state on November 4, 1924, to fill the unexpired term of her late husband, Governor William B. Ross.

**1949**    President Harry S. Truman labels his administration the "Fair Deal" in the course of delivering his State of the Union message to Congress.

**1964**    On the second day of his tour of the Holy Land, Pope Paul VI meets with Patriarch Athenagoras I of Constantinople in Jerusalem, the first such meeting between leaders of the Roman Catholic and Orthodox churches since the 15th century.

## JANUARY 6

**1759**    Martha Dandridge Custis, widow of Daniel Parke Custis of Virginia, is married to George Washington.

**1838**    Samuel F. B. Morse and his partner Alfred Vail demonstrate their telegraph publicly for the first time in a factory room of the Speedwell Iron Works at Morristown, New Jersey. (*See May 24.*)

**1872**    An ugly scandal results in murder as Edward S. Stokes, the spendthrift son of a prominent New York family, shoots and kills Jim Fisk on the stairway of the Grand Central Hotel in New York. (Fisk was a speculator and one of those responsible for the "Black Friday" panic in Wall Street in 1869. Earlier in the day, Stokes had been indicted for attempted blackmail of Fisk.)

**1878**    Birthday of Carl Sandburg, American writer and poet, eminent biographer of Abraham Lincoln. ("Personal freedom, a wide range of individual expression, a complete respect for the human mind and human personality, this is the ideal of the democratic system.")

**1912**    President Taft issues a proclamation admitting New Mexico to the Union as the 47th state.

**1919**    Former President Theodore Roosevelt dies at his home in Oyster Bay, New York.

**1925**    Paavo Nurmi, the "Flying Ghost of Finland," runs at the Finnish-American track matches at Madison Square Garden in New York, smashing two world's records in the greatest double performance to date over an indoor track. (Among other events, he proved that 2 miles could be run in less than 9 minutes.)

**1936**    The Supreme Court rules that the Agricultural Adjustment Act of 1933 is unconstitutional.

**1941**    President Franklin D. Roosevelt, in his annual message to Congress, defines his goals for a world at peace, a world which will guarantee to all the "Four Freedoms": Freedom of Speech, Freedom of Worship, Freedom from Want, and Freedom from Fear.

**1942**    In his first State of the Union message since the declaration of war, President Roosevelt calls for vastly increased production quotas for 1942 to assure ultimate victory over the Axis powers. Specifically, the President asks American industry to produce 60,000 airplanes, 45,000 tanks, 20,000 antiaircraft guns, 8,000,000 tons of shipping. (Many critics of the President claimed these production goals were "fantastic." In each case, however, they were achieved.) (WORLD WAR II)

## JANUARY 7

**1789**    The first election for a President of the United States takes place throughout the nation. (*For electors' choice, see February 4.*)

**1800**    Millard Fillmore, 13th President of the United States, is born in a log cabin in Cayuga County, N.Y.

**1830**    Commercial railroad service gets under way in the United States as a horse-drawn carriage rolls out of Baltimore on the first stretch of track to be completed by the Baltimore & Ohio Railroad Company.

**1896**    Fannie Farmer, "The Mother of Level Measurements," publishes her first cookbook. (Like the Bible, this book is one of the "bestsellers" of all time.)

**1918**    Nikolai Lenin, the Communist leader of Soviet Russia, abolishes the constituent assembly in that country and establishes a dictatorship of the proletariat.

**1920**    Grover Cleveland Bergdoll, the notorious "draft dodger" of World War I, is apprehended and arrested by agents of the Department of Justice as he hides under a window seat in his family's home in Philadelphia.

**1924**    George Gershwin, aged 26, completes the piano score of his *Rhapsody in Blue.*

7

**1931** A report made to President Hoover by the Emergency Committee for Unemployment Relief claims that between four and five million residents of the United States are without jobs and regular sources of income.

**1939** Governor Olson of California frees Tom Mooney from prison after the latter has served 23 years of his life sentence. (Mooney was alleged to have thrown a bomb during the Preparedness Day parade in San Francisco in 1916. His actual guilt has never been proved.)

**1952** General Dwight D. Eisenhower releases a statement at Supreme Headquarters, Allied Powers in Europe, in France, saying that he is a Republican and that he will not reject the Presidential nomination if it is offered to him by the Republican Convention this July, assuming that there is a "clear-cut call to political duty."

**1953** In his State of the Union address to Congress, President Truman announces that the United States has developed a hydrogen bomb. Says the President: "From now on, man moves into a new era of destructive power, capable of creating explosions of a new order of magnitude, dwarfing the mushroom clouds of Hiroshima and Nagasaki...."

**1965** Indonesia President Sukarno, angered because his alleged enemy, Malaysia, has become a member of the United Nation's Security Council, announces in Jakarta that his nation has "walked out" of the international peace organization.

# JANUARY 8

**Jackson Day** A legal holiday in Louisiana. (*See below.*)

**1815** General Andrew Jackson decisively defeats the British at New Orleans, killing some 700 of the enemy, wounding 1,400 and capturing 500. The American casualties are 8 killed, 13 wounded. (This was the closing military engagement of the War of 1812, occurring 2 weeks after the United States and Britain had reached a peace settlement at Ghent, Belgium. Neither the British nor the American combatants were aware of the treaty because the transmission of news in those days was so slow.)

**1824** To commemorate the anniversary of the Battle of New Orleans, President and Mrs. John Quincy Adams give a ball in the White House in honor of General Andrew Jackson. One thousand guests attend the function.

**1882** Oscar Wilde, the visiting English wit and playwright, startles the literary world in New York by appearing at a reception in his honor dressed in a black velvet jacket, silk knee breeches, and long black silk stockings. (The reception, given by Mrs. David G. Croly, better known as the writer "Jennie June," was also given in honor of Louisa May Alcott, but as the New England lady was dressed conventionally in a black bonnet and silk dress, she

8

drew very little attention compared to the spectacular visitor from London.)

**1918** President Wilson's "Fourteen Points": In a speech before a Joint Session of Congress, President Woodrow Wilson specifies the 14 points on which he hopes a "peace of justice" can be based. Most controversial of the proposals is Number 14: "A general association of nations must be formed under specific covenants for the purpose of affording mutual guarantees of political independence and territorial integrity to great and small states alike...." (WORLD WAR I)

**1925** Igor Stravinsky, Russian composer, conducts the New York Philharmonic Symphony Orchestra in a program of his compositions, his first public appearance in America.

**1959** General Charles de Gaulle, 68, becomes the first president of the Fifth French Republic, and begins serving a 7-year term.

**1963** President and Mrs. John F. Kennedy head a group of distinguished guests at Washington's National Gallery of Art to view the first showing of the "Mona Lisa," on loan from the French government. Painted by Leonardo da Vinci more than 450 years ago, this painting has sometimes been described as "the world's greatest painting."

**1965** Senator Everett M. Dirksen (R., Ill.), the Minority Leader of the Senate, reintroduces a bill to make the marigold the national flower of the United States. Senator Dirksen refuses to predict the ultimate success of his bill, noting that the rose, the carnation and the corn tassel are competitors to the marigold." (*See January 10.*)

## JANUARY 9

**1788** Connecticut ratifies the Constitution and is admitted into the Union.

**1793** The first successful balloon flight in the United States takes place over Philadelphia as Jean Pierre Blanchard, a Frenchman, soars up above the courtyard of the Germantown Prison and sets out in the direction of New Jersey. Forty-six minutes later, he makes a safe landing at Woodbury, New Jersey, 15 miles away. (Blanchard's takeoff was witnessed by a large crowd of excited spectators, including President Washington, Thomas Jefferson, John Adams, Henry Clay, and Paul Revere.)

**1861** Mississippi secedes from the Union.

**1873** Victoria Woodhull, the fiery newspaper editor and candidate for the Presidency in 1872, throws Cooper Institute in New York into an uproar as she repeats her speech charging the Reverend Henry Ward Beecher with adultery. At the conclusion of her speech, police officers mount the platform and escort her to the Ludlow Street Jail. (She had been in hiding, evading a police summons issued because she had aired the Beecher case in her paper, technically guilty of sending obscene matter through the mails. In the end, she was acquitted.) *(See January 11.)*

**1882**   All of the First Families of New York society turn out in full force at Delmonico's in New York for the exclusive Patriarchs' Ball. (A society editor reported, the next day, that the "seventy-five top names in the *Social Register* were there, including Astors, Vanderbilts, Iselins, Goelets, Fishes, etc.")

**1945**   General MacArthur's promise "I shall return" is fulfilled as American soldiers invade Luzon in the Philippine Islands. In all, 68,000 men are landed. (WORLD WAR II)

**1964**   Anti-U.S. demonstrations break out in the Panama Canal Zone after Panamanian mobs clash with American troops. The immediate cause of the violence stems from a 1963 agreement between the two nations that their respective flags would be flown together in the Zone. After U.S. students attending the Zone's Balboa High School raise the American flag without the flag of Panama, demonstrators move in on the school. As a result, U.S. troops are called out and the first of the 4-day riots erupts. *(See January 10.)*

# JANUARY 10

**1776**   Thomas Paine publishes his pamphlet, *Common Sense,* in Philadelphia, setting forth the proposition that the colonies should separate from Great Britain and establish their own independent government. (Some historians claim that *Common Sense* was to the American Revolution what *Uncle Tom's Cabin* was to the War between the States.)

**1861**   Florida secedes from the Union.

**1870**   John D. Rockefeller incorporates the Standard Oil Company in Cleveland, Ohio, with a capital of one million dollars.

**1916**   Pancho Villa, the Mexican revolutionary leader, removes and kills 18 American mining engineers from a train at Santa Ysabel, Mexico.

**1917**   William F. ("Buffalo Bill") Cody, frontier scout and showman, dies.

**1920**   The League of Nations comes into being as the Treaty of Versailles goes into effect.

**1925**   A second woman becomes the governor of a state, as Mrs. Miriam ("Ma") Ferguson is sworn into office as governor of Texas. *(See January 5.)*

**1928**   Leon Trotsky, one of the chief architects of the Soviet Union, is ordered into exile by the Communist Politburo.

**1946**   Delegates of 51 nations convene in London for the first session of the General Assembly of the United Nations.

**1952**   The freighter *Flying Enterprise* sinks 35 miles off the southwest coast of England, after a heroic attempt by its captain, Henrik Kurt Carlsen, to save it. (The ship cracked during a storm at sea on December 29, 1951. Carlsen ordered the passengers and crew to abandon it, but he refused to desert the ship until it began to sink.)

**1955** Senator Margaret Chase Smith (R., Me.) and Congresswoman Frances Bolton (R., Ohio) introduce resolutions in Congress proposing that the rose be made the national flower of the United States. The resolutions state: "The rose has long been the favorite flower of the American people, who prefer it by a margin of 18 to 1 over any other." (To date, no action has been taken on these proposals.)

**1961** The first desegregation in public education in Georgia occurs peacefully when two Negro students, Charlayne Hunter and Hamilton Holmes, enroll at the University of Georgia in Athens.

**1964** Panama severs diplomatic relations with the United States after her government charges "unjustifiable aggression" by U.S. troops following the flag incident of January 9. Panamanian President Roberto Chiari says in a broadcast to his people that "complete revision" of the treaties governing U.S. operation of the Panama Canal will be the one condition for resuming relations with Washington. (*See April 3.*)

## JANUARY 11

**1757** Alexander Hamilton, American statesman and first Secretary of the Treasury, is born on the island of Nevis in the West Indies.

**1785** The Continental Congress convenes in New York.

**1861** Alabama secedes from the Union.

**1864** Senator John B. Henderson of Missouri offers a resolution in the Senate to abolish slavery completely throughout the United States by means of an amendment to the Constitution. (The Senate later passed this proposal; the House rejected it 6 months later.)

**1875** Theodore Tilton, lecturer and newspaper editor, sues the Reverend Henry Ward Beecher for alienating his wife's affections, bringing the great Tilton-Beecher scandal out into the open. (This scandal and the subsequent trial seem to have left Dr. Beecher still without peer as the most popular preacher and orator of his day. The jury disagreed without reaching a conclusive verdict, and the public indicated that they thought Mrs. Tilton was guilty, Dr. Beecher innocent. Residents of Brooklyn, Dr. Beecher's home, went right on calling their borough "Beechertown.")

**1878** A Brooklyn, New York, milkman, Alexander Campbell, delivers milk in glass bottles for the first time to his customers. (Up until this time, milk was sold "loose," that is, purchasers brought containers to their milkman and he ladled out the exact quantity they wanted.)

**1913**    Patrons of the National Automobile Show in New York are introduced to a new type of automobile, the "sedan," a luxury model with four doors. At this show, too, there are more than 700 vehicles, the product of 88 automobile manufacturers. A one-passenger "roadster" is available for $395.

**1935**    In an attempt to become the first woman to make a solo across the Pacific Ocean, Amelia Earhart Putnam takes off from Wheeler Field, Honolulu, bound for the United States. (She arrived in Oakland, California, 18¼ hours later.)

**1964**    Luther L. Terry, Surgeon General of the United States, releases a federal report that describes cigarette smoking as a definite "health hazard" that "far outweighs all other factors" as a cause of lung disease. The report was prepared by a federal advisory committee.

## JANUARY 12

**1737**    Birth of John Hancock, American patriot and statesman, onetime president of the Continental Congress.

**1865**    Jefferson Davis, President of the Confederacy, meets with an emissary of President Lincoln in Richmond, Virginia, to discuss peace negotiations. In a letter to Lincoln, the Confederate president says he is willing "to enter into negotiations." (*See February 3.*)

**1910**    At a dinner in the White House, Baroness Rosen, the wife of the Russian ambassador, almost starts a diplomatic incident when she asks President Taft for a cigarette. To make things worse, the President borrows a cigarette from a member of the band and then proceeds to light it for the lady. (This incident placed the Baroness outside the limits of decent society. Not only did well-bred women of 1910 not smoke in public, if they smoked at all, but it was unheard of for women to smoke at White House dinners. Even men smoked in privacy after dinner, away from the delicate nostrils of the ladies, who retired to the drawing room.)

**1932**    Mrs. Hattie W. Caraway (D., Ark.), widow of the late Senator Thaddeus H. Caraway, becomes the first woman in any state to be elected to the U.S. Senate. (She served until 1945. A woman had previously sat in the Senate, but she was an interim appointee, not elected.) (*See October 3.*)

**1943**    Because of the shortage of meat, an official of the Office of Price Administration announces that standard frankfurters will be replaced by "Victory Sausages" for the duration of the war. The wartime sausage will consist of some meat and an unspecified amount of soybean meal or some other substitute. (WORLD WAR II)

**1948**    The Supreme Court, in a unanimous ruling, orders the State of Oklahoma to provide Ada Lois Fisher, a Negro, with the same education in law that it offers white students. Miss Fisher, thus far, has been barred from entering the University of Oklahoma Law School. (Five days later, the Supreme Court of Oklahoma ruled that the State must establish a separate but equal law school for Miss Fisher.)

**1965** Premiers of 13 Arab League nations conclude a 4-day summit meeting in Cairo after issuing a communique that they have agreed to take joint action against any foreign state that establishes diplomatic relations with Israel.

## JANUARY 13

**1733** James Edward Oglethorpe, together with some 130 English colonists, arrives at Charleston, South Carolina, with a charter to establish a settlement in what is now the State of Georgia.

**1834** Horatio Alger, author of "rags-to-riches" stories, is born in Revere, Massachusetts.

**1864** Stephen Foster, found ill in his hotel room 3 days earlier, dies in Bellevue Hospital, New York. (In his pocket the hospital authorities found his worldly goods—35 cents and a little slip of paper on which the composer had written "Dear friends and gentle hearts.")

**1868** The Senate refuses to accept President Johnson's ouster of Secretary of War Edwin M. Stanton. General Grant, acting War Secretary, resigns.

**1877** A literary critic of *The New York Times* finds Mark Twain's *The Adventures of Tom Sawyer* to be "unnecessarily sinister." Says the reviewer: "In the books to be placed into children's hands for purposes of recreation, we have a preference for those of a milder type than *Tom Sawyer.*"

**1898** Georges Clemenceau, editor of the Parisian newspaper *L' Aurore,* publishes Émile Zola's *J'accuse,* a bitter attack against those who are responsible for the court-martial and degradation of Captain Alfred Dreyfus.

**1902** Mrs. Patrick Campbell makes her American debut in New York in the play *Magda.*

**1906** In the current issue of the *Scientific American,* the Electro Importing Company of New York advertises a radio set for the first time. The set is described as "a complete outfit comprising one-inch spark coil, balls, key, coherer with auto coherer and sounder, 50 ohm relay, 4 cell dry battery, send and catch wires and connections with instructions and drawings. Will work up to one mile...." The cost: $7.50.

**1910** Enrico Caruso and Emmy Destinn, singing operatic arias backstage of the Metropolitan Opera House in New York, are heard as far away as Connecticut as technicians of the De Forest Radio-Telephone Company broadcast the impromptu concert by means of a telephone transmitter.

**1953** "Doctors' Plot" in Russia: From Moscow comes the announcement of the arrests of nine physicians, charged with plotting the deaths of Soviet political and military leaders. Because six of the physicians are Jews, observers believe that the Soviet Union is about to embark on another wave of anti-Semitism. (On April 4, in a complete about-face, the Soviet Ministry of Internal Affairs announced that the doctors had been freed after the charges against them had been proved false.)

## JANUARY 14

**1875** Birthday of Albert Schweitzer, medical missionary and philosopher.

**1906** Miss Maude Adams, the well-known actress, is cutting quite a figure for herself as she drives about the country in a "curved dash" Oldsmobile, steered by a stick.

**1909** President Theodore Roosevelt, soon to retire from the Presidency, writes to his son Kermit describing his feelings on leaving the White House: "I have had a great run for my money, and I should have liked to stay in as President if I had felt it was right for me to do so. . . . Mother and I are in the curious and very pleasant position of having enjoyed the White House more than any other President and his wife whom I recall. . . ."

**1914** Henry Ford revolutionizes the manufacture of automobiles by inaugurating his "assembly line," a new technique that permits the assembly of a car while it is in continuous motion. (The effect on automobile production was tremendous: in 1913, before the assembly line, Ford mechanics spent at least 12½ hours putting a car together. Beginning with this date in 1914, complete assembly took only 93 minutes.)

**1940** Agents of the Federal Bureau of Investigation seize 18 persons in New York and charge all of them with conspiring to overthrow the government. Among those arrested is an elevator mechanic, a telegrapher, a baker, a telephone lineman, a tailor, a captain in the National Guard. They are all members of the so-called "Christian Front" and their plot includes plans to overthrow New York's police force, destroy all the Jews in that city, seize Federal gold deposits there, and take over the public utilities. (The Christian Front, before and during World War II, was an organization strongly sympathetic to Nazi Germany and violently opposed to the administration of President Franklin D. Roosevelt.)

**1943** President Roosevelt and Prime Minister Churchill begin a 10-day conference at Casablanca, Morocco, to plan Allied offensives aimed at the "unconditional surrender" of the Axis powers. (WORLD WAR II)

**1953** Premier Tito is elected president of the Federal People's Republic of Yugoslavia by a secret ballot in Parliament. (He was the only person nominated for the office. One deputy refused to vote for Tito, the final count being 568–1.)

**1964**   Mrs. John F. Kennedy, overwhelmed with messages of sympathy from 800,000 persons all over the world, appears on national television to express her gratitude. This is the first time Mrs. Kennedy has made a public statement since the assassination of President Kennedy.

**1964**   For the first time in history, a hootennany * is held in the White House. During a State Dinner given by President and Mrs. Lyndon B. Johnson in honor of President Antonio Segni of Italy, the New Christy Minstrels set hands clapping and feet tapping as they play and sing six folk tunes. (The Italian guests shouted "Bravo!")

## JANUARY 15

**1827**   To test the heat resistance of asbestos, a Frenchman named Chabert enters an oven in Paris clad in an asbestos suit and holding a steak in his hand. In 12 minutes, the steak and Monsieur Chabert emerge, the former cooked—a trifle overdone; the latter undercooked, but a trifle bothered.

**1870**   For the first time in political history, a cartoon appears with a donkey symbolizing the Democratic Party. The cartoon, the work of Thomas Nast, appears in *Harper's Weekly* and bears the caption, "A Live Jackass Kicking a Dead Lion." It is aimed at Democratic press abuse of the late President Lincoln's Secretary of War, Edwin M. Stanton.

**1899**   Edwin Markham, a California schoolteacher, publishes his poem, "The Man with the Hoe" in *The San Francisco Examiner,* inspired by a reproduction of Millet's painting of the same name.

**1919**   Ignace Jan Paderewski, the famous Polish concert pianist, becomes the first premier of the newly created Republic of Poland.

**1922**   The Irish Free State is established.

**1943**   Workmen complete the Pentagon building, the headquarters of the U.S. Department of Defense and the world's largest office building, located on the Virginia side of the Potomac River just outside of Washington. (Among other staggering dimensions, the building covers 34 acres and has 17 miles of corridors.)

**1953**   President Harry S. Truman says farewell to the nation in a radio and television broadcast from the White House, the first outgoing President of the United States to do so. Says the President: "... When Franklin Roosevelt died, I felt there must be a million men better qualified than I to take up the Presidential task. But the work was mine to do, and I had to do it. I have tried

---

* "Hootenanny: an informal party, usually featuring folk dancing and group singing."—*Webster's Dictionary.*

to give it everything that was in me.... As Mrs. Truman and I leave the White House, we have no regrets. I hope and believe we have contributed to the welfare of the nation and to the peace of the world...." (In commenting on the physical demands of the Presidency, Mr. Truman revealed that he had worked "usually seventeen hours a day," signed his name "on the average 600 times a day," shaken hands with "thousands each year," traveled "135,000 miles by air, 77,000 by rail, and 17,000 by ship.")

**1961** Twenty-eight airmen and civilians, working on repairs to a U.S. Air Force radar tower 105 miles off the coast of New Jersey, lose their lives as the tower collapses and sinks during an Atlantic storm.

## JANUARY 16

**1883** The Pendleton Act goes into effect, providing for the U.S. Civil Service Commission.

**1920** War Department officials distribute 4,265,000 "Victory" medals to American soldiers, sailors, nurses, and others who were engaged in the military services during World War I.

**1920** Beginning of the "Noble Experiment": The Volstead Act to enforce the Eighteenth Amendment to the Constitution goes into effect, providing for the prohibition of the manufacture, sale, or transportation of intoxicating liquors. This date marks the birth of the "Era of the Speakeasy." (The amendment had been ratified exactly one year earlier when Nebraska became the 36th state to approve it. One year's grace, however, was allowed before Prohibition became the law of the land. On December 5, 1933, the Twenty-first Amendment went into effect, putting an end to national Prohibition.)

**1920** Charlie Chaplin and an appealing little boy are the stars of *The Kid,* a moving picture released today for public distribution. The child star's name is Jackie Coogan.

**1925** New York's Century Theatre is the setting for an ambitious production of *The Miracle,* produced by Max Reinhardt and acted out by a tremendous cast and a symphony orchestra.

**1942** Screen actress Carole Lombard and her mother and twenty other passengers are killed as a commercial airliner crashes near Las Vegas, Nevada. (Miss Lombard, the wife of actor Clark Gable, was returning to Los Angeles aboard the airplane after leaving Indianapolis where she helped sell more than $2,000,000 worth of war bonds.)

**1952** Soviet Russia orders all foreign diplomats in Moscow to limit their movements to within 25 miles of the city. Twenty-two cities of Russia and Siberia are declared out of bounds for all foreigners, including members of diplomatic missions. (Russia claimed the order was necessary because diplomats had been found spying on military installations.)

16

**1964**  In New York, theatregoers cheer the opening of *Hello, Dolly!*, a musical comedy based on Thornton Wilder's play, *The Matchmaker*. Drama critics agree that the new musical is likely to be the "hit" of the season and applaud in particular the performance of Carol Channing, the star of the play.

**1965**  Willie Mays, center fielder for the San Francisco Giants baseball team, signs his 1965 contract, thus maintaining his status as baseball's highest-paid player. Once more, Mays will earn $105,-000 for the current season.

## JANUARY 17

**1706**  Birthday of Benjamin Franklin, American printer, journalist, scientist, inventor, philosopher, philanthropist, statesman, diplomat, and author. ("Those who would give up essential liberty to purchase a little temporary safety, deserve neither liberty nor safety.")

**1806**  A baby boy is born in the White House in Washington, the first birth to take place in the Executive Mansion. The baby is James Madison Randolph, the son of Thomas Mann Randolph and Martha Jefferson Randolph, the latter being the daughter of President Thomas Jefferson.

**1876**  Etta Morgan, a member of the Berger Family's Ladies' Orchestra, begins her performance at the Olympic Theatre in New York. Miss Morgan delights her audiences as she performs on the saxophone, a musical instrument little known in the United States.

**1917**  The United States buys the Virgin Islands from Denmark for $25,000,000. (Denmark had owned the Islands almost continuously since 1671.)

**1936**  Propaganda Minister Joseph Goebbels tells the German people during a speech in Berlin: "We can do without butter, but despite all our love of peace, not without arms. One cannot shoot with butter but with guns. . . ."

**1949**  The trial of the 11 top-ranking Communists in the United States, charged with plotting the overthrow of the federal government, gets under way in New York City. (The trial was conducted by Judge Harold R. Medina and ran 169 courtroom days, during which time 5,000,000 words of testimony were heard. *See October 14*.)

**1950**  Nine robbers, wearing Halloween masks, hold up Brink's armored car service in Boston and escape with $1,000,000 in cash and $500,000 in checks, the largest cash robbery in the nation's history. (The FBI apprehended the criminals in 1956 but have recovered less than $100,000 of the stolen funds; eight men were sentenced to life imprisonment.)

**1962**  Ten prize-winning contestants on the so-called "rigged" television quiz shows receive suspended sentences in Special Sessions Court in New York City after they plead guilty to perjury charges. The defendants, accused of lying to a grand jury in saying they had not been given quiz questions and answers in advance, include contestants who had won up to $220,500 in cash prizes.

**1963**    According to the Restaurant Association of America, the average American consumes 1600 pounds of food each year. This is broken down as follows: 158 pounds of red meat, 353 eggs, 29.8 pounds of chicken, 348 pounds of milk and cream, 18 pounds of ice cream, 17½ pounds of butter and margarine, almost one hundred pounds of fresh fruits, more than 100 pounds of vegetables, 16½ pounds of coffee, etc.

**1965**    A story in the monthly bulletin of the John Birch Society reveals that the ultra-conservative organization collected $3,-200,000 in donations in 1964, just about twice the amount received in 1963. A signed article in the publication by Robert Welch, Jr., president of the organization, quotes him as saying that 100 John Birch members had attended the 1964 Republican National Convention as delegates and that their influence at the convention had been "strongly felt."

## JANUARY 18

**1782**    Birthday of Daniel Webster, American orator and statesman, onetime Secretary of State. ("God grants liberty only to those who love it, and are always ready to guard and defend it.")

**1871**    William I of the Hohenzollern dynasty is proclaimed Emperor of Germany.

**1912**    Captain Robert F. Scott, an English explorer, accompanied by four companions, reaches the South Pole and is disappointed to find that the Norwegian explorer Roald Amundsen had preceded him barely 5 weeks earlier.

**1919**    President Raymond Poincaré of France formally opens the Peace Conference at Versailles. (WORLD WAR I)

**1924**    W. E. ("Pussyfoot") Johnson, the noted American Prohibitionist, returns to the United States after a 7,000-mile world trip, undertaken to "sell" the idea of Prohibition to foreign countries in Europe and Africa. In all, he has delivered more than 107 speeches, all of them in defense of temperance and the Eighteenth Amendment. (His pleas met with cold receptions wherever he traveled.)

**1943**    Moscow announces the lifting of the German siege of Leningrad, which has lasted since the autumn of 1941. During this period, the only contact of the populace with the outside world has been the ice-road across Lake Ladoga. (WORLD WAR II)

**1943**    To save manpower and steel-cutting equipment, commercial bakers in the United States are directed to stop the sale of sliced bread for the duration of the war. Only whole loaves will be available to consumers in grocery stores. (WORLD WAR II)

**1944**     General Dwight D. Eisenhower, now commander-in-chief of Allied forces for the forthcoming invasion of Europe, explains the purpose of his new post in a worldwide broadcast: "We are going to hit the enemy . . . and keep hitting him until the last measure of Nazi resistance is crushed. . . . There is no other course. Military defeat is the only logic that a Nazi understands." (WORLD WAR II)

**1944**     Jazz music invades the Metropolitan Opera House as the first such concert is performed in the New York citadel of classical music. Among the musicians appearing on the program are Louis Armstrong, Big Sid Catlett, Lionel Hampton, Roy Eldridge, Oscar Pettiford, Barney Bigard, Jack Teagarden, Dave Tough, Benny Goodman, and Artie Shaw.

## JANUARY 19

**1807**     Robert E. Lee, commander-in-chief of the Confederate armies during the War between the States, is born at Stratford, Virginia. His birthday is a legal holiday in 12 Southern states.

**1809**     Edgar Allan Poe, American writer of poems and stories, is born in Boston.

**1861**     Georgia secedes from the Union.

**1886**     Congress enacts legislation stipulating that, in the event of the deaths of both the President and Vice President, the Presidential office will be filled by the Secretary of State.

**1931**     The National Commission on Law Observance and Enforcement, more popularly known as the Wickersham Commission, reports to President Hoover that national Prohibition is not working. (The 11 members of the Commission found it difficult to reach any unanimous decision: two favored outright repeal of the Eighteenth Amendment, four urged modification, and five recommended further trial of the amendment.)

**1937**     Howard Hughes establishes a new transcontinental air record as he flies across the United States in 7 hours, 28 minutes, and 25 seconds.

**1938**     Units of General Franco's Nationalist Air Force bomb Barcelona and Valencia in Spain, killing 700 civilians and wounding hundreds more.

**1943**     Four rooms of the Ottawa Civic Hospital are declared extraterritorial for the birth of Margriet Francisca, third daughter of Crown Princess Juliana of the Netherlands, so that the infant princess can be said to be born on Dutch soil. (The Crown Princess and her children were residing in America during the Nazi occupation of her native land.)

**1949**     A new congressional act increases the salaries of the President and Vice President of the United States and the Speaker of the House of Representatives. As of this date, the President's salary is increased from $75,000 to $100,000, with a tax-free expense allowance of $50,000 annually. Both the Vice President's and Speaker's salaries will be increased from $20,000 to $30,000, each official to receive an annual $10,000 tax-free expense allowance.

**1955** The first Presidential news conference covered by moving picture and television cameras takes place in Washington after President Eisenhower permits his regular meetings with the press to be filmed. White House aides say both newsreel and television cameramen will be admitted to these conferences in the future on the same basis as other accredited reporters.

**1965** A scandal, involving violations of the honor system, rocks the U.S. Air Force Academy at Colorado Springs, Colorado, after Academy officials announce that they are investigating "possible cheating activities" by a group of cadets. (Two months later, Secretary of the Air Force Eugene M. Zuckert reported that he had accepted the resignations of 105 cadets. The official explanation: "They were involved in stealing examination questions after illegal entry to an unauthorized area.")

## JANUARY 20

**Inauguration Day** The day on which, once every 4 years, the Presidents of the United States are sworn into office. (*See March 4.*)

**1801** President John Adams appoints John Marshall of Virginia to be chief justice of the Supreme Court. (One week later, his appointment was confirmed by the Senate.)

**1887** The Senate approves the leasing of Pearl Harbor, in the Hawaiian Islands, as a base for the U.S. Navy.

**1892** Students at the International Y.M.C.A. Training School in Springfield, Massachusetts, play the first official basketball game, invented by Dr. James Naismith to provide indoor exercise and competition between the football and baseball seasons. (Dr. Naismith used peach baskets in the Y.M.C.A. gymnasium and the players were obliged to use ladders to remove the ball from the basket.)

**1934** A new labor code is established by the National Socialist Party in Germany. Collective bargaining is abolished, forced dues are collected, and union elections are banned.

**1936** King George V of Great Britain dies. His eldest son, the Prince of Wales, succeeds to the throne as Edward VIII.

**1937** As a result of the Twentieth or "Lame Duck" Amendment to the Constitution, President Franklin D. Roosevelt is sworn into office for his second term, the first President in our history to be inaugurated in January.

**1941** Franklin D. Roosevelt is inaugurated for his third term of office, the first President of the United States to be so elected.

**1945**  Once again, President Franklin D. Roosevelt breaks the tradition against more than two Presidential terms as he is inducted into office for his fourth term.

**1949**  President Harry S. Truman, who succeeded to the Presidency on the death of Franklin D. Roosevelt in April, 1945, is sworn into office, following his triumph at the polls in last November's national elections.

**1953**  For the first time in 20 years, the nation inaugurates a Republican President, as General Dwight D. Eisenhower takes the oath of office as the 34th President of the United States.

**1957**  Because their first terms come to an end on a Sunday, President Eisenhower and Vice President Nixon are sworn into office privately in the East Room of the White House. (On the day following, the public ceremonies were held on the East Plaza of the Capitol.)

**1961**  The New Frontier of John Fitzgerald Kennedy takes over Washington as he and Lyndon Baines Johnson are inaugurated President and Vice President of the United States. Kennedy, the youngest man ever elected to the Presidency,* is also the first Roman Catholic to occupy that office. The new President stirs the nation with an inaugural address in which he says: "...Let the word go forth from this time and place, to friend and foe alike, that the torch has been passed to a new generation of Americans— born in this century, tempered by war, disciplined by a hard and bitter peace, proud of our ancient heritage—and unwilling to witness or permit the slow undoing of those human rights to which this Nation has always been committed, and to which we are committed today at home and around the world...."

**1964**  President Lyndon B. Johnson, intent on implementing a governmental program of economy, tells reporters that he has started a campaign to cut the cost of electricity in the White House: "I told my maid this morning...to turn out all those lights on those chandeliers when there is no one in the house....Someone told me that the light bill in the White House ran several thousand dollars a month!...."

**1965**  Lyndon B. Johnson and Hubert H. Humphrey are sworn into office as President and Vice President of the nation in the biggest inauguration in history. A record crowd of 1,200,000 people are on hand at the Capitol in Washington and along Pennsylvania Avenue to celebrate the events of the day. In a departure from custom, the President asks his wife, rather than an official of the government, to hold the family Bible as he takes his oath of office from Chief Justice Earl Warren.

* Theodore Roosevelt (42) was actually younger than Kennedy (43), but the former *succeeded* to the Presidency in 1901, following the assassination of President McKinley, rather than being *elected* to the office.

# JANUARY 21

**1824**    Birthday of Thomas Jonathan ("Stonewall") Jackson, Confederate general, second only to Robert E. Lee in popular affection in the South.

**1861**    Twelve days after his state of Mississippi secedes from the Union, Senator Jefferson Davis resigns from the U.S. Senate after telling his former colleagues in that body: "I am sure I feel no hostility to you, Senators from the North. I am sure there is not one of you, whatever sharp discussions there may have been between us, to whom I cannot now say in the presence of my God, I wish you well."

**1874**    Morrison R. Waite of Ohio becomes chief justice of the U.S. Supreme Court, succeeding the late Salmon P. Chase.

**1899**    In the current issue of the *Scientific American,* the editor makes this comment on the automobile: "It looks like a hackney-coach with delirium tremens, but it is a sober-minded, straightforward vehicle. We not only give it our respect but our admiration, for with its big rubber tires, it gets over the ground in a velvety sort of way and reaches its destination without becoming tired."

**1908**    New York City enacts the Sullivan Ordinance which labels smoking by women illegal and makes it an offense for the manager of a public place to allow women to smoke on his premises.

**1918**    Soviet Russia repudiates all of its foreign financial obligations as the Council of People's Commissars rules: "Absolutely and without exception, all foreign loans are annulled."

**1924**    Nikolai Lenin, leader of the Russian Revolution of 1917 and organizer of the Communist government of Russia, dies near Moscow at the age of 54. (He died of a stroke, not by violence, as so many of his fellow Communists did.)

**1943**    Following the fatal shooting of a German policeman in a railway car at Radom, Poland, fifty of the car's passengers, the mayor of the town, and several other local residents are hanged on orders of the Nazi occupation chief. (WORLD WAR II)

**1950**    Alger Hiss, former official in the State Department, is found guilty of perjury by a federal jury in New York City. The jury deliberated 23 hours and 40 minutes. (On January 25, Mr. Hiss was sentenced to 5 years' imprisonment.)

**1954**    The first atomic-powered submarine, the *Nautilus,* is launched at Groton, Connecticut.

# JANUARY 22

**1788**    Birthday of Lord Byron (George Gordon Noel Byron), English lyric and dramatic poet.

**1789**    The first American novel is published in Boston, written by Mrs. Sarah Wentworth Morton who uses the nom de plume of "Philenia." The story, entitled *The Power of Sympathy*, is a chronicle of scandal dealing with illicit love affairs, averted incest, and suicide.

**1901** An era ends in England as Queen Victoria dies in her 82nd year. The Queen has ruled the British Empire since 1837, the longest reign in the history of any civilized nation. She will be succeeded on the throne by the Prince of Wales who is to assume the name of Edward VII.

**1905** "Red Sunday" in St. Petersburg: Russian Cossacks and troops of the Imperial Army fire on 15,000 Russian workingmen as they are marching to the Winter Palace in St. Petersburg to beg the Czar for better living and working conditions. (Scores of the petitioners were killed and wounded, some 5,000 of them arrested and many sent to prison camps in Siberia. Memories of this brutal incident inspired many of the marchers to join up with the Bolsheviks in 1917 and 1918.)

**1907** As a result of the American *première* of Richard Strauss' opera *Salome* and its "Dance of the Seven Veils," vaudeville entertainers in every section of the United States are busy performing their own versions of the "naughty" dance. (The members of the Board of Directors of New York's Metropolitan Opera were so shocked by the opera that they voted to prohibit any further performances of it in their famous opera house.)

**1917** In an earnest plea for a quick end to the war in Europe, President Woodrow Wilson asks the belligerents for a "peace without victory." The President, speaking before the Senate, says that the only peace worth guaranteeing is one "representing security by the organized major force of mankind.... First of all, it must be a peace without victory. Victory would mean a peace forced upon the loser, a victor's terms imposed upon the vanquished. It ... would leave a sting, a resentment, a bitter memory upon which terms of peace would not rest permanently, but only as upon quicksand...."

**1952** For the second time in 2 months, a commercial airliner crashes at Elizabeth, New Jersey, striking a row of apartment houses. Among the 29 persons killed is former Secretary of War Robert P. Patterson.

**1957** George P. Metesky, 54, is arrested in Waterbury, Connecticut, as the "mad bomber" who had planted 32 bombs in the New York City area and injured 15 persons in the past 16 years. (Before he was committed to a hospital for the criminally insane, it was learned that Metesky was motivated by a grudge he bore against the city's leading electrical public utility.)

# JANUARY 23

**1845**   Congress rules that all national elections shall take place on the first Tuesday following the first Monday in the month of November.

**1893**   Eleanora Duse, the Italian tragedienne, makes her American debut in New York, playing the title role in *Camille.*

**1906**   Readers of the *Ladies' Home Journal* are advised that "a shampoo for dark hair consists of a pint of hot rain water, one ounce of spirits of rosemary, and the yolk of one egg."

**1920**   Ignoring a demand made by the delegates to the Versailles Peace Conference, the government of Holland refuses to surrender the ex-Kaiser of Germany to the Allies for punishment as a war criminal. (The Dutch had granted asylum to the Kaiser in November, 1918, and he was living comfortably in Doorn, Holland. This was particularly infuriating to Lloyd George of England who had promised voters there that he would hang the Kaiser from the Tower of London.)

**1937**   The eyes of the world are on Moscow where 17 members of the Communist Party, all of them prominent in Soviet affairs, confess they conspired with Leon Trotsky to undermine the Stalin regime.

**1937**   According to a news story in the *Literary Digest,* the ventriloquist Edgar Bergen has executed a will which makes Charlie McCarthy, his dummy, the beneficiary of a $10,000 trust fund "to forever care for and keep Charlie McCarthy in good and serviceable condition and repair."

**1941**   Charles A. Lindbergh, appearing before the House Foreign Affairs Committee to testify against the proposed Lend-Lease Bill, says he doubts that Germany can be defeated, even if the United States enters the war on the side of the Allies. The prominent aviator also comments: "I would prefer to see neither side win. I'd like to see a negotiated peace."

**1943**   Alexander Woollcott, famous author and dramatic and literary critic, collapses in a radio studio in New York where he is participating in a panel discussion on the subject "Is Germany Incurable?" (He died a few hours later.)

**1948**   Citing the fact that he has promised to serve as president of Columbia University, General Dwight D. Eisenhower tells politicians who hope he will run for the Presidency in the November elections that he will not accept any nomination.

**1964**   South Dakota ratifies the Twenty-fourth Amendment to the Constitution banning the required payment of poll taxes as a condition for participating in federal elections. The South Dakota action thus completes the necessary ratification by two-thirds of the legislatures of the 50 states.

# JANUARY 24

**1848**   Discovery of Gold: James W. Marshall, an employee of John Augustus Sutter, discovers gold in a branch of the Sacramento River near Coloma, California. (Marshall was building a sawmill for Sutter when he made his discovery. The men tried to keep the news a secret, but all over the United States people set out for California, for Sutter's tract of land in particular. By 1852, over 200,000 people had moved into the state to make their fortunes. So many established squatters' rights on Sutter's land that he was left with nothing, although the California legislature finally granted him a pension.)

**1908**   The first Boy Scout troop is organized in England by Sir Robert Baden-Powell, a general in the English Army.

**1922**   Christian K. Nelson of Onawa, Iowa, receives a patent for his "Eskimo Pie," a brick of ice cream encased in a coating of chocolate.

**1932**   A report of the Seabury Investigating Committee, appointed to delve into New York City's crime and its wave of municipal scandals, claims that the city's corrupt government is due to the influence of Tammany Hall.

**1941**   Viscount Halifax, the new British ambassador to the United States, arrives in Chesapeake Bay aboard the battleship *King George V.* President Roosevelt, breaking all diplomatic precedent, drives 33 miles to Annapolis, Maryland, to welcome the British envoy.

**1945**   Russian soldiers cross the Oder River and land on German soil for the first time. (WORLD WAR II)

**1946**   Delegates to the United Nations General Assembly vote to create a United Nations Atomic Energy Commission.

**1949**   To save millions of snowbound cows and sheep isolated on the Great Plains and throughout the West, the U.S. Air Force starts "Operation Haylift," an aerial relay which will drop bales of hay to the stranded livestock.

**1956**   Parents of 27 Negro children in Little Rock, Arkansas, apply for admission of their children in the now-segregated white public schools of the city.

**1965**   The world mourns the death of Sir Winston Churchill, "an Englishman who became the first citizen of the free world, a commoner who dominated a century, a statesman who both made history and wrote it." * *(See January 30.)*

* *New York Herald-Tribune,* January 25, 1965

# JANUARY 25

**1759**   Birthday of Robert Burns, the national poet of Scotland.

**1787**   Shays' Rebellion: Led by Daniel Shays, a captain in the Revolutionary Army, 2,000 debt-ridden and discontented rebels march on the Federal Arsenal in Springfield, Massachusetts, hoping to overthrow the government. (The revolt was broken up, but soon thereafter the Massachusetts legislature passed a series of relief measures.)

**1858**   Mendelssohn's "Wedding March" is played for the first time at the marriage ceremony of Queen Victoria's daughter, the Princess Royal, to the Crown Prince of Prussia.

**1890**   Guns boom a welcome across New York Bay in honor of Nellie Bly, the daring young reporter of *The New York World,* who has just returned from a trip around the world in the astounding time of 72 days, 6 hours, 11 minutes. (*See November 14.*)

**1915**   Transcontinental telephone service is inaugurated as Alexander Graham Bell, using a replica of his first telephone in New York City, again speaks the words, "Watson, come here, I want you" to his assistant, Thomas A. Watson, seated in a room in San Francisco. (*See March 10.*)

**1936**   Al Smith, once an ardent backer of Franklin D. Roosevelt, but now an equally ardent critic of the President and his political ideology, addresses 2,000 guests at a banquet of the anti-New Deal American Liberty League in Washington. In attacking New Dealers, Smith draws thunderous applause as he says: ". . . It is all right with me if they want to disguise themselves as Karl Marx and Lenin . . . but I won't stand for them to march under the banner of Andy Jackson and Grover Cleveland. . . . Let me give this solemn warning: there can be only one capital, Washington or Moscow. There can be only one atmosphere of government, the clean, pure, fresh air of free America, or the foul breath of communistic Russia. . . ."

**1946**   United Mine Workers' members, led by John L. Lewis, rejoin the American Federation of Labor, from which they had bolted 10 years earlier.

**1954**   After Senator Joseph R. McCarthy (R., Wis.) promises to change the rules governing procedure on the Senate Investigations Subcommittee, the three Democrats on the Committee agree to rejoin the Republican majority. The three Democrats, absent since July, 1953, are Senators John L. McClellan of Arkansas, Henry M. Jackson of Washington, and Stuart Symington of Missouri.

**1961**   At his first Presidential press conference, President John F. Kennedy announces that the two surviving crewmen of a U.S. Air Force jet plane shot down in the Barents Sea off northern Russia in July, 1960, have been released from prison in Moscow and will return home within 48 hours. The two airmen are Captain

John R. McKone of Tonganoxie, Kansas, and Captain Freeman B. Olmstead of Elmira, New York.

**1965**   The dramatic growth of the United States is highlighted by President Lyndon B. Johnson as he submits his current budget message to Congress: "Since I sent you my first budget a year ago—4 million Americans have been born; 3.2 million young people have reached college age; 1.7 million new families have been formed; 1.3 million persons have entered the labor force; 1.5 million persons have reached retirement age...."

## JANUARY 26

**1784**   Benjamin Franklin, in a letter to his daugher Sarah Bache, expresses his disapproval of the eagle as a symbol of the United States: "I wish the Bald Eagle had not been chosen as the Representative of our Country; he is a Bird of bad moral Character; like those among Men who live by Sharping and Robbing, he is generally poor, and often very lousy. The Turkey is a much more respectable Bird and withal a true original Native of America."

**1830**   Senator Daniel Webster delivers one of his most brilliant speeches on the floor of the Senate when he replies to Senator Robert Young Hayne's attack on New England and the Southern Senator's recent proposal that the South and West form an alliance to espouse states' rights against the federal government. ("Liberty and Union, now and forever, one and inseparable!")

**1837**   Michigan joins the Union as the 26th state.

**1861**   Louisiana secedes from the United States.

**1918**   To save meats and grain, Food Administrator Herbert Hoover asks Americans to observe voluntarily "wheatless Mondays and Wednesdays, meatless Tuesdays, porkless Thursdays and Saturdays."

**1945**   A syndicate headed by Larry McPhail and Dan Topping, two prominent sportsmen, buy the New York Yankees baseball team for $3,000,000.

**1950**   India ceases to be a British dominion and becomes the Republic of India. Pandit Jawaharlal Nehru, a follower of the late Mohandas K. Gandhi, is the premier of the new republic.

**1952**   Egyptian mobs in Cairo go on a rampage, burning and destroying property in that city belonging to American, British, and French citizens. The embassies of all three governments are stoned and the famous Shepheard's Hotel is set afire. (These "antiforeigner" riots were associated with native demands for Great Britain to withdraw from the Suez area.)

**1954**   Citizens of Norwalk, Connecticut, are engaged in a bitter local controversy, after it is disclosed that the Norwalk post of the Veterans of Foreign Wars has formed a secret committee to turn over to the Federal Bureau of Investigation the names of all local residents suspected of Communist sympathies.

**1965**    A dispatch from Johannesburg reports that an increasing number of South Africans are protesting their government's refusal to let them have television. But Albert Hertzog, the Minister of Posts and Telegraphs, the agency that supervises broadcasting, is standing by his opposition to television on the grounds that it "would be mainly dependent on British and American films which are drenched with liberalistic and demoralizing propaganda." (*See April 24*)

## JANUARY 27

**1756**    Birthday of Wolfgang Amadeus Mozart, great Austrian musician and composer.

**1830**    Senator Robert Young Hayne, continuing his Senate debates with Daniel Webster, insists that any state has the right to nullify legislation and acts of the federal government.

**1832**    Birthday of Lewis Carroll (nom de plume for Charles L. Dodgson), English clergyman and mathematician, creator of the immortal *Alice in Wonderland*.

**1850**    Birthday of Samuel Gompers, American labor leader, one of the organizers of the American Federation of Labor and its president for nearly forty years.

**1862**    President Lincoln issues General War Order Number 1, instructing Northern Army and naval forces to be prepared to move forward not later than February 22.

**1880**    A patent for an electric incandescent lamp is granted to Thomas Alva Edison of Menlo Park, New Jersey.

**1888**    The National Geographic Society is founded in Washington, D.C.

**1924**    Commenting on the recent death of Nikolai Lenin, the *New York Tribune* reports: "Of the dozen possible successors to Lenin as Premier of Soviet Russia, Ivan Stalin appears to lead.... He assumed the name of 'Stalin,' which means 'steel,' out of caprice. He is also known as 'the man who never wore a boiled shirt.' " (This early story seems to indicate that Stalin was known as Ivan rather than Joseph before his rise to fame.)

**1934**    Columnist Walter Winchell writes a highly complimentary story about an all-night "disc jockey" named Arthur Godfrey, the first important mention of the new entertainer in the national press. (After Winchell followed this first column with subsequent notes on Godfrey, the latter received thirty offers from Broadway producers and talent scouts.)

**1943**    The U.S. Eighth Air Force stages the first all-American air raid on Germany, bombing Wilhelmshaven in broad daylight. (WORLD WAR II)

**1964**    France recognizes Communist China.

**1964** Senator Margaret Chase Smith of Maine announces she will seek the Republican nomination for the Presidency in November elections. Mrs. Smith says that she has decided to enter the race even though it has been argued that "no woman should ever dare aspire to the White House—and that this is a man's world and should be kept that way." (Senator Smith thus became the first woman ever to seek the Presidential nomination of a *major* U.S. political party.) (*See May 10.*)

## JANUARY 28

**1871** Paris capitulates to the Prussians in the Franco-Prussian War.

**1878** In New Haven, Connecticut, the first commercial telephone switchboard is set in operation, serving 21 subscribers. The operator is George Willard Coy. Telephone users receiving calls cry out "Ahoy-ahoy" rather than the later greeting of "hello."

**1902** A gift of $10,000,000 from Andrew Carnegie establishes the Carnegie Institution in Washington to "encourage in the broadest and most liberal manner investigation, research and discovery, and the application of knowledge to the improvement of mankind."

**1915** Congress passes legislation creating the U.S. Coast Guard, thereby combining the Life Saving Service and the Revenue Cutter Service, the latter agency dating back to 1790.

**1932** A song symbolizing the plight of millions of Depression-ridden Americans, "Brother, Can You Spare a Dime?" is sweeping all over America.

**1945** A convoy of American trucks from India crosses the Burma-Chinese frontier, thus opening the famous Burma Road. (By this time, however, the thoroughfare was officially called the Stilwell Road.) (WORLD WAR II)

**1954** Because of the rise in prices of coffee imported from Brazil, American restaurants are raising their prices from 10 to 15 cents a cup. In grocery stores, coffee is selling as high as $1.35 a pound, despite the mutterings of angry housewives.

**1955** After a bitter debate, the Senate follows the lead of the House and passes a resolution permitting President Eisenhower to use armed forces abroad to defend Formosa and the Pescadores Islands and "related positions and territories" against possible attacks by the Chinese Communists.

**1963** Harvey B. Gantt, 20, enrolls without incident at Clemson College, Clemson, South Carolina, the first Negro to be permitted to attend school with white students in the history of the state.

**1965** Mr. and Mrs. Leon Gillis of Providence Forge, Virginia, and four of their children, return to the United States after their personal goodwill tour of Europe. For the past 8 months, they have traveled 4,000 miles in a covered wagon. Their trek started in Antwerp, Belgium and ended in Moscow.

**1965** The continuing wave of prosperity sweeping over the United States is reflected today in announcement by General Motors, giant of the industrial world, that the corporation in 1964 made the biggest profit of any company in history. General Motors earnings in the previous year totaled $1,735,000,000, pushing it ahead of American Telephone & Telegraph, which reported earnings of $1,700,967,000.

## JANUARY 29

**1843** William McKinley, 25th President of the United States, is born at Niles, Ohio.

**1845** Edgar Allan Poe's poem, "The Raven," is published for the first time in *The New York Evening Mirror*. (It was not signed by Poe, however, he chose to use the nom de plume of "Quarles.")

**1850** Senator Henry Clay introduces into the Senate his Compromise Bill to "settle and adjust amicably all existing questions of controversy ... arising out of the institution of slavery...." Included in the Senator's proposals is the admission of California into the Union as a free state; a declaration that Congress cannot forbid the slave trade among the slave states; a more effectual arrangement for the capture and return of fugitive slaves.

**1856** Queen Victoria orders the first Victoria Cross to be made from Russian cannon captured in the Battle of Sevastopol in the Crimean War. The decoration, showing the British Crown surmounted by a lion on a Maltese Cross, has been designed by Prince Albert, the Queen's husband, and will be awarded for military bravery.

**1861** Kansas enters the Union as the 34th state.

**1889** Crown Prince Rudolf of Austria-Hungary, heir to the Hapsburg crown, kills his mistress, the Baroness Marie Vetsera, and then takes his own life in a hunting lodge at Mayerling, Austria.

**1891** Hawaii proclaims as its queen Liliuokalani, the composer of the song "Aloha Oe."

**1900** Baseball's American League is organized at Philadelphia, composed of eight teams: Buffalo, Chicago, Cleveland, Detroit, Indianapolis, Kansas City, Milwaukee, and Minneapolis.

**1936** The first five men to be elected to the Baseball Hall of Fame at Cooperstown, New York, are Ty Cobb, Walter Johnson, Christy Mathewson, Babe Ruth, and Honus Wagner.

**1943** Ruth C. Streeter of Morristown, New Jersey, a member of the women's auxiliary of the U.S. Marine Corps, is appointed to the rank of major, the first woman to achieve that distinction in the Marines. (WORLD WAR II)

**1963** France vetoes the application of Great Britain to join the Common Market.

**1798**    A brawl takes place on the floor of the House of Representatives as Congressmen Matthew Lyon of Vermont and Roger Griswold of Connecticut engage in a dispute. (The House voted to expel Lyon, but the motion failed to carry a two-thirds vote.)

**1815**    The Library of Congress, destroyed in 1814 when invading British forces burned the Capitol, is restored as the U.S. government buys Thomas Jefferson's 7,000-volume library for $25,000.

**1835**    Richard Lawrence, a demented painter, attempts to assassinate President Andrew Jackson as the latter visits the Capitol in Washington to attend funeral services for a congressman. Although Lawrence shoots at the President twice, his aim in each case misses. (This was the first instance of an assassination attempt on a U.S. President.)

**1882**    Birthday of Franklin Delano Roosevelt, 32nd President of the United States, and the only U.S. President to be elected to more than two terms of office. ("The test of our progress is not whether we add more to the abundance of those who have much; it is whether we provide enough for those who have too little. . . .")

**1933**    "The Lone Ranger," a radio program destined to become a national favorite, is broadcast for the first time.

**1933**    Adolf Hitler comes into official power as he is named chancellor of the German Reich by President Paul von Hindenburg.

**1934**    The first nationally contributed money to battle polio is raised during balls held in eight cities honoring the birthday of President Franklin D. Roosevelt. (The total receipts of this first FDR Birthday Ball added up to $1,016,443, all of that amount going to the drive to wipe out the crippling disease.)

**1937**    On the fourth anniversary of his accession to power, Chancellor Hitler calls a meeting of the German Reichstag and tells its members that Germany repudiates the war-guilt provision of the Treaty of Versailles.

**1948**    Mohandas K. Gandhi is assassinated by a Hindu extremist, Ram Naturam, in the gardens of Birla House, New Delhi, where Gandhi was leading one thousand of his followers into a summer house for evening devotions. All India is plunged into sorrow. ("Now the light has gone out," says Jawaharlal Nehru, India's prime minister.)

**1964**    The ruling military junta in South Vietnam is toppled in a bloodless coup led by Major General Nguyen Khanh.

**1965**    Britain and the world joins in paying final homage to Sir Winston Churchill. After an extraordinary state funeral * in London, the body of the former prime minister is laid to rest in

* Queen Elizabeth II broke precedent by becoming the first reigning monarch to attend a commoner's funeral. In all, about 350,000,000 people throughout the world watched the funeral ceremonies on television.

the village churchyard at Bladon, near his family's ancestral home, Blenheim Palace. (One of the unique aspects of this moving state funeral was the singing of the American hymn, "Battle Hymn of the Republic" expressly selected by Mr. Churchill himself.)

## JANUARY 31

**1797**    Birthday of Franz Schubert, Austrian composer. ("My compositions spring from my sorrows. Those that give the world the greatest delight were born of my deepest grief.")

**1865**    Jefferson Davis, President of the Confederacy, appoints General Robert E. Lee commander-in-chief of Confederate armies.

**1892**    Eddie Cantor, American entertainer and comedian, is born in New York City.

**1905**    New York's "Four Hundred" are entertained at a Louis XIV Costume Ball given by James Hazen Hyde, vice president of the Equitable Life Assurance Society. Society reporters claim that the ball has cost Mr. Hyde between one hundred and two hundred thousand dollars.

**1917**    Germany announces she is instituting a policy of unrestricted submarine warfare. (WORLD WAR I)

**1926**    President Coolidge, asked by reporters to comment on the recent remarks made by Rupert Hughes, journalist and playwright, to the effect that George Washington was a "profane and irreligious and pleasure-loving man," looks out of his White House windows and replies: "Well, I see that the monument is still there."

**1934**    President Roosevelt, acting under the Gold Reserve Act, devalues the American dollar in its relationship to gold. The President fixes the dollar at 59.06 cents, gold value.

**1943**    The turning point of World War II for Russia comes as Joseph Stalin announces in a triumphant communique that the Soviet Union has destroyed the Nazi German forces formerly encircled around Stalingrad. (*See February 2*)

**1950**    President Truman announces he has ordered the development of the hydrogen bomb, saying: "I have directed the Atomic Energy Commission to continue its work on all forms of atomic weapons, including the so-called hydrogen or super-bomb."

**1952**    Angered over Senator Joseph R. McCarthy's repeated attacks on federal employees as well as his charges that Communists have infiltrated the government, President Truman denounces the Republican senator as pathological, untruthful, and a character assassin who needs no information for his accusations.

**1958**    Explorer I, the United States' first earth satellite, is launched from the Cape Canaveral, Florida, missile test center.

**1961**    Ham, a male chimpanzee, is rocketed into space in a test of the Project Mercury capsule designed to carry ultimately a U.S. astronaut into orbit.

# FEBRUARY

## FEBRUARY 1

**1790**   The Supreme Court of the United States holds its first session, meeting in the Royal Exchange Building in New York City. Chief Justice John Jay presides.

**1861**   Texas votes to secede from the Union.

**1862**   Julia Ward Howe's "Battle Hymn of the Republic" is published for the first time in the *Atlantic Monthly*. (Mrs. Howe was inspired to write the words after reviewing Union troops in a dress parade outside of Washington. All day long she had been hearing soldiers sing "John Brown's Body." While she liked the melody, she thought very little of the words. That night, at her hotel in the nation's capital, she got out of bed and wrote new words for the existing music.)

**1892**   Mrs. William B. Astor gives a ball at her New York town house, limited to four hundred guests, the beginning of the social term, "the Four Hundred." (Mrs. Astor's guests were selected by her counselor, the social arbiter Ward McAllister, who released the sacred list to the press just before the ball. Reporters asked him how he arrived at the figure of four hundred. "Why, there are only about four hundred people in fashionable New York Society," answered McAllister. "If you go outside that number you strike people who are either not at ease in a ballroom or else make other people not at ease.")

**1893**   Thomas A. Edison finishes work on the first moving-picture studio in the world. The building is in West Orange, New Jersey, and cost the inventor $637.37.

**1898**   An insurance policy covering the driver of an automobile, the first such policy in the world, is issued by the Travelers Insurance Company to Dr. Truman J. Martin of Buffalo, New York. (The policy promised protection to Dr. Martin from possible damage suits brought by owners of horses frightened by the sight and noise of his car.)

**1956**   Autherine Lucy, 26-year-old Negro student, is admitted to the University of Alabama on orders issued by a federal court.

She is the first Negro to be admitted to that university. (Miss Lucy, however, was not to remain at the University very long. First she was tormented by segregationist-minded rioters. Later, university trustees suspended her for allegedly making "outrageous, false and baseless accusations" against campus officials. While a federal court ordered her reinstatement on February 29, she did not return to her classes.)

**1958** President Gamal Abdel Nasser of Egypt announces the merger of Egypt and Syria into the United Arab Republic.

**1960** A new technique in fighting discrimination against Negroes is introduced when Negro students quietly occupy lunch-counter seats in Greensboro, North Carolina. Negro leaders describe these demonstrations as "sit-ins" and say they are nonviolent protests aimed at business proprietors who refuse to serve food to Negroes. (The original sit-in protester was James McNeill, a Negro college student, who had been refused food the day before at Greensboro's public bus terminal.)

**1963** The magazine *Time* obviously does not think much of the role being played by Vice President Lyndon B. Johnson in government affairs. In its current issue, the magazine concludes: ". . . In the Kennedy Administration, the Vice-Presidency has again become what is was throughout most of the nation's history: a ceremonial office in which a man stands by to take office in case the President dies. . . ."

## FEBRUARY 2

**Ground Hog Day** "This is the day on which the ground hog, or woodchuck, emerges from his deep-dug burrow and takes a look at the sky. When clouds obscure the sun, he knows that spring can't be far behind. But if the sun is shining, and he can see his shadow, the ground hog ducks underground and curls up for another nap. He knows, and tells the farmers so, that winter will hold spring off for six long weeks."

**1848** Mexico puts her signature upon a treaty with the United States at Guadalupe Hidalgo, Mexico, thereby agreeing to cede Texas, New Mexico, Arizona, and California to the latter upon payments totaling $15,000,000.

**1870** Physicians reveal that the so-called "Cardiff Giant," discovered on the farm of William Newell, near Cardiff, New York, in 1869, is not a petrified human being, as claimed, but is actually a hoax perpetrated by Newell's brother-in-law, George Hull. (The giant figure was exhibited and attracted thousands of curious people who were only too happy to pay admission. Actually, Hull had it cut from a two-ton block of gypsum in Chicago.)

**1876** Eight baseball teams band together to organize the National League. The teams are Boston, Chicago, Cincinnati, Hartford, Louisville, New York, Philadelphia, and St. Louis.

**1882**   Birthday of James Joyce, Irish writer, author of the controversial *Ulysses*.

**1893**   One day after Thomas A. Edison completed his moving-picture studio, in West Orange, New Jersey, a cameraman there takes the first "close-up" in film history. His subject is comedian Fred Ott, shown in the process of sneezing.

**1917**   Former President Theodore Roosevelt writes to Secretary of War Newton D. Baker asking permission to raise an army division made up entirely of volunteers. "If you believe there will be war and a call for volunteers, I respectfully and earnestly request that you notify me at once. I have prepared the skeleton outline of what I have desired the Division to be. . . ." (The War Department was opposed to the volunteer system and finally refused Roosevelt's request on May 11.) (WORLD WAR I)

**1943**   Now that the Battle of Stalingrad has ended, Russian officials announce that the siege of the city cost the Germans 503,650 dead and wounded. Radio Berlin acknowledges the end of the battle. (WORLD WAR II)

**1953**   President Eisenhower, announcing his first change in U.S. Far Eastern policy, says that the Seventh Fleet will no longer block Chinese Nationalist raids from Formosa against the mainland of China.

**1961**   Six hundred passengers aboard the hijacked Portuguese liner *Santa Maria,* 42 of them Americans, land at Recife, Brazil. (This ended a harrowing episode at sea for the vacationers, following capture of the ship at gunpoint in the Caribbean Sea by Portuguese and Spanish exiles who planned to overthrow Premier Salazar's regime in Portugal.)

**1962**   A Marine Corps corporal, John Uelses of Quantico, Virginia, becomes the first pole vaulter to reach 16 feet when he clears the pole at 16 feet, 1/4 inches during the indoor Millrose Games in New York. (A day later, in Boston, Uelses established another record, this time vaulting 16 feet, 3/4 inches. In both instances he used a fiberglass pole and thus set off a heated controversy. One-time record-holder Don Bragg charged that because of the extreme flexibility of fiberglass, the pole "adds six inches to a foot to a vault.") (*See April 28*)

## FEBRUARY 3

**NOTE**   The traditional Festival of Setsubun, officially marking the end of winter, is observed annually in Japan on this date. Japanese spend the day joyfully throwing dried beans at each other, symbolizing an old legend when brave warriors drove away wicked demons by throwing dried soybeans in their eyes. The "wicked demon" in today's festival is lingering winter.

**1811**   Birthday of Horace Greeley, American journalist, founder of the *New York Tribune* in 1841, onetime Presidential candidate.

**1865**   President Lincoln and Secretary of State Seward confer with Alexander H. Stephens, Vice President of the Confederacy, aboard the Union vessel *River Queen* at Hampton Roads, Virginia, in an attempt to bring the War between the States to an end. (The conference was doomed to failure.)

**1869**   Booth's Theatre in New York, built and managed by the well-known actor, Edwin Booth, has its grand opening. The first production is *Romeo and Juliet,* with tickets selling for as high as $125.

**1906**   The name of Woodrow Wilson, president of Princeton College, is proposed for president of the United States by Colonel George Harvey at a dinner given in honor of Wilson at the Lotos Club in New York. (Seven years later, Mr. Wilson was in the White House.)

**1913**   After it is ratified by Wyoming, the 36th state to do so, the Sixteenth, or Income Tax, Amendment becomes the law of the land. ("The Congress shall have power to lay and collect taxes on incomes. . . .")

**1917**   As a follow-up to Germany's announcement of unrestricted submarine warfare, the United States severs diplomatic relations with that nation. (WORLD WAR I)

**1924**   Woodrow Wilson, former President of the United States, dies at his home in Washington.

**1930**   President Hoover appoints Charles Evans Hughes Chief Justice of the U.S. Supreme Court.

**1943**   One of the most heart-warming episodes of World War II is enacted on a sinking ship less than a hundred miles off the coast of Greenland as four chaplains—one, a Jewish rabbi, two of them Protestant ministers, the fourth a Catholic priest—take off their life preservers and hand them to four unequipped soldiers. Moments later, the ship goes down below the icy waters, and with it the four chaplains linked arm in arm, their voices raised in prayer. (The ship was the *Dorchester,* an American transport, and the four clergymen were Rabbi Alexander D. Goode of York, Pennsylvania; the Reverend Clark V. Poling of Schenectady, New York; the Reverend George L. Fox, Gilman, Vermont; and Father John P. Washington of Arlington, New Jersey.)

**1965**   Worried by continuing acts of racial violence, business and civic leaders of Mississippi warn that the state must "adjust" to new federal legislation. A statement issued by the Mississippi Economic Council, the state's largest organization of business leaders, says: "We recognize that the Civil Rights Act of 1964 has been enacted by the Congress as law. It cannot be ignored and should not be unlawfully defied. . . ."

# FEBRUARY 4

**1789**    Presidential electors cast all 69 of their votes for George Washington. John Adams is chosen Vice President.

**1861**    Delegates from six seceding Southern states—South Carolina, Georgia, Florida, Alabama, Mississippi, and Louisiana—form the Confederate States of America at Montgomery, Alabama. (*See February 9.*)

**1901**    A campaign to eradicate the scourge of yellow fever is begun in Cuba by Major William C. Gorgas of the U.S. Army.

**1901**    Ethel Barrymore receives "star" billing for the first time as she opens in New York in *Captain Jinks of the Horse Marines.*

**1926**    The craze for dancing the "Charleston" reaches its peak when John Giola of New York City becomes the champion Charleston endurance dancer of the world. (He danced the new step for 22 hours and 30 minutes!)

**1938**    Adolf Hitler seizes control of the German army, placing trusted Nazi confederates in key positions. At the same time, he announces the appointment of Joachim von Ribbentrop, former wine merchant, as foreign minister of Germany.

**1938**    *Our Town,* a play by Thornton Wilder, opens at the Henry Miller Theatre in New York. (It won the Pulitzer Prize some months later.)

**1941**    The United Service Organizations (USO) is founded to serve the social, educational, religious, and welfare needs of men and women in the armed forces.

**1948**    Ceylon becomes a free and self-governing dominion of the British Empire.

**1950**    Twelve prominent scientists in the United States protest the use of any future hydrogen bomb as "a weapon of war."

**1954**    Senator Joseph R. McCarthy (R., Wis.) begins a schedule of "Lincoln Week" speech-making across the country, his theme being the Democratic Party's "twenty years of treason." (*See February 6.*)

**1962**    The Population Reference Bureau, a private research agency, estimates that 77,000,000,000 persons have lived on the earth since the dawn of mankind. (For the purposes of its study, the bureau called the year 600,000 B.C. as the probable beginning of human life.)

**1964**    Communist China charges Russian Premier Nikita Khrushchev is seeking world domination through his policy of collaboration with the United States.

# FEBRUARY 5

**Constitution Day in Mexico**    This day commemorates the promulgation of the liberal Constitution of 1857 and the present Constitution of 1917.

**1762**    A servant of the Earl of Colchester in England reveals the breakfast tastes of his day: "The family rose at six, took breakfast at seven. My Lord and Lady sat down to a repast of two pieces of salted fish, a half dozen of red herrings, a dish of sprats, a quart of beer, and an equal amount of wine. Then came a half chine of mutton."

**1934**    Senator Huey Long (D., La.) outlines his "Share-the-Wealth" program to members of the Senate. The Senator's proposal includes these features: 1) personal fortunes to be limited to $3,000,-000; 2) every American family would be given $4,000 by the government to help in the purchase of a house, an automobile, etc.; 3) pensions for each individual over the age of 65; 4) a minimum annual wage of not less than $2500; 5) a shorter work week; 6) government-paid college educations for "proven" youths.

**1937**    A bitter controversy begins as President Franklin D. Roosevelt sends a series of proposals to Congress to reorganize the federal judiciary, in particular the Supreme Court. (*See July 22.*)

# FEBRUARY 6

**1843**    "The Virginia Minstrels," the first minstrel show ever produced in America, is staged at the Bowery Amphitheatre in New York by Dan Emmett, starring Emmett, Billy Whitlock, Dick Pelham, and Frank Brown.

**1900**    In answer to those politicians who are mentioning his name as a possible choice for William McKinley's running mate in the coming elections, Theodore Roosevelt issues a statement, saying: "Under no circumstances could I or would I accept the nomination for the Vice-Presidency...." (Four months later, he was pleased to accept the Vice Presidential nomination.)

**1911**    In one of the most celebrated weddings of the pre-World War I era, Miss Vivien Gould, granddaughter of the millionaire Jay Gould is married to Lord Decies of England at St. Bartholomew's Church in New York. Private detectives dressed in formal frock coats are on hand to prevent an enormous crowd of the uninvited from entering the church. (People on both sides of the Atlantic read every word they could about the fabulous wedding: the bride's wedding train was 15 feet long; 225 seamstresses were said to have worked for months on her trousseau; and, according to one reporter, "the wedding cake alone cost $1,000 with its electric lights and tiny bisque cupids bearing the ducal coat-of-arms....")

**1933**    A proclamation by the Secretary of State declares the Twentieth, or "Lame Duck," Amendment to be in effect. (Not only did the amendment provide for ending the old "Lame Duck" holdover terms of office of defeated congressmen, but it set up January 20 as the new day of inauguration for U.S. presidents, beginning in 1937.)

**1941**    Kichisaburo Nomura, the new Japanese ambassador to the United States, arrives in this country and issues a statement, saying: "There is no question whatsoever outstanding between the two countries which cannot be settled in an amicable and satisfactory manner through a timely display of statesmanship by the respective peoples of both sides."

**1943**    General Dwight D. Eisenhower is appointed commander-in-chief of the Allied Expeditionary Forces in North Africa. (WORLD WAR II)

**1952**    King George VI of Great Britain dies after a lengthy illness. He is succeeded to the throne by his daughter, Princess Elizabeth, who will assume the name of Queen Elizabeth II.

**1954**    In Detroit, Senator Joseph R. McCarthy (R., Wis.) infuriates Democrats when he tells a Detroit audience that the Democrats "had well earned and ... still deserved to be labeled 'the party of betrayal.'"

**1964**    Fidel Castro orders his government to cut off the normal water supply to the U.S. Naval Base at Guantanamo Bay. His action is a reprisal for the seizure earlier in the week of four Cuban fishing vessels off the coast of Florida.

## FEBRUARY 7

**1827**    The first ballet group to be formed in the United States performs at the Bowery Theatre in New York. (The ballerina, Madame Francisquy Hutin, was dressed in such flimsy attire that many of the ladies in the audience felt obliged to leave.)

**1885**    Sinclair Lewis, American writer, is born in Sauk Center, Minnesota. (The creator of *Main Street* and *Arrowsmith*, in 1930, became the first American to win the Nobel Prize for literature.)

**1926**    A report on current wage rates in the *New York Tribune* says: "The average rate for common labor for the entire country is 54 cents an hour, as against 53 cents five months ago. The labor situation is favorable to a continuation of the present trend in building."

**1931**    *Peter Ibbetson*, an American opera composed by Deems Taylor, has its world *première* at the Metropolitan Opera House in New York.

**1936**    President Roosevelt issues an Executive Order creating a flag for the office of the Vice President of the United States.

**1942**     In a message to Generalissimo Chiang Kai-shek, President Roosevelt pledges full aid to China: "I extend to you across land and sea the hand of comradeship for the common good, the common goal, the common victory that shall be ours." (WORLD WAR II)

**1948**     General Dwight D. Eisenhower resigns as army chief of staff. He will be succeeded by General Omar N. Bradley.

**1964**     More than 3,000 fans of The Beatles, "England's most successful export since the bowler hat," jam Kennedy International Airport in New York to await the arrival of the internationally famous rock 'n' roll quartet. At least 100 policemen are on hand to protect the English entertainers from their American enthusiasts.

## FEBRUARY 8

**1587**     Mary, Queen of Scots, is beheaded, charged with plotting the murder of Britain's Queen Elizabeth I.

**1820**     Birthday of William Tecumseh Sherman, general in the War between the States, leader of the famous Northern "March to the Sea."

**1907**     A story in *The New York World* by Irvin S. Cobb describes the human drama going on in the courtroom trial of Harry K. Thaw, charged with the murder of the well-known architect Stanford White: "A pale slim little woman on the witness stand this afternoon laid bare the horrors of a life such as few women have led in her effort to save Harry Thaw from the electric chair. The woman was his wife, Evelyn Nesbit Thaw. . . . Men and women wept as this life-story was unfolded, sometimes artlessly, sometimes with thrilling dramatic force and fervor. . . ."

**1910**     The Boy Scouts of America is incorporated in the District of Columbia.

**1912**     To the *New York American,* many of the modern dances are shameful. "New York and Newport society," says the newspaper, "are just at present manifesting a craze for the disgusting and indecent dance known as the 'Turkey Trot.' "

**1918**     *The Stars and Stripes,* the American Expeditionary Forces' official weekly newspaper, is published for the first time. (WORLD WAR I)

**1940**     Every 10th person is shot in two villages near Warsaw, Poland, in reprisal for the deaths of two German soldiers. (WORLD WAR II)

**1944**     All over the United States, war-weary Americans are singing the nonsensical lyrics of "Mairzy Doats," a song telling of mares eating oats and does eating oats and little lambs eating ivy.

**1949**     An Air Force jet bomber flies across the United States in 3 hours, 46 minutes, the fastest transcontinental flight to date.

**1955**    In a surprise move, Soviet Premier Georgi M. Malenkov, in office 23 months following Joseph Stalin's death, resigns as chief of state. An announcement from Moscow says that Malenkov will be succeeded by Marshal Nikolai A. Bulganin.

**1962**    After being pressed for months to enter the Republican race for governor in Michigan, automobile manufacturer George W. Romney, a devout Mormon, makes news by announcing he will not reach a decision until he has concluded a 24-hour fast and session of personal prayer. (Two days later, he threw his hat into the ring and won the election in the following November.)

**1962**    Speaking to alumni of the Harvard, Yale, and Princeton clubs in Washington, Senator Barry M. Goldwater (R., Ariz.) says on the subject of the controversial right-wing John Birch Society: ".... My chief objection is to the Society's leader (Robert H. W. Welch, Jr.). He is intemperate and unwise. I wish he would step out so the fine responsible people who are members could take charge ..."

**1965**    A story in *U.S. News & World Report* assesses the plight of the Republican Party following the 1964 elections and reports that the party "starts its comeback drive from the lowest point it has reached since it was flattened by Franklin D. Roosevelt in the 1930s ..." Of the 435 members of the House of Representatives, the story points out, there are but 140 Republicans, the smallest number since 1936. Of the Senate membership of 100, Republicans occupy only 32 seats, the smallest number since 1940. Republicans in 50 state capitals are represented as governors in 17 state houses.

## FEBRUARY 9

**1773**    Birthday of William Henry Harrison, ninth President of the United States.

**1825**    The House of Representatives elects John Quincy Adams President of the United States, following the national election of December 1, 1824, when not one of the various candidates, including Adams, managed to receive an electoral majority. (The new chief executive's father, former President John Adams, received the momentous news, took pen in hand and sent off this note to his son: "Never did I feel so much solemnity as upon this occasion. The multitude of my thoughts and the intensity of my feelings are too much for a mind like mine, in its 90th year. May the blessing of God Almighty continue to protect you to the end of your life.")

**1849**    Dolley Madison, now 82 years of age, is the honored guest at a reception in the White House given by President and Mrs. James Knox Polk. According to one eyewitness: "... Dolley was there in her customary décolletage and turban. ... Resplendent

41

in white satin, she received with the First Lady, seated on a dais. She left the reception on the President's arm shortly after midnight."

**1861**    Jefferson Davis and Alexander H. Stephens are elected president and vice president, respectively, of the Confederacy by the Confederate Congress.

**1941**    In a speech directed to the United States, Prime Minister Winston Churchill of Great Britain says: "Put your confidence in us. Give us your faith and your blessing, and under Providence all will be well. We shall not fail or falter; we shall not weaken or tire. Neither the sudden shock of battle nor the long-drawn trials of vigilance and exertion will wear us down. Give us the tools and we will finish the job." (WORLD WAR II)

**1942**    The former French liner *Normandie,* in the process of being refitted as a transport ship for the U.S. Navy, burns and capsizes at her pier in New York harbor. (WORLD WAR II)

**1943**    Representative Clare Boothe Luce (R., Conn.) introduces a new word into the language when, in discussing the liberal objectives of Vice President Henry A. Wallace before the House of Representatives, she says: ".... Much of what Mr. Wallace calls his global thinking is, no matter how you slice it, still *globaloney.*"

**1943**    Japan evacuates Guadalcanal in the Solomon Islands in the face of overwhelming American military superiority. (WORLD WAR II)

**1950**    A charge that the State Department is infested with Communists is made by Senator Joseph R. McCarthy (R., Wis.) during a speech delivered before the Republican Women's Club of Ohio County in Wheeling, West Virginia: "I have in my hand fifty-seven cases of individuals who would appear to be either card-carrying members or certainly loyal to the Communist Party."

## FEBRUARY 10

**1840**    All England rejoices as Queen Victoria is married to Prince Albert of Saxe-Coburg-Gotha. (The wedding preparations were jolted when the court physician, Sir James Clark, incorrectly told Her Majesty that she was coming down with the measles.)

**1915**    President Wilson warns Germany that she will be held to "strict accountability" for acts endangering the lives of American citizens during the current European war. (WORLD WAR I)

**1933**    A new feature in telegraphic service is introduced in New York when the Postal Telegraph Company starts to deliver "singing telegrams."

**1936**    In Germany, the secret police agency, the Gestapo, is given control of concentration camps and made independent of administrative courts. By this order, the Gestapo may arrest any individual and hold him indefinitely, even if he has been acquitted by the civil courts.

**1937**    Chinese Communists offer to end their 10-year civil war with the regime of Chiang Kai-shek in favor of a "united front" against the Japanese invaders.

**1941**    Senator Harry S. Truman (D., Mo.) demands that the Senate investigate alleged irregularities in the awarding of government defense contracts. (This led to the Truman Committee, to the Vice Presidency, and finally to the White House.)

**1942**    The last civilian automobiles roll off the assembly lines in Detroit. No further civilian automobiles will be manufactured for the duration of the war, the automotive industry to be converted for war production. (WORLD WAR II)

**1949**    *Death of a Salesman,* written by Arthur Miller and starring Lee J. Cobb, Arthur Kennedy, and Mildred Dunnock, opens at the Morosco Theatre in New York. (The New York Drama Critics overwhelmingly voted it "the best American play of the 1948–49 season.")

**1953**    Premier Mohammed Naguib of Egypt issues a proclamation giving to himself the power of rule of the nation aided by an "Army Council of the Revolution." The Premier promises to restore democratic rule after 3 years.

**1962**    Francis Gary Powers, held by Russia as an American spy, is released in exchange for Soviet spy Rudolf Abel. (Powers was the pilot of the U-2 plane shot down near Sverdlovsk in 1960. Abel, reputed to be the director of a Soviet spy network in the United States, had been in American custody since 1957.) (*See May 5*)

## FEBRUARY 11

**1812**    The word "gerrymander" comes into the English language as the legislature of Massachusetts, at the bidding of the governor, Elbridge Gerry, passes a bill dividing Essex County into a dragon-shaped district in order to draw political support for the Jeffersonian Republicans. (Today, the word is used in politics to describe the act of dividing civil divisions in such a way as to give one political party an unfair advantage over its opponent.)

**1847**    Thomas Alva Edison is born at Milan, Ohio. (At the time of his death in 1931 it was estimated that his 1,097 inventions had brought 25½ billion dollars to the pockets of businessmen around the world. *The New York Times* said this gave Edison's brain the highest cash value in history.)

**1861**    President-elect Lincoln and his wife set out from Springfield, Illinois, bound for the nation's capital. To the more than a thousand friends and neighbors who are assembled at the Great Western depot to wish the Lincolns godspeed, Lincoln says: "Here I have been a quarter of a century and have passed from a young man to an old man. Here my children have been born, and one is buried. I now leave, not knowing when or whether I ever may return, with a task before me greater than that which rested upon Washington." *

**1916**    Germany advises the U.S. ambassador in Berlin, James W. Gerard, that the Central Powers intend to sink all armed enemy merchantmen without warning after March 1. (WORLD WAR I)

**1937**    As a result of the intervention of Governor Frank Murphy of Michigan, the "sit-down" strike of General Motors' workers is ended, the management agreeing finally to a recognition of the CIO United Automobile Workers union.

**1945**    Concluding their week-long conference at Yalta in the Crimea, President Roosevelt, Prime Minister Churchill, and Marshal Stalin sign the Yalta agreements. Russia agrees to enter the war in the Pacific against Japan in return for a share of the Manchurian railways, lease of Port Arthur and rights in Dairen, but with Chinese sovereignty preserved. (WORLD WAR II)

**1952**    For the 3rd time in 2 months, a major air disaster takes place in Elizabeth, New Jersey, resulting in the deaths of 33 persons. (The first accident took place on December 16, 1951, when an airliner crashed in the city, killing 56 persons. The second occurred on January 22, 1952, and resulted in 29 deaths.)

**1961**    In Washington, Robert C. Weaver is sworn in as administrator of the U.S. Housing and Home Finance Agency, the highest federal post ever held to date by a Negro.

**1964**    Commenting on the recent assassination of President John F. Kennedy, the current issue of the ultra right-wing John Birch Society publication, *American Opinion,* claims that his "memory will be cherished with distaste." In an article signed by Revilo P. Oliver, a John Birch member, the author says that if international Communists "succeed in completing their occupation of our country, Americans will remember Kennedy while they live, and will curse him as they face the firing squads or toil in a brutish degradation. . . ."

## FEBRUARY 12

### Lincoln's Birthday

**Georgia Day**    commemorating the day in 1733 when James Edward Oglethorpe landed with his colonists at Savannah.

**1809**    Birthday of Abraham Lincoln, 16th President of the United States. ("I was born February 12, 1809, in the then Hardin County, Kentucky, at a point within the new county of Larue, a mile or a mile and a half from where Hodgen's mill now is.")

---

* Six states of the South had already seceded from the Union.

**1809**    Birth of Charles Darwin, famous British scientist, author of *The Origin of Species* (1859) and creator of the concept of evolution.

**1870**    All women in the Territory of Utah are granted full suffrage.

**1912**    China becomes a republic as the Manchu dynasty is overthrown by Chinese Nationalists led by Dr. Sun Yat-sen.

**1918**    By order of Fuel Administrator Harry A. Garfield, all theatres in New York are shut down to save coal. (WORLD WAR I)

**1924**    A memorable concert takes place in New York at Aeolian Hall as Paul Whiteman conducts a program of "symphonic jazz," highlighted by the first public performance of George Gershwin's *Rhapsody in Blue,* with the composer at the piano. The cheering audience includes such famous musicians as John Philip Sousa, Walter Damrosch, Leopold Godowsky, Jascha Heifetz, Fritz Kreisler, John McCormack, Sergei Rachmaninoff, Leopold Stokowski, Moriz Rosenthal, Mischa Elman, and Igor Stravinsky. (Since the concert took place on Lincoln's birthday, it was described as "the emancipation proclamation of jazz.")

**1942**    The 26,000-ton German battleships *Scharnhorst* and *Gneisenau* and the 10,000-ton *Prinz Eugen* escape from Brest, France, into the North Sea going toward the Kiel naval base at Helgoland. (*See December 26.*) (WORLD WAR II)

**1953**    Soviet Russia breaks off diplomatic relations with Israel after terrorists bomb the Russian Legation in Tel Aviv.

**1957**    After a 4-day national convention of the U.S. Communist Party in New York, members vote to shake off Moscow's ideological control. One speaker states that American Communists no longer agree that ". . . the interpretation of Marxism-Leninism made by the Communist Party of the Soviet Union was ipso facto valid. . . ."

**1963**    At a White House reception observing the centennial of the Emancipation Proclamation, President and Mrs. John F. Kennedy are hosts on Abraham Lincoln's birthday to more than a thousand Negroes and civil rights workers.

## FEBRUARY 13

**1635**    The Boston Latin School, the oldest public school in America, is established in Boston, Massachusetts.

**1741**    Andrew Bradford of Philadelphia publishes the first magazine in the United States, a periodical he calls *The American Magazine, or a Monthly View of the Political State of the British Colonies.* (Benjamin Franklin had hoped to get out the first American periodical, but his magazine, *The General Magazine & Historical Chronicle,* went on sale 3 days after Bradford's.)

**1867** Johann Strauss (the Younger) conducts "The Blue Danube Waltz" publicly for the first time at a concert in Vienna. (Said one enthusiastic music critic of the performance: "Vienna's darling, when he mounted the stage, was clamorously applauded. . . . There is no more popular name in Vienna than Strauss. The Strauss dance music has accompanied and played about thousands of love romances. . . . The air of Vienna is full of it.")

**1914** To protect the rights of musical composers and authors, a group of composers' and publishers' representatives organize the American Society of Composers, Authors and Publishers (ASCAP) in New York City. The new society will seek to protect copyrighted music against illegal public performance.

**1920** The former crown prince of Germany sends a cable to President Wilson offering to surrender himself for trial as a war criminal if the Allies will drop similar charges against 890 prominent German leaders. (President Wilson refused to acknowledge the crown prince's offer.)

**1931** After a heated debate, the English House of Commons defeats a bill to prohibit the manufacture and sale of alcoholic beverages.

**1942** Russian trucks manage to break the German blockade of Leningrad, entering the city with stores of bread for the hungry populace. (The siege was not lifted until the following January, however. (*See January 18.*) (WORLD WAR II)

**1945** Ruined Budapest in Hungary falls to Russian soldiers after 49 days of street fighting that cost the Germans more than 50,000 killed and 133,000 captured. (WORLD WAR II)

**1959** Don Bragg, a 23-year-old Army private from Fort Dix, New Jersey, establishes in Philadelphia the world indoor pole vault record when he leaps over an aluminum pole, clearing it at 15 feet, 9½ inches. Bragg has thus shattered the 16-year record held by Cornelius Warmerdam. (*See February 2, March 20*)

## FEBRUARY 14

### St. Valentine's Day

**1859** Oregon, the 33rd state, is admitted into the Union.

**1861** King Mongkut of Siam, grateful for a gift of books from the United States, writes to President Lincoln offering to give him several elephants to be used for travel through the "jungle." (The President politely declined the gift, saying Americans found steam to be the most efficient agent of transportation.)

**1886** The West Coast citrus industry is born as the first trainload of oranges leaves Los Angeles for eastern markets.

**1894** Benny Kubelsky, later to become famous as the American comedian Jack Benny, is born in Waukegan, Illinois.

**1903**  President Theodore Roosevelt enacts into law an act creating the Department of Commerce and Labor. George B. Cortelyou will join the Cabinet, serving as the Department's first secretary.

**1912**  Arizona becomes the 48th state to be admitted into the Union.

**1918**  A motion picture "thriller," *Tarzan of the Apes,* based on Edgar Rice Burroughs' stories that appeared serially in 1912, is released for the first time.

**1929**  St. Valentine's Day Massacre: in Chicago, seven members of the O'Bannion Gang, hijackers, bootleggers, and rivals of the Capone Gang, are murdered in their garage headquarters by five unidentified gangsters, three of them masquerading as members of the municipal police force.

**1958**  Iraq and Jordan merge into a political union to be known as The Arab Federation.

**1962**  The American public gets its most extensive view of the White House as television networks simultaneously broadcast a tour of the Executive Mansion with Mrs. John F. Kennedy serving as guide and commentator.

## FEBRUARY 15

**1564**  Birthday of Galileo Galilei, great Italian astronomer and mathematician, the creator of experimental science.

**1820**  Birthday of Susan B. Anthony, pioneer crusader for women's rights. ("I have been striving for over sixty years for a little bit of justice ... and yet I must die without obtaining it.")

**1851**  A mob of Boston Negroes break into a federal prison and rescue a Southern slave, jailed under the terms of the Fugitive Slave Act of 1850.

**1862**  The *Monitor,* the first ironclad vessel of the U.S. Navy, is ready for sea duty, her construction completed in only 126 days.

**1879**  President Rutherford B. Hayes signs into law a bill admitting women to practice law before the U.S. Supreme Court. (*See March 3.*)

**1898**  At 9:40 P.M., the U.S. battleship *Maine* is blown up in Havana harbor, resulting in the deaths of 260 members of the crew. (Although it was not possible to prove Spain's guilt for this act, public opinion in the United States was inflamed and the cry, "Remember the *Maine!*" led to a declaration of war in April.)

**1918**  Captain Vernon Castle, a partner in the world-famous dance team of Irene and Vernon Castle, is killed in an airplane accident in Texas where he is instructing British pilots. (WORLD WAR I)

**1933**  President-elect Franklin D. Roosevelt narrowly escapes assassination in Miami, Florida, when a fanatic named Giuseppe

Zangara fires several bullets at him. (Mr. Roosevelt was unharmed, but Mayor Anton J. Cermak of Chicago, who was with him at the time, was fatally injured. )

**1942**    Singapore falls 7 days after the island fortress is invaded and on the 70th day after the Japanese invasion of Malaya. (WORLD WAR II)

**1964**    Toivo Silvo, a 51-year-old Finnish longshoreman of Hamina, Finland, claims the world's record for going without sleep. Silvo, up to this day, has been awake for 276 consecutive hours. One of the reasons he has been conducting this "awakeathon," he says, is due to the fact that "I hate beds."

**1965**    With a 21-gun salute on Parliament Hill in Ottawa, Canada unfurls its new red and white national Maple Leaf flag, thus replacing the old Red Ensign. (The latter was disliked by French-speaking Canadians because it carried a British Union Jack in its upper left corner.)

**1965**    According to an announcement released today, Mickey Mantle of the New York Yankees baseball team has signed a contract with the club awarding him, for the third time, an annual salary of $100,000. Mantle is thus the second-highest salaried player in the game. Willie Mays of the San Francisco Giants will receive $105,000 for the current season.

## FEBRUARY 16

**1607**    Neighborhood children serenade Archdeacon John Sprat of St. David's Church in London:

> "Jack Sprat could eat no fat;
> His wife could eat no lean;
> And so betwixt them both, you see
> They licked the platter clean."

(The archdeacon had a reputation for very dainty eating. His wife, on the other hand, had a keen appetite and people tried very hard to invite the archdeacon out for dinner without asking his wife.)

**1804**    Lieutenant Stephen Decatur of the U.S. Navy, with 75 American sailors, climbs aboard the former U.S. Navy frigate *Philadelphia* in the harbor of Tripoli, sets it afire and makes his escape with only one casualty among his men. (Pirates of Tripoli had captured the *Philadelphia* and the Navy was determined to render it useless. Decatur's feat was described later by Admiral Nelson of the British Navy as "the most daring act of the age.")

**1838**    Birthday of Henry Adams, American historian and writer, best remembered for his autobiography, *The Education of Henry Adams*.

**1862**    General Grant dispatches a note to the Confederate commander of Fort Donelson on the Cumberland River: "No terms except an unconditional and immediate surrender can be accepted. I propose to move immediately upon your works." As a result, the Southern commander, General Simon B. Buckner, surrenders at once his entire force of 14,000 men. (The North, on hearing of Fort Donelson's capitulation, went mad with joy and promptly referred to U.S. Grant as "Unconditional Surrender" Grant.)

**1868**    Members of "The Jolly Corks," a social and benevolent society, organize themselves into a new organization called the Benevolent and Protective Order of Elks. (Their purpose is to practice charity, justice, brotherly love, and faithfulness.)

**1898**    Birth of Katharine Cornell, American actress, in Berlin, Germany.

**1925**    Rescue crews report that Floyd Collins is dead after being trapped in a cave at Cave City, Kentucky, for the past 18 days. (Collins had dislodged a boulder while exploring the cave and one leg was pinned beneath it. While rescuers worked feverishly trying to free him without causing a cave-in, the whole nation waited breathlessly in the hope that the trapped man would come out alive.)

**1938**    Bowing to Nazi pressure, Chancellor Kurt von Schuschnigg of Austria agrees to admit Austrian Nazis into his Cabinet.

**1945**    American paratroopers start landing on Corregidor in the Philippines and manage to plant the flag of the United States on a half-mile stretch of land there. (WORLD WAR II)

**1947**    Admiral Richard E. Byrd, flying over the South Pole for the second time, drops the flags of all the United Nations on the Pole during "Operation High Jump." (Byrd's first flight to the South Pole was in 1929.)

**1959**    Fidel Castro, leader of the Cuban revolution, is sworn in as that country's premier.

**1965**    A bizarre plot to bomb the Statue of Liberty, the Washington Monument, and the Liberty Bell in Philadelphia is frustrated in New York following a series of arrests there by a team of police, Federal Bureau of Investigation agents, and the Royal Canadian Mounted Police. Arrested are three young Negro extremists and a French Canadian young woman. (One of the men seized said that the plot to destroy the three symbols of American freedom was "to draw attention to the conditions of my [Negro] race.")

## FEBRUARY 17

**1801**    After 35 separate ballots, the House of Representatives breaks the electoral tie between Thomas Jefferson and Aaron Burr, electing the former third President of the United States. Mr. Burr will serve as Vice President.

**1817**    For the first time in American history, a city street is illuminated by gas lights. The city is Baltimore.

**1876** The first sardine is canned at Eastport, Maine, by Julius Wolff of the Wolff and Reesing cannery.

**1906** Alice Roosevelt, the eldest daughter of President Theodore Roosevelt, and known all over the nation as "Princess Alice," is married in the East Room of the White House to Congressman Nicholas Longworth of Ohio. (When the bridal couple left for their honeymoon, the President invited some of his Harvard classmates to the White House for an evening of group singing.)

**1913** "Modern art" is introduced to Americans officially as an exhibition of contemporary French painting is opened at the Sixtyninth Regiment Armory in New York. Most viewers are puzzled by the canvases of Picasso, Matisse, Braque, and Marcel Duchamp, but the latter's "Nude Descending a Staircase" evokes the greatest comment. Critics refer to it as "baffling," "scandalous," "ridiculous," "meaningless." (In 1913, Americans were not prepared for "modern" art. Theodore Roosevelt condemned all "modernists" as lunatics. And Enrico Caruso went to the Armory show where he drew caricatures of the cubist paintings on display there and then scattered them to the boisterous crowd.)

**1944** American soldiers land on the Japanese-held base of Eniwetok in the Marshall Islands (WORLD WAR II)

**1964** In an historic decision that goes to the roots of the American Constitutional system, the U.S. Supreme Court, by a 6–3 decision, rules that Congressional districts within each state must be roughly equal in population. (". . . We hold that, construed in its historical context, the command of Article I, Section 2, that Representatives be chosen 'by the people of the several states' means that as nearly as is practicable one man's vote in a Congressional election is to be worth as much as another's. . . ."—Justice Hugo L. Black.)

## FEBRUARY 18

**1678** Bunyan's *Pilgrim's Progress* is published for the first time.

**1861** Jefferson Davis is sworn into office as president of the Confederate States of America. Delivering his inaugural address on the steps of the State Capitol at Montgomery, Alabama, President Davis says "All we ask is to be left alone." (The jubilant Southerners selected as their theme song for the inaugural the popular song "Dixie" and sang it over and over again during the ceremonies.)

**1890** Gilbert & Sullivan's new comic opera *The Gondoliers* is playing at the Park Theatre in New York, to the delight of New Yorkers and theatregoers from out of town alike.

**1915** Virtually unnoticed by the press, Frank James, the brother and confederate of the notorious outlaw Jesse James, dies

50

in Excelsior Springs, Missouri, where he has been living as a respectable farmer.

**1930**    The planet Pluto is discovered by astronomer Clyde W. Tombaugh, working at the Lowell Observatory, Flagstaff, Arizona.

**1939**    Ceremonies in San Francisco mark the opening there of the Goldern Gate Exposition.

**1943**    Madame Chiang Kai-shek of China, addressing a Joint Session of Congress, says: "We in China, like you, want a better world not for ourselves alone but for all mankind, and we must have it." (WORLD WAR II)

**1948**    John A. Costello is elected prime minister of Eire, replacing Eamon de Valera who has served in that office for 16 years.

**1953**    The most costly single television contract to date is signed in Hollywood when Lucille Ball and Desi Arnaz are awarded a contract paying them $8,000,000 to continue their program, "I Love Lucy," through 1955.

**1954**    Because he refuses to reveal the identities of army officers involved in the promotion and honorable discharge of an alleged subversive in the Army Dental Corps, Brigadier General Ralph W. Zwicker, a hero of World War II, is told by Senator Joseph R. Mc-Carthy (R., Wis.) that he is "not fit to wear that uniform" and "should be removed from any command." (General Zwicker had been instructed by the Secretary of the Army not to reveal any such names.)

## FEBRUARY 19

**1473**    Birth of Copernicus (Nikolaj Kopernik), world-famous astronomer, at Torun, Poland.

**1864**    The Knights of Pythias fraternal organization is founded in Washington, D.C., by 13 men, based on the classical story of Damon and Pythias. The new society will seek religious toleration, the social and fraternal well-being of its members, obedience to law, and loyalty to government.

**1878**    Thomas A. Edison receives a patent for his invention of the phonograph. (Edison's mechanics were paid on a piecework basis and when he handed the sketch for his phonograph to John Kreusi, his assistant, the inventor wrote $18 on the drawing, thus advising Kreusi that that was the amount he was to be paid for making it.)

**1881**    Kansas adopts statewide prohibition of all alcoholic beverages.

**1910**    "Diamond Jim" Brady's appetite shows no sign of slowing down. At a dinner party in New York, he eats 7 dozen oysters, 5 servings of roast beef, 2 gallons of stewed fruit, and 3 gallons of orange juice.

**1922** Ed Wynn, "The Perfect Fool" of vaudeville and musical-comedy fame, becomes the first big name in show business to sign up for a regular radio program featuring him as the star performer. (In 1922, stars of theater and music did not consider radio a suitable medium for first-class talent.)

**1941** Radio Berlin's propaganda division short-waves an appeal to the United States to send messages collect to Germany. (More than a thousand Americans took advantage of this offer and sent messages, most of them highly critical to the Nazi regime.)

**1945** U.S. Marines land on Iwo Jima, thus beginning the bloody battle for that Japanese-held island. (*See March 16.*) (WORLD WAR II)

**1945** War Mobilization Director James Byrnes orders a midnight curfew for all places of entertainment, including night clubs, saloons, cafés, and theatres. (WORLD WAR II)

**1959** An "agreed foundation for the final settlement of the problem of Cyprus" is signed in London by the prime ministers of England, Greece, and Turkey. The agreement provides for the creation of a Cypriot republic within a year and a Presidential regime, with the president "being Greek and the vice president Turkish, elected by universal suffrage by the Greek and Turkish communities . . . respectively."

**1965** The American Bar Association asks the Supreme Court to reverse the conviction of Billie Sol Estes, bankrupt Texas financier, for alleged charges of fraud and swindle. The Bar Association argues that television coverage of Estes' trial had violated his constitutional rights. (Estes was convicted on November 7, 1962, on a state charge at Tyler, Texas, of swindling a farmer. *See June 7*)

## FEBRUARY 20

**1792** President George Washington signs the first postal act, thereby establishing the Federal Post Office. The measure provides for rates at 6 cents for letters not exceeding a 30-mile distance; 8 cents for letters traveling 30 to 60 miles; 10 cents for mail carried 60 to 100 miles; and 12½ cents for letters going from 100 to 150 miles.

**1809** The Supreme Court rules that the power of the federal government is greater than that of any individual state of the Union.

**1872** The Metropolitan Museum of Art in New York is opened to the public, using the premises of a rented house at 681 Fifth Avenue.

**1912** Former President Theodore Roosevelt reveals to reporters in Cleveland, Ohio, that he has made up his mind to be a candidate again for the Presidency. He says: "My hat is in the ring! The fight is on and I'm stripped to the buff." (Roosevelt had split with his conservative successor and onetime close friend, President William Howard Taft, who was seeking renomination for a second term.)

**1921**    The hearts of hundreds of thousands of American women are beating faster as they anticipate seeing the latest moving picture starring Rudolph Valentino, *The Four Horsemen of the Apocalypse,* released today for the first time.

**1938**    Anthony Eden resigns as British foreign secretary in protest against the "appeasement" policy of Prime Minister Neville Chamberlain.

**1950**    Senator Joseph R. McCarthy (R., Wis.) speaks on the floor of the Senate for almost 6 hours, in an attempt to give the members of that body details on 81 State Department employees whom he claims are Communists.

**1954**    Secretary of the Army Robert T. Stevens, saying he will not permit army personnel to be "browbeaten or humiliated," defies Senator Joseph R. McCarthy and orders army officers to ignore the Senator's subpoenas.

**1962**    Marine Lieutenant Colonel John H. Glenn, Jr., becomes the first American to go into orbit. After being launched from Cape Canaveral, Florida, the 40-year-old astronaut circles the earth 3 times in a space capsule and then lands safely in the Atlantic. *(See February 23, 26, 28 and March 1)*

**1965**    In a near-perfect expedition, the Ranger 8 spacecraft crashes into its target area on the moon after relaying back to the earth about 7,000 pictures of the lunar surface. Ranger 8 was launched from Cape Kennedy, Florida, and its impact on the moon was within 15 miles of its aiming point.

# FEBRUARY 21

**1846**    Sarah Bagley becomes the first woman telegrapher in history when she reports to work in the newly opened Lowell, Massachusetts, office of the New York and Boston Magnetic Telegraph Company.

**1848**    John Quincy Adams collapses on the floor of the House of Representatives and is carried by his colleagues to the speaker's office where a bed is set up for him. After he is revived, the former President calls for Henry Clay and then cries out, "This is the end of earth, but I am composed." (Adams took his seat in the House in 1831, two years after he left the White House. When he collapsed on February 21, 1848, he went into a coma and finally died 2 days later, still installed on a bed in the speaker's office.)

**1868**    The feud between President Andrew Johnson and Secretary of War Edwin M. Stanton continues at a high pitch as the President orders Stanton to vacate the secretary's office and appoints Adjutant-General Thomas as Secretary of War ad interim.

**1878**    A telephone directory, the first of its kind in the world, is issued by the New Haven Connecticut Telephone Company. The names of 50 subscribers are listed in the directory.

**1885**    After 37 years of construction, the Washington Monument is dedicated in the nation's capital. (The cornerstone was laid on July 4, 1848.)

**1909**    Sixteen battleships of the U.S. Navy, nicknamed "The Great White Fleet," steam into Hampton Roads, completing the first worldwide journey ever undertaken by vessels of our navy. The expedition started December 16, 1907, and lasted 434 days.

**1925**    A new magazine reaches the newsstands as the first issue of *The New Yorker* is published.

**1950**    Hungary sentences an American businessman, Robert A. Vogeler, to 15 years' imprisonment after he had "confessed" to a People's Court there that he was guilty of espionage. (Vogeler served 17 months of his sentence. He was released April 28, 1951.)

**1964**    The *S.S. Exilona* arrives in Odessa with the first cargo of American wheat for the Soviet Union.

**1965**    The Labor Department in Washington releases projected figures that indicate the labor force in the United States will grow to 86 million in 1970 and 101.4 million in 1980. The labor force in 1960 totaled 73 million and was 77 million in 1964.

## FEBRUARY 22

### Washington's Birthday

**1732**    George Washington, "The Father of Our Country," is born at his parents' plantation near Fredericksburg, Virginia.

**1810**    Frédéric François Chopin, Polish composer and pianist, is born in Warsaw.

**1819**    In a treaty with Spain, Florida is ceded to the United States.

**1847**    "General Taylor never surrenders" is the only response received by General Santa Anna at the Battle of Buena Vista, Mexico, after the Mexican had demanded the immediate surrender of General Zachary Taylor and his American troops.

**1879**    The first "five-cent store," forerunner of the modern "five-and-ten," is opened in Utica, New York, by Frank W. Woolworth. (The store was a great disappointment, its sales after a few weeks running as low as $2.50 a day. In June, 1879, Woolworth moved the store to Lancaster, Pennsylvania, where it proved a success.)

**1891**    New York saloon-keeper Steve Brodie, who had made a name for himself in 1886 by jumping off the Brooklyn Bridge, repeats his jumping stunt from a stage bridge at Niblo's Garden in New York.

**1892**   Birthday of Edna St. Vincent Millay, American poet.

**1943**   A horrible air disaster occurs in Portugal when an American commercial airliner crashes into the Tagus River. (The airship was carrying a company of American entertainers abroad, all of them scheduled to perform at military installations. Twenty-four of them were drowned. Among the survivors were the popular radio singer Jane Froman and the accordionist Gypsy Markoff.)

**1957**   Teen-age devotees of "rock 'n' roll," the latest fad in swing music, storm into New York's Times Square area, intent on seeing one of their idols. *The New York Times* reports: "They began lining up at 4 A.M. to see the show at the Paramount Theatre. It wasn't until 18½ hours later. . . . that the last of the line entered the theatre. . . . The show featured Alan Freed, a disc jockey who takes credit for coining the phrase 'rock 'n' roll' . . ." (One expert described rock 'n' roll as essentially a rolling two-beat rhythm with the accent coming on every second beat.)

## FEBRUARY 23

**1633**   Birthday of Samuel Pepys, English public official and author of the most famous diary in the world. (Pepys had no idea the public would someday share his personal entries. Actually, he wrote his diary in shorthand and after his death it was deciphered and then published. The diary was kept by Pepys for 9 years and 5 months.)

**1847**   General Zachary Taylor and his American soldiers defeat General Santa Anna at the Battle of Buena Vista, Mexico.

**1861**   Accompanied by guards, President-elect Lincoln arrives secretly in Washington at 6 o'clock in the morning. (An assassination plot in Baltimore was foiled when Lincoln's guards made him by-pass that city.)

**1870**   Mississippi is readmitted into the Union.

**1871**   The word "vaudeville" appears for the first time at Weisiger's Hotel in Louisville, Kentucky, where a traveling troupe entertains the patrons of the hotel. The troupe is billed as "Sargent's Great Vaudeville Company."

**1905**   After observing that strangers in a city are very often inhospitably received, Paul Percy Harris, a Chicago lawyer, and three friends found the first Rotary Club.

**1927**   President Coolidge signs the Dill-White Radio Act creating a Federal Radio Commission. (This act recognized the fact that radio was now an industry.)

**1942**   During a "Fireside Chat" to the nation by President Roosevelt, a Japanese submarine fires 25 shells at an oil refinery near Santa Barbara, California.

**1945**   Six members of the Fifth Division of the U.S. Marines plant the American flag atop Mount Suribachi in Iwo Jima. (Five of the men's identities were later established: Private René A. Gagnon of Manchester, New Hampshire; Private Ira H. Hayes, Bapchule, Arizona; Sergeant Michael Strank, Conemaugh, Pennsylvania; Pharmacist's Mate John H. Bradley, Appleton, Wisconsin; Sergeant Henry O. Hansen, Somerville, Massachusetts. The feat of these men was equalled by an Associated Press photographer, Joe Rosenthal, who recorded the memorable event in the most famous photograph of World War II.)

**1954** The first mass inoculations of school children with the Salk antipoliomyelitis vaccine begin in Pittsburgh, Pennsylvania.

**1954** Garry Davis, who renounced his U.S. citizenship in 1948 to become "a citizen of the world," announces that he has established an international World Citizens Party.

**1962** Lieutenant Colonel John Glenn, Jr., America's space hero, escorted by Vice President Lyndon B. Johnson, returns to Cape Canaveral, Florida, where he is reunited with his family. Later, President Kennedy joins the astronaut and awards him the Distinguished Service Medal.

**1965** The Associated Press reports that an unnamed German business firm has introduced a radical innovation in its daily routine. From now on, incoming and outgoing telephone calls will be stopped for one hour daily "so everyone can concentrate on work." The hour period will be known as the "Silent Hour" and the prohibition of telephone calls will apply to the president of the corporation as well as his entire staff.

## FEBRUARY 24

**1761** James Otis of Massachusetts, having resigned as advocate general of the king, protests the current English practice of "search and seizure." Otis says: "One of the most essential branches of English liberty is the freedom of one's house. A man's house is his castle, and whilst he is quiet, he is as well-guarded as a prince in his castle."

**1803** In writing a decision on the case of *Marbury* v. *Madison* (concerning Secretary of State James Madison's refusal to honor a political appointment of former President Adams), Chief Justice Marshall hands down what many people claim is the most important decision ever ruled on by the Supreme Court: that "the Supreme Court shall have the power to declare invalid any Act of Congress which, in the opinion of the Court, is unconstitutional."

**1852** A memorial service is held in Metropolitan Hall in New York to mark the recent death of James Fenimore Cooper. Daniel Webster presides over the ceremonies while the main address is delivered by William Cullen Bryant.

**1868** The only impeachment proceedings ever instituted against a President of the United States are started by the House of Representatives when it resolves to impeach President Andrew Johnson for "high crimes and misdemeanors." (Specifically, the action was taken because the President had dismissed Secretary of War Stanton and, it was alleged, declared several laws unconstitutional. *See May 16 and May 26.*)

**1920** A group of German nationalists organize the National Socialist Party, an ominous date for the entire civilized world.

**1922** Henri Désiré Landru, best known to the world as "Bluebeard," is executed at Versailles, France, for murdering 10 of his 13 "fiancées" and then burning their bodies piecemeal in his cookstove. (The women had been lured to his lonely villa. During his trial, "Bluebeard" admitted nonchalantly that he had 250 sweethearts in reserve for similar fates. He described his technique as "win a woman, get her money, rub her out.")

**1931** Economists estimate the current cost of each session of Congress as $1,400 an hour.

**1942** The Voice of America, the worldwide radio network operated by the U.S. government, goes on the air for the first time with these words: "The Voice of America speaks. Today, America has been at war for seventy-nine days. Daily . . . we shall speak to you about America and the war. The news may be good or bad, but we shall tell you the truth."

**1945** American troops liberate Manila completely from Japanese occupation and control. (WORLD WAR II)

**1946** Juan Perón is elected president of Argentina.

**1954** Secretary of the Army Robert T. Stevens yields to Senator Joseph R. McCarthy's demand and agrees to permit army officers to testify in the investigation of Dr. Irving Peress, a former member of the Army Dental Corps and currently under fire by McCarthy as an alleged subversive.

**1963** A play in West Berlin by an unknown playwright is generating a growing and bitter controversy. The play is *The Vicar,* written by 32-year-old Rolf Hochhuth, a German. Its plot is a thinly disguised condemnation of the late Pope Pius XII for his failure to speak out forcefully against Nazi persecution of the Jews of Europe in World War II. (This play, also known as *The Deputy,* opened in New York on February 26, 1964, where it was similarly applauded and attacked.)

## FEBRUARY 25

**1793** Heads of the various government departments meet with President Washington at his home, the first recorded meeting of a President's "Cabinet."

**1820** Felix Walker, a congressman from North Carolina, whose district embraces Buncombe County, refuses to let the House take a vote on the Missouri Bill until he makes another of his long-winded speeches about his beloved county. (From Walker's repeated references to Buncombe County, the word "bunk" evolved, meaning "nonsense," or "hot air.")

**1873** Enrico Caruso, great operatic tenor, is born in Naples, Italy. (His name became so important in Italy that his native city dedicated the world's largest candle to his memory in 1924. The candle, measuring 18 feet in height and 7 feet in circumference, is lit once a year on his birth date and is expected to last 1,800 years.)

**1901** J. P. Morgan incorporates the United States Steel Corporation in New Jersey, the first "billion-dollar corporation."

**1913** The Sixteenth Amendment to the Constitution, empowering the Congress to levy income taxes, goes into effect.

**1919** Oregon becomes the first state to tax gasoline. From now on, motorists will have to pay one percent of the cost to the state.

**1928** Marathon dancing has become a national craze. Almost every sizable city is staging dance-endurance contests. A New York newspaper reports that "wherever you travel today in the United States, crowds of people collect in dingy halls, heavy with the odors of coffee and tobacco, to watch the disheveled couples, not a few of whom manage to remain on their feet for eighty running hours."

**1948** In a bloodless *coup d'état*, the Communists seize complete control of Czechoslovakia. President Beneš is to remain in office. (But on June 7, the little patriot resigned, having taken as much as he could stand.)

**1954** A vote in the Senate defeats the proposed Bricker Amendment which would restrict the treaty-making powers of the President. (This controversial bill was sponsored by Senator John W. Bricker (R., Ohio). A substitute measure was also defeated the next day by a single vote.)

**1956** A strong attack on the late Russian dictator, Joseph Stalin, is made by Nikita Khrushchev at the Communist Party Congress, meeting in Moscow. Khrushchev, now First Secretary of the party, scores Stalin's "intolerance, his brutality and his abuse of power" and accuses him of encouraging the "cult of the individual."

**1964** Cassius Marcellus Clay, 22, of Louisville, Kentucky, wins the world's heavyweight boxing championship in Miami Beach, Florida, after title-holder Charles (Sonny) Liston fails to come out of his corner for the seventh round. (Clay's purse was estimated at $600,000.)

## FEBRUARY 26

**1802** Birthday of Victor Hugo, French novelist, poet, and playwright, one of the greatest figures in French literature, remembered particularly for his novel, *Les Misérables*.

**1815** Napoleon Bonaparte, with a squadron of 1,200 men, flees from the Island of Elba aboard the brig *L'Inconstant* to begin his second conquest of France. (On March 1, he landed in the Bay of Juan and was on his way to Cannes at the head of his troops.)

**1846** William Frederick Cody, better known as "Buffalo Bill" and the man who personified the romance of the frontier West, is born in Scott County, Iowa.

**1861** At the first meeting of the Board of Trustees of Vassar College, its founder, Matthew Vassar, explains why he is anxious to assist in the establishment of a college for women: "It occurred to me that woman, having received from her Creator the same intellectual constitution as man, has the same right as man to intellectual culture and development."

**1870** New York's first subway line is opened to the public. Passengers are admitted at 25 cents apiece and enter the one car from a Broadway store basement. The subway is operated by a rotary blower which propels it like "a sailboat before the wind."

**1907** Congress enacts legislation providing for salary increases for the Vice President, Cabinet members, and the Speaker of the House, bringing their salaries to $12,000 and those of senators and representatives to $7,500.

**1919** Congress establishes Grand Canyon National Park in Arizona.

**1935** Germany starts the operation of its air force under the supervision of Reichsmarshal Hermann Goering.

**1942** A terse radio message is received by the U.S. Navy in Washington from Donald F. Mason, a Navy flier stationed in the Pacific Theater of Operations: "Sighted sub, sank same." (WORLD WAR II).

**1951** James Jones' novel, *From Here to Eternity,* destined to become one of the bestselling books of all time, is published in New York.

**1962** Thousands of people line the streets of Washington, D.C., and extend a tumultuous welcome to Lieutenant Colonel John Glenn, Jr. The astronaut's motorcade stops at the Capitol where he addresses a joint session of Congress.

**1964** President Lyndon B. Johnson signs the tax reduction and reform bill just 6 hours after the legislation clears Congress. The bill provides for tax reductions of $7.7 billion in 1964 and $11.5 billion a year beginning in 1965.

## FEBRUARY 27

**1860** Abraham Lincoln makes his first speech in the East as he addresses the Young Men's Central Republican Union at Cooper Union, in New York City "Wrong as we think slavery is, we can yet afford to let it alone where it is, because that much is due to the necessity arising from its actual presence in the nation; but can we, while our votes will prevent it, allow it to spread into the national territories, and to overrun us here in these Free States? If our sense of duty forbids this, then let us stand by our duty, fearlessly and effectively...." (Fifteen hundred people turned out to listen to his speech, including the great poet and editor, William Cullen Bryant, who introduced him to the audience.)

**1902**    John Steinbeck, American novelist, is born in Salinas, California. (He is famous, in particular, for his *Of Mice and Men* and *Grapes of Wrath*.)

**1931**    Congress passes the Bonus Loan Bill for the aid of U.S. war veterans, overriding President Hoover's veto.

**1933**    Less than a week before the all-important German elections to confirm the appointment of Adolf Hitler as chancellor of Germany, the Reichstag in Berlin is mysteriously gutted by fire. Hitler immediately arrests some five thousand "Communists," charging that the fire is a Communist plot to oust him from power. (The Nazis finally singled out Marinus van der Lubbe, a Dutchman, as the individual responsible for the fire. Actually, they burned the building themselves in an attempt to convince the populace of the Communist menace.)

**1939**    "Sit-down strikes" are outlawed by the U.S. Supreme Court.

**1940**    Jazz terminology is confusing to at least one reader of a Chicago newspaper who addresses a letter to the editor asking for a definition of the phrase "jam session." The writer says: "I feel as though I am living in another world with a completely new language. Just what is a jam session?"

**1942**    Beginning of the Battle of the Java Sea, to be won ultimately by the Japanese who sink 13 warships as compared to a loss of two in their own navy. (WORLD WAR II)

**1963**    Mickey Mantle of the New York Yankees baseball team signs a contract guaranteeing him a 1963 salary of $100,000—just $98,900 more than he earned in 1949 when he signed his first contract with the club. (In all, only five baseball players are understood to have received $100,000 or more in annual salaries: in addition to Mantle, Joe DiMaggio of the Yankees; Willie Mays of the San Francisco Giants; Ted Williams of the Boston Red Sox; and Stan Musial of the St. Louis Cardinals.)

**1964**    The city of Pisa asks the Italian government to spend more than a million dollars to straighten the 184-foot Leaning Tower of Pisa. The world-famous Tower, weighing 14,000 tons, now slants almost 11 feet from true perpendicular and engineers are fearful it may crash to earth.

# FEBRUARY 28

**1844**  An excursion down the Potomac River ends in a national tragedy as a 12-inch gun aboard the U.S. gunboat *Princeton* explodes, killing the Secretary of State Abel P. Upshur, the Secretary of the Navy Thomas W. Gilmer, and several other government officials. (President Tyler and his Cabinet and some two hundred other government officials were aboard the vessel at the time, the guests of the *Princeton's* captain. The party made the trip during an inspection of the ship, the latest and most modern steam warship in our navy.)

**1859**  Readers of the *Savannah* (Georgia) *Republican* are advised that a large slave auction will be held in the near future: "The Negroes will be sold in families, and be seen on the premises of Joseph Bryan in Savannah, three days prior to the day of sale, when catalogues will be furnished. . . ."

**1919**  Senator Henry Cabot Lodge (R., Mass.) speaks for 2½ hours on the floor of the Senate in opposition to President Wilson's support of the Covenant of the proposed League of Nations.

**1933**  Adolf Hitler's government issues a decree suppressing civil liberties in Germany. At the same time, Hitler orders his Storm Troops to continue their wholesale arrests. (The decree of this date was referred to by anti-Nazis in Germany as "The Magna Carta of the Concentration Camp.")

**1942**  Japanese forces land on Java, the last Allied bastion in the Netherlands East Indies. (WORLD WAR II)

**1962**  In Las Vegas, Nevada, a group of local Republicans meet to form a "John Glenn for President Club." In endorsing the astronaut, a spokesman for the new group says: "We don't know if he is a Democrat or Republican,* but we'll take him just like we did with Herbert Hoover and Dwight Eisenhower."

**1963**  In his special civil rights message to Congress, President John F. Kennedy notes that in the 100th anniversary year of the Emancipation Proclamation American Negroes are still the victims of race discrimination: ". . . The Negro baby born in America today—regardless of the section or state in which he is born—has about one-half as much chance of completing high school as a white baby born in the same place on the same day; one-third as much chance of completing college; one-third as much chance of becoming a professional man; twice as much chance of becoming unemployed; about one-seventh as much chance of earning $10,000 a year; a life expectancy which is seven years less; and the prospects of earning only half as much. . . ."

---

* Colonel Glenn answered this question on January 17, 1964, when he declared himself a candidate for the Democratic nomination for U.S. Senator from Ohio. On the following March 30, however, he was forced to withdraw from the race after receiving a severe head injury in a fall.

# FEBRUARY 29

## Leap Year

This extra day comes every four years because it takes the earth $365\frac{1}{4}$ days to revolve about the sun and those four one-quarter days make one whole day every fourth year. Leap Year has long been associated with the tradition of having spinsters propose to bachelors rather than await proposals of marriage from them. In old Scotland, Parliament even went so far as to pass a law forbidding any man to turn down a girl who proposed to him on Leap Year. If he did decline the proposal, he was fined the equivalent of $500.

**1872**    Queen Victoria of Great Britain narrowly misses death at the hands of a would-be assassin, Albert O'Connor, an 18-year-old revolutionary.

**1906**    Readers of the *Ladies' Home Journal* are told by Editor Bok that "women of good birth and breeding long ago discarded the use of perfumes. No well-bred woman will exhale any other scent than that indescribable pure sweet aroma which is the result of the daily bath and clean linen."

**1924**    The former head of the Veterans' Bureau in Washington, Charles R. Forbes, is indicted for defrauding the government of $250,000,000.

**1956**    President Eisenhower puts an end to many months of conjecture when he announces at his press conference that he will run for a second term of office if the Republican National Convention nominates him in August. In the evening, the President appears on a nationwide radio and television broadcast explaining his position to the country, saying that his decision to run after his heart attack in September was made in light of "the favorable reports of my doctors." He adds: "I can now perform as well as I ever have all the important duties of the Presidency."

**1964**    The United States has secretly developed a jet airplane, called the A-11, capable of flying at more than 2,000 miles per hour at altitudes of more than 70,000 feet, according to an announcement made today by President Lyndon B. Johnson.

# MARCH

## MARCH 1

**1781**    The American colonies adopt the Articles of Confederation, thus paving the way for a federal union.

**1803**    Ohio is admitted into the United States as the 17th state.

**1855**    Parisian theatregoers applaud *La Case de l'Oncle Tom,* the French version of Harriet Beecher Stowe's *Uncle Tom's Cabin.*

**1867**    Nebraska becomes the 37th state to join the Union.

**1872**    Congress authorizes the creation of Yellowstone National Park.

**1872**    A Civil Rights Act enacted by Congress provides for the right of Negroes to serve on juries and guarantees them equal rights in public places.

**1918**    A young girl from Noxopater, Mississippi, makes headlines in New York as she submits to a public haircut. She is Marjorie Lawrence and her hair ("the most beautiful hair in Mississippi") is cut off and auctioned, lock by lock, so that she might invest the proceeds in Liberty Bonds "to help Uncle Sam." (WORLD WAR I)

**1932**    The disappearance of a baby shocks the entire world as the 20-month-old son of Colonel and Mrs. Charles A. Lindbergh is kidnapped from his bed in the Lindbergh home on Sourland Mountain near Hopewell, New Jersey. (*See April 3, May 12, September 19.*)

**1945**    Just 30 hours after his return from the Big Three Conference at Yalta, President Franklin D. Roosevelt makes a personal report of the meeting to a joint session of Congress. The President, seated in his wheel chair, says, in opening his remarks: "I know you will pardon me for sitting down, but I've been away on a 14,000-mile trip. . . ." (WORLD WAR II)

**1949**    Joe Louis, world heavyweight boxing champion, announces his retirement from the ring after an all-time record reign of 11 years, 8 months, and 1 week. (His retirement did not last very long, however, for on September 27, 1950, Louis attempted to regain his title by meeting Ezzard Charles in New York City. The match was won by Charles in the 15th round, thus retaining the title he won in 1949 from "Jersey Joe" Walcott. )

**1954** Five congressmen are wounded in Washington as three Puerto Rican nationalists fire wildly from the gallery in the House of Representatives.

**1954** The United States explodes a hydrogen bomb of more than 10 megatons at Bikini, completing its first H-bomb tests in the Pacific.

**1961** The Peace Corps is established by executive order of President John F. Kennedy.

**1962** New York City welcomes Lieutenant Colonel John Glenn, Jr., his family and fellow astronauts with a traditional ticker-tape parade.

**1963** Mrs. Cecil Blaffer Hudson of Houston, Texas, wins a record divorce settlement of $6,500,000 from her former husband, Edward J. Hudson. (*See August 3.*)

## MARCH 2

**1836** At a convention held in Texas, 55 local men issue a proclamation declaring the territory's independence from Mexico. Before the session is adjourned, David Burnett is chosen president of the new state and Sam Houston appointed commander of its military forces.

**1867** Congress enacts the Tenure of Office Bill, overriding the veto of President Johnson. The act prohibits the President from removing any civil official without the express consent of the Senate. (It was this act, or more specifically his dismissal of Secretary of War Stanton, that led to the impeachment charges against President Johnson.)

**1877** Shortly before dawn, the president of the Senate announces to a joint session of Congress the election of Rutherford B. Hayes as President of the United States, following the disputed election of 1876. (A special Electoral Commission made the decision on party lines and agreed to recognize Hayes as victor over Samuel J. Tilden, Democrat. In return, Hayes, a Republican, placated the Democrats by agreeing to withdraw federal troops from some of the Southern states.)

**1899** Congress establishes Mount Rainier National Park, Washington.

**1923** A new weekly newsmagazine entitled *Time* is published for the first time by Briton Hadden and Henry R. Luce.

**1927** Babe Ruth of the New York Yankees becomes the highest-paid baseball player to date when he signs a 3-year contract guaranteeing him $70,000 a year. (Beginning in 1914 and ending in 1938, Ruth's baseball earnings amounted to $925,900. In addition, he collected $41,500 in World Series bonuses.)

**1939** Eugenio, Cardinal Pacelli, is elected Pope on the death of Pius XI. The new Pope announces he will assume the name of Pius XII.

**1945** Units of the U.S. Ninth Army reach the Rhine River at a point opposite Düsseldorf, Germany. (WORLD WAR II)

**1949** The *Lucky Lady II*, an Air Force B-50 Superfortress, completes the first nonstop round-the-world flight at Fort Worth, Texas. (The bomber covered 23,452 miles in 94 hours, 1 minute.)

## MARCH 3

**1837** Congress increases the membership of the U.S. Supreme Court from seven to nine justices.

**1845** Florida enters the Union as the 27th state.

**1847** Alexander Graham Bell, the chief inventor of the telephone, is born in Edinburgh, Scotland.

**1847** Members of both houses of Congress vote to install gas lighting in the Capitol and on the grounds of the building.

**1849** The U.S. Department of the Interior is created by Act of Congress.

**1863** One more justice is added to the Supreme Court by act of Congress, bringing the full membership up to 10. (In 1869, the Court was again reduced to nine justices.)

**1871** Congress authorizes the Civil Service Commission, the first members being appointed by President Grant.

**1879** Mrs. Belva Ann Lockwood of Washington, D.C., becomes the first woman lawyer admitted to practice before the Supreme Court.

**1911** Robert E. Peary receives a decoration and the thanks of the U.S. Congress for his expedition to the North Pole in 1909.

**1915** In New York, the *première* of one of the world's greatest silent motion pictures takes place. The film is David Wark Griffith's *The Birth of a Nation* with a cast that includes Lillian Gish, Mae Marsh, and Wallace Reid.

**1917** President Woodrow Wilson denounces a Senate filibuster, masterminded by 11 senators, aimed at preventing passage of a bill to arm American merchant ships. The angry President charges that "... A little group of wilful men ... have rendered the great Government of the United States helpless and contemptible.... The only remedy is that the rules of the Senate shall be so altered that it can act...."

**1918** Peace is signed by the Russian Bolsheviks and Germany, Austria-Hungary, and Turkey at Brest-Litovsk.

**1931** "The Star-Spangled Banner" is designated by act of Congress and approved by President Hoover to be "the national anthem of the United States of America."

**1945**   German flying bombs are directed against the British Isles in daylight for the first time since the autumn of 1944. (WORLD WAR II)

## MARCH 4

**NOTE**   This was the original Inauguration Day in U.S. history until 1937 when President Franklin D. Roosevelt was sworn in for his second term, thus complying with the terms of the Twentieth Amendment establishing January 20 (which see) as the new inaugural date.*

**1789**   The first U.S. Congress, meeting under the new Federal Constitution, convenes in Federal Hall in New York City. (It had to adjourn, however, a quorum of its members not being present.)

**1791**   Vermont, the 14th state, enters the Union.

**1801**   Thomas Jefferson, the third President of the United States, is the first President to be inaugurated in Washington. The new President takes the oath of office in the Senate Chamber. (In his inaugural address, Jefferson promised "Equal and exact justice to all men, of whatever state or persuasion, religious or political; peace, commerce, and honest friendship with all nations—entangling alliances with none.")

**1829**   A tremendous crowd turns out for the inauguration of Andrew Jackson, the seventh President of the United States. Crowds jam the White House, breaking furniture, china, and glass. Fearful for the President's safety, White House aides persuade him to leave the building and retire to Gadsby's Hotel. (The mob was finally induced to leave the White House after servants placed tubs of punch out on the lawns.)

**1850**   Too ill to speak himself, Senator John C. Calhoun of South Carolina sits by while his bitter attack on Henry Clay's Compromise of 1850 is read to members of the Senate by Senator Mason of Virginia. Calhoun's speech warns the Senate that "the South will be forced to choose between abolition and secession.... The Southern States ... cannot remain, as things now are, consistently with honor and safety in the Union...."

* In addition to those inaugurations singled out above for special interest, the following inaugurals took place on various March 4ths: George Washington, 1793; John Adams, 1797; Thomas Jefferson, second term, 1805; James Madison, 1809; James Madison, second term, 1813; James Monroe, 1817; John Quincy Adams, 1825; Andrew Jackson, second term, 1833; Martin Van Buren, 1837; William Henry Harrison, 1841; James Knox Polk, 1845; Zachary Taylor, 1849; Franklin Pierce, 1853; James Buchanan, 1857; Ulysses S. Grant, 1869; Ulysses S. Grant, second term, 1873; James Abram Garfield, 1881; Grover Cleveland, first term, 1885; Benjamin Harrison, 1889; William McKinley, 1897; William McKinley, second term, 1901; Theodore Roosevelt, 1905; William Howard Taft, 1909; Woodrow Wilson, 1913; Warren G. Harding, 1921; Calvin Coolidge, 1925; Herbert Hoover, 1929.

**1861**   With the nation on the brink of a civil war, a tense Washington crowd witnesses the inauguration of Abraham Lincoln as the 16th President of the United States. The President is solemn as he tells the assembly: "In *your* hands, my dissatisfied fellow countrymen, and not in *mine*, is the momentous issue of civil war. The government will assail *you*. You can have no conflict, without being yourselves the aggressors. *You* have no oath registered in heaven to destroy the government, while *I* shall have the most solemn one to preserve, protect and defend it. . . . I am loath to close. We are not enemies, but friends. We must not be enemies. . . ."

**1865**   Abraham Lincoln, speaking at his second inaugural, pleads for an early end to national strife: "With malice toward none, with charity for all, with firmness in the right, as God gives us to see the right, let us strive on to finish the work we are in, to bind up the nation's wounds, to care for him who shall have borne the battle, and for his widow and his orphan; to do all which may achieve and cherish a just and lasting peace among ourselves and with all nations. . . ."

**1893**   Grover Cleveland is inaugurated for his second, nonconsecutive term of office. (As he took the oath of office, Mr. Cleveland was hardly aware of the fact that his inaugural would plague historians for generations to come. When he was sworn into office in 1885, he had become the nation's 22nd President. In 1889, he was succeeded by Benjamin Harrison, the 23rd President. Now, in 1893, he was the same man who had occupied the White House in 1885, but was he the 22nd or 24th President? The *Congressional Directory* has changed its onetime stand and now lists Cleveland as the 22nd *and* 24th President, much to the consternation of those who claim that one President cannot be both. )

**1896**   Queen Victoria presides at a state dinner in London for a visiting rajah from India. The guests are startled to see the rajah lift up his finger bowl and drink from it, evidently unaware of its real purpose. To save him embarrassment, the Queen picks up her bowl and drinks from it too, all of the guests following the Queen's lead.

**1917**   Jeannette Rankin (R., Mont.) takes her seat in the House of Representatives, the first woman to serve in either house of Congress.

**1933**   As millions of worried Americans sit by their radio 'ets, a hundred thousand more in Washington witness the inauguration of Franklin Delano Roosevelt as the 32nd President of the United States, the first Democrat to move into the White House since Woodrow Wilson left it in 1921. The new President, aware of the fear that has strangled the Depression-ridden American public, offers a refreshing breath of hope and confidence in his inaugural address: "This is pre-eminently the time to speak the truth, the whole truth, frankly and boldly. Nor need we shrink from honestly facing conditions in our country today. This great nation will endure as it has endured, will revive and prosper. So first of all let me assert my firm belief that the only thing we have to fear is fear itself." *

**1942**   The Stage Door Canteen, a war service of the American Theatre Wing for men in the armed forces, opens its doors on West 44th Street in New York City.

**1964**   The powerful head of the International Brotherhood of Teamsters, James R. Hoffa, is convicted by a federal jury in Chattanooga, Tennessee, of attempting in 1962 to influence a jury that was trying him in that year. (On the following July 26, Hoffa was convicted again, this time in Chicago, on charges of fraud in the use of his union's pension fund.)

## MARCH 5

**1770**   The Boston Massacre: British troops, irritated by colonial jeers and taunts, fire on some civilians assembled on King Street in Boston, killing five and wounding half a dozen. (But the American patriots were stirred up. John Adams wrote in 1816: "Not the battle of Lexington, nor the surrender of Burgoyne or Cornwallis, were more important events in American history than the Battle of King Street on March 5, 1770.")

**1821**   President James Monroe, the fifth President of the United States, is inaugurated for his second term of office. (March 4 that year fell on a Sunday.)

**1868**   To decide on the charges leveled against President Andrew Johnson, the U.S. Senate is organized into a Court of Impeachment. Chief Justice Salmon P. Chase will serve as the presiding officer.

**1875**   Andrew Johnson of Tennessee returns to the U.S. Senate, the first former President of the nation to become a Senator after his Presidential term of office had expired. As the new Senator enters the chamber, he is touched when he sees his desk covered with flowers. On hand are 13 of the 35 senators who had voted to impeach him in 1868. (Johnson had been a member of the Senate, 1857–61, before his election as Vice President in 1864.)

**1877**   Rutherford B. Hayes is inaugurated 19th president of the United States. (*See March 2, November 7.*)

**1917**   President Woodrow Wilson is sworn into office for his second term.

**1933**   On his first full day of work as President, Franklin D. Roosevelt proclaims a national "bank holiday" effective the next day, to save the country's tottering banks. Americans find them-

* The President may have taken his famous line, "The only thing we have to fear is fear itself," from Thoreau who, in his *Journal* under date of September 7, 1851, wrote: "Nothing is so much to be feared as fear...."

selves stranded for pocket or household money, but some communities arrange a system of temporary "scrip" payments. Local merchants, in some cases, permit small checks to be cashed. Radio City Music Hall in New York announces it will sell tickets of admission to patrons having "scrip" in their possession.

**1933**  Election returns in Germany give the Nazis and their Nationalist allies 52 percent of the seats in the Reichstag. (This was the last "free" election in Germany until after World War II. The elections under Hitler were merely to indicate a "Ja" or "Nein" for his continued rule, and very few "Neins" were registered.)

**1934**  The first Mother-in-Law Day is celebrated at Amarillo, Texas. The guest of honor is Mrs. W. F. Donald, the mother-in-law of Gene Howe, local newspaper editor and the man responsible for the celebration.

**1946**  Before an audience of 2,000 at Westminster College in Fulton, Missouri, Winston Churchill delivers a memorable address, one of the first to alert the world to the onset of the "Cold War." The former British Prime Minister charges in his speech: ". . . From Stettin in the Baltic to Trieste in the Adriatic, an Iron Curtain has descended across the Continent. . . ."

**1953**  Premier Joseph Stalin of Russia, 73, dies in his apartment in the Kremlin in Moscow after being stricken with a cerebral hemorrhage on March 1. (The body of the dictator was interred beside Lenin's in the Lenin mausoleum on Red Square March 9 after the most spectacular funeral in Soviet history. This was before a wave of anti-Stalinism swept Russia and the Communist Party in 1956, during which time the Party leaders sought to indict Stalin for many intolerant and cruel acts committed during his regime.)

## MARCH 6

**1475**  Birthday of Michelangelo Buonarroti, great Italian painter, sculptor, and architect.

**1836**  On this day, the 13th of the siege of the Alamo, a mission compound in San Antonio, Santa Anna's Mexicans are able finally to overwhelm the tiny but courageous band of Texan defenders. (When it was all over, the 187 Americans, including Davy Crockett, were killed and all that remained was the ringing battle cry, "Remember the Alamo!" a permanent testimonial to one of the most gallant stands in warfare.)

**1857**  The U.S. Supreme Court hands down one of its most controversial rulings when it decides, in the Dred Scott case, that Scott, a Negro slave who had once lived in the "free" state of Illinois, could not sue for his freedom in a federal court. (In effect, the tribunal held that a slave was not a citizen, but was the property of his master. Chief Justice Taney went so far as to say that the Constitution was made by and for white men.)

**1896**     Charles Brady King rides around the streets of Detroit in his "Horseless Carriage," the first automobile to appear on the streets of what subsequently was to become the "Motor Capital of America." (When his vehicle broke down on one of the city's main streets, spectators jeered, "Get a horse!" a cry that was to be heard regularly during the next decade.)

**1938**     To win a bet for 40 dollars, Thomas Garson of Chicago eats 22 hamburgers and 2 quarts of ice cream in 25 minutes.

**1947**     The Supreme Court upholds a lower court's $710,000 fine against John L. Lewis and the United Mine Workers union for their illegal 1946 strike.

**1948**     Mrs. Florence Hubbard of Chicago identifies the comedian Jack Benny as "The Walking Man," thus ending a radio quiz program that has kept the entire nation in suspense. (Mr. Benny was chosen to represent the mystery man because "he is so tight he won't spend the money for cab fare." The 10-week program raised $1,500,000 for the American Heart Association and won for Mrs. Hubbard a "jackpot" of $22,500 in various prizes.)

**1953**     An announcement from Moscow states that Georgi Malenkov has succeeded the late Joseph Stalin as premier of the Soviet Union.

**1957**     The merged former colonies of the Gold Coast and British Togoland in Africa become the independent state of Ghana. The sovereign nation's prime minister is Kwame Nkrumah. On hand to witness the birth of the new Negro nation are Vice President Richard M. Nixon, representing President Eisenhower, and the Reverend Martin Luther King, Jr., the American integration leader.

**1961**     President John F. Kennedy issues an executive order "to insure that Americans of all colors and beliefs will have equal access to employment within the Government and with those who do business with the Government . . ."

**1962**     In his first public appearance since his release from a Russian prison, Francis Gary Powers, pilot of the U-2 reconnaissance plane shot down over the Soviet Union in 1960, tells his story before a hearing of the Senate Armed Services Committee.

# MARCH 7

**1850**     Webster's Seventh of March Speech: Senator Daniel Webster pleads for the preservation of the Union in a brilliant 3-hour speech on the floor of the Senate. The great spokesman for the North, fully aware that he has chosen the unpopular course, comes out in support of Clay's Compromise Bill of 1850: "I wish to speak today not as a Massachusetts man, nor as a Northern man, but as an American and a member of the Senate of the United States. . . . I speak today for the preservation of the Union. . . . I speak today out of a solicitous and anxious heart for the restoration to the country of that quiet and that harmony which makes the blessings of this Union so rich and so dear to us all...."

**1876** Alexander Graham Bell receives a patent for his invention of the telephone.

**1908** A minor controversy breaks out in Cincinnati when Mayor Markbreit of that city tells the City Council that no woman is physically fit to operate an automobile.

**1928** Americans are reading one of the "bestsellers" of the 1920's, Thornton Wilder's *The Bridge of San Luis Rey*. Advertisements claim the novel has sold 100,000 copies in 90 days.

**1932** In the midst of the worst depression ever to hit the United States, 3,000 men riot for jobs at the Detroit plant of the Ford Motor Company, four of them losing their lives in the melee. (Ford had announced that a few plant jobs were available.)

**1933** As the "New Deal" gets under way, a good many Americans are commenting about the first woman to serve in a President's Cabinet. She is Madam Frances Perkins, chosen by President Roosevelt to serve as Secretary of Labor. (She served from March 4, 1933, to June 30, 1945.)

**1936** Adolf Hitler orders his troops to march into the Rhineland, thus breaking the Treaty of Versailles and the Locarno Pact.

**1940** In a mad dash to safety, the British liner *Queen Elizabeth* arrives in New York harbor, safe from Nazi submarine and air attacks. (WORLD WAR II)

**1945** The U.S. First Army crosses the Rhine River at Remagen, south of Cologne, Germany. (WORLD WAR II)

**1957** The Egyptian government reopens the Suez Canal for daylight use by vessels of up to 500 tons. An announcement says that "all ships that pay tolls to Egypt will be allowed transit" through the canal. (*See July 26.*)

**1965** An attempted civil rights protest march to Montgomery, Alabama, comes to a violent end in the Alabama town of Selma, when state troopers and a sheriff's posse advance on hundreds of Negro and white demonstrators. Eighty-four of the marchers are injured after they are attacked by tear gas, whips, and clubs. (Alabama Governor George C. Wallace's comment: "We saved their lives by stopping the march...") (*See March 9*)

## MARCH 8

**1841** Birthday of Oliver Wendell Holmes, foremost American jurist of his time, justice of the U.S. Supreme Court, 1902–32. ("The great dissenter whose dissent now prevails.")

**1864** Ulysses S. Grant, about to be put in command of all the Union armies, arrives in Washington for the first time in his life. (The general was described by a Washington journalist as "a short, round-shouldered man in a very tarnished major-general's uniform. ... He had no gait, no station, no manner. ...")

**1894**    New York State becomes the first state to pass a law requiring dogs to be licensed, the statute providing "for the better protection of lost and strayed animals and for securing the rights of the owners thereof. ...."

**1917**    Riots and strikes in St. Petersburg mark the beginning of the Russian Revolution.

**1923**    As the result of a poll conducted by *The Women's Weekly* in Paris, 14,000 French women reply that of all the men in the world, outside of France, they would prefer American husbands to those of any other nationality. (As twenty thousand answers were tallied in all, American men were obviously the choice of a large percentage of French women.)

**1939**    Department of Agriculture statisticians announce that the annual diet of an average resident of the United States includes 62 pounds of beef, 102 pounds of sugar, 177 pounds of flour, 180 pounds of potatoes, 918 pounds of milk.

**1944**    French authorities in Algiers adopt an ordinance reforming the status of Moslem Algerians, enunciating the principle that French Moslems of Algeria shall henceforth enjoy the same rights and shall submit to the same duties as French non-Moslems.

**1953**    A survey undertaken by the Census Bureau reveals the fact that in 2 years' time the nation's farmers have decreased by some 239,000.

**1961**    The U.S. nuclear submarine *Patrick Henry* arrives at the Scottish naval base of Holy Loch from Charleston, South Carolina, after a record-making underseas journey of 66 days, 22 hours. This is the first American submarine to use the base in Scotland, under terms negotiated between the United States and Great Britain in 1960.

## MARCH 9

**1789**    George Washington, visiting the patriot Benjamin Harrison, comments about his forthcoming inauguration as President of the United States: "... My movements to the chair of government will be accompanied by feelings not unlike those of a culprit who is going to the place of his execution."

**1822**    Charles Graham of New York City receives the first patent for artificial teeth.

**1832**    Abraham Lincoln, a resident of New Salem, runs for his first political office, announcing his candidacy for the Illinois legislature in the columns of the *Sangamo* (Illinois) *Journal:* "I have no wealth or popular relations to recommend me. My case is thrown exclusively upon the independent voters of this county, and if elected they will have conferred a favor upon me, for which I shall be unremitting in my labors to compensate. But if the good people in their wisdom shall see fit to keep me in the background, I have been too familiar with disappointments to be very much chagrined. . . ." (He lost the election that followed.)

**1858** The grandfather of the modern-day soda fountain appears for the first time in Lowell, Massachusetts, the work of Gustavus D. Dows of that city.

**1860** Niimi Buzennokami, the first Japanese ambassador accredited to the United States, arrives in San Francisco, accompanied by a legation of 74 men.

**1862** The ironclad warships, the Northern *Monitor* and the Confederate *Merrimac,* battle for four hours off Hampton Roads, Virginia. (Some historians claim the engagement ended in a draw, but while both ships suffered damages, the *Merrimac's* commander decided to retreat to Norfolk, thus giving the *Monitor* at the very least a moral victory.)

**1916** Mexican soldiers allied with the revolutionary general, Pancho Villa, cross the American border and attack the town of Columbus, New Mexico, killing 8 civilians and 7 U.S. soldiers. In reprisal, American troops pursue the raiders and kill 120 of them, penetrating some 15 miles into Mexico.

**1933** Called into special session by President Roosevelt, Congress begins its "Hundred Days," enacting into law many of the principal proposals and policies of the New Deal.

**1947** One of the longest strikes in American labor history comes to an end after 440 days when members of Local 180, United Automobile Workers of America, settle their differences with the Case Manufacturing Company of Racine, Wisconsin.

**1965** White racists in Selma, Alabama, savagely attack the Reverend James J. Reeb, a white minister from Boston, Massachusetts, one of the many clergymen in Selma aiding the civil rights drive there to insure equal voting rights for local Negroes. (Reverend Reeb died 2 days later. Four white men were arrested as his assailants.) (*See March 13*)

## MARCH 10

**1775** Daniel Boone and a company of frontiersmen are hired by the Transylvania Company to cut a road through the wilderness to the Kentucky River.

**1862** The first paper money of the U.S. government is issued, available in notes valued at $5, $10, $20, $50, $100, $500, and $1000.

**1876** Alexander Graham Bell secures his place in history as he transmits the first clear and distinct telephone message in Boston. (His words, "Come here, Watson, I want you," were directed to his assistant, Thomas A. Watson, located in the same house as Bell, but on another floor. Both men had telephone receivers in their respective rooms, thus enabling them to speak with each other.)

**1880**     The Salvation Army, already functioning in England, begins its work in the United States as Commissioner George Scott Railton and seven women assistants arrive in New York from Britain. The group immediately proceed to Castle Garden on the Battery to hold their first American religious service.

**1888**     John L. Sullivan and his English challenger, Charlie Mitchell, stage an exciting fight at Apremont, France, in a ring pitched on grass at the edge of a woodland. (Sullivan started out in this prizefight by throwing his hat into the ring, thus reviving an old boxing custom. The two men fought for 3 hours, but although Mitchell was knocked down 15 times, the 44-round bout ended in a draw.)

**1938**     Leslie Hore-Belisha, British War Secretary, tells the House of Commons that Great Britain will never again send masses of men to fight and die in the mud of future European battlefields.

**1945**     B-29 bombers of the U.S. Air Force begin their incendiary raids on Japan. A 15-mile area of Tokyo is set afire. (WORLD WAR II)

**1948**     Jan Masaryk, foreign minister of Czechoslovakia, plunges to his death in Prague. The free world debates the question: Did Masaryk commit suicide or was he pushed out the window by Communists?

**1949**     Mildred E. Gillars, better known to former soldiers of World War II as "Axis Sally," is convicted of treason for her wartime broadcasts for the Nazis. (Her sentence: 30 years' imprisonment and a fine of $10,000.)

## MARCH 11

**1810**     Archduchess Marie Louise, the 18-year-old daughter of Emperor Francis I of Austria, becomes the wife of the Emperor Napoleon. (The bride had never met Napoleon; nor did she see him on her wedding day. Napoleon was represented at the brilliant cathedral wedding in Vienna by a proxy, Marshal Berthier.)

**1861**     Delegates to the Confederate Congress meeting at Montgomery, Alabama, adopt the Constitution of the Confederacy.

**1888**     Blizzard of '88: a violent snowstorm raging along the Atlantic Coast begins to cripple New York City, with transportation and communication lines completely disrupted. (The snow kept coming down until March 14, marooning hundreds of thousands in their homes and places of business. More than two hundred persons lost their lives from cold and exposure, and in some city streets the snow piled up as high as the first floor of brownstone houses.)

**1917**    Czar Nicholas II of Russia orders the Duma to disband. Members of that parliamentary body refuse to accede to the Czar's demand.

**1927**    More than six thousand persons cheer veteran showman Samuel ("Roxy") Rothafel as he opens his spectacular new Roxy Theatre in New York. The featured film for the opening week stars Gloria Swanson and John Boles in *The Loves of Sunya.*

**1930**    Former President and Chief Justice William Howard Taft is buried in the National Cemetery at Arlington, Virginia, the first President of the United States to be interred there.

**1941**    President Roosevelt signs into law the hotly debated Lend-Lease Bill, providing for the transfer to Great Britain and other nations at war with the Axis specified military equipment and materials. (Five minutes after he signed the act, the President approved the first list of war goods to be sent immediately to Great Britain and Greece.) (WORLD WAR II)

**1942**    In the dead of night, General Douglas MacArthur and a party of twenty aides leave Bataan Peninsula in four torpedo boats on the first lap of their trip to Australia. (WORLD WAR II)

**1954**    A detailed report prepared by the Department of the Army accuses Senator Joseph R. McCarthy (R., Wis.) and Roy Cohn, chief counsel of the Senate Investigations Subcommittee, of using pressure to obtain favored treatment for Private G. David Schine, a former consultant to the Committee.

**1964**    Senator Carl Hayden (D., Ariz.) establishes the all-time record for service in the U.S. Senate. As of this date, the Arizona lawmaker has been a member of the Senate for 37 years and 7 days. This is one day longer than the previous service record of Senator Francis E. Warren (R., Wyo.) who put in 37 years and 6 days, starting in 1890.

**1965**    After a group of almost one hundred civil rights pickets spend the day marching in front of the White House in Washington, demanding support for equal rights of Negroes in Alabama, a dozen of them march into the mansion and stage a sit-in protest that lasts more than 6 hours. The demonstrators are finally taken to local police stations.


# MARCH 12

**1664**    New Jersey becomes a British colony as King Charles II grants land in the New World to his brother James, Duke of York.

**1912**    Captain Albert Berry performs the first parachute jump from an airplane at Jefferson Barracks, Missouri.

**1912**    The Girl Scouts of America have their beginning in Savannah, Georgia, when Mrs. Juliette Gordon Low of that city organizes the first troop. (Actually, the first troop was called "Girl Guides," but the name was changed to "Girl Scouts" a year later.)

**1932**    Ivar Kreuger, the so-called "Swedish Match King," carefully draws the blinds in his Paris apartment and then commits suicide. (Immediately afterwards, the world learned that Kreuger's mammoth financial empire was nothing but a house of cards and that thousands of investors have been wiped out.)

**1932**    In the Lindbergh kidnapping case, Professor John F. Condon, better known in the Bronx, New York, as "Jafsie," makes the headlines by meeting Bruno Richard Hauptmann, the alleged kidnapper, in Woodlawn Cemetery in that New York borough.

**1933**    President Franklin D. Roosevelt, in office just 6 days, introduces a new feature to American life when he broadcasts his first "Fireside Chat." Speaking from the Diplomatic Reception Room in the White House, the President, in a friendly, informal manner, explains to the nation just how the reopening of the country's banks will be accomplished. (Present at the birth of that first Fireside Chat were Robert Trout, a CBS news commentator; Carleton Smith, an NBC news commentator; and Clyde Hunt, then a CBS engineer.)

**1938**    The tiny country of Austria is invaded by Adolf Hitler's Nazi troops. Chancellor Kurt von Schuschnigg, ousted from office, tells his Austrian countrymen in a radio broadcast: "We are yielding to force. And so I take my leave of the Austrian people with a heartfelt wish: 'God Save Austria!' " (The next day Hitler announced that Austrian Anschluss, or union with Greater Germany, would take place.)

**1940**    Finland surrenders to Russia and a truce between the two nations is signed in Moscow. (WORLD WAR II)

**1945**    Governor Thomas E. Dewey signs a bill in Albany making New York the first state to set up a permanent commission to eliminate discrimination in employment.

**1947**    Truman Doctrine: President Truman asks Congress for $400,000,000 to be used for military and economic aid to Greece and Turkey. The President says that American aid is necessary to help those nations who are trying to withstand the inroads of Communism: "I believe that it must be the policy of the United States to support free peoples who are resisting attempted subjugation by armed minorities or by outside pressures...." (Ten days later, Congress approved the President's request.)

## MARCH 13

**1665**    Samuel Pepys records in his diary: "This day my wife begun to wear light colored locks, quite white almost, which, though it makes her look very pretty, yet, not being natural, vexes me. I will not have her wear them."

**1852**    For the first time, in the New York *Lantern,* a cartoon appears depicting "Uncle Sam" as the symbol of the United States.

In the drawing by Frank Bellew, shipowners of Great Britain and the United States are shown in keen competition, with "John Bull" backing the Cunard Line and "Uncle Sam" standing by observing the scene.

**1868** Impeachment proceedings against President Andrew Johnson get under way in the Senate. Chief Justice Salmon P. Chase of the U.S. Supreme Court is the presiding officer. (*See May 16, May 26.*)

**1923** Advertisement in New York newspapers: "Radio receiving set, latest improved foolproof design, with a concealed tone speaker, three tubes and batteries. Anyone can operate it. You do not need head phones. No permission from landlord necessary."

**1925** The governor of Tennessee signs into law a bill making it unlawful for any teacher in any of the state's universities, normal, and all other public schools, to teach any theory that denies the story of the divine creation of man as taught in the Bible. (This was to forestall the teaching of evolution, the theory that man has descended from a lower order of animals.)

**1933** Banks throughout the United States begin to open following the "bank holiday" proclaimed on March 5 by President Roosevelt.

**1938** In one of the great "purge" trials being conducted in the Soviet Union, several prominent Communist leaders are found guilty of treason against the State. Some of the individuals so convicted are Rykov, former president of the Council of Commissars; Bukharin, former editor of *Pravda;* and Yagoda, former chief of the secret police agency, OGPU.

**1954** On the eve of his 75th birthday, Dr. Albert Einstein sends a message to the Emergency Civil Liberties Conference at Princeton, New Jersey, urging intellectuals "to refuse to cooperate in any undertaking that violates the constitutional rights of the individual."

**1961** At a White House reception for 250 Latin American diplomats and Congressional leaders, President John F. Kennedy calls for a new Alliance for Progress. The President urges South American republics to join the United States in a 10-year, 10-point program that will "transform the American continents into a vast crucible of revolutionary ideas and efforts . . . an example to all the world that liberty and progress walk hand in hand. . . ."

**1965** As hundreds of protest demonstrations are held all over the nation, accompanied by demands for equal rights for the Negroes of Alabama, Governor George C. Wallace of that state flies to Washington for a conference with President Lyndon B. Johnson. The President tells the segregation-minded Governor that all people will be protected in Alabama, by federal troops if necessary, "whether the Governor likes it or not." After the meeting, the President says at a televised news conference: "What happened in Selma,

Alabama, was an American tragedy. The blows that were received, the blood that was shed ... must strengthen the determination of each of us to bring full and equal justice to all of our people...."
*(See March 15, 19, 21)*

## MARCH 14

**1743**   The first town meeting, later to become famous throughout New England, is held in Faneuil Hall, Boston.

**1794**   Eli Whitney receives a patent on his invention, the cotton gin, a contrivance to separate the cotton from its seed. (A year later, cotton farmers observed that Whitney's invention made it possible for one man to clean fifty pounds of cotton a day as compared to a single pound done by hand before the appearance of the gin.)

**1812**   The U.S. government authorizes the issue of the first war bonds, floated for the purchase of military equipment for an enlarged army in preparation for the War of 1812.

**1879**   Birthday of Albert Einstein, world-famous physicist and originator of the theory of relativity.

**1923**   President Harding files his income tax with the Collector of Internal Revenue in Washington, the first President to have to submit an accounting of his income and pay a tax on it. Statisticians estimate that the President's tax amounts to almost $18,000.

**1933**   After receiving a request from President Roosevelt, Congress approves a measure authorizing the sale and manufacture of 3.2 beer. (This meant that beer containing not more than 3.2 per cent of alcoholic content could be manufactured and sold legally.)

**1938**   Adolf Hitler, jubilant over the submission of Austria to his Nazi troops, enters Vienna in triumph.

**1950**   After a prolonged drought, the City of New York, fearful for its scant water supply, hires Dr. Wallace E. Howell, director of the Mount Washington Observatory, as its official "rainmaker." Dr. Howell will receive $100 a day for his efforts to create rainfall. (Whether it was coincidence or not, a snowstorm occurred a month later and then some rain.)

**1964**   A jury in Dallas, Texas, convicts Jack L. Ruby of the "murder with malice" of Lee Harvey Oswald, President John F. Kennedy's alleged assassin. The jury recommends that Ruby's punishment be death, but his defense counsel calls for a new trial outside of Dallas.

## MARCH 15

**1767**   Birthday of Andrew Jackson, seventh President of the United States.

**1820**   Maine, the 23rd state, is admitted into the Union.

**1913**    Just 11 days after his inauguration, Woodrow Wilson holds the first open Presidential press conference in history. All newsmen in Washington who cover White House news are invited to the Executive Offices. (This meeting, attended by some 125 newsmen, was suggested by Joseph P. Tumulty, the President's private secretary. Previously, White House news was distributed by press releases or by calling in specially selected reporters.)

**1916**    General John J. Pershing is given command of 12,000 soldiers and ordered to proceed into Mexico to capture the revolutionary Mexican leader Pancho Villa.

**1917**    The Romanov dynasty comes to an end as Czar Nicholas II abdicates from his throne in favor of the Grand Duke Mikhail. (On the next day, the Grand Duke abdicated, leaving the government in the hands of a provisional body.)

**1919**    One thousand veterans of the American Expeditionary Force meet in Paris to form the American Legion.

**1934**    Samuel Insull, the former American financier, flees from Athens, Greece, dressed as a woman, to evade extradition to the United States for fraud.

**1939**    Despite guarantees given by Germany to France and Great Britain and despite Adolf Hitler's declaration in the Reichstag that Germany had no further territorial claims toward the Czechoslovak Republic, Nazi troops cross the frontiers of Bohemia and Moravia and occupy what remains of Czechoslovakia after the Treaty of Munich. (Hitler entered Prague with his troops and immediately thereafter ordered a program of mass arrests and deportations.)

**1953**    Premier Malenkov of Russia, the successor to Joseph Stalin, says in one of his first public statements that international disputes can be settled by "peaceful means."

**1953**    President Eisenhower is urged by the organization Freedom House to "check the irresponsible tactics of Senator McCarthy" and the "character butchering" by congressional committees. The organization warns that the United States' freedom is being whittled away by "probes which slander the innocent and fail to clarify the crucial distinction between conspiratorial conduct . . . and independent thought and the search for truth. . . ."

**1956**    Cheers and rave reviews greet the first performance in New York of an entrancing new musical play, *My Fair Lady,* based on George Bernard Shaw's play, *Pygmalion.* Playing the star roles of Eliza Doolittle and Henry Higgins are Julie Andrews and Rex Harrison. (It ran for 6½ years in New York and when it closed on September 29, 1962, 3,750,000 people had paid $20,000,000 to see it there. It was the longest-running musical in the history of Broadway theatre and the film rights to the play were sold to Hollywood for the record price of $5,500,000.)

**1961**   At a London conference of British Commonwealth prime ministers, the Union of South Africa announces its decision to withdraw from the Commonwealth when it becomes a republic on the following May 31. (This action was taken after Asian and African Commonwealth member states had denounced South Africa's policies of racial segregation.)

**1965**   Before a specially called night session of Congress and with millions of Americans watching on television, President Lyndon B. Johnson demands immediate action on new legislation which will remove every barrier set up to prevent citizens from trying to register and vote. The President, obviously shaken by weeks of race violence in Alabama, says: "... The harsh fact is that in many places in this country men and women are kept from voting simply because they are Negroes. Every device of which human ingenuity is capable has been used to deny this right...." (The President was interrupted 36 times by applause and two standing ovations.)

## MARCH 16

**1751**   James Madison, fourth President of the United States, is born in Port Conway, Virginia.

**1802**   An Act of Congress authorizes the establishment of the U.S. Military Academy at West Point, New York.

**1825**   Note in the *New York Tribune:* "The Females who have so long been oppressed by their employers propose to meet at Palmo's Opera House this afternoon. An address is to be delivered, and there will be a discourse of excellent music. The Mayor and Common Council have been invited, together with gentlemen of the press."

**1830**   Just 31 shares of stock are traded on the New York Stock Exchange, the slowest day in the history of the Exchange.

**1850**   *The Scarlet Letter,* Nathaniel Hawthorne's great novel, is published for the first time.

**1882**   Senate approval is given to the treaty making the United States a member of the Red Cross.

**1918**   A comparatively unknown girl, Tallulah Bankhead, makes her New York debut in the play *The Squab Farm.* (Many people wanted to know how little Miss Bankhead received her unusual first name. The answer: she was named for a grandmother who was named after Tallulah Falls, Georgia.)

**1935**   Adolf Hitler scraps the Versailles Treaty and reestablishes universal military training in Germany.

**1945**   Japanese resistance on Iwo Jima comes to an end after one of the bloodiest battles in World War II. American casualties total more than 20,000, of which 4,300 were fatal.

**1950**   Despite the protests of dairy farmers, Congress votes to remove federal taxes on oleomargarine.

**1965** Gamal Abdel Nasser wins another 6-year term as president of the United Arab Republic and rolls up a record when he wins 99.999% of the vote. In an official report of yesterday's election in Egypt, President Nasser received 6,950,652 votes. Only 65 ballots in the entire nation were cast against him. (This was the third time Mr. Nasser had stood unopposed for "election" since he seized power in 1952.)

# MARCH 17

## St. Patrick's Day

**1897** James J. (Gentleman Jim) Corbett loses his heavyweight boxing crown to Bob Fitzsimmons in a 14-round match at Carson City, Nevada.

**1898** John P. Holland's submarine, said to be the first practical one in marine history, is submerged off Staten Island, New York, remaining under water for almost an hour and three-quarters.

**1905** Anna Eleanor Roosevelt marries her fifth cousin, Franklin Delano Roosevelt, in New York City. The bride is given in marriage by her uncle, President Theodore Roosevelt.

**1906** President Theodore Roosevelt, speaking before the members of the Gridiron Club in Washington, coins a new word, "muckrake." The practice of muckraking, says the President, is nothing more than the deplorable habit of making sweeping and unjust charges of corruption against public officials and corporations alike.

**1912** Mrs. Luther H. Gulick of Lake Sebago, Maine, announces the formation of a new organization for young girls, to be known as the Camp Fire Girls. The watchword of the new group is "Wohelo," coined from the first two letters of the words, Work, Health, and Love.

**1917** A great many men and women are shaking their heads when they read that the first bowling tournament for women is starting in St. Louis, Missouri. Almost a hundred women from all over the United States are participating.

**1931** Two of New York's most prominent clergymen, Rabbi Stephen S. Wise and the Reverend John Haynes Holmes, call on Governor Franklin D. Roosevelt and hand him a 4,000-word indictment against Mayor James J. Walker of New York City, citing 10 specific accusations of general negligence and misconduct on the Mayor's part. Both men urge the Governor to order an investigation of Walker and alleged corruption in city affairs.

**1938** Generalissimo Francisco Franco starts his bombings of the Loyalist-held city of Barcelona in the Spanish Civil War.

**1940** A ring of professional killers, known as "Murder, Incorporated," is uncovered in Brooklyn, New York.

**1941**    The National Gallery of Art in Washington, including the collections of Andrew W. Mellon and Samuel H. Kress, is opened by President Franklin D. Roosevelt.

**1948**    Brussels Pact: England, France, Belgium, the Netherlands, and Luxembourg sign a 50-year military alliance at Brussels, Belgium, designed primarily as a mutual assistance treaty against Communist aggression.

**1953**    The last price controls set up during World War II in the United States are discarded when the Office of Price Stabilization ends controls on steel, machine tools, sulphur, metal cans, and scarce metal alloys.

**1958**    The U.S. Navy successfully launches Vanguard I, a $3\frac{1}{4}$ pound satellite, into orbit around the earth.

## MARCH 18

**1837**    Birthday of Grover Cleveland, 22nd and 24th President of the United States.

**1902**    In a room in the Hotel di Milano, Milan, Italy, hastily converted into an improvised studio, Enrico Caruso records 10 arias for the Gramophone Company, thus becoming one of the first great artists to recognize the phonograph as an acceptable medium for musicians. (Caruso received a fee of $500 for these 10 records, said today to be the first completely satisfactory phonograph recordings.)

**1923**    A report from Berlin says that because of the inflated cost of butter, it is no longer being served to patrons of restaurants. As a result, Germans who dine out carry their own "butter boxes" with them, complete with a small supply of butter for their bread.

**1931**    The first electric shavers are ready for sale, ushering in a new age for American men who shave themselves at home or in their places of business.

**1937**    A national disaster takes place in New London, Texas, when an explosion in the Consolidated Public School there claims the lives of 426 persons, most of them children.

**1938**    The government of Mexico moves to appropriate all foreign-owned oil properties in that country, including the holdings of American oil companies. (Settlements with American companies were made 3 years later.)

**1944**    After it was announced that 1,500 alarm clocks would be offered for sale, some 2,500 women jam a Chicago department store, pushing aside guards and floorwalkers alike, all of them eager to buy the precious household commodity, almost unobtainable since the war began. (WORLD WAR II)

**1954**    RKO Pictures Corporation stockholders approve the sale of the company to Howard Hughes. After Mr. Hughes writes out a check for $23,489,478, he becomes the first individual ever to be the sole owner of a major motion-picture company.

**1962**    After more than 7 years of warfare, which cost 250,000 lives and $20,000,000,000, France and Algerian rebels reach accord in a truce. The agreement specifically guarantees Algeria the right to hold a referendum for self-determination. (*See July 3.*)

**1964**    Charlie Cooper, a 46-year-old London bachelor and a $29-a-week public utility clerk, wins the equivalent of $630,375.20 after betting 70 cents in an English soccer pool.

**1965**    Former King Farouk of Egypt, deposed from his throne by a military junta in 1952, dies in Rome after collapsing in a fashionable restaurant.

**1965**    During a two-man flight into space, a Russian cosmonaut squeezes out of a hatch in his capsule and "steps into space." He is Lieutenant Colonel Alexei Leonov and he remains outside the craft for 20 minutes, secured only by a long lifeline. While this spectacular feat is undertaken, a fellow cosmonaut, Colonel Pavel Belyayev, remains at the spacecraft's controls.

## MARCH 19

**NOTE**    This is the date when the swallows traditionally return to San Juan Capistrano Mission in California. (A columnist in *The Los Angeles Times* commented on February 18, 1963: "... The legend of the swallows indicates they always arrive on March 19, but that was before the era of the freeways.... The San Diego Freeway now bypasses San Juan Capistrano, and it can hardly be surprising if the great roaring behemoths of traffic along its concrete surfaces should prove confusing to the little birds migrating north from Mexico....")

**1860**    Birthday of William Jennings Bryan, congressman and senator from Nebraska, onetime Secretary of State, nominee on three different occasions for the Presidency.

**1906**    The last word in modern hotel appointments is to be found at the new Hotel Traymore in Atlantic City, New Jersey, which advertises: "Twenty-five private baths; capacity 450."

**1917**    A victory for labor occurs when the Supreme Court rules that the Adamson Act, signed by President Wilson on September 3, 1916, and providing for an 8-hour work day on the railroads, is constitutional.

**1920**    The U.S. Senate rejects the Versailles Treaty, providing for a League of Nations. Some 28 Republicans and 21 Democrats vote "Yea" for the treaty, but their total lacks by seven votes the needed two-thirds majority.

**1942**    All men in the United States between the ages of 45 and 64, estimated to number 13,000,000 in all, are ordered to register with Selective Service for nonmilitary duty. (WORLD WAR II)

**1945**     Members of the Norwegian Underground embark on a program of organized sabotage against German occupation troops in their native land. So effective is the sabotage that Berlin orders 200,000 Nazi soldiers in Norway to stamp out the resistance movement by terrorist methods. (WORLD WAR II)

**1951**     Herman Wouk's novel, *The Caine Mutiny,* is published for the first time. (It won the Pulitzer Prize in 1952.)

**1959**     The Dalai Lama, Tibet's spiritual ruler, flees from his country following a revolt by natives against Communist Chinese troops. (On March 28, the Chinese installed the Panchen Lama as the head of a new "loyalist" Tibetan regime.)

**1965**     After a federal judge approves the petition of the Reverend Martin Luther King, Jr., and his civil rights supporters, to march from Selma to Montgomery, Alabama, Governor George C. Wallace advises President Johnson that his state cannot afford the expense of calling out the state National Guard to provide that protection. As a result, President Johnson federalizes 1800 Alabama guardsmen and sends two battalions of Army military police control troops into the state. (*See March 21*)

## MARCH 20

**1852**     *Uncle Tom's Cabin,* Harriet Beecher Stowe's story of slavery, is published for the first time in book form and promptly becomes one of the all-time sensations of book-publishing history. (By the following May, the novel had appeared in 23 different editions and had sold well over a million copies. By 1878, the British Museum had shelved copies of the book in 20 different languages.)

**1865**     President Lincoln frustrates the first plan of John Wilkes Booth to abduct the President and take him to Richmond, Virginia, as a captive. (Booth was waiting for the President to show up at the Soldiers' Home outside Washington, but a change of plans prevented Mr. Lincoln from putting in an appearance there.)

**1927**     A sordid crime takes place in New York as Albert Snyder, a prominent magazine art editor, is murdered by his wife, Ruth Brown Snyder, and her paramour, Henry Judd Gray, of East Orange, New Jersey. (The murderers confessed and were electrocuted in 1928.)

**1940**     Edouard Daladier resigns as premier of France and is succeeded by Paul Reynaud. The new premier appoints a new Cabinet to prosecute the war against Germany to the limit. (Daladier had been accused of fighting a "phony war," a French term for a passive war.) (WORLD WAR II)

**1942**     In his first statement since landing in Australia to assume command of the military forces in the southwest Pacific, General Douglas MacArthur says: "The President of the United States has ordered me to break through the Japanese lines and proceed from Corregidor to Australia for the purpose, as I understand it, of organizing the American offensive against Japan. A primary purpose of this is relief of the Philippines. I came through and I shall return." (WORLD WAR II)

**1943**    An indoor pole vault record that is to stand for 16 years is chalked up in Chicago as Cornelius Warmerdam, using a bamboo pole, achieves a mark of 15 feet, 8½ inches. (*See February 2, 13*)

**1951**    Juan Perón, dictator of Argentina, seizes control of the opposition Buenos Aires newspaper, *La Prensa*. Perón charges that "international capitalism" is raising a false issue of freedom of the press and using the *La Prensa* case to "damage Argentina's international prestige...."

# MARCH 21

**1685**    Birthday of Johann Sebastian Bach, German composer, musician, and organist.

**1790**    Thomas Jefferson of Virginia becomes the first U.S. Secretary of State in the Cabinet of George Washington.

**1843**    Thousands of Americans are panic-stricken all day as they await the end of the world predicted by William Miller, a preacher in Pittsfield, Massachusetts. (By the next day, everyone sighed and concluded the world would continue its existence for a while.)

**1866**    An act of Congress authorizes the establishment of Homes for Soldiers in certain areas of the United States "for the relief of the totally disabled officers and men of the volunteer forces of the United States."

**1868**    The writer "Jennie June" (real name: Jane Croly) and a few of her friends organize the first club for professional women in New York City. The club will be called "Sorosis."

**1918**    American and German soldiers are engaged in the Battle of the Somme. Meanwhile, Paris is bombarded by long-range German guns, fired at a distance of 75 miles. (WORLD WAR I)

**1939**    King George VI and Queen Elizabeth of Great Britain are hosts at Buckingham Palace to President and Madame Albert Lebrun of France.

**1945**    In one of the war's greatest coordinated air efforts, 7,000 Allied airplanes drop 12,000 tons of explosives on Germany in full daylight. (WORLD WAR II)

**1946**    The United Nations moves into temporary headquarters at Hunter College in New York City.

**1955**    Rocking-chair marathons are sweeping all over the Province of Quebec in Canada. The current champion is Aimé Lavoie, 33, of Cap St. Ignace who recently rocked for 81 hours, 3 minutes, 52 seconds.

**1961**    Six years later, rocking-chairs are in the news again, this time in association with the President of the United States. Photographers report that in the two months he has been President, John F. Kennedy has conducted almost all of his office conferences seated in a rocking-chair. In answer to press queries on this date, the White House physician, Dr. Janet Travell, says that the President, suffering from a chronic back ailment, finds his rocking-chair "provides gentle, constant exercise and helps prevent muscular fatigue."

**1965**    Reverend Martin Luther King, Jr., leads his march of Negro and white civil rights demonstrators out of Selma, Alabama, toward the state's capital, Montgomery. (*See March 19*)

## MARCH 22

**1630**    Colonists in Boston are forbidden to gamble as the result of a statute which stipulates "that all persons whatsoever that have cards, dice or tables in their houses shall make away with them before the next court convenes under pain of punishment."

**1765**    The British Stamp Act becomes law in the American colonies. From now on, the Act of Parliament provides that revenue stamps must be attached to newspapers, playing cards, legal documents, brochures. (From the very beginning, the colonists set out to resist the enforcement of this unpopular act.)

**1775**    Edmund Burke makes a plea in Parliament for conciliation with the American colonies, speaking more than 3 hours and offering 13 resolutions favoring a new policy of amiable relations. (His words were almost completely ignored.)

**1794**    Congress enacts legislation prohibiting slave trading with foreign countries.

**1820**    Commodore Stephen Decatur, American naval hero, is mortally wounded in a duel with Commodore James Barron outside of Washington. (The duel was the result of Barron's belief that Decatur was responsible for the former's removal from active naval service.)

**1874**    The Young Men's Hebrew Association (YMHA) is founded in New York City.

**1917**    Russia's provisional government is recognized by the United States, the first nation to do so. (This government is not to be confused with the Bolshevik regime which came into power later in the year in the so-called "October Revolution.")

**1923**    Residents of Ormond Beach, Florida, turn out in large numbers to watch three generations of Rockefellers play golf— John D. Rockefeller and his son John D., Jr., and the latter's son, John D., III.

**1941**    Grand Coulee Dam on the Columbia River in the Pacific Northwest begins the production of electrical power.

**1948**   Station WNEW, New York, receives hundreds of telephone calls after Jerry Marshall, a master of ceremonies, plays a recording of a brand-new song, "Nature Boy." The song is the work of Eden Ahbez, a young man who has voluntarily chosen the life of a hermit. ("Nature Boy" was a sensational success. It was heard over the radio constantly and sung in night clubs and private homes. Millions of recordings of the song were sold as fast as music shops received them.)

## MARCH 23

**1743**   A London audience hears Handel's *Messiah* for the first time. As the "Hallelujah Chorus" is sung, King George II inaugurates a precedent by rising to his feet. The audience follows suit.

**1775**   Speaking in favor of arming Virginia in case war against England is necessary, Patrick Henry cries out before members of the Virginia Convention: "Is life so dear, or peace so sweet, as to be purchased at the price of chains and slavery? Forbid it, Almighty God! I know not what course others may take, but as for me, give me liberty, or give me death!"

**1901**   Madame Nellie Melba, celebrated opera diva, tells how she prepares toast: Cut the bread paper thin and bake it on an oven rack until dry and crisp. (Her "fans" immediately started a vogue for "Melba Toast," a staple today for those who are trying to lose weight.)

**1929**   Reports from Washington say that President Hoover, in office only 19 days, is "modernizing" the White House. He has had a telephone installed on his desk and has hired five different secretaries. (All previous presidents had gone to an adjoining room on the rare occasions when they used the telephone. And one secretary had been the rule before Mr. Hoover's administration.)

**1933**   The German Reichstag gives Adolf Hitler "blanket powers" for the next 4 years.

**1942**   Japanese-American residents of the Pacific coastal areas, most of whom are native born, are moved from their homes to internment camps in inland communities. (WORLD WAR II)

**1943**   Bravely defying the Germans now occupying their nation, Danes go to the polls to vote for or against Democracy. Ninety-nine percent of the ballots are cast for Democracy as against 1 percent favoring the New Order of Germany. (WORLD WAR II)

**1944**   President Franklin D. Roosevelt confers the first Legion of Merit Medal upon Rudolph Forster, posthumously, in recognition of the former White House aide's services to the government from 1897 until his death in 1943.

**1956**   Pakistan becomes the first Islamic Republic, but will retain her membership in the British Commonwealth of nations.

**1965**  The first two-man American space team is shot into orbit as Major Virgil I. Grissom and Lieutenant Commander John W. Young are launched from Cape Kennedy, Florida, aboard the spaceship *Molly Brown.* (The two astronauts, the 16th and 17th human beings to achieve orbit, accomplished something new: they were the first spacemen to shift their orbits by manual control.)

## MARCH 24

**1603**  The Crowns of England and Scotland are joined under James VI of Scotland who now starts his reign as James I.

**1882**  Professor Robert Koch announces in Berlin his discovery of the pathogenic germs of tuberculosis.

**1902**  One of the earliest "Advice to the Lovelorn" columns appears regularly in *My Queen,* "a weekly journal for young women." In the current issue this query is directed to the editor: "Can two people live comfortably on twelve dollars a week? I am engaged to be married to a young man who earns eight dollars a week while I earn four." (Replied the editor: "We do not approve of marriage on a financial basis. ....")

**1923**  At a dance given in London by the English post of the American Legion, the Prince of Wales delights everyone present by his prowess as a versatile dancer.

**1930**  Religious services are televised for the first time as Station W2XBS, New York, presents a special Easter program conducted by Dr. Samuel McCrea Cavert and accompanied by the Westminster Choir.

**1932**  For the first time in history, a radio "variety" program is broadcast from a moving train as Belle Baker, assisted by Jack Denny's orchestra, broadcasts from a Baltimore & Ohio train as it makes its regular run through Maryland. The program is carried by Station WABC, New York.

**1934**  The United States grants the Philippine Islands its independence, to become effective July 4, 1946.

**1949**  Walter Huston and his son John are the first father-and-son team to receive "Oscar" awards as the Academy of Motion Picture Arts & Sciences honors the elder Huston as the best supporting actor in the film, *The Treasure of Sierra Madre,* and the son for his direction of the picture.

**1953**  England is plunged into mourning as Dowager Queen Mary, 86, grandmother of Queen Elizabeth II and widow of the late King George V, dies in London.

**1960**  The U.S. Court of Appeals rules that the novel *Lady Chatterley's Lover* by the English writer D. H. Lawrence is not an obscene book and can therefore be sent through the mails. The Court's ruling, in effect, thus rebukes Postmaster General Arthur E. Summerfield and scores his powers of censorship. Summerfield, up until now, has banned the mailing of the book from U.S. postoffices.

**1965** Senator Robert F. Kennedy of New York reaches the top of Mount Kennedy in the Yukon Territory, the first person ever to scale the highest (13,000 feet) hitherto unclimbed mountain in North America. At the summit, the Senator plants a black-bordered flag and a copy of his brother's 1961 Inaugural Address. (The Canadian government had named the mountain in honor of the late President of the United States.)

**1965** Led by the Reverend Martin Luther King, Jr., a crowd of 25,000 Negroes and their white sympathizers converge on the state capitol at Montgomery, Alabama, after their 5-day, 54-mile march from nearby Selma. The march was staged in protest of Alabama's denial of equal voting rights to the state's Negroes. ("Walk together, children. Don't you get weary, and it will lead to the promised land. And Alabama will be a new Alabama, and America will be a new America."—Martin Luther King, Jr., addressing the marchers as they left Selma on March 21.)

**1965** Mrs. Viola Liuzzo of Detroit, a white civil rights worker, is killed by racists on the road from Selma to Montgomery, Alabama, following the protest march there to demand equal voting rights for the state's Negroes. Mrs. Liuzzo, accompanied by a Negro man, was murdered in her automobile while driving to the Alabama capital to pick up a group of the marchers for the return trip to Selma. (*See March 26, May 7*)

## MARCH 25

**1821** Greek patriots start their revolt against domination by the Ottoman Empire. (This uprising ended in 1833 with the establishment of the independent kingdom of Greece.)

**1867** Arturo Toscanini, world-famous orchestral conductor, is born in Parma, Italy.

**1882** New Yorkers gape at the first public demonstration of pancake-making on an oversized griddle easily seen behind a plate-glass window.

**1894** Coxey's Army, led by Jacob S. Coxey, starts out from Massillon, Ohio, bound for Washington to arouse public and congressional interest in a plan to "save the country" from the after-effects of the Panic of 1893. (Specifically, Coxey and his army of the unemployed wanted $500,000,000 to be issued by the government for the construction of roads throughout the nation, the laborers to be hired at $1.50 an hour for an 8-hour work day.)

**1900** The Socialist Party of the United States is organized at Indianapolis.

**1911** A disastrous fire, one of the worst ever to occur in the United States, sweeps over the premises of the Triangle Shirt Waist

Company in New York. Blocked exits and locked doors trap many of the women employees in the plant, forcing at least fifty of them to jump from the top floors of the building. In all, 147 lives are lost, many injured.

**1913** The famous Palace Theatre in New York, billed for years as the vaudeville headquarters of America, opens its doors for the first time. On the first bill are Ed Wynn, Hy Meyer, Milton Pollock & Company, The Four Vannis, Otto Gygi, and Taylor Holmes.

**1947** An explosion in a mine in Centralia, Illinois, results in the death of 111 miners, most of them asphyxiated by resulting gas vapors.

**1954** The Radio Corporation of America begins its commercial production of television sets equipped to transmit programs in color. These first sets, now being manufactured at Bloomington, Indiana, will be available to consumers at approximately $1,000.

**1964** As a tribute to the late President John F. Kennedy, the British government donates an acre of land at Runnymede, the site of the signing of the Magna Carta, for a permanent Kennedy Memorial.

# MARCH 26

**1875** Birthday of Robert Frost, American poet, celebrated as one of the poetic interpreters of New England.

**1883** A fancy dress ball launches Mr. and Mrs. William K. Vanderbilt into New York society. For the occasion, the Vanderbilts opened their new château at Fifth Avenue and Fifty-second Street and turned it into a replica of the Château de Blois in France. (An observer of the social scene was to write later: "So far as cost, richness of costume, and newspaper celebrity were concerned, the Vanderbilt ball had, perhaps, no equal in history.")

**1892** America loses a great poet as Walt Whitman, 73 years old, dies in Camden, New Jersey.

**1918** General Ferdinand Foch of France is appointed commander of all Allied armies in the war against Germany and her confederates. (WORLD WAR I)

**1923** Sarah Bernhardt, "the Divine Sarah," 81, dies in the arms of her son Maurice in Paris.

**1925** Inflation is so rampant in Italy that a public bonfire of 100,000,000 lire in bank notes is ignited in Rome in the presence of Minister of Finance de Stefani. The bonfire is the opening event in the government's campaign to reduce the circulation of paper money.

**1937** As a tribute to his well-known fondness for spinach, the residents of Crystal City, Texas, dedicate a statue of "Popeye the

Sailor" during a local Spinach Festival. ("Popeye" is a comic strip character created by Elzie Crisler Segar.)

**1942**    President Manuel L. Quezon and members of the Philippine War Cabinet join General Douglas MacArthur in Australia after a hazardous trip from Corregidor. (WORLD WAR II)

**1953**    A new vaccine capable of immunizing human beings against polio is announced by Dr. Jonas E. Salk of the University of Pittsburgh. (*See April 12.*)

**1962**    In an historic decision with far-reaching implications, the U.S. Supreme Court rules, 6–2, that citizens of Tennessee have the right to challenge the apportionment of their state legislature in the federal courts. (This decision opened a flood of litigation by citizens of other states. *See February 17.*)

**1965**    In a dramatic television appearance, President Lyndon B. Johnson tells the nation that four * members of the Ku Klux Klan have been arrested in Birmingham, Alabama, for the murder of the white civil rights worker, Mrs. Viola Liuzzo. The President says the government will declare war on the Klan and describes its members as "the enemies of justice who for decades have used the rope and the gun and the tar and the feathers to terrorize their neighbors. . . . I shall continue to fight them because I know their loyalty is not to the United States of America but instead to a hooded society of bigots. . . ." (*See March 24, 30*)

## MARCH 27

**1634**    Leonard and George Calvert, English colonists, buy a tract of some 30 acres of land on the St. Charles River and establish the first settlement in what is now Maryland.

**1884**    The *Boston Journal* describes the first long-distance telephone call, made by managers of the Bell Telephone Company in New York and Boston: "The words were heard as perfectly as though the speakers were standing close by. . . ."

**1920**    Hundreds of thousands of American moving-picture fans are excited over the wedding of two of Hollywood's most popular stars, Mary Pickford, better known as "America's Sweetheart," and the swashbuckling actor, Douglas Fairbanks.

**1933**    Japan resigns from the League of Nations. (Five months earlier, the Lytton Commission of the League had branded Japan as the willful aggressor in Manchuria.)

**1946**    Andrei Gromyko, Russian delegate to the United Nations Security Council, stages a "walkout" from that body after a resolution is passed to investigate a complaint by Iran that Soviet troops refuse to depart from Iranian territory.

* One of the four culprits was not a Klansman and was released. Later information revealed that Gary Rowe accompanied the remaining three in his role as a paid informer for the Federal Bureau of Investigation.

**1953**    By a vote of 74–13, the Senate confirms the appointment of Charles E. Bohlen as ambassador to the Soviet Union. (Mr. Bohlen's appointment had been held up since March 18 when Senator Joseph R. McCarthy (R., Wis.) charged that Secretary of State Dulles had not told the Senate the complete truth about the Federal Bureau of Investigation's report on Bohlen. On March 24, a bi-partisan committee of Senator Robert A. Taft (R., Ohio) and Senator John Sparkman (D., Ala.) examined the report and said they had found nothing in it that the Secretary of State had not already reported. )

**1954**    In a letter to *The New York Times,* Lewis Mumford, a prominent writer and critic, makes a strong plea for the end of experimentation and further explosions of the H-bomb: "If as a nation we have become mad, it is time for the world to take note of that madness. If we are still humane and sane, then it is time for the powerful voice of sanity to be heard once more in our land."

**1958**    Nikita Khrushchev, up until now the First Secretary of the Communist Party, replaces Nikolai Bulganin as premier of the Soviet Union. The new Premier tells members of the Supreme Soviet: "I shall do everything to justify your confidence and shall not spare strength, health or life to serve you." (*See October 15.*)

**1964**    An earthquake, one of the worst in modern history, strikes Alaska, leaving behind property damage of some $750,000,-000. One hundred and seventeen persons are either dead or missing.

## MARCH 28

**1797**    Nathaniel Briggs of New Hampshire receives a patent for a washing machine, describing his invention as an "improvement for washing cloaths."

**1905**    In the current issue of the *Ladies' Home Journal,* readers are reminded that "when planning a week's menus, consider that on washing and ironing days there will be a steady fire and select some dish that takes long slow cooking."

**1921**    Designers of beach wear predict that American women will start wearing form-fitting one-piece bathing suits this summer despite "the displeasure of clergymen and Puritans alike."

**1939**    Madrid surrenders to the nationalist forces of Generalissimo Francisco Franco.

**1942**    British naval forces, including a contingent of Commandos, raid Nazi-occupied St. Nazaire, France, and blow up harbor installations there. (The British destroyer, H.M.S. *Campbeltown,* with 5 tons of high explosives, raced at top speed into the great dry dock there and then blew up harbor works, one of the most daring and courageous feats of the war.) (WORLD WAR II)

**1944**    Radio Station WQXR in New York bans "singing commercials" from its broadcast schedules.

**1955** Pierre Poujade and his Union for the Defense of Shopkeepers and Artisans (800,000 members) stage a one-day strike of small shopkeepers in a campaign to force the government to suspend all taxation throughout France.

**1963** A federal jury in El Paso, Texas, convicts Billie Sol Estes on four counts of mail fraud and one of conspiracy. The bankrupt "wizard" of farm finance has been charged with swindling finance companies in mortgage deals involving $24,000,000.

## MARCH 29

**1790** John Tyler, 10th President of the United States, is born in Virginia.

**1812** The first wedding takes place in the White House when Mrs. Lucy Payne Washington is married there to Justice Thomas Todd of the Supreme Court. (The bride was a sister of the First Lady of the land, Mrs. James Madison.)

**1824** The Society for the Reformation of Juvenile Delinquents is incorporated in New York City.

**1847** As General Winfield Scott captures Vera Cruz, Mexico, the Mexican troops march out, to be disarmed and released on parole.

**1848** For the first time in its recorded history, Niagara Falls stops flowing, a phenomenon that fills nearby residents with fear. (By the next afternoon, spectators lined the river banks, exploring the exposed river bed. The explanation of this freak of nature came later: a heavy wind had started the Lake Erie ice field in motion and tons of ice jammed the river's entrance near Buffalo, damming the river for almost thirty hours. When the dam broke up, the water cascaded over the Falls once more and people in nearby areas began to relax.)

**1867** The Act of Confederation is passed by the British Parliament, creating the Dominion of Canada, with a federal parliament of its own, provincial government, and dominion status in the British Empire.

**1927** An automobile driven by Major Henry Segrave at Daytona Beach, Florida, achieves an average speed of 203 miles an hour, the first motor-driven vehicle to exceed the speed of 200 miles per hour.

**1932** Jack Benny, a prominent vaudeville entertainer, makes his radio debut as a guest on the Ed Sullivan program, broadcast over the facilities of the Columbia Broadcasting System.

**1945** As the result of a 55-mile march into Germany, soldiers of the U.S. First Army, assisted by mechanized units, all but cut the Ruhr Basin from the rest of Germany. (WORLD WAR II)

**1961** Citizens of the District of Columbia will henceforth be permitted to vote in Presidential elections, the first time since 1800, as the Twenty-third Amendment to the Constitution goes into effect.

## MARCH 30

**1858**    A pencil equipped with an eraser, the first of its kind, is patented by Hyman L. Lipman of Philadelphia.

**1867**    Secretary of State William H. Seward and the Russian minister to the United States, Baron de Stoeckl, reach agreement on the purchase of Alaska by the United States for $7,200,000 in gold. (Seward was attacked bitterly for the purchase of Alaska, many of his critics referring to the northern territory as "Seward's Folly" and "Seward's Ice Box.")

**1870**    The Fifteenth Amendment to the Constitution is ratified. ("The right of citizens of the United States to vote shall not be denied or abridged by the United States or by any State on account of race, color, or previous condition of servitude.")

**1870**    Texas is readmitted into the Union.

**1923**    The Cunard liner *Laconia,* the first passenger liner to circumnavigate the world, arrives back in New York after a cruise of 130 days.

**1940**    Japan establishes a puppet government in occupied China headed by Wang Ching-Wei.

**1942**    A directive from Washington states that men's suits will be manufactured for the duration of the war without trouser cuffs, pleats, and patch pockets. (WORLD WAR II)

**1945**    Russian troops invade Austria, forcing the retreat of Nazi soldiers on all fronts. (WORLD WAR II)

**1965**    Following President Johnson's denunciation of the Ku Klux Klan, the U.S. House of Representatives' Committee on Un-American Activities votes unanimously to conduct a full investigation into the operations of that secret organization. (*See March 26*)

## MARCH 31

**1776**    Abigail Adams admonishes her husband, John Adams: "In the new code of laws which I suppose it will be necessary for you to make, I desire you would remember the ladies and be more generous and favorable to them than your ancestors." (Mr. Adams was a member of the Continental Congress at this time.)

**1850**    Former Vice President of the United States and South Carolina Senator John C. Calhoun dies murmuring, "The South, the poor South."

**1870**    One day after the ratification of the Fifteenth Amendment, a Negro votes for the first time. He is Thomas Peterson-Mundy of Perth Amboy, New Jersey, who votes in a municipal election.

**1880**   Residents of Wabash, Indiana, celebrate as their town becomes the first incorporated community to be completely illuminated by electrical power.

**1889**   The Eiffel Tower is opened officially in Paris, despite the vigorous protests of one hundred leading writers, composers, and artists. In a petition attacking "this horrid nightmare," authors Guy de Maupassant and Alexandre Dumas condemn the Tower for "looming over Paris like a huge, black factory smokestack, crushing Notre Dame Cathedral, the Arc de Triomphe, overwhelming our architecture." The writers add: "We protest with all our might, all our indignation, in the name of French taste which is outraged. . . ."

**1900**   An automobile company advertises in a periodical with a national circulation for the first time as the W. E. Roach Company of Philadelphia takes space in the current issue of the *Saturday Evening Post.*

**1918**   Daylight saving time goes into effect throughout the United States for the first time.

**1923**   In the first "Dance Marathon" to be held in the United States, Miss Alma Cummings establishes a world's record in New York City by remaining on her feet for 27 hours. (On August 29, 1930, the most celebrated American dance marathon began in Chicago and lasted until the beginning of 1931.)

**1933**   Congress creates the Civilian Conservation Corps to provide vocational training and employment for young men in the United States.

**1943**   *Oklahoma!,* a refreshing and melodious musical comedy by the team of Rodgers and Hammerstein, is cheered by an enthusiastic first-night audience at the St. James Theatre in New York. (This show is said to have rolled up the longest run of any musical up to this time.)

**1949**   Newfoundland becomes Canada's 10th province, following a plebiscite held on July 22, 1948.

**1963**   The first Negro to be selected for training as an astronaut is 29-year-old Air Force Captain Edward J. Dwight, Jr., of Edwards Air Force Base, California.

# APRIL

## APRIL 1

**April Fools' or All Fools' Day**    Believed by many people to have originated in France in 1564 when the reformed calendar was adopted, confusing everybody. Hence, the modern-day custom of playing harmless tricks and jokes upon one's friends.

**1789**    Almost a month after its first meeting, the House of Representatives is able to transact business, a quorum of its members being present for the first time. The first action taken by the members is the election of Augustus C. Muhlenberg of Pennsylvania as Speaker of the House.

**1853**    Cincinnati, Ohio, inaugurates a precedent when the municipal government decides that its Fire Department personnel will be paid a regular salary. Ordinary firemen are to receive $60 a year, lieutenants, $100, captains, $150 and pipemen, $365.

**1861**    William H. Seward, Secretary of State on the new Lincoln administration and himself a disappointed aspirant for the Presidency, submits to President Lincoln a memorandum entitled "Some Thoughts for the President's Consideration" in which he offers to take over the real operation of the government. (The election of Lincoln was considered unfortunate by many Republicans, Seward included. But the new President advised his Secretary of State that he had been elected chief magistrate and that he intended to run the executive branch himself.)

**1896**    The current issue of the *Ladies' Home Journal* describes a twenty-room Dutch Colonial residence which the editors say can be built anywhere in the United States for $5,000.

**1918**    The Royal Air Force is founded in Great Britain. (Two months later, in World War I, the RAF began the strategic bombing of industrial targets in Germany, taking off from bases in eastern France.) (WORLD WAR I)

**1920**    The New York legislature in Albany expels five of its duly elected members after hearing them admit that they are Socialists.

**1931**   For the first time in baseball history, a woman is signed up as a regular member of an otherwise all-male team. The woman is Virne (Jackie) Mitchell, 19 years old, who will pitch from now on for the Chattanooga, Tennessee, Baseball Club.

**1937**   Great Britain separates Burma from India and sets it up as a crown colony with its own legislature and a British governor.

**1939**   Generalissimo Francisco Franco, rebel commander-in-chief, announces that the Spanish Civil War has ended. The government of the United States extends recognition to the Franco regime.

**1945**   American armed forces, supported by a naval armada of more than 1,400 vessels, begin the invasion of Okinawa, the largest of the Ryukyu Islands in the Pacific. (WORLD WAR II)

**1963**   Eight of the nine major daily newspapers in New York City publish their first editions following termination of the strike that had closed them down on December 8, 1962. (*The New York Post* had resumed publication on March 4, 1963. For the other papers, the strike lasted 114 days, the longest in newspaper history to date.)

## APRIL 2

**1792**   Congress enacts legislation authorizing a Mint of the United States to coin money, all coins to be inscribed with the motto, "E Pluribus Unum." At the same time, Congress fixes the price of gold at $19.39 an ounce and orders the coinage in gold of "Eagles" ($10), "Half-Eagles" ($5), and "Quarter-Eagles" ($2.50).

**1805**   Birth of Hans Christian Andersen, Danish writer of fairy tales.

**1865**   President Jefferson Davis and most of his Confederate Cabinet flee from Richmond, Virginia, after General Robert E. Lee abandons Richmond and Petersburg.

**1873**   Birthday of Sergei Rachmaninoff, Russian pianist and composer.

**1896**   Barnum & Bailey Circus opens its season at Madison Square Garden in New York, the stellar attraction of the grand opening parade being not wild animals nor bearded ladies, but a Duryea "Horseless Carriage."

**1902**   Thomas L. Tally opens the first moving-picture theatre at 262 South Main Street in Los Angeles. The proprietor advertises that featured films soon to be seen include *New York in a Blizzard* and *The Capture of the Biddle Brothers*. (Tally's venture was devoted not entirely to moving pictures. He ran it in conjunction with a carnival.)

**1917**   Before a Joint Session of Congress, President Woodrow Wilson calls for a declaration of war against Germany, saying that "The world must be made safe for democracy." Citing various acts of aggression by the German Navy and yet fully cognizant of the seriousness of his request, the President adds: "It is a fearful thing to lead this great peaceful people into war, into the most terrible and disastrous of all wars, civilization itself seeming to be in the balance. But the right is more precious than peace, and we shall fight for the things which we have always carried nearest our hearts —for democracy...."

**1925** George Bernard Shaw tells an American visitor that he will never visit America, saying: "I have waited too long. I might have gone twenty years ago, but not now. They'd kill me with kindness. They'll kill God himself if he came to America." (Nonetheless, he *did* pay a brief visit to the United States in 1933.)

**1932** Charles A. Lindbergh and Dr. John F. ("Jafsie") Condon turn over $50,000 in bills to an unidentified man in St. Raymond's Cemetery in the Bronx, New York, in the hope of regaining Lindbergh's kidnapped son. (The unidentified man was obviously Bruno Richard Hauptmann, later put to death for kidnapping and murdering the child.)

**1947** Islands in the Pacific formerly held by Japan under mandates are assigned by the United Nations Security Council to the trusteeship of the United States.

**1963** Negroes in Birmingham, Alabama, begin mass demonstrations demanding more civil rights and an end to segregation. (*See May 3.*)

## APRIL 3

**1776** Harvard College confers the honorary degree of Doctor of Laws on General George Washington.

**1783** Birthday of Washington Irving, American writer and diplomat, creator of the immortal Rip Van Winkle and Ichabod Crane.

**1800** Congress authorizes Martha Washington, widow of George Washington, to send all of her mail postage free.

**1860** The Pony Express postal service is inaugurated as two riders simultaneously leave St. Joseph, Missouri, and Sacramento, California. (The service continued for about a year and a half, until the Pacific Telegraph Company line was completed, and embraced the services of some 80 riders, working in relays, and almost 500 horses.)

**1865** The Union Army occupies Richmond, Virginia, one-time capital of the Confederacy.

**1882** The famous outlaw, Jesse James, living in St. Joseph, Missouri, under the assumed name of "Thomas Howard," is shot and killed as he is straightening a picture on the wall in his home. The murderer is Robert Ford, a member of James's gang.

**1918** The House of Representatives adopts the stirring words of William Tyler Page as "The American's Creed": "I believe in the United States of America as a Government of the people, by the people, for the people; whose just powers are derived from the consent of the governed; a democracy in a republic; a sovereign nation of many sovereign states; a perfect Union, one and inseparable. . . ."

**1933**      Women reporters attending a press conference with Mrs. Franklin D. Roosevelt rush to the telephones to inform their newspapers of the First Lady's announcement that beer henceforth will be served at the White House. (Congress had legalized 3.2 beer on March 22. The sale of hard liquor came on December 5.)

**1936**      Bruno Richard Hauptmann is electrocuted in Trenton, New Jersey, for the kidnapping and murder of Charles A. Lindbergh, Jr.

**1946**      Lieutenant General Masaharu Homma of Japan, who ordered the "Death March" of the Americans captured in Bataan, is executed by a war crimes tribunal.

**1948**      The Foreign Assistance Act of 1948 creates the European Recovery Program, allocating $5,300,000,000 for some 16 European countries during the next fiscal year.

**1964**      The United States and Panama resume diplomatic relations. Both governments, at odds since the January riots in the Canal Zone, agree to negotiate their differences.

## APRIL 4

**1818**      Congress orders that the flag of the United States be redesigned and that the number of stripes be reduced to the original 13, the number of stars to be 20. It was further ordered that "on admission of every new state into the Union, one star be added . . . and that such addition shall take effect on the Fourth of July next succeeding such admission."

**1841**      Exactly one month after his inauguration, President William Henry Harrison dies in the White House, following an attack of pneumonia. (The First Lady of the land had not even arrived in Washington to take up her residence there.)

**1865**      One day after the Union Army occupied Richmond, Virginia, President Lincoln visits the fallen city, accompanied by his 12-year-old son, Tad, Admiral David D. Porter, and an escort of 12 sailors. (Wherever the President went, crowds of Negroes fell to their knees and broke into tears at the sight of him.)

**1900**      Admiral George Dewey, the hero of the Spanish-American War, creates a sensation when he announces that he is available for the Presidency: ". . . If the American people want me for this high office, I shall be only too willing to serve them. . . . Since studying this subject, I am convinced that the office of President is not such a difficult one to fill, his duties being mainly to execute the laws of Congress . . ."

**1902**    The will of the late Cecil Rhodes, British financier and South African colonizer, bequeaths $10,000,000 to provide scholarships for American young men at Oxford University.

**1914**    The first showing of *The Perils of Pauline,* one of the earliest and certainly the most famous of all moving-picture "serials," takes place in New York. Starring the actress Pearl White, the first film is concluded with an announcement that future installments will feature "flying machine accidents, thrilling rescues, fires at sea, train wrecks, automobile accidents. . . ."

**1917**    In response to President Wilson's war message, the Senate approves a resolution of war against Imperial Germany, by a vote of 82–6. (WORLD WAR I)

**1932**    After 5 years of research, Professor C. G. King of the University of Pittsburgh isolates Vitamin C.

**1933**    The U.S. naval dirigible *Akron* founders in a storm and falls into the sea off Barnegat Bay, New Jersey. Seventy-three members of the crew are lost in the disaster.

**1949**    As representatives of 12 nations * convene in Washington to sign the North Atlantic Treaty, President Truman tells them: "What we are about to do here is a neighborly act. We are like a group of householders, living in the same locality, who decide to express their community of interests by entering into a formal association for their mutual self-protection. . . ." (Article 5 of the NATO Pact states: "An armed attack against one or more of the signatories in Europe or North America shall be considered an attack against them all.")

**1953**    The first chapter of the scholastic fraternity Phi Beta Kappa to be established in a Negro college is activated at Fisk University, Nashville, Tennessee.

## APRIL 5

**1614**    Pocahontas, daughter of the Indian chieftain Powhatan, is married in Virginia to John Rolfe, an English colonist.

**1792**    President George Washington establishes a Presidential precedent when he vetoes a congressional bill for the apportionment of representation.

**1827**    Birthday of Sir Joseph Lister, English surgeon and founder of modern antiseptic surgery. (Listerine, the antiseptic mouth wash, was named after him.)

**1841**    Following the death of President William Henry Harrison in Washington, Fletcher Webster, chief clerk of the State Department, travels to Williamsburg, Virginia, to inform Vice President John Tyler that he will become the 10th President of the

* The document was signed by the United States, Canada, Denmark, Iceland, Portugal, Great Britain, France, Italy, the Netherlands, Norway, Belgium, and Luxembourg.

United States. (The Vice President was roused at sunrise, clad in a nightshirt and cap. He called a conference of his family to tell them the news, ate a hearty breakfast and then set out for Washington. *See April 6.*)

**1869**   Daniel F. Bakeman, 109 years old and the last surviving soldier of the Revolutionary War, dies in Freedom, New York.

**1915**   Jess Willard, an ex-cowpuncher from Kansas, knocks out Jack Johnson in the 26th round at Havana, Cuba, thus winning the world heavyweight boxing championship.

**1916**   Charles Chaplin, not yet 27 years old, becomes the highest-priced film star in the world after signing a contract with the Mutual Film Corporation guaranteeing him $675,000 for one year's work.

**1933**   In order to stop the hoarding of gold, President Franklin D. Roosevelt issues an Executive Order calling for the surrender of all private stores of gold to banks of the Federal Reserve System in exchange for equivalent currency.

**1939**   In Germany the government orders all children aged 10 to 13 to register and serve in the Hitler Youth Organization.

**1951**   Julius and Ethel Rosenberg of New York City are sentenced to death as "atom spies," charged with transmitting secret atomic energy information to agents of the Soviet Union.

**1955**   Prime Minister Winston Churchill, 81 years old, goes to Buckingham Palace and submits his resignation to Queen Elizabeth II, after serving as prime minister 8 years, 7 months, 25 days.* He offers the Queen as his recommendation for a successor the name of Sir Anthony Eden.

## APRIL 6

**1789**   The first Federal Congress of the United States gets under way as a Joint Session of the Senate and House of Representatives convenes in New York City for the express purpose of opening and counting the electoral votes cast on February 4 for President and Vice President. After a tally shows that 69 votes were cast for George Washington and 34 for John Adams, messengers are instructed to set out and notify both men that they have been elected President and Vice President respectively.

**1830**   Joseph Smith, a Vermont-born farmer, organizes the Church of Latter-Day Saints, more familiarly known as the Mormon Church, at Fayette, New York. The new religious group has 30 members.

**1841**   At the stroke of noon, in Brown's Hotel, Washington, Chief Justice William Cranch of the U.S. Circuit Court of the Dis-

* From May 10, 1940, to July 25, 1945, and from October 26, 1951, to April 5, 1955.

trict of Columbia swears in Vice President John Tyler as the 10th President of the United States, following the death of President William Henry Harrison.

**1862**    General Grant is almost routed from his position on the Tennessee River as Confederate soldiers, led by General Albert Sidney Johnson, take the Northerners by surprise in a dawn attack on their camp at Shiloh, Tennessee. (The battle lasted through April 7 and would have resulted in a complete defeat for the Union Army if reinforcements from the Army of the Ohio had not arrived. Even so, Grant suffered 13,000 casualties out of his total force of 63,000 men.)

**1866**    Veterans of the Union Army organize the Grand Army of the Republic (G.A.R.) at Decatur, Illinois.

**1909**    After 23 years of effort, Robert Edwin Peary becomes the first civilized man to reach the North Pole. (While Peary was accompanied by 7 men from the United States and 17 Eskimos when he set out to discover the Pole in 1908, this last lap of his expedition included only Peary, his servant, Matt Henson, and 4 Eskimos. They remained at the Pole for 30 hours and planted the flag of the United States there before leaving. In his diary, Peary reported his joy: "My dream and goal for 20 years. Mine at last! I cannot bring myself to realize it. It seems all so simple and commonplace.")

**1917**    The United States is at war with Germany as President Wilson, advised that the House of Representatives has followed the Senate's lead in voting for a resolution of war, signs a proclamation that "a state of war exists between the United States and the Imperial German Government." (WORLD WAR I)

**1941**    German troops invade both Greece and Yugoslavia. (WORLD WAR II)

**1949**    Herbert A. Philbrick, a former undercover agent for the Federal Bureau of Investigation who masqueraded as a "loyal" Communist in the Boston area, is introduced by the prosecution at the trial of the top 11 Communists in New York City as a witness for the government.

**1954**    Senator Joseph R. McCarthy (R. Wis.) charges in a nationwide telecast that the well-known news commentator and analyst Edward R. Murrow had "engaged in propaganda for Communist causes" as far back as 20 years ago. (The McCarthy speech was in answer to an attack made by Mr. Murrow on March 9, at which time he accused the Senator of stepping over "the line between investigating and persecuting.")

**1955**    Queen Elizabeth II summons Sir Anthony Eden to Buckingham Palace to tell him that she has decided to name him prime minister, successor to Sir Winston Churchill who resigned yesterday.

**1957**    Trolley cars become memories of the past in New York City as the few remaining trolleys complete their last runs.

# APRIL 7

**1770** William Wordsworth, great English poet, is born at Cockermouth, England.

**1891** The legislature of Nebraska introduces a "radical" precedent when it enacts a statute providing for an 8-hour work day.

**1927** An audience gathered in the auditorium of the Bell Telephone Laboratories in New York watches the first successful long-distance demonstration of television. Secretary of Commerce Herbert Hoover, seated in his Washington office, is both seen and heard clearly by the spectators in New York.

**1932** Governor Franklin Delano Roosevelt gives a clue to the theme he will use in his campaign if he wins the Democratic nomination for President at the forthcoming convention in Chicago. Speaking in a radio broadcast, Mr. Roosevelt points to the plight of the "Forgotten Man," describing him as "the forgotten man at the bottom of the economic pyramid." *

**1940** The Socialist Party nominates Norman Thomas for the Presidency, the fourth time that he has received the nomination.

**1943** Advance patrols of the Second United States Army Corps and the British Eighth Army meet on the Gafsa-Gabes Highway in Tunisia as William Brown, a sergeant from Devonshire, England, and Joseph Randall, a sergeant from State Center, Iowa, shake hands and clap each other on the back. The American-British forces in North Africa are thus joined. (WORLD WAR II)

**1949** A smash theatrical "hit" opens in New York as *South Pacific*, a musical play by the team of Rodgers and Hammerstein, makes its bow at the Majestic Theatre. The entrancing songs are sung by Mary Martin and Ezio Pinza, the latter a former star of the Metropolitan Opera Company.

**1953** Dag Hammarskjold of Sweden is elected Secretary General of the United Nations for a 5-year term beginning April 10. (He succeeded Trygve Lie, the first Secretary General of the United Nations.)

**1959** Oklahoma votes to repeal its law prohibiting the sale of liquor, in effect since achieving statehood in 1907. (This left Mississippi as the only remaining "dry" state.)

**1962** A military court in Havana convicts 1,179 Cuban prisoners captured in the 1961 Bay of Pigs invasion. Charged with "crimes committed against the nation in connivance with a foreign power," the prisoners are sentenced to jail terms of 30 years and loss of their Cuban citizenship. (*See December 23.*)

* Mr. Roosevelt was probably familiar with the first famous usage of this phrase in a speech delivered in 1883 by Professor William Graham Sumner of Yale.

# APRIL 8

**1513** Ponce de León, Spanish soldier and explorer, lands in Florida near the present site of St. Augustine, seeking the Fountain of Youth.

**1730** Members of Shearith Israel, the first Jewish congregation to be organized in America, consecrate their synagogue in New York City. (This congregation dates back to 1655 when Sephardic Jews, refugees from Portugal, settled in what was then New Amsterdam.)

**1865** General Grant asks General Robert E. Lee to surrender in the name of his Army of Northern Virginia. General Lee sends a note to Grant asking him to stipulate the terms of peace.

**1904** France and Great Britain sign the "Entente Cordiale," beginning an era of close cooperation between those two powers.

**1913** Despite disapproval of some members of his Cabinet and many members of Congress, President Woodrow Wilson appears in person before Congress to appeal for tariff revision. In his remarks, Mr. Wilson makes it clear that he feels a President has every right to come before the Congress in person: "... I am very glad indeed to. ... address the two houses directly and to verify for myself the impression that the President of the United States is a person, not a mere department of the Government hailing Congress from some island of jealous power. ..."

**1923** Georgia admirers of automobile manufacturer Henry Ford are urging him to become a Presidential candidate in the 1924 elections. Mr. Ford finally issues a statement, saying: "I don't know where this boom started, but I'm not interested in it." Mrs. Henry Ford has the last word on the subject when she says: "If Henry goes to the White House, he will have to go without me!"

**1935** Congress approves an appropriation of $5,000,000,000 to provide "work relief and to increase employment by providing useful projects" under the Works Progress Administration (WPA).

**1943** Wendell Willkie's book *One World* is published, an account of his global trip made in 1942 as a special envoy of President Franklin D. Roosevelt. (Within two months after its publication, the sales of this book topped a million.)

**1946** The League of Nations Assembly begins its final session in Geneva. (On April 18, the organization adjourned, having transferred its assets and powers to the United Nations.)

**1952** President Truman seizes the steel industry to forestall a general strike.

**1964** The body of General of the Army Douglas MacArthur, who died on April 5, lies in state in the Rotunda of the U.S. Capitol in Washington.

# APRIL 9

**1833** The townspeople of Peterborough, New Hampshire, found the first public library in the nation to be supported by municipal taxes.

**1865** General Robert E. Lee surrenders the Army of Northern Virginia to General Ulysses S. Grant, commander-in-chief of the Union Army, at the farmhouse of Wilmer McLean at Appomattox Court House, Virginia. ("The whole country had been so raided by the two armies that it was doubtful whether they would be able to put in a crop to carry themselves and their families through the next winter without the aid of the horses they were then riding. . . . I would, therefore, instruct the officers I left behind . . . to let every man of the Confederate Army who claimed to own a horse or mule take the animal to his home. . . ."—General Grant to General Lee at Appomattox.)

**1929** The troublesome Washington controversy over diplomatic precedence between Mrs. Edward Everett (Dolly) Gann, sister and hostess of Vice President Charles Curtis, and Mrs. Nicholas Longworth, wife of the Speaker of the House of Representatives, is settled by the diplomatic corps who agree to accord Mrs. Gann the rank of a Vice President's wife. (It may seem unimportant today, but this long-time controvery split Washington's governmental and diplomatic society into bitter rival factions.)

**1939** Seventy-five thousand people crowd around the Lincoln Memorial in Washington to hear Marian Anderson sing, after the Daughters of the American Revolution had refused to allow the singer to perform in Constitution Hall because she was a Negro. Among those who have come out to hear Miss Anderson are Chief Justice and Mrs. Charles Evans Hughes, Associate Justice Hugo Black, Secretary of the Treasury Henry Morgenthau, and Secretary of the Interior Harold Ickes. (The First Lady of the land, Mrs. Franklin D. Roosevelt, resigned from the D.A.R. in protest over their action.)

**1940** Germany carries out a "blitzkrieg" invasion of both Denmark and Norway. (WORLD WAR II)

**1941** The Professional Golfers' Association announces the creation of a Golf Hall of Fame, the first players selected for membership being Bobby Jones, Francis Ouimet, Walter Hagen, and Gene Sarazen.

**1942** Fall of Bataan: after more than 3 months of heroic resistance, the American and Filipino forces on Bataan, in the Philippines, are overwhelmed by a Japanese army 10 times their number. From the Voice of Freedom radio station on Corregidor, in Manila Bay, the free world hears this short-wave message: "Bataan has fallen, but the spirit that made it stand, a beacon to all liberty-loving peoples of the world, cannot fail." (WORLD WAR II)

**1953**    The New York State Grand Lodge, Knights of Pythias, becomes the first major fraternal organization in the United States to ban racial or religious restrictions in its membership qualifications.

**1959**    At a press conference in Washington, the National Aeronautics and Space Administration introduces America's first "Astronauts." The seven carefully chosen spacemen are: Navy Lieutenant Malcolm Scott Carpenter, 33; Air Force Captain Leroy Gordon Cooper, Jr., 32; Marine Lieutenant Colonel John Herschel Glenn, Jr., 37; Air Force Captain Virgil Ivan Grissom, 33; Navy Lieutenant Commander Walter Marty Schirra, Jr., 36; Navy Lieutenant Commander Alan Bartlett Shepard, Jr., 35; Air Force Captain Donald Kent Slayton, 35.

**1963**    President Kennedy signs a proclamation making Sir Winston Churchill an honorary citizen of the United States. Speaking at a ceremony in the White House garden, the President says: ". . . In proclaiming him an honorary citizen, I only propose a formal recognition of the place he has long since won in the history of freedom and in the affections of my—and now his—fellow countrymen . . ." (Sir Winston, now 88, watched the ceremony via television at his London home. *See also April 15 and January 30.*)

**1965**    President and Mrs. Lyndon B. Johnson are on hand in Houston, Texas, for the opening of that city's brand-new roofed-over athletic stadium, known locally as the Astrodome. To highlight the occasion, baseball fans in Texas have the added pleasure of seeing the Houston Astros defeat the New York Yankees, 2–1, the first time in major league history that a baseball game is played in daytime under a roof. (For the players, it was less than pleasurable: the dome's 4,596 plastic skylight panels so diffused the sunlight that fly balls were all but untrackable. A team of experts later came up with a solution: paint the panels.)

## APRIL 10

**1847**    Birthday of Joseph Pulitzer, American journalist and philanthropist, founder of the Pulitzer Prizes and the Pulitzer School of Journalism at Columbia University.

**1849**    Walter Hunt of New York City receives a patent for his invention of the safety pin.

**1863**    Because of a serious shortage of food, President Jefferson Davis begs all farmers in the South to plant corn, peas, and beans in place of the regular crops of tobacco and cotton.

**1866**    Henry Bergh, a former secretary of the United States legation in St. Petersburg, Russia, finally succeeds in obtaining recognition for his humane society as the New York State legislature charters the American Society for the Prevention of Cruelty to Animals.

**1869**    The states of Texas, Mississippi, and Virginia are told by Congress that their respective legislatures will have to ratify the Fifteenth Amendment before they are permitted to send representatives to the Senate and House once more.

**1872**    At the suggestion of Governor J. Sterling Morton, who is concerned over the great shortage of trees in the state, residents of Nebraska observe the first Arbor Day celebration in America. At least a million trees are planted all over the state in community observances.

**1938**    In a national election, Austrians vote 99.75 percent for a merger with Germany.

**1945**    The notorious Nazi concentration camp at Buchenwald, near Weimar, Germany, is liberated by soldiers of the U.S. 80th Division. (WORLD WAR II)

**1946**    Women in Japan, now eligible to vote, go to the polls for the first time in the history of their country.

**1948**    General Dwight D. Eisenhower tells reporters in Washington that he means to abide by his letter of January 23 to the publisher of the *Manchester* (New Hampshire) *Evening Leader,* in which he stated his belief that professional soldiers should abstain from seeking high political office.

**1959**    A good many Americans sit by their television sets, entranced as they watch the wedding ceremonies of Crown Prince Akihito of Japan to a young commoner, Miss Michiko Shoda. The Shinto ceremony in Tokyo marks the first wedding of a Crown Prince to a commoner in the 619-year history of the Japanese throne.

**1963**    The nation is shocked by a Navy announcement that the atomic-powered submarine U.S.S. *Thresher* has not surfaced after making a deep dive in the North Atlantic. (This was the worst submarine disaster to date in U.S. history. Lost were 96 enlisted men, 16 officers, and 17 civilian technicians.)

## APRIL 11

**1814**    Napoleon decides to abdicate and signs a proclamation stating: "The Allied Powers having proclaimed that the Emperor Napoleon is the sole obstacle to the reestablishment of peace in Europe, he, faithful to his oath, declares that he is ready to descend from the throne, to quit France, and even relinquish life, for the good of his country...."

**1865**    President Lincoln makes his last public speech, addressing a group of citizens assembled before the White House on his preliminary plans for the reconstruction of the South.

**1898**    President William McKinley sends a message to Congress asking for a declaration of war against Spain. Says the President:

"In the name of humanity, in the name of civilization, in behalf of endangered American interests . . . the war in Cuba must stop. . . ."

**1899** The U.S. government proclaims a treaty of peace with Spain, thus ending the Spanish-American War.

**1941** President Franklin D. Roosevelt creates the Office of Price Administration and Civilian Supply to prevent runaway prices and hoarding. Leon Henderson will serve as chief of the new agency. (WORLD WAR II)

**1945** The British Admiralty announces that as a result of a raid by the Royal Air Force, the *Admiral Scheer,* one of Germany's two remaining pocket battleships, has been bombed and sunk at the Kiel Naval Base. (WORLD WAR II)

**1947** For the first time in baseball history, a Negro plays with a major league team. The player is Jackie Robinson who joined with the Brooklyn Dodgers today in an exhibition game with the New York Yankees.

**1951** President Truman relieves General Douglas MacArthur of his commands in the Far East. A statement issued by the President from the White House states: "I have concluded that General of the Army Douglas MacArthur is unable to give his wholehearted support to the policies of the U.S. government and of the United Nations in matters pertaining to official duties. . . ." Lieutenant General Matthew B. Ridgway has been appointed to succeed MacArthur.

**1953** Mrs. Oveta Culp Hobby is sworn in as the nation's first secretary of the Department of Health, Education, and Welfare. (The Department achieved Cabinet status on that date. Mrs. Hobby was the second woman in history to become a member of a President's Cabinet. The first was Madam Frances Perkins, named as Secretary of Labor in 1933 by President Franklin D. Roosevelt.)

**1961** Adolf Eichmann goes on trial before an Israeli court in Jerusalem, accused of managing the Nazi German slaughter of 6,000,000 Jews. (*See May 31 and December 15.*)

**1962** President Kennedy reacts in cold anger to the news that the United States Steel Corporation and five other major steel-producing firms are going to increase the price of steel by $6 a ton. At his press conference, the President says ". . . (we have asked) union members to hold down their wage requests at a time when restraint and sacrifice are being asked of every citizen. The American people will find it hard, as I do, to accept a situation in which a tiny handful of steel executives, whose pursuit of private power and profit exceeds their sense of public responsibility, can show such utter contempt for the interest of 185,000,000 Americans. . . ." (The President was referring to the labor pact signed on March 31 by major steel companies and the steel-workers union, in which the union agreed to pass up demands for wage increases. As a result, the price increases announced were rescinded April 13–14.)

**1962**   For the first time in history, a ballet company dances in the White House as the Jerome Robbins Ballet entertains the guests of President and Mrs. John F. Kennedy. The performance follows a state dinner in honor of the Shah and Queen of Iran.

**1965**   Jack Nicklaus of Columbus, Ohio, wins his second Masters golf title as he shoots a 69 for a 17-under par 271 score at the Augusta (Ga.) National Course. In chalking up his victory, Nicklaus thus breaks two records: his score is below those established by Ben Hogan in 1953 (274) and in 1955 by Cary Middlecoff (279).

## APRIL 12

**1861**   Civil War comes to the United States as Confederate forces under the command of General P. T. Beauregard open fire on Fort Sumter, the federal citadel in the harbor of Charleston, South Carolina. (The first shot was fired by a 67-year-old Virginian, Edmund Ruffin.)

**1865**   General Robert E. Lee writes to Jefferson Davis, President of the Confederacy, advising him that the Army of Northern Virginia has been surrendered to General Grant: "The enemy were more than five times our numbers. If we could have forced our way one day longer it would have been at a great sacrifice of life, and at its end I did not see how a surrender could have been avoided. We had no subsistence for man or horse, and it could not be gathered in the country...."

**1905**   A brand-new theatrical palace, the Hippodrome in New York, opens its doors with a spectacular musical revue, *A Yankee Circus on Mars.*

**1916**   American soldiers led by General John J. Pershing come to grips with the troops of the Mexican revolutionary leader Pancho Villa in Parral, Mexico. Villa makes his getaway from the Americans.

**1927**   Chiang Kai-shek breaks with the left wing of the Kuomintang and orders a mass purge of Communists in Shanghai.

**1937**   The Supreme Court upholds the National Labor Relations Act of 1935.

**1945**   "The President is dead!" These words are on the lips of people all over the world—in Washington and New York, Baton Rouge and Omaha, in London and Rome and Anchorage, Bombay and Chungking, in foxholes and on the decks of aircraft carriers. The President they are referring to is Franklin Delano Roosevelt, 32nd President of the United States, who died in Warm Springs, Georgia, at 4:35 o'clock in the afternoon. (The tributes were warm and heartfelt and, sometimes, belated, but an observer for the Associated Press reported that the one repeated a thousand times that day was heard on Main Streets all over America: "I never set eyes on him—but I knew him, I knew him.")

**1945**    In the presence of his family, Cabinet officers, and congressional leaders, Harry S. Truman is sworn into office as the 33rd President of the United States at 7:09 o'clock in the evening by Chief Justice Harlan Stone. The ceremony takes place in the executive offices of the White House.

**1948**    On the third anniversary of the death of President Franklin D. Roosevelt, his widow unveils a statue to his memory in Grosvenor Park, London. The ceremonies are attended by the entire Royal Family and Winston Churchill.

**1954**    Dr. J. Robert Oppenheimer, world-famous scientist and often referred to as the "father of the atomic bomb," is suspended by the Atomic Energy Commission as a possible security risk. (Nine years later, the Commission had an obvious change of heart. *See December 2.*)

**1955**    A news flash from Ann Arbor, Michigan, brings joy to the world: "The vaccine works! It is safe, effective, and potent." The reference is to the antipoliomyelitis vaccine developed by Dr. Jonas E. Salk of Pittsburgh, pronounced a success by the University of Michigan Polio Vaccine Evaluation Center. The university's positive report is a result of tests conducted by the National Foundation for Infantile Paralysis a year ago. (The report was deliberately timed to coincide with the 10th anniversary of the death of President Franklin D. Roosevelt, himself a polio victim and the founder of the National Foundation in 1938.)

**1961**    A Russian reserve Air Force pilot becomes the first known human space traveler as he goes into orbit around the earth aboard a Soviet space craft. Radio Moscow goes on the air and announces at regular intervals: "Russia has successfully launched a man into space. His name is Yuri Gagarin. He was launched in a sputnik named Vostok. . . ." (The total time Major Gagarin took to make his single orbit of the earth was 89.1 minutes.)

**1964**    Arnold Palmer of Latrobe, Pennsylvania, wins his fourth Masters golf championship at the Augusta (Ga.) National Golf Club. As a result, his winnings in official U.S. competitions now total $506,496.84.

## APRIL 13

**1743**    Thomas Jefferson, third President of the United States, is born in Albemarle County, Virginia. ("We hold these truths to be self-evident, that all men are created equal; that they are endowed by their Creator with certain unalienable rights; that among these are Life, Liberty and the pursuit of Happiness. . . .")

**1830**    At a dinner in Washington, President Andrew Jackson heads a distinguished group honoring the birthday of Thomas Jefferson. The President's toast brings the diners to their feet, "Our Federal Union—it must be preserved!" Moments later, Jackson's political enemy and ardent advocate of states' rights, Vice President John C. Calhoun, jumps to his feet to respond with another stirring toast, "The Union—next to our liberty, the most dear!"

**1934**   Harry Hopkins, chief of the Civil Works Administration, announces that 4,700,000 families in the United States are on relief. (Less than a year later, on March 6, 1935, some 22,000,000 Americans were receiving relief benefits.)

**1941**   Russian and Japan sign a 5-year neutrality pact.

**1943**   President Franklin D. Roosevelt dedicates the Thomas Jefferson Memorial in Washington as "a shrine to freedom." The dedication ceremonies commemorate the 200th anniversary of the third President's birth.

**1945**   President Truman, in his first full day of office following the death of Franklin D. Roosevelt, is still stunned by the rapid chain of events which has made him President of the United States. To reporters, the new President says: "I don't know if any of you fellows ever had a load of hay or a bull fall on him, but last night the whole weight of the moon and stars fell on me. I feel a tremendous responsibility. . . . Please pray for me! I mean that!"

**1958**   To the cheers of an enthusiastic crowd of Moscow music lovers, 23-year-old Van Cliburn of Kilgore, Texas, is awarded first prize in the Soviet Union's Tchaikovsky International Piano Contest.

**1964**   Sidney Poitier becomes the first Negro to win a top motion-picture Oscar as he is named the best actor of 1963 at the annual ceremonies in Hollywood.

**1965**   Lawrence Bradford, Jr., a 16-year-old boy from New York City, starts work as the first Negro page to ever serve in either house of Congress. Bradford has been appointed to the Senate's page staff by Senator Jacob K. Javits, Republican of New York. *(See April 14)*

# APRIL 14

## Pan American Day

**1775**   The first Abolition Society is organized in Philadelphia under the name of "The Society for the Relief of Free Negroes Unlawfully Held in Bondage." Benjamin Franklin has agreed to serve as president of the Society.

**1789**   Charles Thomson, Secretary of Congress, delivers a message to George Washington at Mount Vernon, advising him of his unanimous election to the Presidency.

**1828**   The first edition of *Noah Webster's Dictionary* is published.

**1861**   The flag of the Confederacy rises above Fort Sumter, South Carolina, as the encircled Union troops there surrender to the Southerners.

**1865**    Four years after the surrender of Fort Sumter, Major General Robert Anderson, the Union officer who was forced to surrender the citadel to the Confederacy at the beginning of the War between the States, is given the honor of hoisting the Stars and Stripes once more over the military base. After the flag is mounted, Anderson turns to the assembled soldiers, saying: "I thank God that I have lived to see this day."

**1865**    John Wilkes Booth, the well-known actor and Confederate sympathizer, creeps into an unguarded box at Ford's Theatre in Washington where a performance of *Our American Cousin* is under way. A moment later, a shot rings out and the fanatical actor, having succeeded in shooting and wounding President Abraham Lincoln, leaps over the box rail to the stage below, shouting "Sic semper tyrannis!" The mortally wounded President is carried to the nearby house of William Petersen, at 453 Tenth Street.

**1865**    At exactly the same time that John Wilkes Booth is stealing into the President's box at Ford's Theatre, Booth's accomplice, Lewis Paine, breaks into the home of Secretary of State William H. Seward, intent on assassinating him. Paine escapes, but not before he has wounded the Secretary and five members of his household.

**1890**    Delegates of 18 republics of North, Central, and South America, meeting in Washington, adopt a resolution creating the First International Bureau of American States, later known as the Pan-American Union.

**1910**    President William Howard Taft inaugurates a precedent by throwing out the first ball at the opening of the baseball season. The President is the honored guest at the American League game between Washington and Philadelphia in the nation's capital.

**1912**    New Yorkers traveling over the Brooklyn Bridge crowd around Frederick R. Law, a moving-picture "stunt" actor, and refuse to budge until they witness his jump off the bridge, a feature of his forthcoming film.

**1931**    King Alfonso XIII and the Spanish Royal Family go into exile after the King signs an instrument of abdication. The affairs of state will rest in the hands of a provisional government.

**1931**    As the 20,000,000th Ford rolls off the assembly line in Detroit, Henry Ford drives the car to the Ford Museum in Dearborn, Michigan, and places it beside Car Number One, manufactured in 1893.

**1965**    A 15-year-old boy is appointed as the first Negro page to serve in the U.S. House of Representatives. He is Frank Mitchell, a high school sophomore from Springfield, Illinois. The boy's appointment was sponsored by Congressman Paul Findley, Republican of Illinois. (*See April 13*)

**1965**    Another feature of American capitalism is appearing in Communist Russia. According to the news agency *Tass*, Russia's first motel is being built in Moscow at the junction of the Minsk and Moscow Circle roads.

*

# APRIL 15

**1837** Abraham Lincoln leaves New Salem, Illinois, and settles down in Springfield, Illinois, where he is forming a law partnership with John T. Stuart.

**1843** Birthday of Henry James, American and British novelist, essayist, and critic.

**1861** President Lincoln sends Congress a message recognizing a state of civil war and calls for 75,000 volunteers to join the Union forces. ("I appeal to all loyal citizens to favor, facilitate and aid this effort to maintain the honor, the integrity, and the existence of our National Union and the perpetuity of popular government. . . .")

**1865** The great heart of Abraham Lincoln, 16th President of the United States, stops beating at 7:22 A.M. Inside the Petersen house, across from Ford's Theatre, where the President's family and members of the government have remained awake in a night-long vigil, Secretary of War Edwin M. Stanton, looking at the dead President, says: "Now he belongs to the ages." (And in New York City, where a saddened crowd had assembled on Wall Street, Congressman James A. Garfield sought to reassure the mourners by speaking to them. "God reigns," said the congressman, "and the Government at Washington still lives.")

**1865** Vice President Andrew Johnson is sworn in as the 17th President of the United States 3 hours after the death of President Lincoln.

**1874** A wedding of international importance takes place at the British Embassy in Paris as Miss Jenny Jerome of New York is married to Lord Randolph Churchill. ("It was not a love-match: it was an attraction-match: and its outcome was momentous, not only for Great Britain and America but for the rest of the civilized world." *—Hesketh Pearson in *The Marrying Americans*)

**1895** An adaptation of George Du Maurier's novel, *Trilby*, is staged in New York at the Garden Theatre. (Immediately thereafter, a Trilby craze swept the country, leaving in its wake a maze of Trilby hats, coats, waltzes, chocolates, children's names.)

**1900** Laborers, working on the new Cornell Dam at Croton, New York, go out on strike in protest over current wage rates. The strikers are demanding a raise from their present daily wage of $1.25 to $1.50.

**1912** After striking an iceberg shortly before midnight during the previous evening, the luxury liner *Titanic*, making her maiden voyage from England to New York, sinks off Cape Race, Newfound-

* A reference to the birth of their first child, Winston Spencer Churchill.

land. Of the 2,223 persons aboard, 1,517 are lost, the remaining passengers rescued a few hours later by the liner *Carpathia.* (The ship's band played steadily until shortly before the great ship sank at 2:27 A.M. Their last selection was the Episcopal hymn, "Autumn," an appropriate choice because of the lines: "Hold me up, mighty waters, Keep my eye on things above....")

**1923** Insulin, discovered by Dr. Frederick Banting of Toronto, Canada, in 1922, becomes available for general use.

**1927** A musical tribute to the popular "Tin Lizzie" automobile highlights a performance of the Boston Symphony. For the first time, Frederick Converse's symphony, *Flivver Ten Million,* is conducted by the orchestra under the baton of Serge Koussevitsky.

**1940** In an attempt to stop the German invaders, British soldiers land in Norway, capturing Narvik as their first objective. (WORLD WAR II)

**1945** The body of Franklin Delano Roosevelt, 32nd President of the United States, is laid to rest in the rose garden of his family estate at Hyde Park, New York. As a Presidential salute is fired from a battery of guns, soldiers, sailors, and marines lift the United States flag from the casket and hand it to the President's widow. Just before the final benediction, the Reverend George W. Anthony, rector of the Roosevelt family's home-town Episcopal church, St. James, Hyde Park, says: "Now the laborer's task is o'er; now the battle-day is past."

**1959** Cuban Premier Fidel Castro arrives in Washington to begin an 11-day goodwill tour of the United States. (*See April 19*)

## APRIL 16

**1787** For the first time in the history of the American theatre, a professional play written by a citizen of the United States is produced in New York. The play is *The Contrast,* written by Royal Tyler, and produced at the John Street Theatre.

**1844** Birthday of Anatole France, French author whose work dominated the field of French literature for 30 years.

**1862** Congress abolishes slavery in the District of Columbia and appropriates $100,000 to be paid to District slaves wishing to emigrate to Liberia or Haiti.

**1862** By order of the Confederate Congress, all white men between the ages of 18 and 35 are to be conscripted into the armed forces of the South.

**1905** Andrew Carnegie places $10,000,000 in the hands of five distinguished men, the income of which is to be used for paying pensions to retired college and university professors. (The fund thus created the Carnegie Foundation for the Advancement of Teaching.)

**1917** Nikolai Lenin, accompanied by his wife and some thirty exiled Bolshevik leaders, arrives in Petrograd from Switzerland, after receiving permission from German war leaders to cross German soil en route to Russia in a "sealed railway car." After being welcomed back to Russia, following his years spent in exile, Lenin addresses the crowd assembled at the railway station: "Dear comrades, soldiers, sailors and workmen, I am happy to greet in you the victorious Russian Revolution, the vanguard of the international proletarian army...." (The Germans who engineered Lenin's return to Russia hoped he would take that country out of the war. Barely a year later, their hopes were realized.)

**1942** The Island of Malta is awarded the George Cross for the heroism and bravery of its inhabitants during daily Fascist air raids. To date, the tiny island has withstood more than 2,000 air raids. (WORLD WAR II)

**1945** President Harry S. Truman, in his first Presidential address to Congress, dedicates his administration to the war and peace ideals of his predecessor, Franklin D. Roosevelt.

**1947** One of the nation's worst disasters strikes at Texas City, Texas, after a nitrate-laden French freighter explodes at a dock and sets off a series of explosions and raging fires. More than five hundred persons lose their lives, thousands are wounded, and property damage amounts to $50,000,000.

**1947** Captain William P. Odom encircles the globe in 78 hours, 55 minutes, and 12 seconds, making his aerial circuit by way of New York, Paris, Cairo, Calcutta, Tokyo, Alaska, and Canada.

**1962** Three Louisiana segregationists are excommunicated by Roman Catholic Archbishop Joseph F. Rummel of New Orleans because of their regular attempts to thwart his order to desegregate parochial schools.

**1964** Sentences of prison terms up to 30 years are handed out to 12 men charged with complicity in the 1963 British mail-train robbery. (*See August 8*)

**1964** A new athletic arena, Shea Municipal Stadium, is dedicated in New York City, one week before the formal opening of the New York World's Fair. (The 55,000-seat stadium, located in Flushing Meadow Park, was built as a home base for the National League's New York Mets baseball team and the American Football League's New York Jets.)

**1965** President Johnson announces that he is sending to the Senate the nomination of a Negro Air Force officer to the rank of lieutenant general, the highest rank ever held by a Negro in the armed forces of the United States. The officer is Major General Benjamin O. Davis, Jr., the only Negro general currently serving on active duty in the armed services. (General Davis was the first Negro to hold the rank of major general. In addition, the Washington officer's father was the first Negro to hold the rank of general in our military forces.)

# APRIL 17

**1521**  The Diet at Worms excommunicates Martin Luther from the Holy Roman Church after the former monk refuses to admit to charges of heresy.

**1777**  Thomas Paine is elected secretary of the Foreign Affairs Committee of the Continental Congress.

**1790**  Benjamin Franklin dies at his home in Philadelphia, aged 84 years.

**1917**  Senator William M. Calder of New York introduces a bill before the Senate which would authorize the adoption of daylight saving time. (The bill was defeated.)

**1933**  Camp Roosevelt, the first camp to be activated under the provisions of the Civilian Conservation Corps, opens near Luray, Virginia.

**1941**  Yugoslavia capitulates to Germany. Partisan forces led by General Draja Mikhailovich continue, however, to wage guerrilla warfare. (WORLD WAR II)

**1944**  The manpower shortage is so acute that a restaurant owner in Seattle, Washington, desperately in need of a woman dishwasher, advertises: "Woman wanted to wash dishes. Will marry if necessary."

**1945**  Prime Minister Winston Churchill, visibly moved, rises to his feet in the House of Commons to pay tribute to the late President Franklin D. Roosevelt: "He died in harness, and we may well say in battle harness, like his soldiers, sailors and airmen who died side by side with ours and carrying out their tasks to the end all over the world. What an enviable death was his...."

**1958**  The Brussels World Fair is opened to the public. (The Fair closed October 19, 1958, with a total attendance of an estimated 42 million persons.)

**1961**  Before dawn, a force of anti-Castro Cuban rebels invades Cuba, landing for the most part in the area of Bahia de Cochinas (Bay of Pigs) in southern Las Villas Province. The attack is directed by the U.S.-based Cuban National Revolutionary Council. (The invasion ended in disaster. Responsibility for its failure is a subject of continuing controversy. The Kennedy Administration was criticized for withholding U.S. air support. Administration supporters, on the other hand, pointed out that planning for the invasion began in the Eisenhower Administration and that, in the face of world opinion, President Kennedy could not justify the use of U.S. military planes or personnel. *See April 7, April 18, April 19, April 24, May 17, December 23.*)

**1964** Mrs. Jerrie Mock, 38-year-old housewife of Columbus, Ohio, becomes the first woman to make a solo flight around the world as she lands at the Columbus airport. She has flown more than 23,000 miles in 29 days, making 21 stops since starting the flight on March 19.

## APRIL 18

**1775** Waiting until he spots a lantern blinking from the North Church in Boston, the patriot Paul Revere starts out on his famous midnight ride to alert the countryside that some eight hundred British soldiers are on their way to confiscate the gunpowder stored in Concord by the American militia. At Lexington, Revere and another patriot, William Dawes, stop long enough to warn John Hancock and Samuel Adams that the British have orders to capture them. Then, Revere is on his way, rousing the sleepy Americans with his message, "The British are coming!"

**1906** While most of the populace is asleep, San Francisco is struck by a violent earthquake at a quarter past five in the morning, the worst earthquake ever to hit the United States. After the tremors have subsided, a new threat follows in the form of raging fires. (By the time it was all over, three days later, half of the city had been wiped out, leaving almost five hundred persons dead, fifteen hundred injured, and more than a quarter of a million homeless.)

**1925** Mrs. Calvin Coolidge, the First Lady of the land, opens the first Woman's World Fair at Chicago.

**1933** The state of Minnesota enacts legislation providing for a mortgage moratorium on farms and residences until the economy of the state is back on its feet. (Farmers in the state, and throughout the entire Middle West, banded together and marched on county sheriffs' offices demanding that foreclosure sales be suspended.)

**1934** The era of the "Laundromat" is born in Fort Worth, Texas, when a local resident opens his "Washateria," a new type of service where electric washing machines can be rented by the hour.

**1942** Americans are thrilled by the daring air raid made by Lieutenant-Colonel James H. Doolittle and his squadron of 16 B-25 bombers on the Japanese cities of Tokyo, Yokohama, Kobe, and Nagoya. (WORLD WAR II)

**1945** Ernie Pyle, the beloved American war correspondent and "GI's columnist," is killed by a bullet from a Japanese machine gun on Ie Shima in the Ryukyu Islands. (WORLD WAR II)

**1949** "An Poblacht Abu!" ("Up the Republic!") is the lusty cry heard all over Dublin, Ireland, as a 21-gun salute from the O'Connell Bridge marks the inauguration of the Republic of Ireland. (The new republic, of course, is that section of Ireland formerly known as Eire. Northern Ireland is still affiliated with the British Empire.)

**1953**  Twenty-one-year-old Mickey Mantle, who succeeded Joe DiMaggio as center fielder for the New York Yankees, hits a home run in Griffith Stadium, Washington, that travels about 565 feet. Baseball fans believe Mantle's hit is the longest ever *measured* in a regular big-league game.

**1955**  Delegates of 29 nations, meeting in Bandung, Indonesia, open the Asia-African Conference. One of the first pieces of business is a resolution rejecting all forms of colonialism.

**1961**  While thousands of angry Russians demonstrate before the U.S. Embassy in Moscow, Premier Khrushchev echoes their protests over the Bay of Pigs invasion. In a message to President Kennedy, he charges that ". . . armed bands invaded Cuba (after being) trained, equipped and armed" by the United States. The Soviet leader goes on to warn that his country will ". . . render . . . all necessary assistance to Cuba to beat back the armed attack . . ."

**1964**  The 17-day strike by Belgian doctors comes to an end when they agree to resume their medical practices pending a negotiation of their differences with the government. (The doctors called the strike in protest against a new national health law which they claimed was a step toward socialized medicine.)

**1965**  The great American contralto, Marian Anderson, ends her formal singing career at a final concert in New York's Carnegie Hall. Her career has spanned thirty years, stretched across the United States, Europe and Asia, and transcended racial barriers. ("There had been fine Negro singers before her . . . It was Miss Anderson who stood as a symbol for the emergence of the Negro. . . . In a way, she was part of the American dream. And her success story was an inspiration to younger Negro musicians. . . ."—*The New York Times'* critic Harold C. Schonberg.)

## APRIL 19

**Patriots' Day**  Commemorating the battles of Lexington and Concord.

**1775**  Beginning of the American War for Independence: about an hour after sunrise, the British, arriving at Lexington, Massachusetts, find awaiting them a small company of Minute Men, those patriots who responded to Paul Revere's warning. "Stand your ground. Don't fire unless fired upon. But if they mean to have war, let it begin here!" With these words, issued by their commander, Captain John Parker, the Americans stand on the village green waiting to see what happens. Major Pitcairn, the British commander, orders them to disperse. A shot is fired and then another. Seven Minute Men are killed instantly, 10 are wounded. The remaining few start to retreat. The American Revolution is on! (But traveling on to Concord, the British found the countryside alive with Minute Men and would not have returned safely to Boston if General Gage had not sent out a British relief force to strengthen their numbers.)

**1783**    Eight years after the Battle of Lexington, Congress announces the end of the Revolutionary War.

**1824**    Lord Byron, English poet, dies at Missolonghi in the fight for Greek freedom.

**1865**    In the great East Room of the White House in Washington, a grief-stricken group of relatives, friends, and government officials sit in hushed silence as funeral services are conducted for President Abraham Lincoln. (Mary Todd Lincoln, the President's widow, was in such a state of shock that she was not permitted to attend.)

**1892**    After working on it for 8 months, Charles E. Duryea of Springfield, Massachusetts, turns the last screw in his horseless carriage and takes it out of his shop for a successful drive. Mr. Duryea calls his vehicle, the first American-made automobile in history, a "buggyaut."

**1933**    The United States abandons the gold standard.

**1951**    General Douglas MacArthur, recalled from Korea by President Truman, closes his military career by addressing a Joint Session of Congress: "The world has turned over many times since I took the oath on the plain at West Point . . . but I still remember the refrain of one of the most popular barracks ballads of that day which proclaimed most proudly that old soldiers never die; they just fade away. And like the old soldier of that ballad, I now close my military career and just fade away. . . ."

**1956**    With more than fifteen hundred press, radio, television, and newsreel reporters covering the event, film actress Grace Kelly of Philadelphia is married to Prince Rainier III, sovereign of Monaco, in the Cathedral of St. Nicholas in Monte Carlo. (Miss Kelly, the first American to marry a reigning sovereign, had been married to the Prince a day earlier in a civil ceremony.)

**1961**    Cuban rebels who invaded their homeland two days ago surrender after they are overwhelmed by Fidel Castro's troops.

## APRIL 20

**1836**    Congress establishes the Territory of Wisconsin.

**1861**    Colonel Robert E. Lee resigns his commission in the U.S. Army with the intention of offering his services to the Confederate cause.

**1889**   Adolf Hitler is born in Braunau, Austria.

**1896**   In New York City, Koster & Bial's Music Hall starts a regular schedule of scenes from Edison's Vitascope along with their customary vaudeville acts and routines.

**1902**   Marie and Pierre Curie isolate one gram of radium salts from about 8 tons of pitchblende and determine the atomic weights and properties of radium and polonium.

**1903**   Andrew Carnegie presents $1,500,000 for the construction of the Hague Peace Palace in the Netherlands.

**1926**   A picturegram of a bank check sent from London to New York by RCA radiophoto is honored and cashed in New York, the first time a bank has so honored a check not actually in its possession.

**1934**   Shirley Temple begins her successful career as a moving-picture child star as the film *Stand Up and Cheer* is released in New York. (The film included the popular "Baby, Take a Bow" song and dance sequence.)

**1947**   The nationally known comedian Fred Allen is cut off the air in the midst of his weekly radio program because of a joke he made about a mythical network vice-president.

**1948**   Walter P. Reuther, president of the United Automobile Workers Union, is seriously wounded as an unidentified assailant fires a shotgun at him through the window of the Reuther home in Detroit.

**1954**   Australian officials prevent Soviet couriers from forcing Madame Yevdokiya Petrov to board a Russian-bound airplane at the Sydney airport. (This was a follow-up to the defection of the woman's husband, Vladimir Petrov, from the staff of the Soviet legation in Australia. Both Petrovs were given asylum by the Australian government.)

**1962**   Segregationists in New Orleans inaugurate a plan to "export" Negroes to the North. Under this plan, the local Citizens Council agrees to provide free bus rides for Negroes without funds who are willing to move to cities in the northern states. (The first local Negroes to accept rides on these so-called "Freedom Buses" were Louis Boyd, his wife and eight children. All 10 arrived in New York City on April 21.)

## APRIL 21

**753 B.C.**   Rome founded by Romulus.

**1789**   Having been advised of his election as Vice President of the United States, John Adams takes his oath of office in New York and assumes his duties as presiding officer of the Senate.

**1816**   Birthday of Charlotte Brontë, English novelist, particularly remembered for her *Jane Eyre.*

**1836**   General Sam Houston, commanding a force of 800 Texans, defeats 3,000 Mexicans led by General Santa Anna on the San Jacinto River near Galveston, Texas.

**1910**   A beloved American figure passes from the scene as Mark Twain dies. William Dean Howells, the famous writer and editor, is so moved by the news that he writes a note to Twain's daughter, Clara Clemens: "You have lost a father. Shall I dare tell you of the desolation of an old man who has lost a friend, and finds himself alone in the great world which has now wholly perished around?"

**1926**   Birthday of Queen Elizabeth II of Great Britain.

**1940**   The phrase, "The sixty-four-dollar question," soon to become a part of the American idiom, is used for the first time in a radio quiz program, "Take It or Leave It." (The reference was to the jackpot question, worth $64 to contestants.)

**1945**   A broadcast from Germany says that Russian troops are already inside the city limits of Berlin, the first Allied soldiers to reach the capital. (WORLD WAR II)

**1953**   The controversial and highly publicized European trip of Roy Cohn and David Schine, two young aides of Senator Joseph R. McCarthy (R., Wis.), comes to an end when the two men return to New York. (During their 18-day tour of France, Germany, Austria, Yugoslavia, Greece, Italy, and Great Britain to investigate alleged subversion, waste, and inefficiency in the U.S. Information Service, Cohn and Schine were subjected to bitter criticism in both the American and European press, and Congressmen James G. Fulton and Robert J. Corbett, both Republicans of Pennsylvania, said "they are doing more harm than good.")

**1954**   Planes of the U.S. Air Force start flying French troops from Paris to Indochina to reinforce the colonial bastion at Dienbienphu.

**1956**   Leonard Ross, a 10-year-old boy from Tujunga, California, makes his mark in television as he wins $100,000 on the quiz program, "The Big Surprise." (Undoubtedly the youngest contestant to win such a large prize, Leonard answered questions related to his specialty, stocks and bonds.)

**1962**   After President John F. Kennedy presses a golden telegraphic key in Palm Beach, Florida, the Century 21 Exposition in Seattle is officially opened to the public.

## APRIL 22

**1707**   Birthday of Henry Fielding, English novelist, best remembered for his tale of *Tom Jones*.

**1793**   Among those attending a performance of Ricketts' Circus in Philadelphia is President George Washington.

**1864**   Congress authorizes the director of the Mint to use the motto "In God We Trust" on all coins of the United States. (The motto was proposed originally by a clergyman, the Reverend M. R. Watkinson.)

**1889**   Twenty thousand homesteaders mass along the central border of the Oklahoma Territory awaiting the signal that will usher in the Oklahoma Land Rush. (By nightfall, a tent city had been laid out, a bank set up, and thousands of men, women, and children had staked out claims to government land.)

**1898**   The U.S. Navy fires the first shot of the Spanish-American War when the U.S.S. *Nashville* opens fire on a Spanish freighter off Key West, Florida.

**1898**   Theodore Roosevelt resigns from his post as Assistant Secretary of War to recruit members for the "Rough Riders," the name popularly assigned to the First Regiment United States Cavalry Volunteers.

**1915**   For the first time in World War I, the German Army starts to use poison gas at Ypres, Belgium, in direct violation of the rules of the Hague Convention. (Specifically, the Germans discharged chlorine gas from mobile cylinders.) (WORLD WAR I)

**1940**   Radio history is made in San Francisco when an all-Chinese program is broadcast. Even the "commercials" are broadcast in Chinese, to the delight of San Francisco's large Chinese colony.

**1944**   Allied soldiers invade New Guinea. (WORLD WAR II)

**1945**   Twenty-one districts in the city of Berlin, one-sixth of the total area of the city, are in the hands of soldiers of the Soviet Army. (WORLD WAR II)

**1946**   Nineteen million Egyptians who live near the Nile River observe the national holiday of Shem-el-Nessim, or "Sniff-the-Breeze Day." (Egyptians believe that there is nothing like a few breaths of the departing spring air to keep away the hot summer's midafternoon drowsiness. This holiday is spent traditionally in picnicking, preferably as near to the Nile as possible.)

**1954**   The Senate Permanent Investigating Subcommittee, Senator Karl Mundt (R., S.D.), Chairman, starts hearings on the controversial quarrel between the Army Department and Senator Joseph R. McCarthy (R., Wis.).

**1964**   The New York World's Fair opens.

## APRIL 23

**1789**   President-elect and Mrs. George Washington move into the first "Presidential Mansion" at the corner of Franklin and Cherry Streets in New York City. Despite the fact that the residence is very large and commodious, the Washingtons are going to be cramped for space since their household includes the First Lady's two grandchildren, several servants, and the President's secretaries.

**1791** James Buchanan, 15th President of the United States, is born in Franklin County, Pennsylvania.

**1792** "La Marseillaise," the national anthem of France, is written by Claude Joseph Rouget de Lisle.

**1843** Followers of the "prophet" William Miller gather throughout the United States to await his prediction that the world will come to an end today. (After much advance fanfare, nothing happened.)

**1860** The Democratic National Convention opens its sessions at Charleston, South Carolina. (No candidates were nominated because of an intraparty dispute.)

**1898** The government asks for 125,000 volunteers to assist in the war against Spain.

**1915** Death of Rupert Brooke, British poet, in Greece while on duty with the Royal Navy in World War I. ("If I should die, think only this of me: that there's some corner of a foreign field that is forever England.")

**1917** At a great mass meeting of theatre personalities in the Palace Theatre in New York, George M. Cohan calls for volunteers to entertain the American Expeditionary Forces overseas. Almost every performer present offers to join the overseas troupes. (WORLD WAR I)

**1932** The Prince of Wales presides at the opening of the Shakespeare Memorial Theatre at Stratford-on-Avon, England. (The first such Memorial had burned 6 years earlier.)

**1941** Six thousand people attending a rally of the America First Committee in New York City hear Charles A. Lindbergh say that "it is obvious that England is losing the war." The famous aviator opposes America's entry into the war. (WORLD WAR II)

**1949** Governor Adlai E. Stevenson of Illinois vetoes a bill that would require cats in that state to be held in leash: "I cannot agree that it should be the declared public policy of Illinois that a cat visiting a neighbor's yard or crossing the highway is a public nuisance. It is in the nature of cats to do a certain amount of unescorted roaming.... In my opinion, the state of Illinois and its local governing bodies already have enough to do without trying to control feline delinquency...."

**1963** William A. Moore, a white man, is shot to death on a road near Attalla, Alabama, while staging a one-man "Freedom Walk" against Negro segregation. Moore started his walk at Chattanooga, Tennessee, and was on his way to Jackson, Mississippi, where he hoped to present a personal appeal for racial integration to Governor Ross Barnett.

# APRIL 24

**1704**   The *Boston News-Letter,* the first American newspaper to be printed on a regular basis, is published for the first time. The publishers are two brothers, John and Duncan Campbell.

**1800**   Congress votes to create a Library of Congress and appropriates $5,000 "for the purchase of such books as may be necessary for the use of both Houses of Congress."

**1877**   Northern rule in the South ends as President Rutherford B. Hayes orders the removal of federal troops from New Orleans.

**1897**   William W. Price reports to work at the *Washington Star,* becoming the first journalist to be known as the "White House reporter." (Before this date, it was the custom for newspapers to "cover" the Capitol regularly and the White House only on specific occasions. Price made the White House his "beat.")

**1898**   Spain declares war on the United States after receiving an American ultimatum to withdraw from Cuba.

**1917**   Congress passes the "Liberty Loan Act," authorizing the Treasury Department to issue war bonds totaling five billion dollars. (WORLD WAR I)

**1933**   Chicago schoolteachers storm Chicago banks demanding back pay amounting to $30,000,000. The teachers have not been paid for ten months, victims of the Depression-ridden city's precarious state of finances.

**1953**   Winston Churchill becomes Sir Winston Churchill as he is knighted at Buckingham Palace by Queen Elizabeth II.

**1953**   Moslem women vote for the first time, the occasion being Karachi's first municipal election. Extra police are on hand to protect the women from male hecklers.

**1961**   As a follow-up to the U.S. government's involvement in the Bay of Pigs disaster, President Kennedy directs his press secretary to release a statement saying: "... As President, I bear sole responsibility for the events of the past days.... The President is strongly opposed to anyone ... attempting to shift the responsibility ..."

**1964**   According to the 1964 edition of *Television Factbook,* the television set count for the world has reached 143,000,000. Of this number, 61,850,000 sets are in the United States. A total of 90 nations now have television broadcasting. Twenty-six of these nations ban television commercials completely.

**1965**   A group of young Army officers and civilians in the Dominican Republic seize control of two radio stations in Santo Domingo and broadcast their intention to oust the military-backed civilian junta ruling the country. Their announced aim is to reinstate Juan Bosch, ousted as President by a military coup in 1963. Within hours, the tiny nation is torn apart by a revolution. (*See April 27*)

# APRIL 25

**1816**  Lord Byron, separated from his wife and a social outcast in England, leaves that country, never to return again.

**1846**  The first shots in the Mexican War are exchanged when Captain Seth B. Thornton and a company of cavalrymen engage the enemy at La Rosia, Mexico.

**1898**  Congress formally declares war on the government of Spain.

**1901**  New York State becomes the first state in the nation to require automobile owners to equip their vehicles with license plates. (Exactly 954 automobiles were registered. Each license plate was inscribed with the owner's initials.)

**1934**  Walter S. Gifford, president of the American Telephone Company, picks up his telephone receiver and places a call to Thomas G. Miller, sitting in an adjacent office. What makes this telephone call unusual is that before the two men speak, the call is routed from New York through San Francisco, Java, Amsterdam, London, and then to Mr. Miller in New York.

**1945**  Benito Mussolini, the former Italian dictator, and his mistress, Clara Petacci, make their escape from Milan, as Allied soldiers converge on that city. (WORLD WAR II)

**1945**  Soldiers of the U.S. First Army and the First Ukrainian Army of the Soviet Union join forces at 4:40 P.M. when advance units of both armies meet on a demolished bridge over the Elbe River at Torgau, Germany. (The celebration that followed was described by a reporter of the Associated Press: "It was a celebration unlike anything seen before in this war. One great party, with doughboys and Russians singing, laughing and dancing and trying to talk to each other in sign language.") (WORLD WAR II)

**1945**  Delegates of 46 nations meet at San Francisco to organize a permanent United Nations. In opening the international conference, President Harry S. Truman of the United States tells the delegates: "We represent the overwhelming majority of all mankind. We speak for people who have endured the most savage and devastating war ever inflicted upon innocent men, women and children. We hold a powerful mandate from our people. They believe we will fulfill this obligation."

**1953**  Senator Wayne Morse (Independent, Ore.,) concludes the longest Senate speech to date * when he argues against the Republican-sponsored bill granting offshore oil lands to certain coastal states. Beginning at 11:40 A.M. on April 24 and winding up at 10:06 A.M. today, the Senator has remained on his feet, speaking

---

* But Senator Morse's record was broken August 28–29, 1957 when Senator Strom Thurmond, then a Democrat of South Carolina, held the floor for a record 24 hours and 18 minutes in a futile attempt to hold up passage of the 1957 Civil Rights Bill.

for 22 hours, 26 minutes. He has sustained himself all during the speech by occasionally eating a few crackers, a candy bar; drinking broth, coffee, and tea, and swallowing ice.

**1959**　The St. Lawrence Seaway, 400-mile waterway enabling ocean vessels to reach inland ports on the Great Lakes, is opened to shipping. (*See June 26*)

**1964**　For the first time since his death in 1923, the papers of former President Warren G. Harding are opened to the public in Columbus, Ohio. The documents and manuscripts number more than 325,000.

## APRIL 26

**1564**　William Shakespeare is baptized in the parish church at Stratford-on-Avon, Warwickshire, England. (Most almanacs list his birth as April 23, 1564, but there is no actual documentary evidence to support that date. His baptism, however, has been recorded as of this date.) (*See below*)

**1607**　The first British colonists to establish a permanent settlement in America land at Cape Henry, Virginia.

**1819**　Lodge Number One of the Independent Order of Odd Fellows is organized at Baltimore, Maryland.

**1865**　After a relentless search, federal troops discover the hiding place of John Wilkes Booth on the farm of Richard Garrett near Port Royal, Virginia. When the assassin of Lincoln refuses to come out of a tobacco barn and surrender, a soldier shoots and kills him, despite orders to capture him alive.

**1877**　People in Minnesota observe this date as a statewide day of prayer, asking for deliverance from a plague of grasshoppers that has ravished thousands of acres of farm crops. (The plague ended the following summer.)

**1910**　At the dedication ceremonies of the Pan-American Union building in Washington, President William Howard Taft and Andrew Carnegie, donor of the structure, plant a "tree of peace" dedicated to friendship among the American republics.

**1944**　The United States takes over the Chicago headquarters of Montgomery Ward & Company, after the company management defies a ruling of the National Labor Relations Board. (The seizure followed a dispute between the management and the Congress of Industrial Organizations. The key figure in the incident was Sewell Avery, Montgomery Ward's New Deal-hating president, who had to be carried out of his office by two soldiers.)

**1951**　William N. Oatis, a correspondent for the Associated Press, is arrested and imprisoned by the government of Czechoslovakia on charges of espionage. (*See May 16*)

**1954**　A nationwide test of the Salk antipoliomyelitis vaccine begins in 171 different districts in 45 states. Nine hundred thousand children are scheduled to receive injections of the vaccine.

126

**1964**   The African nations of Tanganyika and Zanzibar merge to form a single sovereign republic. The official name of the new state is Tanzania.

**1964**   Countries dotted all over the face of the globe start to commemorate the 400th anniversay of William Shakespeare's birth. Commenting on the debt of the United States to the great poet, an editorial in *The Washington Post* says: "... [No one] would have guessed in 1564 that a country across the seas, not yet settled by Englishmen, would one day owe an enormous debt to William Shakespeare of Stratford.... Except for the King James version of the Bible, no other body of literature has had such a pervasive influence upon our civilization as have Shakespeare's plays and poems...."

## APRIL 27

**1822**   Ulysses S. Grant, 18th President of the United States, is born at Point Pleasant, Ohio. (*See below*)

**1844**   Martin Van Buren and Henry Clay announce they oppose President Tyler's proposal to annex Texas, unless Mexico agrees to the annexation.

**1850**   An American-owned steamship, *The Atlantic,* inaugurates a schedule of regular transatlantic passenger service, the first American ship to offer competion to British liners.

**1882**   Ralph Waldo Emerson, essayist, poet, and philosopher, dies at his home in Concord, Massachusetts.

**1897**   The body of former President Ulysses S. Grant is removed to the tomb bearing his name on New York's Riverside Drive. (The mausoleum was built by popular subscription, some ninety thousand citizens contributing $600,000 of the cost.)

**1898**   The American fleet under the command of Commodore Dewey leaves China for the Philippines.

**1906**   The United States Steel Corporation begins to break ground along Lake Michigan for the construction of a new Indiana town, to be known as Gary, Indiana.

**1937**   The first Social Security payment is made in accordance with the provisions of the Social Security Act of 1935.

**1941**   Athens falls to the German invaders. The Nazi swastika is hoisted over the Acropolis after 180 days of heroic Greek resistance to the invaders.

**1947**   Baseball fans observe "Babe Ruth Day" throughout the nation in honor of the seriously ill former "Sultan of Swat." The largest observance is held at Yankee Stadium in New York, where 58,339 persons tender the Babe the greatest ovation in the history of the national pastime. Barely able to speak, Ruth stands up before a microphone to thank the cheering crowd: "Thank you very much, ladies and gentlemen. You know how bad my voice sounds.

Well, it feels just as bad. . . . There's been so many lovely things said about me, I'm glad I had the opportunity to thank everybody. Thank you." (A little over a year later, he was dead.)

**1965** As the revolution in the Dominican Republic grows more intense, the U.S. aircraft carrier *Boxer* and two transports move into offshore positions to begin the evacuation of U.S. civilians there. (*See April 28*)

## APRIL 28

**1758** James Monroe, the fifth President of the United States, is born in Westmoreland County, Virginia.

**1788** Maryland enters the Union as the seventh state.

**1789** Mutiny breaks out on the British ship *Bounty*. As a result, Captain William Bligh and 18 sailors are set adrift in a launch, the *Bounty* sailing to Tahiti under command of the rebel mate, Fletcher Christian. (Captain Bligh and his 18 sailors rowed more than 3,600 miles to Timor. The *Bounty* itself ended up in Pitcairn Island in 1790 where the remnants of the original crew set her afire.)

**1902** *The New York World* is waging a vigorous campaign against the role of the so-called "Beef Trust" in the present-day high cost of living. *The World* cites some "Prices That Stagger Humanity": sirloin steak, 24 cents a pound; lamb chops, 18 cents; pork chops, 18 cents; ham, 18 cents.

**1937** A new feature is added to the attractions of the Great White Way in New York when Douglas Leigh introduces the first electrical animated cartoon on the front of a building in Times Square.

**1941** Charles A. Lindbergh, incensed because President Roosevelt referred to him 3 days earlier as a modern-day counterpart of the "copperhead defeatists of the Civil War," resigns as colonel in the U.S. Army Air Corps Reserve. (Lindbergh, at this time, was an outspoken member of America First, a group opposed to the United States' entry into World War II and equally opposed to military and financial aid to Great Britain.) (WORLD WAR II)

**1945** The end of Benito Mussolini: Italian patriots execute Benito Mussolini, his mistress, Clara Petacci, and 16 other Italian Fascists in the town of Giuliano di Mezzegere, near Lake Como, as they attempt to make their getaway to Switzerland. (Said the Associated Press: "Mussolini was beaten, kicked, trampled upon, riddled, hanged head downward, mutilated and spat upon, his flesh treated as less than carrion, his memory hideously reviled.") (WORLD WAR II)

**1952** The war with Japan officially ends as the treaty signed by the United States and 47 other nations at San Francisco in 1951 goes into effect.

**1959**    The U.S. Senate is in an uproar because of a continuing feud between Senator Wayne Morse (D., Ore.) and Mrs. Clare Boothe Luce. Almost immediately after the Senate confirms the controversial Mrs. Luce as Ambassador to Brazil, she issues a statement offering her explanation of Senator Morse's opposition to her appointment: ". . . My difficulties, of course, go some years back when Senator Morse was kicked in the head by a horse." * (After several senators took to the floor saying they would have voted against her confirmation had she issued the statement before the vote, her husband, Henry R. Luce advised her to resign. She did resign on May 1.)

**1962**    Marine Lieutenant Dave Tork of Camp Pendleton, California, establishes a world outdoor pole vault record of 16 feet 2 inches in Walnut, California, using the controversial fiberglass pole. *(See February 2)*

**1965**    After President Lyndon B. Johnson receives an urgent appeal from U.S. ambassador to the Dominican Republic W. Tapley Bennett to "land troops immediately or [American] blood will run in the streets," the President orders 400 Marines to land in Santo Domingo. *(See May 4)*

## APRIL 29

**1862**    New Orleans, the gateway to the Mississippi and once a stronghold of the Confederacy, falls to Union forces.

**1878**    Readers of Boston newspapers are amused by an advertisement of the latest fad: "A Telephone, Complete $3.00. Guaranteed to Work 1 Mile. One guaranteed to work 5 miles, $5.00."

**1894**    Jacob S. Coxey and his "army" of several hundred unemployed men arrive in the nation's capital to petition Congress for relief legislation. After a demonstration on the steps of the Capitol, Coxey and some of his chief aides are arrested for "walking on the grass" and sentenced to 20 days in jail.

**1913**    The zipper, an indispensable modern-day gadget, becomes a part of everyday life after Gideon Sundback of Hoboken, New Jersey, patents it under the title of a "separable fastener."

**1918**    Captain Edward V. Rickenbacker achieves his first victory over enemy aircraft when he shoots down a German airplane over the Toul sector in France. (WORLD WAR I)

**1923**    The Chinese game of mah-jongg is the current craze in every state of the Union. From Main Street to Park Avenue, the talk from morning to night is of "bamboos," "pung," "flowers," "seasons," "South Wind," and the "Red Dragon."

* In fact, Senator Morse's *jaw* was broken in 1951. His opposition to her was based on his charge that she was unqualified to be a diplomat because of her statement in 1944 that President Franklin D. Roosevelt had "lied us into World War II." During committee hearings, Mrs. Luce said: "I stand by my statement."

**1931**    President Hoover receives King Prajadhipok of Siam at the White House, the first absolute monarch to visit the United States.

**1945**    In his secret bunker in Berlin, Adolf Hitler draws up a last will and testament: "My possessions belong to the Party, or, if this no longer exists, to the State. If the State, too, is destroyed, there is no need for any further instructions." (WORLD WAR II)

**1945**    American soldiers liberate 32,000 Nazi victims at Dachau, the oldest and worst of the German concentration camps. (WORLD WAR II)

**1945**    The bodies of Benito Mussolini and his companions, executed by Partisans the day before, are hung up and displayed to the populace in Milan, Italy. (WORLD WAR II)

**1962**    President and Mrs. Kennedy entertain at the White House 49 past winners of the Nobel Prize. Also invited are 124 other writers, educators, editors, and scientists. Among those present are seven Pulitzer prize winners, including the President. To his guests, the President describes the dinner as "probably the greatest concentration of talent and genius in this house except for perhaps those times when Thomas Jefferson dined alone."

**1964**    Princess Irene, daughter of Queen Juliana and Prince Bernhard of the Netherlands, is married in Rome to Prince Carlos Hugo of Bourbon-Parma. (This event climaxed a crisis in the Netherlands. The Princess, having embraced Catholicism, was obliged to renounce her succession rights to the throne of the Protestant House of Orange. The Royal Family did not attend the wedding but remained at The Hague where they watched the ceremony over television.)

## APRIL 30

**1789**    A great crowd assembles in New York to watch and hear George Washington take the oath of office as the first President of the United States. After Washington is sworn in on the balcony of Federal Hall, Chancellor Robert R. Livingston, who administered the oath, steps forward to the railing and shouts "Long live George Washington, President of the United States!" As the crowd breaks into a great cheer, a 13-gun salute is sounded from the harbor, and the flag of the infant nation is hoisted above the building, a proud symbol of the new republic.

**1803**    Louisiana Purchase: The United States more than doubles its physical area by purchasing from Napoleon Bonaparte all of the French territory west of the Mississippi River. (This transaction, the greatest peacetime acquisition of land in the history of any nation, cost the United States about $15,000,000, roughly four cents an acre, and included enough land for the subsequent addition of 13 states to the Union.)

**1812**     Louisiana is admitted into the Union as the 18th state.

**1889**     Congress fixes this date as a national holiday to celebrate the centennial of the inauguration of George Washington.

**1900**     Casey Jones, the "brave engineer" of the famous American folk song, is killed at Vaughan, Mississippi, on the Illinois Central Railroad, when his Cannonball Express collides with the back end of a freight train.

**1939**     President Franklin D. Roosevelt opens the New York World's Fair, dedicated to "The World of Tomorrow." A half million persons jam the opening, eager to view the exhibits of 60 nations.

**1945**     The end of Hitler: Adolf Hitler, the Nazi dictator of Germany, commits suicide in a bunker 30 feet below the ruins of the Reichschancellery in Berlin. (WORLD WAR II)

**1945**     Russian soldiers capture the Reichstag in Berlin and raise the Communist flag over the former German capitol. (WORLD WAR II)

**1957**     After almost 2 years of study, a special committee headed by Senator John F. Kennedy (D., Mass.) selects five "outstanding Senators of the past." The five men, representing the unanimous choices of the five-man committee of present-day senators, are: Henry Clay of Kentucky, Daniel Webster of Massachusetts, John C. Calhoun of South Carolina, Robert M. La Follette, Sr., of Wisconsin, and Robert A. Taft of Ohio.

**1963**     Governor John W. King of New Hampshire signs into law a bill legalizing two sweepstakes a year. Thus, New Hampshire becomes the first state to authorize a state-run lottery since 1894 when a similar one was ended in Louisiana. *(See September 12)*

# MAY

## MAY 1

### May Day

**1795**   As a result of the addition of Kentucky and Vermont to the Union, making a total of 15 states, Congress authorizes the national flag to increase its stars and stripes to 15 each.

**1844**   At the Whig National Convention in Baltimore, Henry Clay of Kentucky receives the unanimous nomination for President.

**1872**   The newly organized Liberal Republican Party nominates Horace Greeley of New York for the Presidency and B. Gratz Brown of Missouri for the Vice Presidency.

**1873**   Penny postal cards are placed on sale for the first time by the U.S. Post Office.

**1883**   William F. Cody, better known as Buffalo Bill, stages his first "Wild West" show to the complete delight of little boys and grown men all over the nation.

**1884**   Construction crews in Chicago start their work on a 10-story office building at the corner of La Salle and Adams streets, the first structure to be called a "skyscraper."

**1886**   A convention of the Federation of Trades meeting at Washington, D.C., sets a standard for American labor when the delegates vote to adopt the 8-hour work day.

**1898**   Commodore George Dewey, in command of the U.S. Asiatic Squadron, sails into Manila Bay in obedience to an order cabled to him at Hong Kong: "You must capture vessels or destroy." At exactly 5:40 A.M., Dewey leans over the bridge of his flagship, the *Olympia,* and says to Captain Charles V. Gridley: "You may fire when you are ready, Gridley." (Within 5 hours, the Spanish fleet was reduced to scrap iron. The American casualties totaled eight slightly wounded men, no ships lost. The fall of Manila was now assured and so was Dewey in the pages of American history.)

**1901**   The Pan-American Exposition opens in Buffalo, New York.

**1904**   The Louisiana Purchase Exposition, marking the 100th anniversary of the purchase of the Louisiana Territory, opens in St. Louis, Missouri.

**1915** On the same day the Cunard liner *Lusitania* prepares to sail from New York for Liverpool, England, the Imperial German Embassy inserts a warning to the liner's passengers in New York newspapers: ". . . vessels flying the flag of Great Britain, or of any of her allies, are liable to destruction . . . and travelers sailing in the war zone on ships of Great Britain or her allies do so at their own risk." *(See May 7.)*

**1931** The Empire State Building, the world's tallest skyscraper, is dedicated by former Governor Alfred E. Smith in New York. The new skyscraper has 102 floors and soars up into the air to a total height of 1,250 feet.

**1942** The War Production Board restricts the production of ice cream, limiting manufacturers to some twenty different flavors. (WORLD WAR II)

**1945** Radio Hamburg broadcasts an announcement to the German people telling them of the death of Hitler "at his command post" and the succession of Admiral Karl Doenitz as the new leader of Germany (WORLD WAR II)

**1964** President Lyndon B. Johnson predicts that the day will come when a woman will serve as President of the United States. He says: "I can see the day coming when none of the great offices of the Republic will be closed to women of talent, not even the office of President—although I hope you will forgive me for hoping that day is still a few years off."

## MAY 2

**1853** A chariot and ostrich race highlights the opening of Franconi's Hippodrome at Broadway and 23rd Street in New York. The new amusement palace can seat 4,000 persons.

**1863** General Thomas Jonathan (Stonewall) Jackson is shot down by his own Confederate soldiers outside of Chancellorsville, Virginia, as he is reconnoitering in front of his battle station. On hearing of Jackson's wounds and the subsequent loss of his left arm, General Robert E. Lee dispatches a note to the valiant officer, saying: "You are better off than I am, for while you have lost your left, I have lost my *right* arm." (Jackson succumbed to his injuries on May 10.)

**1865** President Andrew Johnson offers a reward of $100,000 to anyone capturing Jefferson Davis, President of the Confederacy.

**1923** Lieutenants Oakley G. Kelly and John A. Macready of the U.S. Navy take off from Roosevelt Field, New York, in a Fokker monoplane, bound for the West Coast. (They landed at Coronado Beach, California, the next day, the first aviators to make a successful nonstop transcontinental flight.)

**1933** Adolf Hitler abolishes labor unions throughout Germany and creates a "Labor Front" to control all German workers.

**1941**   The Federal Communications Commission approves the regular scheduling of commercial television broadcasts beginning July 1.

**1945**   The last organized resistance ends in Berlin as the German garrison there surrenders to soldiers of the Soviet Army. A great part of the city is a mass of debris and crumbled stone. (WORLD WAR II)

**1945**   The Allies announce the unconditional surrender of Nazi troops in Italy and southern and western Austria. (WORLD WAR II)

**1946**   A serious riot breaks out in Alcatraz Prison as convicts there attempt to break out of the fortress in San Francisco Bay. (The riot was suppressed after a 48-hour battle in which 80 Marines assisted local authorities in a siege of the prison. Two guards and 3 prisoners were killed, and 14 guards and one prisoner were wounded.)

**1954**   Stan Musial, a player with the St. Louis Cardinals, establishes a major-league record to date for home runs in a doubleheader when he hits five of them against the New York Giants in St. Louis. (He tied the record for home runs in two consecutive games.)

**1960**   After 12-years of litigation, Caryl Chessman is executed in San Quentin Prison, California. (First convicted in 1948 on counts of kidnapping, robbery, sexual abuses, and attempted rape, Chessman spent his years in prison writing four books. He won eight stays of execution and became the rallying force for foes of capital punishment.)

**1963**   In an historic speech on the floor of the U.S. Senate, Senator Thomas H. Kuchel (R., Calif.) lashes out at American "fright peddlers" and right-wing extremists. He says: "... I have nothing but contempt for the originators of the hoaxes and swindles, from the ludicrous leaders of the Birch Society to any and all of the several hundred similar self-styled 'patriotic' groups. They are anything but patriotic. Indeed, a good case can be made that they are unpatriotic and downright un-American...."

## MAY 3

**1810**   Lord Byron swims the Hellespont in 1 hour and 10 minutes.

**1849**   Birthday of Jacob A. Riis, American journalist and civic reformer, champion of New York's downtrodden immigrants.

**1865**   The body of President Abraham Lincoln arrives back in his home town of Springfield, Illinois, after a 1,700-mile journey from the nation's capital.

**1903**   The editor of the *Ladies' Home Journal* advises his readers that in dining out "One should keep one's plate in as orderly a condition as circumstances will allow. Women should place their gloves in their laps, not in the wineglasses."

**1919** Airplane passenger service is inaugurated when Robert Hewitt flies Mrs. J. A. Hoagland and Miss Ethel Hodges from New York City to Atlantic City, New Jersey.

**1922** The journal of the barber trade, *The American Hairdresser,* is not sure that bobbed hair for women is here to stay, but it concedes that it "will probably last through the summer, anyway."

**1933** A woman becomes a director of the U.S. Mint for the first time as Mrs. Nellie Tayloe Ross is sworn into that office.

**1940** Congress proclaims the third Sunday in May as "I Am an American Day."

**1944** Synthetic quinine is produced in a Harvard University laboratory from coal-tar products by Dr. Robert B. Woodward and Dr. William E. Doering.

**1945** More than 150,000 German soldiers surrender to units of the British Second and American Ninth Armies along the Elbe River. (WORLD WAR II)

**1948** The Supreme Court forbids the states to enforce property "restrictive covenants," those agreements that bind owners not to sell property to racial and religious minorities.

**1963** Thousands of Negroes, many of them school children, stage protest marches for the second straight day in Birmingham, Alabama. On the orders of Eugene (Bull) Connor, the city's Police Commissioner, the marchers are set upon by police dogs or sent sprawling by powerful streams of water from fire hoses. With those arrested today, the total number of adults and juveniles held in local jails is almost 2500.

## MAY 4

**1626** Peter Minuit, Dutch colonizer, lands on Manhattan Island.

**1796** Birthday of Horace Mann, educational reformer, "Father of the public school system," and first president of Antioch College.

**1855** The first hospital in the world to be operated exclusively for the use of women opens its doors in New York City. The new institution, named The Woman's Hospital, has space for 40 bed-patients.

**1863** General Robert E. Lee and his Confederate forces defeat the Northern armies commanded by General Joseph Hooker at Chancellorsville, Virginia.

**1886** Haymarket Square Riot: At an open-air mass meeting in Chicago's Haymarket Square where a demonstration is going on for the 8-hour work day, a bomb explodes as municipal police attempt to break up the meeting. In the riot that follows, seven policemen and four other people are killed, seventy wounded. (No one was able to prove the identity of the bomb thrower, but after order was restored, eight alleged "anarchists" were arrested and convicted for murder. Of this number, one committed suicide in his prison cell, four were hanged in 1887, and the remaining three were pardoned in 1893 by Governor John P. Altgeld of Illinois.)

**1932** Al Capone, vice overlord of the United States and listed by the Justice Department as Public Enemy Number One, is thrown into jail at Atlanta Penitentiary, charged with income-tax evasion.

**1938** The dictators of Germany and Italy pledge "eternal friendship" during a state visit of Adolf Hitler to Benito Mussolini in Rome.

**1941** President Franklin D. Roosevelt dedicates the birthplace of Woodrow Wilson at Staunton, Virginia, as a national shrine.

**1942** Beginning of the Battle of the Coral Sea at which the Japanese fleet suffers a major defeat at the hands of the U.S. Navy. (On May 8, the total losses were 39 ships for Japan, one aircraft carrier for the United States. (WORLD WAR II)

**1954** Corporal Edward S. Dickenson of Cracker's Neck, Virginia, is sentenced by an army court-martial to 10 years at hard labor for collaborating with the Communists in Korea and also for informing on fellow American prisoners while in Korea.

**1961** The first of the so-called "Freedom Riders," a bi-racial group of 13 persons, set out by bus from Washington, D.C., bound for New Orleans, to test segregation barriers in interstate buses and terminals.

**1964** The Pulitzer Prize jury fails to award 1964 prizes in the fields of fiction, drama, and music—the first time that all three categories of art were passed up for awards in a single year.

**1965** President Johnson's contention that American troops are in the Dominican Republic because of knowledge that 58 of the rebel leaders who masterminded the revolt in that country have "Communist backgrounds" sets off a national debate in the United States. Dominican leaders as well as some American newsmen stationed there refute the President's charges. (James W. Goodsell, correspondent for the *Christian Science Monitor,* for example, wrote in his paper's May 19 edition: "A good degree of sloppy intelligence work went into the preparation of the lists, for they contain the names of persons in prison at the time . . . others out of the country . . . and still others who are not Communists. . . .") *(See May 5)*

## MAY 5

**1818** Birthday of Karl Marx, German social philosopher, the chief theorist of modern socialism.

**1821** Napoleon Bonaparte dies in exile on the island of St. Helena.

**1840**   Martin Van Buren is nominated for the Presidency by the Democrats, meeting in convention at Baltimore. The selection of a Vice Presidential candidate is left to the various states.

**1847**   The American Medical Association is organized in Philadelphia.

**1862**   French troops trying to seat the Archduke Maximilian of Austria on the throne of Mexico are repulsed by Mexican soldiers near Puebla. (The anniversary of this battle is celebrated annually in Mexico as Cinco De Maya Day.)

**1863**   A new labor union, the Brotherhood of Locomotive Engineers, is organized in Detroit.

**1864**   General Robert E. Lee routs Union troops led by General Ulysses S. Grant at the first Battle of the Wilderness. (The Wilderness was a wild and tangled woodland about 10 miles west of Fredericksburg, Virginia.)

**1891**   A 5-day music festival gets under way in New York as Carnegie Hall is dedicated, a gift to the city's music lovers by Andrew Carnegie. Peter Ilich Tchaikovsky, the famous Russian composer, is guest conductor.

**1904**   Cy Young, a player with the Boston Red Sox, pitches a perfect no-hit, no-run game against the Philadelphia Americans, during which no man reaches first base. (Young won more games [511], pitched more games [906], and played in the major leagues more years [22] than any other pitcher.)

**1920**   Nicola Sacco and Bartolomeo Vanzetti are arrested, charged with the murder of two payroll guards at South Braintree, Massachusetts.

**1925**   John T. Scopes, a biology teacher in the Dayton, Tennessee, public school system, is arrested for teaching the theory of evolution in violation of a state statute.

**1936**   The war in Ethiopia ends as Addis Ababa, the nation's capital city, falls to the Italians.

**1941**   Five years from the day that Ethiopia fell to the Italian invaders, Emperor Haile Selassie enters his capital of Addis Ababa in triumph, following the liberation of his country by British forces. (WORLD WAR II)

**1942**   Traveling across 8,500 miles of sea lanes, British naval forces invade the island of Madagascar and take over the Vichy-administered naval base there, the first allied invasion of World War II. (WORLD WAR II)

**1955**   The Federal Republic of Germany (West Germany) becomes a sovereign state when the ambassadors of France and Great Britain deposit in Bonn their governments' ratification of the Paris agreements of 1954. (United States' ratification took place on April 21, 1955.)

**1960**   The U-2 incident: Soviet Premier Khrushchev angrily announces that an American airplane had invaded Russian territory on May Day and had been shot down on orders from Moscow. Khrushchev describes it as a U-2 high-altitude jet reconnaissance plane and says it was intercepted during a military intelligence mission. The Premier identifies the pilot as Air Force Lieutenant Francis Gary Powers and insists he is working for the U.S. Central Intelligence Agency. (Later, the National Aeronautics Space Administration admitted Powers was missing but claimed he was engaged in a weather research project.

**1961**    Commander Alan B. Shepard, Jr., 37, is rocketed 115 miles into space from Cape Canaveral, Florida, and thus becomes America's first space explorer. (Fifteen minutes later, as he was picked up in the Atlantic Ocean, he summed up his feat: "Boy, what a ride!")

**1965**    A formal cease-fire truce is signed by the rebels and the military junta in the Dominican Republic civil war. The agreement has been negotiated by a commission of the Organization of American States.

## MAY 6

**1816**    The American Bible Association is organized in New York.

**1835**    The first issue of the *New York Herald* is published by James Gordon Bennett.

**1840**    The famous "penny black" stamp is issued in Victorian England, the first postage stamp in history.

**1856**    Birthday of Sigmund Freud, Austrian neurologist and "father of psychoanalysis."

**1861**    Arkansas withdraws from the Union after a convention of its citizens votes overwhelmingly for secession.

**1884**    The New York investment firm of Grant & Ward goes into bankruptcy, leaving former President Ulysses S. Grant almost penniless.

**1889**    Visitors to the Paris World's Fair are all agog over an "automobile" exhibited by an Austrian, Karl Benz. The vehicle has an internal combustion engine that burns liquid fuel.

**1895**    Rudolph Alfonzo Raffaele Pierre Filibert Guglielmi de Valentina d'Antonguolla is born in Italy. (As Rudolph Valentino, he was destined to become the most famous of all moving-picture lovers.)

**1896**    Professor Samuel P. Langley, secretary of the Smithsonian Institution in Washington, claims he made the first airplane flight earlier in the day when he soared 5,000 feet along the Potomac River at a speed of about 20 miles per hour. (Langley manufactured his own plane. His flight on this date has never been accredited official recognition, although he insisted until his death that his flights preceded those of the Wright brothers.)

**1910** The Edwardian Era comes to an end as King Edward VII of Great Britain dies in Buckingham Palace. (When the news reached New York that evening, Broadway theatres played "God Save the King.")

**1935** The Works Progress Administration (WPA) is created by Congress as a means to provide work for the unemployed through a series of projects supported by federal funds.

**1937** A horrified crowd of people on hand to welcome the German dirigible *Hindenburg* to its mooring mast at Lakehurst, New Jersey, stand by helplessly as the giant airship explodes and bursts into a raging fire. One radio announcer, on hand to report the arrival of the dirigible, describes the holocaust to a coast-to-coast audience: "It's burst into flames! It's falling on the mooring mast! It's one of the worst catastrophes in the world!" (Thirty-six passengers lost their lives in the disaster.)

**1941** Joseph Stalin, Communist dictator of Russia, becomes premier of that nation, succeeding V. M. Molotov, who remains in office as foreign commissar and takes over the duties of vice premier.

**1942** Corregidor's exhausted garrison of 11,574 United States and native troops and some 3,000 civilians surrender to the Japanese. In Washington, Secretary of State Hull issues this statement: "Corregidor and Bataan will live forever in the memory of Americans. They stand for reverses that are but preludes to victory. . . ." (*See February 16*)

**1957** A 39-year-old member of the U.S. Senate, John Fitzgerald Kennedy, is awarded a Pulitzer Prize for his book, *Profiles in Courage*. The book deals with decisive moments in the lives of American statesmen.

**1959** A painting of a Dutch girl by Pablo Picasso is sold in London for $154,000, the highest price ever received to date for the work of a *living* artist.

**1960** Princess Margaret Rose, the sister of Queen Elizabeth II of Great Britain, is married to a commoner, Antony Armstrong-Jones, in Westminster Abbey. (*See October 31*)

## MAY 7

**1789** The first President's Inaugural Ball is held in honor of President George Washington, the festivities taking place in the Assembly Rooms in New York.

**1833** Birthday of Johannes Brahms, one of the world's great composers.

**1840** Birthday of Peter Ilich Tchaikovsky, Russian composer and conductor.

**1912** Final plans for the Pulitzer Prizes, established by Joseph Pulitzer, are approved by Columbia University.

**1915**     A German submarine torpedoes the Cunard liner *Lusi-tania* off the coast of Ireland, the great liner sinking below the waves in less than 22 minutes. Almost 1,200 passengers lose their lives in the sinking, 124 of them citizens of the United States. (WORLD WAR I)

**1939**     The Rome-Berlin Axis: An open military alliance, as well as a political alliance, between Germany and Italy is an-nounced simultaneously in Rome and Berlin.

**1943**     Allied forces win a great victory in North Africa as the British First Army and the U.S. Second Corps, assisted by French troops, liberate Tunis and Bizerte. (WORLD WAR II)

**1945**     Germany surrenders: On the 2,075th day of the biggest, bloodiest, costliest war in history, representatives of the German High Command sign unconditional surrender terms at General Eisenhower's temporary headquarters in Rheims, France. The sign-ing takes place at 2:41 in the morning, Paris time. (WORLD WAR II)

**1945**     The controversial decision regarding "portal to portal" pay for bituminous coal miners is upheld by the U.S. Supreme Court.

**1954**     Rebel forces in Indochina capture the French Union fortress at Dienbienphu. The Communists claim they have captured nearly 10,000 members of the 16,000-man garrison and to have killed or wounded the rest.

**1960**     Premier Khrushchev of Russia announces that Francis Gary Powers, the pilot of the U-2 plane shot down on May 1, has confessed that he was on an intelligence mission for the U.S. Cen-tral Intelligence Agency and will be brought to trial in Moscow. Khrushchev adds that Powers had been ordered to kill himself rather than "fall alive into the hands of Soviet authorities," but that he had failed to use a "poisoned pin" to commit suicide. (On the same day, the U.S. State Department said that "in endeavoring to obtain information now concealed behind the Iron Curtain, a flight by an unarmed civilian U-2 plane" was probably undertaken. The statement added that it is "no secret" that all countries, in-cluding the Soviet Union, are engaged in "intelligence collection activities.")

**1965**     The trial of one of the Ku Klux Klansmen charged with the March 25 murder of the white civil rights worker Mrs. Viola Liuzzo, following the Selma to Montgomery, Alabama, Free-dom March, ends with a hung jury in Hayneville, Alabama. As a result of the deadlock (10 jurors for conviction, 2 holding out for acquittal), the court declares a mistrial and releases the defendant, Collie LeRoy Wilkins, Jr.

# MAY 8

**1541**   Hernando de Soto and a company of Spanish explorers discover the Mississippi River at a point near the present city of Memphis, Tennessee.

**1725**   King George I of Great Britain founds the Order of the Bath, its membership to be limited to a select group of nobles.

**1878**   In a game between the Providence and Boston baseball teams, Paul Hines, a Providence center fielder, makes the first unassisted triple play in the history of the game. (Providence won, 3–2.)

**1879**   George B. Selden of Rochester, New York, files papers for the first automobile patent. (His claim was granted by the Bureau of Patents on November 5, 1895.)

**1884**   Harry S. Truman, 33rd President of the United States, is born on a farm near Lamar, Missouri. ("A man's age depends entirely on his physical set-up. Some are aged at 50 and some are not aged even at 100. I guess the best assurance of a long life is to get yourself a set of long-living parents like I did.") (*See below*)

**1902**   A great volcanic eruption on Mount Pelée on the island of Martinique practically wipes out the town of St. Pierre as molten lava sweeps down from the mountainside leaving 40,000 persons dead and tremendous destruction in its wake.

**1905**   Dwight B. Huss of Detroit, Michigan, sets out on the first transcontinental automobile race, leaving New York City in his Oldsmobile runabout. (He arrived in Portland, Oregon, 44 days later, 40 of which were spent in actual driving time.)

**1914**   The Senate approves a resolution offered by Representative Thomas Heflin of Alabama, and already passed by the House, which provides for the observance of Mother's Day annually on the second Sunday in May. President Wilson issues a proclamation establishing the holiday. (*See May 9.*)

**1942**   Vice President Henry A. Wallace coins a new phrase when he says in a speech: "The century on which we are entering can be and must be the century of the common man."

**1945**   Official V-E (Victory in Europe) Day: President Truman addresses the nation in a radio broadcast, announcing the end of the war in Europe: "The Allied Armies, through sacrifice and devotion and with God's help, have won from Germany a final and unconditional surrender.... This is a solemn but a glorious hour. I only wish that Franklin D. Roosevelt had lived to witness this day." (WORLD WAR II)

**1958**   During an 18-day goodwill tour of South America, Vice President and Mrs. Richard M. Nixon are greeted with hostility in Peru. In Lima, as he seeks to address students at the University of San Marcos, a crowd of 2,000 pelts him with fruit, eggs, and stones.

Later, the Nixons are spat upon as they enter their hotel. (*See May 13*)

**1960**    Russian Premier Khrushchev, in the wake of the May 1 U-2 incident, warns that nations permitting the use of their airfields for U.S. air intelligence missions will run the risk of destruction by Soviet missiles.

**1961**    Franchise owners of the recently organized new National League baseball club in New York announce that their team will be called "The Mets." The selection of the name follows a polling of baseball fans for suggested names. In all, 644 different names were submitted, a majority favoring the name selected. (The Mets played their first game April 11, 1962, meeting the St. Louis Cardinals in that city's Busch Stadium. The Cardinals won, 11–4.)

**1964**    Despite the fact that they are bitterly opposed to his civil rights proposals, President Lyndon B. Johnson is acclaimed by tremendous crowds * in Georgia as he carries the debate on race relations into the South. The President says in Atlanta: "... In our own search for justice, the Constitution of the United States must be your guide. Georgia helped write that Constitution. ... I believe Georgia will join with the entire nation to insure that every man enjoys all the rights secured him by that American Constitution. Because the Constitution requires it, because justice demands it, we must protect the constitutional rights of all of our citizens, regardless of race, religion, or the color of their skin. ..."

**1964**    On the occasion of his 80th birthday, ex-President Harry S. Truman becomes the first former Chief Executive to address a regular session of the U.S. Senate.

**1965**    Randy Matson, a Texas college sophomore, smashes the 70-foot barrier in the shot put, breaking his own pending world record of 69 feet, 3/4 inch. Matson's record throw of 70 feet, 7 inches, made in College Station, Texas, at the Southwest Conference track and field meet, thus surpasses the recognized world record of 67 feet, 10 inches held by Dallas Long of California.

## MAY 9

**1502**    Christopher Columbus, accompanied by his 13-year-old son, sets out from Cadiz, Spain, on his fourth and last voyage. His expedition includes four vessels and one hundred and fifty men. (The explorer reached the easternmost tip of Central America, but the voyage was one of great hardship. Once again, a mutiny broke out among the men and Columbus himself was stranded for an entire year on the island of Jamaica.)

* Crowds were so large and enthusiastic in Atlanta, for example, that the city's police chief said he had not "seen anything like it since Franklin D. Roosevelt and [the opening of the film] *Gone With the Wind*."

**1754** The first newspaper cartoon appears in America when Benjamin Franklin's famous "Join or Die" cartoon is printed in his own newspaper, the *Pennsylvania Gazette.* The illustration depicted a dissected snake, each part representing an American colony.

**1907** Miss Anna Jarvis of Philadelphia suggests at a public meeting that one day a year be set aside to honor the nation's mothers. Miss Jarvis proposes that the second Sunday in each May should be so designated, at which time Americans might wear carnations as a tribute to all mothers. *(See May 8.)*

**1921** For the first time in history, Americans seated comfortably in their homes can *hear* a professional stage show as Station KDKA broadcasts directly from the stage of the Davis Theatre in Pittsburgh.

**1926** Commander Richard E. Byrd of the U.S. Navy and Floyd Bennett become the first men to fly over the North Pole as they soar over the Pole at 9:02 o'clock in the morning, 15½ hours after they left Kings Bay, Spitzbergen. (The two aviators made the flight in a triple-engined Fokker monoplane, the *Josephine Ford.*)

**1933** Twenty-five thousand books, all of them considered *verboten* by Adolf Hitler and Nazi Party leaders, are thrown into a huge bonfire in Berlin. Included in the book burning is a copy of the Bible. (This was the first, but not the last, of the celebrated Nazi book burnings.)

**1936** With the war in Ethiopia over, Benito Mussolini proclaims that nation to be a colony of the Italian Empire.

**1940** Laurence Olivier and Vivien Leigh open in New York in an exciting production of *Romeo and Juliet.* (For Miss Leigh, it was her American debut. Mr. Olivier had played here before.)

**1942** The Russian Academy of Sciences elects three Americans and two Englishmen to membership in the organization, the first foreigners to be so honored by Soviet Russia. (The Americans were: Dr. Walter Bradford Cannon, physiologist; Dr. Gilbert Newton Lewiss, chemist; Dr. Ernest Orlando Lawrence, physicist. The Englishmen: Sir Henry Dale, physiologist; and J. B. S. Haldane, biologist.)

**1946** King Victor Emmanuel III of Italy abdicates, yielding the throne to his son, Crown Prince Humbert.

**1957** Viet Nam President Ngo Dinh Diem, in the United States for a 14-day state visit, addresses a joint session of Congress. *(See November 1)*

**1960** Secretary of State Christian A. Herter, referring to the U-2 plane shot down over Russia, says the United States would be "derelict to its responsibilities" if it failed to take intelligence measures to "overcome this danger of surprise attack" from the USSR.

**1961** Newton N. Minow, chairman of the Federal Communications Commission, minces no words when he tells 2,000 members of the National Association of Broadcasters in Washington what he thinks of television: "... When television is good ... nothing is better. But when television is bad, nothing is worse. I invite you to sit down in front of your television set ... and keep your eyes glued to that set until the station signs off. I can assure you that you will observe a vast wasteland. You will see a procession of game shows, violence, audience participation shows ... blood and thunder, mayhem, violence, sadism, murder, Western badmen, Western goodmen, private eyes, gangsters, more violence ... And, endlessly, commercials—many screaming, cajoling and offending. And most of all, boredom. True, you will see a few things you will enjoy. But they will be very, very few. And if you think I exaggerate, try it...."

**1963** An agreement to halt racial violence in Birmingham, Alabama, is reached in that city. The pact stipulates, as a beginning, a plan of gradual desegregation of facilities.

**1965** One of the most dramatic events in modern musical history takes place in New York's Carnegie Hall as the internationally famous pianist Vladimir Horowitz plays his first public concert in 12 years. (Horowitz, who had interrupted his career following a period of nervous fatigue, received a sustained ovation from the cheering audience that lasted for a half-hour.)

## MAY 10

**Confederate Memorial Day** A legal holiday in North and South Carolina.

**1775** Ethan Allen and his "Green Mountain Boys," the colonial militia of Vermont, storm the British-held fortress at Ticonderoga, New York. "I demand your surrender, Sir!" Allen says to English Commander Delaplace. "By whose authority?" asks the irate and sleepy Englishman. "In the name of the Great Jehovah and the Continental Congress!" Allen replies. (Next day, the banner of the Green Mountain Boys flew over the fort.)

**1865** Jefferson Davis, President of the Confederate States, is captured and arrested as he is fleeing from Irwinville, Georgia. (He spent the next 2 years in prison at Fort Monroe, Virginia.)

**1869** A one-word telegraphic message, "Done!" is flashed all over the United States, as Governor Leland Stanford of California drives a golden spike into the last railway tie at Promontory Point, Utah, thus completing the first transcontinental railway in America. After the Governor completes his task, the Central Pacific's locomotive *Jupiter* and the Union Pacific's *119* move toward each other until their noses touch and the engineers of the two trains exchange bottles of champagne in celebration.

**1871** The Treaty of Frankfort ends the Franco-Prussian War.

**1872** A woman is nominated for the office of President of the United States for the first time in American history as Victoria

144

Claflin Woodhull is chosen the candidate of the National Woman Suffrage Association at their convention in Apollo Hall, New York City. Miss Woodhull is a "lady broker" and also the publisher of *Woodhull and Claflin's Weekly*.

**1876** The Centennial Exposition opens in Philadelphia to commemorate the nation's 100th anniversary. At the Grand Opening ceremonies, a tremendous crowd is on hand to greet President Ulysses S. Grant and the Emperor and Empress of Brazil. Highlight of the day is the singing of John Greenleaf Whittier's "Centennial Hymn," by a chorus of 150, and the first performance of Richard Wagner's "Centennial Inaugural March," written especially for the Exposition by the famous German composer at a fee of $5,000. (When the fair closed in November, more than 9,000,000 persons had paid 50 cents apiece to visit it.)

**1915** In answer to those individuals who are clamoring for a declaration of war against Germany because of the sinking of the *Lusitania,* President Wilson tells an audience in Philadelphia: "There is such a thing as a man being too proud to fight. There is such a thing as a nation being so right that it does not need to convince others by force that it is right...."

**1940** Invasion of the Lowlands: Moving by land, air, and water, 89 divisions of the Germany Army invade the 3 countries of Belgium, Luxembourg, and the Netherlands. In each case, the attacks come without any warning and in each country the invaders are ruthless. Nonmilitary targets are bombed and fleeing refugees machine-gunned. Dozens of villages are set afire and hostages jailed or shot for no valid reason. (WORLD WAR II)

**1940** Britain's serious military situation leads to the resignation of Prime Minister Neville Chamberlain. He is succeeded by Winston Churchill who forms a coalition government made up of Conservatives, Laborites, and Liberals. (WORLD WAR II)

**1941** A startling development in the war occurs when Rudolf Hess, deputy leader of the German National Socialist Party and second in power only to Adolf Hitler, parachutes to earth on the Duke of Hamilton's estate near Glasgow, Scotland. (Three days later, Hess told English authorities that "I have come to save humanity." Most historians believed his mission was to arrange a negotiated peace.) (WORLD WAR II)

**1941** Germany launches its biggest air raid to date on the city of London, damaging the Chamber of the House of Commons, Westminster Abbey, Westminster Hall, the British Museum and the famous tower clock of "Big Ben." (WORLD WAR II)

**1963** Pope John XXIII receives the Balzan Peace Prize, the first peace prize ever awarded to a Pope. (Soviet Premier Nikita Khrushchev surprised almost everyone by writing to the Pope saying that the Pontiff deserved the prize because of his efforts in "the noble cause of the defense of peace.")

# MAY 11

**1768**    Birthday of John Chapman, known in American folklore as "Johnny Appleseed," planter of thousands of apple trees. ("Your labor has been a labor of love, and generations yet unborn will rise up and call you blessed."—General Sam Houston's eulogy in the Senate.)

**1832**    The first political platform is drawn up in Washington, D.C., when delegates from 16 states meet to draw up a series of resolutions to use as the basis for their platform in the campaign to elect Henry Clay President.

**1846**    President Polk sends a war message to Congress, saying: "The cup of forbearance has been exhausted.... Mexico has passed the boundary of the United States, has invaded our territory and shed American blood upon the American soil."

**1858**    Minnesota enters the Union as the 32nd state.

**1864**    Balked by General Lee's Confederate forces at Spottsylvania Court House, Virginia, General Grant sends a dispatch to the War Department in Washington, saying: "I propose to fight it out on this line if it takes all summer."

**1900**    James J. (Gentleman Jim) Corbett, former boxing heavyweight champion of the world, is defeated in his attempt to regain the title when he is knocked out in the 23rd round at Coney Island, New York, by James J. Jeffries.

**1910**    Glacier National Park in Montana is created by an act of Congress.

**1928**    Station WGY, Schenectady, New York, begins the first regularly scheduled television programs. Starting today, WGY will offer telecasts three times each week.

**1934**    Dust storms in Texas, Oklahoma, Kansas, and Colorado, are blowing hundreds of thousands of tons of topsoil eastward into the Atlantic Ocean.

**1943**    American forces land on Attu Island in the Aleutians, the first American soil to be regained by the United States after seizure by the Japanese. (WORLD WAR II)

**1963**    The truce between Negroes and whites in Birmingham, Alabama, is shattered after the home of the Reverend A. D. King, Martin Luther King's brother, is bombed. Later in the day, an integrated motel is bombed.

**1964**    The highest per capita income in the United States in 1963 was in the state of Nevada. Figures released by the U.S. Department of Commerce show that man for man Nevadans brought home $3,372 in earned income in that year. The per capita income is higher only in the District of Columbia, which is not a state. There, residents had an average income of $3,398.

# MAY 12

**1789**    A number of New York mechanics and small tradesmen, tavern-keepers, and minor political leaders form the Society of Tammany or Columbian Order, a revival of the pre-Revolutionary Sons of Liberty. The organization takes its name from Tammany, a legendary chief of the Delaware tribe. (Originally, the Tammany Society was a patriotic order, a club for social events and mutual helpfulness. Later, however, Aaron Burr turned Tammany into a political group and identified it exclusively with the politics of the Democratic Party.)

**1820**    Birthday of Florence Nightingale, famous English nurse who first organized medical services for the wounded on a sanitary basis in the Crimean War.

**1919**    Henry Ford's $1,000,000 editorial libel suit against the *Chicago Tribune* begins at Mount Clemens, Michigan, an outgrowth of the newspaper's reference to the industrialist as an "anarchist." (When it was all over, Mr. Ford won damages of 6 cents plus costs. His prestige, however, suffered badly because of various statements made by him on the stand. Examples: He described Benedict Arnold as a "writer" and made his famous comment that "History is bunk!")

**1922**    The current issue of the magazine *Radio Broadcast* comments on the current interest in radio: "The rate of increase in the number of people who spend at least a part of their evening in listening in (to radio) is almost incomprehensible."

**1932**    Searchers find the body of the baby son of Colonel and Mrs. Charles A. Lindbergh, kidnapped on March 1, in a wooded area 5½ miles from the Lindbergh home in Hopewell, New Jersey.

**1933**    President Franklin D. Roosevelt signs into law the Agricultural Adjustment Act, an attempt to alleviate the distress of the nation's farmers and "to relieve the existing national economic emergency by increasing purchasing power."

**1937**    George VI, who succeeded to the throne on the abdication of his brother Edward VIII, is crowned king in Westminster Abbey, London.

**1949**    After 328 days, the Soviet occupation authorities in Berlin announce the end of the land blockade of the German capital.

**1955**    Eight hundred "mourners" crowd into the six cars of the last train to travel the regular route of the Third Avenue Elevated transit service in New York. To the accompaniment of much whistle hooting, the last train leaves the Chatham Square station in Chinatown at 6:04 P.M., and arrives at 149th Street, in the Bronx, at 7:20 P.M., the last "El" to huff and puff on the Third Avenue Line before it is demolished.

**1963**    Bombings of the previous day, aimed at Negro leaders and integrated facilities, set off new riots in Birmingham, Alabama.

In Washington, President Kennedy announces he has ordered federal troops to bases near the city. Says the President: "This Government will do whatever must be done to preserve order, to protect the lives of its citizens and to uphold the law of the land. . . ."

## MAY 13

**1607**     The first colonists to establish a permanent English settlement in the New World land near the James River, Virginia, and start to build their fortress community. (This was the beginning of Jamestown.)

**1783**     Commissioned officers of the Continental Army organize themselves into the Society of the Cincinnati.

**1846**     Two days after receiving President Polk's war message, Congress follows his recommendations and declares that a state of war exists between the United States and Mexico.

**1854**     Joseph N. White of New York City and George Smith of Watertown, New York, stage the first American billiard match of importance at Malcolm Hall, Syracuse, New York. Mr. White wins the $200 purse by a score of 500 to 484.

**1867**     Jefferson Davis, held in Fort Monroe during the past two years as the "nation's prisoner" because of his leadership of the Confederate cause, is released from prison on $100,000 bail and promptly brought to trial on charges of treason. (Davis' bailers included Cornelius Vanderbilt and Horace Greeley. The government dropped its case against him in 1869.)

**1888**     In a rolling basso profundo voice, the actor DeWolf Hopper recites Ernest L. Thayer's "Casey at the Bat" during the second act of *Prince Methusalem,* a musical comedy playing at Wallack's Theatre in New York. When Hopper is finished, the entire audience rises from its seats and breaks into a roaring cheer, some of them chanting:

> Then from the gladdened multitude
>    went up a joyous yell,
> It bounded from the mountain top
>    and rattled in the dell;
> It struck upon the hillside and re-
>    coiled upon the flat,
> For Casey, mighty Casey, was
>    advancing to the bat.

(Thereafter, no show in which Hopper appeared was complete without his reading of the poem. He estimated years afterwards that he had recited it some 15,000 times.)

**1915**     Six days after the sinking of the Cunard liner *Lusitania,* the government of the United States addresses a note to the Imperial German government holding that government responsible for the loss of American lives. (On May 28, Germany replied to the note, claiming that the *Lusitania* was an armed ship carrying munitions to the European theater of war and therefore was a military target.) (WORLD WAR I)

**1916**    Sholem Aleichem, considered by many people to be the greatest of all Jewish humorists, dies in New York. (As he lay dying, Aleichem made a wish that his fellow-Jews the world over, in moments of depression and melancholia, would remember him and laugh. Each May 13, a sort of memorial service is held for him at his former New York residence, the sole specification for attendance being that laughter must dominate the ceremonial.)

**1940**    The House of Commons votes unanimously to confirm the selection of a new prime minister, Winston Churchill. As Nazi German divisions are heading toward France, the new British leader rises to his feet and to underscore the seriousness of the English military situation tells the legislators: "... I would say to the House, as I said to those who have joined this Government: 'I have nothing to offer but blood, toil, tears and sweat.' * .... You ask, what is our policy? I will say: It is to wage war, by sea, land and air, with all our might and with all the strength that God can give us: to wage war against a monstrous tyranny, never surpassed in the dark, lamentable catalogue of human crime. That is our policy...."
(WORLD WAR II)

**1940**    Queen Wilhelmina, Crown Princess Juliana, and key figures of the Dutch government arrive in England, after fleeing from the Nazi invaders of the Netherlands. (WORLD WAR II)

**1945**    In a victory address to the British Empire, Prime Minister Churchill reassures the United States that Great Britain will throw her entire military might into the war against Japan. (WORLD WAR II)

**1958**    Once again, Vice President Richard M. Nixon is attacked by mobs during his goodwill tour of South America. This time, he is set upon by hundreds of anti-U.S. demonstrators in Caracas, Venezuela, who hurl melon-sized rocks at his limousine. Despite the fact that he is covered by shattered glass, Mr. Nixon escapes injury. (President Eisenhower immediately ordered four companies of marines and paratroopers to fly to Caribbean bases to back White House demands that Venezuela guarantee the Vice President's safety.)

**1958**    In Chicago, Stan (The Man) Musial of the St. Louis Cardinals joins seven other great players in baseball history when he scores his 3,000th major league hit.

---

* Churchill undoubtedly took his famous "blood, toil, tears and sweat" from the Italian patriot Garibaldi who used a similar phrase in one of his speeches.

# MAY 14

**1802**    It rains so hard on the island of Manhattan on this date that the Hudson River overflows.

**1804**    Captain Meriwether Lewis and William Clark set out from St. Louis, Missouri, on their expedition to the Pacific Coast, a fact-finding mission to study specifically what the United States had acquired in the Louisiana Purchase. Accompanying the two explorers are 14 soldiers of the U.S. Army, 9 Kentucky frontiersmen, 2 Frenchmen, an interpreter and hunter, and Clark's personal servant.

**1811**    Paraguay declares its independence from Spanish rule. (This day is observed annually in that country as Independence Day.)

**1904**    The Olympic Games are held in the United States for the first time, the international athletic competitions starting on this date at St. Louis, Missouri, the site of the current Louisiana Purchase Exposition.

**1913**    John D. Rockefeller's donation of $100,000,000, said to be the largest single gift of money to date, establishes the Rockefeller Foundation for the promotion of the "well-being of mankind throughout the world."

**1940**    British authorities establish the Local Defence Volunteers, later known as the Home Guard. (Winston Churchill recalled the valiant work of these men and women when he said: "In that terrible summer of 1940. . . . Shotguns, sporting rifles, and staves were all they could find for weapons.") (WORLD WAR II)

**1940**    Nazi airplanes bomb the Dutch city of Rotterdam, razing entire sections of the city and killing some 30,000 persons, despite the fact that truce negotiations are under way. Later, General H. G. Winkelman, Commander-in-Chief of the Netherlands Army, surrenders to the Germans to prevent further unnecessary bloodshed and destruction. (WORLD WAR II)

**1940**    At regular intervals during the day, announcers for the British Broadcasting Corporation read this announcement: "The Admiralty have made an order requesting all owners of self-propelled pleasure craft between 30 and 100 feet in length to send all particulars to the Admiralty within fourteen days from today." (These privately owned boats were soon to be commandeered for the evacuation of Dunkerque.) (WORLD WAR II)

**1942**    Congress establishes the WAAC's, the Women's Auxiliary Army Corps. (WORLD WAR II)

**1948**    Great Britain ends her 31-year rule in Palestine, followed immediately by a proclamation in Tel Aviv of the birth of the free and independent State of Israel. The boundaries of the new state conform in general to those defined by the United Nations in 1947 for the partition of Palestine into sovereign Jewish and Arab states.

**1961** Two busloads of Negro and white civil rights workers, in the midst of their so-called "Freedom Ride" from Washington to New Orleans to test desegregation of facilities at bus depots, are attacked by mobs of white racists in Anniston and Birmingham, Alabama. U.S. Attorney General Robert F. Kennedy telephones Alabama officials, asking them to guarantee protection for the integrated travelers.

**1965** In a moving and unique ceremony, Queen Elizabeth II dedicates a British shrine in memory of President John F. Kennedy and bequeaths to the American people an acre of ground in the meadow at Runnymede, England, where King John signed the Magna Carta in 1215. In the presence of Mrs. John F. Kennedy and members of the Kennedy family, the Queen describes the late President as one "whom in death my people still mourn and whom in life they loved. . . ."

## MAY 15

**Straw Hat Day in the United States** Considered by many well-dressed men to be the official date on which it is permissible to start wearing straw hats for the summer season.

**1765** Parliament enacts a statute making it mandatory for American colonists to provide housing and supplies for British troops stationed there.

**1862** Congress creates the Department of Agriculture to be administered by a Commissioner of Agriculture and to be included within the framework of the Department of the Interior.

**1869** A group of women meet in New York to form the National Woman Suffrage Association, its main objective being to secure the ballot for women via an amendment to the U.S. Constitution. Elizabeth Cady Stanton is chosen first president of the new organization.

**1918** U.S. government participation in civil aviation gets under way as the Post Office Department launches the first regular air-mail service between Washington, Philadelphia, and New York. The airplanes and pilots to be used have been borrowed from the War Department.

**1924** Both houses of Congress pass the Johnston Act, restricting immigration into the United States. Hereafter, admissions into this nation will be on a quota basis.

**1930** The United Air Lines introduces a new service for its passengers by providing a "stewardess" on its flights from San Francisco to Cheyenne, Wyoming. The first stewardess so employed is Miss Ellen Church.

**1942**    Gasoline rationing starts in 17 eastern states. (WORLD WAR II)

**1942**    Mrs. Oveta Culp Hobby is appointed director of the Women's Army Auxiliary Corps. (WORLD WAR II)

**1948**    Within a few hours after the announcement of the birth of the new State of Israel, that country is attacked by Egyptian planes and invaded in the north and east by troops from Lebanon and Transjordan.

**1953**    In the 44th victory of his professional career, Rocky Marciano, world's heavyweight boxing champion, knocks out former title-holder "Jersey Joe" Walcott, at the Chicago Stadium, after 2 minutes and 25 seconds of the first round.

**1963**    Air Force Major Leroy Gordon Cooper is launched into space from Cape Canaveral, Florida. (By the time his mission was completed the next day, he had successfully orbited the earth 22 times.)

## MAY 16

**1866**    The Treasury Department is authorized to manufacture and place into circulation the first U.S. five-cent piece, more often referred to as the "nickel." Actually, the new coin will be made of 25 percent nickel and 75 percent copper.

**1868**    Chief Justice Salmon P. Chase, presiding in the Senate impeachment trial of President Andrew Johnson, polls each Senator present on the Eleventh Article of Impeachment and then announces: "On this Article, 35 Senators having voted guilty and 19 not guilty, a two-thirds majority not having voted for conviction, the President is, therefore, acquitted under this Article." (But the trial, inspired almost exclusively by political considerations, was not over. A 10-day recess was declared before votes on the other articles were to take place.) (*See May 26*)

**1903**    George A. Wyman leaves San Francisco on the first lap of a trip across the United States by motorcycle. (A little less than 2 months later he cycled into New York City, the first man to cross the continent by motorcycle.)

**1927**    Despite the fact that the manufacture and sale of alcoholic beverages are unlawful, the Supreme Court rules that "bootleggers" must file income-tax forms.

**1929**    For the first time in the history of the film industry, the Academy of Motion Picture Arts and Sciences awards its "Oscars" to actors, directors, and films making the most distinguished contributions to the industry in the 1927–28 season. Among the award winners: Best Actress: Janet Gaynor, for her roles in *Seventh Heaven, Street Angel*, and *Sunrise;* Best Actor, Emil Jannings, for his acting in *The Way of All Flesh* and *The Last Command;* Best Production, *Wings;* Best Director, Frank Borzage, for his direction of *Seventh Heaven.*

**1940**    President Roosevelt, alarmed by the "blitzkrieg" tactics of Nazi Germany in overrunning a large part of the European continent, asks Congress to provide funds for the manufacture of 50,-000 airplanes a year. (This proposal was received critically by many congressional figures, all of whom believed that that production figure was neither possible nor necessary.) (WORLD WAR II)

**1953**    After holding him in prison for nearly 2 years as an American spy, the Government of Czechoslovakia releases William N. Oatis, formerly the chief correspondent in Prague for the Associated Press. The Czechs announce that Oatis' release is the result of a letter written from the United States by his wife, Laurabelle, to Klement Gottwald, the late President of Czechoslovakia.

**1954**    The nationally known entertainer and piano-player, Liberace, often billed as "The Keyboard Casanova" and the idol of an army of fans across the nation, performs at a one-man concert in New York's Madison Square Garden. Sixteen thousand persons crowd into the auditorium for the 3-hour concert and give the pianist a thunderous ovation.

**1960**    The Big Four summit conference of heads of state of the United States, Great Britain, Russia, and France collapses when Premier Nikita Khrushchev refuses to participate until the United States meets his conditions. The Soviet Premier demands, as a result of the U-2 plane incident, that (1) the United States terminate all military flights over Russia; (2) that it apologize for its past "aggressions"; and (3) punish those responsible for such flights. (President Eisenhower had already given his assurance that intelligence flights had already been ended and would not be resumed.) (*See May 18*)

## MAY 17

**1792**    Twenty-four New York brokers meet under a buttonwood tree on the present site of 68 Wall Street and sign an agreement to fix uniform rates of commission in the sale of stocks and bonds. (This was the real beginning of the New York Stock Exchange.)

**1814**    Norwegian Constitution Day, an annual observance marking the signing of the Constitution at Eidsvold, Norway.

**1875**    The first "Kentucky Derby" horse race is held at Churchill Downs, Louisville, Kentucky. The Derby, carrying a purse of $2,850, is won by Aristides, running a mile and a half in 2:37¾.

**1877**    Edwin T. Holmes, operator of the Holmes burglar alarm service, installs the first telephone switchboard in history in his Boston office, to be used by day as a telephone service for his clients and as a burglar alarm system by night.

**1938**    "Information, Please!" a novel radio panel "quiz" program, is broadcast for the first time on the Blue Network of the National Broadcasting Company.

**1954** In a unanimous decision, the U.S. Supreme Court rules that racial segregation in the nation's public schools is unconstitutional: "We then come to the question presented: Does segregation of children in public schools solely on the basis of race, even though the physical facilities and other 'tangible' factors may be equal, deprive the children of the minority group of equal educational opportunities? We believe that it does. . . . To separate them from others of similar age and qualifications solely because of their race generates a feeling of inferiority as to their status in the community that may affect their hearts and minds in a way unlikely ever to be undone. . . ."

**1957** Egypt bars Israel from sending merchant ships through the Suez Canal.

**1961** Premier Castro of Cuba offers to exchange most of the prisoners captured in the Bay of Pigs invasion for 500 U.S. heavy tractors.

## MAY 18

**1812** President James Madison is nominated by a congressional caucus of Democratic-Republicans for a second term.

**1852** Massachusetts becomes the first state in the Union to pass a statute making school attendance compulsory for children between the ages of 8 and 14 years. All such children must attend classes a minimum of 12 weeks in the year, 6 weeks of which must be consecutive.

**1860** Abraham Lincoln is nominated for President by the Republicans meeting in Chicago at a temporary convention hall known as the "Wigwam." (In Springfield, Illinois, where he was awaiting word from the convention at the office of the *Springfield Journal,* Mr. Lincoln tells well-wishers crowding into the office: "Well, gentlemen, there is a little short woman at our house who is probably more interested in this dispatch than I am; and if you will excuse me, I will take it up and let her see it.")

**1910** Halley's Comet passes over the sun, frightening many hundreds of thousands of people throughout the United States, all of whom are certain that the comet's appearance would coincide with the end of the world. (Many farm families camped in cyclone cellars, others crowded churches. New York, said *The New York World,* was "keyed up to a high pitch of expectancy at the prospect of being sprinkled with star dust, and the possibility of being smothered by noxious gases or bombarded by meteorites. . . . But the show did not come off.")

**1926** Aimée Semple McPherson, the nationally known evangelist, disappears completely from sight on the bathing beach at Venice, California. (Her disappearance remained a first-rate mystery until June 23 when she turned up in Agua Priesa, across the

United States-Mexican border from Douglas, Arizona, claiming to be a victim of a kidnapping. When she returned to Los Angeles, 30,000 persons were on hand to greet her. Later, her followers carried her in a wicker chair from her railway car to a waiting automobile. As she drove to her headquarters at Angelus Temple, 100,000 persons lined the streets to welcome "Sister Aimée" home.)

**1933**    President Franklin D. Roosevelt signs into law the Tennessee Valley Authority Act, passed earlier in the day by Congress to develop and curb the waters of the Tennessee River, including the development and sale of electric power by the federal government.

**1941**    Throughout the nation, communities celebrate the first "I Am an American Day," honoring the 300,000 aliens who have become naturalized citizens of the United States within the past year.

**1944**    After 4½ months, the bloody campaign at Monte Cassino, Italy, ends as the Allies capture the town and fortress monastery, site of fierce German resistance. Victory at Cassino will now open up for the Allies the use of Highway Six leading to Rome. (WORLD WAR II)

**1953**    The American aviatrix Jacqueline Cochran becomes the first woman to fly faster than the speed of sound. (Piloting an F-86 Sabrejet fighter plane at Edwards Air Force Base, California, she flew an average of 652.337 miles per hour.)

**1960**    At the Palais de Chaillot in Paris, an enraged Nikita Khrushchev blames the collapse of the Big Four summit conference directly on the United States and President Eisenhower. The Soviet Premier tells the nearly 3,000 reporters present that if the U.S. intelligence flights over Russia are repeated, "we shall administer shattering blows at the bases whence they come.... When we caught them [the United States] red-handed they say they are not thieves. Wouldn't it be better.... to take the American aggressors by the scruff of the neck.... and give them a little shaking....?" (*See May 25*)

## MAY 19

**1536**    Anne Boleyn, married to King Henry VIII of England since January, 1533, is beheaded on Tower Green in London, the execution carried out by an expert imported from France by the King. (Anne, Henry's second Queen and mother of the future Queen Elizabeth of Britain, was charged by His Majesty with acts of adultery.)

**1856**    Senator Charles Sumner, Republican of Massachusetts, rises to his feet in the Senate chamber and delivers a blistering attack on slavery and the people of the South. The Senator calls his speech, "The Crime against Kansas," a reference to the current strife in the Kansas Territory between the free-soil and pro-slave factions. (*See May 22.*)

**1915**    This advertisement is attracting a good deal of attention in a Chicago newspaper: "Modern Dancing Lessons. 3½ Hours Dancing, 25¢."

**1928**    Fifty-one frogs enter the "Frog Jumping Jubilee" staged at Angels Camp, Calaveras County, California. After the competition is over, the judges announce the winner: "The Pride of San Joaquin Valley," a frog owned by L. R. Fischer of Stockton, California. His jump: 3 feet, 4 inches. (This event is held each year, commemorating Mark Twain's story, "The Celebrated Jumping Frog of Calaveras County.")

**1940**    William Allen White, editor of the *Emporia Gazette*, Emporia, Kansas, and a group of men and women dedicated to the overthrow of Fascism throughout the world, organize the Committee to Defend America by Aiding the Allies. (WORLD WAR II)

**1943**    Prime Minister Winston Churchill of Great Britain, in a speech before a Joint Session of Congress, promises a full partnership with the United States in the assault on Japan until "its cities and other munition centers are in ashes, for in ashes they must surely lie before peace comes back to the world." (WORLD WAR II)

**1945**    More than four hundred U.S. Superfortress bombers soar over Japan, attacking Tokyo and laying mines in vital sea lanes. (WORLD WAR II)

**1964**    The State Department in Washington reveals that American diplomats in Moscow have found at least forty secret microphones hidden in various rooms of the U.S. Embassy in the Russian capital. (The microphones, of course, had been installed for espionage purposes.)

## MAY 20

**1506**    Christopher Columbus dies in Spain.

**1830**    Something new in railway service is introduced by the Baltimore & Ohio Railroad as it publishes the first "timetable" in history. (The schedule of departures and arrivals, between Baltimore and Ellicott's Mills, Maryland, was not handed out to passengers but printed in the *Baltimore American*.)

**1834**    The Marquis de Lafayette, who served the cause of freedom in the American and French Revolutions, dies in France.

**1861**    North Carolina votes to secede from the Union.

**1862**    President Lincoln signs into law the Homestead Act, providing 250,000,000 acres of free land to settlers in the West. Under the terms of the law, citizens will be permitted to stake out claims to 160-acre tracts of government land. After the claimants have cultivated the land for 5 years, the government will transfer titles of ownership to them.

**1902** Cuban Independence Day: Cuba becomes a republic as American occupation under General Leonard Wood comes to an end. At 12 noon, a 45-gun salute in Havana hails the new republic and the Stars and Stripes are lowered, replaced on the government buildings by the lone-star banner of the Republic of Cuba.

**1921** President Harding presents to Madame Curie, co-discoverer of radium with her husband, Pierre, a capsule of radium worth $100,000, the gift of the women of the United States.

**1927** At 7:40 A.M., Charles A. Lindbergh climbs into his monoplane *The Spirit of St. Louis* at Roosevelt Field, New York, and takes off for Paris in an attempt to win a $25,000 prize offered for the first solo nonstop flight across the Atlantic. Lindbergh's plane is stocked with 451 gallons of gasoline and 20 gallons of oil, but has no lights, heat, radio, automatic pilot or de-icing equipment. (Thirty-three and a half hours later, the slim aviator landed at Le Bourget Airport, Paris, and was greeted by a cheering crowd of 100,000. During the first 4 days following his departure from New York, American newspapers devoted 27,000 columns of words in reporting the exciting "story.") *(See below)*

**1932** On the fifth anniversary of Charles A. Lindbergh's first solo flight across the Atlantic, Amelia Earhart Putnam takes off from Newfoundland for Ireland. When she lands in Londonderry less than 15 hours later, she becomes the first woman in the history of aviation to fly the Atlantic alone.

**1939** Pan American Airway starts the first regular air passenger service across the Atlantic as the *Yankee Clipper* takes off from Port Washington, New York, bound for Europe.

**1940** A German invasion of the British Isles seems imminent as Adolf Hitler's Nazi troops reach Abbeville, France, on the English Channel. (WORLD WAR II)

**1942** Japanese forces are in command of most of Burma, including the vital Burma Road. In India, General Joseph W. ("Vinegar Joe") Stilwell, American military advisor to the Chinese government, says: "I claim we took a hell of a beating." (WORLD WAR II)

**1957** Thirty years to the day that Charles A. Lindbergh set out to become the first man to make a solo nonstop flight across the Atlantic, an Air Force pilot, Major Robinson Risner, flies the same route in a commemorative flight. (There was one major difference, however. Lindbergh's time totaled 33½ hours, while Major Risner flew the route in 6 hours, 38 minutes.)

**1962** To press for support of a bill to provide medical care for the aged, President Kennedy addresses a rally of 20,000 "senior citizens" at Madison Square Garden, New York. The President says: ". . . The business of government is the business of the people, and the people are right here. . . . This is a problem whose solution

is long overdue. . . . And I believe . . . as inevitably as the tide comes
in . . . this bill is going to pass. . . ."

## MAY 21

**1819**   New Yorkers catch a glimpse of the first bicycle ever to
be propelled on the streets of the city, an importation from England. (The vehicle was considered such a hazard that a few months
later the City Fathers passed a law forbidding "the use of veloci-
pedes in public places and on the sidewalks of the city.")

**1832**   What is considered to be the first Democratic National
Convention gets under way at Baltimore. The delegates not only
nominate President Andrew Jackson for a second term and Martin
Van Buren to be the candidate for Vice President, but pass a rule
requiring all party candidates to receive at least two-thirds of the
votes of the delegates.

**1868**   Republican delegates meeting in Chicago, now organized as the "National Republican Party," nominate General Ulysses S. Grant for President and Schuyler Colfax for Vice President.

**1874**   Nellie Grant, the only daughter of President and Mrs.
Ulysses S. Grant, is married in the White House to a handsome
young Englishman, Algernon Sartoris. The ceremony is performed
under a tremendous floral wedding bell in the gaslit East Room.
(This event provided society reporters with thousands of words of
copy, but most of them didn't know that the President, disconsolate
at the loss of his only daughter, spent a good part of the morning
in his room crying his eyes out.)

**1881**   Clara Barton organizes the first American Red Cross in
Washington and consents to serve as its first president.

**1932**   To promote ticket sales, the Missouri Pacific Railroad
runs the first "Mystery Excursion" between St. Louis and Arcadia,
Missouri. Passengers purchased tickets but were unaware of their
destination until they arrived at Arcadia.

**1941**   A German submarine sinks the U.S. merchant ship
*Robin Moor* in the mid-Atlantic. The crew and passengers are
picked up by rescue ships. (WORLD WAR II)

**1941**   President Franklin D. Roosevelt proclaims "an unlimited state of national emergency." (WORLD WAR II)

**1948**   President Harry S. Truman sends a special message to
Congress proposing statehood for Alaska.

**1955**   Lieutenant John M. Conroy of Van Nuys, California,
achieves a new kind of air record when he spans the United States
twice between dawn and dusk, flying an F-86 Sabrejet 5,085 miles
from Los Angeles to New York and back in a record time of 11
hours, 26 minutes, 33 seconds. (The young man  had breakfast in
Los Angeles, lunch in New York, and supper back in Los Angeles.)

**1961** After "Freedom Riders" had been attacked by white segregationists the day before in Montgomery, Alabama, Governor John Patterson proclaims martial law in that city. Robert F. Kennedy, the U.S. Attorney General, orders U.S. marshals to Montgomery over the protests of the Governor.

## MAY 22

**National Maritime Day** Commemorating the voyage of the *Savannah* across the Atlantic Ocean. (*See below.*)

**1807** Former Vice President Aaron Burr goes on trial for "treason" in Richmond, Virginia. Chief Justice John Marshall of the U.S. Supreme Court is conducting the trial. (Burr was charged with plotting to set up a state independent of the U.S. government. He was completely acquitted in the following August.)

**1813** Richard Wagner, German composer, is born in Leipzig, Germany.

**1819** For the first time in history, an American-made steamship, the *Savannah,* sets out for a transatlantic voyage. (The vessel sailed from Savannah, Georgia, but no passengers signed up for the trip. It arrived in Liverpool on June 20, having relied on its steam engine for only 80 hours during the entire voyage.)

**1856** Official Washington is thrown into an uproar as Representative Preston S. Brooks of South Carolina strides into the Senate chamber, armed with a gold-headed cane, and savagely beats Senator Charles Sumner of Massachusetts. (Brooks was not only enraged by Senator Sumner's attack on the South in his "Crime against Kansas" speech 3 days earlier, but equally infuriated by Sumner's references to Senator A. P. Butler of South Carolina.)

**1868** The Great Train Robbery: Seven members of the Reno Gang hold up the crew of the Indianapolis-bound Jefferson, Madison and Indianapolis train at Marshfield, Indiana. After overpowering the crew, the masked robbers detach the locomotive and the adjoining Adams Express car and speed to a spot outside of Seymour, Indiana, where they make off with $98,000 in cash from a safe in the express car.

**1924** After the body of 13-year-old Bobby Franks is found in a ditch outside of Chicago, police investigations lead to the arrest of Nathan Leopold, Jr., and Richard Loeb, both 19 years of age and students at the University of Chicago. The two young men are charged with kidnapping and murder. (The kidnappers had lured the child into an automobile and sought to obtain a ransom from Mr. Franks, Sr. Before he could oblige, the child was murdered. They were saved from the gallows by Clarence Darrow, who served as defense counsel. Finally, each man was imprisoned for 99 years. Loeb was killed in prison by a fellow convict in 1936. Leopold was paroled in 1958 after serving 33½ years in prison. On his release, he went to Puerto Rico where he started a new life as a hospital technician.)

**1940**    President Franklin D. Roosevelt invites former Governor Alfred M. Landon of Kansas, his Republican opponent in the 1936 Presidential election, to confer with him in the White House with reference to a "coalition" Cabinet to serve for the duration of the European war. Landon refuses his support unless President Roosevelt promises not to seek a third term.

**1943**    Soviet Russia announces the dissolution of the Communist International (Comintern), founded in 1919 to promote world revolution.

**1947**    The "Truman Doctrine" is enacted into law as Congress appropriates $400,000,000 for military and economic aid to Greece and Turkey. (*See March 12.*)

**1953**    President Eisenhower signs the controversial Tidelands Oil Bill, guaranteeing coastal states the rights to all minerals in submerged lands within their historic boundaries.

**1961**    By a 4–3 vote, the U.S. Supreme Court rules that the giant Du Pont Corporation of Wilmington, Delaware, must divest itself of its 63,000,000 shares of General Motors Corporation stock. Du Pont will be permitted to sell these holdings, worth almost $3,000,000,000, within a 10-year period. (This action was a follow-up to a 1957 Court ruling that Du Pont's ownership of 23 percent of all General Motors stock tended to create a monopoly.)

## MAY 23

**1701**    Captain William Kidd is hanged in London, charged with piracy and murder.

**1785**    Bifocal eyeglasses, invented by Benjamin Franklin to save him from the chore of carrying around two separate pairs of spectacles, are described by Mr. Franklin in a letter to a friend: "I have only to move my eyes up and down as I want to see distinctly far or near."

**1788**    South Carolina enters the Union as the eighth state.

**1792**    The birthday of the Democratic Party is usually given as May 23, 1792, the date on which Thomas Jefferson wrote a letter to President George Washington discussing the philosophies of the vigorous but unorganized factions whose spokesman Jefferson had become.

**1904**    European steamship companies transporting immigrants to the United States announce they will reduce their steerage rates to $10 a person.

**1911**    The present main building of the New York Public Library, at Fifth Avenue and 42nd Street, is dedicated by President William Howard Taft.

**1922**    *Abie's Irish Rose,* a new comedy by Anne Nichols, opens at the Fulton Theatre in New York. (The play was reviewed the next day as "bad theatre," but despite its unfavorable reception it ran for 2,327 performances without a break and has been revived time and time again. In fact, *Abie's Irish Rose* has been running somewhere on the face of the earth ever since it opened, performed in faraway places like China and the Scandinavian countries. More than 50,000,000 people have seen the play since it opened on May 23, 1922.)

**1939**    The U.S. Navy's submarine *Squalus* sinks off Portsmouth, New Hampshire, in 240 feet of water. Thirty-three of the 59 men aboard are rescued by a diving bell.

**1941**    Joe Louis defends his heavyweight boxing crown for the 17th time when challenger Buddy Baer is disqualified at the start of the seventh round after his manager refuses to leave the ring.

**1945**    Heinrich Himmler, the sinister chief of the Nazi Secret Police, commits suicide at Lüneburg, Germany, 3 days after his capture by British troops. (WORLD WAR II)

**1949**    A decree in Bonn, Germany, designates the western government of that country as The Federal Republic of Germany. (Eastern Germany, of course, was not included in this new political establishment.)

**1960**    The Prime Minister of Israel, David Ben-Gurion, announces the capture of Adolf Eichmann, the notorious Nazi official accused of causing the death of 6,000,000 European Jews. Ben-Gurion says that Eichmann will be tried in Israel under terms of a 1950 law empowering that nation to hand down death sentences to convicted German war criminals. (Israeli agents had run down Eichmann in Argentina.)

## MAY 24

**Empire Day**    Celebrated throughout the British Empire on the anniversary of Queen Victoria's birthday.

**1626**    Peter Minuit, a director of the Dutch West India Trading Company, buys the island of Manhattan from the Indians for the equivalent of $24 and founds the colony of New Amsterdam.

**1819**    Birthday of Victoria, Queen of Great Britain and Ireland and Empress of India.

**1844**    Birth of the modern telegraph industry: Samuel Finley Breese Morse, sitting in the U.S. Supreme Court room in the Capitol in Washington, sends the first public telegraph message to his associate, Alfred Vail, located in the Baltimore & Ohio railway station in Baltimore. Morse's message reads: "What hath God wrought!" (The government had appropriated $30,000 for the construction of this telegraphic line linking Washington and Baltimore.)

**1859**  "Ave Maria," music composed by Charles Gounod, is sung for the first time at a concert in Paris. The soloist is Madame Caroline Miolan-Carvalho.

**1883**  The Brooklyn Bridge, linking the boroughs of Manhattan and Brooklyn in New York City, is opened for the first time to public traffic. The new bridge, designed by John A. Roebling, is the longest suspension bridge in the world to date and consists of 5,296 galvanized steel wires bound together.

**1899**  Public interest in the "horseless carriage" prompts the Back Bay Cycle & Motor Company in Boston to open the first public garage in America. The owners advertise their garage as a "stable for renting, sale, storage and repair of motor vehicles."

**1941**  H.M.S. *Hood* of the British Navy, the world's largest warship, is sunk by the German battleship *Bismarck* somewhere between Iceland and Greenland. Most of the *Hood's* 1,341 officers and men are lost in the action. (WORLD WAR II)

**1949**  An unknown assailant shoots Victor Reuther, brother of the president of the United Automobile Workers' Union, at his Detroit home. (The attack followed a similar one on Walter Reuther at his home and resulted in the loss of Victor Reuther's eye.)

**1954**  Lieutenant Geneviève de Galard-Terraube, 29, French nurse and the only woman within the besieged fortress of Dienbienphu, Indochina, is released by the victorious Vietminh Nationalists after being held prisoner for 17 days.

**1962**  Lieutenant Commander Malcolm Scott Carpenter of the U.S. Navy becomes the second American to go into orbit as he circles the earth three times.

**1964**  After making a survey of the present day's mobile society, Thomas J. Fleming, writing in *This Week,* reports that some 37,000,000 Americans will have switched homes by the time 1964 is ended. Mr. Fleming also reveals that five million families a year move from one state to another and that only 35 percent of all current heads of families are living in the areas where they were born.

**1965**  Art collectors in the United States and Great Britain participate in the world's first transatlantic art auction, made possible by the facilities of the Early Bird television satellite. While all of the paintings up for sale are in London, they are shown to bidders on both sides of the Atlantic via television. The bidding is done in English pounds, American viewers being provided with a conversion table showing one pound equal to $2.80. (Collectors seated in a New York auction gallery bought a painting by Sir Winston Churchill for $39,200 and a Degas pastel for $56,000.)

# MAY 25

**1787** Delegates to the Constitutional Convention hold their first regular session in Independence Hall, Philadelphia.

**1803** Birthday of Ralph Waldo Emerson, poet, essayist, and philosopher. ("Be an opener of doors to such as come after you, and do not leave the universe a blind alley.")

**1836** Former President John Quincy Adams, now a member of the House of Representatives, opposes the annexation of Texas in a speech delivered on the floor of the House. Adams fears such a move will bring about a war with Mexico.

**1844** A Washington correspondent for the *Baltimore Patriot* becomes the first journalist to send a news dispatch by telegraph as he sends the paper this wire: "One o'clock. There has just been made a motion in the House to go into committee of the whole on the Oregon question. Rejected. Ayes 79; Nays 86."

**1927** Henry Ford announces that he will discontinue the manufacture of his famous Model T Fords. The Detroit automotive manufacturer plans to replace the popular "Tin Lizzie" with his new Model A car.

**1935** Babe Ruth, soon to retire from professional baseball, swats out the last home run of his career—his 714th—at Forbes Field, Pittsburgh, where Ruth's team, the Boston Braves, is playing the Pittsburgh Pirates.

**1940** In Atlanta, Georgia, Oglethorpe University seals its "Crypt of Civilization" after thousands of objects representing daily life in the year 1940 are sealed into it. The crypt is not to be opened until the year 8113.

**1955** A violent series of tornadoes sweeps through Kansas, Oklahoma, Texas, and Missouri, taking the lives of at least 121 persons. Udall, Kansas, the most seriously stricken town, is almost completely demolished.

**1960** Following the collapse of the Big Four summit meeting in Paris, President Dwight D. Eisenhower makes a nationwide radio and television report to the country. The President says that his goal will still be to reduce conflict with the Soviet Union. On the subject of the U-2 flight, he points out: "... Our safety and that of the free world demand ... effective systems for gathering information about the military capability of other powerful nations, especially those that make a fetish of secrecy ... I take full responsibility for approving all the ... programs undertaken by our government to secure and evaluate military intelligence."

**1965** A bizarre prizefight in Lewiston, Maine, for the world's heavyweight boxing championship, between titleholder Cassius Clay and challenger Sonny Liston, comes to an end after 1 minute, 56 seconds * of the first round. Ringside spectators are stunned as Liston is knocked out by a right-hand "phantom" punch from Clay, a punch that is described by one sportswriter as "landing with the thud of a creampuff." (Listed as the fastest knockout in a heavyweight title bout, boxing fans in and out of the arena were quick to cry "fix" and "fraud." The controversy raged over the punch itself, the actual length of the bout, the timekeeper's count on the knockout while the referee was engaged in trying to get Clay back to a neutral corner.)

## MAY 26

**1848**    Delegates to the Democratic National Convention end their proceedings in Baltimore after nominating Lewis Cass of Michigan for President and William O. Butler of Kentucky for Vice President.

**1854**    By a vote of 35–13, the Senate passes the Kansas-Nebraska Act sponsored by Senator Stephen A. Douglas, Democrat of Illinois. The act practically repeals the Missouri Compromise by creating the separate territories of Kansas and Nebraska and permitting the residents there to decide whether or not they want slavery. (This act, in effect, was a challenge to the North by the pro-slavery South and has been called "the most momentous measure that passed Congress from the day the Senators and Representatives first met to the outbreak of the War between the States.")

**1868**    President Andrew Johnson, facing impeachment proceedings in the Senate on charges of "high crimes and misdemeanors," is acquitted, the impeachment forces losing by a single vote. (Thirty-five senators voted for impeachment, 19 against it; a two-thirds majority was therefore not achieved. The charges against the President were inspired largely by political considerations. And yet the radical leader of the House, the Republican Thaddeus Stevens, was so embittered by the final vote that he commented that henceforth no President could be removed from office by process of law. "If tyranny becomes intolerable," Stevens predicted, "the only recourse will be in the dagger of a Brutus.")

**1868**    Immediately after the Senate acquits President Johnson, Secretary of War Edwin M. Stanton, the man primarily responsible for the impeachment charges, submits his resignation from the Cabinet in a letter to the President. (*See January 13 & 15*)

**1886**    Birthday of Al Jolson, stage, screen, radio, and television personality.

**1913**    In Marquette, Michigan, former President Theodore Roosevelt sues a state newspaper for libel after the editor had

* According to newsmen who clocked the match, Liston went down at 1:44 and finally got up at 1:56.

charged that Roosevelt was habitually drunk. Appearing on the stand as his own witness, Mr. Roosevelt testifies that he drank one glass of beer in his life—and that made him ill. He adds that at state and public dinners he sometimes drinks a glass or two of champagne "and I do that in public." (After a parade of well-known witnesses attested to his temperate use of alcoholic beverages, the editor made a public retraction and Mr. Roosevelt said he would be pleased to accept the jury's verdict of "nominal damages"—six cents.)

**1927** A day after announcing the discontinuation of the Model T Ford, Henry Ford and his son Edsel take turns driving the 15,000,000th automobile to be manufactured by the Ford Motor Car Company.

**1937** Members of the Ford factory police attack and brutally beat Walter Reuther and Richard Frankensteen at the company's River Rouge plant where the two officials of the United Automobile Workers Union were supervising the distribution of a pamphlet demanding the end of Ford's policy of guaranteeing an open shop.

**1942** Radio Tokyo, boasting of the military victories over both the United States and Great Britain, announces to the Japanese home front: "America and Britain . . . have now been exterminated. . . . The British and American fleets cannot appear on the oceans. To rebuild their naval strength would require years and a great amount of equipment. . . . The Japanese people can look forward to a triumphal march into London and a victory march into New York." (WORLD WAR II)

**1945** Almost 20 square miles of Tokyo are ablaze following raids by United States B-29 bombers. Four thousand tons of fire bombs have been dropped on the city. (WORLD WAR II)

**1954** The funeral ship of the Egyptian Pharaoh Cheops is unearthed in a limestone chamber near the Great Pyramid of Giza in Egypt.

# MAY 27

**1818** Birthday of Amelia Bloomer, American feminist, whose name was given to a form of woman's dress she recommended, loose trousers gathered in tightly at the ankles.

**1819** Birthday of Julia Ward Howe, leader of antislavery and woman suffrage movements and author of the lyrics of the classic "Battle Hymn of the Republic."

**1844** A splinter group of "Tyler's Democrats" meeting in Baltimore nominates President John Tyler to succeed himself in the December elections. (Tyler, originally a Democrat, had joined forces with William Henry Harrison and the Whigs in the 1840 campaign and had been promptly dubbed "Turncoat Tyler" by the regular Democrats. He was so unpopular with the Democrats in 1844 that he withdrew as a candidate of the "Tyler Democrats" 3 months after he was nominated.)

**1860**     Giuseppe Garibaldi, Italian patriot and onetime candle-maker of Staten Island, New York, invades Sicily with 1,000 "Red Shirts" and captures Palermo in his drive to take over the Kingdom of Naples.

**1933**     The Century of Progress Exposition opens in Chicago.

**1937**     A one-week celebration marks the opening of the Golden Gate Bridge in San Francisco Bay.

**1941**     After a pursuit of 1,750 miles by four British battleships, the German battleship *Bismarck*, the warship responsible for the sinking of H.M.S. *Hood* on May 24, is torpedoed and sunk 400 miles west of Brest, France. Most of the crew of the German battleship is lost at sea. (WORLD WAR II)

**1942**     Reinhard Heydrich, the "Hangman of Czechoslovakia" and Adolf Hitler's Gauleiter in that occupied nation, is murdered by patriots in Prague. (WORLD WAR II)

**1954**     More than 100 crew members of the U.S. aircraft carrier *Bennington* are killed as an explosion rocks the huge warship off the coast of Rhode Island. Another 200 crew members are wounded.

**1955**     At 8:51 A.M., Washington time, the "Census Clock" in the lobby of the Department of Commerce Building registers an even 165,000,000 Americans, the latest census count. The clock indicates that, by current statistic reports, a baby is born every 8 seconds somewhere in the United States, a death occurs every 21 seconds and an immigrant is registered every 2 minutes. (*See July 1*)

**1957**     Senator Theodore F. Green (D., R.I.), at the age of 89 years, 7 months, and 26 days, becomes the oldest man ever to serve in the United States Congress—House or Senate. The record up until today was formerly held by Representative Charles M. Stedman of North Carolina who died in office in 1930 at the age of 89 years, 7 months, and 25 days.

**1961**     For the first time since the Reconstruction, Texas will be represented in the U.S. Senate by a Republican. John G. Tower, 35, an ultra-conservative Republican, wins the seat formerly occupied by Vice President Lyndon B. Johnson.

**1964**     Jawaharlal Nehru, the first and only Prime Minister of the Indian Republic to date since its founding in 1947, dies in New Delhi. The news is broken to Parliament by a Cabinet official who says: "The Prime Minister is no more. Life is out. The light is out . . ." (These were the same words Nehru had used in January, 1948 after the death of Gandhi.)

# MAY 28

**1798** President John Adams is empowered by Congress to recruit an army of 10,000 volunteers.

**1864** Archduke Maximilian, brother of the Emperor Franz Joseph of Austria-Hungary, lands at Vera Cruz to assume the throne as the Emperor of Mexico.

**1892** A budding comedienne, Marie Dressler, makes her debut in New York in the comic opera, *The Robber of the Rhine.*

**1905** Imperial Russia's fleet suffers a disastrous defeat at the hands of the Japanese Navy commanded by Admiral Togo. The Japanese victory seals Russia's ultimate defeat in the Russo-Japanese War.

**1929** For the first time in motion-picture history, the Warner Brothers releases a talking film produced entirely in color. The moving picture, *On with the Show,* starring Ethel Waters, Joe E. Brown, and Betty Compton, is being shown at the Winter Garden Theatre in New York.

**1934** With the assistance of a midwife and Dr. Allan Roy Dafoe, a local country doctor, Mrs. Oliva Dionne gives birth to five baby girls in her farmhouse near Callender, Ontario. (The Dionne quintuplets, claimed to be the first quintuplets to survive infancy, were so tiny at birth that their mother was able to slip her wedding ring over their hands.)

**1937** Prime Minister Stanley Baldwin of Great Britain resigns and is succeeded by Neville Chamberlain.

**1940** The evacuation of British and French forces from Dunkerque, France, begins as the British Admiralty dispatches a hastily improvised fleet to that port in an effort to rescue as much of the Anglo-French military force from the path of the triumphant Germans as possible. (*See June 3.*) (WORLD WAR II)

**1940** King Leopold III of Belgium surrenders the 300,000-man Belgian Army to Nazi Germany. His Cabinet, furious at the King's capitulation, disowns him. (WORLD WAR II)

**1942** Adolf Hitler orders a "blood bath" in Czechoslovakia in reprisal for the murder of Reinhard Heydrich a day earlier. (Before the Nazis were through with this one atrocious campaign, some 2,000 Czechs had been executed, and thousands deported to concentration camps.) (WORLD WAR II)

**1955** Albert Whitehouse, a director of the United Steelworkers of America, tells an audience in Atlantic City, New Jersey, that automation of the nation's factories will lead to a 2-hour work day. (But when?)

**1959** Two monkeys named Able and Baker survive a 300-mile trip into space out of Cape Canaveral, Florida. (They were confined in the nose of a rocket and picked up uninjured later.)

**1962**    The Stock Market's "Blue Monday": On the New York Stock Exchange, a total of $20.8 billion in share values is lost, the biggest one-day drop since the famous "Black Tuesday" of October 29, 1929. (*See October 28, 29, 30*)

## MAY 29

**1453**    Constantinople, the capital of the Byzantine Empire, is captured by the Turks. (Considered one of the greatest events in the history of the world, this date is listed by some historians as the closing of the Middle Ages.)

**1790**    By the close vote of 34–32, Rhode Island ratifies the United States Constitution, the last of the 13 colonies to do so.

**1844**    James Knox Polk of Tennessee becomes the first "dark horse" candidate in American political history to receive the Presidential nomination as the Democrats end their national convention at Baltimore. (Polk, a compromise candidate, was brought forth on the eighth ballot after a deadlock developed between former President Martin Van Buren and Lewis Cass, both aspirants for the nomination. Polk may have been unknown by the delegates but he surprised everyone by winning the election in the following December.)

**1848**    Wisconsin enters the Union as the 30th state.

**1865**    President Andrew Johnson issues a proclamation of amnesty extending a Presidential pardon to all individuals who participated in the southern rebellion against the Union, excepting those in 14 specified classifications. Included in the latter are former officers of the Confederate Army, all ex-Confederates who possess more than $20,000 in taxable property, and certain officials of the Confederate civil government.

**1868**    General Ulysses S. Grant accepts the Republican nomination for the Presidency and issues a statement saying "Let us have peace."

**1898**    Commodore Winfield S. Schley commanding the U.S. fleet, on orders from Admiral William T. Sampson, starts to blockade the Spanish fleet in the harbor at Santiago, Cuba.

**1910**    A prize of $10,000 offered by *The New York World* is won by Glenn H. Curtiss after he completes a successful flight from Albany, New York, to New York City, a distance of 142 miles, in 2 hours and 51 minutes. (He made a stop at Poughkeepsie for additional fuel and, on discovering that none was available at the farm where he landed, he borrowed a few gallons from a passing motorist.)

**1912**    *The New York Sun* reports that 15 young women were dismissed from their jobs at the Curtis Publishing Company in Philadelphia by Edward W. Bok, editor of the *Ladies' Home Journal,* after he observed them dancing the "Turkey Trot" during their lunch period. (Many people, in 1912, considered the "Turkey Trot" to be "not quite nice.")

**1917**    John Fitzgerald Kennedy, the 35th President of the United States, is born in Brookline, Massachusetts, the second child and second son born to Rose (Fitzgerald) and Joseph P. Kennedy.

**1953**    Edmond P. Hillary, 34, a New Zealand bee-keeper, and Tensing Norkay, 42, a tribesman of Nepal, are the first persons in history to reach the top of Mount Everest, the world's highest mountain, more than 29,000 feet above sea level.

**1965**    In Modesto, California, Ralph Boston, a Santa Monica school teacher, establishes a world record in the broad jump as he leaps 27 feet, 5 inches, thus breaking his own previous world mark set a year ago by three-quarters of an inch.

## MAY 30

**Memorial Day (also known as Decoration Day)**    This holiday is a legal observance in those states where it is celebrated. Originally intended as a day to honor the memory of those who fell in the War between the States, it is now observed in memoriam of the nation's dead in all wars. (*See below.*)

**1431**    Joan of Arc, the Maid of Orleans, is burned at the stake in Rouen, France, at the age of 19. (She had been charged and found guilty of sorcery and heresy.)

**1765**    Cries of "Treason!" interrupt Patrick Henry in the Virginia House of Burgesses as he makes a stirring speech denouncing the British Parliament's right to levy taxes on Virginia without its consent. But the lanky Virginia patriot is not to be silenced. "Tarquin and Caesar each had his Brutus, Charles the First his Cromwell, and George the Third may profit by their example. If this be treason, make the most of it!"

**1868**    The first formal observance of Memorial Day takes place following the request of General John A. Logan, national commander of the Grand Army of the Republic, who ordered all G.A.R. posts to "strew with flowers or otherwise decorate the graves of comrades who died in defense of their country during the late rebellion."

**1883**    An unfounded report that the Brooklyn Bridge is about to collapse results in an outbreak of panic among the large crowd of strollers who are inspecting the new bridge, opened to traffic only 6 days ago. Men and women and children jamming the exits trample 12 persons to death and injure 40 more.

**1896**    More than a thousand people congregated at the Ardsley Country Club, in Irvington, New York, see a Duryea automobile come in first to win the $3,000 prize offered by John Brisben Walker, editor of *The Cosmopolitan*. (The car was one of four that started out earlier in the day from New York's City Hall.)

**1901**   At a special ceremony on the campus of New York University in New York City, the Hall of Fame is dedicated officially and opened to the public. Twenty-nine tablets in memory of celebrated Americans have been installed in the monument. (The first bust, that of the educator Horace Mann, was put in place on Memorial Day in 1907.)

**1922**   Chief Justice William Howard Taft of the U.S. Supreme Court dedicates the Lincoln Memorial in the nation's capital while 100,000 persons stand by. Located at the end of the Mall, the memorial is surrounded by 36 columns of white marble, one column for each state of the Union that existed at the time of Lincoln's death.

**1937**   An attempt by 1,000 strikers to force a shutdown at the Republic Steel Corporation in South Chicago leads to a pitched battle between strikers and the police. Order is restored at the gates of the plant only after 10 people are killed and 90 more wounded.

**1942**   Britain's Royal Air Force makes its first "thousand bomber" raid on a German target as 1,130 planes attack Cologne, dropping 1,500 tons of bombs on the city in 90 minutes' time. (WORLD WAR II)

**1961**   Generalissimo Rafael Trujillo Molina, dictator of the Dominican Republic since 1930, is assassinated in Ciudad Trujillo.

## MAY 31

**1819**   Birthday of Walt Whitman, American poet and author of the immortal *Leaves of Grass*.

**1889**   Johnstown, Pennsylvania, suffers a disastrous flood after heavy rains cause the Conemaugh Dam to burst. In the wake of the flood waters, more than two thousand lives are lost and thousands of buildings are razed to the ground.

**1907**   A flotilla of "taximeter cabs," imported from Paris, arrive in New York, the first "taxis" to be seen in an American city.

**1910**   The Union of South Africa is founded as the South African Act welds into a simple union the two former Dutch republics of the Transvaal and the Orange Free State and the two former British colonies of the Cape of Good Hope and Natal.

**1913**   Secretary of State William Jennings Bryan declares the Seventeenth Amendment to the Constitution in effect. (The amendment provides for the popular election of U.S. senators.)

**1916**   Battle of Jutland: In one of the greatest naval engagements in military history, two units of the British Royal Navy, commanded by Admiral Jellicoe and Admiral Beatty, force Admiral von Scheer and his German fleet to make an about-face in the North Sea in an effort to rejoin the main German fleet at the Kiel Naval

Base. Most of Von Scheer's fleet returns to Kiel intact. (WORLD WAR I)

**1926** Philadelphia's Sesquicentennial Exposition, celebrating the 150th anniversary of the founding of the United States, is opened to the public. (It closed the following November 30.)

**1933** Visitors to the Chicago Century of Progress Exposition on Memorial Day are still talking about an unknown entertainer named Sally Rand and her Fan Dance. In Miss Rand's debut yesterday at the Fair, she created a furor by dancing "all white and naked, twisting and turning behind two huge fans." (A few weeks later, a newspaper correspondent reported: "The Adler Planetarium is playing to poor business; the wonders of the Travel and Transport Building are drawing but fair to average crowds; 40 men could toss a medicine ball around in the Hall of Science and never bother the customers.... But Sally Rand, dancing nude on the 'Streets of Paris,' has been jamming the place nightly.")

**1949** Mary Margaret McBride, one of America's leading radio personalities, marks her 15th anniversary as a broadcaster with a gigantic celebration at Yankee Stadium in New York. Thirty-five thousand "fans" are on hand to pay tribute to Miss McBride.

**1951** Radio Moscow claims that television was first invented by a Russian, Professor Boris Rosing, in 1907.

**1962** Adolf Eichmann, the Nazi war criminal who played a major role in the German slaughter of millions of European Jews during World War II, is put to death by hanging in Israel.

**1964** The longest double-header in major league baseball history is played in New York by the New York Mets and the San Francisco Giants, with the Giants winning both games. The total time of play is 10 hours, 23 minutes. (The second game alone lasted 7 hours, 23 minutes, the longest game by time in the major leagues.)

# JUNE

## JUNE 1

**1792**    Kentucky, the 15th state, is admitted into the Union.

**1796**    Another star is added to the flag as Tennessee is admitted into the Union as the 16th state.

**1812**    President James Madison advises Congress that a second war with Great Britain is inevitable. ("Our commerce has been plundered in every sea, the great staples of our country have been cut off from their legitimate markets, and a destructive blow aimed at our agricultural and maritime interests. . . .")

**1813**    "Don't Give up the Ship" becomes the slogan of the U.S. Navy today after Captain James Lawrence, commander of the *Chesapeake,* is carried mortally wounded from his post on the deck, during the battle with the British frigate *Shannon.*

**1856**    Henry Ward Beecher, a Congregationalist clergyman of Brooklyn, New York, and a vigorous foe of slavery, holds a mock public "auction" of a young Negro girl to expose the evils of slavery.

**1881**    Officials of the U.S. Military Academy at West Point, New York, announce that henceforth cadets may not use tobacco in any form.

**1905**    The Lewis and Clark Exposition opens in Portland, Oregon.

**1914**    Josephus Daniels, Secretary of the Navy, stirs up a hornet's nest when he issues an order forbidding the use of all alcoholic beverages in the Navy.

**1933**    A session of the Senate Banking and Currency Committee is thrown into an uproar when a publicity-seeking circus agent lifts a midget onto the lap of the startled New York financier, J. P. Morgan, just before he starts to testify before the committee.

**1939**    The old-age pension plan advocated by Dr. Francis Townsend of California is rejected by the House of Representatives. The Townsend Plan calls for a government monthly pension of $200 to be awarded to all citizens 60 years of age or older, on condition that the entire amount will be spent in the United States within a month after receipt.

**1943**  Leslie Howard, the English-born star of stage and motion pictures, loses his life when the civilian transport plane on which he is traveling from Lisbon to London is attacked by a German plane and sunk in the Bay of Biscay. (WORLD WAR II)

**1944**  The siesta is abolished in Mexico.

**1958**  General Charles de Gaulle becomes premier of France, the 26th man to hold that office since the end of World War II. (*See January 8*)

## JUNE 2

**1851**  For the first time in American history, a state passes a prohibition law. The state is Maine and its law bans the sale of alcoholic beverages in ". . . drinking houses and tippling shops."

**1856**  James Buchanan of Pennsylvania and John C. Breckinridge of Kentucky are nominated for the Presidency and Vice Presidency by delegates to the Democratic Convention meeting in Cincinnati.

**1883**  Two thousand spectators in Fort Wayne, Indiana, see the first baseball game to take place at night, as two local teams play at League Park under light streaming from 17 floodlights.

**1886**  Grover Cleveland, the President of the United States, is married in the White House to his ward, Miss Frances Folsom. (This was the first time that a U.S. President had been married in the executive mansion.)

**1924**  Congress confers citizenship upon all American Indians.

**1932**  Thousands of unemployed war veterans from all over the United States are pouring into Washington, hoping to persuade Congress to grant them the hotly debated soldiers' bonus.

**1941**  In a jubilant mood, Air Marshal Hermann Goering predicts a successful invasion of the British Isles and tells the German Luftwaffe that "there is no unconquerable island." (WORLD WAR II)

**1946**  As the result of a national referendum, the Italian people vote to abolish the monarchy. King Humbert II prepares to go into exile.

**1953**  Queen Elizabeth II, 27 years old, is crowned in Westminster Abbey, London, by the Archbishop of Canterbury. More than a million people from all over the world jam the streets of the city to catch a glimpse of the Queen in the coronation procession. ("I, whose youth was cast in the august, unchallenged and tranquil glories of the Victorian era, may well feel a thrill in evoking once more the prayer and the anthem, 'God Save the Queen!' " —Winston Churchill, on the Queen's accession).

**1957**  American television viewers are treated to a filmed, unrehearsed interview with Russian Communist Party boss Nikita Khrushchev. Appearing on the Columbia Broadcasting System's "Face the Nation" program, produced in his office in the Kremlin,

Khrushchev says: ". . . Your grandchildren in America will live under socialism . . . and will not understand how their grandparents did not understand the progressive nature of a socialistic society. . . ."

**1960**    A dispute between Actors Equity and New York theatre owners results in a blackout of Broadway theatres, the first such shutdown in 41 years. (The dispute settled, the curtains went up again on June 12.)

**1961**    America's First Lady, Mrs. John F. Kennedy, is the hit of Paris. Huge crowds cheer her appearances, crying "Jackie! Jackie!" President Kennedy, who is in Paris for talks with French President De Gaulle, delights luncheon guests when he says: "I do not think it altogether inappropriate to introduce myself. I am the man who accompanied Jacqueline Kennedy to Paris, and I have enjoyed it."


## JUNE 3

**Confederate Memorial Day**    A legal holiday in Kentucky, Louisiana, and Tennessee.

**1808**    Birthday of Jefferson Davis, President of the Confederate States of America. His birthday is a public holiday in 10 Southern states.

**1871**    The 24-year-old outlaw Jesse James and his gang rob the newly opened Obocock Bank in Corydon, Iowa, escaping with $15,000, the total cash on hand in the bank.

**1888**    "Casey at the Bat," the immortal baseball classic written by Ernest L. Thayer, is published for the first time in *The San Francisco Examiner*.

**1898**    Lieutenant Richmond P. Hobson of the U.S. Navy, together with seven volunteers, attempts to sink the old collier *Merrimac* in Santiago harbor, Cuba, in the hope of bottling up the Spanish fleet for the remainder of the Spanish-American War. (The attempt was doomed to failure and the men were taken prisoner by the enemy, but nonetheless Hobson's audacity thrilled the American home front.)

**1935**    The French liner *Normandie* makes her maiden voyage across the Atlantic in 4 days, 11 hours, and 42 seconds, establishing a new record.

**1937**    The Duke of Windsor, formerly King Edward VIII of Great Britain, is married to Mrs. Wallis Warfield Simpson of Baltimore in Monts, France. (The long-awaited marriage was described by H. L. Mencken as "the greatest news story since the Resurrection.")

**1940**    The Allied evacuation in Dunkerque, France, which began on May 28, is completed, some 337,000 British, French, and Belgian troops having reached English ports safely. (The evacuation, one of the miracles of World War II, was accomplished by ships of the Royal Navy and 665 other British craft, including yachts, fishing trawlers, barges, and motor launches. British casualties were 13,000 killed, 40,000 wounded. The Royal Air Force engaged the main strength of the German Luftwaffe and inflicted losses of at least four to one.) (WORLD WAR II)

**1948**  The world's largest telescope is dedicated at Mount Palomar Observatory, California.

**1963**  The world mourns the death of Pope John XXIII.

**1963**  A survey of marriage and divorce in the United States reveals these statistics: "Out of 111,600,000 American men and women 20 years old or older, 88.6 million are married or have been married and never divorced. Single persons who have never married total 12.5 million. Approximately 10.5 million have been divorced." *

**1965**  Two American astronauts, Major James A. McDivitt and Major Edward H. White of the U.S. Air Force, are launched into orbit from Cape Kennedy, Florida, aboard their Gemini 4 spacecraft. (During their exciting 4-day orbital flight, Major White became for a while a human satellite as he floated about in space for 20 minutes, tethered to the spacecraft by a 25-foot "umbilical" line carrying a supply of oxygen and lines of communications.)

# JUNE 4

**1070**  After returning to a cave, near Roquefort, France, where he had left an uneaten lunch of barley bread and sheep's milk cheese several weeks earlier, an anonymous shepherd finds the bread covered with heavy black mold but the cheese only slightly so. On tasting the cheese, he finds it has a delicious new flavor and rushes to a local monastery to share it with the monks. (Shortly thereafter, the monks started to cure their cheese in this cave, the first Roquefort cheese in the world.)

**1800**  There is great excitement in the nation's capital as James Hoban, the architect of the President's house, directs a crew of workmen in putting the finishing touches on the Executive Mansion. At the same time, President and Mrs. John Adams arrive in Washington to prepare to move into the Mansion.

**1811**  The first talk of secession from the Union is heard on the floor of Congress, following a debate on the disposition of the Orleans Territory. Says Representative Josiah Quincy of Massachusetts: "It will be the right of all and the duty of some of the states definitely to prepare for a separation, amicably if they can; violently, if they must..."

* *U.S. News & World Report*, June 3, 1963

**1893**    The Anti-Saloon League of America is organized in Ohio.

**1896**    Henry Ford wheels the first Ford car from a brick shed at 58 Bagley Avenue, Detroit, and drives it around the darkened city streets in a successful trial run.

**1924**    An eternal light is set into operation in Madison Square, New York, to "shine forever" in memory of the New York soldiers who died in World War I.

**1936**    Headed by Premier Leon Blum, the first Socialist government in France takes office.

**1940**    Speaking before a solemn House of Commons, assembled to hear a report on the evacuation of Dunkerque and the flight of the British Army from the European continent, Prime Minister Winston Churchill says: "We shall not flag or fail. We shall go on to the end. We shall fight in France, we shall fight on the seas and oceans, we shall fight with growing confidence and growing strength in the air, we shall defend our Island, whatever the cost may be. We shall fight on the beaches, we shall fight on the landing grounds, we shall fight in the fields and in the streets, we shall fight in the hills; we shall never surrender." (WORLD WAR II)

**1941**    Wilhelm II, former Kaiser of Germany, dies in Doorn, Holland, where he has lived in exile since 1918.

**1942**    The Battle of Midway begins as ships of the U.S. Navy meet a Japanese fleet, near Midway Islands, 1,200 miles northwest of Hawaii. (When it was all over, the Japanese suffered their first decisive defeat of World War II, the United States losing 2 vessels to the 10 lost by Japan, including 4 aircraft carriers.)

**1943**    Seven thousand army troops, marching from their barracks outside Buenos Aires to government headquarters, overthrow the regime of President Ramon S. Castillo of Argentina.

**1944**    Soldiers of the U.S. Fifth Army and the British Eighth Army occupy Rome, the first Axis capital to fall to the Allies. (WORLD WAR II)

**1946**    Juan Perón is inaugurated President of Argentina after having staged a coup d'etat in 1945. His ambitious wife, now First Lady, decrees that her official title will be Doña Maria Eva Duarte de Perón.

**1961**    President Kennedy and Russian Premier Khrushchev confer in Vienna.

## JUNE 5

**1865**    The hymn "Onward, Christian Soldiers," is sung for the first time at a parish festival held in Horbury, England. The words are by the Reverend Sabine Baring-Gould, a clergyman and novelist, and the music adapted from Haydn's *Symphony #15 in D*. (Six years later, Sir Arthur Sullivan wrote a new melody for the hymn.)

**1872** At the Republican National Convention meeting in Philadelphia, Ulysses S. Grant and Henry Wilson are nominated for the Presidency and Vice-Presidency.

**1876** Visitors to the Centennial Exposition at Philadelphia are delighted with the first bananas they have ever tasted. Refreshment stands are selling the bananas, individually wrapped in foil, for 10 cents apiece. (Before this time, bananas were rarely seen or eaten in the United States.)

**1884** While Republicans at the national convention in Chicago are hopeful that they can persuade General William T. Sherman to accept their Presidential nomination, the former Union commander refuses to submit to pressure and sends the meeting a curt telegram of rejection: "If nominated, I will not accept; if elected, I will not serve."

**1888** Grover Cleveland and Allen G. Thurman are nominated by the Democratic Convention at St. Louis for President and Vice President.

**1917** More than 9½ million American men, between the ages of 21 and 30, register for the draft under the Selective Military Conscription Act. (WORLD WAR I)

**1927** Clarence Chamberlain and Charles A. Levine arrive in Eisleben, Germany, in their monoplane *Columbia,* after flying from Mineola, New York, across the Atlantic Ocean, a total distance of 3,905 miles, in 42 hours, 31 minutes.

**1933** President Franklin D. Roosevelt signs a bill abrogating the gold standard. Henceforth, the U.S. government will be permitted to pay its obligations in any currency that is legal tender at the time of payment.

**1940** The Germans begin the Battle of France. (WORLD WAR II)

**1947** Speaking at the Commencement exercises held at Harvard University, Secretary of State George C. Marshall outlines his plan for the recovery of Europe's economy. Evening newspapers refer to the Secretary's speech as the "Marshall Plan." ("Our policy is directed not against any country or doctrine but against hunger, poverty, desperation and chaos.")

**1950** The U.S. Supreme Court rules unanimously that segregation practices in Southern railroad dining cars and in two Southern universities (University of Texas Law School and the University of Oklahoma) are invalid.

**1954** Greece, Yugoslavia, and Turkey announce they are joining forces in a new Balkan military alliance.

**1961** The Supreme Court orders the U.S. Communist Party to register with the Justice Department.

## JUNE 6

**1816**   Ten inches of snow falls in New England, beginning "the year in which there was no summer."

**1852**   After casting 49 ballots, the Democratic Convention at Baltimore nominates Franklin Pierce of New Hampshire for President and William R. King of Alabama for Vice President.

**1884**   James G. Blaine is nominated for President by the Republicans meeting at Chicago. General John A. Logan of Illinois will be his running mate. (The nomination of Blaine was unacceptable to the "Mugwumps," the liberal wing of the party, and that group promptly bolted the convention.)

**1904**   Newspapers in Philadelphia campaign for a drop in the cost of living, citing the "outrageous prices" of everyday food staples: eggs, 17 cents a dozen; cream, 10 cents a pint; chickens, 40 cents apiece, half a ham, 70 cents.

**1932**   Samuel Insull, Chicago utilities magnate, resigns as president or chaiman of the board of no less than 85 companies. As word leaks out that his financial empire is collapsing, the financier flees to Europe.

**1933**   A motion picture "drive-in" theatre, the first of its kind, opens in Camden, New Jersey. Room is provided for 500 cars and patrons can view and hear films from a screen measuring 40 by 50 feet.

**1934**   The Securities and Exchange Commission (SEC) is established by Congress, with full powers to police the stock exchange and investment markets of the nation.

**1944**   D-Day: In the greatest invasion the world has ever seen, the Allies, commanded by General Dwight D. Eisenhower, hurl an armada of 4,000 ships, 11,000 airplanes and whole divisions of airborne troops across the English Channel to France and start to make landings on the beaches of Normandy. ("Our sons, pride of our nation, this day have set upon a mighty endeavor, a struggle to preserve our Republic, our religion and our civilization, and to set free a suffering humanity."—President Franklin D. Roosevelt.)

**1963**   Scandal rocks Great Britain as John Profumo resigns as Secretary of State for War, after admitting he lied to the House of Commons when he denied earlier that he had been intimate with model Christine Keeler.

## JUNE 7

**1769**   Daniel Boone starts his exploration of Kentucky.

**1776**   Richard Henry Lee of Virginia introduces a series of resolutions before the members of the Continental Congress. (These resolutions were the forerunners of the Declaration of Independence, the most famous one stating "That these united colonies are, and of right ought to be, free and independent states.")

**1778** Birthday of George Bryan Brummell, English man of fashion, known as "Beau Brummell."

**1848** The Whigs hold their national convention at Philadelphia and nominate Zachary Taylor of Louisiana for President and Millard Fillmore of New York for Vice President.

**1860** The "dime novel" makes its first appearance when a New York publisher issues *Malaeska, the Indian Wife of the White Hunter,* written by Mrs. Ann Stevens. (The tale was advertised as "a dollar book for only a dime! 128 pages complete, only ten cents!!!")

**1864** President Abraham Lincoln is renominated by the Republicans for a second term. The convention delegates, meeting in Baltimore, choose Andrew Johnson of Tennessee to run for Vice President. ("I will [not] conceal my gratification . . . that the Union people, through their convention, in their continued effort to advance the nation, have deemed me not unworthy to remain in my present position."—Lincoln).

**1909** Mary Pickford makes her motion-picture debut as Biograph Pictures releases her first film, *The Violin Maker of Cremona.*

**1933** Great Britain, France, Italy, and Germany sign a 10-year peace pact.

**1939** George VI and Queen Elizabeth of Great Britain, the first British monarchs to visit the United States, cross over onto American soil from Canada as they arrive at Niagara Falls, New York.

**1940** After 62 days of heroic and bitter fighting against the German invaders, organized resistance in Norway ceases. King Haakon VII and the Royal Family, and members of the government, leave the homeland for England. Before he boards the British cruiser *Devonshire,* the King issues a proclamation to his people promising to "use all our strength, our life and all we possess for Norway's cause. . . ." (WORLD WAR II)

**1942** Japanese forces occupy Attu and Kiska in the Aleutian Islands. (WORLD WAR II)

**1948** General Dwight D. Eisenhower takes up his duties as president of Columbia University in New York.

**1948** President Eduard Beneš of Czechoslovakia resigns after refusing to sign a new Communist-dictated national Constitution.

**1964** Thomas Paine, the colonial patriot whose writings helped set the stage for the American Revolution, is honored by the people of Thetford, England, where he was born 227 years ago. (This ceremony was not without irony. Paine's writings, particularly *The Rights of Man,* led to a British indictment before the Revolution broke out, charging him with seditious libel.)

**1965**    The U.S. Supreme Court strikes a blow at courtroom television when it reverses, by a 5-to-4 decision, the swindling conviction of Texas financier Billie Sol Estes on the grounds that his trial in Tyler, Texas, had been televised despite his repeated objections. (This ruling, however, had no bearing on Estes' other convictions for mail fraud and conspiracy.)

## JUNE 8

**1786**    An advertisement inserted in a New York newspaper by a Mr. Hull of 76 Chatham Street announces that he will start manufacturing ice cream on a commercial basis.

**1861**    Tennessee secedes from the Union.

**1869**    Ives W. McGaffey of Chicago obtains a patent for his vacuum cleaner, described by the inventor as a "sweeping machine."

**1880**    James A. Garfield is nominated for President on the 36th ballot by delegates to the Republican Convention at Chicago. The Vice Presidential nomination goes to Chester Alan Arthur.

**1905**    President Theodore Roosevelt offers his services as mediator to the belligerents in the Russo-Japanese War.

**1915**    Secretary of State William Jennings Bryan, an outspoken pacifist, resigns his office in protest against the firm notes sent by President Woodrow Wilson to the Imperial German government in connection with the sinking of the *Lusitania*. (Fifteen days later, the President appointed Robert Lansing to succeed Mr. Bryan.)

**1928**    Station WGY, Schenectady, New York, starts a regular schedule of television programs. People with television receivers will now be able to see programs emanating from WGY studios three times a week, from 1:30 to 2 o'clock in the afternoons and from 11:30 to midnight in the evenings.

**1931**    New York newspapers break the news of the discovery of the body of Starr Faithfull, 25-year-old New York girl reported missing for some days, off Long Beach, Long Island. (This sordid case provided headlines for weeks for readers of big-city tabloids, but the girl's disappearance and murder have never been solved.)

**1939**    The king and queen of Great Britain, George VI and Queen Elizabeth, arrive in Washington to begin their visit of state to President and Mrs. Franklin D. Roosevelt at the White House.

**1947**    Eva Perón, the wife of the President of Argentina, receives a tumultuous reception in Madrid, the first such reception permitted by General Francisco Franco since 1940 when the Spanish chief of state welcomed the Nazi secret police leader, Heinrich Himmler.

**1953**    Reversing a previous ruling of the U.S. Court of Appeals on January 22, the U.S. Supreme Court rules, 8—0, that restaurants in the District of Columbia may not legally refuse to serve "well-behaved and respectable" Negro patrons.

# JUNE 9

**1791**    Birthday of John Howard Payne, author of the ballad "Home, Sweet Home."

**1815**    The Congress of Vienna, called to settle the problems of territory and government resulting from the Napoleonic Wars, holds its last session.

**1877**    Samuel Langhorne Clemens explains the origin of his pen name in a letter to the editor of the *Daily Alta Californian*: " 'Mark Twain' was the nom de plume of one Captain Isaiah Sellers, who used to write river news over it for the *New Orleans Picayune*. He died in 1863 and as he could no longer need that signature, I laid violent hands upon it without asking permission of the proprietor's remains. That is the history of the nom de plume I bear. Yours, Samuel L. Clemens."

**1890**    Theatre audiences in Chicago's Grand Opera House are thrilled by the *première* of Reginald DeKoven's operetta *Robin Hood*. The greatest applause follows the singing of "O Promise Me" by Jessie Bartlett Davis. (One contemporary columnist has made the claim that "O Promise Me" is sung at wedding ceremonies at least once daily somewhere in the United States.)

**1899**    The heavyweight boxing championship is won at Coney Island, New York, by James J. Jeffries, after he knocks out Bob Fitzsimmons in the 11th round.

**1915**    President Woodrow Wilson sends a second note to Germany following the sinking of the *Lusitania* demanding a pledge from that government guaranteeing freedom of the seas. (WORLD WAR I)

**1943**    After several years of debate, Congress passes an act providing for "Pay-As-You-Go" income-tax deductions. Employers will now be authorized to withhold income-tax payments from weekly salary checks of their employees.

**1948**    President Harry S. Truman stirs up a controversy when he declares in a Spokane, Washington, speech that the present Eightieth Congress is "the worst we have ever had."

**1956**    Americans are both shocked and worried when the White House announces that President Eisenhower has undergone surgery for an intestinal ailment at Walter Reed Army Hospital in Washington.

**1965**    Michel Jazy, a Frenchman, establishes at Rennes, France, a world track record for the mile run with a time of 3 minutes and 53.6 seconds. Jazy's time is thus five-tenths of a second faster than the recognized world record scored in 1964 by Peter Snell of New Zealand.

## JUNE 10

**1776**    The Continental Congress appoints a committee to draft a Declaration of Independence. Members of the committee are Thomas Jefferson, John Adams, Benjamin Franklin, Roger Sherman, and Robert R. Livingston.

**1864**    The Confederate Congress enacts legislation authorizing the conscription of men into the army between the ages of 17 and 18 and 45 and 50.

**1892**    President Benjamin Harrison is renominated for President on the first ballot by the Republicans convening in Minneapolis. Whitelaw Reid of New York is chosen to be the President's running mate.

**1898**    U.S. Marines begin the invasion of Cuba in the Spanish-American War.

**1916**    Charles Evans Hughes of New York and Charles W. Fairbanks of Indiana are nominated for President and Vice President, respectively, by the Republican National Convention in Chicago. (Mr. Hughes resigned as Associate Justice of the Supreme Court to accept the nomination.)

**1931**    Mrs. Ernest Simpson, an American woman living in London, is presented at Court in Buckingham Palace and meets the Prince of Wales for the first time. (Six years later Mrs. Simpson was married to the former prince.)

**1939**    King George VI and Queen Elizabeth of Great Britain make a triumphal tour of New York City and pay a visit to the New York World's Fair.

**1940**    Choosing a moment when France is almost prostrate, Italian dictator Benito Mussolini declares war on France and Great Britain. When news of this declaration reaches President Franklin D. Roosevelt at Charlottesville, Virginia, the President says in a speech at the University of Virginia: "On this tenth day of June, 1940, the hand that held the dagger has struck it into the back of its neighbor." (WORLD WAR II)

**1942**    The German Gestapo burns to the ground the tiny village of Lidice, in Czechoslovakia, after shooting the 173 male inhabitants of the town, and deporting the women and children to concentration camps. Nazi officials say Lidice has been wiped off the map in retaliation for the assassination in Prague of Gauleiter Reinhard Heydrich known as "The Hangman of Czechoslovakia." (WORLD WAR II)

**1958**    The House of Representatives Subcommittee on Legislative Oversight releases records indicating that Sherman Adams, the powerful White House assistant to President Eisenhower, had interceded with government agencies for "preferred treatment" for Boston industrialist Bernard Goldfine. Further evidence proves that

Mr. Goldfine had also paid various hotel bills amounting to $1,642 for Mr. Adams. (*See June 11, June 18, September 22*)

**1964**    The U. S. Senate, by a vote of 71–29, invokes closure on further debate on the pending civil rights bill, following a 75-day filibuster. Never before has the Senate given up its rights to unlimited talk on a civil rights bill. (*See June 19, July 2*)

## JUNE 11

**1859**    Henry Tompkins Paige Comstock, known to local prospectors as "Old Pancake," lays claim to a silver deposit in Six Mile Canyon, Nevada. (Comstock sold his rights for $11,000, completely unaware of the fact that the Comstock Lode was to prove to be the greatest silver bonanza discovered by man, yielding some $340,000,-000 in riches to a few "silver millionaires.")

**1910**    The Printers' Association of America decides to campaign against the portrayal of women's skirts on billboards. (This was rather a surprising move, since women's skirts in 1910 were just a trifle above the ground.)

**1920**    Senator Warren G. Harding of Ohio is summoned to a "smoke-filled room" in the Hotel Blackstone, Chicago, and told that he will be the Republican Party's nominee for President. (Harding was a dark horse, chosen only because of the deadlock that had developed on the floor of the convention between Governor Frank O. Lowder of Illinois and General Leonard Wood of New York. The Vice Presidential nomination went to Governor Calvin Coolidge of Massachusetts.)

**1927**    Charles A. Lindbergh is welcomed home in the nation's capital by the President of the United States after the young aviator's historic flight across the Atlantic Ocean. President Coolidge presents the first Distinguished Flying Cross to Lindy.

**1936**    Russian authorities submit a draft of the proposed new Constitution of the Soviet Union to the people. Fifteen million copies of the document are being circulated, printed in one hundred languages.

**1936**    Cheering Republicans nominate Governor Alf Landon of Kansas for the Presidency on the first ballot, during the nominating convention's proceedings at Cleveland, Ohio. Frank Knox of Illinois is the Vice Presidential candidate.

**1937**    The Supreme Military Tribunal of the Soviet Union sentences Marshal Tukhachevsky and seven other ranking generals of the Red Army to death on charges of "military conspiracy with an unfriendly power" (Germany). (The former heroes of the Russian Revolution promptly "confessed" and were shot to death within 24 hours.)

**1939**    The King and Queen of Great Britain taste their first "hot dogs" at a picnic given by President and Mrs. Franklin D.

Roosevelt at their estate in Hyde Park, New York. The King is so pleased with "this delightful hot-dog sandwich" that he asks Mrs. Roosevelt for another one. (".... I had corralled two friends to cook hot dogs on an outdoor fireplace, and we had smoked turkey ... several kinds of ham, salads, baked beans and a strawberry short-cake ..."—Mrs. Franklin D. Roosevelt).

**1950**     Ben Hogan wins the U.S. open golf championship at the Merion Cricket Club, Ardmore, Pennsylvania, in a miraculous comeback after suffering near-fatal injuries in an automobile accident 16 months ago.

**1958**     Sherman Adams, President Eisenhower's chief assistant in the White House, admits that he was guilty of "imprudence" in his relationship with industrialist Bernard Goldfine. *(See June 18, September 22)*

**1963**     Governor George Wallace tries to prevent the admission of two Negro students to the University of Alabama, but steps aside when he is confronted by the federalized National Guard. As a result, the Negroes register as part of the undergraduate body.

**1963**     Following the above incident, President John F. Kennedy addresses the nation from the White House. In discussing the situation in Alabama and the general subject of race discrimination, he says: "... This nation was founded by men of many nations and backgrounds. It was founded on the principle that all men are created equal, and that the rights of every man are diminished when the rights of one man are threatened.... We are confronted primarily with a moral issue. It is as old as the Scriptures and is as clear as the American Constitution. The heart of the question is whether all Americans are to be afforded equal rights and equal opportunities; whether we are going to treat our fellow Americans as we want to be treated...."

# JUNE 12

**1630**     John Winthrop, first governor of The Massachusetts Bay Company, enters the harbor of Salem in the *Arbella*.

**1776**     George Mason of Virginia drafts the Virginia Bill of Rights.

**1839**     If legend is to be believed, this is the day that Abner Doubleday is supposed to have created a new ball game while studying at Cooperstown, New York. Doubleday calls it "baseball" and his rules of play call for a diamond-shaped field and 11 players. (Many baseball historians insist, however, that there is no proof of Doubleday's invention.)

**1912**     Lillian Russell, the queen of the musical-comedy stage in New York, marries her fourth husband, Alexander P. Moore of Pittsburgh. At the same time, the actress announces that she is retiring from the stage and will become "just another housewife in Pittsburgh, Pennsylvania."

**1923**     In an open-air exhibit in New York, the internationally known magician Harry Houdini thrills a large audience by struggling free from a straitjacket, head downward, 40 feet above the ground.

**1924**     President Calvin Coolidge receives the Presidential nomination from the Republican Convention meeting in Cleveland, Ohio. Charles G. Dawes of Illinois is chosen to run for Vice President. (Politically speaking, this was a cut-and-dried convention. But the Republican Convention of 1924 made history in another direction: it was the first political convention to be covered by a radio broadcasting network. Millions of Americans listened to the proceedings via a special network of 16 radio stations in 12 cities across the land.)

**1934**     President Franklin D. Roosevelt signs the Reciprocal Trade Agreements Act, authorizing him to negotiate trade treaties with other governments without the express permission of Congress.

**1957**     The *Mayflower II,* replica of the original vessel bearing that famous name, arrives from England in Provincetown Harbor, Massachusetts. The 92-foot *Mayflower* has crossed the Atlantic in 53 days, 14 days faster than the original ship that brought the Pilgrims to the New World. *(See September 6, November 11)*

**1961**     The U.S. Army officially rebukes Major General Edwin A. Walker for "taking injudicious actions and for making derogatory public statements about prominent Americans." (Walker had named many well-known Americans as either Communists or "pinks" and had, it was charged, disseminated the views of the John Birch Society among his troops while he was commander of the 24th Division.)

**1963**     Medgar W. Evers, a Mississippi Negro civil rights leader, is murdered in front of his home in Jackson. (Eleven days later, Byron de la Beckwith, a white segregationist of Greenwood, Mississippi, was charged as the murderer. But as late as 1965, he remained free after two hung juries were unable to seal his conviction.)

**1963**     Ten thousand people mass around the Rivoli Theatre in New York City, eager to see the celebrities who have turned out for the premiere of *Cleopatra.* Starring Elizabeth Taylor, Richard Burton, and Rex Harrison, the film has been described as "the longest, costliest, and most publicized motion picture ever made." (The film was produced at a cost of $40,000,000 and originally ran for 4 hours, 3 minutes.)

# JUNE 13

**1789** Mrs. Alexander Hamilton gives a dinner party for General George Washington and completely delights her guests by serving ice cream for dessert.

**1917** General John J. Pershing and his headquarters staff arrive in Paris. (WORLD WAR I)

**1927** Millions of New Yorkers turn out to welcome Charles A. Lindbergh after he flies to their city from Washington accompanied by an army air escort of 23 planes. At City Hall, Mayor James J. Walker, complimenting the young aviator on his recent transatlantic flight, tells him: "You can hear the heartbeats of the six million people that live in this City. . . . New York City is yours —I don't give it to you, you won it!"

**1935** Jim Braddock wins the world heavyweight boxing title from Max Baer in a 15-round decision at Long Island City, New York.

**1935** Senator Huey Long (D., La.) speaks 15 hours, 35 minutes, during his filibuster on the floor of the Senate against the extension of the National Recovery Administration.

**1942** *Yank,* the new U.S. Army newspaper of World War II, is published in New York for the first time.

**1942** President Franklin D. Roosevelt creates the Office of War Information (OWI) and names Elmer Davis, radio commentator and journalist, to serve as the agency's director. (WORLD WAR II)

**1944** Germany's highly publicized "secret weapon," the flying bomb, is dropped on English targets for the first time. Prime Minister Churchill describes the new weapon as "literally and essentially indiscriminate in its nature, purpose, and effect." (WORLD WAR II)

# JUNE 14

## Flag Day in the United States

**1775** The U.S. Army is founded when Congress authorizes the recruiting of 10 companies of riflemen to serve the colonies for one year.

**1777** The Stars and Stripes becomes our national flag as the Continental Congress, sitting in Philadelphia, resolves: "That the flag of the thirteen United States shall be of thirteen stripes of alternate red and white, with a union of thirteen stars of white in a blue field, representing a new constellation."

**1811** Birthday of Harriet Beecher Stowe, internationally famous author of *Uncle Tom's Cabin.*

**1827**   The Journeymen House Carpenters of Philadelphia shock their employers by demanding a 10-hour day. (They had to wait until 1860, however, before this "short" working day was put into effect.)

**1846**   A group of American settlers raise the Bear Flag at Sonoma, California, and proclaim the free and independent Republic of California. (Part of the flag included a piece of red flannel, torn from a woman's petticoat.)

**1898**   Thousands of American troops sail from Tampa, Florida, bound for Cuba and the Spanish-American War, singing "There'll Be a Hot Time in the Old Town Tonight."

**1922**   President Warren G. Harding becomes the first President of the United States to broadcast. At the dedication of the Francis Scott Key memorial at Fort McHenry, Maryland, the President's speech is picked up and broadcast over the facilities of Station WEAR, Baltimore.

**1940**   The Germans enter Paris: at 6:30 in the morning, battalions of German soldiers march through the streets of the city. German airplanes fly ceaselessly overhead and two of them land on the Place de la Concorde. By 11 A.M., the swastika flies from the Ministry of Marine, the Chamber of Deputies, and the Eiffel Tower. (WORLD WAR II)

**1949**   The legislature of the state of Missouri adopts the "Missouri Waltz" as the official state song.

**1951**   Senator Joseph R. McCarthy (R., Wis.), speaking on the floor of the Senate, attacks Secretary of Defense George C. Marshall, charging that the General had made "common cause" with Joseph Stalin during and after World War II.

**1953**   President Dwight D. Eisenhower, speaking at Dartmouth College, assails "book burners," saying: "Don't join the book burners. Don't think you are going to conceal thoughts by concealing evidence that they ever existed. . . . How will we defeat communism unless we know what it is and why it has such an appeal for men?"

**1963**   The Soviet Union sends its fifth astronaut into space. He is Lieutenant Colonel Valery F. Bykovsky. (*See June 16, June 19*)

## JUNE 15

**1215**   King John of England, under pressure from his barons, sets his seal on the Magna Carta at Runnymede. (This document has been hailed as "the cornerstone of American liberty.")

**1752**   Benjamin Franklin and his son demonstrate the relationship between electricity and lightning when he launches a kite at Philadelphia during a summer storm. A pointed wire is attached to the end of the kite and an iron key is suspended from the string held in Franklin's hand.

**1775**    George Washington is appointed commander-in-chief of the Continental Army.

**1836**    Arkansas, the 25th state, is admitted into the Union.

**1876**    Robert G. Ingersoll makes his impassioned nominating speech in behalf of James G. Blaine before the Republican Convention meeting in Cincinnati: "Like an armed warrior, like a plumed knight, James G. Blaine marched down the halls of the American Congress and threw his shining lance full and fair against the brazen foreheads of the defamers of his country and the maligners of his honor. For the Republicans to desert this gallant leader now is as though an army should desert their general upon the field of battle...." (Mr. Ingersoll's use of the term "plumed knight" made history, but he made little impression on the delegates. Mr. Blaine did *not* win the nomination.)

**1904**    A pleasure excursion comes to a tragic end when the steamboat *General Slocum*, carrying some 1,400 passengers up the East River off Manhattan Island, bursts into flame. Before the fire is put out, 1,021 persons lose their lives.

**1919**    Competing for the $50,000 prize offered by the *London Daily Mail* for the first airplane nonstop translantic flight, Captain John Alcock, an Englishman, and Lieutenant Arthur W. Browne, an American, successfully fly from Newfoundland to Ireland, in 16 hours, 12 minutes.

**1922**    The Permanent Court of International Justice opens its first session at The Hague in Holland.

**1928**    The Republican Convention at Kansas City comes to an end after nominating Herbert Hoover, the Secretary of Commerce, for President and Senator Charles Curtis of Kansas for Vice President.

**1944**    American troops invade the Marianas Islands, landing on Saipan about 1,500 miles south of Tokyo. (WORLD WAR II)

**1964**    The Supreme Court rules that the various states must apportion their legislatures on the basis of equal population. Writing for the majority, Chief Justice Earl Warren said: "Legislators represent people, not trees or acres. Legislators are elected by voters, not farms or cities or economic interests...."

## JUNE 16

**1858**    Delegates to the Illinois State Convention of the Republican Party at Springfield, Illinois, listen attentively to Abraham Lincoln as he tells them that the issue of slavery must be resolved: " 'A house divided against itself cannot stand.' I believe this government cannot endure permanently half slave and half free. I do not expect the Union to be dissolved—I do not expect the house to fall —but I do expect it will cease to be divided. It will become all one thing or all the other...."

**1876**    On the seventh ballot at the Republican Convention in Cincinnati, Rutherford B. Hayes of Ohio is nominated for President, and William A. Wheeler of New York receives the Vice Presidential nomination.

**1890**    An inaugural concert marks the opening of the new Madison Square Garden in New York City. The building has been designed by the architect Stanford White.

**1916**    The Democratic Convention at St. Louis votes to renominate President Woodrow Wilson and Vice President Thomas Marshall for a second term.

**1923**    The Prince of Wales is selected by the National Institute of Social Dancing as the best dancer in the world.

**1932**    President Herbert Hoover and Vice President Charles Curtis are both renominated for second terms by the delegates of the Republican Convention meeting at Chicago.

**1933**    The National Recovery Administration (NRA) comes into existence as President Franklin D. Roosevelt signs the National Industrial Recovery Act. After signing the statute, the President says: "History probably will record the National Industrial Recovery Act as the most important and far-reaching legislation ever enacted by the American Congress."

**1940**    Marshal Henri Pétain becomes premier of France and asks Adolf Hitler to submit his terms of peace. (WORLD WAR II)

**1941**    The United States orders Germany to close all 24 of her consulates in the United States by July 10, charging that they have carried on activities ". . . inimical to the welfare of this country."

**1955**    Widespread riots break out all over Buenos Aires as the Argentine Navy seeks unsuccessfully to oust President Juan Perón.

**1960**    A state visit to Japan by President Eisenhower, slated to begin on June 19, is cancelled following weeks of anti-American riots in that Asian nation. (The riots were inspired by left-wing opposition to ratification of the Japanese-U.S. security treaty.)

**1963**    The world's first woman space traveler, Lieutenant Valentina Tereshkova, is launched into orbit from a base in Russia. (*See June 19*)

**1964**    In a unique social event, Mrs. Endicott Peabody, wife of the Governor of Massachusetts, is the guest of honor at a tea-party given by the scrubwomen of the State House in Boston. During the party, a spokesman for the cleaning women presents the Governor's wife with a plaque which reads: "For her gracious and kind understanding of the problems of others. . . . She is our proven friend."

# JUNE 17

## Bunker Hill Day

**1775**    Thirty-five hundred British soldiers attack one thousand American patriots on Bunker Hill * across the Charles River from Boston. Because of the serious shortage of ammunition, the colonial troops are told: "Don't fire until you see the whites of their eyes!" Twice, the British are repulsed, but the outnumbered Americans finally retreat across Charlestown peninsula. (British casualties, 1,054; American losses, 441.)

**1825**    The cornerstone of the Bunker Hill Monument is set in place by the Marquis de Lafayette during memorial ceremonies on the 50th anniversary of the battle. Daniel Webster is the featured speaker.

**1858**    After listening to his "House Divided" speech the day before, enthusiastic Republicans gathered in Springfield, Illinois, for their state convention, nominate Abraham Lincoln to run for a seat in the U.S. Senate, against the incumbent Stephen A. Douglas, Democrat of Illinois.

**1928**    Amelia Earhart becomes the first woman to fly across the Atlantic Ocean when she takes off from Newfoundland as a passenger in a plane piloted by Wilmer Stultz. (A little more than 20 hours later they were in Wales.)

**1930**    President Herbert Hoover signs into law the Hawley-Smoot Tariff Bill, providing for the highest rates in American history and described by angry free-traders as "a declaration of economic war against the whole of the civilized world."

**1942**    The term "GI Joe" appears for the first time, a reference to the principal soldier depicted in Lieutenant Dave Breger's comic strip in *Yank,* the army weekly. (WORLD WAR II)

**1953**    Residents of the Russian-occupied zone of Berlin stage mass anti-Communist riots, protesting against the working and living conditions imposed by their Soviet overlords. As the rioting increases, more than 40,000 East Berliners mob government buildings, tear down Russian flags, overturn squad cars, and jeer Communist officials.

**1954**    The Senate Subcommittee investigation of the clash between the U.S. Army and Senator Joseph R. McCarthy (R., Wis.) comes to an end after 36 days, 187 hours of television coverage, and 2,000,000 words of testimony. (*See April 22.*)

**1954**    Rocky Marciano retains the world heavyweight boxing championship after winning a 15-round decision in New York over former champion Ezzard Charles.

* Actually, the battle was fought at Breed's Hill.

**1959**    Eamon de Valera, after serving as prime minister of the Irish Republic (Eire) for 21 years, is elected president of that nation.

**1963**    The Supreme Court rules by a vote of 8–1 that no state or locality may require recitation of the Lord's Prayer or verses from the Bible in the public schools. The Court's majority holds that required prayers in public schools is a violation of the First Amendment to the Constitution.

# JUNE 18

**1778**    Colonial forces enter Philadelphia as the British, under the command of Sir Henry Clinton, evacuate the city.

**1798**    "Millions for defense, but not one cent for tribute!" is the toast proposed by Robert Goodloe Harper * at a dinner honoring John Marshall in Philadelphia. (Mr. Harper's reference was to a French proposal that a money payment might bring to an end acts of piracy against our merchant ships on the high seas.)

**1812**    For the second time in American history, the United States is at war with Great Britain, as Congress declares war on that power.

**1815**    Napoleon is defeated at the Battle of Waterloo in Belgium by British forces commanded by the Duke of Wellington and Prussian troops led by Field Marshal von Blücher. (Waterloo was Napoleon's final struggle to dominate Europe. Four days later, he dictated to his brother Lucien his act of abdication.)

**1896**    The nominees of the Republican Convention at St. Louis are William McKinley of Ohio for President and Garret A. Hobart of New Jersey for Vice President.

**1898**    The career of George Bernard Shaw shows no promise to a critic on the staff of *The New York Times* who writes: "This voluble jack-of-all-trades, this so-called Socialist, this vociferous advocate of plain fare and industrial reform . . . who devotes all his time to word-juggling about the arts of music and the drama . . . this carnivorous vegetarian cannot be judged by his own standards when he puts his wares in the open market. . . ."

**1935**    Adolf Hitler signs a treaty with Great Britain promising not to expland the German Navy beyond 35 percent of the strength of the Royal Navy.

**1940**    Prime Minister Churchill addresses the House of Commons and warns its members that the Battle of Britain is about to start: "Let us therefore brace ourselves to our duties, and so bear ourselves that, if the British Empire and its Commonwealth last

---

* No worthwhile purpose is served here by entering into the age-old controversy of whether this toast originated with Harper or two years earlier in Paris when Charles C. Pinckney, our American minister to France, is alleged to have said the same thing. My own research points in the direction of Harper.

for a thousand years, men will say, 'This was their finest hour.' "
(WORLD WAR II)

**1945**   General Dwight D. Eisenhower returns in triumph to Washington and is greeted by a million persons. (WORLD WAR II)

**1953**   Egypt is proclaimed a republic by the "Army Council of the Revolution." Premier Mohammed Naguib becomes the country's first president.

**1958**   While a political controversy rages around Sherman Adams and his acceptance of an oriental rug and a vicuna coat from Boston industrialist Bernard Goldfine for alleged preferential treatment by federal regulatory agencies, President Eisenhower discusses his executive assistant at a press conference. The President admits that Adams may have acted "imprudently," but adds: "... Anyone who knows Sherman Adams has never had any doubt of his personal integrity and honesty; no one has believed that he could be bought ... I personally like Governor Adams. I admire his abilities. I respect him.... I need him...." (*See September 22*)

# JUNE 19

**1756**   At Calcutta, India, natives herd 146 British prisoners into a dungeon, the infamous "Black Hole of Calcutta," thus suffocating all but 23 who managed to survive.

**1846**   The first baseball game between organized teams takes place at the Elysian Field in Hoboken, New Jersey. After four innings, the New York Baseball Club trounces the Knickerbocker Club, 23–1.

**1856**   The Republicans adjourn their first national convention at Philadelphia, having nominated John C. Frémont of California for President and William L. Dayton of New Jersey for Vice President.

**1862**   Congress passes an act prohibiting slavery in the various territories of the United States.

**1867**   The Emperor Maximilian of Mexico, brother of Emperor Franz Josef of Austria-Hungary, is executed in Mexico by the rebel Benito Juarez after France withdraws her military support from Maximilian's regime.

**1903**   Birthday of Lou Gehrig, one of the greatest players in American baseball history.

**1910**   The first observance of Father's Day takes place in Spokane, Washington. The idea originated with a local woman, Mrs. John Bruce Dodd. ("Poor father has been left out in the cold. He doesn't get much recognition. But regardless of his breadwinning proclivities, it would be a good thing if he had a day that would mean recognition of him."—Jane Addams).

**1912**   The U.S. government adopts the 8-hour day for all of its employees.

**1934**    The U.S. Congress creates the Federal Communications Commission (FCC) to regulate interstate communications by wire and radio, including radio and television broadcasting.

**1936**    The German boxer Max Schmeling knocks out Joe Louis in the 12th round at Yankee Stadium, New York.

**1945**    Millions of New Yorkers and out-of-town visitors line the streets of the city to catch a glimpse of General Dwight D. Eisenhower during the day-long reception in his honor.

**1953**    At Sing Sing Prison, Ossining, New York, Ethel and Julius Rosenberg are executed for betraying secret information about atomic energy to agents of the Soviet Union. The Rosenbergs are the first spies ever executed in the United States on the orders of a civil court.

**1959**    The Senate rejects President Eisenhower's appointment of Lewis L. Strauss to become Secretary of Commerce. Strauss thus becomes the eighth man in U.S. history to be turned down by the Senate for a Cabinet post.

**1963**    The Russian man-and-woman team of astronauts land safely by parachute in Kazakhstan. (When it was all over, Colonel Bykovsky had orbited the earth 81 times and Lieutenant Valentina Tereshkova had circled the globe 48 times.)

**1963**    President John F. Kennedy sends a message to Congress asking that body to enact the most far-reaching civil rights legislation to date. In further asking the Congress not to adjourn until a civil rights bill is passed, the President appeals to every member "to set aside sectional and political ties. . . . to look at this issue from the viewpoint of the nation . . . to look into your hearts—not in search of charity, for the Negro neither wants nor needs condescension—but for . . . a sense of justice. . . ."

**1964**    After the longest legislative debate in the history of the U.S. Senate, * the 1964 Civil Rights bill is passed by a vote of 73–27 in that body. Senator Barry M. Goldwater of Arizona, one of the six Republicans to vote against the bill, says: ". . . I am unalterably opposed to discrimination of any sort, and I believe that though the problem is fundamentally one of the heart, some law can help—but not law . . . (with) provisions which fly in the face of the Constitution and which require for their effective execution the creation of a police state . . ." (". . . This bill goes further to invest the rights of man with the protection of law than any legislation in this century . . ."—President Lyndon B. Johnson).

**1964**    Senator Edward M. Kennedy (D., Mass.) is seriously injured as an airplane carrying him to Springfield in his home state crashes outside of Southampton, Massachusetts. (After months of hospitalization, the young Senator made good his vow to be on hand for the opening of the Eighty-ninth Congress in January, 1965.)

* 736 hours, 10 minutes

## JUNE 20

**1782**   Congress adopts the Great Seal of the United States. The seal, designed by William Barton, depicts an eagle clutching an olive branch in one talon and 13 arrows in the other. In its beak is a ribbon bearing the legend "E Pluribus Unum."

**1837**   Beginning of the Victorian Age: At 6 o'clock in the morning, the Archbishop of Canterbury and Lord Conyngham, the Lord Chamberlain of the Court, rouse Princess Victoria of Kent at Kensington Palace in London to tell her that her uncle, King William IV, is dead and that she is the Queen of England. (One of the first acts of the 18-year-old queen was to demand a room of her own. Up until this day, she had always shared a room with her mother, the Duchess of Kent.)

**1863**   West Virginia becomes the 25th state to be admitted to the Union.

**1874**   Congress becomes responsible for the administration of the affairs of the District of Columbia.

**1893**   Spectators cheer as the foreman of the jury in Superior Court, New Bedford, Massachusetts, announces that the jurors find Miss Lizzie Borden "Not Guilty" of murdering her father and step-mother. The bodies of the elder Bordens were found hacked to death in their home in Fall River, Massachusetts, on August 4, 1892.*

**1898**   The U.S. Navy seizes Guam, the largest of the Marianas Islands, in the Spanish-American War. (On August 1, 1950, President Harry S. Truman signed a bill, granting U.S. citizenship to the people of Guam.)

**1908**   At the Republican National Convention meeting in Chicago, William Howard Taft of Ohio is nominated for President and James S. Sherman of New York for Vice President.

**1910**   A new name comes to the attention of Broadway critics as Fanny Brice makes her debut in the *Ziegfeld Follies of 1910*.

**1931**   President Herbert Hoover summons reporters to the White House and tells them that he will propose a one-year international moratorium on all payments on intergovernmental debts, including principal and interest.

**1949**   President Truman signs a bill authorizing a reorganization of the federal government as proposed by the Hoover Commission.

---

\* Apparently most of the nation did not share the sympathies of the cheering spectators in the courtroom, for one of the most familiar doggerels of the day ran something like this:

> "Lizzie Borden took an ax
> And give her mother forty whacks.
> When she saw what she had done
> She gave her father forty-one."

194

**1959**  American prizefighter Floyd Patterson is the world's heavyweight champion once more as he knocks out Ingemar Johansson of Sweden in the fifth round at their match in New York's Polo Grounds. *(See June 26)*

**1963**  The United States and the Soviet Union sign an agreement in Geneva to establish a so-called "hot line" emergency communication system, linking Washington and Moscow. (The idea was and is to reduce the risk of accidental war by an exchange of views between the chiefs of state of the two nations.)

## JUNE 21

**1788**  The U.S. Constitution goes into effect as the legislature of New Hampshire ratifies it, the ninth state to do so. (The last Article of the Constitution reads: "The Ratification of the Conventions of nine States shall be sufficient for the Establishment of this Constitution between the States so ratifying the Same.")

**1852**  The Whig National Convention ends in Baltimore having nominated Winfield Scott of New Jersey for President on the 53rd ballot. William A. Graham of North Carolina is the candidate for Vice President.

**1877**  Ten "Molly Maguires" are captured and sent to the gallows in Pennsylvania. (The Molly Maguires were members of a secret Irish terrorist society active in the anthracite coal regions of Pennsylvania. Their name was derived from Ireland where the agitators frequently dressed as women before starting out on their marauding expeditions.)

**1892**  Democrats at Chicago organize their national convention before nominating former President Grover Cleveland for the Presidency once more. His running mate will be Adlai E. Stevenson of Illinois.

**1900**  President William McKinley is renominated for a second term by the Republican Convention at Philadelphia. Theodore Roosevelt of New York is chosen to run for Vice President. (Mark Hanna, the powerful Republican boss, was bitterly opposed to Roosevelt and pleaded with party kingmakers to select another Vice Presidential nominee. Said Hanna: "Don't any of you realize that there is only one life between this madman and the White House?" Much to Hanna's chagrin, his fears materialized: 15 months later, Theodore Roosevelt was the occupant of the White House. *See September 14).*

**1932**  Sixty-two thousand fans watch Jack Sharkey win the world heavyweight boxing title from Max Schmeling in a 15-round bout at the Long Island City Bowl in New York.

**1941**  In response to a reporter's question asking him if he will support the Soviet Union in the case of a German attack on that country, Prime Minister Winston Churchill answers bluntly:

"I have only one purpose, the destruction of Hitler, and my life is much simplified thereby. If Hitler invaded Hell, I would make at least a favorable reference to the Devil in the House of Commons." (WORLD WAR II)

**1942**   Tobruk, the Libyan stronghold held by the British since January 22, 1941, surrenders to German forces led by Field Marshal Erwin Rommel. Thirty thousand British soldiers are taken prisoner. (WORLD WAR II)

**1945**   The struggle for Okinawa Island in the southwest Pacific comes to an end at 10 o'clock in the evening as the Japanese forces there surrender to the American command. (Control of Okinawa was costly to both the United States and Japan. American casualties were more than 12,000 killed, 33,769 wounded. Japan lost 90,401 in dead alone.) (WORLD WAR II)

**1948**   Dr. Peter Goldmark of the Columbia Broadcasting System demonstrates his "long-playing" record, soon to revolutionize the entire recording industry.

**1954**   The American Cancer Society reports that "heavy" cigarette smokers, aged 50 to 70, have a death rate up to 75 percent higher than nonsmokers.

**1954**   John Landy, of Melbourne, Australia, establishes a new world's record when he runs a mile in 3 minutes, 58 seconds in Turku, Finland.

**1960**   Birth of the Chinese-Russian ideological split: At the Communist Party Congress in Rumania, Premier Khrushchev angers the Chinese by saying that "... under present conditions, war [with capitalistic nations] is not inevitable...." The delegate of Communist China then rises and tells the Congress that war *is* inevitable as long as Western "imperialism" exists.

**1963**   Cardinal Giovanni Battista Montini, Archbishop of Milan, is elected Pope by the College of Cardinals. He will assume the name of Paul VI.

**1964**   Jim Bunning of the Philadelphia Phillies pitches a perfect game, the first one in the National League in 84 years, defeating the New York Mets, 6–0.

## JUNE 22

**1868**   Arkansas is readmitted into the Union.

**1870**   The U.S. Department of Justice is created by an act of Congress. (Before this time, the attorney general was the government's prosecution agent, but he did not head an executive department. )

**1874**   Dr. Andrew Taylor Sill, of Macon, Missouri, founds the science of osteopathy.

**1906**   King Haakon and Queen Maud are crowned king and queen of Norway in Oslo.

**1911**   Representatives of almost every royal dynasty in the world congregate in Westminster Abbey to witness the coronation of George V, King of Great Britain and Ireland, and his consort, Queen Mary.

**1912**   After a bitter floor fight between Republican Party conservatives and progressives, delegates to the nominating convention meeting at the Coliseum in Chicago renominate President William Howard Taft and Vice President James S. Sherman. The "Bull Moose" wing of the party bolts the convention.

**1937**   Joe Louis becomes the heavyweight boxing champion of the world after knocking out Jim Braddock in the eighth round at Comiskey Park in Chicago. (He retained the title until he retired in 1949.)

**1938**   Max Schmeling, the boxing pride and joy of Nazi Germany, is knocked out by world champion Joe Louis at Yankee Stadium, New York. (Before he sailed from Germany, Adolf Hitler entertained Schmeling at lunch and Propaganda Minister Joseph Goebbels issued a statement saying that the fight in New York would prove Aryan supremacy forever. As it turned out, however, "Aryan supremacy" did not go beyond the first round.)

**1940**   The fall of France: Adolf Hitler and his staff summon the French armistice envoys to the same railway car in the forest of Compiègne where Marshal Foch had presented the armistice terms to the defeated Germans in 1918. The Germans present their demands to the Frenchmen and the armistice is signed, thus making it possible shortly for Adolf Hitler to assume a position on French soil overlooking the English Channel. (WORLD WAR II)

**1941**   Germany invades Russia and later issues a declaration of war against that nation. Still later, a proclamation from Adolf Hitler is read over Radio Berlin charging the Soviet Union with having "miserably betrayed the stipulations of our friendly agreement" of August, 1939. In Moscow, Foreign Secretary V. M. Molotov accuses the Nazis of "perfidy unparalleled in the history of civilized nations." (WORLD WAR II)

**1942**   The U.S. Post Office sends its first filmed "V Mail" to American soldiers stationed in England. (WORLD WAR II)

**1943**   The nation's worst race riot since 1918 is checked as federal troops patrol the streets of Detroit, Michigan, after arresting at least 1,300 persons. Thirty-four persons are dead and hundreds wounded as a result of the fighting, which broke out June 20 between white and Negro mobs.

**1962**   The Soviet Union casts its 100th veto in the United Nations Security Council as it supports India against Pakistan on the question of a proposed plebiscite for Kashmir.

**1964**   The U.S. Supreme Court, by a vote of 5 to 4, rules that Henry Miller's book, *Tropic of Cancer,* may not constitutionally be banned. The Court thus has reversed an earlier Florida Supreme Court decision outlawing the controversial book, written in 1934, on the grounds of obscenity.

## JUNE 23

**1683** William Penn signs a treaty of peace and friendship with the Leni-Lenape Indians at Shackamaxon on the Delaware River.

**1836** As the result of a surplus in the U.S. Treasury, 26 states divide up $28,101,644.91.

**1845** The Congress of Texas agrees to its annexation by the United States.

**1860** Regular Democrats who split with Southern delegates at the national convention in April convene at Baltimore and nominate Stephen A. Douglas of Illinois for President and Herschel V. Johnson of Georgia for Vice President.

**1868** Christopher Latham Sholes, Wisconsin journalist and state senator, receives a patent for his "Type-Writer," his machine having capital letters only.

**1876** Irvin S. Cobb, American humorist, is born in Paducah, Kentucky.

**1894** Birthday of the Duke of Windsor, King Edward VIII of Great Britain and Ireland before his abdication.

**1904** President Theodore Roosevelt and Vice President Charles W. Fairbanks are nominated by acclamation for another term by Republican delegates to the national convention meeting in Chicago.

**1924** Lieutenant R. L. Maugham of the U.S. Army makes his "dawn to dusk" flight from New York City to San Francisco, flying 2,700 miles in 18 hours, 52 minutes.

**1931** Wiley Post and Harold Gatty take off for a round-the-world flight in their plane, the *Winnie Mae*. (Their trip lasted 8 days, 15 hours, 51 minutes.)

**1938** Congress creates the Civil Aeronautics Authority to regulate air traffic.

**1947** By a vote of 268–25, the House overrides the veto of President Harry Truman and thus enacts the Labor-Management Act of 1947, familiarly known to the nation as the Taft-Hartley Act.

**1959** After serving 9 years of his 14-year sentence for turning over atomic bomb secrets to Russia, Dr. Klaus Fuchs is released from prison in England. British authorities then permit him to fly to East Germany.

**1964** The burned empty station wagon of three civil rights workers, missing since June 21, is found near Philadelphia, Mississippi. The three integrationists—Michael Schwerner, 24, and Andrew Goodman, 20, of New York City, and James Chaney, 21, of Meridian, Mississippi—were part of a group recently arrived in the state to aid in a voter-registration drive among Negroes. (President Johnson directed Allen W. Dulles, former Director of the Central Intelligence Agency, to make an on-the-spot investigation for him. *See August 4.*

## JUNE 24

**1647**    Mistress Margaret Brent, a niece of Lord Baltimore, appears before the Maryland Assembly to demand both voice and vote for herself in that body. (Mistress Brent, probably the first "suffragette" in American history, completely shocked the all-male Assembly.)

**1665**    Thomas Willett, the first mayor of the City of New York, is installed in office.

**1880**    The Democratic nominees of the national convention meeting at Cincinnati are General Winfield S. Hancock of Pennsylvania for President and William H. English of Indiana for Vice President.

**1924**    The first issue of the *New York Daily Mirror* predicts that the American saloon is gone forever. In an editorial entitled "Gone, Thank God!" the *Mirror* says: "The WIDE OPEN saloon, the 'What'll you have?' the 'Here's How!' and the echoing conclusion, 'Here's how to ruin a young life,' are gone forever."

**1940**    Traveling under the code name of "Fish," more than one-half billion dollars of England's financial treasure is shipped to Canada for safe-keeping in face of an imminent German invasion of the British Isles. The treasure is stowed aboard H.M.S. *Emerald*, sailing out of Greenock, Scotland, and consists of 2,229 bullion boxes, each containing four bars of gold and 488 boxes of securities. (On July 8, a convoy carrying one and three-quarter billion dollars of treasure sailed from Britain for Canada. In all, seven billion dollars of assets were shipped to Canada, not one penny of which was lost in transit.) (WORLD WAR II)

**1942**    The Royal Family of the Netherlands, in exile since the Nazi occupation of their homeland, arrives in the United States to establish temporary residence here. (WORLD WAR II)

**1947**    The first "flying saucers" are reported by Kenneth Arnold of Boise, Idaho, who claims he observed nine "shining saucer-like objects" flying in formation over Mount Rainier, Washington, earlier in the day. (So many reports of "flying saucers" followed in the next eight years that the U.S. Air Force set up a top-secret "Project Saucer" to investigate them. On October 25, 1955, the Air Force concluded that flying saucers were illusions or explainable as "conventional phenomena.")

**1948**    The Soviet Union blockades the western zones of Berlin, banning all rail and road traffic between those sectors of the city and western Germany.

**1948**    For the second time in his political career, Governor Thomas E. Dewey of New York is chosen by the Republicans to run for the office of President of the United States. His running mate, nominated by the convention at Philadelphia, is Governor Earl Warren of California.

**1964**    The U.S. Federal Trade Commission announces that it will start requiring cigarette manufacturers to print on their packages a warning that cigarette smoking can be injurious to health. (So strong was the opposition of tobacco-raising states to this ruling, however, that by mid-1965 the warning was still missing from cigarette packets.)

## JUNE 25

**1630**    Governor John Winthrop introduces the table fork to America, bringing it to Massachusetts in a leather case with a bodkin and a knife.

**1868**    The former Confederate states of North and South Carolina, Georgia, Florida, Alabama, and Louisiana are readmitted into the Union.

**1876**    "Custer's Last Stand": General George Armstrong Custer and his force of 208 men are killed in the Battle of Little Big Horn River, Montana, by Sioux Indians led by their chieftain, Sitting Bull. (The Indians were enraged over the federal government's attempts to move them to a reservation.)

**1886**    A 19-year-old cellist in the orchestra of the Rio de Janeiro Opera House picks up the baton and conducts the orchestra in a performance of *Aïda* when the regular conductor fails to make an appearance. The cellist's name: Arturo Toscanini. (His success in Rio de Janeiro that night prompted him to abandon his cello for a conductor's career.)

**1888**    Republican delegates to the nominating convention meeting in Chicago select Benjamin Harrison of Indiana as their candidate for President and Levi P. Morton of New York for Vice President.

**1906**    Stanford White, America's most famous architect, is killed by Harry K. Thaw on the roof of Madison Square Garden during the opening performance of *Mamzelle Champagne,* a new musical revue. (Thus began one of the most sensational murder cases in American history, brought on by Thaw's charge that the architect had "ruined" the former's wife, Evelyn Nesbit.)

**1918**    U.S. Marines finally drive the Germans out of Belleau Wood, France, after a bitter two weeks' battle. (WORLD WAR I)

**1938**    President Franklin D. Roosevelt signs the Wage and Hours Act, providing a minimum hourly wage of 25 cents, rising to 40 cents at the end of 6 years. The work week is limited to 44 hours for the next year, dropping to 40 hours 3 years after the bill is enacted.

**1941** Executive Order Number 8802 is issued by President Franklin D. Roosevelt, creating a Fair Employment Practices Committee to prohibit discrimination in defense industries because of race, color, creed, or national origin.

**1942** The U.S. War Department announces the formal establishment of a European theater of operations for American forces under the command of Major General Dwight D. Eisenhower. (WORLD WAR II)

**1950** Five years after World War II ends, war breaks out once more in Asia, as Communist soldiers of North Korea invade the Republic of Korea.

**1951** The Columbia Broadcasting System presents the first commercial color broadcast in television history. Emanating from New York City, the hour-long program features such television personalities as Arthur Godfrey, Faye Emerson, Sam Levenson, and Ed Sullivan.

**1962** The Supreme Court rules, by a vote of 6–1, that a prayer used in the public schools of New York State and described as "nondenominational" is nonetheless unconstitutional.

## JUNE 26

**1284** The Pied Piper of Hamelin, Germany, lures 130 children of the town into oblivion. (The piper thus received his revenge against the town fathers who refused to pay him a fee of 1,000 guilders after he charmed the rats and mice out of the city into the Weser River.)

**1844** President John Tyler, a widower, marries Miss Julia Gardiner secretly in New York City. (Americans knew nothing about the President's marriage until the next day. He was so intent on keeping it a secret that, on arriving in New York on June 25, he persuaded the owner of Howard's Hotel to lock up his servants for the night to prevent them from leaking the news of his presence in the city.)

**1870** The first boardwalk in the world is completed at the resort town of Atlantic City, New Jersey.

**1900** Dr. Walter Reed and three other U.S. Army doctors begin their campaign to wipe out the dread disease, yellow fever.

**1902** The coronation of King Edward VII is postponed when the King undergoes surgery after an attack of acute appendicitis.

**1917** The first troops of the American Expeditionary Force reach France. (WORLD WAR I)

**1941** President Risto Ryti of Finland announces that his country is at war with the Soviet Union for the second time in 2 years. (WORLD WAR II)

**1944**    Cherbourg, France's third greatest port, is liberated from Nazi control by the Allies. (One of the moving incidents of this liberation took place when Major General Lawton Collins, commander of the American troops, presented Cherbourg with a Tricolor made from the red, white, and blue parachutes in which the vanguard of the invasion attacked from the skies beginning on June 6.) (WORLD WAR II)

**1945**    Delegates of 50 nations conclude their meeting in San Francisco and sign a charter establishing the United Nations Conference on International Organization. The charter, effective October 24, pledges "to save succeeding generations from the scourge of war, which twice in our lifetime has brought untold sorrow to mankind."

**1948**    As an answer to the Russian blockade of West Berlin, the U.S. occupation forces in that city announce the organization of a "Berlin Airlift." Daily cargo flights to West Berlin will now be stepped up from 50 to at least 100 daily.

**1959**    President Eisenhower meets Queen Elizabeth II of Great Britain at St. Lambert, Quebec, where they jointly dedicate the St. Lawrence Seaway.

**1959**    Ingemar Johansson of Sweden is the new world's heavyweight boxing champion after he knocks out Floyd Patterson in the third round in their New York match. (*See June 20*)

**1959**    A report by the U.S. Office of Civil and Defense Mobilization estimates that a nuclear attack on the United States, using 263 hydrogen bombs, would kill 19,651,000 Americans the first day, injure another 22,179,000 fatally, and result in less serious injuries for still another 17,191,000 persons.

**1962**    Fifty-two prominent Americans form a committee to raise $62,000,000 to ransom the 1,178 Cuban rebels held by Fidel Castro following the Bay of Pigs invasion.

**1963**    President John F. Kennedy receives a tumultuous welcome in West Berlin. He tells cheering Berliners that the Berlin Wall is an "offense against humanity" and adds: "... Freedom is indivisible and when one man is enslaved, who are free? .... All free men, wherever they may live, are citizens of Berlin. And therefore as a free man, I take pride in the words: 'Ich bin ein Berliner.' ...."

## JUNE 27

**1787**    Edward Gibbon, English historian, lays down his pen, having completed the last page of his monumental work, *The Decline and Fall of the Roman Empire.*

**1844**    Joseph and Hyrum Smith, Mormons, are murdered by a mob in Carthage, Illinois. Brigham Young becomes head of the Mormon Church.

**1847**  People in New York and Boston will be able to communicate with each other by telegraph from now on, following the completion of connecting wires between the two cities.

**1880**  Birthday of Helen Keller, blind and deaf American author and lecturer, born on this day in Tuscumbia, Alabama. ("Literature is my Utopia. Here I am not disfranchised. No barrier of the senses shuts me out from the sweet, gracious discourse of my book-friends. They talk to me without embarrassment or awkwardness."—*The Story of My Life,* Helen Keller).

**1893**  A major economic depression begins as prices on the New York Stock Exchange collapse. (Before the year was over, some 74 railroads declared bankruptcy.)

**1936**  President Franklin D. Roosevelt and Vice President John Nance Garner are renominated for second terms of office by the delegates of the Democratic Convention at Philadelphia. In making his acceptance speech in person once more, the President says: "The economic royalists complain that we seek to overthrow the institutions of America. What they really complain of is that we seek to take away their power. Our allegiance to American institutions requires the overthrow of this kind of power."

**1941**  The biggest airplane bomber the world has ever seen thus far, the U.S. Army's four-engined B-19, passes its first test flight successfully in a 56-minute cruise in California.

**1942**  J. Edgar Hoover, director of the Federal Bureau of Investigation, announces in New York that eight highly trained saboteurs, all of them former German-American Bundists, landed from German submarines in two groups of four each on the Long Island, New York, and Florida coasts on June 13 and 17. The eight men who landed at Amagansett Beach, New York, and Ponte Vedra Beach, Florida, have all been taken into custody, carrying with them $169,748.76 for expenses and bribes and a set of forged draft registration and social security identification cards. (On August 8, after a special military commission had found the eight men guilty, six of the saboteurs were electrocuted and two given prison sentences of life and 30 years respectively.) (WORLD WAR II)

**1947**  Automobile workers receive the first pension provision in automotive history as the Ford Motor Company in Detroit agrees to contribute $200,000,000 to start and $15,000,000 a year thereafter to the plan.

**1950**  President Harry S. Truman orders the U.S. air and naval forces under General Douglas MacArthur to help repel the North Korean invaders. At the same time, the United Nations Security Council invokes military sanctions against North Korea.

**1963**  President Kennedy is in the midst of another triumphal tour, this time in Ireland where he is the guest of President Eamon de Valera. After a rousing welcome in Dublin, he goes to visit cousins in Dunganstown. (At New Ross, the President joined some serenading school children in singing, "Kelly, The Boy from Killane.")

## JUNE 28

**1778**   Mary Ludwig Hays, better known as Molly Pitcher, takes her mortally wounded husband's place at a cannon at the Battle of Monmouth, New Jersey. As a recognition of her heroism, the valiant woman is commissioned a sergeant by General George Washington.

**1881**   American "fans" of Lily Langtry, the famous English actress, are disturbed by a London dispatch reporting her personal misfortunes: "The property of Mrs. Langtry has been sold at auction. She had an income of 1,200 pounds a year, but demands of the social season were so great that she and her husband have been overwhelmed in debt."

**1894**   Congress makes Labor Day a holiday for federal employees, designating the first Monday in September to be so observed.

**1902**   The uncompleted Panama Canal is bought from France by the United States.

**1914**   The spark that fires World War I is ignited at Sarajevo, Bosnia, when a young Serbian fanatic, Gavrilo Princip, assassinates the heir to the throne of Austria-Hungary, the Archduke Francis Ferdinand, and his wife.

**1919**   Five years after the beginning of World War I at Sarajevo, the end of the war is symbolized by the signing of the Treaty of Versailles at Versailles, France. (While the United States signed the document, the Senate failed to muster the two-thirds majority needed for ratification.)

**1927**   Lieutenants Lester J. Maitland and Albert F. Hegenberger of the U.S. Army Air Corps make the first successful air flight from San Francisco to Hawaii.

**1931**   In reply to suggestions that he become a Presidential candidate, Will Rogers in his daily column writes: "I not only 'don't choose to run' but I don't want to leave a loophole in case I am drafted, so I won't 'choose.' I will say 'won't run' no matter how bad the country will need a comedian by that time."

**1938**   To help Pennsylvania farmers dispose of an egg surplus, slot machines dispensing hard-boiled eggs for a nickel apiece have been installed in cafés and taverns throughout the state.

**1939**   Regular transatlantic air service gets under way as the *Dixie Clipper*, flying for the Pan-American Airways, leaves Port Washington, New York, bound for Lisbon, Portugal.

**1940**   Wendell L. Willkie of Indiana and Senator Charles L. McNary of Oregon are chosen by the delegates to the Republican

Convention at Philadelphia to head the party's ticket in the forthcoming November Presidential elections.

**1944** Two state governors, Thomas E. Dewey of New York and John W. Bricker of Ohio, are nominated by the Republican Convention at Chicago for President and Vice President respectively.

**1945** General Douglas MacArthur announces the reconquest of Luzon in the Philippines. (WORLD WAR II)

**1962** Eight thousand supporters of the Christian Anti-Communism Crusade stage a rally in New York's Madison Square Garden. The main speaker is Dr. Fred C. Schwarz, an Australian physician, who tells the crowd that the Communists will take over the United States in less than twenty years unless their timetable is upset.

**1962** A New York State Supreme Court jury awards $3,500,000 to John Henry Faulk, a radio and television performer, the largest libel verdict in history. (The decision came after 11 weeks of testimony, during a trial in which Faulk charged that he had been dismissed by the Columbia Broadcasting System and subsequently blacklisted by the broadcasting industry because of charges that linked him to a Communist conspiracy. The defendants were an organization known as Aware, Incorporated, Vincent W. Hartnett, its founder, and another anti-Communist crusader, Laurence A. Johnson.)

## JUNE 29

**1852** Henry Clay, former U.S. Senator, Speaker of the House, and Secretary of State, dies in Washington. ("If anyone desires to know the . . . paramount objective of my public life, the preservation of the Union will furnish the . . . key.")

**1861** Birthday of William James Mayo, distinguished American surgeon and cofounder with his brother Charles of the famous Mayo Clinic in Rochester, Minnesota.

**1876** The Democratic National Convention in St. Louis adjourns after having nominated Samuel J. Tilden of New York for President and Thomas A. Hendricks of Indiana for Vice President.

**1928** Unlike the stormy proceedings that characterized their convention 4 years ago, the Democrats meeting in Houston, Texas, conclude their business peacefully after nominating on the first ballot Governor Alfred E. Smith of New York for President. Senator Joseph T. Robinson of Arkansas is selected to run for Vice President.

**1946** In an attempt to stamp out alleged terrorism, the British arrest 2,718 Jews in Palestine.

**1954** Controversy follows the decision of the Atomic Energy Commission not to grant Dr. J. Robert Oppenheimer access to restricted information. (Dr. Oppenheimer, the physicist who directed the development of the atom bomb, was suspended by the AEC in December, 1953, as an alleged security risk.)

**1954**    One of the most bitter libel trials ends as the writer and journalist Quentin Reynolds is awarded damages of $175,001 in his suit against the columnist Westbrook Pegler.

## JUNE 30

**1859**    Five thousand persons watch Émile Blondin, a professional French acrobat, cross Niagara Falls on a tightrope. The French daredevil, dressed in pink tights and a spangled tunic of yellow silk, manages to accomplish his feat in 5 minutes' time.

**1870**    Ada H. Kepley of Effingham, Illinois, is graduated from the Union College of Law in Chicago, the first woman to be graduated from an accredited law school.

**1899**    Charles M. (Mile-a-Minute) Murphy rides his bicycle in a mile race in 57⅘ seconds, paced by a special railway car, from Farmingdale, to Maywood, Long Island. (The railway car, built by the Long Island Rail Road, created a powerful suction for Murphy to pedal in.)

**1918**    Eugene V. Debs, militant Socialist leader and pacifist, is arrested in Cleveland, charged with willful interference with army and navy recruiting.

**1921**    President Warren G. Harding names William Howard Taft chief justice of the U.S. Supreme Court, the first man in the nation to serve both as President of the United States and as chief justice.

**1924**    The Teapot Dome scandals result in the indictment of Secretary of the Interior Albert B. Fall and oilmen Harry F. Sinclair and Edward L. Doheny; all three men being charged with bribery and conspiracy to defraud the government in the leasing of the Teapot Dome, Wyoming, and Elk Hills, California, naval oil reserve areas. (The Secretary of the Interior had persuaded the Secretary of the Navy, Edwin Denby, to transfer the naval oil reserves to Interior Department jurisdiction, and, once having obtained that control, negotiated a series of leases with private oil interests headed by Sinclair and Doheny. The latter were acquitted, but Fall was fined $100,000 and handed a jail sentence of one year, the first Cabinet officer to be convicted of a penal offense.)

**1934**    Adolf Hitler begins his great "blood bath" throughout Germany, thus "purging" that nation of hundreds of political and military leaders, many of them former close associates of the Reichsfuehrer.

**1936**    *Gone with the Wind,* a lengthy novel of the War between the States, is published in New York. (Written by Margaret Mitchell, of Atlanta, Georgia, the novel became an immediate best seller, more than a half-million copies being sold within 3 months' time. In fact, a record was achieved during the following October when 50,000 copies were sold in one day. By 1955, six million copies of the book had been sold, including translations into almost every know language throughout the world. A film version of the novel was produced in 1939 and the book subsequently was printed in Braille and recorded for use among the blind.)

**1936**     Emperor Haile Selassie of Ethiopia pleads before the League of Nations in Geneva for help against the Italian invaders.

**1950**     President Harry S. Truman announces he has ordered U.S. troops stationed in Japan to Korea to assist in the war against the North Korean invaders.

**1960**     The former Belgian colony of the Congo in Africa becomes an independent republic following a proclamation issued by King Baudouin of Belgium.

**1960**     Liberal Democrats, worried by various moves to run Senator Lyndon B. Johnson (D., Texas) for the Presidency, warn delegates to the forthcoming Democratic National Convention not to nominate him for the top spot on the party's ticket. A statement issued over the name of the chairman of Americans for Democratic Action says: "(A Johnson nomination) would make a mockery of the Democratic Party's professions of liberalism..." (*See July 5*)

# JULY

## JULY 1

**Dominion Day in Canada**   Observing the establishment of the Canadian confederation under the British North America Act in 1867.

## The United States government begins its fiscal year today

**1859**   The first intercollegiate baseball game is played between Amherst and Williams at Pittsfield, Massachusetts, Amherst winning by a score of 66 to 32.

**1867**   "The Beautiful Blue Danube" waltz, by the Viennese composer Johann Strauss (the Younger), is played in America for the first time at a concert of Theodore Thomas' Orchestra in New York.

**1874**   Americans are shocked to learn of the kidnapping of 4-year-old Charlie Ross from his home in Germantown, Pennsylvania. (The disappearance of the child has never been solved satisfactorily. In 1939, an Arizona carpenter won the recognition of the Superior Court of Phoenix as the long-lost man, but members of the Ross family refused to recognize him as such.)

**1898**   Lieutenant Colonel Theodore Roosevelt and the First Voluntary Cavalry, popularly known as the "Rough Riders," stage a victorious assault on San Juan Hill in Cuba in the Spanish-American War.

**1922**   Four hundred thousand railroaders throughout the United States go out on strike in protest against a 12.5 percent wage cut ordered by the Railroad Labor Board. (The strike lasted until September 15, when it collapsed after Federal Judge James Wilkerson of Chicago issued an injunction banning all strike activities against the railroads.)

**1931**   Wiley Post and Harold Gatty, flying in the monoplane *Winnie Mae,* complete their round-the-world air flight, having traveled 15,474 miles in 8 days, 15 hours, 51 minutes.

**1932**  Franklin Delano Roosevelt, Governor of New York, is nominated for the Presidency by the Democrats, meeting at convention in the Chicago Stadium. John Nance Garner of Texas is named the party's Vice Presidential nominee.

**1936**  Pastor Martin Niemoeller of Berlin is arrested by the Nazis in Germany, and, along with other anti-Hitler Protestant clergymen, is thrown into prison.

**1943**  The "Pay-as-you-go" Income Tax Bill goes into effect, as individual employers and business firms start to withhold 20 percent of their employees' salaries.

**1948**  The nickel subway fare disappears in New York as all of the underground lines begin to collect 10 cents for each ride.

**1957**  The International Geophysical Year for study of the earth's phenomena begins.

**1962**  Doctors in the Canadian province of Saskatchewan go out on strike in protest against the government's compulsory medical care plan. (The strike was settled July 23 after the government promised to amend the so-called Medical Care Insurance Act.)

**1964**  Estimates released by the U.S. Census Bureau show the nation's population to be approximately 191,334,000. (Four years earlier, on this date, it was 179,323,175.)

**1965**  The national debt of the United States is expected to reach $316,900,000,000 today. This means that every American man, woman, and child's share amounts to $1,624.


# JULY 2

**1776**  The Continental Congress meeting in Philadelphia passes a resolution that "these United Colonies are, and of right, ought to be, Free and Independent States" and that "they are absolved from all allegiance to the British Crown." (This resolution, therefore, was the official Declaration of Independence; the signing of it on July 4 was a proclamation to the world that the colonies were free and independent.)

**1867**  New Yorkers are excited over the opening of the Elevated Railroad, the first "El" in the city's history.

**1881**  President James A. Garfield is shot in the back while passing through Washington's Baltimore & Ohio Railroad Station. (The shot was fired by Charles J. Guiteau, an unsuccessful office-seeker. *See September 19.*)

**1912**  On the forty-sixth ballot, Democrats meeting in Baltimore nominate Woodrow Wilson of New Jersey for President and Thomas R. Marshall of Indiana for Vice President.

**1921**  Heavyweight boxing champion Jack Dempsey knocks out Georges Carpentier in the fourth round at Boyle's Thirty Acres in Jersey City. (Because the box-office proceeds of the bout totaled

$1,789,238, boxing historians refer to this fight as "The Million Dollar Gate." )

**1926**    The U.S. Army Air Corps is created.

**1932**    Franklin D. Roosevelt flies from Albany to Chicago to deliver his acceptance speech before the members of the Democratic Convention, the first time in the political history of the United States that a candidate accepts his nomination in person. ("I pledge you, I pledge myself, to a new deal for the American people. Let us all here assembled constitute ourselves prophets of a new order of competence and of courage. This is more than a political campaign; it is a call to arms. Give me your help, not to win votes alone, but to win in this crusade to restore America to its own people.")

**1937**    The famous American aviatrix, Amelia Earhart, and her co-pilot, Frederick J. Noonan, are lost in the Pacific Ocean, somewhere between New Guinea and Howland Island, in the midst of their round-the-world flight. (Their disappearance is still an unsolved mystery.)

**1941**    Joe DiMaggio hits a home run in the fifth inning of the New York-Boston game in Yankee Stadium, thus extending his hitting streak to 45 consecutive games and breaking the all-time record of 44 games set by Wee Willie Keeler in 1897.

**1945**    With the war in Europe over, the lights go on in the British Isles for the first time since September 3, 1939.

**1946**    As a result of two decisions handed down by the U.S. Supreme Court in 1944, both upholding the right of Negroes to vote in primary elections, Negroes in Mississippi vote for the first time in that state's Democratic primary elections. (The 1960 census listed Mississippi's Negro population at 915,743. Five years later, out of 550,000 registered voters in that state, about 29,000 were Negroes.)

**1955**    Senator Lyndon B. Johnson (D., Texas), the Majority Leader of the Senate, suffers a heart attack. (He returned to his Senate duties on December 12.)

**1961**    Ernest Hemingway, winner of both the Nobel and Pulitzer prizes in literature, dies in Ketchum, Idaho, after suffering a gunshot wound in the head.

**1963**    President Kennedy calls on the newly elected Pope, Paul VI, at the Vatican in Rome.

**1964**    President Johnson signs into law the 1964 Civil Rights Act, the most far-reaching piece of race relations legislation passed by the U.S. Congress since the days of the Reconstruction. ("... This law's purpose is not to punish. Its purpose is not to divide, but to end divisions—divisions which have lasted too long. Its purpose is national, not regional.... Let us close the springs of racial poison."—President Johnson).

# JULY 3

**1775**  George Washington assumes command of the Continental Army at Cambridge, Massachusetts.

**1819**  The first savings bank in America, the Bank for Savings in New York City, opens its doors to the public. (Eighty depositors opened accounts the first day, depositing a total of $2,807.)

**1863**  Battle of Gettysburg: On the third day of fighting, General George G. Meade and his Union forces recapture Culp's Hill. Shortly thereafter, the Confederate General George E. Pickett makes his famous charge, leading an army of five thousand men. But the withering northern artillery fire proves to be too much for Pickett's men and two-thirds of his troops are either killed, wounded, or captured. (Gettysburg was the turning point of the war; after this battle, the fortunes of the Confederacy began to decline.)

**1890**  Idaho becomes the 43rd state to enter the Union.

**1892**  After two days of demonstrations, workers at the Carnegie Steel Company in Homestead, Pennsylvania, go out on strike, protesting wage cuts and the action of the management in bringing in 300 Pinkerton guards to maintain order. (The strike, one of the most violent in labor history, came to an end on November 20, but not before 7 guards and 11 strikers and spectators were shot to death.)

**1898.**  The U.S. Navy completely defeats the Spanish fleet in the harbor of Santiago, Cuba, in the Spanish-American War.

**1919**  An order from the Office of the Judge Advocate of the U.S. Army forbids marriages between American soldiers, serving in the Rhine occupation zone, and women of German citizenship.

**1941**  For the first time since the German invasion of Russia, Premier Joseph Stalin addresses his countrymen by radio and instructs them in the "scorched earth" policy: "In areas occupied by the enemy, guerrilla units, mounted and foot, must be formed, diversionist groups must be organized to combat enemy troops, to foment guerrilla warfare everywhere, to blow up bridges, roads, damage telephone and telegraph lines, and to set fire to forests, stores and transports." (WORLD WAR II)

**1945**  American occupation troops, made up of the Second Armored Division, start to enter Berlin. (The American flag was raised over Berlin the next day.) (WORLD WAR II)

**1945**  The first postwar civilian passenger automobile made since February, 1942, leaves the Ford Motor Company's Detroit assembly line.

**1950**  U.S. soldiers meet the North Koreans in battle for the first time.

**1957**  In a struggle for power, Nikita Khrushchev, First Secretary of Russia's Communist Party, persuades the party's all-powerful Central Committee to oust his rivals from the committee. The most prominent individuals to be purged are: former Premier Georgi M. Malenkov, former Foreign Minister Vyacheslav M. Molotov, and Lazar M. Kaganovich.

**1962**    After 132 years of French rule, the independent state of Algeria comes into existence. (This action followed a July 1 referendum in which the Algerians overwhelmingly voted for their independence from France.)

## JULY 4

### Independence Day

**1776**    The Continental Congress, sitting in Philadelphia, adopts the Declaration of Independence. The document is signed by John Hancock, President of the Congress, and Charles Thomson, Secretary. (The other members of Congress signed it beginning August 2, 1776. *See July 19.*)

**1802**    The U.S. Military Academy at West Point, New York, is opened formally with the arrival of the first 10 cadets.

**1826**    Birth of Stephen Collins Foster, America's first great composer of music, at Lawrenceville, Pennsylvania.

**1826**    John Adams and Thomas Jefferson, the second and third Presidents of the United States, both die on this day, the 50th anniversary of the signing of the Declaration of Independence.

**1831**    Former U.S. President James Monroe dies in New York City.

**1832**    The song "America" is sung publicly for the first time by the children of Boston at a Fourth of July celebration in the Park Street Church. (The words, written in a half-hour's time by Dr. Samuel Francis Smith, a clergyman, were set to the music of "God Save the King.")

**1845**    Henry David Thoreau, American writer and naturalist, starts his sojourn in the woods at Walden Pond near Concord, Massachusetts.* ("I went to the woods because I wished to live deliberately, to front only the essential facts of life, and see if I could not learn what it had to teach, and not, when I came to die, discover that I had not lived.")

**1855**    The poet Walt Whitman publishes in Brooklyn, New York, the first edition of his *Leaves of Grass,* a collection of 12 poems. (Whitman was his own publisher and had about a thousand copies of this edition printed. The title page omitted any reference to the author, but he did include as frontispiece a portrait of himself in workingman's clothing. Several years later, the poet commented on the publication of the little volume: "I don't think

* Although Thoreau lived at Walden from July 4, 1845, to September 6, 1847, he really used his hut there as a workshop and returned to Concord whenever it was necessary.

one copy was sold, not a copy. The books were put in the stores but nobody bought them. They had to be given away.")

**1872** Calvin Coolidge, 30th President of the United States, is born in Plymouth, Vermont.

**1895** The verses of "America, the Beautiful," written by Katherine Lee Bates, appear for the first time in the Boston magazine, *The Congregationalist*. (The words were later set to the music of Samuel A. Ward, and on many occasions it has been suggested that the patriotic song be adopted as the national anthem of the United States.)

**1917** After leading a parade in Paris of the first American soldiers to reach France, General John J. Pershing places a wreath on the grave of the Marquis de Lafayette. The American Colonel Charles E. Stanton concludes the ceremony by saying, "In time of our peril France came to our rescue. We have not forgotten. Lafayette, we are here!" (WORLD WAR I)

**1919** Jack Dempsey, the "Manassa Mauler," wins the heavyweight boxing championship at Toledo, Ohio, when he knocks out the present titleholder, Jess Willard.

**1942** *This Is the Army*, an all-soldier revue featuring the songs of Irving Berlin and directed by Sergeant Ezra Stone, opens at the Broadway Theatre in New York. (President Franklin D. Roosevelt, seeing the show when it played later in Washington, said it was the greatest musical play he had ever seen. Thousands of Americans agreed with the President, because at the end of its 12-week run in New York, *This Is the Army* had accumulated a net profit of $780,000.)

**1946** The Philippine Republic comes into existence at 10 o'clock in the morning, after 47 years of U.S. sovereignty.

**1954** For the first time since 1939, meat rationing ends in England.

**1959** A 49th star is added to the flag of the United States following the admission into the Union of the state of Alaska.

**1960** The U.S. flag, starting today, has 50 stars, as a result of Hawaii's admission into the Union.

## JULY 5

**1811** Venezuela declares her independence from Spain, the first of the South American countries to do so.

**1865** William Booth founds the Salvation Army in London.

**1900** Delegates to the Democratic National Convention in Kansas City, Missouri, unanimously nominate William Jennings Bryan of Nebraska for the Presidency, and Adlai E. Stevenson of Illinois for Vice President. (Stevenson had already served as Vice President during the second administration of Grover Cleveland.)

**1920**    To run against the Harding-Coolidge ticket adopted by the Republicans, the Democrats at their convention in San Francisco nominate James M. Cox of Ohio for President, and Franklin D. Roosevelt of New York for Vice President.

**1935**    One of the most far-reaching attempts ever made by legislative process to adjust labor relations to 20th century conditions becomes law when President Franklin D. Roosevelt signs the Wagner-Connery Bill, officially called the National Labor Relations Act of 1935. The act sets up a National Labor Relations Board (NLRB) and guarantees labor's right of collective bargaining.

**1942**    A news dispatch from Detroit reports that Edsel Ford, whose family has manufactured 30,000,000 automobiles since 1903, cannot get a new car for his own use until a local rationing board considers his application. (WORLD WAR II)

**1945**    General Douglas MacArthur announces that the "entire Philippine Islands are now liberated and the Philippine campaign can be regarded as virtually closed." (WORLD WAR II)

**1948**    The Labor Government in England adopts the National Health Service Act, providing free medical service for any citizen who requires it. Included in the act are additional benefits for unemployment, sickness, motherhood, widows, orphans, old age, and death.

**1959**    President Achmed Sukarno dissolves the Parliament of Indonesia and assumes dictatorial powers for himself.

**1960**    Six days before the Democratic National Convention is to get under way in Los Angeles, Senator Lyndon B. Johnson (D., Texas) announces he is a candidate for the Presidential nomination. To reporters who want to know where he stands in the political spectrum, Johnson says: "I am progressive and prudent without being radical. I am conservative without being reactionary . . ." (*See July 13, 14*)

# JULY 6

**1699**    The notorious pirate, Captain William Kidd, is seized in Boston and deported to England.

**1854**    After several organizational meetings, the Republican Party has its formal beginning at a statewide convention held in Jackson, Michigan. (Several hundred persons attended the meeting, including a number from outside the state. The most significant resolution adopted by the delegates stated: "Resolved, that . . . in view of the necessity of battling for the first principles of Republican government, and against the schemes of an aristocracy, the most revolting and oppressive with which the earth was ever cursed, or man debased, we will cooperate and be known as REPUBLICANS until the contest be terminated.")

**1885**   In Paris, the bacteriologist Louis Pasteur inoculates the first human being, a boy who had been badly bitten by an infected dog. (The boy, Joseph Moister, thanks to Pasteur, did not develop an infection, and later became superintendent of the Pasteur Institute. On the day the Germans entered Paris in World War II, however, he committed suicide at the Institute.)

**1904**   Because they have no faith in the political promises of either the Democrats or Republicans, Negroes form the National Liberty Party and hold a nominating convention in St. Louis. Delegates from 36 states select George E. Taylor to be their Presidential candidate in the November elections. (Mr. Taylor may well have been the first Negro to run for the Presidency.)

**1924**   Senator Robert M. La Follette of Wisconsin is chosen as the Presidential nominee of the Progressive Party, meeting in convention at Cleveland. Burton K. Wheeler of Montana receives the nomination for Vice President.

**1928**   A preview of the first all-talking motion picture, *The Lights of New York,* produced by Warner Brothers, takes place at the Strand Theatre in New York.

**1933**   An All-Star baseball game is played for the first time when the American League defeats the National League in Chicago, 4 to 2.

**1944**   The most disastrous circus fire in history takes place in Hartford, Connecticut, as the main tent of the Ringling Brothers and Barnum & Bailey Circus goes up in flames during a performance. As a result of burns and panic, 168 persons are killed and almost 350 more are injured.

**1945**   Nicaragua becomes the first nation to accept formally the United Nations Charter drawn up at the San Francisco Conference.

**1947**   Voters in Spain approve the dictatorship of General Francisco Franco by a wide margin. At the same time, the Spaniards vote to restore the monarchy ultimately, although Franco is to remain chief of state as long as he lives.

**1952**   The liner *United States,* en route to England from New York, establishes a new speed record across the Atlantic, crossing it in 3 days, 10 hours, and 40 minutes.

**1959**   Queen Elizabeth II of Great Britain leaves Canada and pays a visit to Chicago, the first such to that city by a reigning British monarch.

## JULY 7

**1754**   King's College in New York City (renamed "Columbia College" in 1784), chartered by King George II of England, opens its doors with eight undergraduates and Dr. Samuel Johnson, its president, the sole member of the faculty.

**1840**   Daniel Webster, campaigning for the Whig ticket of "Tippecanoe and Tyler, Too" (William Henry Harrison and John

Tyler), delivers an election speech before 15,000 persons on Stratton Mountain, Vermont.

**1846**    Commodore J. D. Sloat, of the U.S. Navy, raises the American flag at Monterey upon the surrender of the Mexican garrison there, and proclaims the annexation of California by the United States.

**1865**    Four persons, named as accomplices of John Wilkes Booth in the assassination of President Abraham Lincoln, are hanged. They are: Mrs. Mary E. Surratt, David E. Harold, George A. Atzerodt, and Lewis Payne.

**1898**    President William McKinley signs a joint resolution of Congress authorizing the annexation of Hawaii by the United States. (*See August 21*)

**1932**    Fearful that both of the major political parties will support legislation to repeal the Eighteenth Amendment after the November elections, the Prohibition Party Convention, at Indianapolis, nominates William D. Upshaw of Georgia for President and Frank S. Regan of Illinois for Vice President.

**1937**    A clash between Japanese and Chinese soldiers on the Marco Polo Bridge near Peiping is used by the Japanese as a pretext for proceeding to capture Peiping, the first major assault on China proper in the Sino-Japanese War.

**1941**    President Franklin D. Roosevelt announces to Congress that U.S. naval forces, to forestall a Nazi invasion, have landed earlier in the day in Iceland, with the full agreement of the government of that country. (WORLD WAR II)

**1953**    A national controversy rages over the refusal of Senator Joseph R. McCarthy (R., Wis.) to dismiss J. B. Matthews, staff director of the Senate Investigating Subcommittee, after the latter's charge that "the largest single group supporting the Communist apparatus in the United States today is composed of Protestant clergymen." (Despite the fact that McCarthy insisted he had complete authority in hiring and firing nonprofessional staff members, he yielded to public and congressional protests and accepted Matthews' resignation on July 9.)


## JULY 8

**1776**    As the Liberty Bell tolls in Philadelphia, calling out the residents to Independence Square, Colonel John Nixon reads the Declaration of Independence to the crowd, the first time the document has been read publicly.

**1796**    Thomas Pickering, Secretary of State, issues the first passport to an American citizen. The recipient is Francis M. Barrere, "a citizen of the United States having occasion to pass into foreign countries about his lawful affairs . . ."

**1822**    The English poet Percy Bysshe Shelley is drowned in the Gulf of Spezzia, Italy, when the boat he was sailing capsizes in a squall. (Ten days later, Shelley's friends, Edward John Trelawny and Leigh Hunt, found the poet's body on the beach at Viareggio and, accompanied by Lord Byron, they burned the corpse. As the flames consumed the body, Trelawny snatched Shelley's heart from the fire and arranged to have it buried in the English Protestant Cemetery in Rome.)

**1835**    The Liberty Bell in Independence Hall, Philadelphia, cracks as it is being rung during the funeral of John Marshall, Chief Justice of the Supreme Court.

**1839**    John D. Rockefeller is born in Richford, New York.

**1853**    An American expedition, headed by Commodore Matthew Perry, arrives in Yokohama harbor, Japan, hoping to establish American relations with that nation.

**1872**    Johann Strauss (the Younger), world famous for his Viennese waltzes, conducts the first of four concerts in New York at the Academy of Music. (He followed his New York visit with one in Boston, where he conducted more than a dozen concerts.)

**1889**    John L. Sullivan fights the last bare-knuckle heavyweight championship boxing bout as he takes on Jake Kilrain in Richburg, Mississippi. (Sullivan defeated Kilrain in the 75th round, the time being 2 hours, 16 minutes, 23 seconds.)

**1896**    William Jennings Bryan of Nebraska, pleading for his silver money policy, makes his famous "Cross of Gold" speech before the delegates of the Democratic National Convention at Chicago. ("You shall not press down upon the brow of labor this crown of thorns! You shall not crucify mankind upon a cross of gold.")

**1907**    The theatrical producer Florenz Ziegfeld stages the first Ziegfeld Follies on the roof garden of the New York Theatre.

**1919**    President Woodrow Wilson, returning from the Peace Conference at Versailles, France, receives a tumultuous welcome from the city of New York.

**1940**    After 62 days of fierce fighting against the invading Nazis, the government of Norway moves to London to continue the struggle from that city. (WORLD WAR II)

**1944**    Saipan Island in the Marianas is taken from Japan by U.S. forces. (WORLD WAR II)

**1950**    General Douglas MacArthur is appointed United Nations commander in Korea.

**1951**    The City of Paris celebrates the 2,000th anniversary of its founding.

**1964**    American military headquarters in Saigon announces that U.S. casualties in South Vietnam now total 1,387 since the nation became involved in the war there in December, 1961. Of this total, 152 American servicemen have been killed in combat.

# JULY 9

**1776**    News of the signing of the Declaration of Independence
reaches New York. At 6 o'clock in the evening, General George
Washington summons his soldiers and has the Declaration read to
them.

**1778**    Delegates from seven states in Congress—Massachusetts,
Rhode Island, Connecticut, New York, Pennsylvania, Virginia, and
South Carolina—sign the Articles of Confederation. (Delegates from
North Carolina, Georgia, New Hampshire, New Jersey, and Dela-
ware signed the document later.)

**1832**    Henry Clay's resolution for a National Fast Day for
prayers to bring an end to the current epidemic of cholera is defeated in the House of Representatives. (Clay wanted Congress to
recommend to President Jackson that he issue a proclamation setting aside this national day of prayer. The President had previously
declined and Congressman Gulian Verplanck of New York had
supported the President, saying: "Let us leave prayer and humilia-
tion to be prompted by the devotion of the heart, and not the
bidding of the State.")

**1850**    After serving only one year and four months of his term,
President Zachary Taylor dies in the White House of a typhus
infection.

**1868**    The Democratic ticket, drawn up in New York at the
party's nominating convention, is Horatio Seymour of New York
for President, and Francis P. Blair of Missouri for Vice President.

**1872**    At Baltimore, delegates to the Democratic National Convention nominate Horace Greeley for President and B. Gratz Brown
for Vice President.

**1924**    Breaking all records for the length of time taken to
decide on a political candidate, the Democrats meeting in New
York's Madison Square Garden nominate John W. Davis for President on the 103rd ballot. The Vice Presidential nominee is Charles
W. Bryan, Governor of Nebraska. (The convention began on June
24 and did not adjourn until July 10. Davis, a dark-horse candidate,
received the nomination only after the rival candidates, William
G. McAdoo and Governor Alfred E. Smith, agreed to release their
delegates on July 8. Far more important than the candidates were
the forces at work behind closed doors in the convention. Many of
the Southern delegates were outspokenly in favor of the Ku Klux
Klan, and therefore bitterly opposed to the nomination of Smith,
a Catholic. McAdoo, while certainly not sympathetic to the Klan,
refused to attack it or its purposes, hoping to maintain the strong
support that the South was willing to give him.)

**1943**    A united American, British, and Canadian air and naval
force, including parachute troops, invades the east and south coasts
of Sicily in World War II. (". . . The time has come for you to de-

cide whether Italians shall die for Mussolini and Hitler—or live for Italy and civilization . . ."—From the joint communique issued by President Franklin D. Roosevelt and Prime Minister Winston Churchill).

**1945**    Because the current newspaper strike in New York prevents readers, particularly children, from following their favorite comic strips, Mayor Fiorello LaGuardia reads them to the public over the facilities of radio Station WNYC. (The artists supplied him with their unpublished drawings and captions.)

**1955**    Nine prominent scientists throughout the world warn that "a war with H-bombs might quite possibly put an end to the human race." Led by Lord Bertrand Russell, British mathematician and philosopher, the scientists call for the "abolition of war" and a conference of scientists to examine the dangers of mass-destruction weapons.

**1960**    Premier Nikita Khrushchev threatens the United States with Soviet rockets if Washington attempts to oust the Castro regime in Cuba.

## JULY 10

**1850**    Vice President Millard Fillmore succeeds to the Presidency on the death of President Zachary Taylor, thereby becoming the 13th President of the United States.

**1867**    Birthday of Finley Peter Dunne, American journalist and humorist, creator of the mythical philosopher and critic, "Mr. Dooley."

**1871**    Marcel Proust, French writer, born in Paris.

**1890**    Wyoming is admitted into the Union as the 44th state.

**1904**    The Democratic Convention, meeting in St. Louis, Missouri, nominates Alton B. Parker of New York for President and Henry G. Davis of West Virginia for Vice President.

**1908**    For the third time, William Jennings Bryan is nominated as the Presidental candidate of the Democrats. His running mate, selected by the delegates at the Denver convention, is John W. Kern of Indiana.

**1913**    In Death Valley, California, the thermometer hits 134° F., the highest temperature ever recorded in the United States. (*See September 13*)

**1917**    Emma Goldman, long identified as a leading American anarchist, is sentenced to 2 years' imprisonment and fined $10,000 for "conspiring to obstruct the operation of the military laws of the United States." (Specifically, she was guilty of trying to slow down the draft quotas.)

**1918**    The Fifth All-Russian Congress of Soviets adopts the written Constitution of Russian Socialist Federated Soviet Republics.

**1938**    Howard Hughes, accompanied by a crew of four, completes his flight around the world in a total of 91 hours.

**1953**    The minority Democrats on the Senate Investigating Subcommittee resign in protest after the four Republicans on the committee vote to give Senator Joseph R. McCarthy (R., Wis.), the chairman, sole power to hire and fire nonprofessional staff members. (The three Democrats were: Senator John L. McClellan, Arkansas; Senator Stuart Symington, Missouri; Senator Henry M. Jackson, Washington.)

**1953**    Lavrenti P. Beria, chief of internal security forces in Soviet Russia, is purged from the Communist hierarchy, accused of "criminal and anti-State activities."

**1962**    Telstar, an experimental communications satellite privately owned and developed by the American Telephone & Telegraph Company, is launched into orbit from Cape Canaveral, Florida. As it spins around the earth, it relays the sounds and pictures of American television programs to the people of Europe.

**1964**    For the third time in a year, a New York court considers the question of whether the 215-year-old English novel *Fanny Hill* is or is not obscene and concludes that the book is not obscene and can be sold in the state. (This ruling upheld an earlier one made by Supreme Court Justice Arthur G. Klein and overruled the Appellate Division of the same court which had reversed Justice Klein's decision on February 27, 1964.)

## JULY 11

**1767**    Birthday of John Quincy Adams, sixth President of the United States.

**1804**    The Vice President of the United States, Aaron Burr, challenges Alexander Hamilton to a duel and, after meeting him at Weehawken, New Jersey, mortally wounds him. (Hamilton had long claimed that Burr was involved in a plot to set up a rival empire.)

**1864**    American economists claim that war-bred inflation is so serious that a dollar bill is worth only 39 cents.

**1878**    President Rutherford B. Hayes stirs up a political tempest when he dismisses Chester A. Arthur as Collector of the Port of New York. (The future President was not removed for dishonesty. Hayes, a year earlier, had issued an order forbidding federal civil servants from taking active roles in political parties. When Arthur refused to resign from his post as chairman of the Republican Central Committee of New York, the President demanded his resignation.)

**1884**    The Democratic Convention at Chicago nominates Governor Grover Cleveland of New York for the Presidency and Thomas A. Hendricks of Indiana for Vice President.

**1896**   After listening to his moving "Cross of Gold" speech, enthusiastic Democrats, attending their national convention in Chicago, nominate William Jennings Bryan of Nebraska for President. Arthur Sewall of Maine receives the Vice Presidential nomination. (Bryan was only 36 years of age at the time.)

**1933**   All schoolteachers in Germany are ordered to read Adolf Hitler's *Mein Kampf* and to make themselves thoroughly familiar with the Nazi creed.

**1944**   President Franklin D. Roosevelt, the first Chief Executive to be elected to a third term of office, announces he is available for a fourth term, saying: "If the (Democratic) Convention should nominate me, I shall accept. If the people elect me, I will serve." *

**1945**   Eamon de Valera, Premier of Eire, announces that Eire is a republic, despite the fact that the British government considers it a dominion.

**1954**   Two months after the U.S. Supreme Court hands down its ruling ordering the desegregation of public schools, 75 men meet in Indianola, Mississippi, to form the first White Citizens' Council. The new organization, soon to attract thousands of members throughout the South, will take steps to fight integration and the National Association for the Advancement of Colored People.

**1955**   The new U.S. Air Academy is dedicated at Lowry Air Base, Colorado. The 306 cadets of the Academy's first class are sworn into the Air Force.

**1961**   President and Mrs. John F. Kennedy score a social triumph as they entertain President Mohammed Ayub Khan of Pakistan on the lawns of Mount Vernon, George Washington's home on the Potomac. (The Kennedys' 140 guests were transported down the river on four yachts. Dinner was served in a tent pavilion and entertainment provided by the National Symphony Orchestra, the Lester Lanin Trio and the U.S. Air Force's "Strolling Strings.")

## JULY 12

**100 B.C.**   Birth of Caius Julius Caesar.

**1810**   Members of the Journeymen Cordwainers, a shoemakers' union, go on trial in New York City for having called a strike to win a wage increase. (The court found the union guilty and fined each member a dollar plus legal costs.)

**1862**   The Medal of Honor is authorized by the U.S. Congress, "to be presented in the name of the Congress to such noncommissioned officers and privates as shall most distinguish themselves by their gallantry in action and other soldier-like qualities during the present insurrection." (The last reference, of course, was to the War

---

* The President thus used General William T. Sherman's famous words in reverse ("If nominated, I will not accept, if elected, I will not serve.") (*See June 5*)

between the States. The following March, Congress extended the awarding of the medal to commissioned officers.)

**1912**    For the first time in American film history, movie fans see a foreign-made feature picture. The picture, made in France, is entitled *Queen Elizabeth* and stars Sarah Bernhardt and Lou Tellegen.

**1933**    A new industrial code establishes a minimum wage of 40 cents an hour throughout the nation.

**1941**    Invading armies of Nazi Germany crack the "Stalin Line" in Russia and march toward Kiev, Moscow, and Leningrad. (WORLD WAR II)

**1957**    A 20-year-old Prince and student at Harvard becomes the new Aga Khan, succeeding his grandfather who died yesterday. Prince Karim, the new leader of twenty million Ismaili Moslems, was designated to be his grandfather's choice as successor because "he has been brought up in the midst of the atomic age."

**1960**    At a news conference in Moscow, Premier Nikita Khrushchev says that "the Monroe Doctrine has outlived its time . . . has died a natural death . . ." (Two days later, the State Department in Washington releases a statement saying that the Government of the United States considers the Monroe Doctrine as valid in 1960 as it was when proclaimed in 1823.)

**1960**    In a last-ditch move to slow the bandwagon of Massachusetts Senator John F. Kennedy at the Democratic National Convention in Los Angeles, Senator Lyndon B. Johnson of Texas arranges a nationally televised "debate" with his front-running opponent. The exchange takes place before the Texas and Massachusetts delegations. The Texas Senator says he should be nominated because he is the man best qualified to be "the trustee for you and your children. . . ." Senator Kennedy answers that, even at this late stage of the contest, "I strongly support Senator Johnson—for majority leader of the U.S. Senate."

**1964**    The rift between Republican moderates and conservatives comes to a head in San Francisco when a letter bearing the name of Governor William W. Scranton of Pennsylvania is sent to Senator Barry M. Goldwater of Arizona. The letter calls for a joint appearance by the two men before the delegates of the Republican National Convention to define their respective stands on various issues. Goldwater, however, refuses and returns the letter in anger because of the charges made against him in the text. (Scranton said the next day that he took full responsibility for the letter even though he had not seen it before some zealous supporters had sent it to the Senator.)

# JULY 13

**1859**   Brigham Young, president of the Mormon Church, who rarely receives members of the press, grants an interview to Horace Greeley, editor of the *New York Tribune,* and throws some light on his marital status: "I have fifteen wives; I know no one who has more."

**1863**   Opposition to the Federal Conscription Act of 1863 inspires an outburst of draft riots in New York City. (The riots lasted through July 16 and resulted in 1,000 persons killed, several Negro lynchings, and a property damage of almost $2,000,000. Feeling against the draft law was inflamed because of the fact that men who could afford it could "buy" their way out of military service. Also, Democrats claimed that government officials in charge of the draft had "stuffed" the public lists with the names of their party members.)

**1865**   In an editorial in the *New York Tribune,* Horace Greeley offers a word of advice to federal civil servants who are complaining about low government salaries and the high cost of living in the nation's capital: "Washington is not a place to live in. The rents are high, the food is bad, the dust is disgusting and the morals are deplorable. Go West, young man, go West and grow up with the country." (When the expression "Go West, young man, go West" became popular all over the country, Mr. Greeley admitted he had first read it in an article written by J. L. Soule in 1851 in the *Terre Haute* [Indiana] *Express.*)

**1878**   The Russo-Turkish War ends.

**1925**   Broadway columnists are commenting about the temporary replacement of W. C. Fields in the *Ziegfeld Follies* by Will Rogers. Fields is on leave because of the death of his mother and the Oklahoma cowboy has taken over the comedian's role on almost no advance notice. One columnist writes: "He has acquitted himself with eminent success."

**1942**   The underground Free French Movement changes its name to "Fighting France." Recognition of the seriousness of the resistance movement prompts German occupation authorities to order all male relatives of French "saboteurs" shot immediately, their women sent to forced-labor camps, their children to Nazi institutions. (WORLD WAR II)

**1960**   John Fitzgerald Kennedy, 43-year-old Senator from Massachusetts, wins the Presidential nomination at the Democratic National Convention in Los Angeles. The young Senator's triumph comes on the first ballot when he captures 806½ votes, far ahead of his strongest opponent, Senator Lyndon B. Johnson of Texas, who receives 409. Kennedy is one of the youngest men ever to be nominated by either party, the wealthiest man ever to be nominated, and the first Senator to win a Presidential nomination since

Warren G. Harding in 1920. (*See July 14, July 15, November 8, November 22, January 20*)

**1964**   With its delegates torn between conservatism and moderation, the Republican National Convention gets underway at the Cow Palace in San Francisco. (*See July 14, July 15, July 16, July 17*)

## JULY 14

**Bastille Day in France**   The national holiday is observed in commemoration of the storming of the Bastille Prison by the citizens of Paris on July 14, 1789, and the release of the monarchy's political prisoners. (During World War II, *The New York Times,* on July 14, 1942, commented: "Bastille Day is the holiday of all free men. It is a day given us in trust by the people of France, against the day of their liberation, the restoration of the rights of man.") *

**1798**   Congress passes the Sedition Act of 1798, making it a crime to publish any "false, scandalous and malicious" writing against the government, the Congress, or the President. (The act imposed on persons found guilty of the above a fine of $2,000 and 2 years' imprisonment.)

**1853**   President Franklin Pierce opens the World's Fair in New York City, the exhibits housed in a replica of the Crystal Palace of London.

**1853**   Commodore Matthew C. Perry is received by the Lord of Toda on Kurihama Beach, Japan, and gives him a letter for the Emperor from former President Fillmore, requesting the establishment of Japanese-American trade relations. (Less than a year later, Perry's mission bore fruit and Japan opened her ports to American commercial interests for the first time in history.)

**1870**   The U.S. Congress passes an act "granting a pension to Mary Lincoln" and awards the widow of Abraham Lincoln an annual grant of $3,000.

**1908**   The first motion picture to be directed by David Wark Griffith is shown at Keith & Proctor's Union Square Theatre in New York. The film is entitled *The Adventures of Dolly,* a sentimental story of a melodramatic kidnapping.

**1940**   The English people, fighting the war alone and expecting a Nazi invasion momentarily, are cheered by the words of their prime minister, Winston Churchill, as he makes a nationwide broadcast: "We are fighting by ourselves alone; but we are not fighting

---

* Coming so soon after the American war of independence, the storming of the Bastille was backed enthusiastically by public opinion in the United States. One year after the Bastille fell, on July 14, 1790, a group of American and French patriots held a dinner in Philadelphia. A pig's head, symbolizing the deposed king's person, was carried around the banquet table and after each man present tried on his head the Cap of Liberty, he looked the pig's head in the eye and cried out "Tyrant!" Then, each guest carved a slice of the pig's head for himself until none of it remained.

for ourselves alone. Here in this strong City of Refuge which enshrines the title-deeds of human progress and is of deep consequence to Christian civilization; here, girt about the seas and oceans where the Navy reigns; shielded from above by the prowess and devotion of our airmen—we await undismayed the impending assault." (WORLD WAR II)

**1940**    Estonia, Latvia, and Lithuania are annexed by Russia and voted into the Soviet Union. (WORLD WAR II)

**1960**    In a move calculated to win Southern support for the Democratic ticket in November, Presidential nominee John F. Kennedy persuades Senator Lyndon B. Johnson (D., Texas) to be his running-mate. Johnson is nominated for the Vice Presidency and tells the Convention in Los Angeles: "... In admiration, and in envy, I want to say to you quite frankly ... I know when I see political genius and I have seen it in my friend John Kennedy. The Democratic party is going all the way with J.F.K. and L.B.J. ...." (The Kennedy-Johnson ticket was the first in U.S. history composed of two incumbent Senators.)

**1963**    Governor Nelson A. Rockefeller (R., N.Y.) declares war on the "radical right wing" of the Republican Party and charges, without mentioning the Senator by name, that the major strategy of the Goldwater-for-President partisans "would not only defeat the Republican Party in 1964, but would destroy it altogether. ...." (*See July 19*)

**1964**    Conservatives are firmly in control of the Republican National Convention in San Francisco as moderate delegates are defeated in their bid to have the party platform include a condemnation of political extremist groups, citing them by name. Moderates also lose out when they seek to have the platform support the constitutionality of the 1964 Civil Rights Act.

**1964**    Former President Eisenhower addresses delegates to the Republican National Convention in San Francisco and tells them that they must support the convention's choice of Presidential nominee or "drown in a whirlpool of factional strife. ...." The former President evokes loud boos and catcalls directed at the corps of newspaper, radio, and television representatives in the hall when he says: "... Let us particularly scorn the divisive efforts of those outside our family, including sensation-seeking columnists and commentators, because, my friends, I assure you that these are people who couldn't care less about the good of our party ...."

# JULY 15

**St. Swithin's Day**    Associated in the popular mind with rain. The old rhyme, associating St. Swithin, the Bishop of Winchester, with rainfall runs as follows:

> "St. Swithin's Day, if thou dost rain,
> For forty days it will remain;
> St. Swithin's Day, if thou be fair,
> For forty days it will rain nae mair."

**1606**    Birthday of Rembrandt Harmensz van Rijn, famous Dutch painter and etcher.

**1789**    At two o'clock in the morning, the Duke of Liancourt wakes King Louis XVI to tell him his authority fell with the Bastille. "But this is a great revolt!" the King exclaims. "No, Sire," answers the Duke, "it is a great Revolution!"

**1876**    George Washington Bradley, playing for the St. Louis baseball team, pitches the first no-hit game in history. The losing team was Hartford and the final score was 2–0.

**1912**    The United States wins the 1912 Olympic Games in Stockholm, Sweden, King Gustav of that nation commenting that Jim Thorpe, a member of the American team, is "the most wonderful athlete in the world." (Thorpe won both the pentathlon and decathlon, field contests comprising 5 and 10 events respectively, the first athlete in history to do so) *

**1919**    The War Department announces that, as of this date, 337,649 American men have been classified as World War I "draft dodgers." Of this total, law-enforcement officials have already arrested 163,738 men accused of evading the Selective Service law.

**1945**    Italy declares war on her former axis partner, Japan. (World War II)

**1948**    The Democratic National Convention in Philadelphia nominates President Harry S. Truman as its Presidential candidate in the November elections, giving him 947½ votes to 263 votes cast for Senator Richard B. Russell of Georgia. While many Southern delegates bolt the convention, President Truman accepts the nomination and announces he will call a special session of Congress to convene on July 26. The Democratic candidate for the Vice Presidency is Senator Alben Barkley of Kentucky.

**1958**    Because he is convinced that yesterday's coup in Iraq, which resulted in the murder of King Faisal, could possibly spread into Lebanon, President Eisenhower orders 3,500 U.S. Marines to

---

* Shortly after his return to the United States, however, Mr. Thorpe was deprived of his honors when the Amateur Athletic Union discovered that he had once played professional baseball, thereby sacrificing his amateur standing.

that country after receiving a request for American military aid from the President of Lebanon. Mr. Eisenhower tells the nation in a radio and television broadcast that American troops are necessary because of evidence that the Soviet Union and the United Arab Republic were planning to overthrow the present regime in Lebanon. (The American troops were withdrawn October 25.)

**1960** An article in the *New York World-Telegram* points out that the average white-collar citizen during his lifetime will be worth $200,000. This figure is reached by adding lifetime income, plus the value of property owned, plus life insurance, etc. The article adds: "The prospective lifetime income of a man whose education ends in grade school figures out to $178,000 . . . A high school diploma raises it to $243,000. . . ."

**1960** Senator John F. Kennedy (D., Mass.) accepts the Democratic nomination for the Presidency and tells cheering Democrats in Los Angeles: ". . . The New Frontier of which I speak is not a set of promises . . . it is a set of challenges. It sums up not what I intend to offer the American people, but what I intend to ask of them. It appeals to their pride, not their pocketbooks. It holds out the promise of more sacrifice instead of more security. . . ."

**1964** Delegates to the Republican National Convention in San Francisco nominate Senator Barry M. Goldwater of Arizona for the Presidency. Senator Goldwater's victory of 883 votes (655 needed for nomination) comes on the first ballot. His only serious competitor, Governor William W. Scranton of Pennsylvania, receives 214 votes. (Before the voting began, a reporter asked the Senator whether the civil rights issue would help the Democrats in the November elections. His answer: "After Lyndon Johnson—the biggest faker in the United States? He opposed civil rights until this year. Let them make an issue of it. I'll recite the thousands of words he has spoken down the years against abolishing the poll tax and the Fair Employment Practices Commission. He's the phoniest individual who ever came around." *See November 8).*

# JULY 16

**1790** Congress establishes the District of Columbia on the Potomac River, voting to set up there the permanent seat of the government of the United States.

**1821** Mary Baker Eddy, founder of the Church of Christ, Scientist, is born at Bow, New Hampshire.

**1862** David Glasgow Farragut becomes the first admiral in the U.S. Navy as Congress passes an act conferring the rank of rear admiral upon him.

**1882** Mary Todd Lincoln, the widow of President Abraham Lincoln, dies in Springfield, Illinois.

**1912** Herman Rosenthal, the biggest gambler in New York, is murdered on the streets of the city, shortly before he was to testify on the connection of the underworld with members of the police force. (Rosenthal's death set off an investigation into police corruption that resulted, on July 29, in the arrest of police Lieutenant Charles Becker, an officer who had amassed a fortune by providing "protection" for operators of gambling and vice establishments. Becker was convicted of the murder of Rosenthal on October 24 and finally executed on July 30, 1915.)

**1918** The Royal Family of Russia, the Czar Nicholas II, the Czarina Alexandra and their children, and members of their household staff, are murdered by Bolsheviks in Ekaterinburg.

**1945** At 5:30 o'clock in the morning, the first experimental test of an atomic bomb takes place at Alamogordo Air Base, New Mexico.

**1951** Leopold III of Belgium abdicates, after serving as king of his country for 17 years. He will be succeeded on the throne by his son Baudouin. (The King's abdication was the sequel of 11 years of national disorders occasioned by his surrender in 1940 to the Germans.)

**1957** A young Marine officer, Major John Glenn, Jr., of New Concord, Ohio, establishes a transcontinental speed record when he flies a jet plane from California to New York in 3 hours, 23 minutes, 8.4 seconds. (*See February 20*)

**1962** Commenting on the "outrageous criticism" that is directed at every U.S. President, *Newsweek Magazine* says that President Kennedy is "being subjected to a torrent of adverse comment, quips, scorn and ridicule, much of it witheringly personal. Not since the days of Franklin D. Roosevelt and the New Deal [has] the level of attack on a President, his family, and his policies seemed quite so heated...."

**1963** Congressman Carl Vinson of Georgia establishes a service record in the U.S. House of Representatives—48 years, 8 months, 13 days. The 79-year-old Democrat thus has served in Congress one day longer than the record held by the late House Speaker Sam Rayburn of Texas.

**1964** Most delegates to the Republican National Convention in San Francisco applaud, but not a few are disturbed by Senator Barry M. Goldwater's speech of acceptance of the Presidential nomination. The most controversial section of the speech occurs when the Senator says: "...Anyone who joins us in all sincerity we welcome. Those who do not care for our cause, we don't expect to enter our ranks in any case. And let our Republicanism so focused and so dedicated not be made fuzzy and futile by unthinking and stupid labels. I would remind you that extremism in the defense of liberty is no vice. And let me remind you also that moderation in the pursuit of justice is no virtue! ...." (*See July 17*)

# JULY 17

**1821**   Florida is formally ceded by Spain to the United States.

**1841**   *Punch,* the English periodical of humor, publishes its first issue in London.

**1917**   The British Royal House changes its family name from Saxe-Coburg and Gotha to Windsor.

**1920**   Sinclair Lewis, a little-known American writer, delivers a manuscript of a novel he calls *Main Street* to publisher Alfred Harcourt. (Lewis told Harcourt that he was hopeful the book would sell 10,000 copies. Harcourt said he thought that figure was conservative and predicted that it would sell 20,000. They were both wrong: in the first 6 months of 1921, 180,000 copies of *Main Street* were sold. Afterwards, the sales soared into the millions.)

**1936**   Beginning of the Spanish Civil War: General Francisco Franco leads army forces in a revolt against the Republican government of Spain. Uprisings break out all over Spain.

**1945**   The Chamber of Deputies in Belgium votes to continue the regency of Prince Charles and, at the same time, resolves to prohibit the return of King Leopold III to the throne without parliamentary consent. (On the following day, the Deputies voted to make Leopold an exile.)

**1948**   Southern Democrats from 13 states meet in Birmingham, Alabama, and organize a States' Rights Party to oppose the Truman-Barkley ticket adopted by the regular Democratic Convention in Philadelphia on July 15. Six thousand delegates nominate Governor J. Strom Thurmond of South Carolina for President and Governor Fielding L. Wright of Mississippi for Vice President.

**1955**   Arco, Idaho, a town of 1,350 persons, becomes the first community in the world to receive all its light and power from atomic energy. For a single hour, electricity from an experimental nuclear plant, 20 miles away, is transmitted to all users over conventional power lines.

**1962**   The U.S. Senate, by a vote of 52–48, kills a bill backed by President Kennedy that would provide, through Social Security financing, health insurance for the aged. The President calls the defeat of the so-called Medicare bill "a most serious defeat for every American family...."

**1964**   Many Republican moderates are disturbed by Senator Barry Goldwater's acceptance speech of the Presidential nomination at the Cow Palace in San Francisco. Governor Nelson A. Rockefeller of New York says flatly that some of the Senator's remarks are "dangerous, irresponsible and frightening." Senator J. Glenn Beall of Maryland tells reporters that "I want from [Goldwater's] own lips.... what he really meant when he said that 'extremism in the defense of liberty is no vice'."

# JULY 18

**A.D. 64**    Rome burns; Nero fiddles.

**1914**    The U.S. Army creates an aviation section within the Signal Corps. Six airplanes are made available for aerial training.

**1932**    A treaty is signed between the United States and Canada for the development of the St. Lawrence River into an ocean lane and power project. (Strong opposition to the project, however, delayed actual construction until the summer of 1954.)

**1938**    Douglas Corrigan, who left Floyd Bennett Field, New York, on July 17 ostensibly on a flight to California, arrives at Baldonnel Airport, Dublin. (Amused Americans immediately tagged him with the nickname of "Wrong Way Corrigan.")

**1940**    President Franklin D. Roosevelt is nominated unanimously for a third term by delegates to the Democratic Convention at Chicago. Henry A. Wallace of Iowa is the candidate for Vice President.

**1947**    President Harry Truman signs the Presidential Succession Act. Under this act, when there is no Vice President, the Speaker of the House of Representatives will succeed to the Presidency, in the case of death. Next in line of succession is the president pro tempore of the Senate, followed by the members of the Cabinet, beginning with the Secretary of State.

**1951**    The world heavyweight boxing championship is won by Joseph ("Jersey Joe") Walcott in Pittsburgh, Pennsylvania, as he knocks out Ezzard Charles in the seventh round.

**1964**    The killing of a 15-year-old Negro boy by an off-duty white policeman in New York leads to an outbreak of racial violence in the city's Negro neighborhoods, particularly the Harlem area. Despite the fact that the patrolman claims the boy had threatened him with a knife, crowds of Negroes riot in the streets and hurl rocks and bottles at scores of policemen. (After 4 days, the riots ended, with one man dead, 81 civilians and 35 policemen wounded, 112 stores and commercial establishments damaged or looted.)

# JULY 19

**1776**    Congress resolves "that the Declaration adopted on the fourth be fairly engrossed on parchment with the title and stile of 'The unanimous Declaration of the thirteen united States of America' and that the same, when engraved, be signed by every member of Congress."

**1848**    "Bloomers," a radical departure in women's dress, are introduced to the delegates of the First Woman's Rights Convention, meeting in Seneca Falls, New York. (The daring costume took its name from Mrs. Amelia Jenks Bloomer, a reformer who sought to "emancipate" women from conventional and feminine modes of dress.)

**1870**    The Franco-Prussian War begins after King William I of Prussia refuses to guarantee France that the Hohenzollern dynasty will not seek the Spanish throne.

**1918**    German armies begin to retreat across the Marne River in France, after their last great offensive in that country is successfully repulsed by the Allies. (WORLD WAR I)

**1941**    The "V for Victory" campaign in Europe is launched at midnight with a broadcast by Prime Minister Churchill of Great Britain. The Prime Minister says: "The V sign is the symbol of the inconquerable will of the occupied territories and a portent of the fate awaiting Nazi tyranny." (The idea spread rapidly throughout Europe. In Holland, the V meant not "Victoire" as it did to French-speaking peoples, but "Vryheid," or "freedom.")

**1942**    Arturo Toscanini conducts the National Broadcasting Company's Symphony Orchestra in the first American performance of the *Seventh Symphony* by Dmitri Shostakovich. (The Soviet composer's famous symphony was dedicated to the beleaguered city of Leningrad.)

**1955**    Russian farmers, touring midwestern farms in the United States, stop at the "Milky Way Dairy" just outside of Oskaloosa, Iowa, and sample their first ice-cream sodas and sundaes. (The Russians' favorite sundae was a concoction called a "Tummy Buster"— six scoops of strawberry, cherry, and vanilla ice cream, marshmallow, pineapple, and chocolate sauce, fresh strawberries, pecans, and maraschino cherries!)

**1963**    Governor Nelson A. Rockefeller (R., N.Y.) calls upon Senator Barry M. Goldwater (R., Ariz.) to disavow the "radical right wing" that is supporting him in his bid for the 1964 Presidential nomination. Says Rockefeller: "... The great threat is whether the radical right wing ... will be able to capture its leader...."

## JULY 20

**1859**    Baseball fans are charged an admission fee for the first time, as 1,500 spectators pay 50 cents each to see Brooklyn play New York. (Baseball players did not receive remuneration until 1863, when they were paid a share of the gate receipts.)

**1861**    The Congress of the Confederate States starts holding its sessions in Richmond, Virginia, the new capital of the Confederacy.

**1894**    Federal troops are withdrawn from Chicago as the power of the Pullman strikers is broken. (The Pullman Strike was one of the most bitter strikes in U.S. history. It was called on June 26,

1894, after the Pullman Car Company reduced wages. When the American Railway Union, led by its president, Eugene V. Debs, inaugurated a boycott, the Justice Department issued an injunction against Debs and the union, ordering them not to interfere with trains carrying mail. When Debs defied the decree, he was sentenced to 6 months' imprisonment.)

**1917**    Secretary of War Newton D. Baker draws the first draft number, 258, from a glass bowl containing 10,500 serial numbers. (The Secretary started the conscription lottery in the public-hearing room of the Senate Office Building, the drawings continuing for the next 16 hours.) (WORLD WAR I)

**1942**    The first detachment of WAACs * (members of the Women's Army Auxiliary Corps) start their basic training at Fort Des Moines, Iowa.

**1944**    Radio Berlin reports that Adolf Hitler narrowly escaped death when a bomb exploded in his headquarters. Hitler himself goes on the air to describe the attack to the German people, saying the bomb "exploded two meters away from me, but I am entirely unhurt apart from negligible grazes, bruises, or burns." (The plot was engineered by a group of high military and civil officials.)

**1945**    The flag of the United States is raised over Berlin as the first American troops prepare to participate in the occupation government. President Harry Truman, in Berlin for the Potsdam Conference, speaks at the flag-raising ceremony, saying: "We are not fighting for conquest. There is not a piece of territory or one thing of a monetary nature we want out of this war."

**1946**    A majority report of the Congressional Pearl Harbor Investigating Committee praises former President Franklin D. Roosevelt, former Secretary of State Cordell Hull, former Secretary of War Henry L. Stimson, and former Secretary of the Navy Frank Knox for their efforts to avert war with Japan. The investigators place chief blame for the Pearl Harbor disaster upon Major General Walter C. Short and Rear Admiral Husband E. Kimmel, army and navy commanders there at the time of the Japanese attack.

**1964**    Senator Barry M. Goldwater, back home in Phoenix, Arizona, after having been nominated by the Republicans for the Presidency, explains how he interprets the word "equality": "Here's where a great many Americans make a mistake about the words of Thomas Jefferson that all men are created equal. [Jefferson] meant all men—Americans, Africans, Mexicans or Cubans—are created equal at the instant of birth. But that's the end of equality. From then on, it depends pretty much on what a man does. It doesn't mean that Government has the responsibility to maintain all men equal."

* The name was changed later to WACs (Women's Army Corps).

# JULY 21

**1831**   Belgian Independence Day: Leopold I, formerly Prince Leopold of Saxe-Coburg, is proclaimed King of the Belgians, following the separation of Belgium from Holland.

**1861**   The first major military engagement in the War between the States takes place at Bull Run Creek, Virginia, about 35 miles southwest of Washington. Despite supreme optimism on the part of the Union Army, the Northerners are defeated by 22,000 Confederate troops led by General Pierre Gustave Beauregard. (It was a strange battle, this encounter at Bull Run. The Northern Army set out bedecked with flowers, armed with bottles of whiskey, and accompanied by hundreds of sight-seers, including many congressmen who drove to the battlefield in carriages equipped with basket lunches and champagne!)

**1873**   The world's first train robbery takes place at Adair, Iowa, when the notorious outlaw Jesse James holds up the Rock Island Express and escapes with $3,000.

**1884**   The so-called "vilest" political campaign in U.S. history gets under way. A story that first originated in the *Buffalo Evening Telegraph,* charging that Democratic Presidential nominee Grover Cleveland is the father of an illegitimate child, rocks the nation. Mr. Cleveland admits that he had lived with a Buffalo widow and that he had contributed to the child's support even though there was no proof that he was the father. Republican rallies ring with the marching cry, "Ma, Ma, where's my pa?" (Despite weeks of regular mud-slinging, Mr. Cleveland was elected in a tight race. *See October 29, November 4*).

**1918**   Allied soldiers retake Château-Thierry on the Marne River in France. (WORLD WAR I)

**1925**   John T. Scopes, a biology teacher in the Dayton, Tennessee, high school, is found guilty of teaching the theory of evolution, contrary to state law, and fined one hundred dollars. (The Scopes trial, beginning on July 10, was the biggest news story of 1925. Tennessee law forbade the teaching of any theory that "denies the story of Divine Creation of man as taught in the Bible, and to teach instead that man has descended from a lower order of animals." The state was assisted in its charges by William Jennings Bryan and Scopes was defended by the liberal attorney Clarence Darrow.)

**1930**   The U.S. Veterans' Administration is established.

**1944**   President Franklin D. Roosevelt is renominated for a fourth term by the Democratic Convention meeting in Chicago. Senator Harry S. Truman is the party's candidate for the Vice Presidency.

**1954**   Armistice agreements ending the 7½-year Indo-Chinese War are signed in Geneva, Switzerland. Under the truce terms,

France surrenders to the Communist Vietminh the northern half of Viet Nam, a total area of about 60,000 square miles and a population of some 14,000,000 people.

**1961**  Air Force Captain Virgil I. Grissom, riding a Mercury capsule, becomes the second American to rocket into the outer reaches of space. His flight lasts 16 minutes.

## JULY 22

**1587**  The second "Lost Colony" is reestablished on Roanoke Island, off the northeast coast of North Carolina. (The first English settlement in America was founded on the island in 1585. When the second expedition of 91 men, 17 women, and 9 children landed there on July 22, 1587, the first settlement had disappeared. Three years later, when a third group arrived, the island was again completely deserted.)

**1864**  The first Battle of Atlanta, Georgia, takes place in the War between the States as the Confederate troops under General John B. Hood are defeated by General William T. Sherman's forces from the North.

**1916**  A "Preparedness Day" parade in San Francisco is interrupted by the explosion of a bomb as the marchers near the corner of Market and Stewart streets. Ten spectators are killed and 40 wounded. (Thus began the long ordeals of labor leaders Tom Mooney and Warren K. Billings, who were charged with murder and sentenced respectively to death and life imprisonment. In 1918, President Wilson commuted Mooney's sentence to life imprisonment. And after 23 years of demonstrations and repeated court appeals the two men were pardoned and released by Governor C. L. Olson of California in 1939.)

**1920**  Members of the Republican National Committee, assembled in the town park of Marion, Ohio, notify Senator Warren G. Harding of Ohio that he has been nominated for the Presidency. Harding accepts the nomination, saying: "I would not be my natural self if I did not utter my consciousness of my limited ability to meet your full expectations, or to realize the aspirations within my own breast, but I will gladly give all that is in me, all of heart, soul and mind and abiding love of country."

**1931**  A moratorium on taxes is put into effect in Kansas to help the thousands of distressed farmers in the state.

**1932**  Congress passes the Home Loan Bank Act, providing for federal loans to private mortgage-lending institutions.

**1933**  Flying in his plane, the *Winnie Mae,* Wiley Post completes the first round-the-world solo flight. (Post flew 15,596 miles in 7 days, 18 hours, and 45 minutes.)

**1934**  John Dillinger, "Public Enemy Number One," is shot and killed by a group of 27 Federal Bureau of Investigation agents, led by Melvin H. Purvis, as he leaves the Biograph Movie Theatre in Chicago. (The ruthless murderer, bank robber, and jail-breaker was betrayed by one of his theatre companions that evening, a Rumanian refugee named Mrs. Anna Sage, later to become famous all over the nation as "The Woman in Red.")

**1937**    President Franklin D. Roosevelt's proposal to reorganize and enlarge the Supreme Court is defeated when the Senate, by a vote of 70 to 21, votes to substitute for it a bill to liberalize the federal judiciary in general, but not including the Supreme Court.

**1960**    On the eve of the Republican Convention, Vice President Richard M. Nixon, the favorite son candidate to succeed President Eisenhower, flies to New York and meets secretly with Governor Nelson A. Rockefeller. Out of the meeting emerges a "Fourteen Point" policy agreement, in which Nixon pledges to press for a liberal party platform. The Governor, in exchange, promises to throw New York support to Nixon and to undertake an active role for Nixon in the forthcoming campaign. (It was this meeting that Senator Barry M. Goldwater of Arizona, leader of the Republican conservative forces, branded as "the Munich of the Republican Party.")

# JULY 23

**1829**    William A. Burt of Mount Vernon, Michigan, receives a patent for his "typographer," claimed by many to be the first typewriter in history.

**1886**    Steve Brodie, proprietor of a New York saloon, claims he jumped off the Brooklyn Bridge into the East River earlier in the day. (Brodie's stunt, performed for publicity, left a permanent record in the history of American slang. To this day, Americans still refer to a spectacular exploit as "pulling a brodie.")

**1892**    Alexander Berkman, a Russian-born anarchist, shoots and stabs Henry Clay Frick, acting head of the Carnegie Steel Company, in the latter's office in Pittsburgh, Pennsylvania. (Berkman's sympathies, of course, were with the strikers in the current riots at the Homestead plant and Frick represented to him everything that was evil in industrial management. Frick recovered, however, and was able to crush the power of the strikers.)

**1904**    The ice-cream cone is born! Charles E. Menches of St. Louis, Missouri, calls on a young lady, carrying in one hand a bouquet of flowers and an ice-cream sandwich in the other. Looking about for a vase for the flowers, the young lady fashions one of the sandwich layers into a vase, thereby suggesting to her caller a novel way of serving a dip of ice cream.

**1914**    Austria presents a series of harsh demands to Serbia as a follow-up of the assassination of the Archduke Francis Ferdi-

nand and his wife at Sarajevo on June 28. (The tiny kingdom of
Serbia rejected the ultimatum a day later.)

**1945**    Marshal Henri Philippe Pétain, charged with treason,
goes on trial in Paris. The former chief of state issues this statement
as the trial gets under way: "I sacrificed my prestige for the French
people. If I treated with the enemy, it was to save you."

**1947**    The President of the United States takes the Senate by
surprise by walking unheralded into their chamber on Capitol Hill
in Washington, taking the seat he held as senator from Missouri.
Called on by the presiding officer to speak, President Truman says:
"I sometimes get homesick for this seat. I spent what I think were
the best ten years of my life in the Senate." (Capitol historians
claimed later that the last President to pay a surprise visit to the
Senate was George Washington, who paid a visit to that body on
August 22, 1789.)

**1958**    Four English women are named by Queen Elizabeth II
to baronial rank and, as a result, become the first women members
of the House of Lords. They are: Baroness Ravensdale, the Dowager Marchioness of Reading, Dame Katherine Elliott, and Mrs.
Barbara Wootton Wright.


## JULY 24

**1679**    New Hampshire becomes a royal colony of the British
crown.

**1783**    Birthday of Simón Bolivar, Venezuelan general, patriot,
and statesman, often called the Liberator of South America.

**1847**    Brigham Young and his Mormon followers arrive at
Great Salt Lake Valley, Utah. (This event is celebrated today
throughout Utah as Pioneer Day.)

**1866**    Tennessee becomes the first seceding state to be readmitted into the Union following the termination of the War between
the States.

**1929**    In the presence of representatives of 43 nations, President Herbert Hoover declares the Kellogg-Briand Treaty in force.
Under the terms of the pact, these nations have agreed to renounce
war as an instrument of national policy.

**1937**    The state of Alabama frees five of the defendants in the
famous Scottsboro case. (Originally, nine Negro boys were indicted
at Scottsboro, Alabama, for alleged rape of a white woman in a
railroad car. One of them was sentenced to death and the rest given
long prison sentences. After many years of court appeals, all of the
defendants but one were freed, the latter escaping from jail and
missing as a fugitive from justice.)

**1948**    Henry A. Wallace and Senator Glen H. Taylor of Idaho
are nominated, by acclamation, for President and Vice President,

respectively, by 3,240 delegates attending the national convention of the Progressive Party in Philadelphia.

**1959** Vice President Nixon and Premier Khrushchev, at the opening of the American Exhibition in Moscow, conduct a running debate on the pros and cons of capitalism and communism. The debate, covered by television cameras, is seen and heard all over the world.

## JULY 25

**1866** Ulysses S. Grant receives the rank of general of the U.S. Army, the first American officer to be so designated.

**1878** The first Chinese diplomatic mission to the United States arrives in Washington, the staff of 35 persons headed by Envoy Extraordinary Chen Lan Pin.

**1909** The French aviator Louis Blériot flies across the English Channel from Calais to Dover, making the 31-mile trip in 37 minutes. Observers point out that this is the first time a visitor has ever set foot in England who did not come by water.

**1934** Chancellor Engelbert Dollfuss of Austria is assassinated by troops of the Nazi Black Guards, as Adolf Hitler stages his unsuccessful attempt to take over the country.

**1943** King Victor Emmanuel of Italy summons Benito Mussolini to Quirinal Palace in Rome and hands him a prepared letter of resignation, demanding that the dictator sign it immediately. When Mussolini refuses, the King dismisses him and announces that Marshal Pietro Badoglio will head the new Italian government. (Mussolini was taken immediately to Lake Bracciano, 75 miles north of Rome, where he was held in custody by Italian troops.)

**1952** Puerto Rico becomes a self-governing free commonwealth after Governor Luis Muñoz Marin proclaims the island's constitution to be in effect.

**1956** Shortly before midnight the luxury liners *Andrea Doria* and the *Stockholm* collide 45 miles off Nantucket.

**1957** A vote by the National Assembly establishes Tunisia as a sovereign republic. Premier Habib Bourguiba becomes the state's first president.

## JULY 26

**1847** Liberia, the only sovereign Negro democracy in Africa, is declared a republic.

**1945** As a result of the previous day's national elections in the British Isles, the Labor Party rolls up a 2-to-1 victory over the Conservatives. Prime Minister Winston Churchill submits his resignation and King George VI appoints Clement Attlee, head of the Labor Party, as the new British Prime Minister. ("All our enemies having surrendered unconditionally, or being about to do so, I was immediately dismissed by the British electorate from all further conduct of their affairs."—Churchill).

**1945**   An ultimatum issued from Potsdam, Germany, over the signatures of the United States, Great Britain, and China * demands that Japan surrender unconditionally or suffer "prompt and utter destruction." In listing their terms, the three allied nations say they are final and absolute: "We shall not deviate from them. There are no alternatives. We shall brook no delay." (Three days later, Prime Minister Suzuki of Japan declared that the terms of the ultimatum were not worthy of his notice or response.) (WORLD WAR II)

**1945**   Unknown to the peoples of the world, the U.S.S. *Indianapolis* is streaming toward Saipan, carrying the atom bombs to be used in the destruction of Hiroshima and Nagasaki, Japan.

**1947**   Congress passes a bill to merge the U.S. armed services under a single Secretary of Defense. (Originally, the name of the agency was National Military Establishment, but on August 10, 1949, it was changed to the Department of Defense.)

**1952**   In the early morning hours, Governor Adlai E. Stevenson of Illinois is chosen Presidential nominee of the Democrats at their nominating convention in Chicago. Senator John J. Sparkman of Alabama is the Vice Presidential nominee.

**1952**   King Farouk of Egypt boards his royal yacht in Alexandria and sails away into exile. (The King had some parting words of caution to the rebels who had deposed him: "It is one thing to run a revolution, but you will find Egypt a very difficult country to govern.")

**1953**   Fidel Castro, son of a wealthy sugar planter, begins the revolution in Cuba against the government of dictator Fulgencio Batista as he leads 165 raiders in an attack on army barracks at Santiago. The raid fails, however, and Castro is thrown into prison. ("Our first fight is for political rights, and after that for social rights and freedom of the people."—Castro, after the raid. *See December 2, January 1*).

**1956**   Egyptian crowds hail President Gamal Abdel Nasser in Alexandria as he issues a decree nationalizing the internationally owned Suez Canal.

**1963**   President John F. Kennedy addresses the nation on the subject of the nuclear-test ban treaty with the Soviet Union: ". . . This treaty is not the millennium. It will not resolve all conflicts, or cause the Communists to forgo their ambitions, or eliminate the dangers of war . . . But it is an important first step—a step toward peace—a step toward reason—a step away from war. . . ." (*See August 5, October 7*)

---

* Russia's name was not attached to the ultimatum because that nation did not declare war on Japan until August 8.

# JULY 27

**1789**  The Department of Foreign Affairs, forerunner of the Department of State, is established by an act of the U.S. Congress.

**1909**  Orville Wright sets a world record by staying aloft in an airplane over Fort Myer, Virginia, for 1 hour, 12 minutes, and 40 seconds.

**1931**  A swarm of grasshoppers decends over the states of Iowa, Nebraska, and South Dakota, destroying thousands of acres of crops.

**1939**  Angered by moves to amend the National Labor Relations Act, labor leader John L. Lewis testifies before a House committee that one of the most prominent "enemies" of labor in the country is Vice President John Nance Garner. Says Lewis: ". . . The genesis of this campaign against labor . . . is not hard to find. It is within the Democratic Party. It . . . emanates from a labor-baiting, poker-playing, whisky-drinking evil old man whose name is Garner. . . ."

**1945**  At a convention of delegates of the Communist Political Association, members vote to disband the organization and reestablish the Communist Party of the United States. (The Party had formed the Association in 1944 to abandon its regular program in the United States in favor of cooperating with the government in its prosecution of the war against Germany and Japan.)

**1953**  Following the longest truce negotiations in the history of warfare (2 years, 17 days, and some 575 meetings between the belligerents), the war in Korea is over. An armistice is signed at Panmunjom by William K. Harrison for the United Nations and Lieutenant General Nam Il for the Korean Communists. (The war had been waged for 3 years and 32 days.)

**1954**  Great Britain and Egypt agree on terms ending the 72-year British occupation of the Suez Canal Zone.

**1955**  Austria regains her sovereignty after 17 years of occupation by foreign troops.

**1960**  Richard M. Nixon is nominated for the Presidency at the Republican National Convention in Chicago, the first Vice President to be nominated from that office since Martin Van Buren in 1835. Nixon is nominated on the first ballot, receiving 1,321 votes. (Earlier, Senator Barry M. Goldwater (R., Ariz.) had been nominated, too, but he asked that his name be withdrawn.)

# JULY 28

**1821**  Independence Day in Peru, commemorating General San Martín's proclamation of freedom from Spanish rule.

**1868**  Bells ring in many American towns and cities as the Secretary of State certifies that the Fourteenth Amendment to the

Constitution is ratified. (There are five sections to the Amendment, but the most important one is Section 1 providing that "all persons born or naturalized in the United States ... are citizens of the United States and of the State wherein they reside. ...")

**1869** Members of the Daughters of St. Crispin, a union of woman shoemakers, hold their first convention at Lynn, Massachusetts.

**1914** Austria declares war on Serbia, marking the real beginning of World War I.

**1915** U.S. Marines land in Haiti to combat a series of revolutionary coups.

**1932** More than 15,000 unemployed war veterans camping in Washington are driven out of the city by federal troops commanded by General Douglas MacArthur. The ex-service men are in the capital demanding immediate payment of "war bonuses." (General MacArthur described the Bonus Army as "a bad-looking mob animated by the spirit of revolution." But Will Rogers praised their behavior, saying, "Just think what 15,000 clubwomen would have done in Washington even if they wasn't hungry." And Congressman Fiorello La Guardia of New York wired President Hoover: "Soup is cheaper than tear bombs and bread better than bullets in maintaining law and order in these times of depression, unemployment, and hunger.")

**1941** After negotiating with the Vichy government of France, Japanese troops swarm into Indochina and begin their occupation of that French colonial outpost. (WORLD WAR II)

**1945** The U.S. Senate, by a vote of 89–2, ratifies the Charter of the United Nations. The two negative votes are cast by Senator William Langer (R., N.D.) and Senator Henrik Shipstead (R., Minn.).

**1945** An Army B-25 bomber, piloted by Lieutenant Colonel William F. Smith, Jr., crashes into the Empire State Building in New York, ripping a hole in the side of the skyscraper 915 feet above the street. (The crash took place in a fog after the pilot decided to reroute the plane to the Newark, New Jersey, airport. Thirteen persons were killed in the disaster and 25 injured.)

**1960** Henry Cabot Lodge, former Senator from Massachusetts and currently U.S. ambassador to the United Nations, is nominated for the Vice Presidency by acclamation at the Republican National Convention in Chicago.

**1960** Vice President Richard M. Nixon, accepting the nomination for the Presidency, tells the delegates to the Republican National Convention in Chicago that, if elected, his Administration would "... build an America in which we shall see the realization of the dreams ... of millions of people ... throughout the world for a fuller, freer, richer life than men have ever known in the history of mankind. ..."

# JULY 29

**1588**   Queen Elizabeth I of England, fearful of a Spanish invasion of her island empire, travels to Tilbury to spur on her troops. ("I am come amongst you at this time, not as for my recreation or sport, but being resolved, in the midst and heat of the battle, to live or die amongst you all.")

**1754**   The first international boxing match in history takes place as the British champion Jack Slack knocks out the French contender Jean Petit in 25 minutes.

**1883**   Birthday of Benito Mussolini, founder of fascism and for more than 20 years the dictator of Italy.

**1914**   A successful telephone conversation between two people in New York and San Francisco heralds the construction of the first transcontinental telephone line in the United States.

**1935**   Governor Herbert H. Lehman of New York appoints Thomas E. Dewey a special prosecutor to investigate the wave of racketeering sweeping over the state.

**1945**   An armada of U.S. B-29 bombers drops 3,500 tons of fire bombs on six Japanese cities, following a warning broadcast to Japan earlier in the week by Major General Curtis LeMay. (WORLD WAR II)

**1945**   The Communist Party in the United States ousts Earl Browder as its chief and names William Z. Foster to succeed him.

**1947**   Three mountain climbers, Gordon Herreid, Frank Mills, and Henry Daub, plant a tobacco tin containing their names on the 20,270-foot southern peak of Mount McKinley in Alaska, the fifth group of mountain climbers to reach the top.

**1959**   As a result of Hawaii's first election as one of the 50 states of the Union, voters there elect the first Orientals to be seated in the U.S. Congress. Hiram L. Fong, Republican, of Chinese-American extraction, wins a seat in the U.S. Senate and Daniel K. Inouye, Democrat, becomes the first Congressman of Japanese ancestry.

**1962**   A poll conducted among 75 noted American historians and political scientists rates the presidents * of the United States in five categories: Great, Near Great, Average, Below Average, Failure. The poll's findings: *GREAT:* Lincoln, Washington, Franklin D. Roosevelt, Wilson, Jefferson; *NEAR GREAT:* Jackson, Theodore Roosevelt, Polk, Truman, John Adams, Cleveland; *AVERAGE:* Madison, John Quincy Adams, Hayes, McKinley, Taft, Van Buren, Monroe, Hoover, Benjamin Harrison, Arthur, Eisenhower,

---

* Because of the shortness of their terms, Presidents William Henry Harrison and James A. Garfield were not considered in the survey. President John F. Kennedy, the incumbent President, was also not included because he was only in the middle of his term of office.

Andrew Johnson; *BELOW AVERAGE:* Taylor, Tyler, Fillmore, Coolidge, Pierce, Buchanan; *FAILURE:* Grant, Harding

## JULY 30

**1619** The first representative assembly in America convenes at Jamestown, Virginia, attended by two delegates from each of the 11 Virginia plantations.

**1818** Birth of Emily Brontë, English novelist and poet.

**1866** One of the earliest riots takes place in the South over proposals to extend the vote to Negroes, as residents of New Orleans stage mass demonstrations protesting moves to grant Negro suffrage in the state legislature.

**1877** The Reverend Henry Ward Beecher, the best-known clergyman in America, strikes out against the current railroad strikes and labor unions alike from his pulpit in Plymouth Church, Brooklyn, New York: "I do not say that a dollar a day is enough to support a workingman, but it is enough to support a man! ... Not enough to support a man and five children if a man would insist on smoking and drinking beer. ... But the man who cannot live on bread and water is not fit to live. ..."

**1914** Czar Nicholas II orders general mobilization of manpower. (WORLD WAR I)

**1916** German saboteurs blow up a munitions plant at Black Tom Island, outside Jersey City, New Jersey. Two people lose their lives in the explosion and property damage is estimated at more than $22,000,000. (WORLD WAR I)

**1918** Sergeant Joyce Kilmer, promising young poet, whose "Trees" is among the best-known American verses, is killed in action in France while on patrol duty with the 165th United States Infantry. (WORLD WAR I)

**1919** Annoyed by a sudden increase of airplanes in the skies, Fred Hoenemann, a farmer in Missouri, gets a temporary injunction prohibiting pilots from flying over his farm. (Many Americans, in 1919, were not happy over the development of aviation. Farmers, in particular, claimed that livestock reacted badly to the "mechanical birds.")

**1937** The American Federation of Radio Artists (AFRA) is organized as a unit of the American Federation of Labor. The new union will embrace all radio performers except musicians.

**1942** President Franklin D. Roosevelt signs the bill creating the WAVES, "Women Appointed for Voluntary Emergency Service" in the U.S. Navy. The auxiliary agency will be staffed by 11,000 women and Miss Mildred McAfee, president of Wellesley College, will serve as director. (WORLD WAR II)

**1948** Former Communist Elizabeth Bentley charges before two congressional committees that former U.S. wartime government officials helped her get classified information for Russia when she was a member of a Communist spy ring.

**1953** Race riots break out in Chicago's Trumbull Park housing project, up until now an all-white community, after a Negro family moves in to take up residence. (For 3 years following this date, the community was under a practically permanent police guard.)

## JULY 31

**1777** The Marquis de Lafayette is commissioned a major general in the Continental Army by Congress.

**1792** David Rittenhouse, Director of the Mint, lays the cornerstone of the building being built in Philadelphia for the Mint, the first building of the U.S. government.

**1845** The saxophone, invented by the Belgian musical instrument maker Adolphe Sax some 5 years earlier, is officially introduced into the military bands of the French Army.

**1939** The Federal Theatre Project of the Work Projects Administration, originated by the New Deal in 1936, goes out of existence.

**1940** Adolf Hitler bans the practicing of Christian Science throughout Germany.

**1943** The French Committee of National Liberation appoints General Henri Giraud commander-in-chief of all French military forces and General Charles de Gaulle permanent chairman of the Committee of National Defense. (WORLD WAR II)

**1945** The French traitor Pierre Laval, denied refuge in Spain, flies to Austria where he surrenders to U.S. occupation authorities in Linz. (WORLD WAR II)

**1947** The Smugglers' Union in Hendaye, France, goes on strike in protest against customs guards who are permitting French citizens to cross into Spain to buy fruit and wine. The union claims this action is "sabotaging the smuggling business."

**1948** As 900 airplanes fly overhead, President Harry S. Truman dedicates the New York International Airport at Idlewild Field in New York City. (NOTE: Following the assassination of President John F. Kennedy, the Airport was renamed Kennedy International Airport.)

**1949** The current interest in uranium prospecting prompts a New York sporting-goods store to advertise "a large stock of Geiger Counters at $54.50 each. Operates on flashlight batteries and fits in a coat pocket. Carry it with you to detect uranium deposits."

**1953** Senator Robert A. Taft of Ohio, majority leader of the U.S. Senate, dies in New York City.

# AUGUST

## AUGUST 1

**1659** William Prynne, English Puritan and Member of Parliament, starts his crusade against women's bobbed hair. Prynne accuses English gentlewomen of "... gonne so farre past shame, past modesty, grace and nature, as to clip their haire like men with lockes and foretops...."

**1790** Seventeen U.S. marshals, aided by 600 assistant marshals, start tabulating the first U.S. Census. When the work is completed, the totals show a national population of 3,929,214 in 17 states. (Many citizens dodged the census-takers, thinking they were to be interviewed for future tax-listings.)

**1794** Beginning of the Whiskey Rebellion in Pennsylvania as 7,000 armed men assemble in Allegheny County, demonstrating against the excise tax imposed on the manufacture of alcoholic beverages. (The insurrection came to an end when President George Washington dispatched two divisions of militia to Fayette County. The tax was repealed in 1801 when Thomas Jefferson became President.)

**1876** Colorado Day is established as an annual holiday in that state, commemorating the day when President Ulysses S. Grant signed the proclamation admitting Colorado into the Union as the 38th state.

**1907** The U.S. Air Force traces its beginning to this date when an Aeronautical Division is set up in the Office of the Chief Signal Officer, U.S. Army. The new division will supervise all matters pertaining to military ballooning, air machines, and kindred subjects.

**1914** As a follow-up to Austria's declaration of war on Serbia on July 28, Germany declares war on Russia. German and French border patrols exchange shots. Formal mobilization orders are issued in France and Germany, and transatlantic liner service between New York and continental Europe is suspended. (WORLD WAR I)

**1933**    Carl Hubbell, the New York Giants' southpaw pitcher, pitches his 45th consecutive scoreless inning.

**1938**    The craze for "jitterbug" dancing brings out 7,500 "jive" enthusiasts to New York's Madison Square Garden for the Jitterbug Jubilee. The music is supplied alternately by the bands of Benny Goodman and Count Basie.

**1940**    John Fitzgerald Kennedy, who graduated from Harvard in June, publishes his first book, *Why England Slept,* a study of that nation's recent appeasement policies. (He was 23 years old.)

**1943**    Americans are disturbed by race riots in New York's Harlem district, after 5 Negroes are killed, 500 injured, and 500 more jailed. The riots followed exaggerated reports that a Negro soldier had been shot by a policeman.

**1946**    The U.S. Atomic Energy Commission is established.

**1955**    The Georgia Board of Education orders all Negro teachers in the state holding membership in the National Association for the Advancement of Colored People to resign from that organization by September 15 or have their teaching licenses revoked for "life." (The Negro organization had incurred the displeasure of Georgia officials because of its campaign against segregated schools in the state.)

## AUGUST 2

**1824**    The City Fathers of New York open a new avenue, from Art Street to 13th Street, that is destined to rank among the world's most celebrated thoroughfares. Its name: Fifth Avenue.

**1858**    Boston and New York install the first street letter boxes for the collection of mail.

**1914**    Russia invades Germany, and Germany invades France, Belgium, and Luxembourg, ignoring the neutrality of the latter two countries. In Berlin, crowds march up and down Unter den Linden roaring, "War! War! War with Russia!" (WORLD WAR I)

**1923**    The nation is shocked by the sudden death of President Warren G. Harding in a San Francisco hotel, on his return from a trip to Alaska.

**1927**    President Calvin Coolidge summons reporters to the Summer White House at Black Hills, South Dakota, and makes history with his one-sentence statement: "I do not choose to run for President in 1928."

**1934**    On the death of President Paul von Hindenburg, Adolf Hitler proclaims himself Reichsfuehrer of Germany, thus becoming that nation's absolute dictator. (Commenting on Hitler's coup, the *Paris Temps* said on this date: "There is no longer a German Republic; no longer a German constitution; no longer a German government. There is only the Fuehrer Hitler with absolute powers, of which the Hohenzollerns never dreamed, sole master after God of the German people.")

**1936**    Jesse Owens, with a time of 0:10:2, sets a new world's record for the 100-meter run in the Olympic Games at Berlin, Germany.

**1939**    The search for an atom bomb begins as Dr. Albert Einstein writes a letter to President Franklin D. Roosevelt advising him that German scientists are trying to find methods of manufacturing such bombs. Dr. Einstein begs the President to start an atomic research project in the United States. Roosevelt decides to initiate the project at once.

**1939**    President Franklin D. Roosevelt signs into law the Hatch Act, a statute that limits expenditures in national political campaigns and restricts the roles of civil servants in political conventions, campaigns, and elections.

**1943**    Lieutenant (j.g.) John F. Kennedy of the U.S. Navy becomes a hero in combat in the Solomon Islands. When his PT-109 boat is split by a Japanese destroyer, the young skipper swims to a nearby island, towing one of his injured men to safety by gripping the straps of the crewman's life preserver belt in his teeth. ("This is how it feels to be killed."—Kennedy's later account of the words that went through his mind during this ordeal.)

**1944**    Lieutenant Joseph P. Kennedy, Jr., a Navy pilot, is killed as his plane explodes over the coast of Belgium. ("Joe was the star of our family. He did everything better than the rest of us. If he had lived, he would have gone on into politics . . ."—John F. Kennedy).

**1945**    At the Potsdam Conference in Germany, which began on July 17, the United States, Britain,* and Russia establish a Council of Foreign Ministers to prepare treaties of peace with Germany, Italy, Rumania, Bulgaria, Austria, Hungary, and Finland. At the same time, the Big Three sets up a control council to govern Germany, carry out the terms of German demilitarization, and establish the conditions of German reparation. (WORLD WAR II)

**1954**    The U.S. Senate votes, 75 to 12, to form a select committee to weigh a motion of censure against Senator Joseph R. McCarthy (R., Wis.).

**1959**    Despite the fact that they live behind the Iron Curtain, 100,000 residents of Warsaw line the route of Vice President Richard Nixon's motorcade and give him an enthusiastic welcome during his visit to Poland.

* The top-ranking conferees at Potsdam originally were President Harry Truman, Prime Minister Winston Churchill, and Premier Joseph Stalin. On July 25, however, as a result of the Labor Party victory in the British elections, the new Prime Minister, Clement Attlee, flew to the Conference to replace Mr. Churchill.

# AUGUST 3

**1492**   Christopher Columbus sails from Palos, Spain, for the New World, with a convoy of three tiny vessels, the *Santa María,* the *Niña,* and the *Pinta,* and not quite a hundred men.

**1907**   As part of President Theodore Roosevelt's policy of "trust busting," the Standard Oil Company of Indiana is indicted for receiving rebates, a violation of the Elkins Law of 1903. Judge Kenesaw Mountain Landis, of the U.S. District Court in Chicago, rules the corporation guilty and fines it $29,240,000. (The fine was set aside in 1908.)

**1914**   Germany declares war on France. England announces she will protect France from naval attack. (WORLD WAR I)

**1923**   As the follow-up to the death of President Warren G. Harding, Vice President Calvin Coolidge, vacationing at his father's farm in Plymouth, Vermont, takes the oath of office from his father, a justice of the peace, at half-past two in the morning.

**1948**   Whittaker Chambers, a senior editor of *Time Magazine* and an admitted ex-Communist, names Alger Hiss, former U.S. Department of State official, as a onetime key member of the Communist underground operating in Washington.

**1951**   Scandal rocks the U.S. Military Academy at West Point, New York, when authorities there dismiss 90 cadets, including most of the members of the football team, for cheating in examinations.

**1954**   The largest known divorce settlement in history to date is awarded to Mrs. Barbara (Bobo) Rockefeller as her marriage to Winthrop Rockefeller is terminated. Mrs. Rockefeller receives a $5,500,000 settlement—about two million dollars short of the sum the United States paid Russia in the purchase of Alaska. (Mrs. Rockefeller no longer holds the record, however. *See March 1.*)

**1957**   The British Royal Family is the target of outspoken criticism from Lord Altrincham, a Tory reform leader. The peer attacks the monarchy for "failing to move with the times" and describes the speeches of Queen Elizabeth II as "a pain in the neck."

**1958**   The atomic-powered U.S. submarine *Nautilus* makes history's first underseas crossing of the North Pole.

# AUGUST 4

**1735**   Freedom of the press is established in the United States when John Peter Zenger, publisher of the *New York Weekly Journal,* wins an acquittal of libel charges preferred by Governor William Crosby. The royal governor had sought to censor Zenger's attacks on the Crown. ("The question before the court and you, gentlemen of the jury, is not of small or private concern. It is not the cause of a poor printer, nor of New York alone, which you are trying. It is the best cause. It is the cause of liberty."—Andrew Hamilton, who defended Zenger.)

**1790**    The beginning of the U.S. Coast Guard: The United States is provided with its first naval protection when the Revenue Cutter Service is organized on this date by an act of the first Congress. Alexander Hamilton, first Secretary of Treasury, was authorized to develop a 10-ship antismuggling fleet at a cost not to exceed $10,000. (The service received the name of Coast Guard on January 28, 1915.)

**1912**    Theodore Roosevelt, arriving in Chicago for the nominating convention of the newly formed Progressive Party, answers a reporter's question about the state of his health: "I feel as strong as a bull moose." (The next day, the Progressive Party was nicknamed the Bull Moose Party.)

**1914**    As a result of the violation of Belgium's neutrality, England declares war on Germany. At the same time, the United States issues a proclamation of neutrality. (WORLD WAR I)

**1916**    In a treaty with Denmark, the United States acquires the Virgin Islands for $25,000,000.

**1944**    Nazi police kick open the door of a hidden room in the heart of Amsterdam and capture 14-year-old Anne Frank and 7 other Jews. All 8 are carried off to the notorious Belsen concentration camp. (The 8 persons had lived together in one room concealed from the Nazis for 728 days. All were put to death, except Anne's father, Otto Frank, who came back to the house after the war and found his daughter's famous diary, since read by millions of people throughout the world.)

**1955**    After more than 2½ years spent as prisoners of the Chinese Communists, 11 U.S. Air Force fliers are released and reach Hong Kong. (The airmen had been captured during the Korean War on January 12, 1953, and charged with espionage.)

**1963**    Newspapers report that Joseph Valachi, a former longtime member of the so-called "Cosa Nostra," has been supplying the Federal Bureau of Investigation with information about a national crime syndicate. U.S. authorities, fearful of attempts to murder Valachi, are holding him in secret protective custody.

**1964**    The bodies of the three missing civil rights workers—Michael Schwerner, Andrew Goodman of New York, and James Chaney of Mississippi—are found by federal agents in a newly built earth dam near Philadelphia, Mississippi. Investigation shows that all three had been murdered. (*See June 23*)

## AUGUST 5

**1858**    Through the persistent efforts of Cyrus W. Field, the first cable across the Atlantic Ocean is completed, stretching between Trinity Bay, Newfoundland, and Valentia, Ireland—a distance of 1,950 statute miles. (Eleven days later, Queen Victoria and President Buchanan exchange messages.)

**1861** For the first time in its history, the U.S. government levies a tax on income, all income in excess of $800 to be taxed at a rate of 3 percent.

**1861** Congress abolishes flogging in the Army.

**1864** Out to control the Confederacy's last port on the Gulf of Mexico, the federal fleet fights the Battle of Mobile Bay in the War between the States, to the accompaniment of Commander David G. Farragut's historic words: "Damn the torpedoes, full speed ahead."

**1867** President Andrew Johnson asks for the resignation of Secretary of War Edwin M. Stanton, suspecting that the Secretary is conspiring with congressional leaders to balk his Reconstruction Policy. Stanton, however, refuses to tender his resignation.

**1876** "Wild Bill" Hickok, U.S. marshal and one of the most colorful figures of the Wild West, is killed in a saloon in Deadwood, South Dakota, by Jack McCall, whose brother had been shot down by Hickok.

**1912** The Progressive Party holds its first political convention at the Coliseum in Chicago. Eighteen hundred disgruntled Republicans, having bolted the regular Republican party convention which nominated William Howard Taft in June, choose Theodore Roosevelt as candidate for the Presidency and Hiram Johnson for Vice President.

**1917** The entire National Guard of the United States is drafted into the Army. (WORLD WAR I)

**1936** General John Metaxas, Premier of Greece, proclaims a dictatorship in Greece under King George II.

**1949** A violent earthquake in Ecuador razes 50 towns and kills about 6,000 people.

**1953** "Operation Big Switch"—the exchange of prisoners of war between the United Nations command and the Chinese and North Koreans—takes place at Panmunjom, Korea. (By September 6, the exchange was completed, all prisoners who desired repatriation having been returned by that date.)

**1963** In Moscow, U.S. Secretary of State Rusk, Britain's Foreign Secretary Lord Home, and the Soviet Foreign Minister Gromyko sign the treaty outlawing nuclear tests in the earth's atmosphere, in space and underseas.

## AUGUST 6

**1809** Birth of Alfred, Lord Tennyson, longtime poet laureate of England.

**1825** Bolivia's Independence Day, marking the date on which that nation secured her independence from Peru.

**1890** William Kemmler is electrocuted at the State Prison in Auburn, New York, the first person in the United States to be so punished for a murder charge. (Kemmler had been convicted of murdering Tillie Ziegler in Buffalo, New York.)

**1914** Mrs. Woodrow Wilson, the first wife of the President of the United States, dies in the White House.

**1914** Austria and Russia declare war. President Woodrow Wilson of the United States offers to serve as peace mediator between the belligerents. (WORLD WAR I)

**1926** Miss Gertrude Ederle of New York becomes the first American woman to swim the English Channel. While accomplishing this feat, Miss Ederle floats on her back on seven different occasions while she is served chicken broth from a trailing tugboat. Her total swimming time is 14 hours, 31 minutes.

**1926** Talking moving pictures are seen for the first time today when two different short films, produced by Warner Brothers, are exhibited at the Warner Theatre in New York. (The first film presented in clear sound the New York Philharmonic-Symphony Orchestra and the voices of Marion Talley, Anna Case, and Giovanni Martinelli. In the second film, however, the voices of John Barrymore and the other members of the cast were inaudible.)

**1930** At 9:15 P.M., Joseph Force Crater, a justice of the New York State Supreme Court, steps into a taxicab on West 45th Street in New York City and disappears into complete oblivion. (The disappearance of Crater has never been cleared up and ranks with the great unsolved mysteries of all times.)

**1940** Battle of Africa starts as the Italians invade British Somaliland. (WORLD WAR II)

**1945** The White House announces that an atomic bomb, the first of its kind to be used on a military objective, has been dropped on Hiroshima, Japan. Of a population of 343,969, the casualties reported were: 78,150 killed, 37,425 injured, and 13,083 missing. President Harry Truman, in making the announcement of the bomb attack to the world, says in part: "It is an atomic bomb. It is a harnessing of the basic power of the universe. The force from which the sun draws its power has been loosed against those who brought war to the Far East." (WORLD WAR II)

**1961** Major Gherman Stepanovich Titov, Russia's second astronaut, makes 17½ orbits around the earth.

## AUGUST 7

**1782** The Order of the Purple Heart, a decoration for military merit, is established by George Washington.

**1789** Congress creates the U.S. War Department.

**1861** Thaddeus S. C. Lowe, pioneer aviator and organizer of the nation's first balloon corps, is named official "military aeronaut" of Union forces in the War between the States. Lowe's strongest supporter is President Lincoln who instructed him to build a balloon for field service at a salary of five dollars a day during construction.

**1912**   Governor Woodrow Wilson of New Jersey accepts the Democratic nomination for President but warns the Democratic Party that he will conduct a dignified campaign: "A presidential campaign may easily degenerate into a mere personal contest and so lose its real dignity. There is no indispensable man."

**1928**   The American dollar bill begins to shrink, appearing today in a size one-third smaller than bills issued previously by the Treasury.

**1934**   The U.S. Court of Appeals in Washington strikes a heavy blow at censorship when it rules against the government's attempt to confiscate and ban all copies of James Joyce's controversial book, *Ulysses*. (The court pointed out that if the book could be banned for its erotic passages, so could *Romeo and Juliet, Hamlet*, and parts of the *Odyssey*.)

**1942**   U.S. Marines launch America's first offensive battle of World War II when they land on Guadalcanal in the Solomon Islands. (WORLD WAR II)

**1945**   In the Philippines, a 45-day furlough in the United States is offered by General MacArthur to American soldiers who capture any "live Japanese general."

**1947**   The Pacific Raft Expedition, led by the Norwegian scientist Thor Heyerdahl on the raft *Kon-Tiki*, ends on a reef in Tuamotu Archipelago, having drifted 4,000 miles in 15 weeks. (The scientist and five associates set out on April 29 from Peru to prove that pre-Incan Indians could have colonized the Polynesian Islands by drifting to them on ocean currents.)

**1954**   Dr. Roger Bannister, 25, of England, defeats John Landy, 24, of Australia, in the "mile of a century" race in the British Empire Games at Vancouver, British Columbia. Bannister is timed at 3 minutes, 58.8 seconds; Landy at 3 minutes, 59.6 seconds.

**1955**   *The New York Times* reports that John D. Rockefeller, Sr., and his son, John D. Rockefeller, Jr., contributed two-and-a-half to three billion dollars during the past hundred years "to promote the well-being of mankind."

**1957**   Col. Rudolf Abel, described as the director of a Russian spy ring operating in the United States, is indicted in New York on espionage charges and sentenced to 30 years in prison. (*See February 10*)

**1963**   Mrs. John F. Kennedy becomes the first President's wife since the days of Mrs. Grover Cleveland to give birth to a baby during her husband's term of office. The President's second son is to be named Patrick Bouvier Kennedy. (*See August 9*)

# AUGUST 8

**1588**    Near the French port of Gravelines, Sir Francis Drake destroys the Spanish Armada, his English fleet accomplishing what he calls "singeing the King of Spain's beard."

**1911**    The membership of the House of Representatives in the United States is fixed at 435, one member for each 211,877 inhabitants.

**1923**    Benny Goodman, only 14 years old, begins a musical career that is to bring him an international reputation. The youngster is hired for his first professional job as the band leader on a Chicago excursion boat tells him to pick up his clarinet and report for work.

**1940**    The German Luftwaffe begins the great daylight attacks on the British Isles which will continue unabated until October 31 and which will cost her 2,375 aircraft destroyed, many hundreds more damaged. The RAF loses 733 aircraft, 375 pilots killed, 358 wounded. (This carefully planned assault was intended to knock out the Royal Air Force and was known throughout the war as the Battle of Britain, not to be confused with the London Blitz which began on the following September 7 and which was an unsuccessful attempt to demoralize the populace of that city.) (WORLD WAR II)

**1945**    President Harry Truman signs the ratification of the United Nations Charter.

**1945**    The Soviet Union declares war on Japan 7 days before that nation agrees to unconditional surrender. (WORLD WAR II)

**1950**    Florence Chadwick, 31, of San Diego, California, swims the English Channel in 13 hours, 28 minutes, a new speed record for women.

**1953**    The United States signs a mutual security pact with the Republic of Korea.

**1955**    Delegates from 72 nations open the First International Conference on the Peaceful Uses of Atomic Energy in Geneva, Switzerland.

**1963**    A gang of masked robbers halt and rob a Glasgow to London mail train of the equivalent of $7,368,095 near Cheddington, England. Police call the holdup the largest armed robbery ever carried out. (*See April 16*)

# AUGUST 9

**1593**    Birth of Izaak Walton, "The Father of Angling," and author of the fisherman's handbook, *The Compleat Angler*. ("Doubt not but angling will prove to be so pleasant that it will prove to be, like virtue, a reward to itself.")

252

**1638** Jonas Bronck becomes the first European settler in what is now the Bronx, New York, having emigrated from Holland to the New World.

**1831** The first train in the United States to be drawn by a steam locomotive makes its run between Albany and Schenectady, New York.

**1848** Chanting their slogan of "Free soil, free speech, free labor and free men," the antislave Free Soil Party nominates Martin Van Buren for President of the United States and Charles Francis Adams for Vice President.

**1902** Queen Victoria's son, the Prince of Wales, is crowned King Edward VII of Great Britain, following his mother's death.

**1942** Mohandas K. Gandhi is arrested by the British and interned until 1944. (Gandhi had offered to cooperate with the British in World War II if India was given immediate independence. When the British rejected his offer, the Mahatma organized resistance programs, resulting in his arrest.)

**1945** The second atom bomb is dropped on Japan, this one on the city of Nagasaki. More than half of the city is wiped from the map and 18,000 buildings completely destroyed. Of the city's 250,000 population, almost 40,000 are killed and some 80,000 injured. (WORLD WAR II)

**1954** French troops arrest over 1,000 Moroccans after 13 persons had been killed and 30 wounded during a 2-day period of rioting by Nationalist forces at Port Lyautey and Fez. The outbreaks followed a general strike called by the Nationalists to protest the exile of the former Sultan, Sidi Mohammed ben Youssef.

**1963** Americans grieve with President and Mrs. John F. Kennedy when their infant son, born on August 7, dies in a Boston children's hospital.

## AUGUST 10

**1776** A committee, made up of Benjamin Franklin, John Adams, and Thomas Jefferson, suggests "E Pluribus Unum" as the motto for the Great Seal of the United States.

**1792** In France, the monarchy is overthrown when the Paris Commune attacks the Royal Palace, driving King Louis XVI to the French Legislative Assembly for sanctuary.

**1809** Independence Day in Ecuador: while complete independence will not be achieved until 1822, the first blow for freedom from Spain is struck today in this South American country.

**1821** Missouri, the 24th state, is admitted into the Union.

**1833** Chicago, population about 200, is incorporated as a village.

**1846** Congress creates the Smithsonian Institution in Washington, naming it for an English scientist, James Smithson, who bequeathed his fortune to the United States in 1826 for the establishment of an institution that would "increase and diffuse knowledge among men." (Smithson's legacy had been shipped over to the United States in 105 bags, each containing one thousand sovereigns, the American equivalent of more than $500,000.)

**1874** Birth of Herbert Clark Hoover, 31st President of the United States, at West Branch, Iowa. (On his 80th birthday, in 1954, an estimated 12,000 persons greeted the former President at his birthplace.)

**1921** The beginning of Franklin Roosevelt's ordeal: After swimming in the icy water of the Bay of Fundy, Franklin D. Roosevelt is stricken with poliomyelitis at his summer home in Campobello Island, Canada.

**1943** Beginning of the sixth war conference between President Franklin D. Roosevelt and Prime Minister Winston Churchill, in Quebec. (The two leaders ended their talks on August 24, at which time they issued a statement saying that their meeting "turned very largely upon the war against Japan and the bringing of effective aid to China....") (WORLD WAR II)

**1945** The Japanese offer to surrender to the Allies if their Emperor is left on the throne. (On August 11 the Allies reply that the Emperor might keep his throne if he will bow to the orders of an occupation commander.) (WORLD WAR II)

**1947** William P. Odom flies alone around the world at a record speed of 19,645 miles in 73 hours, 5 minutes, 11 seconds.

**1954** Workers of the Studebaker automobile manufacturing plant at South Bend, Indiana, vote to accept wage cuts of $12 to $20 a week to help the corporation recover from a sales slump.

## AUGUST 11

**1894** Kelly's Hobo Army, led by an unemployed agitator named "Hobo" Kelly and composed of some 1,200 unemployed and discontented men from the western states, is driven across the Potomac River by federal troops after encamping in the nation's capital since early July.

**1902** Oliver Wendell Holmes is appointed associate justice of the U.S. Supreme Court by President Theodore Roosevelt.

**1909** The first radio SOS in history is sent when the liner *Araphoe*, with its engines disabled, radios for help off Cape Hatteras, North Carolina.

**1919** Germany becomes a republic as the Weimar Constitution is promulgated.

**1919** Andrew Carnegie, retired ironmaster and philanthropist, dies. His will makes news when it is learned that the industrialist had provided annuities for the Prime Minister of Great Britain David Lloyd George, former President of the United States

William Howard Taft, and for the widows of former Presidents Grover Cleveland and Theodore Roosevelt.

**1924**   For the first time, all of the nominees for the Presidency in the November elections are photographed for newsreel motion-picture shorts. President Calvin Coolidge, running on the Republican ticket, is photographed at the White House; Senator Robert LaFollette, Progressive, on the Capitol steps; and John W. Davis, Democratic nominee, at Locust Valley, New York.

**1928**   After being advised officially that he has been named the Republican candidate for President in the November elections, Secretary of Commerce Herbert Hoover accepts the nomination in Palo Alto, California, saying: "We in America today are nearer the final triumph over poverty than ever before in the history of any land."

**1935**   Nazi Storm Troopers stage mass demonstrations against the Jews of Germany. Adolf Hitler's newspaper writes: "A Jew who permits himself to be seen with a German (Aryan) woman publicly, a Jew who in a public dancing place arrogantly shakes his limbs, or who in German bathing places behaves in a loud or conspicuous manner, creates a public nuisance and endangers public order."

**1954**   A formal peace announcement in Indochina ends the 7½-year war in that nation between the victorious Vietminh forces and the government of France.

**1962**   Russia sends a cosmonaut, Andrian G. Nikolayev, into orbit for a long-duration flight. (*See August 12*)

**1963**   Civil rights leaders who have often accused Vice President Lyndon B. Johnson, a native Texan, of being opposed to integration movements are heartened by his words before a Los Angeles audience: "... We know today, as we have known for a hundred years, that it is wrong for tax-paying, vote-casting Americans to be unable to find a bed for the night or meals for their children along the highways of our free and decent society...."

## AUGUST 12

**1658**   A "Rattle Watch" of eight men is established in the Colony of New Amsterdam, the first police force in America.

**1851**   Isaac Singer is granted a patent on his sewing machine and organizes his business in Boston with a capital of 40 dollars.

**1867**   President Andrew Johnson, continuing his feud with Secretary of War Edwin M. Stanton, suspends the Secretary from office and names General Ulysses S. Grant Secretary of War.

**1877**   Thomas Alva Edison works out the principle of the "talking machine" (phonograph) and turns his crude model over to John Kreusi, an assistant, with instructions to manufacture one for demonstration. (Mr. Kreusi was skeptical and told the inventor "Next you will make one to think and eat, I suppose! But, I bet you, Mr. Edison, I bet you two dollars, that it won't work." When the machine was completed and Kreusi heard it work, Edison reminded him of the bet and collected the two dollars.)

**1898**     The peace protocol ending the Spanish American War is signed after hostilities with Spain lasting 3 months and 22 days. As a result of the war, the United States annexes Hawaii, at the request of its government, and eliminates Spain from lands in the New World discovered by Columbus. In addition, the United States will acquire Puerto Rico, Guam, and the Philippines, paying $20,-000,000 for all Spanish claims in the latter territories.

**1941**     Marshal Henri Philippe Pétain, virtual dictator of France, summons the full support of his countrymen in behalf of Nazi Germany, saying that Germany is fighting "in defense of civilization." The Marshal says bluntly that "authority no longer comes from below but is that which I give or which I delegate." (WORLD WAR II)

**1947**     Violent controversy in the United States attends the showings of autumn and winter women's wear featuring the "New Look," a design stressing unusually full dresses reaching nearly to the ankles.

**1948**     Madame Oksana Kasenkina, teacher of children of Russian diplomats stationed in the United States, jumps out a third-story window of the Russian consulate in New York. At Roosevelt Hospital in New York, the Russian teacher claims she has been held prisoner in the consulate pending her forcible return to the Soviet Union. (Madame Kasenkina later received asylum in the United States and subsequently became an American citizen.)

**1959**     Despite the presence of jeering crowds, token desegregation of its public schools is accomplished in Little Rock, Arkansas, after six Negro students are permitted to enroll in that city's senior high schools.

**1960**     Echo I, a balloon satellite measuring 100 feet in diameter, is launched at Cape Canaveral, Florida, and directed into orbit, the largest man-made object thus far thrust into space. The satellite has been designed to aid worldwide communications by reflecting radio and television waves.

**1962**     While his fellow spaceman Nikolayev is still spinning around the earth, another Russian cosmonaut, Pavel R. Popovich, is launched into orbit. (Both men landed back on Russian soil on August 15, Nikolayev having made 64 orbits and Popovich 48.)

## AUGUST 13

**1867**     Augustin Daly's *Under the Gaslight,* one of the most successful melodramas to be staged in the American theatre, opens in New York. A feature of the play is an express train bearing down on a man lashed to the tracks.

**1923**    "Yes, We Have No Bananas" is the Number One hit song of the nation. Written by orchestra leader Frank Silver and his piano player, Irving Conn, the song is such a hit that 500,000 copies of the sheet music have been sold during the first 12 weeks of its publication, a record to date.

**1930**    A new aviation speed record is established when Captain Frank Hawks flies from Los Angeles to New York City in 12 hours, 25 minutes.

**1936**    Delegates arrive in Cleveland for the first convention of Father Charles E. Coughlin's National Union for Social Justice. At the convention, the world is astounded to hear the priest, pastor of Detroit's Shrine of the Little Flower, demand of his followers that they approve a platform that endorses "without any exception whatsoever, all the acts of our ... great leader, Father Charles E. Coughlin. ... His teachings have come to us as manna. ..." Thirty thousand delegates and guests hear Coughlin attack both the Republican and Democratic parties and cheer his plea to support Representative William Lemke of North Dakota as the Union's candidate for the Presidency in the 1936 elections. (*See September 25*)

**1961**    To halt the flow of refugees out of her territory, East Germany seals off the border between East and West Berlin. More than 2,000,000 East Germans have fled the country since 1949. (*See August 15*)

**1963**    Miners David Fellin, Henry Throne, and Louis Bova are trapped 331 feet underground by a mine cave-in near Sheppton, Pennsylvania. (Fourteen days later, drillers were able to reach Fellin and Throne and they were lifted to safety. Mr. Bova lost his life.)

## AUGUST 14

**1900**    Two thousand United States Marines assist in the capture of Peking, China, ending the Boxer Rebellion.

**1911**    As a follow-up to Irving Berlin's "Alexander's Ragtime Band," the craze for "ragtime" music is sweeping all over America, producing a host of new dance steps. According to a Chicago newspaper, the most popular of the new dance steps are "The Kangaroo Dip," "The Crab Step," "The Fish Walk," "The Texas Tommy," "The Grizzly Bear," and the ever-popular "Turkey Trot."

**1929**    The dirigible *Graf Zeppelin* starts out from Friedrichshafen, Germany, on its round-the-world trip with 20 passengers. (The dirigible returned to its home base on September 4, 1929, after visiting Tokyo, Los Angeles, and Lakehurst, New Jersey.)

**1935**    The Social Security Act, establishing old-age benefits and unemployment insurance, is passed by the U.S. Congress.

**1941**    The Atlantic Charter: Washington and London announce simultaneously that President Franklin D. Roosevelt and

Prime Minister Churchill have met "at sea" and agreed on an eight-point plan for world peace to follow "the final destruction of the Nazi tyranny."

**1945**    At 7:00 P.M., Eastern War Time, President Harry S. Truman announces to the nation that Japan has accepted the terms of unconditional surrender and that the hostilities of World War II have come to an end. (Before this day dawned, the fate of every nation under the sun and some two billion people was at stake. The Axis and its five satellites were opposed by the United Nations, an association ultimately of some fifty countries. Only five nations were neutral in the war and the armed forces of the belligerents totaled more than 100,000,000 men and women. United States casualties totaled 1,125,369, almost 400,000 of them dead. Direct cost in dollars to the United States: $330,500,000,000.)

**1964**    A number of Negro grade-school children register at formerly all-white elementary schools in Biloxi, Mississippi, thus becoming the first of their race to break public school segregation barriers in that state.

## AUGUST 15

### Traditional beginning of hay-fever season

**1769**    Birth of Napoleon Bonaparte, French leader and emperor.

**1771**    Birth of Sir Walter Raleigh, Scottish poet and master of the historical romance.

**1914**    With the passage of the government vessel *Ancon* from the Atlantic to the Pacific, the Panama Canal is opened officially to traffic after 10 years of construction.

**1935**    Will Rogers, humorist and cowboy philosopher, and Wiley Post, aviator, are killed when their airplane crashes near Point Barrow, Alaska.

**1940**    Reichsmarshal Hermann Goering of Germany launches the latest Nazi air attack on Great Britain when his fliers begin their "Eagle Attack" from occupied Norway, hoping once more to wipe out the British Air Force. (When it was all over, of the 1,800 German planes thrown into the attack, 76 were lost by the Luftwaffe, 34 by the RAF.) (WORLD WAR II)

**1943**    Sergeant Edward M. Dzuba, of the 305th U.S. Medical Battalion, is awarded the Legion of Merit by the War Department for "originating many unusual and appetizing recipes for the utility of leftover scraps. This ingenuity has greatly reduced food losses from waste and spoilage."

**1944**    Invasion of southern France: United States General Alexander Patch's Seventh Army, supported by British airborne troops, the RAF, and other Allied fliers, and covered by British,

American, and French warships, lands near Toulon, France, on the French Mediterranean Coast. (WORLD WAR II)

**1947** Great Britain ends her 200-year-old rule over India. At the same time, two new sovereign states come into existence, India and Pakistan.

**1948** The Independent Republic of Korea is proclaimed with Seoul named as its capital.

**1961** East German laborers start the construction of the Berlin Wall, 28 miles of concrete and steel girders, surmounted by barbed wire. The wall seals off the border between East and West Berlin. (*See August 13*)

**1962** American newspapers are reporting the biggest cash robbery in U.S. history as they describe the holdup of a mail truck near Plymouth, Massachusetts. (The gang of robbers included five men and one woman and their haul amounted to more than $1,500,000.)

**1963** It is announced in Washington that 2,600 books have been selected as the nucleus for an official White House library. This is the result of a request made by Mrs. John F. Kennedy a year ago for a collection of "the books most essential to an understanding of our national experience." The committee selecting the books has been headed by James T. Babb, Yale University librarian.

# AUGUST 16

**1777** Today is a legal holiday in Vermont, commemorating the Battle of Bennington and the victory of the American forces led by Colonel John Stark over the British.

**1861** The federal government prohibits the states of the Union from trading with the seceding states of the Confederacy.

**1896** Great excitement follows the discovery of gold in the Klondike at Bonanza Creek, Alaska.

**1922** Station WEAF starts to broadcast radio programs from its studios atop the Western Electric Building in New York.

**1923** Steel workers hail the decision of the Carnegie Steel Corporation establishing the 8-hour work day.

**1939** The last stage performance takes place at New York's famous Hippodrome. Demolition crews are to start work tomorrow to tear down the world-famous vaudeville hall.

**1945** Winston Churchill tells the House of Commons that the atom bomb saved the lives of 1,000,000 American and 250,000 British soldiers because the bomb had made an invasion of Japan unnecessary.

**1948** Babe Ruth, the idol of millions of baseball fans, dies in New York.

**1955** There is deep gloom in Brooklyn, New York, as the Brooklyn Dodgers baseball team announces it will play at least seven "home" games in Jersey City's Roosevelt Stadium in 1956 because of decreasing attendance at the Dodgers' Ebbets Field in Brooklyn.

**1956** Adlai E. Stevenson becomes a Presidential contender for the second time as the Democratic National Convention in Chicago nominates him to head the ticket in the forthcoming November elections. An unusual situation develops when Stevenson declines to dictate the choice of his running-mate and calls instead for an "open choice" in the selection of the Vice Presidential nominee. Despite a boom for the candidacy of Senator John F. Kennedy of Massachusetts, the vote finally favors Senator Estes Kefauver of Tennessee.

**1960** The former British crown colony of Cyprus becomes the Republic of Cyprus, with the Cypriote Archbishop Makarios chosen as the tiny state's first president.

## AUGUST 17

**1786** Birth of Davy Crockett, Indian fighter, scout, politician, congressman, and most famous as "The King of the Wild Frontier."

**1790** New York City ceases to be the federal capital as the government moves its headquarters to Philadelphia. (At various times, Congress has met in New York City; Philadelphia, York, and Lancaster, Pennsylvania; Baltimore and Annapolis, Maryland; Trenton and Princeton, New Jersey; and finally in Washington.)

**1807** Robert Fulton's steamboat, the *Clermont,* makes its first run up the Hudson River. The trip from New York to Albany, a distance of about 150 miles, is made in 32 hours.

**1812** At their convention meeting in New York, the Federalist Party nominates DeWitt Clinton to run against James Madison, Republican, for the Presidency.

**1915** A great hurricane strikes at Galveston, Texas, causing the death of 275 persons.

**1915** An ugly story comes to an uglier ending with the lynching and hanging of Leo Frank by a mob in Marietta, Georgia. (This was the most famous American crime of its day. Frank had been sentenced to death for the alleged rape-murder of Mary Phagan, an employee in his Atlanta factory. Because of a good deal of doubt as to his guilt, Georgia's governor had commuted his sentence to life imprisonment. An irate mob broke into prison and kidnapped Frank and then murdered him in Marietta. As bad as the crime itself were the overtones of anti-Semitism, one Atlanta editorial branding the young manufacturer as "that filthy perverted Jew from New York...")

**1933** Lou Gehrig of the New York Yankees' baseball team breaks the record for consecutive games played by one man when he plays in his 1,308th game at St. Louis. Up to this day, the record had been held by Everett Scott, a former Yankee, who played in 1,307 straight games.

**1940**    Wendell L. Willkie, accepting the Republican nomination for the Presidency at his farm in Elwood, Indiana, challenges President Franklin D. Roosevelt to a national debate.

**1945**    Provisional President Charles de Gaulle commutes the death sentence of Marshal Henri Pétain to life imprisonment, after the 89-year-old French hero of World War I had been found guilty of treason for collaborating with the German Nazis during World War II.

**1948**    Alger Hiss, identified as a Communist while he was an important member of the federal government, confronts his accuser, Whittaker Chambers, at a hearing before the House Un-American Activities Committee. Hiss denies emphatically that he was a Communist.

**1962**    An 18-year-old East Berlin boy, Peter Fechter, is shot by East German police as he attempts to make his way across the Berlin Wall. Fechter is left to die on the ground unattended, within full sight of thousands of West Berliners.

## AUGUST 18

**1587**    Virginia Dare is born at Roanoke Island, North Carolina, the first child born in America of English parents.

**1823**    Political campaigning in Maryland is marked by frank intolerance as Benjamin Galloway announces his candidacy for a seat in the state legislature on the "Christian ticket." Mr. Galloway seeks only Christian support and says he does not want the votes of "Jews, Deists, Mohammedans, or Unitarians." (He won the election.)

**1856**    The first milk to be condensed is patented on this date, but the Patent Office doubts the commercial value of the invention.

**1896**    On taking over control of *The New York Times,* Adolph S. Ochs says: "It will be my earnest aim that *The New York Times* gives the news, all the news, in concise and attractive form, in language that is permissible in good society, and give it early, if not earlier, than it can be learned through any other medium."

**1914**    Germany declares war on Russia in World War I.

**1914**    President Woodrow Wilson issues his Proclamation of Neutrality to the nations at war in World War I. ("The United States must be neutral in fact as well as in name. . . . We must be impartial in thought as well as in action.")

**1916**    The birthplace of Abraham Lincoln at Hodginsville, Kentucky, is given to the United States for a national shrine.

**1919**    The Anti-Cigarette League of America is organized in Chicago.

**1923** Helen Wills, 18-year-old Californian, becomes the Women's National Tennis Singles Champion, winning that title from Mrs. Molla Mallory at Forest Hills, New York.

**1924** As a follow-up to the Versailles Peace Treaty ending World War I, French troops begin to evacuate the Ruhr Valley.

**1940** The United States and Canada establish a joint defense plan against possible enemy attack. (WORLD WAR II)

**1954** Assistant Secretary of Labor James E. Wilkins attends a meeting of President Eisenhower's Cabinet, in the absence of Labor Secretary James P. Mitchell. Wilkins is the first Negro ever to attend a Cabinet meeting.

**1963** James H. Meredith is graduated from the University of Mississippi, the first Negro to win a degree from the 115-year-old university. There are no incidents on the campus at Oxford, where 11 months earlier Meredith had been the central figure in race riots that followed his enforced admission into the university. (*See September 30*)

## AUGUST 19

**1812** The U.S. frigate *Constitution* (*Old Ironsides*) fights its famous victorious battle with the British frigate *Guerrière* eastward of Nova Scotia. The American vessel had been lampooned previously by the British Navy as "a bundle of pine boards sailing under a bit of striped bunting."

**1862** Hoping to get the President to come out strongly for full emancipation of Negroes, Horace Greeley, editor of the *New York Tribune* and one of his severest critics, addresses an open letter to Abraham Lincoln: "We think you are strangely and disastrously remiss in the discharge of your official and imperative duty with regard to the emancipation provisions of the new Confiscation Act...." (On August 22, Lincoln replied to Greeley: "My paramount objective in this struggle is to save the Union, and is not either to save or destroy slavery." )

**1890** The Daughters of the American Revolution are organized, membership in the society restricted to those who have at least one ancestor who aided in establishing American independence.

**1918** *Yip Yip Yaphank,* a musical comedy about army life in World War I and written by Sergeant Irving Berlin, opens at the Century Theatre in New York. The musical score of the show includes "Oh, How I Hate to Get Up in the Morning" and "Mandy."

**1934** Germany votes on whether Adolf Hitler shall be the official successor to President von Hindenburg. (Of the 43,500,000 persons who voted, 38,362,763 voted "Ja," and 4,294,654 voted "Nein.")

**1942**    Canadian Commandos, assisted by the British and a few American Rangers, stage a costly raid on Nazi forces stationed in Dieppe, France. (WORLD WAR II)

**1945**    Lieutenant General Jonathan W. Wainwright, hero of the Battle of Corregidor in World War II, is found safe and sound in a Japanese prisoner compound in Sian, Manchuria.

**1953**    Premier Mohammed Mossadegh of Iran, in office for the past 20 months, is ousted in a revolt that climaxes a 3-day feud between the Premier's Nationalists and Iranian Royalists.

**1955**    The worst flood in the history of the northeastern United States strikes 10 states, leaving behind almost 200 dead, 20,000 destroyed or damaged homes, 40,000 homeless people, and 75,000 people without jobs. The total dollar damage amounted to $1.67 billions, more than half that amount being suffered by Connecticut.

**1960**    On the third day of his trial before a three-man tribunal in Moscow, Francis Gary Powers, pilot of the American U-2 plane shot down in the Soviet Union on May 1, is convicted of having "collected information of a strategic significance which constitutes a state . . . secret of the Soviet Union" and sentenced to 10 years confinement. (*See February 10, May 5*)

## AUGUST 20

**1741**    Alaska is discovered by Vitus Jonas Bering, Danish navigator.

**1776**    George Washington eludes the British in Brooklyn, New York, in a dense "London-like fog," and transports his army across the East River to Manhattan during the Revolutionary War.

**1833**    Birthday of Benjamin Harrison, 23rd President of the United States.

**1885**    Theatregoers applaud *The Mikado* by Gilbert & Sullivan as it starts a run at the Fifth Avenue Theatre in New York.

**1914**    Germany occupies Brussels, the capital of Belgium. (WORLD WAR I)

**1940**    Great Britain offers to lend sea-air bases to the United States in return for American naval aid. (WORLD WAR II)

**1940**    In a moving tribute to the courageous men of the Royal Air Force, Prime Minister Winston Churchill tells the House of Commons: "Never in the field of human conflict was so much owed by so many to so few." (WORLD WAR II)

**1941**    The Russians blow up their Dnieper Dam as German troops sweep across the Ukraine. (WORLD WAR II)

**1953**    France forces the nationalist Sultan of Morocco, Sidi Mohammed ben Youssef, off his throne into exile.

**1955**    On the second anniversary of the removal of the nationalist Sultan of Morocco, Sidi Mohammed ben Youssef, natives of Morocco and Algeria start street riots and demonstrations against the French, leaving a reported thousand people dead, and many hundreds wounded.

**1955** Colonel Horace A. Hanes, U.S. Air Force, flies 40,000 feet up in the air, attaining an average speed of 822.135 miles per hour in a Super Sabrejet, a record to date for high-altitude flights.

**1964** As a start toward the beginning of his domestic legislative program aimed at creating "The Great Society," President Lyndon B. Johnson signs the "anti-poverty" bill. Says the President: "... The days of the dole in our country are numbered ..."

## AUGUST 21

**1621** "1 Widow and 11 Maides" are sent from London to Virginia to be sold to wife-seeking bachelors for 120 pounds of tobacco each.

**1858** The Lincoln-Douglas debates begin, marking the start of a political contest between Abraham Lincoln and Stephen A. Douglas for a seat in the U.S. Senate. (The debates, seven in number, lasted until October 15. Despite Lincoln's skill as an orator, Douglas won the election in November.)

**1887** In a game with the New York Giants baseball team, Dan Casey, southpaw pitcher for the Phillies, strikes out in the ninth inning, thus inspiring Ernest L. Thayer's immortal "Casey at the Bat." (*See May 13,* for DeWolf Hopper's first recitation of the poem.)

**1940** The first English children arrive in the United States, seeking temporary haven from German air attacks during World War II.

**1940** Leon Trotsky, 61, Communist revolutionary and one of the principal founders of Soviet Russia, dies in Mexico City, where he had resided in exile since 1937, after receiving wounds at the hands of an alleged agent of Joseph Stalin, Jacques van den Dreschd, alias "Frank Jackson."

**1944** Representatives of the United States, Great Britain, Russia, and China meet at Dumbarton Oaks in Washington, D.C., to plan for the establishment of a postwar international peace organization.

**1950** Members of the United Nations staff move into their new permanent Secretariat Building in New York City.

**1951** The United States orders construction of the world's first atomic submarine.

**1959** For the second time in the year 1959 a new state is admitted into the Union as President Eisenhower officially proclaims Hawaii the 50th state of the United States. Immediately thereafter a new 50-star flag is unfurled at the White House. (*See January 3*)

**1963**    South Vietnam orders martial law after troops and civil police attack Buddhist pagodas and arrest hundreds of Buddhists.

## AUGUST 22

**1762**    The first American woman newspaper editor, Ann Franklin, assumes her duties on *The Newport Mercury*, Newport, Rhode Island.

**1787**    Spectators are amused as John Fitch pilots his side-paddled steamboat on the Delaware River. Most of the observers doubt that Fitch's boat will prove practical.

**1851**    The U.S. yacht *America* outraces the British yacht *Aurora* off Cowes, England, and thus wins the silver trophy offered by the Royal Yacht Society of England. (This trophy has since remained in the United States, successfully defended in many meets.)

**1903**    Barney Dreyfuss, onetime owner of the Pittsburgh Pirates baseball team, addresses a letter to Henry J. Killilea, president of the Boston Red Sox, saying: "The time has come for the National and American Leagues to organize a World Series." This letter is followed by a meeting between the two men in Pittsburgh, where they draw up plans for the first World Series, with the first three games to be played in Boston and the next four in Pittsburgh. The opening game will be October 1, 1903.

**1911**    The world of art is shocked by the theft from the Louvre Museum in Paris of Leonardo da Vinci's famous painting, "Mona Lisa." (The painting was recovered by the museum in 1913.) (*See December 10.*)

**1941**    Nazi troops reach the outskirts of Leningrad, Russia. (WORLD WAR II)

**1956**    At the Cow Palace in San Francisco, President Dwight D. Eisenhower and Vice President Richard M. Nixon are renominated by the Republican National Convention for second terms. (*See November 6*)

**1959**    A story-book romance is climaxed by the marriage of Stephen C. Rockefeller, son of the Governor of New York, to Anne Marie Rasmussen at her parents' home in Soegne, Norway. (For weeks, Americans followed every development in the romance between the young heir to the Rockefeller fortune and the young lady who had recently worked as a maid in his family's household.)

## AUGUST 23

**1500**    Because he was accused of mistreating the natives of Haiti, Christopher Columbus is arrested there and ordered sent back to Spain in chains.

**1630**    For the first time in America, legislation controlling labor is passed in the Massachusetts Bay Colony by Governor John Winthrop and his Court of Assistants who decree that construction laborers be paid at the rate of one shilling a day.

**1775**    King George III of England proclaims the existence of open rebellion in the American colonies.

**1858**    *Ten Nights in a Barroom,* a melodrama with a temperance theme, opens in New York at the National Theatre.

**1879**    Followers of Mary Baker Eddy obtain a charter in Lynn, Massachusetts, giving them permission to organize as "The Church of Christ, Scientist."

**1902**    Fannie Farmer opens her School of Cookery in Boston.

**1914**    Japan declares war on Germany in World War I.

**1923**    The first real comedians of radio broadcasting, Billy Jones and Ernie Hare, go on the air for the Happiness Candy Company, billed as "The Happiness Boys."

**1924**    Mrs. Miriam A. Ferguson, known as "Ma" Ferguson, wins the Democratic nomination for governor of Texas by more than 80,000 votes. (She was elected the following November and became the first woman to serve as a state governor.)

**1926**    Throughout the nation, hundreds of thousands of women mourn the death in New York of the Great Lover of the films, Rudolph Valentino.

**1927**    Sacco and Vanzetti are executed. (Nicola Sacco and Bartolomeo Vanzetti, two Italian workmen residing in the Boston area, were convicted in 1921 of shooting, robbing, and killing two payroll guards in South Braintree, Massachusetts. Despite the fact that both defendants produced alibis, a jury convicted them and they were sentenced to die. Their sentence was protested by thousands of citizens who formed "Sacco and Vanzetti Committees," with the result that the condemned men's cases were reviewed until 1927 when, on this date, they were finally put to death.)

**1937**    The Japanese land at Shanghai. One hundred and seventy-three residents are killed as a shell explodes in the international quarter of that city.

**1947**    Fifteen thousand people attend a concert in Hollywood Bowl to hear Miss Margaret Truman, daughter of the President of the United States, give her first public concert.

**1955**    Two English pilots, John Hackett and Peter Moneypenny, make the first London-New York round trip in one day, flying 6,920 miles in 14 hours, 21 minutes, 45.4 seconds. The fliers left London at 7:17 A.M. and returned to English soil at 9:41 P.M.

**1961**    Communist East Germany imposes new curbs on travel between West and East Berlin. In retaliation, the Western Powers place tanks along the East-West border and the United States warns Russia that continued travel curbs will be interpreted as "an aggressive act."

# AUGUST 24

**A.D. 79**    Thousands of people are killed and the cities of Pompeii and Herculaneum are buried following the eruption of Mt. Vesuvius in Italy.

**1814**    The British capture Washington, D.C., burning the Capitol and the Executive Mansion. President James Madison flees the capital, returning on the evening of August 27.

**1857**    The Panic of 1857 begins, following the failure of the Ohio Life Insurance & Trust Company.

**1909**    Construction crews start to pour concrete in Gatun Locks, the Panama Canal.

**1932**    Amelia Earhart Putnam becomes the first woman to make a transcontinental nonstop flight, taking off from Los Angeles and landing at Newark, New Jersey, after flying approximately 2,600 miles in 19 hours, 5 minutes.

**1939**    While President Franklin D. Roosevelt appeals to Germany to avoid war, Germany and Russia sign a 10-year nonaggression pact.

**1939**    Louis "Lepke" Buchalter, "president" of "Murder, Incorporated," the ruthless organization of vice, racketeering, extortion, and murder that has held New York in its grip from 1928 until the present, surrenders by arrangement to columnist Walter Winchell at Madison Square in New York City. The columnist takes him to Fifth Avenue and 28th Street where J. Edgar Hoover of the Federal Bureau of Investigation is waiting.

**1948**    The Soviet Union closes its consulates in the United States. The next day, the American consulate in Vladivostok is closed, the final act in the current diplomatic breach caused by the defection of Madame Oksana Kasenkina. (*See August 12.*)

**1954**    President Getulio Vargas of Brazil kills himself after the federal army overthrows his regime.

**1954**    President Dwight D. Eisenhower signs into law the Communist Control Act of 1954, outlawing the Communist Party in the United States.

# AUGUST 25

**1718**    The city of New Orleans, Louisiana, is founded and named in honor of the Duke of Orleans of France.

**1829**    The famous steam engine, the "Tom Thumb," races with a horse-drawn car. (The horse won after the engine broke down.)

**1835**    Ann Rutledge, said to be Abraham Lincoln's true love, dies in New Salem, Illinois, at the age of 22.

**1879**    Gilbert & Sullivan's *Pinafore* is performed on a real ship floating in a gigantic tank of water in New York's Madison Square Garden.

**1921** The United States signs a treaty of peace with Germany in Berlin, thereby ending officially the state of war with that nation.

**1924** Divers locate $35,000,000 of the treasure lost on the British cruiser *Laurentic* when that vessel was sunk off the coast of Ireland in World War I.

**1925** The Florida boom is at its height. Property speculation is reaching an all-time high with an estimated 2,000 real estate offices and 25,000 agents operating feverishly in the Miami area alone.

**1928** The Byrd Antarctic Expedition leaves New York in *The City of New York*.

**1939** As British diplomats sign a defense pact with Poland, the first "Anderson Shelters" are installed in the gardens of Buckingham Palace in London to provide safety for the Royal Family from enemy air attacks.

**1942** The Duke of Kent, the youngest brother of King George VI of Great Britain, is killed in an airplane crash en route to Iceland on a mission of war.

**1944** U.S. troops liberate Paris in World War II.

**1950** To forestall a general strike, President Harry S. Truman seizes all railroads throughout the nation.

**1964** At the Democratic National Convention in Atlantic City, New Jersey, the majority of the Mississippi delegation walks out of Convention Hall rather than sign a "loyalty" oath promising to support the national ticket in November. Four members of the delegation remain after signing the pledge. (On August 26, the majority of the Alabama delegation also staged a walkout.)

## AUGUST 26

**1842** The U.S. Congress establishes the beginning of the government's fiscal year as July 1.

**1873** Birthday of Dr. Lee De Forest, physicist, whose invention of the three-element vacuum tube in 1906 made possible modern electronics technology, including radio, television, and radar.

**1883** Beginning on this date and continuing the next day, the great volcano at Krakatoa in the Netherlands East Indies erupts with a violent explosion, destroying two-thirds of the island. Sea waves occur as far away as Cape Horn. (An estimated 36,000 persons lost their lives in the disaster.)

**1918** *Lightnin'*, starring Frank Bacon, the first play to run more than a thousand performances, opens at the Gaiety Theatre in New York.

**1920** Sex rears its head constitutionally as the Nineteenth Amendment to the U.S. Constitution, providing for suffrage for women, is declared operative by the Secretary of State. ("The right of citizens of the United States to vote shall not be denied or abridged by the United States or by any State on account of sex.")

**1932**   The U.S. government proclaims a moratorium on foreclosures by the holders of first mortgages, thereby attempting to ease the plight of householders during the dark days of the Depression.

**1934**   Adolf Hitler says he seeks peace with France and, at the same time, demands the return of the Saar to Germany.

**1942**   Wendell L. Willkie, unsuccessful Republican candidate for President in the 1940 elections, leaves New York for his "One World" trip as a special envoy for President Franklin D. Roosevelt.

**1948**   Mildred Elizabeth Gillars, known to thousands of American soldiers in World War II as "Axis Sally," is flown to the United States from Berlin by the Department of Justice to face charges of espionage and treason because of her wartime propaganda broadcasts for the Germans.

**1964**   President Lyndon B. Johnson becomes the second Presidential candidate in the history of the Democratic Party to be nominated by acclamation.* Jubilant delegates to the Democratic National Convention in Atlantic City nominate him for the Presidency and Senator Hubert H. Humphrey of Minnesota for the Vice Presidency. (*See November 3*)

## AUGUST 27

**550 B.C.**   Birth of Confucius, Chinese sage and philosopher.

**1660**   The published books of John Milton are burned in London because of his attacks on King Charles II.

**1859**   Colonel Edwin L. Drake drills the first oil well in the United States near Titusville, Pennsylvania, the beginning of the commercial development of the American petroleum industry.

**1862**   The Italian patriot Giuseppe Garibaldi is seized as he is on his way to capture the city of Rome.

**1894**   Despite the veto of President Grover Cleveland, Congress votes to assess a 2 percent tax on incomes over $4,000.

**1904**   The first automobile driver to be jailed for speeding is given a 5-day sentence in the Newport (Rhode Island) County Jail.

**1908**   Lyndon Baines Johnson, 36th President of the United States, is born near Stonewall, Texas.

**1912**   A new literary hero is introduced to the American public as Edgar Rice Burroughs' *Tarzan of the Apes* appears in a magazine. (Since its first appearance, the various sagas of Tarzan have sold at least 25,000,000 copies in 56 different languages.)

---

* President Franklin D. Roosevelt had also been nominated by acclamation by the 1936 Democratic Convention.

**1918** Because of the fuel shortage in the United States, owners of automobiles, motorcycles, and motorboats are asked not to use them for pleasure trips on Sundays. (WORLD WAR I)

**1928** The Kellogg-Briand Pact to outlaw war is signed by representatives of 5 nations at Paris. (The pact was ratified by the U.S. Senate on January 15, 1929.)

**1939** Adolf Hitler serves notice on England and France that Germany wants Danzig and the Polish Corridor.

**1945** Admiral William F. Halsey, aboard the battleship *Missouri,* leads the U.S. Third Fleet into Sagami Bay, 30 miles south of Tokyo, the first step in General MacArthur's occupation of Japan. (WORLD WAR II)

**1949** Eight persons are injured when a hostile anti-Communist mob breaks up a Paul Robeson concert outside of Peekskill, New York. (A more serious riot at Peekskill occurred 8 days later, on September 4, as 15,000 people showed up at a second concert scheduled by Mr. Robeson, many of them members of war veteran groups. Almost 150 persons were injured.)

**1964** At the Democratic National Convention in Atlantic City, New Jersey, Mrs. John F. Kennedy, widow of the late President, is the guest of honor at a reception attended by thousands of people. Later, President Johnson makes his speech of acceptance for the nomination and pledges "answers, not retreats; unity, not division; hope, not fear...."

## AUGUST 28

**1749** Birth of Johann Wolfgang von Goethe, German poet, dramatist, and philosopher.

**1828** Birth of Count Leo Tolstoy, Russian novelist, essayist, philosopher, and social reformer.

**1830** The Baltimore & Ohio Railroad tries out the first American-built locomotive, the "Tom Thumb," built by Peter Cooper.

**1833** The British Parliament bans slavery throughout the Empire. Seven hundred thousand slaves are to be liberated on August 1, 1834.

**1917** Hoping to win the sympathy of President Woodrow Wilson, 10 suffragettes picket the White House in Washington, and are finally arrested for disturbing the peace.

**1922** The first "commercial" in radio broadcasting is heard over Station WEAF in New York. The sponsor of the radio advertisement is the Queensboro Realty Company of Jackson Heights, New York, who paid the radio station $100 for 10 minutes of air time.

**1941** Ambassador Kichisaburo Nomura delivers a note from Japanese Premier Konoye to President Franklin D. Roosevelt, saying that Japan wishes to "pursue courses of peace in harmony with the fundamental principles to which the people and Government of the United States are committed."

**1947**  Because of her shaky economic condition and shortage of foodstuffs, England cuts her meat ration to the equivalent of 20 cents a person a week and orders an end to nonessential automobile driving after October 1.

**1950**  A storm of protests follows the action taken today by the General Foods Corporation in dropping actress Jean Muir from the cast of their sponsored television program, "The Aldrich Family." Miss Muir had been accused by the editors of *Red Channels*, a book listing alleged Communist and Communist sympathizers in radio and television, of being a "fellow traveler."

**1961**  Opera lovers are assured of an uninterrupted season at the Metropolitan Opera House in New York as Secretary of Labor Arthur J. Goldberg successfully arbitrates a rift between management and labor.

**1962**  Seventy-five Northern clergymen of all religious faiths are arrested in Albany, Georgia, after holding a prayer demonstration there against racial discrimination. For the past month, the Reverend Martin Luther King, Jr., has been leading Negro protests against Albany segregation practices.

**1963**  The March on Washington: 100 years and 240 days after Abraham Lincoln appealed to the slaves he had emancipated to "abstain from all violence," 200,000 Negroes and whites from all over the United States hold an orderly and peaceful rally in the nation's capital, demanding full civil rights. (It was the greatest assembly for a redress of grievances ever held in Washington.)

## AUGUST 29

**1852**  Brigham Young proclaims the "celestial law of marriage," thus signifying his approval of the practice of polygamy among Mormons.

**1864**  The Democrats, meeting at Chicago, nominate General George B. McClellan for President and George H. Pendleton of Ohio for Vice President.

**1901**  Carrie Nation, Kansas temperance agitator, creates a stir in New York City as she belabors City Hall officials and then, armed with her hatchet, descends on the saloon operated by the former boxing champion John L. Sullivan. The brawny pugilist declines to see Mrs. Nation, instructing a messenger to "tell her I'm sick in bed."

**1921**  Newspapers report that members of the Ku Klux Klan have tarred and feathered 43 Texans in the past 7 days.

**1945**    Missing for 25 months after participating in an air bat-tle over New Guinea, U.S. Marine hero Major Gregory (Pappy) Boyington is found alive in a prisoner-of-war camp in Japan.

**1948**    Henry A. Wallace, Presidential candidate of the Pro-gressive Party, is heckled and pelted with eggs at a political rally in Durham, North Carolina.

**1957**    As the filibuster over the 1957 Civil Rights Bill comes to an end, Senator Strom Thurmond (then Democrat, South Car-olina) establishes the record to date for the longest speech by one Senator, 24 hours, 18 minutes. Despite his efforts and those of other Southern senators, the bill is passed on this date, the first Civil Rights Bill since the Reconstruction.

## AUGUST 30

**30 B.C.**    Cleopatra commits suicide by permitting an asp to bite her.

**1637**    Ann Hutchinson is banished from Massachusetts, hav-ing been charged with "traducing the ministers and the ministry."

**1780**    Benedict Arnold, general in the Revolutionary Army, decides to sell his honor for a "pot of gold." Specifically, Arnold promises the British General Sir Henry Clinton that he will sur-render the American fort at West Point, which is under his com-mand. (Arnold's treachery was discovered by the capture of Major John André, a British spy, who was carrying a message from Arnold to Clinton. The hapless André was tried and hanged, but Arnold escaped.)

**1830**    The Baltimore & Ohio Railroad abandons the horse-powered locomotive for steam.

**1862**    The Union Army commanded by Major General John Pope is defeated by Confederate troops in the Second Battle of Bull Run.

**1893**    Huey Long's birthday; legal holiday in Louisiana.

**1924**    Diplomats in London sign the Dawes Plan, an agreement calling for the payment of reparations by Germany to her former enemies in World War I.

**1932**    Hermann Goering, often referred to as the "Number Two Nazi," is elected president of the German Reichstag.

**1945**    General Douglas MacArthur arrives in Japan and sets up headquarters in the New Grand Hotel in Yokohama. At the same time, U.S. Marines land in Tokyo Bay and take over the Yokosaka Naval Base there. (WORLD WAR II)

**1961**    The long stalemate between the United States and the Soviet Union revolving around the question of a proposed limita-tion of nuclear experimentation results in an announcement by Russia that she will resume the testing of nuclear weapons. (*See September 1*)

# AUGUST 31

**1886**   The first major earthquake to hit the United States jolts Charleston, South Carolina, causing 41 deaths there.

**1887**   Thomas A. Edison receives a patent for Kinetoscope, a mechanism he has devised "to produce pictures representing objects in motion throughout an extended period of time."

**1903**   A Packard automobile ends a 52-day journey from San Francisco to New York, the first time an automobile has crossed the continent under its own power.

**1935**   President Franklin D. Roosevelt signs the Neutrality Act of 1935, prohibiting the export from the United States of arms, ammunition, or implements of war to any belligerent state or to any neutral port for transshipment to, or for the use of, a belligerent country.

**1939**   Adolf Hitler promises peace if Poland will accept 16 conditions. Poland rejects Hitler's terms.

**1947**   The United Nations Investigating Committee recommends that Great Britain give up control of Palestine and that Arab and Jewish states be established within that country.

**1954**   The Permanent Senate Subcommittee on Investigations releases a majority (Republican) and minority (Democrat) report on the recent quarrel between Senator Joseph R. McCarthy (R., Wis.) and the U.S. Army. In the findings, the Democrats assail the Senator and the Republicans mildly criticize him. Secretary of the Army Robert T. Stevens is also rebuked, but the strongest criticism is reserved for Roy Cohn, former chief counsel of the McCarthy investigating committee.

**1954**   New England and coastal areas of New York and New Jersey are lashed by Hurricane "Carol," resulting in a casualty loss of 68 persons dead and some $500,000,000 damages.

**1955**   Argentine President Juan Perón offers to resign from office in an effort to end political unrest in the country. Later in the day, Perón withdraws offer and tells 100,000 followers in the Plaza de Mayo in Buenos Aires to "answer violence with greater violence."

**1958**   The Census Bureau, in a Labor Day analysis of the nation's working force, reports that among more commonplace occupations there are currently 902 female sailors and deck hands in the United States. Other unusual findings in the report: 2,737 American women earn their livings as funeral directors and embalmers; 2,365 men are "male laundresses" and another 6,408 men are employed as midwives and practical nurses.

**1964**   After months of speculation, the Bureau of the Census announces officially that the state of California has passed New York and is now the most populous state of the Union. The Census Bureau's calculations give California a population of 18,084,000 as compared with 17,915,000 for New York.

# SEPTEMBER

## SEPTEMBER 1

**1806**    Captain Zebulon Pike and his exploring party, having purchased horses with much difficulty and accompanied by only three Pawnee and four Osage Indians, start out on their journey to explore the West.

**1807**    A circuit court in Richmond, Virginia, acquits Aaron Burr of charges of treason. (Burr, Vice President of the United States during Thomas Jefferson's administration, was accused of plotting to set up an independent empire in the South and West, establishing himself as emperor.)

**1878**    A woman is employed as a telephone "operator" for the first time when Miss Emma Nutt takes over the switchboard at the Telephone Despatch Company in Boston, Massachusetts. Before Miss Nutt's employment, young men served as operators, but their rudeness to telephone subscribers caused the company owners to replace them with women.

**1896**    Chop suey is concocted and served for the first time—in the United States. The dish is created by a chef working for the Chinese statesman Li Hung-Chang, now visiting the United States. When Li's guests ask what the tasty concoction is called, the chef is summoned and he tells them that "I call it chop suey—that's what we call 'hash' in China." As a result, chop suey "parlors" spring up all over America.

**1918**    Because of grain shortages brought on by World War I, the U.S. Food Administration orders bakeries to use 20 percent wheat substitutes in each loaf of bread.

**1923**    The worst earthquake in Japan's history shakes the eastern seaboard of that nation, inflicting particularly heavy damage to the cities of Tokyo and Yokohama. At least 150,000 persons lose their lives in the disaster and many thousands more suffer injuries.

**1932**    As a result of the Seabury Committee's investigation of corruption in New York City's government, James J. (Jimmy) Walker, the city's popular mayor, resigns and goes to Europe.

**1938** Adolf Hitler demands autonomy for the Sudeten Germans living in Czechoslovakia.

**1939** For the second time in 25 years, Europe is plunged into war as Germany breaks the peace. At dawn, without any formal declaration of war, Germany invades Poland. Great Britain and France serve an ultimatum on Adolf Hitler, demanding the immediate cessation of German hostilities.

**1946** In a plebiscite supervised by American and British forces, the people of Greece vote to recall their king, George II, to the throne. The King has been living in exile in England, following the outbreak of civil war in his country in 1944.

**1961** The Soviet Union, angered because her proposals for a nuclear treaty have been rejected by the United States, explodes an atomic bomb above ground in central Asia. (*See August 30*)

## SEPTEMBER 2

**1666** The Great Fire of London, spreading over 436 acres, destroys 13,000 houses, 89 churches, including St. Paul's, and leaves in its wake damages of ten million pounds. (The fire raged on for 4 more days.)

**1789** Congress establishes the U.S. Department of the Treasury.

**1864** Before starting his famous "March to the Sea," General William T. Sherman occupies Atlanta, Georgia, and Northerners receive the jubilant message: "Atlanta is ours, and fairly won!" ("War is cruel and you cannot refine it."—Sherman's reply to the protest of Atlanta city officials on his troops' invasion.)

**1901** The "Big Stick" becomes a trademark of Vice President Theodore Roosevelt following a speech he makes at the Minnesota State Fair: "There is a homely adage which runs, 'Speak softly and carry a big stick; you will go far.' If the American nation will speak softly and yet build and keep at a pitch of the highest training a thoroughly efficient navy, the Monroe Doctrine will go far."

**1919** One hundred and forty delegates representing 58,000 members of the Communist Labor Party of America (organized 2 days earlier) hold a convention in Chicago, Illinois, and form the Communist Party of America.

**1922** Henry Ford posts notices in his factory in Detroit, Michigan, warning each employee that he will lose his job if he has "the odor of beer, wine or liquor on his breath" or possesses any intoxicants on his person or in his home. The poster adds: "The Eighteenth Amendment is a part of the fundamental laws of this country. It was meant to be enforced."

**1924** In New York City, theatregoers cheer the opening of Rudolf Friml's operetta, *Rose Marie,* and particularly one song in its musical score, "The Indian Love Call."

**1930**   Flying in their airplane, *The Question Mark,* the French aviators Captain Dieudonne Coste and Maurice Bellonte complete the first nonstop flight from Europe to the United States, arriving in Valley Stream, New York, from France after a flight of 37 hours, 18½ minutes.

**1940**   The United States and Great Britain sign an agreement whereby the United States receives a 99 years' lease of air and sea bases in Newfoundland and Bermuda. In addition, bases in Jamaica, St. Lucia, Trinidad, Antigua, and British Guiana are leased in exchange for 50 over-age American naval destroyers.

**1945**   The Japanese sign the terms of unconditional surrender ending World War II aboard the U.S. battleship *Missouri* in Tokyo Bay. General Douglas MacArthur signs the documents for the United States and, at the conclusion of the ceremonies, informs the Japanese envoys: "As supreme commander for the Allied powers, I announce it is my firm purpose in the tradition of the countries I represent, to proceed in the discharge of my responsibilities with justice and tolerance, while taking all necessary dispositions to insure that the terms of surrender are fully, promptly and faithfully complied with." A few moments after the signing, President Harry Truman broadcasts to the world from the White House in Washington, saying, "We shall not forget Pearl Harbor. The Japanese will not forget the U.S.S. *Missouri.*"

**1949**   Vice President Alben W. Barkley, writing to a friend, explains the origin of his popular nickname, "The Veep": "... It is a name that my children gave to me in connection with the Vice Presidency. They just took the two letters, *V* and *P,* and put a couple of small *E*'s between, and it spelled *Veep,* and it has now become rather familiar over the country as a new title for the Vice President."

**1957**   Despite the fact that the school board of Little Rock, Arkansas, had adopted a plan for gradual integration of the city's schools to start on September 3, Governor Orval E. Faubus announces over radio and television that he has ordered the National Guard and the State Police to surround Central High School to prevent the entry of Negroes. (*See September 3, 4, 5, 14, 20, 23, 24, 25*)

**1963**   In Tuskegee High School, Alabama Governor George C. Wallace stops public school integration by encircling the building with a cordon of state troopers. (*See September 10*)

## SEPTEMBER 3

**1783**   The Revolutionary War between the United States and Great Britain is ended officially with the signing of the Treaty of Paris. The treaty is signed for the United States by John Adams, Benjamin Franklin, and John Jay.

**1826**    The U.S.S. *Vincennes,* an American warship commanded by William Bolton Finch, leaves New York harbor to circumnavigate the globe. (When the ship returned to New York on June 8, 1830, she became the first warship to accomplish that feat.)

**1852**    Commenting on the popularity in England of Harriet Beecher Stowe's novel, *Uncle Tom's Cabin,* the *London Times* writes: "Mrs. Stowe has received $10,000 as her copyright premium on three months' sales of the work—we believe the largest sum of money ever received by any author, either American or European, from the sale of a single work in so short a period of time."

**1916**    The Allies turn back the Germans at Verdun. (WORLD WAR I)

**1919**    President Woodrow Wilson starts out on a speaking tour throughout the western areas of the United States to rouse popular support for the Treaty of Versailles and the League of Nations.

**1925**    The U.S. naval dirigible *Shenandoah,* which had set out from Lakehurst, New Jersey, on September 2, bound for St. Paul, Minnesota, is torn to pieces in a thunder squall while traveling over Ava, Ohio. Fourteen crew members are killed.

**1939**    At 11 o'clock in the morning, when her ultimatum to Adolf Hitler to cease hostilities in Poland expired, Great Britain declares war on Germany. France follows Britain's lead 6 hours later. In quick succession, war declarations against Germany are proclaimed by Australia, New Zealand, South Africa, and Canada. (WORLD WAR II)

**1939**    Prime Minister Neville Chamberlain goes before the House of Commons, following the British declaration of war on Germany, and says: "This is a sad day for all of us and to no one is it sadder than to me. Everything that I have worked for ... has crashed into ruins." (WORLD WAR II)

**1939**    Prime Minister Chamberlain names Winston Churchill First Lord of the Admiralty and a message is flashed to His Majesty's Navy: "Winston is back." ("So it was that I came again to the room I had quitted in pain and sorrow almost exactly a quarter of a century before."—Churchill.)

**1943**    The Allies invade the Italian mainland, landing on the west coast of the Province of Calabria at 4:30 in the morning. Later in the day, fighting in Sicily ends as the Allies sign a military armistice with representatives of Marshal Badoglio, the successor to Premier Mussolini. (WORLD WAR II)

**1945**    Singapore, occupied by the Japanese since 1942, is returned to British control.

**1945**    With World War II barely over, at least 10 Frenchmen are killed in Indochina as a result of Annamese nationalist uprisings in Hanoi.

**1957**    Little Rock, Arkansas, is tense as 270 armed National Guardsmen ring Central High School to prevent the enrollment of

Negro students in that school. When none of the Negroes appear, Federal District Judge Ronald N. Davies orders the school board to integrate forthwith.

## SEPTEMBER 4

**1609**    Sailing in his vessel, the *Half Moon,* the explorer Henry Hudson discovers the Island of Manhattan.

**1781**    Los Angeles, California, is founded by Spanish settlers who name the community "El Pueblo de Nuestra Señora La Reina de Los Angeles de Porcicincula."

**1833**    Barney Flaherty, a 10-year-old New York boy, becomes the first known newsboy in the United States after he is hired by the publisher of *The New York Sun.*

**1870**    In Paris, the Third French Republic is proclaimed.

**1885**    The forerunner of today's modern cafeteria, the self-service restaurant, opens its doors to the public at 7 New Street in New York City. The restaurant is known as the Exchange Buffet.

**1931**    Major James H. Doolittle establishes an aviation record when he flies from Burbank, California, to Newark, New Jersey, in 11 hours, 16 minutes.

**1938**    Fashion experts in London reveal that coats made of mouse skins will be popular in the winter of 1939. Furriers say that a full-length coat will require about four hundred skins, the cost amounting to about the equivalent of $350. The cost can be lowered considerably if customers will catch and supply their own mice.

**1940**    Speaking in Berlin, Adolf Hitler promises the German people that he will invade Great Britain: ". . . no matter what happens, England will be broken one way or another. And if today, in England, people are very inquisitive and are asking, 'But why doesn't he come?' they may rest assured he'll come all right." (WORLD WAR II)

**1941**    A German submarine attacks the U.S. destroyer *Greer* off the coast of Ireland. (WORLD WAR II)

**1944**    Allied soldiers liberate Antwerp, Belgium, from the German invaders. (WORLD WAR II)

**1957**    A crowd of 400 jeering white men and women are on hand at Central High School in Little Rock, Arkansas, as troopers bar nine Negro students from entering the building.

**1962**    New Orleans Catholics peacefully integrate the city's parochial schools.

# SEPTEMBER 5

**1670** William Penn, arrested for holding a Quaker meeting in Grace Church Street, London, and thereby causing a "great terror and disturbance" of the people, is acquitted of that charge by a jury in London's Old Bailey court. Penn's arrest and trial is part of Charles II's war against religious nonconformists.

**1774** The first Continental Congress assembles in Carpenter's Hall, Philadelphia, organized to secure united action in behalf of common rights and liberties. Forty-four delegates represent 12 colonies, Georgia being the only colony not participating. The session lasts until October 26 and is held in secret.

**1882** Members of labor unions hold the first Labor Day parade in the United States as 10,000 workmen parade in New York City. The paraders carry placards and banners reading "Less Work and More Pay," "Less Hours More Pay," "To the Workers Should Belong the Wealth," etc.

**1885** Jake D. Gumper of Fort Wayne, Indiana, buys the first gasoline pump to be manufactured in this country.

**1896** The vaudeville team of Joe Weber and Lew Fields opens the Weber & Fields Music Hall in New York City.

**1896** Because of the Gold Rush in the Klondike, the first beefsteak to reach Circle City, Alaska, is selling today at $48 a pound, the highest known price ever paid for beef.

**1905** Through President Theodore Roosevelt's efforts, a treaty of peace between Russia and Japan is signed at Portsmouth, New Hampshire, thus ending the Russo-Japanese War which started February 10, 1904. Japan, having defeated Russia, emerges from the war as one of the world's major powers.

**1939** The U.S. goverment proclaims its neutrality in the European war. (WORLD WAR II)

**1942** The Czechoslovak government in exile in London announces that Germans have executed 1,568 Czechs, regardless of sex or age, in reprisal for the killing on May 27 of the German deputy governor of Czechoslovakia, Reinhard Heydrich, known as the "Butcher of Prague." (WORLD WAR II)

**1945** The American flag is raised on Wake Island after Rear Admiral Shigamatsu Sakaibara surrenders his Japanese forces there. (WORLD WAR II)

**1957** In the wake of Arkansas Governor Faubus' moves to bar integration of the public schools in Little Rock, President Eisenhower warns the Governor that he will uphold the Federal Constitution by every legal means.

**1963** At the order of Alabama Governor George C. Wallace, the Board of Education of Birmingham closes three white schools scheduled for imminent integration. (*See September 10*)

# SEPTEMBER 6

**1620**   One hundred and forty-nine Pilgrims sail from Plymouth, England, aboard the *Mayflower,* bound for the New World.

**1837**   Women students at Oberlin Collegiate Institute (now Oberlin College) at Oberlin, Ohio, are granted equal academic status with men, thus making it the first coeducational institution in this country.

**1899**   U.S. Secretary of State John Hay proposes his Open Door Policy with reference to China, outlining a policy of maintaining equal opportunities for trade by foreign powers in that nation. (On March 2, 1900, the Secretary announced that all of the major powers have agreed to his proposal.)

**1901**   While attending the Pan-American Exposition in Buffalo, New York, President William McKinley is shot and critically wounded by an anarchist, Leon Czolgosz.

**1909**   The world receives the news that 5 months earlier, on April 6, Admiral Robert E. Peary had discovered the North Pole, accompanied by a small expedition consisting of his personal attendant, Matthew Henson, four Eskimos, and 40 dogs. (Peary's claim, challenged by Dr. Frederick A. Cook who claimed he had discovered the Pole in 1908, was upheld by the National Geographic Society in 1910.)

**1919**   New Yorkers are going to the theatre again as the month-old actors' strike is ended. Almost all of the city's theatres have been closed since August 7 when actors deserted the footlights following a dispute with Broadway producers.

**1923**   "Player pianos," operated by foot pedals turning perforated rolls of paper, are in great demand all over the United States. Manufacturers report that Americans are expected to buy 343,000 pianos by the end of the year, at least half of them being these new "player pianos."

**1940**   King Carol II of Rumania abdicates as the Germans prepare to occupy his country. (WORLD WAR II)

**1945**   Fritz Kuhn, pro-Nazi leader of the German-American Bund in the United States, is ordered deported to Germany by Attorney-General Tom C. Clark.

**1948**   In the presence of Europe's royal families and the diplomatic corps, the coronation of Queen Juliana of the Netherlands takes place in Amsterdam. The Queen's mother, Queen Wilhelmina, announced her abdication and retirement last May 12.

**1954**   President Dwight D. Eisenhower announces that the United States and five other nations (Great Britain, France, Canada, Australia, and South Africa) have decided to form an international atomic pool to develop atomic energy for peaceful uses. The Soviet Union has declined to participate in the pool.

**1533** Birthday of Elizabeth I, Tudor queen of England.

**1813** The nickname "Uncle Sam" stems from this day when a writer for the *Troy* (New York) *Post* uses it as a symbolic reference to the United States.

**1822** Brazilian Independence Day: freedom from Spanish rule is proclaimed.

**1825** The Marquis de Lafayette makes his last farewells at the White House, having come to this country on the invitation of Congress. When he left for France the next day, he had completed a tour of all 24 states, received honorary American citizenship, a gift of $200,000 from Congress, and 23,000 acres of land in Florida —testimonials of gratitude for his services in the fight for American independence.

**1892** John L. Sullivan is knocked out by James J. (Gentleman Jim) Corbett in the 21st round in the first major prize fight to be fought under the Marquis of Queensberry rules. The New Orleans match has excited boxing fans all over the nation because for the first time two first-rate fighters have used gloves, rather than bare knuckles, and observed the rule of 3-minute rounds. Corbett's purse totaled $35,000.

**1899** There is great excitement in Newport, Rhode Island, as social leaders in that resort parade in the first automobile parade to be held in this country. Nineteen automobiles are in the parade, all of them decorated with flowers, but the prize was awarded to Mrs. Herman Oelrichs without any dissenting votes. Mrs. Oelrichs' car was covered with sprays of wisteria and fastened to the radiator was a flock of white doves!

**1936** Boulder Dam (now Hoover Dam) begins its operations. Located at the Nevada-Arizona border, on the Colorado River, the mammoth dam was authorized to provide hydroelectric power, irrigation, and flood control.

**1940** The Nazis start the London Blitz to terrorize the British public. Before it is over, the brave city will be bombed 82 out of 85 consecutive nights, and in 8 months' time, its residents will suffer 87,403 casualties, almost half of that number killed. (WORLD WAR II)

**1944** French Provisional President General Charles de Gaulle repudiates the Vichy government of Marshal Henri Pétain and all its statutes. The General promises his countrymen and the rest of the world that France will remain a true republic.

**1960** The Reverend Norman Vincent Peale, a prominent Protestant minister, sets off a political and religious controversy when he releases a statement in the midst of the Presidential campaign saying that a Roman Catholic President would be under "extreme pressure from the hierarchy of his church" to align U.S.

policy with that of the Vatican. (Senator John F. Kennedy, the Democratic candidate, was a Roman Catholic.)

**1963** The government of South Vietnamese President Ngo Dinh Diem arrests 800 high school students for demonstrating against his rule. (Two days later, another 1,000 students were arrested.)

## SEPTEMBER 8

**1565** A Spanish expedition headed by Don Pedro Menendez de Avilés lands at what is now St. Augustine, Florida, and founds the first permanent settlement of Europeans on the continent of North America. (A more famous Spaniard, Ponce de Léon, had explored this area as early as 1513, but after failing to find his "Fountain of Youth," he moved on.)

**1664** Peter Stuyvesant surrenders the Province of New Netherland and the City of New Amsterdam to the British Colonel Richard Nicolls, representing James, Duke of York and Albany. As Stuyvesant and his soldiers sail for Holland, the English rename both the province and city "New York" in honor of the Duke.

**1855** The Crimean War ends.

**1858** Abraham Lincoln makes a speech at Clinton, Illinois, and one sentence becomes a timeless maxim: "You can fool all of the people some of the time; some of the people all of the time; but not all of the people all of the time."

**1900** The eyes of the world are on Galveston, Texas, where a tornado and tidal wave smash the city and leave behind 6,000 dead and millions of dollars of property damage. In New York, the celebrated composer and conductor Victor Herbert leads 420 musicians in a benefit concert for the stricken city.

**1917** The *manufacture* of whiskey is stopped on this date to conserve grain. No restrictions are placed on the *sale* of alcoholic beverages.

**1934** The U.S. liner *Morro Castle* burns off Asbury Park, New Jersey, causing the loss of 137 lives. News of the burning ship attracts a crowd of almost 250,000 people to the New Jersey resort, some 15,000 of them buying standing room in the ocean-front Convention Hall allowing them to catch a glimpse of the wreck from second-story windows.

**1935** Senator Huey Long of Louisiana, known throughout his state as a virtual political dictator, is shot in the State House, Baton Rouge, Louisiana, by Dr. Carl A. Weiss, the son-in-law of a Long political opponent. (The Senator died 2 days later.)

**1939** Beginning of the siege of Warsaw: German mechanized units reach the outskirts of the Polish capital and open fire on the city with heavy artillery. (WORLD WAR II)

**1941**     The 17-month siege of Leningrad begins as 23 German armies encircle the Russian city. (WORLD WAR II)

**1943**     General Dwight D. Eisenhower announces the unconditional surrender of Italy. (WORLD WAR II)

**1945**     General Douglas MacArthur enters Tokyo to begin the American occupation of Japan. At a ceremony in the American Embassy, he instructs Lieutenant General Robert L. Eichelberger, commander of the Eighth Army: "General Eichelberger, have our country's flag unfurled and in Tokyo's sun let it wave in its full glory as a symbol of hope for the oppressed and as a harbinger of victory for the right."

**1951**     The United Nations officially terminate the war with Japan by signing a treaty of peace with that nation in San Francisco.

**1954**     The eight-nation Southeast Asia Defense Treaty sponsored by the Western Powers is signed at Manila in the Philippine Islands.

**1963**     A 34-year-old grandmother, Mrs. Ines Cuervo de Priete, gives birth to quintuplets, all boys, in Maracaibo, Venezuela.

## SEPTEMBER 9

**1776**     The term "United States" becomes official: the Second Continental Congress rules "that in all Continental commissions and other instruments, where heretofore the words 'United Colonies' have been used, the style be altered, for the future, to the 'United States.'"

**1830**     Charles Durant, known today as the first professional American aeronaut, makes a balloon flight from Castle Garden in New York City to Perth Amboy, New Jersey, the first time such a flight was made by a native-born American.

**1836**     Abraham Lincoln receives his license to practice law.

**1850**     California is admitted into the Union as the 31st state.

**1893**     For the first time in the history of the United States, a child is born to the First Lady of the land in the White House, as Mrs. Grover Cleveland becomes the mother of a baby girl. (This was not the first child to be born in the White House, however, since Thomas Jefferson's granddaughter was born there in 1806.)

**1894**     Sun Yat-sen leads his first attempt at revolution in China, 17 years before its successful culmination in 1911.

**1919**     For the first time in U.S. history, a great American city is virtually without police protection as almost the entire police force of Boston walks out on strike. Out of a total force of 1,544 policemen, 1,117 men have struck over the Police Commissioner's refusal to recognize their newly organized union. (The strike was ended on September 12, but not before Governor Calvin Coolidge ruled that the strikers would not be permitted to return to their jobs. Coolidge made history in the terse wire he sent to President

Samuel Gompers of the American Federation of Labor: "There is no right to strike against the public safety by anybody, anywhere, any time.")

**1923** The word "fascism" is beginning to make the headlines in German newspapers. A news dispatch from Munich says the Bavarian Fascists, under the leadership of Adolf Hitler, are in open rebellion against the republican government in Berlin. Hitler's followers declare they will thwart the government's attempt to live up to the provisions of the Treaty of Versailles.

**1926** The National Broadcasting Company is organized in New York City as a service of the Radio Corporation of America to produce nationwide network radio broadcasts.

**1945** The formal surrender of about 1,000,000 Japanese soldiers in China takes place in Nanking. (The Japanese invaders surrendered to Chinese General Ho Ying-chin.)

**1945** U.S. troops land in South Korea and the Russians take over the northern half of the country from Japan. The 38th Parallel will serve as the dividing line between the two occupation forces.

**1963** A federal injunction against Governor George C. Wallace of Alabama is issued after he orders state policemen to block Negroes from enrolling in the segregated public schools of Birmingham, Tuskegee, and Mobile. (Despite the Governor's defiance, token integration was later accomplished.)


## SEPTEMBER 10

**1813** The first defeat in the history of an English squadron takes place as Captain Oliver H. Perry, American naval officer in the War of 1812, defeats the British at the Battle of Lake Erie, and then sends his famous report to General William Henry Harrison: "We have met the enemy and they are ours: two ships, two brigs, one schooner, and one sloop."

**1846** After 5 years of experimentation, Elias Howe of Spencer, Massachusetts, receives a patent for his invention of the sewing machine.

**1898** The Empress Elizabeth of Austria-Hungary is assassinated in Geneva by the anarchist Luigi Lucheni.

**1919** General John J. Pershing, America's World War I military leader, and 25,000 soldiers of the U.S. First Division, are welcomed home by the City of New York in one of the greatest parades and receptions ever tendered by that city.

**1923** The Japanese ambassador presents to Secretary of State Charles Evans Hughes a message from the prime minister of Japan expressing the gratitude of the nation's Emperor and people for the "precious gift of American sympathy" and help in the recent earthquake.

**1927**   An American meat-packing firm announces that it has perfected a frankfurter with a zipper. Consumers are advised to boil the "hot dog" in its zippered casing and then discard it.

**1944**   At 3:30 in the afternoon, guns of the U.S. First Army on the western front fire the first American shells to reach German soil, at a point near Aachen, Germany. (WORLD WAR II)

**1945**   President Harry Truman, both houses of Congress, and the populace of Washington turn out to welcome home General Jonathan Wainwright, the gallant hero of the fortress on Corregidor. (WORLD WAR II)

**1962**   Cuba discloses that she has granted permission to the Soviet Union to use Havana harbor as a base for a fishing fleet. Western diplomats warn that in reality the Russians are planning to base nuclear submarines there.

**1963**   Negroes enter the white public schools of Birmingham, Tuskegee, and Mobile, Alabama, after President Kennedy federalizes that state's National Guard as a move toward integrating the public schools.

## SEPTEMBER 11

**1777**   General George Washington's troops defending Philadelphia are badly defeated by the British, led by General William Howe, at the Battle of Brandywine.

**1841**   All of the members of President John Tyler's Cabinet resign, except Secretary of State Daniel Webster, in protest over the President's veto of the Banking Bill.

**1847**   The proprietor of Andrews' Eagle Ice Cream Saloon in Pittsburgh, Pennsylvania, advertises in the Pittsburgh *Daily Commercial Journal* that entertainers in his emporium will sing Stephen Foster's "Oh! Susanna" this evening, the first public performance of the song.

**1850**   Jenny Lind, "The Swedish Nightingale," in the United States under the management of P. T. Barnum, opens her American concert series at Castle Garden in New York.

**1923**   The ZR-1, the biggest dirigible now in active service, flies over New York's tallest skyscraper, the Woolworth Tower. The mighty airship is only 102 feet shorter than the height of the skyscraper.

**1940**   Prime Minister Winston Churchill, in a world broadcast, describes Adolf Hitler and the effect he has had on British morale: "This wicked man, the repository and embodiment of many forms of soul-destroying hatred, this monstrous product of former wrongs and shame, has now resolved to try to break our famous Island race by a process of indiscriminate slaughter and destruction. What he has done is to kindle a fire in British hearts, here and all over the world, which will glow long after all traces

of the conflagration he has caused in London have been removed."
(WORLD WAR II)

**1941**    After German U-boats have attacked or sunk three U.S.
vessels in one week's time, President Franklin D. Roosevelt orders
the U.S. Navy to shoot on sight in American defense waters. (WORLD
WAR II)

**1941**    Speaking at an America First rally in Des Moines, Iowa,
Colonel Charles A. Lindbergh charges that the possible entry of
the United States into World War II against Germany is being
pushed by "the three most important groups which have been
pressing this country toward war . . . the British, the Jewish and the
Roosevelt Administration." Lindbergh adds: ". . . instead of agi-
tating for war, the Jewish groups in this country should be oppos-
ing it in every possible way, for they will be among the first to
feel its consequences. . . ."

**1944**    Prime Minister Churchill and President Franklin D.
Roosevelt hold their second Quebec Conference, discussing plans
for the prosecution of the war and the restoration of the peace.
(WORLD WAR II)

**1945**    Former Japanese Premier Hideki Tojo attempts to commit suicide in his Tokyo home as General Douglas MacArthur
seeks to round up Japanese war criminals. (Tojo was hospitalized,
recovered, and lived to be executed by the War Crimes Tribunal.)

**1963**    Three Negroes are enrolled at the University of South
Carolina without incident, ending an 86-year history of segregation
at that university.

## SEPTEMBER 12

**1609**    Henry Hudson, English navigator in the service of Holland, enters the river which is to bear his name.

**1814**    Defenders' Day in Maryland; a legal holiday marking
the successful defense of Baltimore by American forces against the
British in the War of 1812.

**1866**    *The Black Crook,* by Charles M. Barras, probably the
most spectacular melodrama ever staged in the American theatre,
opens at Niblo's Garden in New York. (The production ran on
for 16 months and has been revived in 9 different theatre seasons.)

**1922**    The Protestant Episcopal House of Bishops votes 36 to
27 to take the word "obey" out of the marriage ceremony.

**1938**    H. V. Kaltenborn, news commentator for the Columbia
Broadcasting System, begins his vigil in the network's Studio Nine
covering the crisis in Czechoslovakia. (Millions of Americans listened regularly to Mr. Kaltenborn's newscasts of the developments
of the crisis. From September 12 until September 30, when Prime
Minister Chamberlain returned from Munich, Kaltenborn lived
and slept in CBS, adjacent to the studio. In 18 days, he made 85
extempore broadcasts exclusively on the Czech situation.)

**1943**    Benito Mussolini, the former dictator of Italy, is kidnapped by German paratroopers from a hotel in Lake Bracciano, Italy, where he has been held prisoner by the government. (On September 15, after he was in German custody, Mussolini organized a new government of "Fascist Republican Italy," named himself president and declared King Victor Emmanuel dethroned.) (WORLD WAR II)

**1944**    American troops on German soil: Spearheads of Lieutenant General Courtney Hodges' U.S. First Army push 5 miles into German territory northwest of Trier, the first Americans to reach German soil. (WORLD WAR II)

**1945**    General Douglas MacArthur orders the secret terrorist Black Dragon Society dissolved in Japan and arrests many of its leaders.

**1953**    A social event of the year takes place in Newport, Rhode Island, where a young member of the U.S. Senate, John Fitzgerald Kennedy, is married to Miss Jacqueline Lee Bouvier.

**1960**    Senator John F. Kennedy, the Democratic candidate seeking the Presidency, meets the anti-Catholic issue openly when he appears before the Protestant Ministerial Association in Houston, Texas. He says: "I believe in an America where the separation of church and state is absolute ... where no public official either requests or accepts instructions on public policy from ... [any] ecclesiastical source ... I do not speak for my church on public matters, and the church does not speak for me. ..."

**1964**    Six individuals holding tickets in New Hampshire's legalized sweepstakes win $100,000 each after the first race is run at Rockingham Park in Salem, New Hampshire.

## SEPTEMBER 13

**1759**    In the French and Indian War, the British defeat the French on the Plains of Abraham overlooking the city of Quebec.

**1788**    The U.S. Congress authorizes the first national election, to be held "the first Wednesday in January next [1789]."

**1851**    Birth of Walter Reed, doctor and bacteriologist, the "... Army surgeon who planned and directed in Cuba the experiments which have given man control over that fearful scourge, yellow fever." *

**1872**    George Francis Train, an adventurer, world traveler, railroader, and newspaper publisher, is out campaigning for the Presidency, telling the American voter what his qualifications are: "I am that wonderful, eccentric, independent, extraordinary genius and political reformer of America, who is sweeping off all the poli-

---

* The citation quoted here was read at the Harvard commencement of 1902 when Dr. Reed was awarded an honorary degree.

ticians before him like a hurricane. I am your modest, diffident, unassuming friend, the future President of America—George Francis Train." (In the November elections, he received no votes.)

**1909**    Oskar Straus' operetta, *The Chocolate Soldier,* with its unforgettable waltz song, "My Hero," opens at the Casino Theatre in New York.

**1918**    General John Joseph Pershing, commander of the American Expeditionary Force, celebrates his birthday as U.S. troops capture St. Mihiel for him as a present. (WORLD WAR I)

**1922**    The world's highest recorded temperature—136° F.—is registered at Azizia, Libya, in North Africa. (*See July 10*)

**1943**    Generalissimo Chiang Kai-shek is elected president of the Chinese National Government, succeeding President Lin Sen who died on August 1.

**1954**    Maine elects its first Democratic governor in 20 years as voters in that state sweep Edmund S. Muskie into office.

**1955**    The Federated German Republic (Western Germany) and the Soviet Union establish diplomatic relations, the first since the end of World War II.

**1960**    Speaking in Portland, Oregon, Vice President Richard M. Nixon, the Republican nominee for President, says that American voters should accept "without any further questioning" Senator John F. Kennedy's Roman Catholic faith. (Kennedy was Nixon's opponent in the 1960 Presidential campaign.)

**1964**    A sermon by an eminent clergyman sets off a heated controversy as the Very Reverend Francis B. Sayre, Jr., Dean of Washington Cathedral in the nation's capital, makes it clear he does not think much of the Presidential nominees of the two major political parties. Referring to the recent nominating conventions, Dean Sayre says: "... We beheld a pair of gatherings at the summit of political power, each of which was dominated by a single man—the one, a man of dangerous ignorance and devastating uncertainty; the other, a man whose public house is splendid in its every appearance, but whose private lack of ethic must inevitably introduce termites at the very foundation ..." (Dean Sayre, the grandson of President Woodrow Wilson, was referring in the first instance to Senator Barry M. Goldwater, the Republican nominee, and in the latter to President Lyndon B. Johnson, candidate for reelection.)

## SEPTEMBER 14

**1741**    The composer George Frederick Handel, having worked without interruption for 23 days, finishes the *Messiah.*

**1778**    Benjamin Franklin is sent to France as minister plenipotentiary, instructed to negotiate a treaty to end the Revolutionary War.

**1812** After Napoleon and his French troops invade Russia, residents of Moscow set fire to the city causing the destruction of some 30,000 houses.

**1814** The words of "The Star-Spangled Banner" are written by Francis Scott Key, a Baltimore lawyer, while a prisoner on the British warship *Supreme* during the bombardment of Fort Mc-Henry, Maryland.

**1847** General Winfield Scott, American commander in the war with Mexico, occupies Mexico City. On his staff are Captain Robert E. Lee and Lieutenant George B. McClellan. (U.S. soldiers, in this war, nicknamed General Scott "Old Fuss and Feathers," because of meticulous concern for military etiquette and discipline.)

**1891** The New York Central train "Empire State Express" establishes a current record by making its run from New York to East Buffalo, a distance of 436 miles, in 7 hours and 6 minutes.

**1901** President William McKinley dies in Buffalo from wounds he received 8 days earlier at the hands of anarchist Leon Czolgosz. Vice President Theodore Roosevelt is sworn in as President at three o'clock in the afternoon in Buffalo.

**1923** After knocking Jack Dempsey out of the ring in the first round, Luis Angel Firpo of Argentina is defeated by Dempsey, the heavyweight boxing champion of the world, in the second round of a thrilling match staged in the Polo Grounds in New York. ("The Manassa matador dropped the Wild Bull of the Pampas, but not until the matador was gored by the bull so that he will remember it for many a day." W. O. McGeehan in the *New York Herald*.)

**1942** American aviators raid Kiska in the Aleutian Islands, sinking two enemy mine sweepers, three large cargo ships, three submarines, and damaging several auxiliary naval vessels. (WORLD WAR II)

**1945** Premier Higashi-Kuni of Japan makes a peace overture to the American public, saying: "People of America, won't you forget Pearl Harbor? We Japanese people will forget the picture of devastation wrought by the atomic bomb and will start entirely anew as a peace-loving nation."

**1957** Governor Orval E. Faubus of Arkansas flies to Newport, Rhode Island, to confer with President Eisenhower on the explosive situation in Little Rock, Arkansas. After discussing the barriers to integration of the Arkansas public schools, Governor Faubus pledges to obey federal laws.

**1963** Mrs. Andrew Fischer, the wife of a $76-a-week shipping clerk in Aberdeen, South Dakota, and already the mother of five children, gives birth to quintuplets. Four of the infants are girls, one a boy. (Seven other sets of quintuplets had been born in the United States between 1776 and 1959, but the Fischer quintuplets were the first to survive.)

# SEPTEMBER 15

**Felt Hat Day**    Traditional day for men to resume wearing winter-weight hats.

**1789**    The U.S. Department of Foreign Affairs, created in 1781, changes its name to the "Department of State."

**1821**    Independence Day of the Central American republics: Costa Rica, El Salvador, Guatemala, Honduras, Nicaragua.

**1857**    Birthday of William Howard Taft, 26th President of the United States, and the only American who ever served in both the Presidency and the office of chief justice of the Supreme Court.

**1887**    The city of Philadelphia inaugurates a 3-day celebration marking the one hundredth anniversary of the U.S. Constitution.

**1935**    In Germany, the Nazis enact the Nuremberg Laws, starting off a program of violent religious and racial persecution. All Jews are deprived of their citizenship, ghettos are revived, and the Swastika becomes the national flag.

**1938**    Prime Minister Neville Chamberlain flies to Berchtesgaden, Germany, in an attempt to mediate the German-Czech crisis.

**1940**    Climax and turning point in the Battle of Britain: On their greatest day, in a running fight with 500 German planes, the Royal Air Force, aided by Free Polish and Czech pilots, destroyed 185 enemy aircraft. (WORLD WAR II)

**1942**    German armies start to attack Stalingrad, thus beginning the bitter siege of that Russian city. (WORLD WAR II)

**1949**    Dr. Konrad Adenauer becomes the first chancellor of the German Federated Republic.

**1959**    Premier Nikita Khrushchev of the Soviet Union, accompanied by members of his family and official aides, arrives in Washington to begin his 13-day visit in the United States. (In addition to being the guest of President and Mrs. Eisenhower in the nation's capital, the Russian Premier visited New York, Los Angeles, San Francisco, Des Moines, and Coon Rapids, Iowa. Later, he told newsmen that he was enjoying his trip immensely and cited, in particular, his first ride in a helicopter and tasting his first American hot dog.)

**1963**    A bomb explodes in a Negro church in Birmingham, Alabama, killing four girls as they are attending Sunday school classes. President Kennedy issues a statement expressing a "deep sense of outrage and grief."

# SEPTEMBER 16

**1630**    The village of Shawmut, Massachusetts, changes its name to Boston, taking its new name from Boston, England.

**1638**    Birthday of Louis XIV, one of the most famous of the kings of France.

**1776** Congress offers $20 and 100 acres of land to all army privates who agree to remain in military service for the duration of the Revolutionary War.

**1810** Independence Day in Mexico, marking the date of the Mexican revolution against Spanish rule.

**1893** Cherokee Strip Day in Oklahoma: More than 100,000 homesteaders rush into the Strip, between Oklahoma and Kansas, to claim shares of the six million acres of land opened up by the U.S. government to new settlers.

**1901** Aboard the funeral train bearing the body of the late President William McKinley, en route from Buffalo, New York, to Washington, political boss Mark Hanna bemoans the fact that Theodore Roosevelt is now the President of the United States. To the editor of the *Chicago Times-Herald,* Hanna cries out: "I told William McKinley it was a mistake to nominate that wild man at Philadelphia. . . . Now, look! That damned cowboy is President of the United States!"

**1917** Premier Alexander Kerensky, head of the provisional government in Russia, proclaims that nation a republic.

**1920** A tremendous bomb explosion outside the building housing J. P. Morgan & Company on New York's Wall Street kills 30 people outright, wounds at least 100, and causes damage amounting to almost $2,000,000. (Police have never been able to discover who planted the bomb, but at the time it was believed to be the work of anarchists.)

**1922** The Hall-Mills murder case: A New Brunswick, New Jersey, clergyman, the Reverend Edward Wheeler Hall, and the choir leader in his church, Mrs. James Mills, are found murdered on a lonely farm lane 2 miles outside the town.

**1940** Congressman Sam Rayburn (D., Texas) becomes Speaker of the House of Representatives. (In all, he scored a record by serving in that post for 17 years, as follows: 1940–47; 1949–53; 1955–61.)

**1940** President Franklin D. Roosevelt signs into law the Burke-Wadsworth Selective Training and Service Act, providing for the registration and eventual conscription of all able-bodied men between the ages of 21 and 35.

**1945** British warships fire a 21-gun salute as the Japanese surrender the crown colony of Hong Kong and the Union Jack is raised over Government House.

**1963** Malaya, Singapore, Sarawak, and North Borneo unite into the new Federation of Malaysia.

# SEPTEMBER 17

**Citizenship Day**    Observed each year by Presidential proclamation on the anniversary of the adoption of the U.S. Constitution by the delegates to the Constitutional Convention in 1787.

**1787**    The Constitution of the United States is completed and signed by a majority of the 55 delegates attending the Constitutional Convention in Philadelphia. Delegates were sent from 12 of the original 13 colonies, Rhode Island alone failing to attend. (The Convention was in session 4 months, drawn out by extreme differences of opinion among the delegates. At last, just before the final vote was taken, Benjamin Franklin addressed some remarks to the presiding officer, George Washington: "I agree to this Constitution with all its faults, if they are such; because I think a general Government necessary for us, and there is no form of Government but what may be a blessing to the people if well administered.... Thus I consent, Sir, to this Constitution because I expect no better, and because I am not sure that it is not the best. The opinions I have had of its errors, I sacrifice to the public good.")

**1796**    In his Farewell Address, President George Washington counsels his fellow-citizens: " 'Tis our true policy to steer clear of permanent alliances with any portion of the foreign world.... Harmony, and a liberal intercourse with all nations, are recommended by policy, humanity and interest." *

**1862**    General George B. McClellan, commander of the Union forces, hurls back General Robert E. Lee's invasion of Maryland in the Battle of Antietam.

**1873**    One of the celebrated "Black Fridays" of American financial history takes place following the failure of the banking firm of Jay Cooke & Company in New York. (It was this spark that set off the Panic of 1873.)

**1894**    *Arms and the Man,* the first George Bernard Shaw play to be produced in the United States, opens at the Herald Square Theatre in New York.

**1935**    Manuel Quézon is elected the first president of the Commonwealth of the Philippines.

**1936**    The debut of the radio program, "Major Bowes' Amateur Hour," starts the trend toward "talent contests" in American radio programming.

**1939**    Russia invades Poland in World War II.

**1944**    Airborne troops of the Allies land behind German lines at Arnheim, Holland, only to be encircled by the enemy. (By Sep-

---

* This quotation is very often confused with the admonition of Thomas Jefferson who, in his first inaugural address in 1801, advised "... peace, commerce and honest friendship with all nations, entangling alliances with none...."

tember 25, the Allied troops were trapped and 2,000 survivors began to filter back through the German lines. Besides 1,200 wounded left behind, possibly 4,800 more men were killed or captured.) (WORLD WAR II)

**1947** On the 160th anniversary of the signing of the Constitution, the Freedom Train sets out from Philadelphia carrying documents tracing U.S. history from the discovery of the American mainland by Christopher Columbus to the creation of the United Nations. (The commemorative railroad caravan returned to Philadelphia on January 8, 1949, after a 35,000-mile tour of 324 cities in the 48 states. In all, 3,800,000 Americans visited the train to view the documents.)

**1947** As a result of the newly organized U.S. Department of Defense, merging into one administrative agency all of the branches of the armed services, James V. Forrestal is sworn in as the nation's first Secretary of Defense.

**1948** Count Folke Bernadotte of Sweden, the United Nations mediator in the war between Israel and the Arab countries, is murdered near Jerusalem while conducting a fact-finding mission. He is succeeded by Dr. Ralph J. Bunche of the United States.

**1960** The White House announces that President Eisenhower has ordered the flag of Panama to be flown with the flag of the United States in the public plaza of the Canal Zone. The President's move is a means of placating the feelings of anti-U.S. Panamanians.

**1963** A young white lawyer and civic leader shocks his fellow-citizens in Birmingham, Alabama, as Charles Morgan, Jr., rises to his feet and charges that the white community must bear guilt in the September 15 murder of four little Negro girls, following the bombing of their church. Addressing the Young Men's Business Club of Birmingham, Morgan asks "Who is guilty?" In his ringing denunciation, he says: "Who is guilty? A business community which shrugs its shoulders.... A newspaper which ... finds it necessary to lecture Negroes every time a Negro home is bombed? A Governor who offers a reward—but mentions not his own failure to preserve either segregation or law and order? And what of lawyers and politicians who counsel people to what the law is not when they know full well what the law is? ...."

## SEPTEMBER 18

**1769** The *Boston Gazette* reports that the first piano made in this country is a spinet manufactured by one John Harris.

**1793** President George Washington lays the cornerstone of the Capitol building of the United States in Washington, D.C.

**1810** Chilean Independence Day, marking the liberation of that South American country from Spanish rule.

**1850**   Congress passes the Fugitive Slave Act, permitting a slave-owner possessing a certificate of ownership to reclaim any slave who has escaped into another state.

**1851**   The first issue of *The New York Times* is published.

**1881**   The *Chicago Tribune* reports on an experiment that sounds very much to present-day readers like our modern television. Says the *Tribune:* "The excursion of electricians to the town of Aurora, 42 miles west . . . to witness the testing of Televide on a 42-mile trial wire, was an event more startling and sensational in interest than any scientific episode that ever occurred in the West. Televide is the new electric apparatus for conveying the human eyesight, by conducting wire and optic appliances to any conceivable distance. The European electricians promise that we will be able to see church steeples from London in the not very remote future. . . ."

**1916**   A reporter for the *London Daily Sketch* describes a new instrument of war, the "tank": "When our soldiers first saw these strange creatures lolloping along the roads and over old battle-fields, taking trenches on the way, they shouted and cheered wildly, and laughed for a day afterwards." (WORLD WAR I)

**1927**   The Columbia Broadcasting System goes on the air with a basic network of 16 stations.

**1928**   Residents of the West Indies and Florida begin to dig out of the debris left by the worst hurricane to strike that section of the earth. (September 12–17.) More than 3,000 persons lost their lives and property damage in Florida amounted to $25,000,000 and $7,000,000 in the West Indies.

**1931**   Japan begins the military occupation of Manchuria by moving troops into the ancestral capital of the Manchu dynasty, Mukden, an act of aggression that marks the beginning of the Sino-Japanese War. (This invasion of Chinese territory took place despite Japan's signature on the League of Nations Covenant, the Nine-Power Treaty of 1922, and the Kellogg-Briand Pact of 1928.)

**1949**   Sir Stafford Cripps, Chancellor of the Exchequer, announces in a radio broadcast from London that the British pound is being devaluated from $4.03 to $2.80 because of an acute shortage of American dollars needed in international trade.

**1959**   Russian Premier Khrushchev, in the United States for a 13-day visit, addresses the United Nations General Assembly and calls for disarmament of all nations within the next 4 years.

**1961**   Dag Hammarskjold, the Secretary General of the United Nations, is killed in a plane crash in Northern Rhodesia, while on a mission trying to arrange a cease-fire between troops of the United Nations and Katanga in the Congo.

**1768**    Bostonians are talking about an advertisement that appears today in the *Boston Gazette:* "Whereas many persons are so unfortunate as to lose their fore-teeth by accident and other ways, to their great detriment, not only in looks but speaking both in public and in private, this is to inform all such that they may have them replaced with artificial ones that look as well as natural, and answers the end of speaking to all intents, by Paul Revere, Goldsmith—near the head of Dr. Clarke's Wharf, Boston."

**1777**    American soldiers in the Revolutionary War fight and win the first battle of Saratoga, New York.

**1846**    Elizabeth Barrett, accompanied by her faithful maid Wilson and her spaniel Flush, flees from 50 Wimpole Street, London, and the tyranny of her father, and elopes to Paris with Robert Browning. (The two poets had been married in secret at St. Marylebone Parish Church on September 12.)

**1859**    The famous Confederate war song, "I Wish I Was in Dixie," is sung for the first time at a minstrel show in New York by Daniel Decatur Emmett, the actor. (Emmett claimed he had composed the song, but many musical historians insist he merely popularized it.)

**1863**    In Georgia, Union and Confederate soldiers meet in the Battle of Chickamauga. (The Southerners defeated the Union troops the next day.)

**1881**    President James A. Garfield dies in Elberon, New Jersey, after being wounded by a disgruntled office-seeker in the Baltimore & Ohio Railroad station on July 2.

**1928**    Americans are introduced for the first time to Mickey Mouse, the lovable creation of Walt Disney, when the animated cartoon feature *Steamboat Willie* opens at the Colony Theatre in New York.

**1934**    Bruno Richard Hauptmann is arrested in the Bronx, New York, charged with kidnapping the baby son of Colonel and Mrs. Charles A. Lindbergh.

**1938**    Britain and France, weakening under pressure from Adolf Hitler, urge Czechoslovakia to cede the Sudetenland to Germany.

**1944**    The German occupation authorities dissolve the Danish police force, deporting 1,250 policemen to German concentration camps. Six thousand Danish policemen escape and "go underground." (WORLD WAR II)

**1945**    William Joyce, the notorious "Lord Haw Haw" of the Nazi radio during World War II, is convicted of treason in London and sentenced to hang. (His execution was carried out on January 3, 1946.)

**1955**   President Juan Perón of Argentina is ousted from office following the army and navy revolts of the past 3 days. (Two days later, Perón was permitted to seek asylum aboard a gunboat owned by the government of Paraguay.)

**1960**   Cuban Premier Fidel Castro throws New York into a furor after he stages a noisy "walkout" from a midtown hotel. He then leads his staff to a hotel in the predominantly Negro district of Harlem which he tells reporters is "humble, a humble hotel of the Negroes in Harlem, but it offered us shelter" when all over the city, he claims, there was hostility. (Castro charged that the first hotel made exorbitant "cash demands" on him, but the hotel management claimed that the Cuban party had been asked to leave after they had been discovered plucking chickens and preparing them for cooking in the various rooms.)

## SEPTEMBER 20

**1519**   The Portuguese navigator Ferdinand Magellan with 5 vessels and some 270 men begins his global voyage to find a western passage to the Indies.

**1797**   The U.S. frigate *Constitution* (*Old Ironsides*) is launched at the Boston Navy Yard.

**1850**   Congress votes to ban slave trading in the District of Columbia after January 1, 1851.

**1870**   *The New York Times* runs its first editorial attacking the corruption of Boss Tweed and Tammany Hall in New York City. (This campaign by the *Times* and the subsequent investigation of a citizens' committee finally led to the downfall of the Tweed Ring in 1871.)

**1873**   The Panic of 1873 reaches a climax when the New York Stock Exchange closes its doors. (Financial chaos in Wall Street was so acute that the Exchange did not reopen until September 30.)

**1881**   Vice President Chester A. Arthur takes the oath of office as the 21st President of the United States at his home on Lexington Avenue in New York City, following the death of President James A. Garfield.

**1884**   Delegates to the National Equal Rights Party convention in San Francisco nominate Mrs. Belva Lockwood, an attorney, for the Presidency of the United States.

**1918**   Battle of the Meuse-Argonne begins in World War I.

**1921**   One of the earliest radio newscasts in the United States gets under way as Station KDKA, Pittsburgh, introduces a daily news program emanating from the city desk of the *Pittsburgh Post*.

**1946**   President Harry S. Truman asks Secretary of Commerce Henry A. Wallace for his resignation following a speech made by the Secretary on September 12 criticizing the current U.S. policy toward Russia.

**1955**   In Argentina, General Eduardo Leonardi, one of the rebel leaders responsible for the ouster of the Perón regime, announces he will assume the duties of provisional president of the nation.

**1957**   Governor Orval E. Faubus of Arkansas obeys a federal court order and withdraws the National Guard troops who have been barring Negro students from entering Central High School in Little Rock.

**1962**   As a crowd of 2,000 stands by jeering and taunting him, James H. Meredith, a Negro Air Force veteran, is blocked from enrolling at the University of Mississippi in Oxford by the state's Governor, Ross R. Barnett. (*See September 24, 25, 26, 30, October 1*)

**1963**   President John F. Kennedy addresses the United Nations General Assembly and proposes a joint U.S.-Russian expedition to the moon.

## SEPTEMBER 21

**1784**   The *Pennsylvania Packet & Daily Advertiser,* the first daily newspaper to be published in the United States, makes its appearance in Philadelphia.

**1792**   With the Royal Family deposed, France is proclaimed a republic.

**1893**   Using the designs of Charles E. Duryea, his brother, Frank Duryea, a toolmaker, operates on the streets of Springfield, Massachusetts, the first successful gasoline-propelled motor vehicle made in America. (Duryea's vehicle was a single-cylinder horseless carriage, incorporating for the first time an electric ignition and a spray carburetor.)

**1896**   A first-night audience at the Herald Square Theatre in New York applauds the French actress Anna Held as she makes her American debut in *A Parlor Match.*

**1897**   The editor of the *New York Sun* writes an editorial entitled "There Is a Santa Claus" in response to 8-year-old Virginia O'Hanlon of New York who had written to the paper's editor asking him if there was a Santa Claus. ("Yes, Virginia, there is a Santa Claus. He exists as certainly as love and generosity and devotion exist, and you know that they abound and give to your life its highest beauty and joy.")

**1925**   Dennis King opens in Rudolph Friml's operetta, *The Vagabond King,* at the Casino Theatre in New York.

**1931**   Great Britain abandons the gold standard.

**1938**   The government of Czechoslovakia issues a communiqué announcing that, as a result of British and French pressure, it has agreed to cede the Sudeten German area of the nation to Nazi Germany.

**1942**    The Inter-Allied Information Committee in London reports that from the beginning of World War II the Nazis have executed 207,373 Europeans, of whom 200,000 were Poles.

**1949**    The German Federal Republic (West Germany) comes into formal existence when the Allied High Commission transfers to it the administration of the American, British, and French zones of occupation.

**1953**    Following an offer made on April 27 by General Mark Clark, United Nations commander in the Korean War, to pay $100,000 to the first Communist pilot to deliver a Russian-designed MIG airplane to United Nations forces, Lieutenant Noh Keun Suk, a North Korean pilot, lands near Seoul and surrenders his plane to the Fifth Air Force.

**1955**    Rocky Marciano defends his heavyweight boxing title for the sixth time when he knocks out Archie Moore in the ninth round at Yankee Stadium, New York. The bout is Marciano's 49th professional victory.

**1964**    Testifying before the Special Committee on Aging of the U.S. Senate, J. Fred Talley, an official of the state of Arizona, says that a "staggering number of Americans...are finally taking Horace Greeley's advice: 'Go West, young man, go West.'" Talley tells the committee that "more than 100,000 new residents are pouring into Arizona each year." California, he adds, is getting 1,700 new residents each day of the week.


## SEPTEMBER 22

**1656**    The General Provincial Court, meeting at Patuxent, Maryland, orders the first jury composed entirely of women to convene in the case of Judith Catchpole charged with murdering her child. (The jury, made up of seven married women and four single women, brought in a verdict of "not guilty.")

**1692**    The last persons are hanged in the American colonies for "witchcraft." (Nineteen persons in all were hanged up to this date, but more than 250 persons were arrested on charges of witchcraft.)

**1776**    Captain Nathan Hale is hanged as a Revolutionary spy by the British at their artillery headquarters in New York City. His last words on the scaffold were: "I only regret that I have but one life to lose for my country." (Hale was asked to obtain information for the Continental Army about British operations on Long Island. He entered British lines near Huntington Bay disguised as a Dutch schoolmaster, but he was apprehended and turned over to the British General Howe.)

**1789**    Congress authorizes the creation of the office of postmaster general of the United States. (Four days later, President

George Washington appointed Samuel Osgood to be the first post-master to fill the office.)

**1908**    In a commentary on Boston baked beans, the *New York Tribune* comments: "Taking the average height of a Bostonian at 5′ 6″ and the height of a beanpot at ten inches, one can easily figure that a Bostonian in a year eats more than two and five-sevenths times his own height in baked beans and more than his own weight. Boston pays for baked beans in a year the price of two of Uncle Sam's modern battleships."

**1927**    In a second bout with Gene Tunney, former heavy-weight boxing champion Jack Dempsey attempts to get back his title, but Tunney wins in the 10th round by decision. (So intense was the interest in this fight that almost 105,000 fans crowded into Soldiers Field, Chicago, to witness it and millions more followed it over radio. Five radio fans dropped dead of heart failure awaiting the results of the controversial and drawn-out "long count" in the seventh round.)

**1937**    A United Front is established in China when the Chinese Communist Party announces its support of the National Government and the principles of Dr. Sun Yat-sen and declares the "Government of the Soviet Republic of China" dissolved.

**1943**    Kate Smith, the popular star of stage and radio, completes her radio War Bond Marathon at two o'clock in the morning. As a result of her 13-hour appeal, radio listeners have pledged to buy bonds totaling $39,000,000. (WORLD WAR II)

**1949**    The Soviet Union explodes its first atom bomb, 4 years after the United States' first detonation.

**1955**    Commercial television begins in England, sponsors being permitted only 6 minutes of advertising for each hour of air time. Unlike the practice in the United States, no advertiser is allowed to select the program he is going to sponsor. Instead, his sales message is rotated in different spots according to the convenience of the program agencies who rent television facilities from the Independent Television Authority. No television is permitted on Sunday mornings, thus eliminating the possibility of competing with church-going.

**1958**    Sherman Adams makes a nationwide radio-television broadcast to announce that he has resigned as President Eisenhower's executive assistant. Adams repeats that he had never sought to use his influence with government agencies to secure favors for his friend Bernard Goldfine. He charges that "a calculated and contrived effort has been ... made to attack and discredit me ... and ... in so doing embarrass the Administration and the President." (*See June 10*)

**1961**    The Interstate Commerce Commission orders an end to racial discrimination against bus travelers.

## SEPTEMBER 23

**63 B.C.**    Birth of Augustus Caesar, first Roman Emperor.

**1642**    Harvard College holds its first commencement exercises.

**1779**    The American naval hero, Commodore John Paul Jones, commanding the *Bonhomme Richard,* wins the naval battle with the British frigate *Serapis,* commanded by Captain Richard Pearson, off the coast of Scotland. (It was at this Revolutionary War engagement that Jones, in answer to Pearson's query "Have you struck?" uttered his famous words, "I have just begun to fight.")

**1806**    The Lewis & Clark Expedition, after an absence of 2 years, 4 months, and 10 days, arrives at St. Louis, having successfully accomplished its mission. (The explorers had traveled over 8,000 miles in boats, on horseback, and on foot through a wilderness peopled only by savages.)

**1912**    The first Mack Sennett "Keystone Comedy" film is released, starring Mabel Normand, Fred Mace, Ford Sterling, and Mack Sennett.

**1926**    Jack Dempsey loses his heavyweight championship title to Gene Tunney before 120,000 spectators in Philadelphia. (Tunney did not achieve a knockout, however; he won the title in the 10th round by decision.)

**1938**    The Time Capsule is buried on the grounds of the World's Fair in Flushing Meadows, New York City. (The 7½ foot long metal capsule is to be unearthed in the year 6,939 to show people of that day an assortment of objects representing the culture of the 1930's in America. Among the items buried in the capsule: a woman's hat [circa 1938], a man's pipe, a mail-order catalogue, a Bible, newsreels of President Franklin D. Roosevelt and the Yale-Harvard football game of 1938, a message from Albert Einstein, copies of paintings by Pablo Picasso.)

**1950**    The Internal Security Act is adopted by Congress over President Harry Truman's veto. The act provides for the registration of Communists and their internment in times of emergency.

**1952**    A disclosure by a New York newspaper that Senator Richard M. Nixon, now campaigning on the Republican ticket for the Vice Presidency, had accepted an $18,235 "expense fund" from 76 wealthy and prominent Californians, prompts Nixon to go on a nationwide radio-television broadcast to refute the allegations of wrong-doing. With some 55,000,000 American voters listening to him, Nixon says that the money was used for "political expenses which I believe should not be charged to the Federal government ... Not one cent. ... ever went to me for my personal use." (In the end, Dwight D. Eisenhower, the Presidential nominee, said Nixon had vindicated himself and refused to dump him from the national ticket.)

**1952**  A new heavyweight boxing champion wins his title at Municipal Stadium, Philadelphia, as Rocky Marciano knocks out former champion Joe Walcott in the 13th round.

**1955**  A jury in Sumner, Mississippi, acquits Roy Bryant and J. W. Milam of the murder of Emmett Till, a 14-year-old Chicago Negro boy. (The two men admitted kidnapping the boy, claiming he had whistled at Bryant's wife and then tried to molest her in the Bryant store in Money, Mississippi. The jury based its verdict on a claim that the slain boy's body was too badly decomposed for positive identification.)

**1957**  A menacing crowd of white supremacists gather in front of Central High School in Little Rock, Arkansas, intent on barring nine Negro students from enrolling in the school. Despite the fact that the children enter the school almost unnoticed, mob violence breaks out on the streets and school grounds. As a result, the school superintendent is forced to withdraw the Negroes from the school under heavy police protection.

## SEPTEMBER 24

**1789**  The first Judiciary Act is passed by the U.S. Congress, providing for an attorney general and for a Supreme Court consisting of a chief justice and five associate justices.

**1869**  "Black Friday" in New York: An attempt by financiers Jay Gould and James Fisk to corner the gold market results in complete panic in Wall Street. The price of gold rises from 137 to 162 and then collapses as the government starts selling gold.

**1906**  Victor Herbert's operetta, *The Red Mill*, starring Fred Stone, has its *première* at the Knickerbocker Theatre in New York.

**1915**  The Triangle Film Corporation, formed by D. W. Griffith, Thomas H. Ince, and Mack Sennett, presents its first moving pictures at the Knickerbocker Theatre in New York. Among the films on the bill is one entitled *The Lamb,* starring a comparatively unknown actor, Douglas Fairbanks.

**1934**  Babe Ruth makes his farewell appearance as a regular player with the New York Yankees at Yankee Stadium, New York.

**1941**  Nine Allied governments in London—Belgium, Free France, Czechoslovakia, Greece, Luxembourg, the Netherlands, Norway, Poland, and Yugloslavia—pledge adherence to the Atlantic Charter drafted by President Roosevelt and Prime Minister Churchill during their recent meeting in mid-Atlantic.

**1953**  Twenty-three U.S. Korean prisoners of war who had refused to be repatriated during the prisoner exchange supervised by the United Nations, are turned over to neutral Indian custody by the North Korean command. Immediately afterwards, the Americans issue this statement: "We love our country and our people. . . . Unfortunately, under present conditions in America, the voices of those who speak out for peace and freedom are rapidly being silenced. We do not intend to give the American government a chance of silencing our voices too."

**1955**    President Dwight D. Eisenhower is stricken with a heart attack while on vacation in Denver, Colorado. The President is removed from the residence of his mother-in-law to Fitzsimmons General Hospital in Denver.

**1957**    As a result of yesterday's violence at Little Rock, Arkansas, President Eisenhower federalizes the state's National Guard and dispatches 1,000 paratroopers to the city under the command of Major General Edwin A. Walker. In a speech to the nation from the White House, the President describes "the sadness I feel in the action I was compelled to take today.... Our personal opinions about the (Supreme Court's desegregation) decision have no bearing on the matter of enforcement...."

**1962**    The Fifth Circuit Court of Appeals in New Orleans orders the University of Mississippi to admit James H. Meredith, a Negro, to its student body.

**1963**    The Senate, by an 80 to 19 vote, approves the ratification of the U.S., British, Russian treaty banning all nuclear tests except those conducted under the surface of the earth.

## SEPTEMBER 25

**1513**    Vasco Nuñez de Balboa, Spanish explorer, crosses the Isthmus of Panama and discovers the Pacific Ocean, the first European to set eyes on that body of water.

**1690**    *Publick Occurrences,* the first newspaper to be published in America, is printed in Boston. (No second issue ever appeared, however, because the publisher incurred the displeasure of the royal governor.)

**1789**    The first Congress of the United States, meeting in New York, adopts 12 amendments to the Constitution and submits them to the states for ratification. (Ten of these amendments, making up what we call the Bill of Rights, were subsequently ratified; the other two were rejected.)

**1804**    The Twelfth Amendment to the U.S. Constitution, providing for separate electoral ballots for the offices of President and Vice President, goes into effect.

**1890**    Congress establishes Yosemite National Park in California.

**1917**    Governor James E. Ferguson of Texas is removed from the governor's office, after impeachment proceedings confirm the fact that he had attempted to dictate educational policies to officials of the University of Texas and sought to overrule the university's Board of Regents.

**1926**    The Ford Motor Company establishes an 8-hour day and a 5-day week.

**1936**    The Reverend Charles Coughlin, the controversial head of the National Union for Social Justice and bitterly opposed to a second term of office for President Franklin D. Roosevelt, charges in Cincinnati that the President is "anti-God" and advocates using bullets when an "upstart dictator in the United States succeeds in making a one-party government and when the ballot is useless."

**1942**    Sports fans in the United States are critical of the decision of Secretary of War Henry L. Stimson to cancel the scheduled heavyweight championship bout between Sergeant Joe Louis and Corporal Billy Conn scheduled for October 12 at Yankee Stadium, New York. (The Secretary said, in announcing his decision, "The standards and interests of the Army do not permit the proposed contest to be carried out. There is no reflection upon the principals.")

**1945**    At Saigon, Indochina, nationalist forces incite violent uprisings against French colonial rule.

**1957**    Under guard of 300 U.S. Army troops, armed with rifles and bayonets, the nine Negro children who have thus far been unable to study at white schools are escorted into Central High School in Little Rock, Arkansas. The troops patrol the school grounds and building corridors.

**1961**    President John F. Kennedy addresses the General Assembly of the United Nations and tells the delegates that the West is ready to defend its obligations in West Berlin. "We shall," says the President, "be remembered either as the generation that turned this planet into a flaming pyre or as the generation that met its vow 'to save succeeding generations from the scourge of war.' "

**1962**    Mississippi Governor Ross Barnett again personally bars James H. Meredith, a Negro student, from registering as an undergraduate at the University of Mississippi.

## SEPTEMBER 26

**1777**    British troops occupy Philadelphia in the American Revolution.

**1789**    President George Washington appoints John Jay to be the first chief justice of the U.S. Supreme Court.

**1815**    The sovereigns of Russia, Austria, and Prussia form the Holy Alliance binding the peoples of those three nations to "remain united by the bonds of a true and indissoluble fraternity."

**1831**    The first political party convention on a national basis takes place in Baltimore as the Anti-Masonic Party nominates William Wirt of Maryland for the Presidency. Delegates from 13 states are attending the convention.

**1892** John Philip Sousa and his band present their first public concert, playing for the first time the bandmaster's *Liberty Bell March*.

**1907** New Zealand becomes a self-governing dominion within the British Commonwealth of Nations.

**1914** The U.S. Federal Trade Commission is established.

**1919** After making 40 speeches in behalf of the Treaty of Versailles, President Woodrow Wilson collapses in his private train en route to Wichita, Kansas. (The President was taken back to the White House where he suffered the stroke that incapacitated him for months and from which he never fully recovered.)

**1945** Constitutional guarantees of freedom of speech, freedom of the press, and right to assembly are suspended in Argentina by executive decree. President Edelmiro Farrell tells the nation that the state of siege is a temporary measure.

**1950** United Nations troops capture Seoul, capital of South Korea, from the North Koreans.

**1955** As a result of the news of President Dwight D. Eisenhower's heart attack, the New York Stock Exchange suffers its worst price break since 1929. During the day, 7,720,000 shares are traded on the floor of the Exchange. (By September 28, 58 percent of the loss had been recovered.)

**1960** The first in a series of four one-hour televised campaign debates * between Senator John F. Kennedy (D., Mass.) and Vice President Richard M. Nixon (R., Calif.), contenders for the Presidency, takes places in Chicago. (*See October 7, October 13, October 21*)

**1962** James H. Meredith, so far unable to study at the University of Mississippi because he is a Negro, tries for the third time to register at the university's Administration Building. This time, he is halted by Lieutenant Governor Paul B. Johnson and 20 unarmed state troopers.

## SEPTEMBER 27

**1779** John Adams is appointed to negotiate peace terms with Great Britain.

**1825** In England, George Stephenson operates the first locomotive to haul a passenger train.

**1904** Crying "You can't do that on Fifth Avenue!", a New York policeman arrests a woman he has observed smoking a cigarette in the rear of an automobile on New York's famous thoroughfare.

---

* In the strict sense of the word, these were not "debates." The form followed was actually an exposition, followed by questions from a panel of newsmen.

**1939**    After 19 days of stubborn resistance to heavy air raids and regular artillery bombardment, the heroic defenders of Warsaw, Poland, surrender to the Germans. Until the very last, Radio Warsaw continues to identify itself by the first three notes of the Chopin *Polonaise in A Major*. (WORLD WAR II)

**1940**    In Berlin, representatives of Germany, Italy, and Japan sign the Tripartite Pact, a 10-year mutual assistance agreement.

**1945**    Breaking all precedents, Emperor Hirohito of Japan calls on General Douglas MacArthur, Supreme Commander of the Allied Powers, in the U.S. Embassy in Tokyo. (This was the first time in history that a Japanese sovereign had made a call on a foreign dignitary.)

**1950**    Former heavyweight boxing champion Joe Louis is defeated by Ezzard Charles at Yankee Stadium, New York, after a 15-round decision. (Louis had retired from the ring 18 months previously but had agreed to meet Charles in an attempt to stage a comeback.)

**1954**    A select committee of the U.S. Senate, headed by Senator Arthur V. Watkins (R., Utah), recommends unanimously a Senate vote of censure against Senator Joseph R. McCarthy (R., Wis.) for contempt of the Senate Privileges and Elections Subcommittee and for unwarranted abuse of Brigadier General Ralph W. Zwicker.

**1963**    At approximately 10:59 A.M., the census clock in the lobby of the U.S. Department of Commerce building in Washington, records a national population of 190,000,000 men, women and children. (The nation's net growth in 1963 was computed on the basis of one birth each 7½ seconds; a death every 18½ seconds; the arrival of an immigrant every 1½ minutes; and the departure of an emigrant every 23 minutes.)

**1964**    After conducting a 10-month investigation of the events attending the assassination of President John F. Kennedy, the Warren Commission releases its report. Its most important conclusion: Lee Harvey Oswald was responsible for the murder of the late President and he acted alone.

## SEPTEMBER 28

**1745**    English theatregoers sing "God Save the King" for the first time in history, following the defeat of English forces under Sir John Cope by the Jacobites led by Bonnie Prince Charlie.

**1781**    Backed by the French fleet, General George Washington, with 9,000 colonial troops and 7,000 French soldiers, begins the siege of 7,000 British and Hessian troops at Yorktown Heights, Virginia.

**1850**    The flogging of sailors in the U.S. Navy is abolished.

305

**1920**    Baseball's biggest scandal: a Grand Jury in Chicago indicts eight players of the Chicago White Sox for "throwing" the 1919 World Series games between their team and the Cincinnati Reds. (It was this incident that led to the appointment of Judge Kenesaw Mountain Landis to serve as the "Czar" of baseball.)

**1937**    President Franklin D. Roosevelt dedicates Bonneville Dam on the Columbia River in Oregon.

**1939**    Germany and the Soviet Union agree on a plan to partition Poland. (WORLD WAR II)

**1941**    Reinhard Heydrich, the newly named "Reich Protector of Bohemia and Moravia," starts a program of terror throughout Czechoslovakia. (WORLD WAR II)

**1953**    Robert C. Greenlease, Jr., 6-year-old son of a wealthy automobile dealer in Kansas City, Missouri, is kidnapped from school by a woman who pretends to be his aunt. (Subsequently, the largest ransom ever paid to kidnappers in the United States, $600,-000, was authorized by the Greenlease family, but the child was found dead in St. Louis, Missouri, on October 7. The day before, police arrested as kidnappers and murderers Carl Austin Hall and Mrs. Bonnie Brown Heady, both of whom were eventually executed for their roles in the shocking crime.)

**1957**    Mrs. Franklin D. Roosevelt interviews Nikita Khrushchev for 2½ hours at his vacation home in Yalta. (At times, as the former First Lady firmly told Khrushchev what she did not like about Communism, the conversation grew heated. When it was all over, the Russian leader commented: "At least we didn't shoot at each other.")

**1962**    Ex-Major General Edwin A. Walker, who resigned from the Army in 1961, makes a radio appeal from Dallas, Texas, for segregationists to go to Oxford, Mississippi, to back up Governor Ross Barnett in his fight to bar Negro James H. Meredith from entering the state university there. Says Walker: ". . . Rally to the cause of freedom! The battle cry of the Republic: Barnett, Yes! Castro, No! Bring your flag, your tent, and your skillet. It's now or never!" (*See September 30, October 1, November 4*)

## SEPTEMBER 29

**1789**    The U.S. War Department establishes a regular army with a strength of 700 men to serve 3 years.

**1862**    Prince Otto von Bismarck-Schönhausen, the new Premier of Prussia, summons a few deputies and ministers of state to his office and tells them what his policy will be: "Not by speeches and decisions of majorities will the greatest problems of the time be decided . . . but by blood and iron. . . ." (From that time on, Bismarck was known as the "Blood and Iron Chancellor.")

**1899**  New York City welcomes Admiral George Dewey, hero of the Spanish-American War, back from Manila. The returning hero is greeted by Dewey flags, Dewey banners, the legend "Welcome, Dewey" spelled out in electric lights across the span of the Brooklyn Bridge, and, most magnificent of all, a Dewey Arch, straddling Fifth Avenue at 23rd Street.*

**1902**  The theatrical impresario, David Belasco, opens his own theatre in New York.

**1917**  To publicize the current food conservation program, U.S. Army authorities point with pride to a company chef at Fort Dix, New Jersey, who manages to feed 212 men 3 meals a day at a total cost of $48. (WORLD WAR I)

**1918**  The Central Powers in the European war are beginning to collapse as Bulgaria signs an armistice and surrenders to the Allies. (WORLD WAR I)

**1922**  Sigmund Romberg's operetta, *Blossom Time,* has its *première* at the Ambassador Theatre in New York.

**1923**  Great Britain begins to govern Palestine under a mandate from the League of Nations.

**1936**  Political leaders of both the Democratic and Republican parties point out that the current campaign between President Franklin D. Roosevelt and Governor Alf Landon of Kansas is the first political campaign to utilize the facilities of radio stations on a nationwide basis. The two major parties have set aside a total of $2,000,000, providing them with broadcast time on radio networks and local stations.

**1941**  At a three-power conference in Moscow, the United States and Great Britain agree to send large stores of war supplies to the Soviet Union to help that nation continue her resistance to the Nazi invaders. (WORLD WAR II)

**1945**  New York office-workers are getting elevator service for the first time in 6 days, following a settlement of a strike called by the AFL Building Service Employees International Union.

**1963**  Pope Paul VI opens the second session of the Ecumenical Council in St. Peter's Basilica, Rome.

## SEPTEMBER 30

**1846**  Dr. William Morton, a dentist of Charleston, Massachusetts, extracts a tooth for the first time with the help of anesthesia (ether). (Dr. Morton subsequently recorded the episode, writing: "Toward evening, a man residing in Boston came in, suffering great

---

* The Admiral had no way of knowing on this day of his triumphal return that months later the arch, really a plaster-of-paris model intended to represent one of marble to be paid for by popular subscription, was to be carted away by garbage collectors. The permanent memorial project came to nothing because of a change of public opinion toward Dewey.

pain, and wishing to have a tooth extracted. He was afraid of the operation, and asked, if he could be mesmerized. I told him I had something better, and saturated my handkerchief, gave it to him to inhale. He became unconscious almost immediately. It was dark, and Dr. Hayden held the lamp while I extracted a firmly rooted bicuspid tooth. . . . He recovered in a minute and knew nothing of what had been done for him.")

**1913**    The U.S. Army reports it has 17 airplanes, with 23 officers and 91 enlisted men on aeronautical duty.

**1935**    *Porgy and Bess,* music by George Gershwin and book by DuBose Heyward, has its world *première* at the Colonial Theatre in Boston.

**1938**    As millions of people all over the world wait breathlessly for a word from the conferees meeting in Munich, Germany (Prime Minister Neville Chamberlain of Britain, Premier Edouard Daladier of France, Chancellor Adolf Hitler of Germany, Premier Benito Mussolini of Italy), the conference ends with an announcement that Britain and France have agreed to Hitler's demand for annexation of Czechoslovakia's Sudetenland. At the same time, Britain and Germany sign a peace compact promising never to war on each other again. Prime Minister Chamberlain flies home and tells crowds welcoming him at Heston Airdrome that the decisions reached at Munich will provide Englishmen with "peace in our time." *

**1939**    For the first time in history, a football game is televised as the cameras of Station W2XBS, New York, photograph the game played between Fordham University and Waynesburg College at Randall's Island, New York.

**1942**    Adolf Hitler says in a Berlin speech: "The occupation of Stalingrad . . . will be a gigantic success . . . and no human being shall ever push us away from that spot." (WORLD WAR II)

**1946**    The International Military Tribunal in Nuremberg, Germany, finds 22 top German Nazi leaders guilty of war crimes and sentences 11 of them to death.

**1953**    President Dwight D. Eisenhower names Governor Earl Warren of California chief justice of the U.S. Supreme Court.

**1955**    The entire French delegation walks out of the United Nations Assembly after that body decides, by the margin of one vote (28–27), to include on its agenda the question of unrest in Algeria.

**1962**    After three futile appeals by telephone to Mississippi Governor Ross Barnett to comply with a federal court order to admit Negro James H. Meredith to the University of Mississippi,

---

* Mr. Chamberlain's "peace in our time" lasted exactly 337 days. As for Hitler, the Munich Conference turned over to him, at Czechoslovakia's expense, 11,000 square miles of territory, with a population of 3,500,000, and the vital Skoda Armament Works.

President Kennedy calls that state's National Guard into federal service and sends army troops to Oxford to restore order. A heavy guard of U.S. marshals escorts Meredith as he takes up residence on the campus. A violent riot breaks out, in part led by ex-Major General Edwin A. Walker of Texas, who had commanded the federal troops dispatched by President Eisenhower to Little Rock, Arkansas, in the 1957 school crisis there. (*See October 1*)

**1962** As the riot in Oxford, Mississippi, goes on, President Kennedy addresses the nation, but his words are aimed directly at the students and people of Mississippi: "... Americans are free ... to disagree with the law, but not to disobey it ... Show that you are men of patriotism and integrity. ... It lies in your courage to accept those laws with which you disagree as well as those with which you agree. ..."

# OCTOBER

## OCTOBER 1

**1873**　John Wanamaker, prominent merchant of Philadelphia, says he has complete faith in the American public despite the seriousness of the Panic of 1873. Mr. Wanamaker inserts an advertisement to this effect in the Philadelphia newspapers, saying: "Checks taken from buyers. Change given in cash."

**1880**　John Philip Sousa becomes conductor of the famous U.S. Marine Band.

**1885**　Beginning today, special-delivery mail service goes into effect throughout the United States. The service is restricted to towns of at least 4,000 residents and an additional charge of 10 cents a letter is collected for this special handling.

**1903**　The first baseball World Series gets under way at Boston as the Boston Americans and the Pittsburgh Nationals start a competition of not more than nine games. (When the Series ended on October 13, Boston won with five victories to Pittsburgh's three. Apparently, the Series attracted very little attention for the total attendance at all games was only a little more than 100,000 and the total receipts amounted to approximately $50,000.)

**1908**　Henry Ford introduces his famous Model T Ford. ("Few inventions have had a more profound social effect on American life than the Model T. The 'motel,' the roadside hamburger stand, the consolidated country schoolhouse—all grew up with the Model T. ... As roads were improved, Ford owners thought nothing of traveling half across the continent. Florida became a kind of winter Coney Island for the North. There were hundreds of jokes about the old 'Lizzie' and her drivers, but somehow indestructible Lizzie doggedly went through the mud and the sand...."—Editorial in *The New York Times* on the 50th anniversary of the founding of the Ford Motor Company.)

**1910**　Twenty-one persons are killed when an explosion rocks the plant of the *Los Angeles Times*. It is generally agreed that the explosion is the result of the bitter running feud between the paper's management and local labor unions. (This assumption was entirely correct. Harrison Gray Otis, owner of the paper, was an outspoken foe of the labor union movement. A year later, two active unionists, J. J. and J. B. McNamara, pleaded guilty to charges of dynamiting the building and were subsequently sentenced to long prison terms.)

**1921** Featuring news bulletins of the current baseball games in the World Series, radio Station WJZ, New York, goes on the air for the first time.

**1928** The first Five-Year Plan is launched by the Soviet Union. The objective of this gigantic economic program is to develop a gradual but progressive increase in industrial and agricultural production.

**1932** A Babe Ruth legend is born. Whether it actually happened or not is beside the point, for many Babe Ruth fans insist that on this date at Wrigley Field, Chicago, the Babe pointed to the exact spot where he would knock the next pitch—and then lined a homer right over the spot.

**1936** General Francisco Franco is proclaimed head of Spain's nationalist government.

**1938** Troops of Adolf Hitler cross into the so-called Sudeten area of Czechoslovakia, bringing about the enslavement of nearly one million Czechs by the Germans. (This next step toward World War II followed a sequence of acts of international aggression by the Fascist powers; Manchuria in 1931, Ethiopia in 1935, Spain in 1936, China in 1937, and Austria in 1938.)

**1943** Soldiers of the U.S. Fifth Army, commanded by General Mark Clark, capture the city of Naples in Italy. (WORLD WAR II)

**1946** The International War Crimes Tribunal at Nuremberg, Germany, sentences 12 top German Nazi leaders to die by hanging. Seven others are handed prison sentences, three are acquitted.

**1949** Under a red flag with five gold stars, Mao Tse-tung, Chinese Communist leader, takes office in Peking. His title is Chairman of the Central People's Government Council. Chou En-lai will serve as premier of the new regime.

**1961** On the last day of the current baseball season, Roger Maris of the New York Yankees establishes a new record for the 162-game season when he hits his 61st home run. (Babe Ruth's 60 home runs in 1927 remained the record for the 154-game season of his day.)

**1962** James H. Meredith, previously barred from entering the University of Mississippi because he is a Negro, is enrolled at the university as the town of Oxford is embroiled in violent riots. The riots are finally quelled by 3,000 army troops and National Guardsmen and 400 federal marshals. (When it was all over that day, two men had been killed, almost 70 injured. Authorities arrested 150 rioters, including the controversial and ultraconservative ex-Major General Edwin A. Walker of Texas.)

# OCTOBER 2

**1780**    Major John André, arrested as a British spy in connection with the treason of Benedict Arnold, is convicted and hanged at Tappan, New York.

**1869**    Birth of Mohandas K. Gandhi, Hindu nationalist, leader, and reformer.

**1882**    William H. Vanderbilt, the railroad tycoon, gives newspaper reporters headline material when he is asked whether he operates his railroads for the public benefit. Says Mr. Vanderbilt: "The public be damned! What does the public care for the railroads except to get as much out of them for as little consideration as possible!" (His words were quoted all over the United States the next day.)

**1905**    Former President Grover Cleveland aligns himself with those who are opposed to giving women the right to vote. In the current issue of the *Ladies' Home Journal,* he writes: "... We all know how much further women go than men in their social rivalries and jealousies. Sensible and responsible women do not want to vote. The relative positions to be assumed by man and woman in the working out of our civilization were assigned long ago by a higher intelligence than ours."

**1915**    Great crowds of people all over America turn out for the gospel meetings of the famous American evangelist, the Reverend Billy Sunday. The former baseball player's favorite admonition is: "I'll give you hell enough before you get through with this meeting. I'll give you all the hell in the Bible. The Lord put it there, and if you don't like it, fix it up with the Lord, not with me."

**1919**    The White House in Washington is converted into a hospital as President Woodrow Wilson suffers a stroke completely paralyzing the left side of his body.

**1921**    Former teammates of the great baseball player, Christy Mathewson, play a benefit game at the Polo Grounds in New York for the old master. The game realizes $40,000 to be used to defray the expenses of Mathewson's year-old illness at Saranac Lake, New York.

**1938**    Bobby Feller, pitcher for the Cleveland Indians baseball team, achieves a record when he strikes out 18 players at bat for the Detroit Tigers.

**1962**    The longest nine-inning game in major league baseball history is played in Chavez Ravine Stadium, Los Angeles, between the San Francisco Giants and the Los Angeles Dodgers. After 4 hours and 52 minutes of play, the Dodgers win by a score of 8–7.

# OCTOBER 3

**1863**    President Abraham Lincoln issues a proclamation designating the last Thursday in November as Thanksgiving Day.

**1876**    Johns Hopkins University in Baltimore, Maryland, is opened.

**1914**    Commenting on German atrocities in Belgium, the London periodical *John Bull* says: "It is our bounden duty to call up before the eye of imagination the scenes of butchery, rape and rapine which everywhere have marked the progress of the German armies." (WORLD WAR I)

**1917**    Congress doubles the income-tax rates of 1916.

**1918**    Americans at home are reading of the heroism of the "Lost Battalion" in France. The unit is made up of U.S. soldiers of the First Battalion of the 308th Infantry and sections of the 306th and 307th Infantry Machine Gun Battalions of the 77th Division, commanded by the valiant Major C. W. Whittlesey. (This battalion was trapped and encircled by Germans near Binarville, France, and was believed lost, but after several days of stout fighting was able to withstand the enemy until relieved by the 154th Brigade.) (WORLD WAR I)

**1919**    The City of New York tenders an official reception to King Albert and Queen Elizabeth of Belgium during their state visit to the United States.*

**1922**    Mrs. Rebecca L. Felton (D., Ga.) is the first woman in the United States to be seated in the Senate, having received a temporary appointment from the governor of Georgia to fill a vacancy caused by the death of Senator Thomas E. Watson.

**1935**    Italy invades Ethiopia, completely ignoring her obligations under the Covenant of the League of Nations. (The only pretext Benito Mussolini could find for this unprovoked aggression was a few unimportant clashes between his soldiers and those of Haile Selassie.)

**1941**    In a jubilant mood, Adolf Hitler announces to a German audience that Russia is defeated and "will never rise again." (WORLD WAR II)

**1942**    President Franklin D. Roosevelt sets up the Office of Economic Stabilization and authorizes controls on prices, wages, and rents. (WORLD WAR II)

**1952**    The Soviet Union demands the recall from Moscow of U.S. Ambassador George F. Kennan.

---

* It was during this visit that the apocryphal story concerning the Queen and the wife of New York's mayor was born and circulated with such glee. According to this legend, the Queen commented proudly on the exuberance of the crowds gathered to greet Their Majesties and Mrs. John F. Hylan's reply was: "Queenie, you said a mouthful!"

**1957** Riots break out in Warsaw after the Polish Communist Party shuts down a popular weekly periodical because ". . . its propaganda views [are] entirely alien to socialism." (The riots were led by students and continued for three more days before police subdued them.)

**1962** Navy Commander Walter M. Schirra, Jr., orbits the earth almost six full times in his Project Mercury capsule. Later, he lands safely near Midway Island in the Pacific.

**1962** The U.S. government closes its ports to all ships carrying cargoes to Cuba.

## OCTOBER 4

**1822** Rutherford B. Hayes, 19th President of the United States, is born in Delaware, Ohio.

**1854** Abraham Lincoln makes his first great political speech at the State Fair in Springfield, Illinois. Without coat or collar, the little-known Illinois lawyer answers Senator Stephen Douglas' speech of the day before and attacks the repeal of the Missouri Compromise.

**1878** Chen Lan-pin, the first Chinese diplomatic envoy ever accredited to the U.S. government, presents his credentials to President Rutherford B. Hayes in Washington.

**1892** After much litigation, the U.S. Circuit Court of Appeals upholds the claim of Thomas Alva Edison that he is the sole inventor of the incandescent lamp.

**1917** The Department of War in Washington announces that it will build 20,000 airplanes for use in the war against Germany. (Most people, in 1917, thought this was a shameful waste of the taxpayers' money.)

**1918** Diners in New York's Delmonico's Restaurant sing "Auld Lang Syne" just before the famous dining place shuts its doors permanently. (At its peak, Delmonico's had more than 200 chefs and waiters and boasted that it was the favorite eating place of the celebrities of America and Europe.)

**1933** The freedom of the press is suspended in Germany by Adolf Hitler. All newspapers are placed under the supervision of Propaganda Minister Joseph Goebbels.

**1940** The dictators of Germany and Italy, Adolf Hitler and Benito Mussolini, meet at the Brenner Pass in the Tyrol and make their plans for a long war. (WORLD WAR II)

**1945** American occupation authorities in Japan order the Imperial Government to end all restrictions on freedom of speech, religion, and assembly, disband the "thought police" and release some 3,000 political prisoners.

**1957** The Russians are jubilant as they announce to the world that they have launched Sputnik I: ". . . The first [man-made space] satellite was successfully launched in the U.S.S.R. on October 4. ... It is fitted with ... radio transmitters continuously emitting signals...."

**1961** For the first time in history, excerpts from the plays of William Shakespeare are enacted in the White House, following a State Dinner given by President and Mrs. John F. Kennedy in honor of President Ibrahim Abboud of the Sudan. (The actors were members of the American Shakespeare Festival and their performances were given on an improvised stage in the East Room of the Executive Mansion.)

## OCTOBER 5

**1830** Birthday of Chester Alan Arthur, 21st President of the United States.

**1853** Antioch College opens its doors for the first time in Yellow Springs, Ohio, the first nonsectarian college to grant equal scholastic opportunities to men and women. The president of the college is Horace Mann.

**1881** Birth of the Spanish painter Pablo Nepomuceno Crispiniano de la Santissima Trinidad Ruiz y Picasso, more familiarly known as Pablo Picasso.

**1918** The end of World War I is near as allied headquarters announces that the Hindenburg Line is broken.

**1921** Baseball lovers are excited over the first radio broadcasts of a World Series. For the first time, fans who are not able to attend the Series can hear an on-the-scene description of the plays by the sports writer Grantland Rice.

**1931** Clyde Pangborn and Hugh Herndon, Jr., complete the first nonstop flight across the Pacific Ocean after arriving in Wenatchee, Washington, 41 hours after they left Japan.

**1937** At Chicago, President Franklin D. Roosevelt calls for a national policy that will "quarantine" aggressor nations. Comparing the steady march of Fascist aggression to an outbreak of disease, the President says: "When an epidemic of physical disease starts to spread, the community approves and joins in a quarantine of the patients in order to protect the health of the community against the spread of the disease...."

**1938** In a speech before the House of Commons in London, Winston Churchill appraises the results of the Munich Agreement concluded by Prime Minister Chamberlain and Premiers Hitler and Mussolini: "... All is over. Silent, mournful, abandoned, broken Czechoslovakia recedes into the darkness...."

**1945** Admiral Chester W. Nimitz, wartime commander of the Pacific Fleet, is honored by the city of Washington and the U.S. Congress.

**1947** To build up a stockpile of grain for Europe, President Harry S. Truman speaks to the nation asking Americans to observe voluntarily meatless Tuesdays and eggless and poultryless Thursdays. (This speech emanating from the White House was the first one to be televised there.)

**1954** Italy, Yugoslavia, the United States, and Great Britain sign a pact amicably settling the partition of Trieste.

**1957** At least one American is irate over the news of the Soviet Union's launching of the first man-made satellite into space. James T. Mangan, who claims outer space as his private domain, charges in Chicago that the Soviet Union was "trespassing" and adds: "I refuse to issue any license to Russia for use of outer space...." (Mr. Mangan filed a formal charter proclaiming the formation of his own outer-space "nation" of Celestia with the Cook County (Illinois) Recorder of Deeds on January 4, 1949.) (*See October 4*)

**1958** The Clinton, Tennessee, high school, integrated in 1956 despite bitter segregationist opposition, is almost completely destroyed by three dynamite explosions. (Because these explosions took place on a Sunday, no lives were lost.)

## OCTOBER 6

**1766** The Irish actor, John Henry, becomes the first matinee idol in America following his appearance in Philadelphia in *The Roman Father.*

**1857** Chess players are agog over the first important chess tournament to be held in the United States. The tournament is going on in New York under the sponsorship of the New York Chess Club.

**1863** While the public is curious about the first "Turkish Baths" to open in America, only one hardy soul ventures to try them out. The baths are located in Brooklyn, New York, and the proprietor is Dr. Charles H. Shepard.

**1884** The Naval War College is established at Newport, Rhode Island, under the supervision of Commander Stephen Bleecker Luce of the U.S. Navy.

**1890** Mormons in the state of Utah renounce the practice of polygamy.

**1917** An editor of the *Literary Digest* comments: "A strange word has gained widespread use in the ranks of our producers of popular music. It is 'jazz,' used mainly as an adjective descriptive of a band. The group that plays for dancing ... seems infected with the virus that they try to instil as a stimulus in others. They shake and jump and writhe in ways to suggest a return to the medieval jumping mania."

**1923** Adolf Hitler, Fascist leader in Bavaria, having lost his first tests of power with the German government, orders his followers to go underground and await his call at a more favorable opportunity.

**1927**   The first spoken words in a full-length motion picture mark the birth of "talking" films. The film is *The Jazz Singer* and the star is Al Jolson. (Actually, there were only 291 spoken words in this Warner Brothers' hit, but nonetheless it was the beginning of a modern film era.)

**1938**   Under the pressure of a German ultimatum, Dr. Eduard Beneš resigns the presidency of Czechoslovakia and leaves for Great Britain and the United States in order to continue his fight for a free Czechoslovakia.

**1947**   Russia revives the Communist International in Warsaw. The new organization will bear the name "Cominform," a shortened version of "Communist Information Bureau."

**1958**   The nuclear submarine *Seawolf* establishes an underseas record when it comes to the surface of the Atlantic Ocean near Block Island, off the coast of New England, after having cruised submerged for 60 days.


## OCTOBER 7

**1765**   Delegates from nine colonies meet in New York to attend the Stamp Act Congress. (The representatives drew up a bill of rights and dispatched a list of grievances to the British Crown and the two houses of Parliament.)

**1849**   Just a few days before his forthcoming marriage to Mrs. Sarah Helen Whitman, Edgar Allan Poe dies under mysterious circumstances at Washington College Hospital in Baltimore.

**1903**   An experiment by Samuel P. Langley, secretary of the Smithsonian Institution in Washington, to launch an airplane and prove that man can fly, ends in failure on the Potomac River. (Langley's plane was launched from a houseboat equipped with a runway. According to observers on hand to see the takeoff, the plane merely slid over the edge of the houseboat and sank into the river.)

**1916**   The most staggering intercollegiate football defeat in history takes place at Atlanta, Georgia, as Georgia Tech trounces Cumberland University, 222–0.

**1918**   President Woodrow Wilson receives a request for armistice terms from the new chancellor of Germany, Prince Max of Baden. (WORLD WAR I)

**1940**   Troops of Nazi Germany occupy Rumania. (WORLD WAR II)

**1942**   Following new German demands for anti-Semitic legislation in occupied Denmark, King Christian X attends a service in the Copenhagen synagogue and tells the congregation that "If the

317

Jews are to wear the Star of David, then we shall all wear it. You are all Danes. You are all my people." (WORLD WAR II)

**1950**   The General Assembly of the United Nations approves an allied advance north of the 38th parallel in Korea.

**1960**   Presidential candidates Senator John F. Kennedy and Vice President Richard M. Nixon hold their second televised campaign debate, originating this time in Washington.

**1963**   President Kennedy signs the nuclear test-ban treaty between the United States, Britain, and the Soviet Union.

**1963**   Mrs. Ngo Dinh Nhu, sister-in-law of South Vietnamese President Diem, arrives in the United States for a visit to win the support of the American people for her family's authoritarian regime. (*See November 1*)

**1963**   Robert G. Baker, Secretary to the Democratic majority in the U.S. Senate since 1955, resigns his post following charges that he is guilty allegedly of "influence peddling."

## OCTOBER 8

**1871**   The great fire of Chicago breaks out after a cow kicks over a lanern in a barn owned by a Mrs. O'Leary at 137 De Koven Street. (One of the great disasters in United States history, the fire swept over 2,100 acres, burned more than 17,000 buildings, killed several hundred people, and left 98,000 persons homeless. The damage amounted to $196,000,000.)

**1904**   The first automobile race for the Vanderbilt Cup starts at Hicksville, Long Island, over a 30-mile course. Included among the entries are 5 Mercedes', 3 Panhards, 2 Fiats, 2 Popes, 1 Renault, 1 Packard, 1 Simplex. The winner is George Heath, driving a Panhard.

**1904**   *Little Johnny Jones,* a musical play by George M. Cohan, opens in Hartford, Connecticut. The score includes the immortal song, "Give My Regards to Broadway."

**1918**   In the heart of the Argonne Forest, France, Sergeant Alvin C. York of the U.S. Army, separated from his patrol, captures a hill, kills 20 enemy soldiers, and captures 132 others. In the words of Marshal Foch, the hero's feat was "the greatest thing accomplished by any private soldier of all the armies of Europe.") (WORLD WAR I)

**1923**   Germany's shaky postwar economy has produced a wave of such disastrous inflation that one penny in U.S. currency buys 6,250,000 paper marks.

**1940**   Congress passes an act levying taxes on excess profits of corporation earnings.

**1942**   The first contingent of WAVES (Women Appointed for Voluntary Emergency Service) start their naval training at Smith College, Northampton, Massachusetts. (WORLD WAR II)

**1951**   Egyptian Premier Mustafa el-Nahas Pasha denounces the Anglo-Egyptian Pact of 1936 and asks Parliament to oust the British from the Suez Canal Zone.

**1953**   A new crisis arises in the much-disputed Free Territory of Trieste when the United States and Great Britain announce they plan to withdraw their occupation forces and permit Italy to assume the administration of Zone A. (*See October 5*)

**1956**   In the fifth game of the World Series in New York, Don Larsen of the New York Yankees pitches a perfect game against the Brooklyn Dodgers, winning by 2–0. Larsen does not yield a hit, a run, or pass a batsman. No Brooklyn player reaches first base. (This was the first no-hitter in the history of the World Series.)

## OCTOBER 9

**Leif Ericsson Day**   Celebrated by the Norwegians to honor the landing of the Norsemen on the coast of North America (probably somewhere in New England) about A.D. 1000. The expedition was headed by Leif Ericsson.

**1701**   Yale College is founded.

**1781**   George Washington sets off the first gun at the siege of Yorktown.

**1855**   Joshua C. Stoddard of Worcester, Massachusetts, receives a patent for the first calliope in history, a steam organ with a simple eight-note keyboard. Mr. Stoddard plans to sell his calliopes to churches for use in bell towers as a novel way of calling people to worship. (As a musical instrument for churches, the new invention failed, but it was taken up enthusiastically by river steamers and circuses.)

**1858**   Mail by overland stagecoach reaches St. Louis, Missouri, after a trip of 23 days and 4 hours out of San Francisco.

**1894**   An invited audience at the Carbon Studio in New York City is delighted with a showing of the first "Magic Lantern" feature picture. The picture is called "Miss Jerry," the principal leads being played by Blanche Bayliss and William Courtenay.

**1910**   Forest fires in northern Minnesota destroy 6 towns with a loss of 400 lives and property damage estimated at $100,000,000.

**1934**   King Alexander of Yugoslavia, on a state visit to France, is assassinated by a member of a Croatian terrorist organization at Marseilles. The King is succeeded to the throne by his young son, Peter II.

**1939**   A Nazi submarine seizes the U.S. merchant vessel, *City of Flint,* and forces it into port at Murmansk, in the Soviet Union. The ship is released 17 days later. (WORLD WAR II)

**1940**    The British Air Ministry announces that the roof of St. Paul's Cathedral in London has been pierced by a German bomber and that the high altar was left in ruins. (WORLD WAR II)

**1958**    Pope Pius XII, 82, dies after a reign of 19 years.

**1963**    President Kennedy approves the sale of $250 million worth of wheat to the Soviet Union, on the condition that the grain will be used only inside Russia and Eastern Europe. The wheat—150 million bushels—will be sold through private commercial channels at the world price for cash or short-term credit.

## OCTOBER 10

**Oklahoma Historical Day**    A legal holiday in that state.

**China's National Day**    Commemorating the anniversary of the overthrow of the Manchu dynasty. (*See below.*)

**1845**    The U.S. Naval Academy, organized by Congress "on an unostentatious and frugal plan," is opened formally at Fort Severn, Annapolis.

**1886**    A tailless dress coat for men, introduced from England, is worn for the first time in the United States at the Tuxedo Club, New York. The coat is worn by a club member, Griswold Lorillard. (Most of the guests at the club that evening were shocked at such informality, but the "tuxedo" eventually became more commonplace in the United States than the tailcoat.)

**1911**    Chinese revolutionaries under Dr. Sun Yat-sen strike at Wuchang and overthrow the Manchu dynasty.

**1913**    In Washington, President Woodrow Wilson presses a button which blows up the last remaining obstruction in the Panama Canal.

**1943**    Generalissimo Chiang Kai-shek is sworn in as president of China on the 32nd anniversary of the founding of the republic.

**1957**    Embarrassed by the racial discrimination suffered by a foreign dignitary, President Eisenhower and Vice President Nixon invite Komala Agbeli Gbdemah, the Finance Minister of Ghana, to have breakfast with them at the White House. (The Finance Minister, during his current visit to the United States, had been denied a glass of orange juice at a Dover, Delaware, restaurant, after being told that "colored people are not allowed to eat here.")

## OCTOBER 11

**Pulaski Memorial Day**    Authorized by President Harry S. Truman in 1946 to honor Brigadier General Casimir Pulaski, Polish nobleman, who died October 11, 1779, fighting for American independence during the Battle of Savannah, Georgia.

**1811**    The first steam-propelled ferry in the world starts its run between New York City and Hoboken, New Jersey.

**1868**  Thomas Alva Edison files papers for his first invention, an electrical vote recorder designed to tabulate floor votes in Congress in a matter of minutes. (Congress rejected it.)

**1884**  Eleanor Roosevelt, wife of President Franklin D. Roosevelt and the only woman in the history of the nation to serve as First Lady of the land for 12 years, is born in New York City. (Space does not permit a more complete listing here of the achievements of Mrs. Roosevelt. President John F. Kennedy called her "one of the great ladies in the history of this country." And in countless polls, both national and international, she was selected as "the world's most admired woman.") *(See November 7, 10)*

**1899**  Winston Churchill sails to South Africa to cover the Boer War as chief correspondent of the *London Morning Post*.

**1900**  Winston Churchill wins his first seat in the House of Commons, representing the constituency of Oldham.

**1921**  The name of Vaughn De Leath is becoming familiar throughout America as she introduces a new type of singing, called "crooning," during her regular radio broadcasts.

**1932**  The Democratic National Committee sponsors a television program emanating from New York, the first political telecast in the United States.

**1936**  "Professor Quiz," the first "quiz" program on radio to attract national attention, starts its long-time run over the facilities of the Columbia Broadcasting System.

**1944**  The American First Army begins its task of capturing the German city of Aachen after Nazi authorities refuse to surrender within the 24-hour ultimatum period. (WORLD WAR II)

**1945**  Chiang Kai-shek and Communist leader Mao Tse-tung issue a joint statement pledging their mutual desires for peace and unity. (The pledge was short-lived, however, as clashes between the Nationalists and Communists caused a resumption of the civil war. Within a month, fighting between the two forces had spread into 11 provinces.)

**1962**  Pope John XXIII opens the Second Vatican Ecumenical Council in St. Peter's Basilica in Rome, the first meeting of the Council since the one held in 1869–70. Attending the sessions in Rome are 2700 Catholic prelates and Protestant observers.

**1963**  A report from Washington says there are now 96,000,000 women in the United States, outnumbering men by nearly four million. Among those making up this total: 44,000,000 are housewives, 24,000,000 are paid workers, 3,250,000 are labor union members, 234 are state legislators, 11 are members of the U.S. House of Representatives and 2 are members of the U.S. Senate.

# OCTOBER 12

## Columbus Day

**1492**  At two o'clock in the morning, Roderigo de Triana, a sailor aboard the *Pinta,* one of the three vessels in the expedition led by Christopher Columbus, sights land. Landing, Columbus takes possession in the name of Ferdinand and Isabella of Spain. (This landing probably took place on the east coast of the Bahamas, in the vicinity of the present Watling Island.)

**1870**  General Robert E. Lee, Confederate hero, dies in Lexington, Virginia.

**1895**  Charles Blair MacDonald wins the first official amateur golf tournament played in the United States. (The contest was staged at the Newport, Rhode Island, Country Club, and MacDonald defeated 31 competitors for the title.)

**1915**  Edith Cavell, heroic English nurse, is shot by a German firing squad in Brussels after admitting she had assisted some 200 English, French, and Belgian patriots to gain their freedom from occupied Belgium. (Miss Cavell faced the firing squad with a dignity which moved the world. To a British chaplain who administered a final sacrament, she remarked, "Patriotism is not enough.") (WORLD WAR I)

**1920**  Construction begins on the twin tunnels under the Hudson River linking New York City and Jersey City, New Jersey. The project will be named the Holland Tunnel.

**1940**  Adolf Hitler postpones "Operation Sea Lion," the projected German invasion of the British Isles, until the spring of 1941. (The Reichsfuehrer was disappointed, but he was convinced, quite correctly, that the Royal Air Force was still undefeated.) (WORLD WAR II)

**1945**  The Allied Control Council in Germany orders the dissolution of the National Socialist (Nazi) Party and all of its agencies and affiliated organizations.

**1950**  The Senate Subcommittee to investigate Interstate Crime starts its hearings in New York City, under the chairmanship of Senator Estes Kefauver (D., Tenn.).

**1960**  The regular decorum of the United Nation's General Assembly is shattered by Premier Nikita Khrushchev as he angrily denounces Assembly President Frederick H. Boland and some delegates for not voting on the Soviet draft declaration against colonialism. After interrupting several speakers, Khrushchev removes one of his shoes and repeatedly pounds his desk with it. (President Boland was so infuriated that he lost his Irish temper and split his gavel trying to maintain order.)

# OCTOBER 13

**1775**   The Continental Congress orders the construction of a naval fleet, thus originating the U.S. Navy. The first vessels to be built will be two cruisers, one equipped with 10 guns and the other with 14 guns.

**1792**   The cornerstone of the President's House, the first public building to be built in Washington, is laid by George Washington. When completed, the executive mansion will be a replica of the Duke of Leinster's Palace in Ireland. (Note that the term "White House" is not used at this period. That designation was not used until after 1818 when the mansion was restored and painted white, following its burning in 1814 by the British.)

**1862**   All over the North, people are singing and whistling "John Brown's Body," an anonymous song sung to the tune of "Glory, Glory, Hallelujah." (The reference, of course, was to the hanging of the noted abolitionist in 1859.)

**1912**   In a move to increase the population, the government of Australia announces a $25 bonus will be paid to the parents of every newborn baby.

**1924**   Alfred Lunt and Lynn Fontanne begin their joint stage careers in New York at the opening of *The Guardsman.*

**1937**   Nazi Germany promises Great Britain and France that, in the case of a future European war, she will not violate Belgian neutrality.

**1943**   Italy declares war on her former Axis partner, Germany. (WORLD WAR II)

**1949**   Pandit Jawaharlal Nehru, Prime Minister of India, in the United States on a state visit, addresses a joint session of Congress.

**1960**   Senator John F. Kennedy, in New York, and Vice President Richard M. Nixon, in Hollywood, are linked by television as they discuss the issues of their campaigns for the Presidency, the third "debate" they have conducted in the last three weeks.

**1962**   Drama critics applaud the opening in New York of the first full-length play by Edward Albee, a 34-year-old writer. In reviewing his play, *Who's Afraid of Virginia Woolf?,* Howard Taubman of *The New York Times* says the new drama is one that "towers over the common run of contemporary plays" and predicts that Albee will become "a major figure of our stage."

# OCTOBER 14

**1066**   At the Battle of Hastings, King Harold and his English forces are defeated by the Normans, led by William, Duke of Normandy. (William, therefore, earned the nickname of "William the Conqueror.")

**1890**   Dwight D. Eisenhower, 34th President of the United States, is born in Denison, Texas.

**1899**   The *Literary Digest* predicts a dim future for the "horseless carriage," saying that "at present it is a luxury for the wealthy; and although its price will probably fall . . . it will never, of course, come into as common use as the bicycle."

**1912**   Former President Theodore Roosevelt, campaigning for a third term, is shot by a would-be assassin in Milwaukee. Colonel Roosevelt refuses to have his breast wound treated at a hospital until he speaks at a scheduled political rally, saying, "It may be the last speech I shall deliver, but I am going to deliver this one." (He was treated at a local hospital after he made his long speech and then insisted on completing his trip to Chicago.)

**1930**   A young singer, making her debut on Broadway, brings down the house at the *première* of George Gershwin's musical comedy, *Girl Crazy*. Her name: Ethel Merman. (One of the things that first-night audience remembered was the way she held a high C for 16 bars during the second chorus of "I Got Rhythm.")

**1933**   Nazi Germany announces she will withdraw from the League of Nations at the end of 1934.

**1937**   "The March of Time," a new type of radio program featuring the news in dramatic form, makes its bow over a coast-to-coast network.

**1939**   The British Admiralty announces the sinking of the battleship *Royal Oak* by a German submarine in Scapa Flow Bay in North Scotland. Eight hundred crewmen lose their lives in the disaster. (WORLD WAR II)

**1944**   British and Greek troops liberate Athens after converging by sea and air on the Greek capital which has been in German hands since April 21, 1941. (WORLD WAR II)

**1947**   Flying in an army rocket-powered research airplane at Muroc Air Base, California, Captain Charles E. Yeager of the U.S. Air Force becomes the first person to fly faster than the speed of sound.

**1949**   Russian occupation authorities set up an East German puppet state with headquarters in East Berlin. Soviet Premier Joseph Stalin hails the new state as "a turning point in the history of Europe."

**1949**   A jury in New York finds 11 leaders of the Communist Party in the United States guilty of a criminal conspiracy against the government. (Prison sentences were handed down on October 21. This trial, which started on January 17, 1949, cost the government $1,000,000 to prosecute and is believed to be the longest criminal case in U.S. history.)

# OCTOBER 15

**1714**   King Charles XII of Sweden is seen buttering his bread with the royal thumb. This conforms to the best practices of etiquette, however, because table knives have not as yet been invented.

**1858**   Abraham Lincoln and Stephen A. Douglas hold their seventh and final debate at Alton, Illinois, before an audience of 6,000 people.

**1914**   The Clayton Anti-Trust Act, supplementing the Sherman Anti-Trust Act of 1890, becomes law. (This act has many provisions, but it became famous as the statute that exempted labor from the anti-trust laws, declaring that "labor is not a commodity.")

**1917**   The most famous spy of World War I, Mata Hari (Gertrud Margarete Zelle), is executed at Vincennes Barracks outside Paris by a firing squad of Zouaves. (The Dutch-born spy, an agent for the German government, adopted the name of "Mata Hari," meaning "Eye of the Morning," in Java some years before the war.)

**1917**   All privately owned ocean-going vessels are requisitioned by the government for the duration of the war. (WORLD WAR I)

**1928**   The German dirigible *Graf Zeppelin* arrives in the United States on its first commercial flight, 4½ days after it left Germany.

**1945**   In accordance with the directives of the allied occupation authorities, Japan completes her military demobilization and, for the first time in history, is without an armed force.

**1945**   Pierre Laval, former French premier, is executed by a firing squad at Fresnes prison for betraying his country to Nazi Germany during World War II. (The Vichy collaborator almost cheated his executioners by swallowing poison a few hours before he was scheduled to die, but he was revived and forced to face his captors.)

**1946**   Reichsmarshal Hermann Goering, sentenced to death by the Nuremberg allied military tribunal, commits suicide by taking poison in his prison cell a day before his scheduled execution.

**1950**   President Harry S. Truman flies to Wake Island in the Pacific to confer with General Douglas MacArthur on matters pertaining to the prosecution of the Korean War. (The two men had never met each other before this date.)

**1958**   An impressionist painting brings a record price at an art auction conducted by Sotheby's in London. Paul Cézanne's "Boy In A Red Vest" is sold to Georges Keller, a New York art dealer, for $616,000, the highest price for any painting ever sold to date at auction.

**1964**   The eyes of the world are turned on Moscow after an announcement is released there stating briefly that Nikita S. Khrushchev has "resigned" as premier and First Secretary of the Central Committee of the Soviet Communist Party. Khrushchev is succeeded as premier by Aleksei N. Kosygin, while the new party First Secretary is Leonid I. Brezhnev. (The replacement of Khrushchev was explained "for reasons of health," but within 24 hours a series of critical denunciations were directed at his leadership. *Pravda,* the party organ, said bluntly that he was guilty of "harebrained scheming.")

## OCTOBER 16

**1829**   The Tremont House in Boston celebrates its opening with a lavish banquet and announces that its rooms will rent for $2.00 a day, including four meals. (This famous Boston establishment is considered by many to be the first modern first-class hotel in America. Its 170 rooms were equipped with soap, wash bowl and pitcher, and gas lights. Bathing facilities were provided in the basement.)

**1846**   The first operation with the patient under ether anesthesia is performed at Massachusetts General Hospital in Boston. (The operation was performed by Dr. John C. Warren and the ether administered by Dr. William T. Morton, a dentist, as many Boston physicians looked on from the gallery. When the operation was completed, Dr. Warren told the physicians, many of whom were skeptical about the value of ether, "Gentlemen, this is no humbug!")

**1859**   The fanatical Abolitionist, John Brown of Osawatomie, Kansas, stages a raid on Harper's Ferry, Virginia, seizing the Wagner House Hotel, the federal arsenal, the town firehouse, and some thirty townspeople. Brown's objective, he says, is to free the nation's Negroes and establish them in an independent Negro republic. (Several comic incidents took place during this otherwise serious and tragic event. On the morning of the next day, Brown needed breakfast for his own band of 18 men and 30 prisoners. One of his prisoners was the bartender in the Wagner House and the hotel's management offered to serve Brown 40 dishes of ham and eggs in exchange for their bartender's release. Brown accepted the offer.)

**1911**   At the National Conference of Progressive Republicans, meeting in Chicago, Senator Robert M. La Follette of Wisconsin is endorsed for the Presidency in the 1912 elections.

**1934**   Chinese Communists, dislodged from southeast China, begin the "Long March," establishing their headquarters in the northwest province of Shensi where they plan to continue their fight against the Nationalist forces of Chiang Kai-shek.

**1939**   Monty Woolley is the star of the hilarious comedy, *The Man Who Came to Dinner,* which opens tonight at the Music Box Theatre in New York.

**1940**   The United States bans all shipments of steel and scrap iron to Japan.

**1944**   Lloyd Douglas' book, *The Robe,* is published—a best seller from the day of its publication.

**1944**  The Macmillan Company brings out *Forever Amber,* a first novel by Kathleen Winsor.

**1946**  Ten top German Nazi war criminals are hanged in Nuremberg. Those executed are: Hans Frank, Wilhelm Frick, Colonel Alfred Jodl, Ernst Kaltenbrünner, Field Marshal Wilhelm Keitel, Alfred Rosenberg, Fritz Sauckel, Arthur Seyss-Inquart, Julius Streicher, Joachim von Ribbentrop.

**1957**  Queen Elizabeth II of Great Britain and her husband, Prince Philip, Duke of Edinburgh, arrive in Jamestown, Virginia, to help celebrate the 350th anniversary of the first permanent English settlement in the New World. While the Queen has visited the United States before, this is her first visit as British sovereign.

**1963**  Because Mississippi Democrats are worried about the growth of the two-party system in their state, some 3,000 of them hold a rally in Jackson and pledge to start a campaign to "bury Republicanism in Mississippi for the next 100 years." (NOTE: In 1964, Mississippi cast its electoral vote for Senator Barry Goldwater, the Republican Presidential candidate.)

**1964**  As the result of yesterday's national elections, Harold Wilson, leader of Britain's Labour Party, becomes the new prime minister of the United Kingdom. This is the first British Labour Government since 1951.

**1964**  Communist China announces it has tested its first nuclear bomb, the fifth known world power to do so.

## OCTOBER 17

**1777**  The British General John Burgoyne surrenders his forces to the Americans at Saratoga, New York, one of the great turning points of the American Revolution. (Perhaps the most significant result of the American victory at Saratoga was that it assured the colonials of prompt French assistance.)

**1824**  Boardinghouse keepers in New York band together because of the high cost of living and vote to serve boarders only four prunes apiece at breakfast.

**1845**  The editor of the *Boston Transcript* reports that the "singularly didactic excordium" of Edgar Allan Poe's reading of "The Raven" the night before at the Lyceum had caused the audience to walk out on him. (Poe answered by saying he was ashamed of having been born in such a city.)

**1855**  Henry Bessemer, successful English engineer and factory owner, patents his process for making steel.

**1869**  James Gordon Bennett, publisher of the *New York Herald,* directs Henry M. Stanley, the Anglo-American explorer and journalist, to find the missing Scottish missionary, David Livingstone, in darkest Africa.

**1920**    John Reed, 33, American journalist and enthusiastic admirer of the Soviet regime in Russia, dies in Moscow of a typhus infection. (The young radical writer was buried in Red Square, near the Kremlin wall, and is considered by the Russians to be one of the few American heroes of the Soviet Union.)

**1923**    Serious riots are sweeping all over Berlin, Germany, as the result of an increase in the prices of bread. Mobs besiege the Town Hall demanding the resumption of food price controls.

**1931**    The best-known bootlegger and racketeer in the United States, Al Capone, is convicted of income-tax evasion by a federal court in Chicago and sentenced to a prison term of 11 years and a fine of $50,000.

**1933**    Dr. Albert Einstein, a refugee from Nazi Germany, arrives in the United States and establishes his residence in Princeton, New Jersey.

**1941**    A German submarine torpedoes the U.S. destroyer *Kearney* off the coast of Iceland, killing 11 members of the crew. WORLD WAR II)

**1945**    After addressing a great mass meeting in Buenos Aires' Plaza de Mayo, Colonel Juan Perón stages a surprise *coup d'état* and overthrows the government of Argentina, thus becoming that nation's absolute dictator.

**1957**    The streets of Washington are lined with 1,000,000 people who have come out in the rain to greet Queen Elizabeth II of Great Britain and her husband, The Duke of Edinburgh, as they arrive in the nation's capital to visit President and Mrs. Eisenhower.


## OCTOBER 18

### Alaska Day (*See Page 329.*)

**1767**    The boundary line between Maryland and Pennsylvania, popularly called the Mason-Dixon Line, is finally settled, based on computations by two English astronomers, Charles Mason and Jeremiah Dixon. The two surveyors mark the border line with the arms of William Penn on one side and those of Lord Baltimore on the other.

**1842**    Samuel Finley Breese Morse lays the first telegraph cable in New York harbor, stretching between the Battery and Governors Island.

**1859**    U.S. troops under the command of Colonel Robert E. Lee storm the firehouse at Harper's Ferry, Virginia, and arrest John Brown and his last ten followers. Brown issues a statement explaining his raid on the town: "I justify my acts upon the Golden Rule. I pity the poor in bondage that have none to help them."

**1867**    At ceremonies marking the formal transfer of Alaska from Russia to the United States, the Russian flag is lowered in front of the governor's residence in Sitka and the flag of the United States raised in its place. General Lovell H. Rousseau takes formal possession of the territory for the Government of the United States. *(See January 3)*

**1873**    Representatives of four eastern colleges—Princeton, Yale, Rutgers, and Columbia—meet in New York and draw up the first rules to govern intercollegiate football matches.

**1892**    The first commercial long-distance telephone line is opened between New York and Chicago after messages are exchanged between the mayors of the two cities.

**1898**    The flag of the United States is raised over the island of Puerto Rico, shortly before Spain formally cedes the island to American control.

**1901**    President Theodore Roosevelt infuriates many sections of the South when it is learned that Booker T. Washington, the famous Negro educator, is to be his dinner guest at the White House. (This news caused several Southern newspapers to engage in shameful attacks upon the President and Mr. Washington. The *Memphis* (Tennessee) *Scimitar,* for example, said Roosevelt had committed "the most damnable outrage ever perpetrated by any citizen of the United States when he invited a nigger to dine with him at the White House.")

**1924**    The Lambs Club in New York establishes a precedent by electing Thomas Meighan their Shepherd. Meighan is the first motion-picture actor to be elected to the supreme office in the famous theatrical club.

**1950**    Connie Mack, manager of the Philadelphia Athletics baseball team, announces his retirement. The Grand Old Man of Baseball has been associated with baseball affairs for 67 years.

**1963**    The Earl of Home succeeds Harold Macmillan as Prime Minister of Great Britain. (The new Prime Minister renounced his title 5 days later, thus becoming Sir Alec Douglas-Home.)

## OCTOBER 19

**1744**    The Earl of Sandwich, inventor of the sandwich, says in London that sandwiches should be eaten with "a civilized swallow and not a barbarous bolt."

**1781**    The Revolutionary War is almost over as Lord Cornwallis, the Lieutenant General of the British Army, surrenders at Yorktown, Virginia, to an allied force of American and French troops. Says General George Washington: "The work is done and well done." And the band of the defeated British soldiers breaks out into a mournful rendition of an old English song entitled "The World Turned Upside Down."

**1814**    "The Star-Spangled Banner" is sung in Baltimore for the first time.

**1860**    To an 11-year-old girl, Grace Bedell, who wrote to him on October 15, saying that she would try to persuade her four brothers to vote for him for President if he grew a beard, Abraham Lincoln writes: "My dear little Miss— . . . As to the whiskers, having never worn any, do you not think people would call it a piece of silly affectation if I were to begin it now?" (But by November 26, 1860, soon after he won the election, a newspaper portrait showed Lincoln with the beginnings of his beard.)

**1936**    A round-the-world airplane race between three newspaper reporters comes to an end when H. R. Elkins of the *New York World Telegram* flies into Lakehurst, New Jersey, after covering some 25,600 miles in 18 days, 11 hours, 14 minutes, and 33 seconds. (Elkins nosed out Dorothy Kilgallen and Leo Kiernan.)

**1943**    A woman serves as the presiding officer of the U.S. Senate for the first time in history as Senator Hattie W. Caraway (D., Ark.) acts as president pro tempore on the invitation of Vice President Henry A. Wallace.

**1944**    Marlon Brando makes his New York stage debut in the new Broadway hit, *I Remember Mama*.

**1953**    The well-known radio and television personality Arthur Godfrey creates a nationwide controversy when he fires Julius La Rosa, one of his singers, from his supporting cast. (Godfrey's explanation was that the young singer showed a "lack of humility.")

**1954**    Great Britain and Egypt sign a new Suez Pact, providing for the withdrawal of British troops from the Suez Canal Zone during the next 20 months. The new pact replaces the Anglo-Egyptian Treaty of 1936 and guarantees Egyptian control of the Suez at the end of 7 years.

**1957**    Queen Elizabeth II, the reigning monarch of Great Britain, does something she has always wanted to do. She leaves Washington for Maryland and witnesses there her first American football game. (The game was between the Universities of Maryland and North Carolina.)

**1960**    As a result of the hostile relations between the U.S. government and the regime of Cuban Premier Fidel Castro, the State Department embargoes shipment of all goods to Cuba with the exception of foodstuffs and medicines.

**1960**    The Reverend Martin Luther King, Jr., is arrested with 52 other Negroes in an Atlanta, Georgia, department store restaurant for staging a sit-down demonstration. Later, he is whisked away to the state penitentiary. (*See October 26*)

# OCTOBER 20

**1873**   P. T. Barnum opens his Hippodrome in New York City, built to house the impresario's "Greatest Show on Earth."

**1910**   Woodrow Wilson resigns as president of Princeton University to run for his first elective office, that of governor of New Jersey.

**1918**   In their third peace note, the Germans accept President Woodrow Wilson's terms to end the war and issue orders recalling all submarines to their home bases. (WORLD WAR I)

**1924**   Lovers of jazz music are flocking to the Cinderella Ballroom in New York to listen to the music of The Wolverines, a popular band recently arrived from Chicago. The greatest attraction in the orchestra is a young cornetist from Davenport, Iowa, Leon (Bix) Beiderbecke.

**1944**   American troops land on the eastern coast of Leyte Island in the Philippines. General Douglas MacArthur, who was forced to leave the islands 2½ years ago, issues this proclamation to the Filipinos: "I have returned. ... Rally to me. Let the indomitable spirit of Bataan and Corregidor lead on. As the lines of battle roll forward to bring you within the zone of operations, rise and strike." (WORLD WAR II)

**1953**   Corporal Edward S. Dickenson of Big Stone Gap, Virginia, one of the 23 American prisoners of war who originally refused to be repatriated after the Korean War, changes his mind and asks to be returned to the United States.

**1955**   Thousands of people in Tokyo cheer the New York Yankees baseball team as they arrive in Japan to play 16 exhibition games in 10 cities against Japanese professional teams.

**1962**   Chinese Communist troops launch an offensive against India in the area of the Kechilang River, north of India's eastern border with Tibet. The official Chinese Communist news agency says that the attack was necessary because "Indian aggressive troops" had "launched a ... frenzied attack on China's frontier guards ..."

# OCTOBER 21

**1805**   The English fleet under the command of Lord Nelson defeats the allied French and Spanish fleets off the Cape of Trafalgar, Spain, thus ending Napoleon's power on the seas. (It was at the beginning of this battle that Lord Nelson signaled his immortal words: "England expects that every man will do his duty.")

**1879**   Thomas Alva Edison invents a workable electric incandescent lamp after 14 months of experimentation at his Menlo Park, New Jersey, laboratory. ("The longer it burned, the more fascinated we were ... There was no sleep for any of us for 40 hours."—Edison.)

**1907**   The New York *première* of *The Merry Widow*, starring Ethel Jackson and Donald Brian, takes place at the Amsterdam Theatre. (This operetta by Franz Lehár had been running in Europe since 1905, so its entrancing score was thoroughly familiar to American theatregoers in 1907. Drama critics present at this New York opening reported that the audience sang, whistled, and hummed the songs along with the cast.)

**1917**   Soldiers of the First Division of the U.S. Army are the first Americans to see action on the front lines. They are training in a sector near Lunéville, France. (WORLD WAR I)

**1925**   The Treasury Department in Washington announces that 29,620 violators of the prohibition enforcement laws paid the government $5,000,000 in fines during the last fiscal year.

**1940**   Prime Minister Winston Churchill twits Adolf Hitler during a radio broadcast, saying: "We are waiting for the long-promised invasion. So are the fishes." (WORLD WAR II)

**1944**   After 10 days of fighting, the U.S. First Army captures Aachen, the first large German city to fall into Allied hands. (WORLD WAR II)

**1960**   The two major Presidential candidates, Senator John F. Kennedy and Vice President Richard M. Nixon, meet in New York for the last of their televised debates on the leading issues of the campaign.

## OCTOBER 22

**1746**   The College of New Jersey, now Princeton University, is granted its charter by the royal governor of New Jersey.

**1836**   General Sam Houston, the hero of the Battle of San Jacinto waged against the Mexicans led by Santa Anna, is sworn into office as the first president of the Republic of Texas. The ceremony takes place at Columbia, Texas.

**1883**   The Metropolitan Opera House in New York celebrates its grand opening with a performance of Gounod's opera *Faust*. The new music center can seat more than three thousand persons.

**1907**   Thousands of people line up in front of the Knickerbocker Trust Company in New York as a "run" on the bank gets under way. All day long, the bank tellers pay out money to panic-stricken depositors, some of whom have been standing in line for 5 and 6 hours. (At noon the next day, with its cash reserves almost depleted, the bank suspended payments and the news of this, more than anything else, spurred on the Panic of 1907.)

**1918**   A dread word is uppermost in the minds of Americans from Maine to California—"flu," an abbreviated form of "influenza," the contagious disease that is striking out at people in every state of the Union. (Nearly one fourth of the people in the nation were stricken with the virus; the total deaths were between 400,000 and 500,000.)

**1919**   A woman named Nan Britton gives birth to a baby girl in Asbury Park, New Jersey, and claims the infant is the daughter of Senator (later President) Warren G. Harding of Ohio. (This scandalous charge was later enlarged, but not conclusively proved, in a book that rocked the nation, *The President's Daughter*.)

**1928**   A phrase in a speech by Secretary of Commerce Herbert Hoover, delivered as part of his campaign to win the Presidency in the November elections, serves to identify him as the exponent of "rugged individualism." (The complete quotation reads: "Rugged individualism is basic to the American System.")

**1942**   Frenchmen conscripted by the Nazis to work on German farms and in German industries fail to appear in Paris. General Otto von Stulpnagel, German Commander for Greater Paris, threatens to use force if the quota is not filled within 24 hours. (WORLD WAR II)

**1953**   Representatives of France and the Indochinese state of Laos sign a treaty in Paris making Laos "fully independent and sovereign." It is agreed that Laos will remain within the structure of the French Union.

**1962**   President Kennedy orders U.S. air and naval forces to establish a "quarantine" of Cuba after he concludes that Fidel Castro, with the help of the Soviet Union, is building missile bases there. The President addresses the nation from the White House, saying: "This Government has maintained the closest surveillance of the Soviet military buildup on the island of Cuba. Within the past week, unmistakable evidence has established the fact that a series of offensive missile sites is now in preparation on that imprisoned island. The purpose of these bases can be none other than to provide a nuclear striking capability against the Western Hemisphere. . . ."

## OCTOBER 23

**1910**   Residents of Fort Wayne, Indiana, are all agog over the first woman to make a public airplane flight by herself. She is Blanche S. Scott and her flight today is taking place over a local park. (Miss Scott rose to a height of 12 feet, a thrilling performance in 1910.)

**1915**   Twenty-five thousand women march in New York City demanding the right to vote in all 48 states.

**1917**   Soldiers of the First Division of the U.S. Army fire their first shots against the Germans in World War I. The actual firing started with Battery C of the Sixth Field Artillery, not far from Lunéville, France.

**1929**    Over six million shares of stocks are traded on the New York Stock Exchange, the average loss for 50 leading railroad and industrial stocks reaching 18.24 points. (Nonetheless, a headline on the financial page of a Chicago newspaper predicted that stock prices had reached "what looks like a permanently high plateau.")

**1935**    The world of crime is unnerved by the murder of "Dutch" Schultz (real name: Arthur Flegenheimer) in Newark, New Jersey. (For 6 years, the murder of this notorious bootlegger and racketeer remained unsolved. But on June 10, 1941, a court in Newark charged Charles [The Bug] Workman with the crime and sentenced him to life imprisonment.)

**1942**    The British Eighth Army, led by General Bernard Montgomery, launches a huge offensive against Axis forces at El Alamein, Egypt. (This was the beginning of the Battle of Egypt and the start of the campaign that was to sweep German and Italian forces out of North Africa.) (WORLD WAR II)

**1947**    The state of Maine is declared a disaster area as forest fires sweep over a large section of the state, destroying thousands of acres of timberland and a considerable part of the resort town of Bar Harbor. Damage is estimated at $30,000,000.

**1955**    Voters in the Saar reject overwhelmingly a proposed statute that would "Europeanize" the tiny country and draw it more closely to France which has controlled its economy since the end of World War II. The referendum indicates clearly that a large majority of Saarlanders want ultimate reunification with Germany.

**1955**    In the first election ever to take place in South Viet Nam, Indochina, the people oust Bao Dai as chief of state and replace him with Ngo Dinh Diem, currently serving as premier. (Diem received 98.2 per cent of the votes cast.)

**1956**    The Hungarian Revolution: Students in Budapest start a series of demonstrations demanding the relaxation of Stalinist terror, as practiced by the Communist regime. At the same time they demand that former Premier Imre Nagy be named as the head of a new government. These demands are rejected by Erno Gero, First Secretary of the Communist Party and street violence breaks out. (Gero appealed to the Russians for help, with the result that Russian tanks swarmed into the city. Order was not restored until November 4).

**1958**    Boris Pasternak, Russian poet and author, wins the 1958 Nobel Prize for literature for his novel, *Dr. Zhivago*. (His selection, however, was greeted in the Soviet Union by scorn and abuse. Various periodicals, reflecting the views of the government, branded Pasternak as anti-Communist and on October 28 he was expelled from the Soviet Writers Union. The next day he wired his "voluntary refusal" of the prize to the Swedish Academy because ". . . of the meaning given to this honor in the community to which I belong.")

**1962**   Despite the fact that both the Soviet Union and Cuba are enraged over President Kennedy's "quarantine" of Cuba, the Organization of American States unanimously votes in Washington to stand behind the United States.

# OCTOBER 24

## United Nations Day

**1667**   King Charles II of England tastes his first cranberries and takes an immediate fancy to them. Ten barrels of the berries have been presented to the English court by explorers returning from Cape Cod, Massachusetts, in the New World.

**1861**   For the first time in history, telegrams are sent across the United States as Stephen J. Field, chief justice of California, sends a message to President Abraham Lincoln in Washington. At the same time, the mayor of San Francisco sends a telegraphic message to the mayor of New York City. (The transcontinental telegraph had been authorized by Congress in June, 1860.)

**1901**   In a stunt to raise money to repay a loan due on her Texas ranch, Mrs. Anna Edson Taylor goes over Niagara Falls in a barrel, the first person to survive such an attempt. (The barrel was equipped with a harness and cushions, leading a reporter on the *Denver Republican* to quip that Mrs. Taylor "seems to be taking a lot of credit that belongs to the barrel.")

**1922**   At a convention of Italian Fascists meeting in Naples, their leader, Benito Mussolini, serves an ultimatum on the Italian government: "Either the government of the country is handed to us peaceably or we shall take it by force, marching on Rome and engaging in a struggle to the death with the politicians now in power."

**1929**   Prices on the New York Stock and Curb Exchanges collapse as over 19,000,000 shares change hands. A pool of six major banking institutions agree to put up $40,000,000 apiece to steady the market, and, after meeting at the offices of J. P. Morgan & Company, issue a statement saying that business is fundamentally sound. (Mr. Thomas W. Lamont, of the Morgan firm, described the day's activities on the market by telling a group of reporters: "There has been a little distress selling on the Stock Exchange.")

**1929**   Rudy Vallee, a saxophone-playing "crooner" from Maine, begins a series of weekly radio programs over the National Broadcasting Company, accompanied by his band, "The Connecticut Yankees." (For the next 10 years, he was one of the most popular performers in the country.)

**1931**   The George Washington Bridge, spanning the Hudson River between New York City and New Jersey, is opened to traffic.

**1939**    Women's hosiery made of nylon is placed on sale for the first time in a Wilmington, Delaware, department store. (Just one year earlier, in October, 1938, the E. I. du Pont de Nemours Company of Wilmington announced that it had patented nylon, describing it as a revolutionary fiber of coal, air, and water. When "nylons" were released for the national market in May, 1940, 780,-000 pairs were sold the first day.)

**1941**    President Franklin D. Roosevelt sets up the Office of Facts and Figures, naming Archibald MacLeish as the agency's director. The new bureau will disseminate news and information at home and abroad as a major instrument in the war effort. (WORLD WAR II)

**1945**    Secretary of State James F. Byrnes announces in Washington that the Charter of the United Nations is in force, following the ratification of the document by the Soviet Union, the 29th nation to do so.

**1952**    General Dwight D. Eisenhower, Republican candidate for the Presidency, tells an audience at the Masonic Auditorium in Detroit that, if elected, he will go to Korea to seek "an early and honorable" end to the war there.

**1955**    An 18-day siege of "smog" * in Los Angeles ends when strong winds clear the air.

**1963**    After he concludes a United Nations Day speech in Dallas, Texas, Ambassador Adlai Stevenson is spat upon, shoved, and jeered by right-wing demonstrators who are opposed to the United Nations. The ugly incidents occur as Mr. Stevenson is leaving Municipal Auditorium. (His comment: "For my part, I believe in the forgiveness of sin and the redemption of ignorance.")

## OCTOBER 25

**St. Crispin's Day**    Dedicated to the patron saint of shoemakers, saddlers, and tanners. This is the prayer usually offered by *pedestrians* to St. Crispin:

> "Dear Saint, the saint of those who make good shoes,
> Thee for my patron saint I also choose.
> Whene'er I walk in highway, trail or street,
> Bring thou *unblistered* home my grateful feet."

**1854**    "The Charge of the Light Brigade": Some 670 men of an English light cavalry brigade, fighting in the Crimean War, charge a heavily protected Russian artillery post at Balaklava, 8 miles away from besieged Sevastopol. (The famous charge was one

---

\* *Smog*, n. (A blend of smoke and fog. ) A fog made heavier and darker by the smoke of a city. *U.S.—Webster's New International Dictionary.*

of the most heroic episodes in British military history, but nonetheless the Russians killed or wounded two-thirds of the entire force and succeeded in capturing the only good road between British forces and their base at Balaklava.)

**1892** Caroline Lavinia Scott Harrison, wife of President Benjamin Harrison, dies in the White House after returning to Washington from a sanatorium in New York State.

**1923** The Teapot Dome scandals begin to unfold as Senator Thomas J. Walsh (D., Mont.) demands a public hearing on the Department of the Interior's leasing of two naval oil reserves to private corporations.

**1929** The Stock Market in New York goes through another day of heavy selling, with 8,655,120 shares traded before the day is over. At the White House, President Herbert Hoover comments: "The fundamental business of the country, that is, the production and distribution of commodities, is on a sound and prosperous basis."

**1936** The Fascist governments of Germany and Italy form the so-called "Rome-Berlin Axis," providing for common opposition to Communism and mutual assistance in case of another European war.

**1938** The Chinese Nationalist government flees to Chungking in the interior of China as the Japanese invaders capture Hankow. (By the end of 1938, the Japanese controlled all of coastal China as far south as Canton.)

**1940** John L. Lewis, president of the Congress of Industrial Organizations, and vehemently opposed to the reelection of President Franklin D. Roosevelt, says in a speech delivered over the facilities of three radio networks: "President Roosevelt will not be re-elected for a third term unless he has the overwhelming support of . . . labor. If he is, therefore, re-elected . . . I will accept the result as a vote of no confidence, and will retire as president of the CIO at its convention in November." (He did, too.)

**1954** For the first time in the nation's history, a session of the President's Cabinet is televised and observed by millions of people in the 48 states. (The occasion was prompted by a special report to President Dwight D. Eisenhower and the Cabinet by Secretary of State John Foster Dulles on his return from a meeting of the foreign ministers of 15 nations in Paris.)

## OCTOBER 26

**1369** Charles V, King of France, known as "Charles the Wise," dedicates a monument to his personal chef, Benkels, who recently invented a recipe for pickled fish that is particularly favored by His Majesty.

**1760** George III is crowned king of England.

337

**1825**   The Erie Canal, the first of the great man-made water-ways of the United States, is opened for traffic. As the highlight of the opening of the canal, which extends from Buffalo to Albany, New York, and connects Lake Erie with the Hudson River, Governor De Witt Clinton and a party of state officials board the canal boat *Seneca Chief* and set out for a trip to New York City. (They arrived there November 4, after witnessing town and village celebrations all along the route.)

**1916**   President Woodrow Wilson, speaking in Cincinnati, says: "I believe that the business of neutrality is over. The nature of modern war leaves no state untouched." (WORLD WAR I)

**1920**   Terence MacSwiney, the lord mayor of Cork, Ireland, dies in his prison cell after fasting for 75 days. (MacSwiney's "hunger strike," said to be the longest in history, was aimed at the British government and represented his demand for complete independence for Ireland. He was imprisoned on charges of conspiring against the Crown.)

**1942**   A major air, land, and sea attack opens in the Solomon Islands between Allied and Japanese forces. The U.S. aircraft carrier *Hornet* is sunk by the enemy. (WORLD WAR II)

**1947**   The first war dead of World War II are returned to this country aboard the transport *Joseph V. Connolly*. Four hundred thousand New Yorkers line the streets in silence as the bodies of the dead heroes are moved up Fifth Avenue to Central Park for memorial services.

**1949**   A shortage of coffee in the United States sets off a wave of price rises and subsequent hoarding. The shortage is due to crop failures in Latin America.

**1951**   Former heavyweight champion Joe Louis is knocked out by Rocky Marciano in 2 minutes, 36 seconds of the 8th round of their bout at Madison Square Garden in New York.

**1951**   As a result of the national elections in Great Britain, the Conservatives are back in power again. Prime Minister Clement Attlee, head of the Labour government, is succeeded by 76-year-old Winston Churchill.

**1960**   Following the arrest of Reverend Martin Luther King, Jr., in Georgia, Senator John F. Kennedy (D., Mass.) puts through a long-distance call to Mrs. King, telling her how concerned he is over the civil rights' leader's unjust arrest and imprisonment. (This occurred in the midst of the Presidential campaign. Vice President Nixon, the GOP candidate, made no comment and after the election, President Eisenhower said that "a couple of phone calls" (by the Senator and his brother Robert) had swung the Negro vote into the Democratic column.)

# OCTOBER 27

**Navy Day**   Celebrated each year on the anniversary of the birth of former President Theodore Roosevelt, onetime Assistant Secretary of the Navy, thus recognizing his special interest in the U.S. Navy.

**1775**   John Adams, drawing up some of the first rules for the new U.S. Navy, stipulates that "each man be allowed for Sunday rations one pound bread, one pound beef, one pound potatoes or turnips."

**1787**   Alexander Hamilton, John Jay, and James Madison, writing over the common pen name of "Publius," begin their series of essays in the *New York Independent Journal* to gain support for the ratification of the Constitution. (These essays, 94 in all, were later published in one volume under the title of *The Federalist*.)

**1858**   Theodore Roosevelt, 26th President of the United States, is born in New York City.

**1871**   William Marcy Tweed, better known as "Boss" Tweed, the corrupt political dictator of Tammany Hall in New York City, is arrested on charges of defrauding the city of millions of dollars.

**1904**   The first subway to prove practical starts its operations in New York, running from the Brooklyn Bridge to midtown Manhattan. ("Men fought and pummeled one another in their mad desire to reach the subway ticket office or to ride on the trains. Women were dragged out, either screaming, in hysterics or in a swooning condition. . . ."—From a newspaper report describing the opening of the subway.)

**1916**   One of the earliest references to the word "jazz" appears in the theatrical periodical *Variety* in a news story reporting the formation of "jazz bands" in Chicago.

**1917**   An enthusiastic audience in Carnegie Hall, New York, cheers the debut of a 16-year-old violinist, Jascha Heifetz. While this is his first public appearance in New York, the young violinist has been playing for concert audiences since he was 5 years old.

**1920**   Radio Station KDKA receives its license from the U.S. Department of Commerce and is making plans to broadcast regularly from its studio atop the tallest building of the Westinghouse Electric Company in Pittsburgh, Pennsylvania.

**1942**   James F. Byrnes, Director of the Office of Economic Stabilization, issues a regulation limiting individual salaries, beginning in 1943, to a high of $25,000 after the payment of federal income taxes and other usual deductions. (President Franklin D. Roosevelt, whose salary of $75,000 was fixed by law, immediately announced he would take a cut to comply with the new regulation.) (WORLD WAR II)

## OCTOBER 28

**1636**   Harvard College is founded in Massachusetts.

**1774**   The Continental Congress recommends a suspension of all public amusements. (Nothing came of this, however, and with the exception of a general observance of the Sunday Blue Laws, the colonists continued to enjoy social and recreational events in public.)

**1886**   Amid pomp and circumstance and oratory and parades and the stirring music of many bands, the Statue of Liberty is dedicated on Bedloe's Island in New York harbor. Just before President Grover Cleveland accepts the statue in the name of the American people, Frédéric Auguste Bartholdi, the statue's designer, pulls the French Tricolor from Liberty's face. In his speech, the President promises: "We will not forget that Liberty has here made her home; nor shall her chosen altar be neglected."

**1918**   The Czechoslovak National Committee in Prague proclaims the establishment of the Republic of Czechoslovakia and the independence of the new nation from Hapsburg control. (WORLD WAR I)

**1919**   The Senate follows the lead of the House of Representatives and passes the Volstead Prohibition Enforcement Act over the veto of President Woodrow Wilson. (In defining what was an alcoholic beverage, the Volstead Act ruled that any beverage containing $\frac{1}{2}$ of 1 per cent of alcohol was "intoxicating.")

**1922**   Black-shirted Italian Fascists set out from their headquarters in Naples and begin their march on Rome. The Fascist leader, Benito Mussolini, follows his legions discreetly and comfortably installed in a railway train. (The next day, after the mob had occupied Rome, King Victor Emmanuel asked Mussolini to form a new Cabinet, thus marking the recognized beginning of Fascism in Europe.)

**1929**   Losses in quoted values on the New York Stock and Curb Exchanges exceed $10,000,000,000. Some of the high-priced bank stocks fall from 100 to 500 points.

**1953**   The U.S. Army charges that a minimum of 29,815 persons have been murdered, tortured, or subjected to other forms of brutality by the Communists in Korea.

**1958**   Angelo Guiseppe, Cardinal Roncalli, 76, Patriarch of Venice, is elected Pope. He takes the name of John XXIII.

**1962**   Soviet Premier Khrushchev, following the U.S. quarantine of Cuba, backs down and informs President Kennedy that he has ordered the withdrawal of Soviet missiles from Cuba. He further promises that Soviet bases on the island will be dismantled under United Nations' inspection.

**1963**   Senator Barry Goldwater (R., Ariz.), an unannounced candidate for next year's Republican Presidential nomination, stirs up a controversy when it is learned that he believes the Tennessee Valley Authority "... would be better operated and ... be of more benefit for more people if it were part of private industry." (The Senator was roundly criticized for his proposal to "sell the TVA." On November 14, he amplified his original statement by saying that he thought some of the TVA services should be turned over to the states and to other appropriate federal agencies, as well as to private industry.)

## OCTOBER 29

**1618**   Sir Walter Raleigh is executed in London, charged with participating in a treasonable plot to oust King James I from the throne.

**1884**   The Democratic Party unites in anger against a statement made by the Reverend Samuel D. Burchard during a speech endorsing the Republican candidate for President, James G. Blaine. In praising Mr. Blaine, the clergyman says: "We are Republicans, and don't propose to leave our party and identify ourselves with the party whose antecedents have been Rum, Romanism, and Rebellion."

**1901**   Leon Czolgosz is electrocuted for the assassination of President William McKinley.

**1918**   Units of the German fleet stationed at Kiel begin a mutiny to underscore their demands for prompt peace negotiations with the Allies. (WORLD WAR I)

**1919**   Governor Alfred E. Smith of New York addresses an overflow audience at Carnegie Hall in New York City, defending himself and his political record against charges made by William Randolph Hearst and the Hearst newspaper chain. (The governor had challenged Hearst to debate on this date, but the publisher declined the invitation.)

**1923**   Turkey becomes a republic, its first president being the nationalist leader Mustafa Kemal. The new President announces he will be known henceforth as Kemal Atatürk.

**1929**   Pandemonium reigns on the New York Stock Exchange as prices virtually collapse. Huge blocks of stock are thrown on the market, but there are few buyers. By the time the gong rings ending the day's trading, billions of dollars of open market values have been wiped out. (In all, 16,410,030 shares were sold that day. But the statistics were not so frightening as the realization that the bottom had fallen out of the boom and the great Depression of the 1930's was under way.)

**1940**   The first peacetime compulsory military service in the United States is inaugurated when Secretary of War Henry L. Stimson draws Number 158, the first draft serial number, from a bowl in the War Department Auditorium in Washington. (The drawings continued until 5:47 o'clock in the morning of the next day, at which time there were serial numbers for all the men who had registered under the Selective Service and Training Act.)

**1955**     An inventory published by the Department of Defense reveals that the military wealth of the United States in property and equipment amounts to almost $124 billion.

**1956**     Now barred from using the Suez Canal, Israel launches an attack on Egypt's Sinai Peninsula and starts her drive toward the Canal.

**1964**     A spectacular gem robbery takes place in New York's American Museum of Natural History. The greatest loss is the Star of India, the largest star sapphire in the world. Also missing are the 100-carat DeLong Star Ruby, the 15-carat Eagle Diamond and several other irreplaceable gems. (Later, it was discovered that the robbery had been ingeniously carried out by three Miami beach boys. The Star of India and eight of the gems were found and returned to New York the following January.)

## OCTOBER 30

**1581**     The Meat Carvers' Guild of Venice tightens up its working conditions and announces that hereafter each carver will not perform for more than six guests. (Professional meat carvers were hired in those days by the gentry to carve for them at dinner parties. )

**1735**     John Adams, the second President of the United States, is born in Braintree, Massachusetts.

**1912**     Vice President James S. Sherman, a candidate for reelection on the Republican ticket with President William Howard Taft, dies before the election takes place in November. (He was replaced on the ticket by Nicholas Murray Butler of New York, but the Democrats won the election.)

**1929**     Heavy selling marks the first day's transactions after the "big bust" of October 29 on the New York Stock Exchange. Despite the fact that 10,727,320 shares are unloaded, John D. Rockefeller and his son announce that they are buying "sound common stocks" for investment. (The Rockefellers hoped this announcement would restore confidence in the market, but they were unable to stem the continued decline.)

**1930**     American economists, summarizing the first 10 months of this depression-ridden year, report that all listed stocks have dropped almost $23,000,000,000 since the previous April. The profits of 200 leading industrial corporations are down 45.9 percent.

**1938**     Orson Welles, the popular young actor, causes a national panic when he produces over the Columbia Broadcasting System a radio dramatization of H. G. Wells' *The War of the Worlds.* Simulating typical news broadcasts of the day, the program is interrupted regularly by "bulletins" describing the invasion of New Jersey by men from Mars. (Even though a clear explanation of the program had preceded the broadcast, thousands of radio listeners rushed out of their homes, many of them setting out for remote spots in the country. Hysterical people tied up the telephone lines, and police stations and hospitals were besieged by terror-stricken crowds.)

**1941**    The U.S. naval destroyer *Reuben James* is torpedoed by a German submarine and sunk off the coast of Iceland, despite the fact that the United States is not at war with Germany. (WORLD WAR II)

**1948**    An army transport from Bremerhaven, Germany, lands 813 European displaced persons in New York City, the first refugees to arrive in the United States under the Displaced Persons Act of 1948.


## OCTOBER 31

### Halloween

**1517**    Martin Luther nails his 95 theses against the abuse of the practice of Indulgence to the door of the Castle Church in Wittenberg, Germany.

**1864**    Nevada, the 36th state, is admitted into the Union.

**1903**    John Barrymore, the youngest member of a family long identified with the theatre, makes his first stage appearance in Chicago, playing at the Cleveland Theatre in *Magda*, a new play by Herman Sudermann.

**1931**    The Treasury Department announces that the financial condition of the nation is so grave that 522 banks closed their doors in the past month. In September, 305 bank failures took place.

**1932**    Nevada orders a 12-day bank holiday to save the state's tottering banks.

**1932**    President Herbert Hoover, campaigning for reelection on the Republican ticket, warns an audience in Madison Square Garden, New York, that if the Democrats come into power they will promptly repeal the high protective tariff, with the result that "the grass will grow in the streets of a hundred cities, a thousand towns; the weeds will overrun the fields of millions of farms."

**1951**    President Harry S. Truman welcomes Princess Elizabeth and Prince Philip of the British Royal Family to Washington during their visit to the United States and Canada.

**1955**    Princess Margaret, the sister of the Queen of England, ends 3 weeks of worldwide suspense and answers the question of whether she will marry Captain Peter Townsend of the Royal Air Force. At eight o'clock in the evening, the British Broadcasting

Corporation reads a statement released by the Princess: "I would like it to be known that I have decided not to marry Group Captain Peter Townsend. . . . Mindful of the Church's teaching that Christian marriage is indissoluble, and conscious of my duty to the Commonwealth, I have resolved to put these considerations before any others. I have reached this decision entirely alone, and in doing so I have been strengthened by the unfailing support and devotion of Group Captain Townsend." (The captain, a former royal equerry to King George VI, was divorced from his first wife.)

**1956**　　After Egypt rejects a cease-fire demand by Britain and France, in connection with the Israeli-Egyptian war, the two European nations bomb Egypt.

**1959**　　Lee Harvey Oswald, an ex-Marine from Texas, tells reporters in Russia where he has been living: "I will never return to the United States. . . . I would like to spend the rest of my life here and get a normal life . . ." (*See September 27, November 22, 24*)

**1961**　　The body of Joseph Stalin, the Soviet Union's longtime dictator, is removed from public display within a mausoleum in Red Square, Moscow, and buried in a simple grave alongside the Kremlin wall. (This was in line with the new so-called "destalinization" policy instigated by Premier Khrushchev who led the attack on Stalin's autocratic one-man rule.)

# NOVEMBER

## NOVEMBER 1

**1765** The Stamp Act, levied by the British Crown to raise revenue within the colonies and providing for stamps on newspapers, legal documents, pamphlets, playing cards, etc., goes into effect. Colonists defy their royal governors and lower their flags to half-mast as proclamations authorizing the act are read publicly.

**1788** The final session of the Continental Congress, which met for the first time in Philadelphia on September 5, 1774, is declared adjourned. (The first Congress under the federal Constitution met on March 4, 1789.)

**1857** The first installment of Oliver Wendell Holmes' *The Autocrat of the Breakfast Table* appears in the introductory issue of the *Atlantic Monthly*. ("Boston State-house is the hub of the solar system.")

**1864** The Post Office Department introduces the money-order system as a means of providing convenience and safety for individuals who want to make payments through the mails.

**1890** A clause in the new constitution adopted by the state of Mississippi restricts Negro suffrage in that state to those individuals who can read and interpret the Constitution of the United States.

**1913** One of the most important games in the history of football takes place at West Point as a virtually unknown Notre Dame team defeats Army, 35 to 13, the latter's first defeat of the season. (This game not only brought Notre Dame and its team captain, Knute Rockne, to the attention of the sports world, but it dramatized a new play called the "forward pass.")

**1918** The Hapsburg monarchy of Austria-Hungary comes to an end as a Hungarian Republic is proclaimed in Budapest and a Republic of Austria is set up in Vienna. (WORLD WAR I)

**1929** After being convicted of accepting a bribe from Edward L. Doheny in the leasing of the Elk Hills naval oil reserve, former Secretary of the Interior Albert B. Fall is sentenced to one year in prison and a fine of $100,000.

**1931** Eugene O'Neill's play, *Mourning Becomes Electra,* is the talk of New York. According to the drama critic of *The New York Times,* the play brings "the cold splendors of Greek tragedy off the sky-blue limbo of Olympus down to the gusty forum of contemporary life."

**1944** An invisible rabbit charms the opening-night audience of *Harvey* at the Forty-eighth Street Theatre in New York. (The play charmed the Pulitzer Awards committee, too. In 1945, the play by Mary Chase was awarded the Pulitzer Drama Award.)

**1948** Barely 24 hours before tomorrow's Presidential elections, most political pollsters and commentators agree that Governor Thomas E. Dewey, Republican of New York, will defeat Democratic President Harry S. Truman by a landslide. The syndicated columnist, David Lawrence, says this morning: "Governor Dewey will be elected by a substantial majority in the Electoral College...." And the well-known radio and television commentator, H. V. Kaltenborn, reports: "...I recall no election in which pollsters and dopesters were so completely unanimous....Dewey will carry from 20 to 29 states. Truman will carry from 9 to 11.... The Dewey electoral vote is predicted as from 274 to 345....The Truman electoral vote is estimated as from 96 to 122...." (President Truman remained calm. The polls, he said, were highly inaccurate.) *(See November 2)*

**1950** Two Puerto Rican Nationalists try to force their entrance into Blair House, in Washington, to assassinate President Harry S. Truman. (Guards killed one of the fanatics; the other was sentenced to death, the President later commuting the sentence to life imprisonment.)

**1963** A military coup deposes the government of South Vietnam and results in the murder of President Ngo Dinh Diem and his powerful brother, Ngo Dinh Nhu.

## NOVEMBER 2

**1795** James Knox Polk, the 11th President of the United States, is born in Mecklenburg County, North Carolina.

**1824** Presidential election: Andrew Jackson, Democrat, receives 99 electoral votes, John Quincy Adams, Democratic Republican, 84 electoral votes, William Harris Crawford, Democrat, 41 electoral votes, and Henry Clay, Republican, 37 electoral votes. (Since 131 electoral votes were needed for election, the contest was carried to the House of Representatives where a decision was made on February 9, 1825. See the 1825 entry under February 9, heading.)

**1852** Presidential election: Franklin Pierce and William R. King, Democrats, are elected President and Vice President respectively, winning 254 electoral votes to 42 received by General Winfield Scott and William A. Graham, Whigs.

**1865**    Warren Gamaliel Harding, 29th President of the United States, is born in Corsica, Ohio.

**1880**    Presidential election: James A. Garfield and Chester A. Arthur, Republicans, are elected President and Vice President respectively, winning 214 electoral votes to 155 received by General Winfield S. Hancock and William H. English, Democrats. (James B. Weaver and B. J. Chambers, running on the Greenback ticket, received no electoral votes.)

**1889**    North and South Dakota are admitted into the Union, ranked as the 39th and 40th states, respectively.

**1917**    Foreign Secretary Arthur James Balfour submits to the British Cabinet a proposal to establish a Jewish homeland in Palestine.

**1920**    Presidential election: Warren G. Harding and Calvin Coolidge, Republicans, are elected President and Vice President, respectively, winning 404 electoral votes to 127 received by James M. Cox and Franklin D. Roosevelt, Democrats. (Eugene V. Debs, running on the Socialist ticket, received no electoral votes.)

**1920**    Station KDKA, Pittsburgh, begins the first regular schedule of radio broadcasting as it reports the returns of the Harding-Cox (see above) Presidential election. (Comparatively few people heard this series of broadcasts, but those who were fortunate enough to own receiving sets kept their earphones on for hours on end, thrilled by the transmission of the news through the air.)

**1929**    The Embassy Theatre, a new type of motion-picture theatre specializing only in newsreels, opens in New York City, the first of its kind in film history.

**1930**    Haile Selassie is crowned emperor of Ethiopia at Addis Ababa.

**1936**    The *Literary Digest's* poll on the following day's Presidential election predicts that Republican Governor Alf Landon of Kansas will defeat President Franklin D. Roosevelt. Landon, says the *Digest,* will carry 32 states with 370 electoral votes against 16 states with 161 electoral votes for Roosevelt. (But James Farley, the astute chairman of the Democratic National Committee, made his own prediction to the President: "After looking these polls over carefully . . . I am still definitely of the opinion that you will carry every state but two, Maine and Vermont.") (*See November 3*)

**1948**    President Harry S. Truman confounds the "experts" and, with his running-mate, Senator Alben W. Barkley (D., Ky.), handily wins his campaign for election. (The President was not only faced with the usual Republican opposition, but he overcame two other tickets, that of the States' Rights Democrats, headed by J. Strom Thurmond, and the Progressive Party slate, headed by Henry A. Wallace. Despite predictions to the contrary, the Truman-Barkley ticket captured 303 electoral votes and 28 states, while the Dewey-Warren ticket won 189 electoral votes and 16 states. The

States' Rights party rolled up 39 electoral votes in 4 states. Wallace's Progressives won over a million popular votes but took no electoral votes.)

**1948** Lyndon B. Johnson, who had barely squeaked through a Democratic run-off primary last August by just 87 votes, defeats his Republican opponent and is elected to the U.S. Senate.

**1962** President John F. Kennedy announces that Russian missile bases in Cuba are being dismantled.

## NOVEMBER 3

**1814** European powers, seeking to resolve the problems left in the wake of the Napoleonic wars, open their discussions at the Congress of Vienna.

**1837** Housewives in Illinois are up in arms over the high cost of living. A pound of butter costs as much as 8 cents, a dozen eggs 6 cents, beef is 3 cents a pound and pork 2 cents. Coffee and sugar are luxuries at 20 cents and 10 cents a pound. A good hired girl costs $2 a week besides her keep. (But an acre of good farm land in those days cost only $1.25.)

**1868** Presidential election: General Ulysses S. Grant and Schuyler Colfax, Republicans, are elected President and Vice President, respectively, winning 214 electoral votes to 80 received by Horatio Seymour and Francis P. Blair, Jr., Democrats.

**1883** Delegates from all over the United States conclude their convention at Detroit after organizing the World Woman's Christian Temperance Union.

**1896** The state of Idaho grants full suffrage to women by popular vote.

**1896** Presidential election: William McKinley and Garret A. Hobart, Republicans, are elected President and Vice President, respectively, winning 271 electoral votes to 176 received by William Jennings Bryan and Arthur Sewall, Democrats.

**1900** The first National Automobile Show opens its doors at Madison Square Garden in New York. Thirty-one manufacturers have cars on display and a daily highlight of the exposition is a series of test drives on obstacle courses. (But automobile expositions did not mean most people had "accepted" cars. Within a few days of this opening at Madison Square Garden, Boston passed an ordinance forbidding automobiles to enter city parks between 10 in the morning and 9 at night. Its purpose: to protect women and children from these dangerous vehicles.)

**1908** Presidential election: William Howard Taft and James S. Sherman, Republicans, are elected President and Vice President, respectively, winning 321 electoral votes to 162 received by William Jennings Bryan and John W. Kern, Democrats. (Eugene V. Debs, running on the Socialist ticket, received no electoral votes.)

**1917**   Americans back home learn of the first deaths of U.S. soldiers in combat. They are Corporal James B. Gresham of Evansville, Indiana, and Private Thomas F. Enright of Pittsburgh, Pennsylvania, and Merle D. Hay of Glidden, Iowa. All three soldiers were attached to the First Division and met their deaths after a German raid near Nancy, France. (WORLD WAR I)

**1935**   A plebiscite in Greece brings about the recall of King George II to the throne. The King has been living in exile since the nationalist uprising of 1923.

**1936**   Presidential election: The New Deal is given an enthusiastic vote of confidence as President Franklin D. Roosevelt and Vice-President John N. Garner, Democrats, are reelected, winning 523 electoral votes to 8 received by Governor Alfred M. Landon and Frank Knox, Republicans. (The Republicans carried only Maine and Vermont.)

**1964**   President Lyndon B. Johnson and his running-mate, Senator Hubert H. Humphrey (D., Minn.), defeat the Republican ticket of Senator Barry M. Goldwater of Arizona and Congressman William E. Miller of New York by the largest percentage of the total vote accorded any candidate since the popular vote was first counted in 1832. The President receives 61 percent of the total vote and runs 15,975,924 votes ahead of Goldwater. (In all, the Democratic President carried 44 states and the District of Columbia, and won 486 of the 538 electoral votes. The six states Goldwater carried were: Alabama, Arizona, Georgia, Louisiana, Mississippi, and South Carolina.)

## NOVEMBER 4

**1842**   Abraham Lincoln, 33, is married to Mary Todd, 23, at the residence of Miss Todd's brother-in-law, Ninian Edwards, in Springfield, Illinois. (The bridegroom, said one guest, looked as "pale and trembling as being driven to slaughter.")

**1856**   Presidential election: James Buchanan and John C. Breckinridge, Democrats, are elected President and Vice President, respectively, winning 174 electoral votes to 114 received by John C. Frémont and William L. Dayton, Republican, and 8 received by Millard Fillmore and A. J. Donelson, candidates of the American Party.

**1879**   Birthday of Will Rogers, American humorist, philosopher, actor, and author. ("All I know is just what I read in the papers.")

**1884**   Presidential election: Grover Cleveland and Thomas A. Hendricks, Democrats, are elected President and Vice President, respectively, winning 219 electoral votes to 182 received by James G. Blaine and John A. Logan, Republicans.

**1890**   Because of the unpopularity of the Republican-sponsored McKinley Tariff Act, the nation's voters swing over to Democratic candidates in the congressional elections, leaving the Republicans with only 88 seats in the House of Representatives. The Democrats win 244 seats.

**1905**  Edward William Bok, editor of the *Ladies' Home Journal,* begins his campaign to elevate American taste in furniture and aims one of his first attacks at the so-called "Morris Chair." This chair, Mr. Bok charges ". . . cost $31 with gaping carved lion heads for arms, and ball-and-claw feet, heavy to move, carved out of all proportion to size, a hideous piece of furniture."

**1924**  Presidential election: Calvin Coolidge and Charles G. Dawes, Republicans, are elected President and Vice President, respectively, winning 382 electoral votes to 136 received by John W. Davis and Charles W. Bryan, Democrats, and 13 received by Robert M. LaFollette and Burton K. Wheeler, candidates on the Progressive and Socialist tickets.

**1931**  The League of Nations cites Japan for willful aggression in Manchuria.

**1947**  Tennessee Williams' play, *A Streetcar Named Desire,* is well received by an opening-night audience at the Henry Miller Theatre in New York.

**1952**  Presidential election: For the first time since the national elections of 1932, the voters of the United States elect a Republican President and Vice President. General Dwight D. Eisenhower and Senator Richard M. Nixon, Republicans, win 442 electoral votes to 89 received by their Democratic opponents, Adlai E. Stevenson and Senator John J. Sparkman.

**1952**  Despite the fact that the Republican Presidential candidate, Dwight D. Eisenhower, sweeps the state of Massachusetts by a plurality of 209,000 votes, Representative John F. Kennedy, 35, defeats incumbent Senator Henry Cabot Lodge by 71,000 votes. (Kennedy was a Democrat, Lodge a Republican who had been in the Senate since 1937.)

**1958**  Senator John F. Kennedy (D., Mass.) is reelected to his seat in the U.S. Senate by a vote majority of 875,000, the largest margin to date ever gained by any candidate for any office in the political history of Massachusetts.

**1960**  While making a campaign appearance in Dallas, Texas, in his bid for election as Vice President, Senator Lyndon B. Johnson (D., Texas), the Majority Leader of the U.S. Senate, accompanied by his wife and aides, is jostled and taunted by a hostile crowd of right-wing extremists in the lobby of the city's Adolphus Hotel. (The Senator described the ugly scene on television the next night in Houston: "We were hissed at and spat upon, and two women were hurt in a mob scene that looked like some other country. It was hard to believe that this was happening in Dallas and in Texas.") (*See October 24, November 22*)

350

**1961** The U.S. Army accepts the resignation of Major General Edwin A. Walker, previously rebuked for his attempts to indoctrinate his troops in Germany with the views of the John Birch Society and other right-wing political ideologies. *(See June 12, September 28, September 30, October 1)*

## NOVEMBER 5

**1605** Guy Fawkes, hired by conspirators against King James I and Parliament, is seized as he is about to blow up the House of Lords. (In British history, this frightening incident is known as the Gunpowder Plot.)

**1733** John Peter Zenger, a freedom-loving German who emigrated from the Palatinate to the American colonies in 1710, starts to publish a newspaper, the *New York Weekly Journal*. The new journal is opposed to the autocratic rule of the royal governor of New York, William Cosby.

**1862** President Lincoln, impatient for a military offensive, relieves General George B. McClellan of the command of the Army of the Potomac and entrusts the Army to General Ambrose E. Burnside.

**1872** Presidential election: President Ulysses Grant is reelected, receiving with his Republican running mate, Henry Wilson, 286 electoral votes, and carrying every state in the Union but 6. Horace Greeley and B. Gratz Brown, the candidates of the Democrats and the so-called "Liberal Republicans," win only 66 electoral votes. (Greeley died on November 29, before his electors could cast these votes for him.)

**1895** George B. Selden, a Rochester, New York, attorney, is notified that the U.S. Patent Office has granted him the automobile patent for which he applied in 1879. (The Selden patent covered every essential feature of the modern gasoline automobile, but the inventor realized only $200,000 in all when he sold out his rights in 1899.)

**1911** Calbraith P. Rogers completes the first American transcontinental airplane flight, arriving in Pasadena, California, 49 days after he set out from Sheepshead Bay, New York, in his Burgess-Wright biplane. (Twenty-four of these days were lost due to bad weather and mechanical difficulties. In 1911, however, the Rogers' flight was considered just short of miraculous.)

**1912** Presidential election: Woodrow Wilson and Thomas R. Marshall, Democrats, are elected President and Vice President, respectively, winning 435 electoral votes to 88 received by former President Theodore Roosevelt and Hiram Johnson, candidates of the Progressive wing of the Republican Party. President William Howard Taft, a candidate for reelection on the regular Republican ticket, wins 8 electoral votes.

**1940**    Presidential election: President Franklin D. Roosevelt is reelected, the first President of the United States to be elected for three terms of office. The President and Henry A. Wallace, Democrats, receive 449 electoral votes to 82 won by the Republican candidates, Wendell L. Willkie and Senator Charles McNary.

**1942**    General Bernard L. Montgomery, commander of the British Eighth Army, announces that his troops have won complete and absolute victory over Axis forces in Egypt. (WORLD WAR II)

**1946**    A new career in politics gets under way as 29-year-old John F. Kennedy (D., Mass.) is elected to a seat in the U.S. House of Representatives.

**1955**    Austria formally opens the reconstructed Vienna State Opera House, celebrating at the same time her liberation from 17 years of occupation by foreign troops. The opera chosen for the grand opening is Beethoven's *Fidelio*. (Vienna was occupied by the French when *Fidelio* had its *première* there 150 years earlier.)

**1956**    Britain and France start landing forces in Egypt.

## NOVEMBER 6

**1860**    Presidential election: Abraham Lincoln and Hannibal Hamlin, Republicans, are elected President and Vice President, respectively, winning 180 electoral votes. The remaining electoral votes are distributed as follows: John C. Breckinridge and Joseph Lane, Democrats, 72; John Bell and Edward Everett, Constitutional Union Party, 39; Senator Stephen A. Douglas and Herschel V. Johnson, Democrats, 12. (An internal party dispute resulted in two sets of Democratic candidates in this election.)

**1869**    The first formal intercollegiate football game is played at New Brunswick, New Jersey, between the teams of Princeton and Rutgers. (Each team was made up of 25 men. The final score was Rutgers 6, Princeton 4.)

**1882**    Lily Langtry, known in England as "The Jersey Lily," makes her American debut at Wallack's Theatre in New York, playing in Tom Taylor's play, *An Unequal Match*.

**1888**    Presidential election: Benjamin Harrison and Levi P. Morton, Republicans, are elected President and Vice President, respectively, winning 233 electoral votes to 168 received by President Grover Cleveland and Allen G. Thurman, Democrats.

**1899**    At the Garrick Theatre, in New York, the curtain goes up for the first time on *Sherlock Holmes*, starring William Gillette. (Gillette also dramatized the famous Conan Doyle classic.)

**1900**    Presidential election: President William McKinley is reelected on the Republican ticket. The President and the new Vice President, Theodore Roosevelt, receive 292 electoral votes. Their Democratic opponents, William Jennings Bryan and Adlai E. Stevenson, win 155 electoral votes. (Mr. Stevenson had served as Vice

President of the United States in the second administration of President Grover Cleveland, starting in 1893.)

**1903** Maude Adams launches a stage classic when she opens in New York in Sir James Barrie's delightful fantasy, *Peter Pan.* (This original run went right through June 8, 1906.)

**1928** Presidential election: Herbert Hoover and Charles Curtis, Republicans, are elected President and Vice President, respectively, winning 444 electoral votes to 87 received by Governor Alfred E. Smith and Senator Joseph T. Robinson.

**1940** To show the world that the United States is united despite the partisan sentiments expressed all during the Presidential campaign that ended on November 5 with the reelection of President Franklin D. Roosevelt, 3,000 people stage a United American Rally at Carnegie Hall in New York. (The promoters of this rally wanted to make it crystal clear to the Axis powers in Europe that the overwhelming majority of Democrats and Republicans in this country shared a mutual dislike for Fascism.)

**1953** The Attorney General of the United States, Herbert Brownell, Jr., sets off a bitter national controversy when he charges in a speech in Chicago that former President Harry S. Truman promoted the late Harry Dexter White to become U.S. Executive Director of the International Monetary Fund in 1946 with the alleged full knowledge that White was "a Russian spy." The charge is immediately denied by Mr. Truman.

**1956** The Republican ticket, headed by President Dwight D. Eisenhower and Vice President Richard M. Nixon, is reelected by a landslide over the Democratic ticket of Adlai E. Stevenson and Senator Estes Kefauver. The Republicans carry 41 states and win 457 electoral votes to the Democrats' 7 states and 73 electoral votes.

**1962** Thirty-year-old Edward M. Kennedy, President Kennedy's youngest brother, wins the same seat in the U.S. Senate occupied by the President until he was elected to the White House.

## NOVEMBER 7

**1805** Lewis and Clark sight the Pacific Ocean for the first time at the mouth of the Columbia River in the "Oregon Country," thus proving that America is a vast continent stretched between two oceans. (One of the great explorations in American history, the Lewis & Clark Expedition was authorized by President Jefferson as a fact-finding mission about the vast tract of land purchased from France in 1803, the so-called Louisiana Purchase. Congress appropriated $2,500 to defray the expenses of Lewis and Clark during their travels.)

**1811** General William Henry Harrison, governor of the Indiana Territory, defeats Chief Tecumseh's Shawnee Indians at the Battle of Tippecanoe on the Wabash River. (The General won more than a battle; the fame gained here was directly responsible for his election to the Presidency in 1840.)

**1820**    The record for political success in a Presidential election is achieved by President James Monroe who, in running for his second term, receives 231 out of a total 232 electoral votes. (William Plumer, a New Hampshire elector, refused to make Monroe's election unanimous, not because he was opposed to the President but because he felt the honor of a unanimous election should go to no one but George Washington. Accordingly, Plumer cast his vote for John Quincy Adams.)

**1848**    Presidential election: General Zachary Taylor and Millard Fillmore, Whigs, are elected President and Vice President, respectively, winning 163 electoral votes to 127 received by Lewis Cass and William O. Butler, Democrats.

**1874**    *Harper's Weekly* runs the first cartoon depicting an elephant as the symbol of the Republican Party. (In the drawing by Thomas Nast entitled "The Third Term Panic," a reference to President Grant's possible bid for a third term, the elephant was labeled "Republican vote" and about to fall into a pit marked "Chaos.")

**1876**    Presidential election: The most bitterly-contested election in U.S. history takes place between Rutherford B. Hayes, Republican, and Samuel J. Tilden, Democrat. (When the ballots were counted, Tilden appeared to have carried all the Southern states, New York, Connecticut, New Jersey, and Indiana, a total of 184 electoral votes, one less than the total required for election. To make things worse, the Republicans charged that the Democrats had prevented Negroes from voting in South Carolina, Florida, and Louisiana, thereby depriving them of the electoral votes of those three states. Finally, Congress created an Electoral Commission to determine the winner of the election, but the decision did not reflect credit on either Congress, the Commission, or the two major political parties. A "deal" was worked out whereby Hayes was to be declared President of the United States if he would promise to withdraw federal troops from the three Southern states. Hayes kept his promise after he was inaugurated.) (*See December 6.*)

**1910**    Victor Herbert's latest operetta, *Naughty Marietta*, draws cheers on its opening-night performance in New York. As the audience streams out of the New York Theatre, at least half of them are humming the entrancing "Ah, Sweet Mystery of Life."

**1916**    Presidential election: President Woodrow Wilson and Vice President Thomas R. Marshall are reelected on the Democratic ticket, winning 277 electoral votes to 254 received by former Supreme Court Justice Charles Evans Hughes and Charles W. Fairbanks, Republicans. (But nonetheless Mr. Hughes went to bed in his suite at the Hotel Astor on election night, thinking *he* had won. And one of his aides told a newspaper reporter seeking an interview: "The President has retired and is not to be disturbed." This was 4 hours before the California vote was tallied and added 12 more electoral votes to President Wilson's column.)

**1917**    Russian Revolution * : Bolshevik troops occupy government buildings in Petrograd and overthrow the provisional regime of Premier Alexander Kerensky. Nikolai Lenin, assuming power as the new head of the government, issues this statement: "Comrades, the workers' and peasants' revolution, about the necessity of which the Bolsheviks have always spoken, has taken place.... From now on, a new phase in the history of Russia begins...."

**1918**    A cable received by United Press headquarters in New York from its president, Roy W. Howard, in Brest, France, sets the United States off on a cross-country celebration of the "False Armistice." (Mr. Howard, learning later that his "scoop" could not be confirmed, sent a second cable to his New York office explaining the error, but it was impossible to convince people that the war was not over until they were confronted with the following morning's headlines.) (WORLD WAR I)

**1940**    The third largest suspension bridge in the world, spanning the strait between Tacoma, Washington, and the Olympic Peninsula, collapses during a particularly strong windstorm. (The bridge, completed earlier in the year, was known to local residents as "Galloping Gertie.")

**1944**    Presidential election: President Franklin D. Roosevelt is reelected to his fourth term of office, the first United States President to be so named. On a Democratic ticket that includes Senator Harry S. Truman of Missouri, the President wins 432 electoral votes to 99 received by Governor Thomas E. Dewey and Governor John W. Bricker, Republicans.

**1956**    The cease-fire order issued by the United Nations, in connection with the fighting in Egypt between that country, Israel, and the British and French forces, goes into effect.

**1962**    Mrs. Franklin D. Roosevelt, widow of the 32nd President of the United States and for a quarter of a century herself known as "The First Lady of the World," dies in New York City. (During the next few days, she was the subject of countless eulogies, but no one surpassed the words of her friend, Adlai E. Stevenson, who said simply: "She would rather light candles than curse the darkness, and her glow has warmed the world....") (*See October 11, November 10*)

**1962**    Tired and angry over his defeat the day before by Democratic Governor Edmund G. Brown in their race for Governor of California, former Vice President Richard M. Nixon bitterly attacks some members of the press. In a news conference in Los

* This is known in Russia as the October Revolution because it occurred in October, according to the Julian Calendar.

Angeles, he says: "Now that all the members of the press are so delighted that I have lost, I'd like to make a statement. . . . I think it's time our great newspapers have the same objectivity, the same fairness of coverage, that television has. Thank God for television and radio for keeping the newspapers a little more honest. . . . But as I leave you, I want you to know—just think how much you're going to be missing. You won't have Nixon to kick around any more. . . ."

**1962**    Billie Sol Estes, the Texas financier, is convicted in Tyler, Texas, for fraud and sentenced by a jury to 8 years in prison. Estes still faces four other state and federal indictments.

## NOVEMBER 8

**1793**    The Louvre Museum in Paris is opened to the public for the first time. (The construction of the Louvre, originally intended for a royal residence, was started in 1204 by Philippe Auguste, King of France. This building, with its fine art collection begun by Francis I in the sixteenth century, was given to the people by decree of the "Convention" of the First Republic of France.)

**1837**    Mount Holyoke Female Seminary, in South Hadley, Massachusetts, starts classes with 80 students, each of whom have agreed to pay $64 a year for tuition and board. Mary Lyon is the first principal of the school. (This was the first college founded exclusively for women.)

**1864**    Presidential election: President Abraham Lincoln, Republican, is reelected, receiving with his Democratic running mate, Andrew Johnson, 212 electoral votes to 21 received by General George B. McClellan and George H. Pendleton, candidates on the regular Democratic ticket. (The Lincoln-Johnson ticket was bipartisan.)

**1880**    Sarah Bernhardt, the internationally famous French actress, makes her American debut in New York, playing the leading role in *Adrienne Lecouvreur*.

**1889**    Montana is admitted into the Union as the 41st state.

**1892**    Presidential election: Former President Grover Cleveland and his Democratic running mate, Adlai E. Stevenson, win the national election, defeating President Benjamin Harrison and Whitelaw Reid, Republicans. The President-elect wins 277 electoral votes to 145 received by President Harrison. James B. Weaver, running on the Populist ticket, receives 22 electoral votes.

**1904**    Presidential election: President Theodore Roosevelt and Charles W. Fairbanks, Republicans, are elected by 336 electoral votes to 140 received by Alton B. Parker and Henry G. Davis, Democrats. Eugene V. Debs, running on the Socialist ticket, receives no electoral votes.

**1923** During a celebration honoring the dead of World War I, Adolf Hitler and his National Socialist Storm Troopers march into the Bürgerbrau Keller, a beer hall in Munich, and force the prime minister and chief of police of Bavaria to swear loyalty to a Nazi revolution. The "putsch" is short-lived, however, as soldiers of the German Army break up the meeting and force Hitler and his followers to flee.

**1932** Presidential election: Governor Franklin D. Roosevelt and John Nance Garner, Democrats, are elected President and Vice President, respectively, winning 472 electoral votes to 59 received by President Herbert Hoover and Vice President Charles Curtis, Republicans. Norman Thomas, running on the Socialist ticket, receives no electoral votes.

**1939** A classic of the stage, an adaptation of Clarence Day's book, *Life with Father*, has its *première* in New York. (Eight years later, it was still running and topping the original runs of both *Abie's Irish Rose* and *Tobacco Road*.)

**1942** Four hundred thousand Allied soldiers, transported by an armada of 500 U.S. and British transports, invade North Africa. In all, 10 separate landings are made in the area of Algiers, Oran, and Casablanca. Recordings of a message broadcast to the French people by President Franklin D. Roosevelt are transmitted to occupied France. Despite the fact that the Vichy government immediately severs diplomatic relations with the United States, thousands of Frenchmen cheer the news as a sign of the ultimate defeat of the Axis powers. (WORLD WAR II)

**1960** Senator John F. Kennedy (D., Mass.) and Senator Lyndon B. Johnson (D., Texas) * are elected President and Vice President, defeating the Republican ticket of Vice President Richard M. Nixon and Ambassador Henry Cabot Lodge. Kennedy won 303 electoral votes, Nixon 219. The Democratic popular-vote plurality was 112,803, the smallest margin since the Presidential election of 1888.

## NOVEMBER 9

**1805** At a victory banquet in London, following the news of the French defeat at Trafalgar, Prime Minister William Pitt is toasted as "the savior of Europe." The Prime Minister responds to the toast by saying: "I return you many thanks for the honor you have done me. But Europe is not to be saved by any single man. England has saved herself by her exertions, and will, as I trust, save Europe by her example."

* In the same election, since he was listed twice on the Texas ballot, Johnson defeated John G. Tower, Republican, for reelection to the Senate, by a margin of 379,972 votes. On January 3, 1961, Johnson was sworn in as the newly elected Senator from Texas and then promptly resigned in favor of a gubernatorial appointee to his seat.

**1872**   In the early evening, fire breaks out in a Boston warehouse and soon sweeps over the greater part of the city, thus beginning the most devastating fire in the city's history. (By the next day, 800 buildings had been destroyed and the total damage amounted to $75,000,000.)

**1918**   Kaiser Wilhelm II of Germany announces from his military headquarters in Spa, Belgium, that he has agreed to abdicate his throne. (Actually, the Kaiser offered to abdicate as emperor of Germany, while returning the title of King of Prussia, but the Imperial government in Berlin refused to grant his wish.) (WORLD WAR I)

**1923**   One day after the attempted "beer-hall putsch," General Erich Ludendorff and Adolf Hitler decide to test the intent of the German government toward the Bavarian Fascists. Accordingly, the two men lead a second march on the streets of Munich, accompanied by 3,000 Storm Troopers. As the demonstrators threaten to get out of hand, the federal army opens fire, killing 14 Nazis, wounding many others. (Hitler fled, but he was soon arrested and sentenced to Landsberg Fortress, where he proceeded to write *Mein Kampf*.)

**1933**   President Franklin D. Roosevelt creates the Civil Works Administration (CWA) as an emergency agency to provide jobs for more than four million unemployed men and women. The new bureau will be administered by Harry L. Hopkins.

**1935**   Led by John L. Lewis, president of the United Mine Workers, a group of labor leaders affiliated with the American Federation of Labor hold a meeting to organize a Committee for Industrial Organization within the framework of the parent organization. The new committee will seek to organize workers who are not eligible for membership in the various craft unions of the American Federation of Labor.

**1938**   In preplanned attacks, bands of Nazis roam the streets of Germany burning and destroying Jewish synagogues, homes, and stores. (After this vicious anti-Semitic demonstration ended, the streets of the big cities were so littered with broken glass that the date became known in Germany as "Crystal Night.")

**1938**   A relatively unknown actress and singer "brings down" the house" as Mary Martin makes her debut in the musical comedy, *Leave It to Me* at the Imperial Theatre in New York. (Miss Martin introduced a song that was soon to take the nation by storm, "My Heart Belongs to Daddy.")

**1953**   Confirming a decision handed down in 1922, the Supreme Court rules that big-league baseball does not come "within the scope of the Federal antitrust laws."

**1965**   A massive power failure, starting at 5:17 P.M. in western New York and reaching New York City at 5:27 P.M., plunged 80,000 square miles of the Northeast in darkness and confusion at the height of the rush hour. Thirty million people in New Hampshire, Vermont, Massachusetts, Rhode Island, Connecticut, New York, and the Province of Ontario were affected for two to thirteen hours.

# NOVEMBER 10

**1775**   The U.S. Marine Corps is authorized by the Continental Congress sitting in Philadelphia. The new fighting service is to be known as "The First and Second Battalions of American Marines."

**1871**   Henry M. Stanley, a newspaperman and explorer, discovers the missing Scottish missionary and explorer, David Livingstone, in a small settlement in "darkest Africa." Coming face to face with the missing man in Ujiji, Central Africa, Stanley says, "Dr. Livingstone, I presume?" And the joyous Scotsman answers: "Yes, and I feel thankful that I am here to welcome you." (Livingstone was seeking to trace the source of the river Nile. He continued his explorations until the year of his death in 1873. At that time, natives carried his body to the coast where it was sent to England and then buried in Westminster Abbey.)

**1888**   A 13-year-old boy from Vienna makes his American debut as a concert violinist at Steinway Hall in New York. His name: Fritz Kreisler.

**1900**   The musical hit of the year opens at the Casino Theatre in New York as *Floradora,* by Leslie Stuart, plays to a cheering audience. The highlight of the musical play is the "Floradora Sextette," featuring six beautiful young ladies singing "Tell Me Pretty Maiden."

**1914**   The name "Pollyanna" seems to have become a household word, familiar to millions of people because of the popular book of that name written a year ago by Eleanor H. Porter. There are Pollyanna Tea Rooms, Pollyanna Apartment Houses, Pollyanna milk, babies named Pollyanna, the Pollyanna hairdo and the famous Pollyanna smile.

**1917**   Forty-one women from 15 states of the Union are arrested outside the White House in Washington for suffragette demonstrations. Included among those arrested are the wife of a former California congressman and a 70-year-old woman. (The women did nothing more than picket the White House with their placards and posters demanding the vote, but nonetheless they drew sentences ranging from 6 days to 6 months.)

**1918**   Kaiser Wilhelm II and his suite of about thirty persons cross from Belgium onto Dutch soil at Eysden, where the Emperor asks for asylum. Frontier guards are ordered to detain the imperial party until Queen Wilhelmina and her ministers are consulted. Finally, the Dutch government agrees to give him sanctuary somewhere within the tiny nation. (It was to be outside the village of Doorn, about 7 miles from Amerongen.)

**1919** The American Legion, organized by American war veterans in Paris earlier in the year, holds its first national convention in Minneapolis.

**1938** Following the assassination in Paris of a Nazi diplomat by a Polish refugee, Herschel Grynszpan, Adolf Hitler orders reprisals against the Jews of Germany. All over the Reich, Jews are arrested and interned in concentration camps and the entire Jewish population of Germany is fined $400,000,000.

**1962** A sorrowing nation bids farewell to Mrs. Franklin D. Roosevelt as she is laid to rest beside the body of her husband in the rose garden of their onetime family estate at Hyde Park, New York. At the gravesite are President and Mrs. Kennedy and former Presidents Truman and Eisenhower.

## NOVEMBER 11

### Veterans' Day, formerly Armistice Day

**1620** Forty-one Pilgrims aboard the *Mayflower,* anchored off the coast of Cape Cod, Massachusetts, sign a compact agreeing to "... combine ourselves together into a civil Body Politick, for our better Ordering and Preservation ... and to enact, constitute, and frame, such just and equal Laws, Ordinances, Acts, Constitutions and Offices from time to time, as shall be thought most meet and convenient for the General Good of the Colony...."

**1854** The music publishing firm of Firth, Pond & Company in New York advertises that it has sold, to date, the following number of copies of Stephen Foster's songs: "Old Folks at Home," more than 130,000; "My Old Kentucky Home," 90,000; "Massa's in de Cold Ground," 74,000; "Old Dog Tray," 48,000.

**1876** With the outcome of the Presidential election still in doubt, the Republican candidate, Rutherford B. Hayes, is sure he has lost the Presidency to Samuel J. Tilden. Writing in his diary, in his home in Fremont, Ohio, he says: "... The election has resulted in defeat ... after a very close contest.... I went to bed at 12 to 1 o'clock. Talked with Lucy [his wife], consoling her with such topics as readily occurred of a nature to make us feel satisfied on merely personal grounds with the result...." (*See December 6*)

**1889** The state of Washington, the 42nd state to join, is admitted to the Union.

**1918** Hostilities cease at 11 o'clock in the morning following the signing of an armistice between the Allied and Central Powers in Marshal Foch's railway car in the Forest of Compiègne, France. Worldwide celebrations mark the end of World War I, while millions of men in trenches and on battlefields chant the happy words,

"The war is over!" In Washington, President Woodrow Wilson pens a note to his fellow countrymen: "The Armistice was signed this morning. Everything for which America fought has been accomplished. It will now be our fortunate duty to assist by example, by sober, friendly counsel, and by material aid in the establishment of just democracy throughout the world."

**1918**   The independence of Poland is proclaimed with Marshal Josef Pilsudski named as first president of the republic.

**1921**   At solemn ceremonies attended by some 100,000 people at Arlington National Cemetery, President Warren G. Harding dedicates the tomb in which America's Unknown Soldier is buried. The monument bears the inscription "Here rests in honored glory an American Soldier known but to God."

**1933**   The "Great Black Blizzard," the first of the great dust storms to lay waste thousands of acres of land in the Great Plains, sweeps over North Dakota, leaving devastation and terror in its wake. (So intense was this storm that the sky over Chicago was blackened the next day and a similar condition was observed in Albany, New York, the day following. But the most serious result of this and subsequent dust storms was the army of migrant families that took to the roads, searching for fertile fields and the means to earn a living.)

**1939**   As a highlight of her Armistice Day radio broadcast, Kate Smith sings Irving Berlin's song, "God Bless America," the first time that it has been heard by the American public. (Although Miss Smith introduced the song, it was written as long ago as 1917, intended, but not used, for the score of Mr. Berlin's World War I soldier show, *Yip Yip Yaphank*. Ever since 1939, "God Bless America" has almost assumed the status of another national anthem, and the accumulated royalties have been turned over by the composer to the Boy Scouts and Girl Scouts of America.)

**1953**   President Eisenhower says he doubts that former President Harry S. Truman knowingly appointed an alleged Communist spy, Harry Dexter White, to high government office. As the controversy over the former President rages, Attorney General Herbert Brownell modifies his original charges against Mr. Truman. But Senator Joseph R. McCarthy (R., Wis.) heaps coals on the fire by calling the former President a "liar" and adds that he "deliberately, knowingly and without regard for the interests of the country appointed, promoted and advanced a Communist" spy.

## NOVEMBER 12

**1854**   All over the nation people are reading the popular temperance novel by Timothy Shay Arthur, *Ten Nights in a Bar-Room and What I Saw There.* (Its sales in the 1850's are said to have run second only to Harriet Beecher Stowe's *Uncle Tom's Cabin.*)

**1920**    Judge Kenesaw Mountain Landis is appointed the first "Czar" of baseball, empowered to regulate players and codes of conduct and other policy matters that pertain to big-league baseball. Judge Landis' term of office will last 7 years and his jurisdiction will cover the 16 teams making up the American and National Leagues.

**1927**    Joseph Stalin becomes undisputed dictator of the Communist Party in the Soviet Union as Leon Trotsky, one of the founders of Communist Russia, is expelled from the Party. (Until this time, many political observers were certain that Trotsky would inherit the powers of the late Nikolai Lenin, but they failed to reckon with the ambitious Stalin.)

**1928**    One hundred and ten persons lose their lives at sea as the British liner *Vestris* sinks in a heavy gale off the coast of Virginia.

**1941**    Nazi soldiers are halted by the Russians at the outskirts of Moscow. (WORLD WAR II)

**1948**    The war crimes' tribunal in Japan sentences former Premier Hideki Tojo and six colleagues to die by hanging. Eighteen other Japanese wartime leaders are handed prison sentences.

**1954**    A session of bitter debate over the proposed motion to censure Senator Joseph R. McCarthy (R., Wis.) is interrupted by Senator Barry Goldwater (R., Ariz.) who rises to the defense of the controversial right-wing Senator from Wisconsin. Says Goldwater: "Like him or not, McCarthy is the strongest voice now speaking in America against Communism.... All the discredited and embittered figures of the Hiss-Yalta period of American dishonor have crawled out from under their logs to join the effort to get even. The news columns and the airwaves have been filled with their pious talk about 'civil liberties,' 'ethical codes,' and 'protection of the innocent,' while at the same time these people have dipped into the smut pot to discredit Senator McCarthy and his work against Communism ..."

## NOVEMBER 13

**1921**    Hollywood releases *The Sheik*, starring the great lover of the films, Rudolph Valentino. (Half a dozen women in New York are said to have swooned at the opening of the picture, carried away by the masculinity of the Italian-born hero of the picture.)

**1927**    The Holland Tunnel, running under the Hudson River between New York City and Jersey City, New Jersey, is opened to public traffic after 7 years of construction. The new tunnel can accommodate 1,900 motor vehicles every hour.

**1933**    Workers in the Hormel Packing Company in Austin, Minnesota, stage a "sit-down" strike on the premises of the plant following a dispute with the company management. (This was the first recorded "sit-down" strike in the United States.)

**1937** The music critic of *The New York Times* warmly praises the first radio concert of the newly organized National Broadcasting Symphony, conducted by Pierre Monteux.

**1942** The Japanese fleet suffers a heavy naval defeat while attempting to retake U.S. positions in the Solomon Islands. The Japanese are repulsed in their efforts to reinforce Guadalcanal. (WORLD WAR II)

**1948** In a nice gesture of "cultural reparation," Luther D. Evans, Librarian of Congress, turns over to the Archbishop of Canterbury in Washington the original manuscript of *Alice in Wonderland*, written by the English clergyman Charles L. Dodgson (Lewis Carroll) in 1862. (An American had acquired the manuscript for $50,000 by outbidding the British Museum. A move to restore it to English ownership resulted in its purchase through donations, and the Archbishop of Canterbury, representing the trustees of the British Museum, visited Washington for the express purpose of carrying it back home.)

**1956** The Supreme Court rules that segregation of the races on public buses is unconstitutional.

**1961** Pablo Casals, the Spanish cellist, joins other musicians playing chamber music in the East Room of the White House. The concert follows a State Dinner given by President and Mrs. John F. Kennedy in honor of Governor Luis Muñoz-Marin of Puerto Rico.

## NOVEMBER 14

**1832** The first streetcar in the world makes its appearance on the streets of New York. Actually, New Yorkers are referring to the new conveyance as a "horse car," because the car is drawn by two horses on tracks laid on Fourth Avenue between Prince and 14th Streets. A total of 30 persons can be accommodated in the 3 compartments of each car.

**1851** Herman Melville's story, *Moby Dick,* is published by Harper and Brothers in New York. (While the book made very little of a stir in the publishing trade when it came out, it has since sold 2,000,000 copies and is required reading in almost every college English course in the country.)

**1881** The trial of Charles Guiteau, charged with the assassination of President James A. Garfield, opens in Washington. (He was convicted and hanged on June 30, 1882.)

**1889** To prove that she can outdo the record of Jules Verne's hero in *Around the World in Eighty Days*, Nellie Bly, a reporter for the *New York World,* sets out from Hoboken, New Jersey, on the first stage of her world tour. ("Nellie Bly" was the pen name of

Elizabeth Cochrane, credited as the first person to make America conscious of the woman reporter. Her trip was startling in itself, but to most ladies of 1889 it was not the journey that seemed unbelievable; the fact that she was traveling without an umbrella was considered "not quite nice.") (*See January 25.*)

**1918** Professor Thomas G. Masaryk is elected the first president of the Republic of Czechoslovakia. The new president receives the news of his election on his way home from the United States, following last-minute conversations with his close friend, President Woodrow Wilson. (In all, Masaryk served four terms as president.)

**1935** President Franklin D. Roosevelt proclaims the Philippine Islands to be a free commonwealth.

**1940** German airplanes drop 225 tons of bombs on Coventry, England, damaging or destroying 69,000 of the town's 75,000 buildings, including the local cathedral. (WORLD WAR II)

**1942** Captain Edward ("Eddie") Rickenbacker, World War I ace, and currently engaged in a special mission for the government, is rescued in the Pacific along with 7 members of the armed forces, after drifting 23 days on a life raft. The men have been missing since October 21 following their flight from Hawaii. (WORLD WAR II)

**1954** A new organization, "Ten Million Americans Mobilized for Justice," starts a 10-day campaign for ten million signatures to a petition demanding that the Senate refrain from censuring Senator Joseph R. McCarthy, Republican, of Wisconsin. (On December 1, an armored car delivered the petitions with some 1,000,816 signatures to the Capitol in Washington. And 4 days later, a rival group was organized on Long Island, New York, this one bearing the name "Twenty Million Americans for Censure of Joe McCarthy.") (*See December 2*)

**1963** President Kennedy, asked at his news conference to comment on the rumored candidacy of a woman who might run against him in next year's Presidential elections, has warm words of praise for Senator Margaret Chase Smith (R., Maine): "I would think that if I were a Republican candidate I would not look forward to campaigning against Margaret Chase Smith. . . . I think she is very formidable, if that is the appropriate word to use about a very fine lady. . . ."

# NOVEMBER 15

**1492** Christopher Columbus notes in his journal the use of tobacco among the Indians of the New World, the first recorded reference to tobacco.

**1777** The Articles of Confederation and Perpetual Union, uniting the states under a common government, are adopted by the Continental Congress and submitted to the states for ratification.

**1806**    Zebulon Pike, exploring the West in an attempt to discover the source of the Mississippi River, sights the mountain peak that is later to be called "Pike's Peak."

**1806**    The first magazine to be published by college undergraduates appears in New Haven, Connecticut. The periodical is the Yale *Literary Cabinet,* edited by members of the senior class.

**1904**    Ethel Barrymore creates a line that is to become her trademark in years to come. At the final curtain in her new play, *Sunday,* appearing now in New York, the actress responds to the enthusiastic applause of the audience by saying: "That's all there is; there isn't any more."

**1909**    Sitting before the mirror in his dressing room in a Brooklyn, New York, theatre, Al Jolson starts to experiment with grease paint and ends up devising the "blackface" routine that is to become his trademark.

**1920**    The knock of a gavel calls to order the first meeting of the Assembly of the League of Nations in Geneva, Switzerland. Delegates of 41 nations are on hand for the opening session. The United States is the only major world power to remain aloof from the organization.

**1926**    To inaugurate the debut of the National Broadcasting Company, Merlin H. Aylesworth, the president of the company, introduces a 4-hour broadcast from the Grand Ballroom of the Hotel Waldorf-Astoria in New York. One thousand guests in the hotel and a vast unseen radio audience are entertained by Mary Garden, Will Rogers, Tito Ruffa, Weber and Fields, the New York Symphony Orchestra with Dr. Walter Damrosch conducting, Edwin Franko Goldman's Band, Vincent Lopez and his orchestra, and the orchestras of Ben Bernie and B. A. Rolfe.

**1935**    Manuel Quézon and Sergio Osmeña are inaugurated in Manila as the first President and Vice President, respectively, of the Commonwealth of the Philippines.

**1942**    After three days of bitter fighting in the Guadalcanal-Tulagi area, the Japanese are routed and control of the sea and air in the southern Solomon Islands passes to the United States. (WORLD WAR II)

**1948**    William Lyon MacKenzie King retires as prime minister of Canada, after serving in that office 21 years, 5 months, and 5 days, an all-time record for the British Commonwealth.


## NOVEMBER 16

**1864**    Convinced that the Confederate General John B. Hood has abandoned the entire state of Georgia, General William T. Sherman and his Union army of about 60,000 men start their celebrated "March to the Sea."

**1901**    Three automobile racers in Brooklyn, New York, speed over Ocean Parkway at a rate of better than a mile a minute, the first automobile drivers to achieve these records. The fastest speed is achieved by Henry Fournier who drives a mile in 51⅘ seconds.

**1907**    Oklahoma is the 46th state to enter the Union.

**1908**    Arturo Toscanini, Italian operatic conductor, makes his U.S. debut, conducting the opera *Aïda* at the Metropolitan Opera House in New York.

**1914**    The 12 Federal Reserve Banks are opened formally in accordance with the Glass-Owen Bill passed in 1913 to "... establish a more effective supervision of banking in the United States."

**1922**    Premier Benito Mussolini addresses the Italian Chamber of Deputies for the first time since his *coup d'état* in October: "The country cheers and waits. We will give it not words but facts. ... We intend to give the nation a discipline.... Let none of our enemies of yesterday, of today, of tomorrow, cherish illusions in regard to our permanence in power. Foolish and childish illusions, like those of yesterday!"

**1928**    The Woman's Home Missionary Society of Oak Park, Illinois, cancels a lecture date with Miss Maude Royden, English preacher and Bible teacher, after members of the Society learn that Miss Royden smokes cigarettes!

**1932**    The most famous vaudeville theatre in America, the Palace in New York, closes its doors. The theatre will be opened shortly for the showing of moving pictures.

**1933**    At 11:50 o'clock in the evening, Washington time, the United States and the Soviet Union establish diplomatic relations. Earlier in the day, President Franklin D. Roosevelt sent this letter to Maxim Litvinov, Russian Commissar for Foreign Affairs: "I am very happy to inform you that as a result of our conversations the Government of the United States has decided to establish normal diplomatic relations with the Government of the Union of Soviet Socialist Republics and to exchange ambassadors. I trust that the relations now established between our peoples may forever remain normal and friendly, and that our Nations henceforth may cooperate for their mutual benefit and for the preservation of the peace of the world."

**1953**    Former President Harry Truman makes a nationwide radio-television broadcast to refute charges that he appointed an alleged Communist spy, Harry Dexter White, to high government office: "I have been accused, in effect, of knowingly betraying the security of the United States. This charge is ... a falsehood, and the man who made it had every reason to know it is a falsehood."

**1963**    Professor Frederick Barghoorn of Yale University who has been imprisoned by the Russians during a visit to Moscow, on charges of espionage, is released following an appeal by President Kennedy.

# NOVEMBER 17

**1734**   John Peter Zenger, who began to edit the *New York Weekly Journal* a little more than a year ago, is arrested by the royal governor of New York, William Cosby, charged with libel.

**1800**   Congress convenes in Washington for the first time. The session is held in the north wing of the Capitol, the only portion of the building that is completed.

**1869**   The Suez Canal in Egypt, between the Arabian Desert and the Sinai Peninsula, is opened formally with considerable pomp and circumstance. Egypt plays host to 6,000 foreign guests, led by Emperor Franz Josef of Austria-Hungary and the Empress Eugénie of France. As the canal is declared officially open to traffic, a display of fireworks is set off on each bank and a squadron of yachts pass through the locks, the first one bearing the Emperor Franz Josef, the Empress Eugénie and the Khedive of Egypt.

**1877**   The first production of the D'Oyly Carte Opera Company is Gilbert and Sullivan's opera, *The Sorcerer*, presented tonight for the first time in London's Opera Comique Theatre.

**1881**   Samuel Gompers organizes the Federation of Organized Trades and Labor Unions of the United States and Canada at a meeting held in Pittsburgh. (This organization was really the forerunner of the American Federation of Labor, formed 5 years later.)

**1891**   The Polish concert pianist, Ignace Jan Paderewski, makes his American debut at New York's new Carnegie Music Hall.

**1938**   The popular orchestra leader Kay Kyser delivers the first in a series of lectures on "swing" music before an audience of 2,300 people in the auditorium of the College of the City of New York. The lecture series is being presented to show the "inner workings and artistic features of swing music."

**1941**   Premier Hideki Tojo of Japan tells members of the Japanese Diet that Japanese foreign policy aims at peace in East Asia. (On the same day, Joseph C. Grew, U.S. ambassador to Japan, warns the State Department that a sudden Japanese attack may come before the embassy in Tokyo can issue a warning. Mr. Grew's message was transmitted some 20 days before Pearl Harbor.)

**1948**   The House of Commons votes to "nationalize" the steel industry in England, thus ending private ownership of the mills and distribution outlets.

# NOVEMBER 18

**1805**   Thirty women meeting at the home of Mrs. Silas Lee in Wiscasset, Maine, organize the Female Charitable Society, the first woman's club in America.

**1852**   More than a million people line the streets of London to view the public funeral of the Duke of Wellington, "England's greatest soldier." (The funeral had been held up 2 months after His Grace's death to await the opening of Parliament.)

**1883**   The United States adopts standard time, the nation henceforth to be divided into the four zones designated as Eastern, Central, Mountain, and Pacific.

**1903**   Panama and the United States sign a treaty reaching agreement on the proposed Panama Canal. The United States agrees to recognize the independence of the Republic of Panama and the latter grants a 10-mile strip of land to the United States for $10,-000,000 in gold and an annuity of $250,000.

**1905**   Following a national Norwegian plebiscite, Prince Carl of Denmark is elected King Haakon VII of Norway. (The Danish prince has been invited to assume the crown without an election, but he insisted that one be held in order to be certain that the people of Norway wanted him as their king.)

**1919**   New York stages an enthusiastic reception for the Prince of Wales on his first visit to the United States. Ticker tape is used for the first time as the Prince's motorcade moves up Broadway, while every type of boat in the harbor salutes him with whistle blasts. (Later, at the Woolworth Tower, then the highest building in the world, office girls surrounded him as he entered the foyer for a tour of inspection. One girl jumped from her place on some crowded steps, attempting to throw her arms around the royal neck. She missed him by several feet but was close enough to cry out hysterically, "God, what a man!")

**1936**   The regime of General Francisco Franco in Spain is recognized by the Fascist governments of Germany and Italy.

**1939**   The Congress of Industrial Organizations, successor to the original Committee for Industrial Organization, elects John L. Lewis as its president.

**1949**   Vice-President Alben W. Barkley, a widower since 1947, is married in St. John's Church in St. Louis, Missouri, to Mrs. Carleton S. Hadley. Mr. Barkley is the first Vice President in history to marry while in office. (The reception that followed the church wedding was televised.)

**1961**   In Los Angeles, President John F. Kennedy speaks out against the rising tide of political extremism across the nation: "... Men who are unwilling to face up to the danger from without are convinced that the real danger is from within. They look suspiciously at their neighbors and their leaders ... They find treason in our churches, in our highest court, in our treatment of water. They equate the Democratic Party with the welfare state, the welfare state with Socialism, Socialism with Communism...."

**1962**   Three Presidents—Presidents Kennedy, Truman, and Eisenhower—sit side by side at the funeral in Bonham, Texas, of veteran Speaker of the House Sam Rayburn. Mr. Rayburn, when he died on November 16, had served in the House of Representatives nearly 49 years and as House Speaker for 17 years.

**1964**    J. Edgar Hoover, the director of the Federal Bureau of Investigation, creates a sensation when he characterizes the civil rights leader, the Reverend Martin Luther King, Jr., "the most notorious liar in the country." Hoover said that King had accused FBI agents in Georgia of failing to act on Negroes' complaints because they were Southerners. (The next day, the Negro leader made a temperate reply, saying that Mr. Hoover ". . . has apparently faltered under the awesome burden, complexities and responsibilities of his office.")

## NOVEMBER 19

**1831**    James Abram Garfield, 20th President of the United States, is born near Mentor, Ohio.

**1863**    President Abraham Lincoln, speaking at ceremonies dedicating the battlefield of Gettysburg, Pennsylvania, as a national cemetery, surprises his listeners by talking for just 2 minutes, confining his remarks to some 10 sentences: ". . . we here highly resolve that these dead shall not have died in vain; that this nation, under God, shall have a new birth of freedom; and that government of the people, by the people, and for the people, shall not perish from the earth." (The President's speech was considered so insignificant that most newspapers the next day carried it on inside pages, in contrast to the 2-hour oration delivered by Edward Everett, which was printed all over the country on page one.)

**1874**    William Marcy Tweed, political "boss" of Tammany Hall in New York City, is convicted of defrauding the city of about $6,000,000 and sentenced to 12 years' imprisonment.

**1874**    The National Woman's Christian Temperance Union (WCTU) is organized in Cleveland, Ohio. The new organization's chief objective is to promote the prohibition of all alcoholic beverages.

**1903**    Frustrated in her attempt to interview President Theodore Roosevelt at the White House, Carrie Nation, the famous prohibitionist, creates a stir in the gallery of the Senate after attempting to make a speech and sell replicas of her celebrated hatchet.

**1919**    The Treaty of Versailles, drawn up by the Paris Peace Conference at the end of World War I, is rejected by the U.S. Senate.

**1944**    The best-known little boy in America is 3-year-old Forest Hoffman, nicknamed "Nubbins," who is celebrating Christmas in his Cheyenne, Wyoming, home. Because of an incurable disease, Nubbins' parents decided to observe a premature Christmas because some 10 doctors have predicted that the child will not live for another month. Thousands of Americans, hoping to make his last "Christmas" a happy one, have sent Nubbins cards, candy, and toys. (For a while, it looked as though Nubbins might respond to hospitalization, but he finally passed away on March 31, 1949.)

**1948**    Newspapers are reporting the startling acts of King Farouk of Egypt and his brother-in-law, Shah Riza Pahlevi of Iran, who have announced that they are divorcing their wives. (Both monarchs were said to have so acted because their royal spouses had failed to produce male heirs.)

**1962**    For the first time in history, a jazz concert is presented at the White House when Mrs. John F. Kennedy entertains the teen-age children of diplomats assigned to Washington from 59 countries. (Jazz bands had played in the White House at dances and receptions, but only for background music.)

## NOVEMBER 20

**1620**    A baby girl, Peregrine White, is born aboard the *Mayflower* in Massachusetts Bay, the first child to be born in the New England colonies.

**1863**    Edward Everett, the famous orator who delivered the principal speech at the dedication of Gettysburg National Cemetery yesterday, writes to President Lincoln to congratulate him on his brief remarks at Gettysburg: "I should be glad if I could flatter myself that I came as near to the central idea of the occasion in two hours, as you did in two minutes." * (The President acknowledged Everett's note, saying "In our respective parts yesterday, you could not have been excused to make a short address, nor I a long one.")

**1866**    The Grand Army of the Republic, composed of the veterans of the Union Army in the War between the States, holds its first national encampment at Indianapolis, Indiana. The delegates elect General Stephen A. Hurlbut of Illinois as their first commander-in-chief.

**1914**    From now on, all American citizens who request passports from the State Department will be required to submit photographs to be attached to their official papers.

**1923**    An article in the woman's magazine, *Pictorial Review,* bemoans the fact that the maiden aunt, once the mainstay in thousands of American homes, is going out to find a job. The article

* Mr. Everett's judgment was not typical of many people. The Republican-owned *Chicago Times* on this date ran an editorial commenting on the Gettysburg Address as follows: "The cheek of every American must tingle with shame as he reads the silly, flat and dishwatery utterances of the man who has to be pointed out to intelligent foreigners as the President of the United States."

reports that "8,549,511 women are earning money in the United States."

**1929**    A new dramatic radio program is heard for the first time, as "The Goldbergs," written by and starring Gertrude Berg, makes its bow over the Columbia Broadcasting System.

**1943**    *Winged Victory*, a salute to the U.S. Air Forces written by Moss Hart, opens in New York City. (In the 27 weeks that the play ran on Broadway, it grossed a total $1,057,318 for the Army Emergency Relief Fund. Mr. Hart donated both his services and his royalties to the Fund.)

**1945**    Twenty-four top German leaders go on trial at Nuremberg, Germany, before the International War Crimes Tribunal. Associate Justice Robert H. Jackson of the U.S. Supreme Court is serving as prosecutor.

**1947**    In Westminster Abbey, London, Princess Elizabeth of England and Lieutenant Philip Mountbatten are married before an assemblage that includes six kings and seven queens and representatives of almost all of Europe's royal dynasties. The wedding ceremony is transmitted by loudspeakers to the streets of London where hundreds of thousands of people are lined up to greet the royal couple on their return to Buckingham Palace.

**1953**    Hugh Roy Cullen, chairman of the Board of Regents of Houston University, in Houston, Texas, gives $2,250,000 to the university because of its football team's 37-7 victory over Baylor University on November 14.

**1962**    President Kennedy instructs the Secretary of Defense to lift the naval quarantine of Cuba.

**1962**    By the stroke of a pen, President Kennedy signs an Executive Order forbidding racial and religious discrimination in housing built or purchased by federal aid.

**1962**    Newspaper reports reveal that President John F. Kennedy is contributing his White House salary to charity.* The White House also tells reporters that every dollar he has earned since going on the government payroll as a Congressman in 1947 has been contributed to charity.

## NOVEMBER 21

**1800**    Abigail Adams, wife of our second President, John Adams, who arrived in the new city of Washington only 5 days ago, sits down and writes a letter to her sister back home in Massachusetts, describing life in the Executive Mansion: "...Not one room

---

* President Kennedy was not the first Chief Executive to contribute his salary to charity. President Herbert Hoover is the first known President to have disposed of his salary by distributing it to various charities.

is finished of the whole.... It is habitable by fires.... thirteen of which we are obliged to keep daily, or sleep in wet or damp places. ...We have not the least fence-yard.... and the great unfinished audience-room I make a drying-room of, to hang the clothes in...."

**1864** President Lincoln sends a letter of condolence to Mrs. Bixby, whose five sons were killed in battle: "I pray that our Heavenly Father may assuage the anguish of your bereavement and leave you only the cherished memory of the loved and lost, and the solemn pride that must be yours to have laid so costly a sacrifice upon the altar of freedom."

**1877** Thomas A. Edison announces in Menlo Park, New Jersey, that he has invented a "talking machine."

**1925** Harold E. ("Red") Grange, the best-known football player of the year, plays his last varsity game with the University of Illinois team. Grange will turn professional in another day or so when he signs up with the Chicago Bears. (In the space of 2 months, this man became so famous that petitions were circulated nominating him for Congress, a real-estate firm offered him a salary of $120,000 a year and a moving-picture corporation signed him up with a $300,000 contract, and President Coolidge received him at the White House.)

**1933** William C. Bullitt begins his service as the first U.S. ambassador to the Soviet Union.

**1938** The western border areas of Czechoslovakia are forcibly incorporated into the Reich and all their inhabitants made German citizens. (In spite of the fact that Adolf Hitler had declared before the Munich Conference that he "wanted no Czechs," some 800,000 Czechs were engulfed by this act of aggression.)

**1940** Philip Murray becomes head of the Congress of Industrial Organizations, succeeding John L. Lewis who resigned 3 days ago.

**1945** Two hundred thousand members of the United Automobile Workers' Union go out on strike at all plants of the General Motors Corporation, following a dispute with management over wage rates and vacation allowances. (The strike wasn't settled until the following May, 1946.)

**1962** In the wake of the Oxford, Mississippi, race riots, the Mississippi Senate approves a resolution expressing defiance and "utter contempt for the Kennedy Administration." The resolution blames the "ruthless and corrupted Administration..." for the riots and asks the separate states to join with Mississippi "in ridding this once great nation of ours of the Kennedy family dynasty and accompanying evils..."

**1963** President and Mrs. John F. Kennedy fly to Texas to begin a 2-day tour of that state. Political observers believe the real reason for the trip is the President's hope that he can heal the bitter rift between the conservative and liberal wings of the Democratic Party there. Mrs. Kennedy is excited over the prospects of her first visit to the state of Texas.

**1963**  President and Mrs. Kennedy are greeted by cheering crowds in San Antonio, Houston and Fort Worth. During a speech in San Antonio, he says: ".... We stand on the edge of a great new era, with both crisis and opportunity.... It is an era which calls for action and for the best efforts of all those who would test the unknown and the uncertain in phases of human endeavor. It is the time for pathfinders and pioneers...." *(See November 22)*

## NOVEMBER 22

**1880**  A beautiful newcomer to the stage, Lillian Russell, makes her debut in vaudeville at Tony Pastor's Theatre in New York.

**1906**  Delegates to the International Radio Telegraphic Convention meeting in Berlin, Germany, adopt the SOS distress signal as the warning to be used by disabled ships at sea.

**1909**  Miss Helen Hayes makes her New York stage debut at the Herald Square Theatre. The young actress from Washington, D.C., has a role in the play, *In Old Dutch*. (On November 21, 1955, to mark Miss Hayes' long association with the theatre, the old Fulton Theatre in New York was rededicated as the Helen Hayes Theatre.)

**1918**  New York City's Great White Way, encompassing the Broadway area adjacent to Times Square, breaks out in a blaze of lights as Fuel Administrator Harry A. Garfield lifts the ban on "lightless nights." (WORLD WAR I)

**1928**  The most popular hair style worn by women who have cut their hair short is the "boyish bob."

**1930**  Radio fans in England hear their first broadcast of a football game in the United States as the British Broadcasting Corporation transmits a description of the Yale-Harvard game playing at New Haven, Connecticut. (Harvard won, 13–0.)

**1935**  The "China Clipper" leaves San Francisco for the first official trans-Pacific airmail flight from that city, loaded down with more than 100,000 letters and official mail. (The 8,000-mile flight, making stops in Honolulu, Midway, Wake, and Guam, arrived in Manila seven days later. President Franklin D. Roosevelt in Washington told the Postmaster-General of the government: "Even at this distance I thrill at the wonder of it all.")

**1943**  President Roosevelt, Prime Minister Churchill, and Generalissimo Chiang Kai-shek open a 5-day conference at Cairo, Egypt, to discuss the defeat of Japan and the establishment of a free Korea. (WORLD WAR II)

**1963**                 The nation's gallant young leader, John Fitzgerald
                          Kennedy, the 35th President of the United States, is
*12:31 p.m.,*             struck down by an assassin's bullets as he rides in a
*C.S.T.*                  motorcade on a street in Dallas, Texas. A half hour
                          later, the 46-year-old President is pronounced dead
at Dallas' Parkland Hospital. (The Governor of Texas, John B.
Connally, riding in the same car with the President, is seriously
wounded.)

*2:15 p.m.,*              After a struggle inside a local movie theatre, Dallas
*C.S.T.*                  police capture an accused suspect. He is Lee Harvey
                          Oswald, 24, an avowed Marxist and embittered mal-
content. Later, he is arraigned on charges of murdering President
Kennedy.

*2:38 p.m.,*              With his wife and Mrs. John Kennedy by his side,
*C.S.T.*                  Vice President Lyndon B. Johnson takes the oath of
                          office aboard the Presidential jet plane at Dallas' Love
Field and thus becomes the 36th President of the United States.
The oath is administered by Federal Judge Sarah T. Hughes.

*5:58 p.m.,*              President Johnson arrives at Andrews Air Force Base,
*E.S.T.*                  outside of Washington, and goes before microphones
                          and television cameras to speak his first words to the
nation: "This is a sad time for all people. We have suffered a loss
that cannot be weighed. For me, it is a deep personal tragedy. I
know the world shares the sorrow that Mrs. Kennedy and her family
bear. I will do my best. That is all I can do. I ask for your help—
and God's."

## NOVEMBER 23

**1804**   Franklin Pierce, 14th President of the United States,
is born in Hillsborough, New Hampshire.

**1863**   Beginning of the "Battle above the Clouds" on Look-
out Mountain, Tennessee, in the War between the States. (When it
was all over two days later, the Northern armies had established
control over the entire state of Tennessee.)

**1876**   Representatives of three eastern colleges—Columbia,
Princeton, and Harvard—form the first intercollegiate football association at a meeting held in Springfield, Massachusetts.

**1896**   The current issue of the *Home Maker's Magazine* says
"The barbecue is to Georgia what the clambake is to Rhode Island,
what a roast beef dinner is to our English cousins, what canvasback
duck is to the Marylander, and what a pork-and-beans supper is to
the Bostonian."

**1903**   Enrico Caruso, celebrated Italian tenor, makes his American debut in New York, singing the role of the Duke in *Rigoletto*
at the Metropolitan Opera House.

**1924**    Playing before a crowded house, Vincent Lopez and 40 jazz musicians stage a concert at New York's staid old Metropolitan Opera House.

**1930**    Although England is a "wet" country, Henry Ford says he will not allow his English workmen to drink, even in their homes. The American industrialist is an ardent supporter of the Prohibition movement.

**1942**    Congress authorizes the creation of a woman's auxiliary of the U.S. Coast Guard. The new service will be known as the SPARS, an abbreviation of the first initials of the Coast Guard motto, "Semper Paratus—Always Ready." (WORLD WAR II)

**1945**    All food rationing in the United States comes to an end, sugar excepted. (WORLD WAR II)

**1954**    The Chinese Communist government at Peiping announces that 11 U.S. airmen captured during the Korean War have been convicted on charges of espionage.

**1963**    As the body of John Fitzgerald Kennedy lies in state in the East Room of the White House, the nation remains in a state of shock. For the most part, the streets of American cities, towns, and villages are almost deserted. And all across the face of the earth, people mourn the loss of the 35th President of the United States. ("Everything in one cried out in protest. This young, gay and brave statesman, killed in the full vigor of his manhood, when he bore on his shoulders all the cares and hopes of the world."—British Prime Minister Sir Alec Douglas-Home.)

# NOVEMBER 24

**1784**    Zachary Taylor, 12th President of the United States, is born in Orange County, Virginia.

**1832**    A state convention of South Carolina, called to protest the Tariff Act of 1832, adopts an Ordinance of Nullification stating that the federal tariff statute is "null, void and no law, nor binding upon this state, its officers or citizens." (Another convention met in March, 1833, and rescinded the Ordinance after Congress had passed a new compromise tariff bill.)

**1859**    Maurice Strakosch, the theatrical impresario, presents his 17-year-old sister-in-law, Adelina Patti, to music lovers at the Academy of Music in New York. Miss Patti receives a tremendous ovation after the curtain comes down on her performance in the title role of *Lucia di Lammermoor,* her world debut as an opera singer.

**1869**    Women representing 21 states of the Union convene in Cleveland to draw up plans calling for the organization of the American Woman Suffrage Association. The chairman is the vigorous Woman's Rights' leader, Lucy Stone, and the principal speaker of the day is Julia Ward Howe.

**1923** The French Parliament approves a bill providing for an annual allowance of 40,000 francs for Madame Curie, the co-discoverer of radium.

**1930** For the first time in history, a woman starts out on a transcontinental air flight across the United States. The aviator is Miss Ruth Nichols who set out today from Mineola, Long Island, in a Lockheed-Vega plane. (She arrived in California 7 days later.)

**1944** Superfortress bombers of the U.S. Air Force make their first raids on Tokyo, taking off from the American base established on Saipan. (WORLD WAR II)

**1953** Senator Joseph R. McCarthy (R., Wis.), in a nationwide radio and television broadcast, answers former President Truman's charge that "it is now evident that the present (Eisenhower) Administration has fully embraced, for political advantage, 'McCarthyism.'" The Wisconsin senator not only attacked Mr. Truman, calling him a "discredited politician" whose administration was "crawling with Communists," but takes issue with President Eisenhower, saying that Communism is an issue and will be an issue in 1954,* despite the President's wish to avoid it.

**1963** The body of President John F. Kennedy leaves the White House for the Capitol where it lies in state in the great rotunda, reposing on the same catafalque that bore the body of Abraham Lincoln 100 years ago. The doors of the Capitol are opened to the American people. (At times, the line of waiting mourners stretched out two miles long.)

**1963** As Lee Harvey Oswald, the alleged assassin of President Kennedy, is led through a basement corridor of the Dallas police building, en route to an armored car that is to transfer him to a county jail, an assailant presses through the crowd and fires at him. Oswald is seriously wounded and dies less than 2 hours later. His murderer is identified as Jack Ruby, a local night-club owner. (Millions of American witnessed this event as it occurred over their television screens. The most incredible aspect of the crime was that Ruby apparently had no difficulty in getting close to Oswald, this despite the fact that the prisoner was surrounded by 60 policemen and deputy sheriffs.)

**1964** Residents of the District of Columbia, it is announced today, cast more ballots in the 1964 Presidential election, than the total rolled up in either Alaska, Nevada, or Wyoming. Of Washington's registered voters, 90.4 percent turned out at the polls, casting 169,796 votes for President Johnson and 28,801 for Senator Goldwater. (This was the first time the District had been permitted to vote for President since 1800.)

---

* This was a reference to the 1954 congressional and gubernatorial elections.

# NOVEMBER 25

**1780** The British frigate *Hussar* sinks in New York harbor with 900,000 gold guineas stored below deck. (Was it recovered? Reader, I have found no record.)

**1834** The proprietor of Delmonico's, one of New York's finest restaurants, advises the public that a meal of soup, steak, coffee, and half a pie costs but 12 cents. Dinner for two can be served for 25 cents, the extra penny providing for a second cup of coffee.

**1844** An enthusiastic audience applauds the first performance of Michael W. Balfe's opera, *The Bohemian Girl*, at the Park Theatre in New York. The most popular song in the score is "I Dreamt I Dwelt in Marble Halls."

**1874** The "Greenback" Party is organized in Indianapolis, its supporters made up of those individuals who are demanding the substitution of legal-tender paper money for all outstanding bank currency.

**1903** Robert (Bob) Fitzsimmons becomes the first man in history to win three different boxing championships after capturing the light heavyweight title in a bout with George Gardner in San Francisco. Fitzsimmons won the middleweight title in 1891 and the heavyweight crown in 1897.

**1913** Miss Jessie Wilson, the daughter of President and Mrs. Woodrow Wilson, is married in the East Room of the White House to Francis B. Sayre, before three hundred guests.

**1920** Station WTAW of College Station, Texas, broadcasts the first play-by-play description of a football game in radio history, as it reports the plays of the Texas University-Texas Aggie game.

**1936** The German-Japanese Anti-Comintern Agreement is signed in Berlin. (It was later signed by Italy, Hungary, Spain, and the puppet government of Manchukuo.)

**1944** In a carefully documented report, the U.S. War Refugee Board charges Germany with mass murder. The report says: "It is a fact beyond denial that the Germans have deliberately and systematically murdered millions of innocent civilians." (WORLD WAR II)

**1957** The American public is stunned by an announcement from the White House, revealing that President Dwight D. Eisenhower has suffered a "mild stroke." (Fortunately, the President made a fast recovery, following a period of rest and limited schedules of work.)

**1963** As a crowd of approximately one million grieving citizens line the streets of Washington, the long cortege escorting the body of President John Fitzgerald Kennedy moves from the U.S. Capitol to the White House to St. Matthew's Cathedral and finally to Arlington National Cemetery. There, the 35th President of the United States, assassinated in Dallas, Texas, 3 days ago, is laid to rest. Just before the funeral ceremony is ended, Mrs. John F. Kennedy places an "Eternal Flame" at the head of his grave. On hand to pay final homage to the fallen leader are obscure citizens and important officials of the government, kings and presidents, and high-ranking representatives of nearly one hundred sovereign nations. ("... Our nation is bereaved. The whole world is poorer because of his loss. But we can all be better Americans because John Fitzgerald Kennedy has passed our way ... And now that he is relieved of the almost superhuman burdens we imposed on him, may he rest in peace."—Chief Justice Earl Warren, November 24, 1963).

## NOVEMBER 26

**1789**   President George Washington sets this date aside as a day of national thanksgiving for the adoption of the U.S. Constitution.

**1825**   Students at Union College in Schenectady, New York, organize the first collegiate social fraternity. The new Greek-letter society will be called "Kappa Alpha."

**1832**   The first streetcar railway in America starts its public service, operating in New York from City Hall to 14th Street. (The streetcar was drawn by a horse, the first driver being Lank O'Dell. The fare was 12½ cents.)

**1864**   A young mathematics instructor at Oxford University, England, sends an early Christmas gift to 12-year-old Alice Liddell, the daughter of a country clergyman. The gift is his hand-written manuscript of a story he has written for Alice. The instructor is Charles L. Dodgson and he calls his story, *Alice's Adventures Underground*. (We know the story today as *Alice In Wonderland* and the instructor by his pen name, Lewis Carroll.)

**1882**   People out in Laramie, Wyoming, are chuckling over Bill Nye's comments on napkins in his local newspaper, *The Boomerang:* "The law of the napkin is vaguely understood. It is poor taste to put it in your pocket and carry it away. The rule of etiquette is becoming more and more thoroughly established that napkins should be left at the house of the hostess. It should be left beside the plate where it may be easily found by the hostess and returned to the neighbor from whom she borrowed it for the occasion."

**1925**   A great many people in the United States who have never owned an automobile are sorely tempted to buy one of the popular Ford "roadsters" now selling for $260.

**1940**   The 500,000 Jews of Warsaw, Poland, are forced by their Nazi overlords to live within a ghetto district surrounded by an 8-foot concrete wall. (WORLD WAR II)

**1941**   Secretary of State Cordell Hull submits American proposals to the Japanese "peace" envoys in Washington outlining methods by which tension can be eliminated in American-Japanese relations.

**1964**    As a follow-up to President Johnson's war on poverty, the Federal Welfare Administration reports that the nation's poorest county is rural Tunica, Mississippi, where the median family income is $1,260. The government agency lists Mississippi at the head of 10 states with the highest percentage of impoverished families.

## NOVEMBER 27

**1889**    Curtis P. Brady receives the first permit issued by the Commissioner of Parks of New York City to drive an automobile through Central Park. The permit is subject to Mr. Brady's pledge "to exert the greatest care to avoid frightening horses" in the park.

**1890**    Residents of the Boston suburbs have sent a complaint to police authorities charging that it is unsafe to drive their horses and buggies on country lanes because of "racing bicyclists attired in black tights and long mustaches."

**1910**    Pennsylvania Station in New York, the world's largest railway terminal to date, is opened to traffic. The mammoth station covers some 28 acres and occupies a site on which 500 houses and commercial buildings formerly stood.

**1911**    A number of theatregoers critical of the Irish Players visiting this country from Dublin's Abbey Theatre try to stop the performance of J. M. Synge's *Playboy of the Western World* at the Maxine Elliott Theatre in New York. The hecklers pelt the Irish cast with fruit, vegetables, and eggs, and order is restored only after policemen arrest 10 men and women.

**1937**    Members of the International Ladies' Garment Workers' Union in New York produce a musical revue entitled *Pins and Needles*, a clever and tuneful plea for organized labor. First-night spectators and critics alike are impressed by the originality of the show and particularly like a song called "Sing Me a Song of Social Significance." (The cast may have been made up of amateurs but the lively little revue continued until sometime in 1939.)

**1942**    Officers and men of the French fleet stationed in Toulon scuttle a major part of the fleet to prevent it from falling into the hands of Nazi forces in "occupied" France. Among the warships sunk are 10 cruisers, 28 destroyers, and 14 submarines. (WORLD WAR II)

**1945**    President Truman names General George C. Marshall as his special representative to China. General Marshall's mission, in the main, is to effect a cessation of hostilities between the Chinese Nationalists and Communists. (On January 10, 1946, both factions in China agreed to end hostilities, but fighting resumed on the following April 15 and the Marshall Mission was doomed to failure.)

**1957**    Because much of the disorder that accompanied the integration of Central High School in Little Rock, Arkansas, has died down, army paratroopers are withdrawn from that city. Federalized National Guardsmen, however, will remain until the end of the current school year.

**1963**    President Lyndon B. Johnson makes his first appearance before a joint session of Congress since he succeeded to the Presidency on November 22. The President, obviously shaken, says: "All I have I would have given gladly not to be standing here today. The greatest leader of our time has been struck down by the foulest deed of our time. Today John Fitzgerald Kennedy lives on in the immortal words and works that he left behind. He lives on in the mind and memories of mankind. He lives on in the hearts of his countrymen. . . ."

## NOVEMBER 28

**1520**    Ferdinand Magellan enters the Pacific Ocean on his way around the world, the first European to sail that body of water from the east.

**1863**    The nation observes the first Thanksgiving set aside by national proclamation. (President Lincoln had asked Americans on October 3 to celebrate the last Thursday in November as a day of general thanksgiving.)

**1895**    America's first automobile race gets under way when 6 cars start on a 55-mile round-trip course from Chicago's Jackson Park to Evanston, Illinois. Two of the cars are electrically driven, four are powered by gasoline engines. The winner is J. Frank Duryea, who drove an automobile invented by his brother Charles E. Duryea. (The winner traveled an average speed of 7 miles per hour. His total driving time, apart from time out for motor repairs, was 7 hours, 53 minutes. The Duryea car used 3½ gallons of drugstore gasoline and 19 gallons of water. Mr. Duryea's prize, offered by the *Chicago Times-Herald,* was $2,000.)

**1929**    Lieutenant Commander Richard E. Byrd, USNR, takes off from his base in "Little America" in Antarctica to attempt a flight over the South Pole. With Byrd are three crew members, including Bernt Balchen as his pilot. (*See November 29.*)

**1942**    The rationing of coffee begins in the United States. (WORLD WAR II)

**1942**    A disastrous fire and stampede break out in the "Cocoanut Grove" night club in Boston after a busboy's match accidentally ignites some artificial palm trees in the café. (More than 800 people were in the club at the time, celebrating the day's local football games. When it was all over, almost 500 people had lost their lives.)

**1943**   For the first time in his life, President Franklin D. Roosevelt meets Premier Joseph Stalin of the Soviet Union as the two men, joined by Prime Minister Winston Churchill, begin a series of discussions at Teheran, Iran. (Among the items on which agreement was reached was the approximate date of the invasion of Western Europe and a promise to recognize Iran's independence and sovereignty both during and after the war.) (*See December 1.*) (WORLD WAR II)

**1963**   President Lyndon B. Johnson, in office 6 days, makes a Thanksgiving Day address to the nation from the White House, saying: ".... A great leader is dead [John F. Kennedy], a great nation must move on. Yesterday is not ours to recover, but tomorrow is ours to win or lose. I am resolved we shall win the tomorrows before us..."

**1963**   President Johnson announces that Cape Canaveral, Florida, will be renamed Cape Kennedy and its space installations will henceforth be called "The John F. Kennedy Space Center."

**1964**   An editorial in the *Washington Post* points out that the "costly flirtation" of the Republican Party with Senator Barry Goldwater (R., Ariz.) and the extreme right-wing political movements has resulted in a serious loss of Republicans in the various state legislatures. Says the *Post:* ".... A survey by the *Congressional Quarterly* shows that the GOP lost more than 500 legislative seats in the states—96 in state senates, and 445 in the houses.... This gives the Democrats legislative control in 32 states...."

# NOVEMBER 29

**1701**   A good many people in London are very excited over an announcement in the *Flying Post* stating that "There is lately arrived a large elephant, the biggest that ever was in Europe, and one that performs varieties of exercise for Diversion and Laughter.... It is to be seen at the White Horse Inn in Fleet Street from 10 in the Morning till 6 at Night."

**1887**   Josef Hofmann, 11 years old but already a famous Polish pianist, makes his American debut at a concert held in the Metropolitan Opera House in New York.

**1890**   The football teams of the U.S. Military Academy and the U.S. Naval Academy hold the first so-called Army-Navy game, playing at West Point, New York. The final score: Navy 24–Army 0.

**1904**   President Theodore Roosevelt sits down at his desk in the White House and writes to a distant cousin, Franklin D. Roosevelt, telling him he approves of his engagement to the President's niece, Eleanor. "Dear Franklin," writes the President, "We are greatly rejoiced over the good news. I am as fond of Eleanor as if she were my daughter; and I like you, and trust you, and believe in you. . . . You and Eleanor are true and brave, and I believe you love each other unselfishly. . . . Golden years open before you . . ."

**1922**   Lord Carnarvon of England and his American assistant, Howard Carter, discover the tomb of King Tutankhamen in Egypt. Their accomplishment is being hailed by the newspapers of the world as "the greatest archaeological discovery of all time." (The average American wasn't much concerned with the archaeological importance of the mission, but he was fascinated by the treasure in the tomb and particularly with the King's unpronounceable name. To people in the United States, in 1922 and 1923, the King was just "King Tut.")

**1929**   In his tri-motored Fokker plane, Lieutenant Commander Richard E. Byrd sends out his famous radio message: "My calculations indicate that we have reached the vicinity of the South Pole." Byrd and his crew of three are thus the first men to fly over the South Pole, and Byrd himself is the only man to date to have flown over both the North and the South Poles. (He flew over the North Pole on May 9, 1926.)

**1932**   The audience at the *première* of Cole Porter's musical comedy, *The Gay Divorce,* at the Ethel Barrymore Theatre in New York, likes the play and its theme and its cast, but the "hit" of the show is a song that will soon have the nation rocking on its heels, "Night and Day."

**1945**   Yugoslavia becomes a federated republic after Marshal Tito reads a proclamation to the Constituent and National Assemblies. The monarchy is abolished and King Peter II is deprived of all his vested rights.

**1948**   Opera is telecast directly from the stage of the Metropolitan Opera House in New York for the first time. The opera is Verdi's *Otello,* transmitted over the facilities of Station WJZ-TV, New York.

**1963**   President Johnson appoints a seven-man bipartisan commission, to be headed by Chief Justice Earl Warren, to investigate the assassination of President John F. Kennedy.

## NOVEMBER 30

**1782**   Preliminary peace articles ending the Revolutionary War between the United States and Great Britain are signed in Paris.

**1804**   For the first time in U.S. history, a justice of the Supreme Court goes on trial to face impeachment proceedings as the trial of Samuel Chase, charged with criticism of government and misconduct in office, begins in Washington.

**1835**   Birthday of Samuel Langhorne Clemens, better known as Mark Twain, author of the internationally read stories, *Tom Sawyer* and *Huckleberry Finn.*

**1874**  Birthday of Sir Winston Spencer Churchill, twice Britain's prime minister, and indomitable leader of the British Empire during World War II. (On November 30, 1954, Great Britain hailed Sir Winston on his 80th birthday in a public celebration believed to have surpassed any honoring a British subject. At the celebration in London's Westminster Hall, however, Churchill disclaimed the credit for inspiring Britain during World War II, saying that victory came because of "the nation and the race . . . that had the lion's heart. I had the luck to be called upon to give the roar.")

**1920**  Charles Ponzi of Boston pleads guilty to charges, preferred against him by the district attorney of Boston, of defrauding thousands of people who turned their life savings over to him for "investment." (The bogus financier was imprisoned in this country until 1934, when he was released and deported to Italy.)

**1922**  Sarah Bernhardt makes her last appearance on any stage, playing in a final performance of *Daniel* in Turin, Italy.

**1939**  Beginning of the Russo-Finnish War: After failing to obtain territorial concessions from Finland, the Soviet Union attacks that nation from land, sea, and air.

**1949**  Chinese Communists capture Chungking, China.

**1955**  In a decree signed by President Pedro Aramburu of Argentina, the Buenos Aires newspaper *La Prensa*, seized by the Perón regime in 1951, is restored to its owner, Dr. Alberto Gainza Paz.

**1962**  General U Thant of Burma is elected to serve a 4-year term as Secretary General of the United Nations. General Thant's election as successor to the late Dag Hammarskjold is by unanimous vote of the United Nations' Security Council and the General Assembly.

# DECEMBER

## DECEMBER 1

**1824** A deadlock develops among the various Presidential candidates when electoral ballots are cast as follows: John Quincy Adams, 84; Andrew Jackson, 99; William H. Crawford, 41; Henry Clay, 37. Since no one candidate has received an electoral majority, the election will be resolved by the House of Representatives. (*See February 9*.)

**1879** One of the greatest evenings in the history of the American theatre takes place at the Fifth Avenue Theatre in New York as Arthur Sullivan steps into the pit to conduct the score of *H.M.S. Pinafore,* the operetta he has composed in collaboration with William S. Gilbert. The other half of the famous team of Gilbert and Sullivan is portraying a sailor's role in the chorus.

**1909** Something new in banking, a "Christmas Club," is introduced in Carlisle, Pennsylvania, as the first member of the Club hands a deposit to the cashier of the Carlisle Trust Company. The idea behind the Club is to encourage individuals to set aside a nest egg for Christmas shopping.

**1913** The world's first drive-in gasoline station opens for business in Pittsburgh, Pennsylvania. (Up until this date, motorists bought gasoline in livery stables and garages and continued to do so until the "gas station" caught on. On opening day, the Pittsburgh establishment sold only 30 gallons.)

**1917** With a fund of less than one hundred dollars, Father Edward Flanagan founds Boys Town, the "City of Little Men," some 11 miles west of Omaha, Nebraska. The new community will be inhabited by and administered for orphans or otherwise homeless boys.

**1919** For the first time in Britain's history, a woman takes her seat in Parliament when Lady Astor is sworn into the House of Commons as a representative of the Plymouth constituency. (She was American born, one of the famous Langhorne sisters of Virginia.)

**1924**   The music of George Gershwin and the dancing of Fred and Adele Astaire combine to make a memorable evening at the Liberty Theatre in New York where the curtain goes up on the first performance of *Lady Be Good.*

**1925**   Representatives of Great Britain, France, Italy, Belgium, and Germany sign the Locarno Pact in London, an attempt to outlaw willful aggression anywhere on the continent of Europe.

**1940**   Census Bureau officials in Washington report that the excess of males over females in the United States is being reduced by nearly 100,000 a year and that in about 5 years there will be a female majority in the nation.

**1942**   Sir William Beveridge makes public in London the Beveridge Plan, providing for social security "from the cradle to the grave." ("The proposals of this Report . . . are a sign of the belief that the object of government is . . . the happiness of the common man.")

**1943**   A communiqué to the world summarizing the agreements reached at Teheran, Iran, by President Roosevelt, Prime Minister Churchill, and Premier Stalin is released by the three Allied leaders: "No power on earth can prevent our destroying the German armies by land, their U-boats by sea, and their war plants from the air. . . . Emerging from these friendly conferences we look with confidence to the day when all the peoples of the world may live free lives untouched by tyranny. . . . We came here with hope and determination. We leave here friends in fact, in spirit, and in purpose." (WORLD WAR II)

**1953**   The New York Stock Exchange announces that for the first time in history investors will be permitted to buy stocks on an installment plan.

**1955**   Mrs. Rosa Parks, a Negro seamstress of Montgomery, Alabama, is arrested when she refuses to give up her front-section bus seat so that a white man might be seated. (*See December 5*)

**1964**   Writing in his organization's monthly magazine, Robert H. W. Welch, Jr., founder of the ultra-conservative John Birch Society, evaluates the November 3 election in which President Johnson roundly defeated the right-wing candidate, Senator Barry Goldwater: "All of these 42 million [Johnson voters], supposedly responsible adults, voted for scrapping the U.S. Constitution entirely, as an absurd and useless antique; and for replacing it with whatever modernistic pieces of legislative furniture might appeal to the taste of the Supreme Court. . . ."

## DECEMBER 2

**1804**   In a glittering ceremony at the Cathedral of Notre Dame in Paris, Napoleon Bonaparte is crowned Emperor of France. (In fact, Napoleon crowned himself. Just as Pope Pius VII raised

385

the large imperial crown and prepared to place it on Napoleon's head, the latter reached out and snatched it from him, and with his own hands placed it on his head.)

**1812**  James Madison is reelected President of the United States, winning an electoral vote of 128 to 89 received by De Witt Clinton. Elbridge Gerry is the new Vice President of the nation.

**1823**  The Monroe Doctrine: In his annual message to Congress, President James Monroe presents to the world the doctrine that is to bear his name, a warning to those antidemocratic forces in Europe which are seeking to spread their despotic power in the New World: "In the wars of the European powers, in matters relating to themselves, we have never taken any part, nor does it comport with our policy to do so. It is only when our rights are invaded, or seriously menaced, that we . . . make preparations for our defense. . . . We should consider any attempt on their part to extend their system to any portion of this hemisphere, as dangerous to our peace and safety."

**1840**  William Henry Harrison and John Tyler, running on the Whig ticket, are elected President and Vice President with an electoral vote of 234 to 60 received by former President Martin Van Buren, the Democratic nominee.

**1851**  Louis Napoleon, nephew of Napoleon Bonaparte, seizes power in a *coup d'état* in France, overthrows the republic, and proclaims himself Emperor Napoleon III.

**1859**  John Brown is hanged in the public square at Charlestown, Virginia, for his raid on Harper's Ferry in October. (The old man remained completely calm before and during his ordeal. As a matter of fact, as he was driven to the gallows, he looked about the countryside and said to his captors: "This *is* a beautiful country.")

**1927**  Henry Ford unveils his Model A Ford, successor to his famous Model T, in some 36 cities of the United States, Canada, and Europe. There is so much interest in the new model that one million people—so the *New York Herald Tribune* estimates—try to crowd into Ford headquarters in New York to catch a glimpse of it. The Model A will be available in a variety of colors (the Model T came in black only) but some of the new cars will be sold at an increased price. The price of the roadster, for example, has climbed to $385.

**1940**  A seat on the New York Stock Exchange is sold for $33,000, the lowest price since 1899 when a seat sold for $29,500.

**1942**  Birthday of the Atomic Age: a self-sustaining nuclear chain reaction is demonstrated for the first time by a group of scientists working in great secrecy below the football stadium at the University of Chicago. (When the demonstration was over, certain key scientists in other parts of the United States were advised of the achievement by this code message: "The Italian navigator has landed; the natives are friendly." The Italian navigator was a reference to Professor Enrico Fermi, Italian physicist who played a major role in the development of atomic energy.)

**1952**    President-elect Dwight D. Eisenhower arrives in Korea, thus keeping a campaign promise to visit that war-torn nation in the hope of effecting an end to the hostilities there.

**1954**    As a follow-up to the recommendation of the Watkins Committee on September 27 to censure Senator Joseph R. Mc-Carthy (R., Wis.), the U.S. Senate votes 67 to 22 to "condemn" the Senator for contempt of a Senate Elections Subcommittee that investigated his conduct and financial affairs, for abuse of its members, and for his insults to the Senate itself during the censure proceedings. (Every one of the 44 Democrats present voted against McCarthy; the Republicans were evenly divided—22 for condemnation and 22 against.)

**1956**    Fidel Castro, intent on overthrowing the government of Fulgencio Batista, lands with 82 men on the coast of Oriente Province in Cuba. Most of his followers are wiped out, but he escapes into the Sierra Maestra mountains. *(See July 26, January 1)*

**1960**    The Archbishop of Canterbury visits Pope John XXIII, the first time in more than 500 years that the head of the Anglican church has visited a Pope.

**1961**    Premier Fidel Castro, in a nationwide radio-television address to the people of Cuba, announces he is forming a single political party and through it will lead his country down the path to Communism. Castro says of himself: "I am a Marxist-Leninist and will be one until the day I die." He goes on to admit candidly that he had concealed his Communist beliefs from Cubans and American friends "because otherwise we might have alienated the bourgeoisie and other forces which we knew we would eventually have to fight."

**1963**    In the White House, President Johnson presents the Fermi Award, the highest honor the Atomic Energy Commission can bestow, to the distinguished physicist Dr. J. Robert Oppenheimer. (This ceremony had been arranged by the late President Kennedy and, in part, it made up for the abuse Dr. Oppenheimer suffered 10 years earlier when the Eisenhower Administration had declared him a security risk.)

## DECEMBER 3

**1750**    A visiting English troupe presents John Gay's opera, *The Beggar's Opera,* to its first American audience at the Nassau Street Theatre in New York.

**1818**    Illinois enters the Union as the 21st state.

**1828**    Andrew Jackson is elected President and John C. Calhoun Vice President, the Democrats receiving 178 electoral votes to 83 received by President John Quincy Adams, the National Republican candidate.

**1833**    Oberlin College at Oberlin, Ohio, the first truly coeducational institution of higher learning in the United States, opens its doors with a total enrollment of 44 students, 29 of them men and 15 women.

**1868**    The trial of Jefferson Davis, former President of the Confederate States, and now charged with treason against the United States, gets under way in the U.S. Circuit Court of Virginia. (*See February 19.*)

**1925**    George Gershwin, the young American composer, appears as a soloist at a concert in Carnegie Hall, New York, playing his *Concerto in F,* the first jazz concerto for the piano in musical history.

**1929**    Despite the collapse of the Stock Market, Edsel Ford announces in Detroit that employees of the Ford Motor Car Company will get an increase in the minimum daily wage, from $6 to $7.

**1935**    Mrs. Franklin D. Roosevelt, the First Lady of the land, Mayor Fiorello H. La Guardia, and Governor Herbert Lehman of New York participate in the dedication in New York City of the New Deal's first low-cost housing project.

**1948**    Representative Karl E. Mundt (R., S.D.), Chairman of the House Un-American Activities Subcommittee, tells reporters in Washington that microfilm copies of secret State, War, and Navy Department documents have been discovered hidden away in a hollow pumpkin on the Maryland farm of Whittaker Chambers, the former Communist underground agent currently involved in the Alger Hiss case. (Chambers said later he had concealed the documents in the pumpkin to foil Communist agents who might search his farmhouse in his absence.)

**1953**    Senator Joseph R. McCarthy (R., Wis.), in a coast-to-coast telecast asks the nation to write or wire President Eisenhower stating whether they consider the President or the Senator right in McCarthy's repeated attacks on the Administration's policy of sending aid to countries trading with Communist China.

**1962**    A heavy fog, one of the worst in years, envelops the city of London, paralyzing almost all transportation. (When it lifted, 4 days later, the fog had caused 106 deaths in the city, most of them due to the abnormally high content of sulphur dioxide in the air.)

## DECEMBER 4

**1783**    George Washington, soon to resign his commission as command-in-chief of the Continental Army, bids farewell to his officers at Fraunces Tavern in New York. ("With a heart full of gratitude, I now take leave of you....")

**1816**    James Monroe, Republican, is elected President by an electoral vote of 183 to 34 received by Rufus King, Federalist.

**1839**    The Whig Party holds its first national convention, meeting in Baltimore. Before the convention adjourns, General William Henry Harrison of Ohio is nominated for the Presidency on the 24th ballot. John Tyler of Virginia is the Vice Presidential nominee. (Thus began a campaign that swept the two candidates into office largely because of a political slogan that caught the fancy of the nation, "Tippecanoe and Tyler, too.")

**1844**    Electors cast 170 votes for the Democratic ticket of James Knox Polk, for President, and George M. Dallas, Vice President. Henry Clay and Theodore Frelinghuysen, Whigs, receive only 105 electoral votes.

**1851**    A workers' rebellion breaks out in Paris in protest to the seizure of power on December 2 by Louis Napoleon. The latter suppresses the uprising and suspends the vote, muzzles the press and forbids freedom of assembly and speech. (In French history, the events of this day are known as the "December 4 Massacre.")

**1915**    In an attempt to end the war in Europe and "get the boys out of the trenches by Christmas," a private peace expedition, headed by Henry Ford, sails from Hoboken, New Jersey, aboard the chartered liner *Oscar II.* (The idealistic group broke up in dissension soon after arriving in Europe.) *(See December 24.)*

**1918**    President Woodrow Wilson sails for France to attend the peace conference at Versailles, the first Chief Executive of the United States to visit a foreign country while still in office.

**1933**    *Tobacco Road,* a dramatization of the novel of the same name by Erskine Caldwell, opens in New York at the Masque Theatre. (It ran for 3,182 performances before closing in 1941 and has been revived countless times.)

**1942**    President Roosevelt orders the liquidation of the Works Progress Administration, created in 1935 to provide work projects for the unemployed. (The WPA cost the nation $10\frac{1}{2}$ billions of dollars, but it provided work for $8\frac{1}{2}$ million victims of the Depression.)

**1943**    Second Cairo Conference: President Roosevelt and Prime Minister Churchill confer at Cairo, Egypt, for the second time, meeting this time with President Ismet Inonu of Turkey with reference to Turkey's entrance into the war. (WORLD WAR II)

**1946**    Justice T. Alan Goldsborough of the U.S. District Court in Washington fines the United Mine Workers $3,500,000 and its leader, John L. Lewis, $10,000 for refusing to call off the 17-day soft-coal strike. (Lewis ordered the strikers back to work 3 days later. On March 6, 1947, the Supreme Court reduced the fine against the Union to $700,000.)

**1963**   The second session of the Ecumenical Council comes to an end in Rome after approving, among other reforms, the use of the vernacular in some rituals of the Roman Catholic church.

## DECEMBER 5

**1776**   Fifty men at the College of William and Mary in Williamsburg, Virginia, organize Phi Beta Kappa, the first scholastic fraternity in America.

**1782**   Birthday of Martin Van Buren, eighth President of the United States. (He was the first of our Presidents to be born a citizen of the United States.)

**1831**   Former President John Quincy Adams takes his seat in the House of Representatives. (Some people intimated that it would be degrading for a former President of the United States to serve in the lower House of Congress. Adams answered them bluntly: "No person could be degraded by serving the people as a Representative in Congress. Nor, in my opinion, would an ex-President of the United States be degraded by serving as a Selectman of his town.")

**1832**   President Andrew Jackson is reelected for a second term, winning 219 electoral votes to 49 received by Henry Clay, the nominee of the National Republican Party. Martin Van Buren is the new Vice President.

**1848**   In his annual message to Congress, President Polk confirms the discovery of gold in California, thus making the Gold Rush of '48 and '49 inevitable.

**1851**   Louis Kossuth, the Hungarian patriot who has been in exile in Turkey since his uprising for Hungarian independence failed, lands in New York aboard an American naval vessel. (His tremendous welcome was described in one of New York's newspapers as follows: "The roar of cannon and the huzzas of immense multitudes honored his disembarkation at Castle Garden, and the subsequent military and civic parade through the city . . . exceeded any demonstration of a similar nature in honor of heroic virtues or public worth.") (*See December 6.*)

**1906**   President Theodore Roosevelt writes to his son Kermit, explaining why he cannot accept the money that goes with the Nobel Prize for peace he has just been awarded: ". . . It appears that there is a large sum of money—they say about $40,000—that goes with it. Now, I hate to do anything foolish. . . . But Mother and I talked it over and came to the conclusion that. . . . I could not accept money given to me for making peace between two nations, especially when I was able to make peace simply because I was President. . . ."

**1933**   At exactly 3:32 P.M. (Mountain Time), national Prohibition comes to an end when Utah, the 30th state, ratifies the

Twenty-first Amendment to the Constitution, thus repealing the Eighteenth (or Prohibition) Amendment. Eight states have voted to remain dry, but the "Noble Experiment" that went into effect in 1920 is now just a matter of controversial history.

**1934** Sixty-six persons are executed in Russia as a follow-up to the current "purge" trials, all of them charged with "plotting" against the Stalin regime.

**1940** An announcement from Brussels itemizes the property damage inflicted on Belgium by the 18-day German "Blitzkrieg" in May: 9,832 houses razed; 24,156 houses severely damaged; 116,710 houses slightly damaged; 352 factories destroyed; 1,455 bridges and tunnels blown up, and 100 railway depots demolished. (WORLD WAR II)

**1955** Negroes of Montgomery, Alabama, start a boycott of city buses, in support of Mrs. Rosa Parks, who was arrested on December 1 for refusing to yield her bus seat to a white man. Now the city's Negroes vow to stay off the buses until they are able to be seated on an equal basis with white passengers. (It was in this year-long boycott that the Reverend Martin Luther King, Jr., began his rise to prominence as a nationally recognized civil rights leader. The strategy for the boycott and other later demonstrations was planned by the minister and his colleagues at his Montgomery church.)

## DECEMBER 6

**1847** Abraham Lincoln takes his seat in the thirtieth Congress as a member of the Illinois delegation in the House of Representatives.

**1876** The special commission appointed by Congress to decide the disputed Hayes-Tilden election of November 7 selects Rutherford B. Hayes, Republican, as the rightful winner. The vote is conducted entirely along party lines: eight Republicans voting for Hayes, seven Democrats for Tilden. (Many historians believe that the election was unmistakably won by Tilden.)

**1889** People throughout the South are saddened by the news of the death of Jefferson Davis in New Orleans.

**1916** Because of a political crisis in England, King George V asks David Lloyd George to head a new government and thus succeed Herbert H. Asquith as British prime minister.

**1917** As the result of a collision between two munitions ships, one Belgian and one French, in the harbor at Halifax, Nova Scotia, a violent explosion rocks the port, killing some 1,630 people, wounding 4,000 more. Twenty thousand residents of the city are left without homes.

**1917** Finland declares its independence from Russia. (WORLD WAR I)

**1933**  Americans crowd into liquor stores and cafés to buy their first legal alcoholic beverages in 13 years.

**1939**  Winston Churchill tells the House of Commons what he thinks the slogan of every Englishman should be in the war against Nazi Germany: "For each and for all, as for the Royal Navy, the watchword should be, 'Carry on, and dread nought.'" (WORLD WAR II)

**1941**  President Roosevelt sends a personal note to Emperor Hirohito "in the fervent hope that Your Majesty may, as I am doing, give thought in this definite emergency to ways of dispelling the dark clouds." (Japan's attack on Pearl Harbor took place the next day.)

**1943**  A note from President Roosevelt informs Premier Stalin of Russia that the combined American-British Command in the European Theatre of Operations has agreed on the selection of General Dwight D. Eisenhower as the commander-in-chief of Operation Overlord, the forthcoming invasion of the continent of Europe. (WORLD WAR II)

**1957**  Members of the AFL-CIO vote to oust from their parent union the International Brotherhood of Teamsters, on charges that that union is dominated by corrupt elements.

## DECEMBER 7

**1787**  Delaware becomes the first state to ratify the U.S. Constitution.

**1808**  James Madison wins the Presidential election, receiving 122 electoral votes to 47 received by Charles C. Pinckney. The Vice President is George Clinton.

**1836**  Martin Van Buren, Vice President in the current administration of President Jackson, wins the Presidential election on the Democratic ticket, defeating General William Henry Harrison, the Whig candidate, by an electoral vote of 170 to 73.

**1842**  The New York Philharmonic Society gives its first public concert, performing Beethoven's *Fifth Symphony,* the *Overture* from Weber's opera *Oberon,* and part of the score from Beethoven's *Fidelio.*

**1917**  Soldiers of the 42nd or "Rainbow" Division of the U.S. Army have arrived in France. (WORLD WAR I)

**1930**  Services at the Cathedral of St. John the Divine in New York are thrown into an uproar when Judge Ben Lindsey of Denver rises from his seat and shouts at Bishop William T. Manning in the pulpit, "Bishop Manning, you have lied to me!" (Judge Lindsey was famous as an advocate of "companionate marriage" and resented Bishop Manning's demand that the New York Churchmen's Association cancel its invitation to him to lecture on this controversial subject.)

**1931**    President Hoover refuses to receive a delegation of "hunger marchers" at the White House. (The marchers had hoped to present a petition to the President asking for employment with a guarantee of minimum wages.)

**1941**    While her envoys are negotiating with the State Department, Japan strikes suddenly in the Pacific, bombing Pearl Harbor, the Philippines, Wake and Guam Islands, and the British possessions of Singapore and Honolulu. At the same time, Japanese forces invade Thailand and Malaya by land and sea. Then, at four o'clock in the afternoon, Eastern Time, the Japanese government declares war against the United States and Great Britain. The news of this action is broadcast to the Japanese public by Premier Hideki Tojo who claims that both the attacks and war declarations were necessary as a measure of "self-protection" against the two Western Powers. (For the United States, the Japanese attack was extremely serious: according to Secretary of the Navy Knox, the fleet lost six warships by sinking: the battleship *Arizona,* the target ship *Utah,* the destroyers *Cassin, Shaw,* and *Downes,* and the minelayer *Ogala.* In addition, the military forces at Pearl Harbor suffered the loss of 2,897 dead, 879 wounded, 26 missing, and a further "tremendous loss" of Army planes on the ground and in hangars.) (WORLD WAR II)

**1963**    With the departure of Mrs. John F. Kennedy and her children, President and Mrs. Lyndon B. Johnson move into the White House. Mrs. Johnson establishes a new precedent when she releases a statement to the American people. The new First Lady says: "I will try to be balm, sustainer, and sometimes critic for my husband; to help my children look at this job with all the reverence due it; to get from it the knowledge their unique vantage point gives them, and to retain the lightheartedness to which every teenager is entitled. For my own self, my role must emerge in deeds, not words."

## DECEMBER 8

**1776**    George Washington crosses the Delaware River, near Trenton, New Jersey, and lands on Pennsylvania soil.

**1863**    President Lincoln announces his plan for Reconstruction of the South. The most important features of the plan provide for an amnesty to all those who participated in the Southern rebellion except Confederate officers above the rank of colonel and those who occupied high positions in the Confederate government. Further, new civil governments will be recognized when one-tenth of the citizens of a Southern state who had voted in the election of 1860 take an oath of allegiance to the federal government. (Emancipation of slaves was expected in each state.)

**1886**    Delegates from 25 labor unions and organizations found the American Federation of Labor at a convention in Columbus,

Ohio. The new union, an outgrowth of the Federation of Organized Trades and Labor Unions, will be headed by Samuel Gompers.

**1903**   Professor Samuel P. Langley, aviation enthusiast and secretary of the Smithsonian Institution, fails in his attempt to fly for the second time when a power-driven airplane built by himself at a cost of $70,000 plunges into the Potomac River. (*See October 7*)

**1940**   Almost four hundred German bombers raid London. The House of Commons suffers its first serious damage. (WORLD WAR II)

**1941**   A solemn Joint Session of Congress hears President Roosevelt castigate Japan for her attack on Pearl Harbor in his message asking for a declaration of war on that nation: "Yesterday, December 7, 1941—a date that will live in infamy—the United States of America was suddenly and deliberately attacked by naval and air forces of the empire of Japan. The United States was at peace with that nation, and, at the solicitation of Japan, was still in conversation with its government and its Emperor looking toward the maintenance of peace in the Pacific. . . . I ask that the Congress declare that since the unprovoked and dastardly attack by Japan on Sunday, December 7, 1941, a state of war has existed between the United States and the Japanese Empire." (By 4:10 P.M. the same afternoon, both the Senate and House had passed declarations of war and the President put his signature to the official declaration. The resolution was passed by the Senate, 82–0; the House approved its resolution by a vote of 388–1, the lone dissenting vote coming from Congresswoman Jeannette Rankin of Montana who had cast a similar vote against war with Germany in 1917.) (WORLD WAR II)

**1949**   The Chinese Nationalist government moves its headquarters from the mainland to Taipei, Formosa.

**1953**   President Eisenhower, speaking before the United Nations General Assembly, proposes that the major powers of the world develop a pool of atomic energy for peaceful purposes and thus demonstrate to the world that the "Great Powers . . . are interested in human aspirations first rather than in building up the armaments of war."

**1953**   The City of Los Angeles announces that it has ousted Philadelphia as the nation's third largest city. The result of a special census places Los Angeles' population at 2,104,663. In the 1950 census, the population of Philadelphia was listed at 2,071,605.

**1962**   A strike called by the International Typographical Union shuts down nine newspapers in New York City. The papers have a total daily circulation of 5,700,000. (Twenty thousand employees were out of work for 114 days, until the papers resumed publication on April 1, 1963.)

# DECEMBER 9

**1608**    Birthday of John Milton, one of the great poets in literary history.

**1793**    Noah Webster establishes *The America Minerva*, New York's first daily newspaper. Webster says that his paper will be "The Friend of Government, of Freedom, of Virtue, and every Species of Improvement."

**1907**    Christmas seals, designed by Emily P. Bissell of Wilmington, Delaware, are placed on sale in the Wilmington post office, the proceeds to be devoted to the campaign against tuberculosis.

**1917**    Turkish troops surrender the city of Jerusalem to British troops commanded by General Viscount Allenby. (WORLD WAR I)

**1934**    Ethiopian and Italian soldiers clash at Wal Wal, thus providing the pretext for the subsequent Italian invasion of Ethiopia.

**1941**    China declares war against Japan, Germany, and Italy. (WORLD WAR II)

**1941**    Within 48 hours after the Japanese attack on Pearl Harbor, the American Theatre Wing organizes to provide entertainment for members of the armed services. The playwright Rachel Crothers has been named president of the project. (WORLD WAR II)

**1958**    At a meeting in Indianapolis, Robert H. W. Welch, Jr., of Massachusetts, and 11 other men, organize a new ultra-conservative political movement that they call the John Birch Society. The organization takes its name from a young Georgia missionary and U.S. intelligence officer who was killed in China by Communist troops at the end of World War II.

# DECEMBER 10

**1817**    Mississippi is admitted into the Union as the 20th state.

**1832**    President Andrew Jackson, taking note of South Carolina's action of November 24 in nullifying the federal tariff acts of 1828 and 1832, issues a proclamation stating firmly his intention of enforcing the law. The President makes it clear that he will not recognize South Carolina's Ordinance of Nullification: "I consider, then, the power to annul a law of the United States, assumed by one State, incompatible with the existence of the Union, contradicted expressly by the letter of the Constitution."

**1898**    Spain signs the Treaty of Paris officially concluding the Spanish-American War and cedes to the United States Guam, Puerto Rico, and the Philippine Islands. In addition, the Spanish government agrees to give up her claims to Cuba.

**1901**    The distribution of the Nobel Prizes is begun for the first time on the anniversary of the death of Alfred Nobel.

**1903**    Jane Cowl makes her New York stage debut in the play *Sweet Kitty Bellairs.* (Later on, Miss Cowl broke all records by playing Juliet in Shakespeare's *Romeo and Juliet* for more than 900 performances.)

**1910**    Giacomo Puccini, the famous Italian composer, is present at the Metropolitan Opera House in New York for the world *première* of his opera *The Girl of the Golden West,* featuring Enrico Caruso, Pasquale Amato, and Emmy Destinn in the stellar singing roles. (Arturo Toscanini conducted the score.)

**1913**    Art lovers throughout the world are overjoyed as they learn that Leonardo da Vinci's "La Gioconda" ("Mona Lisa"), stolen from the Louvre Museum in Paris 2 years ago, has been recovered. (The world-famous painting, valued at $5,000,000, was returned to Italian authorities by Vincenzio Perugia who confessed he stole it "for love and for Italy.")

**1941**    Japanese planes sink the British battleships *Prince of Wales* and *Repulse* in the South China Sea, 150 miles north of Singapore. (WORLD WAR II)

**1941**    Troops of Japan land on northern Luzon in the Philippines. (WORLD WAR II)

**1955**    The largest prize in the annals of radio and television "give-away" programs to date, $100,000, is won by Mrs. Ethel Park Richardson, 72, of Los Angeles, after she correctly answers a 6-part question about folk songs on the National Broadcasting Company's television program, "The Big Surprise."

**1964**    The Reverend Martin Luther King, Jr., famous throughout the world for his nonviolent leadership in the fight for American civil rights, is awarded the Nobel Peace Prize in ceremonies at Oslo, Norway. Dr. King thus becomes the 12th American and the 3rd Negro to win this peace award. In accepting his prize, he says: "I accept this award today with an abiding faith in America and an audacious faith in the future of mankind. . . ."

## DECEMBER 11

**1700**    Matrons of Flatbush (Brooklyn), New York, famous for their waffles served daily at teatime, tell visiting New Englanders how to prepare them: "1 pound butter, 1 pound flour, 1 pound sugar, 10 eggs. Bake in window-pane waffle irons and when slightly cool, sprinkle with powdered sugar."

**1816**    Indiana, the 19th state, is admitted into the Union.

**1899**    Governor Theodore Roosevelt of New York writes to his friend Senator Henry Cabot Lodge of Massachusetts, explaining why he does not want to run for the Vice Presidency in 1900: "The Vice Presidency is a most honorable office, but for a young man there is not much to do.... If I am Vice President I am 'planted' for four years...." (In the end, however, he submitted to Republican pressures and was nominated and elected Vice President.)

**1907** President Theodore Roosevelt disappoints his followers when he states publicly, "I will not ... accept another nomination" for the Presidency. (Four years later, when he was out of the White House, he changed his mind.)

**1929** Designers of the skyscraper to be known as the Empire State Building in New York release this announcement: "The directors of Empire State, Incorporated, believe that in a comparatively short time the Zeppelin airships will establish transatlantic, transcontinental and transpacific lines, and possibly a route to South America from the Port of New York. Building with an eye to the future, it has been determined to erect a mooring tower atop the Empire State Building."

**1936** "King Edward VIII Abdicates" is the headline featured on the first page of every newspaper in America. And when the announcement is made that the former king, now to be known as "His Royal Highness, the Duke of Windsor," is to broadcast to the world, the business of the day stops while people across the nation cluster around their radios to hear his words of farewell: "I have found it impossible to carry the heavy burden of responsibility and to discharge my duties as King as I should wish to do, without the help and support of the woman I love.... And now we all have a new King. I wish him and you, his people, happiness and prosperity with all my heart. God bless you all! God save the King!" (The Duke of York, the former king's brother, succeeded to the throne as George VI.)

**1941** Four days after Japan's attack on Pearl Harbor, Germany and Italy declare war on the United States. A few hours later, Congress unanimously resolves that a state of war exists between the United States and Germany and Italy. (WORLD WAR II)

**1941** With the United States declarations of war against Japan and the Axis powers, the strongly isolationist America First Committee announces in Chicago that it is disbanding and urges "all those who have followed its lead to give their full support to the war effort of the nation, until peace is attained ..."

**1946** John D. Rockefeller, Jr., announces that he has offered to donate a six-block parcel of land along the East River in New York to the United Nations as a site for its world headquarters. (The offer was accepted the next day.)

**1963** Almost one million dollars of the more than $7,000,000 stolen during the great British train robbery in August has been recovered. So far, 21 persons have been arrested in connection with the crime. (*See August 8*)

397

# DECEMBER 12

**1792**  Ludwig van Beethoven, aged 22, pays 19 cents for his first music lesson from Franz Joseph Haydn in Vienna.

**1831**  Delegates of the National Republican Party, meeting in Baltimore, nominate Henry Clay for President and John Sergeant for Vice President. (This political party is not to be confused with today's Republican Party.)

**1850**  Susan Warner's highly emotional novel, *The Wide, Wide World,* is published, although the author lists herself on the title page as "Elizabeth Wetherell." (By 1852, this book was in its 14th edition. Many publishers consider it to be the first "bestseller" in the United States.)

**1901**  The Atlantic Ocean is bridged by the miracle of wireless! Guglielmo Marconi and an assistant, seated in an improvised receiving station near St. John's, Newfoundland, intercept the letter "S" sent by Morse code by an operator stationed at Poldhu in the British Isles.

**1924**  Guests at the Hotel Savoy in London dance to the music of a band playing in New York City. (The music was broadcast over Station WNYC, New York, picked up by Station KDKA, Pittsburgh, and relayed to a receiving set in the London hotel.)

**1937**  Japanese planes bomb and sink the U.S. gunboat *Panay* in the Yangtze River above Nanking, China, killing 2 and wounding almost 30 crew members. At the same time, the British warships *Ladybird, Bee, Cricket,* and *Scarab* are damaged by Japanese gunfire. (The Japanese government apologized for these incidents, claiming mistaken identity. In the case of the *Panay,* the United States received an indemnity of $2,214,000.)

**1937**  The Federal Communications Commission reprimands the National Broadcasting Company for permitting Mae West to "sex up" a skit based on the biblical story of Adam and Eve. (All was forgiven and the public's indignation quieted when the network, advertising agency, and sponsor involved in the program offered their apologies.)

**1947**  John L. Lewis withdraws his United Mine Workers union from the American Federation of Labor for the second time. Lewis' announcement is contained in a terse two-word telegram to President William Green of the AFL: "We disaffiliate."

**1953**  Major Charles (Chuck) Yeager flies a Bell X-1A jet research plane at more than two-and-a-half times the speed of sound at Edwards Air Force Base, California.

**1955**  The Ford Foundation announces a gift of a half-billion dollars to the nation's private hospitals, colleges, and medical schools, the largest single philanthropic act in world history.

**1642** New Zealand is discovered and named by Abel Tasman, Dutch navigator.

**1862** Union troops commanded by General Ambrose E. Burnside are severely defeated by the Confederates on Marye's Heights, outside of Fredericksburg, Virginia. In broad daylight, the Union general sends wave after wave of his soldiers across the open plain in the hope of taking the Southerners stationed behind a stone wall. But by nightfall, the North's casualties are almost 11,000 men in dead and wounded and Burnside is obliged to retreat back across the Rappahannock River.

**1918** American soldiers attached to the Third Army cross the Rhine River at Coblenz, Germany. (WORLD WAR I)

**1927** Charles A. Lindbergh, bound for a "goodwill" tour of Latin American countries, sets out from Washington on a nonstop flight to Mexico City, where he will be the guest of American Ambassador Dwight W. Morrow.

**1927** Yehudi Menuhin, a 10-year-old child violinist, makes his New York debut at a concert in Carnegie Hall. (When it was all over, the enthusiastic audience wanted nothing more than to flock backstage and congratulate the little boy. The little boy wanted nothing more than a big dish of ice cream.)

**1928** George Gershwin's tone poem for orchestra, *An American in Paris,* is performed for the first time by the New York Philharmonic Symphony Orchestra, Walter Damrosch conducting.

**1937** Japanese soldiers capture Nanking, China, and begin their systematic looting of the city's homes and shops.

**1941** The Japanese issue an ultimatum to British forces to surrender the Crown Colony of Hong Kong. The British promptly reject the ultimatum and the Japanese start a concentrated program of air raids on the city. (WORLD WAR II)

**1948** James C. Petrillo's 11½-month ban on phonograph recordings by members of his American Federation of Musicians comes to an end when Attorney General Tom C. Clark agrees that the union's welfare-fund contract with the nation's 13 major record makers is not a violation of the Taft-Hartley Act.

**1958** Senator Lyndon B. Johnson (D., Texas), the Majority Leader of the Senate, gives a frank rejection to those supporters who are urging him to run for the Presidency in 1960: "I don't think anybody from the South will be nominated in my lifetime. If so, I don't think he will be elected."

**1799**    George Washington, the first President of the United States, dies at Mount Vernon after telling his doctors, "I thank you for your attention, you had better not take any more trouble about me, but let me go off quietly."

**1819**    Alabama enters the Union as the 22nd state.

**1861**    All England is plunged into grief as Prince Albert, the husband of Queen Victoria, dies at Windsor Castle, the victim of typhoid fever. The Queen is inconsolable and refuses to see anyone except her children. (This was the beginning of Victoria's long life of seclusion. For months, for years, dressed in severe mourning attire, she passed dolefully from Windsor to Osborne, from Osborne to Balmoral, seeing only a few of her ministers and then for very brief periods of time.)

**1902**    The cableship *Silverton* sets out from San Francisco to lay the first cable between that city and Honolulu. (By January 1, 1903, Honolulu was reached and the cable was ready for business.)

**1910**    A gift of $10,000,000 from Andrew Carnegie establishes The Carnegie Endowment for International Peace. The purpose of the new organization is to work toward international peace through research, publications, and other educational activities.

**1911**    Roald Amundsen, a Norwegian explorer, discovers the South Pole.

**1929**    Garnet Carter, a Tennessee promoter, is hard at work in Florida establishing a new national pastime—miniature golf. (By the time the summer of 1930 rolled around, hundreds of thousands of Americans were knocking golf balls around on roadside courses.)

**1935**    Thomas G. Masaryk, President of Czechoslovakia since 1918, announces that he has decided to resign from that office because of ill health.

**1936**    A delightful play by Moss Hart and George S. Kaufman, *You Can't Take It with You,* settles down for a long run at the Booth Theatre in New York.

**1940**    Premier Henri Philippe Pétain of France ousts Vice Premier Pierre Laval from office and announces that Laval is no longer a member of the Cabinet. Pétain charges that the former Vice Premier was plotting to set himself up as the dictator of France. (WORLD WAR II)

**1953**    Testifying before an investigating committee of the New York State Legislature, F. Emerson Andrews, a representative of the Russell Sage Foundation, states flatly that of the more than four billion dollars contributed to charity in the United States during the current year at least $120,000,000 of it went into the pockets of charity "racketeers."

# DECEMBER 15

## Bill of Rights Day

**1791** The Bill of Rights, the term applied to the first 10 amendments to the Constitution, goes into effect following ratification by the state of Virginia.

**1890** Sitting Bull, chief of the Sioux Indians, is shot and killed in South Dakota following a skirmish with federal troops.

**1932** All over the United States people are talking about Howard Scott and his theory of Technocracy. Scott's idea is based on the premise that the Depression is the result of an outmoded economic system and that the whole system must be overhauled. Specifically, the Technocrats suggest that our price system should be based on energy, in units like ergs and joules. (The whole fuss over Technocracy died down in a year's time. One strike against its popular acceptance was the language used by the Technocrats themselves. Mr. Scott, for example, liked to describe Technocracy as "a synthetic integration of the physical sciences that pertain to the determination of all functional sequences of social phenomena.")

**1944** U.S. forces, led by General Douglas MacArthur, land at Mindoro, in the Philippine Islands. (WORLD WAR II)

**1945** To avoid facing trial as a war criminal, Prince Fumimaro Konoye, a former Japanese premier, commits suicide in his home.

**1948** A Federal Grand Jury in New York indicts Alger Hiss, former State Department official, on two perjury counts. The charges are that Hiss lied when he claimed he had never given any State Department documents to Whittaker Chambers and had not seen Chambers after entering the State Department in September, 1936.

**1961** Adolf Eichmann, former Nazi head of the Bureau of Jewish Affairs, is sentenced to death for his role in causing the deaths of millions of Jews during World War II. The sentence is handed down in Jerusalem, where a special Jewish tribunal has been hearing his case.

# DECEMBER 16

**1770** Birthday of Ludwig van Beethoven, German composer and pianist, "the unsurpassed master of instrumental music."

**1773** Boston Tea Party: In protest against the British tax on tea, a half hundred Boston patriots, disguised as Indians, board a British vessel at anchor in the harbor and break open 342 chests of tea in the hold, and then throw the contents into the water.

**1835**    Fire breaks out in New York and before long sweeps over whole city blocks. Because of the bitter cold weather, fire fighters are obliged to chop through the ice in the East River before they can tap the water supply there. When it is finally subdued, at least 600 buildings have been razed and the total property loss is set at more than $20,000,000. (So serious was this fire that fire engines were summoned from as far away as Philadelphia.)

**1893**    The New York Philharmonic Symphony Orchestra offers the first performance of Anton Dvořák's *New World Symphony* at Carnegie Hall in New York. The composer attends the *première,* well pleased by the enthusiastic applause of the large audience.

**1905**    *Variety,* a weekly periodical devoted to all phases of show business, is published for the first time by its founder, Sime Silverman. The first issue contains 16 pages and sells for 5 cents.

**1916**    In a setting that would do justice to a lurid cloak-and-dagger "thriller," Gregory Rasputin, the "mad Monk" who wields such a powerful influence over the Czar and Czarina of Russia, is lured to the palace of a Petrograd nobleman where he is poisoned and then murdered. Later, his body is sunk beneath the ice of a local canal.

**1944**    Battle of the Bulge: the Germans launch a great counteroffensive in the Ardennes Forest in Belgium. (WORLD WAR II)

**1947**    A campaign to check inflation gets under way in the Soviet Union as the government there devalues the ruble and abolishes rationing, the latter step taken to wipe out the Black Market in commodities.

**1960**    One of the worst disasters in the history of commercial aviation takes place in New York during foggy weather, when two airliners collide over New York harbor and then crash to the earth. One hundred and thirty-one persons are killed immediately.

## DECEMBER 17

**1878**    The term "Solid South," a political reference to the bloc of 13 states of the former Confederacy, is added to the American vocabulary for the first time when Senator Morgan of Alabama uses it in a speech on the floor of the Senate.

**1903**    Orville and Wilbur Wright make the first successful airplane flights in history as they soar over the sand dunes near Kitty Hawk, North Carolina. The first flight, with Orville at the controls, lasts just 12 seconds. At 12 noon, Wilbur takes off and manages to stay aloft for 59 seconds. (Later, the Wright brothers recalled this historic morning: "The first flights with the power machine were made on December 17, 1903. Only five persons besides ourselves were present. . . . Although a general invitation had been extended to the people living within five or six miles, not many were willing to face the rigors of a cold December wind in

402

order to see, as they no doubt thought, another flying machine not fly.")

**1925** General William (Billy) Mitchell, an outspoken advocate of a separate air force, is found guilty by a court-martial in Washington, charged with violating the 96th Article of War, which concerns conduct prejudicial to the good of the armed services. (As a result, Mitchell was sentenced to suspension from the Army for 5 years. The charges against him stemmed from a statement he gave out to newspaper reporters in San Antonio, Texas, following two major air disasters. In these statements he accused the War and Navy Departments of "incompetence, criminal negligence and almost treasonable administration of our national defense." Twenty years later, in 1945, the Senate voted to confer on him posthumously the Congressional Medal of Honor and, at the same time, promoted him to the rank of major general.)

**1936** Following his spectacular success at the Rainbow Room in New York, Edgar Bergen, a ventriloquist featuring a precocious dummy named "Charlie McCarthy," makes his first appearance on a national radio program.

**1939** With British warships in hot pursuit, the Nazi vessel *Graf Spee* is scuttled off the coast of Uruguay following express orders to the crew by Adolf Hitler himself. (WORLD WAR II)

**1940** Verne Marshall, editor of the *Cedar Rapids* (Iowa) *Gazette,* announces the formation of the "No Foreign War Committee," organized to combat war propaganda in the United States and to fight against the influence of William Allen White's "Committee to Defend America by Aiding the Allies." Marshall's committee will cooperate with the "America First" committee, headed by General Robert E. Wood.

**1941** Ten days after Pearl Harbor, the Japanese news agency Domei quotes Admiral Isoroku Yamamoto, commander-in-chief of the Japanese fleet, as saying: "I shall not be content merely to capture Guam and the Philippines and occupy Hawaii and San Francisco. I am looking forward to dictating peace to the United States in the White House at Washington." *

**1941** President Franklin D. Roosevelt addresses a letter to "the President of the United States in 1956" suggesting a West Point appointment for Colin P. Kelly, III, the 18-months-old son of Captain Colin P. Kelly, Jr., "as a token of appreciation of the heroic services of his father who met death in line of duty" when he bombed and sank the Japanese battleship *Haruna* a few days after Pearl Harbor. (The letter was filed away in the National Archives and delivered to President Eisenhower in January, 1956.) (WORLD WAR II)

* On January 10, 1946, Fleet Admiral Nimitz claimed this quotation to be a hoax and that it was invented for propaganda purposes by Japanese militarists.

**1962**    While seated in his rocking chair in his White House office, President John F. Kennedy gives a report to the American people on the actions of his Administration during his first 2 years in office. The President is interviewed by three newsmen from the major radio-television networks.

**1963**    According to the Associated Press, a record 54,373,386 persons bet $3,807,082,319 at U.S. race tracks in the year 1963.

## DECEMBER 18

**1787**    By a unanimous vote, New Jersey ratifies the proposed Constitution of the United States.

**1865**    Slavery is abolished in the United States by the adoption of the Thirteenth Amendment to the Constitution, declared in effect as of this date by Secretary of State Seward. ("Neither slavery nor involuntary servitude, except as a punishment for crime whereof the party shall have been legally convicted, shall exist within the United States, or any place subject to their jurisdiction.")

**1915**    President Woodrow Wilson, a widower for a little over a year, is married to Mrs. Edith Bolling Galt, widow of a Washington jeweler, in a ceremony at the bride's home in Washington.

**1923**    Charles Evans Hughes, U.S. Secretary of State, turns down a request of the Soviet Union for American recognition of that nation.

**1924**    Theatrical note: "Joe Weber and Lew Fields, comedians, whose carefully broken English has cheered two generations of theatregoers, arrive in Los Angeles to begin translating their humor into motion pictures."

**1935**    Dr. Eduard Beneš, Czechoslovakia's minister of Foreign Affairs and the candidate recommended by former President Masaryk as his successor, is unanimously elected president of that country by the national Parliament.

**1935**    In her debut at the Metropolitan Opera House in New York, the Australian operatic soprano Marjorie Lawrence, singing the role of Brünnhilde in *Die Götterdämmerung,* sends her horse through a ring of real flames burning on the stage, the first time this has ever been attempted by an opera singer.

**1936**    The first giant panda to be imported into the United States arrives at San Francisco from China. Zoo officials say the curious animal is a cross between a bear and a raccoon.

**1941**    A committee to investigate the military disaster at Pearl Harbor is appointed by President Roosevelt. Associate Justice Owen Roberts of the U.S. Supreme Court will serve as chairman. (WORLD WAR II)

**1963**    Some 500 African students, enrolled in various Russian colleges and institutes, riot in Moscow's Red Square, protesting alleged racial discrimination. The Africans claim that a student from Ghana was killed by Soviet police to prevent him from marrying a Russian girl.

# DECEMBER 19

**1732** Benjamin Franklin begins to publish his *Poor Richard's Almanac.*

**1776** The first installment of Thomas Paine's *The American Crisis* appears in *The Pennsylvania Journal,* the beginning of some 13 essays designed to keep up the morale of American patriots during the Revolutionary War. ("These are the times that try men's souls. The summer soldier and the sunshine patriot will, in this crisis, shrink from the service of their country; but he that stands it now, deserves the love and thanks of man and woman. Tyranny, like hell, is not easily conquered. . . . What we obtain too cheap, we esteem too lightly; it is dearness only that gives everything its value. . . .")

**1777** George Washington and his Continental Army troops start their winter encampment at Valley Forge, Pennsylvania.

**1924** Members of the American Federation of Labor elect William Green as their president to succeed Samuel Gompers who died 6 days ago.

**1939** Crew members of the German liner *Columbus* scuttle the vessel in mid-Atlantic to escape capture by ships of the British Royal Navy. (WORLD WAR II)

**1941** Faced with declining military fortunes on the Russian front, Adolf Hitler dismisses his chief of staff, General von Brauchitsch, and assumes supreme command of the German Army himself. ("The consciousness of an inner call and the will to take the responsibility that was his were of importance when Adolf Hitler resolved to be his own supreme military leader."—From the official text of the announcement released by Hitler's headquarters.) (WORLD WAR II)

**1941** Japanese short-wave broadcasts claim that Hong Kong fell at eleven o'clock in the morning. The British War Office, however, insists that a small force of Englishmen, Canadians, and Indians is still holding out within the Crown Colony. (WORLD WAR II)

**1946** War breaks out in Indochina as troops under the Nationalist leader Ho Chi Minh launch widespread attacks in north and south Indochina and begin a bitter assault on the French garrison at Hanoi.

**1950** General Dwight D. Eisenhower is appointed commander of military forces operating under the North Atlantic Treaty Organization (NATO).

**1959** Walter Williams, said to be 117 years old and reputed to be the last surviving veteran of the Civil War, dies in Houston, Texas. Williams served with the Confederate forces in the Texas Brigade.

# DECEMBER 20

**1790**    Samuel Slater, an English expert in textile machinery, starts the first successful American cotton mill at Pawtucket, Rhode Island. (Slater has been called the "Father of American manufacturers" and is considered the most important influence in introducing the machine age into the United States.)

**1803**    In a ceremony in the heart of New Orleans, the flag of France is replaced by the flag of the United States, thus symbolizing the official transfer of the lands making up the Louisiana Purchase from French to American control.

**1820**    The state of Missouri levies a tax against bachelors. The statute orders unmarried men between the ages of 21 and 50 to pay a tax of a dollar a year.

**1860**    A momentous decision is made by the state of South Carolina when it votes unanimously, at a special convention held in Charleston, to secede from the United States of America, the first state to do so. (". . . the union now subsisting between South Carolina and other States, under the name of the 'United States of America,' is hereby dissolved.")

**1864**    General William T. Sherman's "March to the Sea" comes to an end as his Union troops occupy the city of Savannah, Georgia.

**1880**    Broadway, New York's main thoroughfare, becomes the "Great White Way" as it is illuminated by electricity for the first time between 14th and 26th Streets.

**1912**    Laurette Taylor writes her name in theatrical history when she opens in J. Hartley Manner's play *Peg o' My Heart* at the Cort Theatre in New York. (Not only did Miss Taylor score an enormous hit but the play itself was an instantaneous success and achieved a run of 603 performances, remarkable for the theatre of that day.)

**1917**    The Communist dictator of Russia, Nikolai Lenin, orders the creation of the Cheka, to serve as the secret police agency of his regime. Felix Dzerzhinsky has been named to serve as the bureau's first director.

**1922**    Fourteen republics of Russia combine, in convention at Moscow, as the Union of Soviet Socialist Republics.

**1928**    Ethel Barrymore becomes the first living actress of the United States to have a theatre named after her as the Ethel Barrymore Theatre is opened in New York.

**1952**    Eighty-seven service men are killed and 28 injured as a huge air force "Globemaster" plane crashes at Moses Lake, Washington, the worst disaster to date in the history of aviation.

**1954**    One of the largest talent contracts ever executed by an entertainer, if not the largest, is drawn up between television comedian Jackie Gleason and the Buick Motor Company. Under the terms of the contract, Mr. Gleason agrees to produce and star in 78 half-hour television programs for Buick during the next 2 years. His fee: $6,142,500.

**1963** The Berlin Wall is opened temporarily for the first time during the Christmas holiday season, thus permitting East and West Berliners to hold 17 days of joyous and tearful reunions. (On January 6, 1964, the wall was sealed once more.)

## DECEMBER 21

**1620** Although their tiny ship, the *Mayflower,* had reached Cape Cod on November 11, the Pilgrims set foot on American soil for the first time, landing at what is now Plymouth, Massachusetts.

**1804** Birthday of Benjamin Disraeli, Earl of Beaconsfield, English statesman, onetime prime minister of Great Britain, novelist and poet.

**1844** Birth of the Cooperative movement: Charles Haworth and 27 poverty-stricken associates, set up a tiny store in the cotton-textile town of Rochdale, England, calling themselves "The Rochdale Society of Equitable Pioneers." (This project, based on the theory of ownership by consumers, was very successful and led ultimately to other cooperative ventures.)

**1914** Marie Dressler's performance in the motion picture *Tillie's Punctured Romance* is described as "uproariously funny." Appearing with her in the Mack Sennett comedy are Mabel Normand, Charles Chaplin, and Mack Swain.

**1919** About 250 aliens, arrested as radical agitators on the order of the Secretary of Labor, are deported to Russia aboard the transport ship *Buford.*

**1937** A charming motion picture animated cartoon, *Snow White and the Seven Dwarfs,* produced by Walt Disney and based on Grimms' famous fairy tale, is shown in Los Angeles for the first time. (To one observer, this film was "the happiest thing that has happened in this world since the Armistice.")

**1942** The U.S. Supreme Court upholds the validity of 6-week divorces granted throughout the state of Nevada.

**1944** Horse racing is banned in the United States for the duration of the war. (WORLD WAR II)

**1953** Ex-Premier Mohammed Mossadegh of Iran is convicted by a military court of having attempted to foment and lead a revolt against the Shah.

## DECEMBER 22

**1650** New England colonists pass a law requiring bakers to make standard weight loaves and to use only pure wheat or rye flour. (This was to silence complaints about the leanness of the common loaf of bread.)

**1775**    The Continental naval fleet is actively organized under the command of Ezek Hopkins, a former New England sea captain. The fleet consists of two frigates, two brigs, and three schooners. Each sailor will be paid eight dollars a month during his period of service.

**1864**    A message is received by President Lincoln at the White House from General William T. Sherman in Georgia which reads: "I beg to present you as a Christmas gift the city of Savannah."

**1869**    Congress passes an act which stipulates that the state of Georgia must ratify the Fifteenth Amendment to the Constitution before she can be readmitted into the Union.

**1886**    Henry Woodfin Grady, editor of the *Atlanta Constitution,* introduces the phrase the "New South" in a speech before the members of the New England Club of New York City: "There is a New South, not through protests against the old, but because of new conditions, new adjustments, and, if you please, new ideas and aspirations."

**1894**    A French court-martial finds Captain Alfred Dreyfus, an officer of the French General Staff, guilty of treason and sentences him to degradation and imprisonment on Devil's Island. (The Dreyfus Affair inflamed public opinion in France and throughout the world. The charges grew out of allegations that Dreyfus had passed on military intelligence to the attaché of the German embassy in Paris. Two years later, it was proved conclusively that Dreyfus was the victim of an anti-Semitic cabal in the French Army and that the information actually was turned over to the Germans by another French officer. Dreyfus himself was vindicated on July 12, 1906, by the Supreme Court of Appeals, and restored to the Army with the rank of major.) (*See January 5, January 13.*)

**1939**    Premier Edouard Daladier of France coins a catch-phrase when he complains to the Chamber of Deputies in Paris that critics of his administration and war effort are referring to the war against Germany as a "phony war." Says Daladier: "A phrase has spread from civilian to soldiers and back again: 'This is a phony war.' " (WORLD WAR II)

**1944**    General Anthony McAuliffe, commander of the American 101st Airborne Division, has but one word for the Germans when he is served with a demand for immediate surrender of his troops at Bastogne, Belgium. The General's answer: "Nuts!" (The German emissary who was given this terse message was puzzled. "What does that mean?" he asked the General's courier. "It means 'go to hell,' " the American replied. That the German understood. He saluted and marched off.) (WORLD WAR II)

**1963**    The nation's month of official mourning for President John F. Kennedy ends as 14,000 men, women, and children hold a candlelight ceremony at the Lincoln Memorial in Washington. President Lyndon B. Johnson says to the silent crowd: "We buried

Abraham Lincoln and John Kennedy, but we did not bury their dreams or their visions. They are our dreams and our visions today, for President Lincoln and John Kennedy moved toward those nobler dreams and those larger visions where the needs of the people dwell. . . ."

## DECEMBER 23

**1783**    George Washington resigns from his army commission and retires to his estate at Mount Vernon.

**1852**    The Chinese colony of San Francisco turns out in force to witness the opening of its own threatre, the first such in the United States.

**1925**    William Allen White, the editor of the *Emporia* (Kansas) *Gazette,* reports the death of the celebrated publisher, Frank Munsey, in an outspoken and hard-hitting obituary notice: "Frank Munsey, the great publisher, is dead. Frank Munsey contributed to the journalism of his day the great talent of a meat packer, the morals of a money changer and the manners of an undertaker. He and his kind have succeeded in transforming a once noble profession into an eight per cent security. May he rest in trust!"

**1928**    The National Broadcasting Company establishes a permanent coast-to-coast radio network.

**1938**    Jazz history is made in Carnegie Hall, New York, when two pianists, Meade Lewis and Albert Ammons, introduce a new kind of popular music which they call "boogiewoogie." (The best example of boogiewoogie composition is "Beat Me Daddy, Eight to the Bar." Eight-to-the-bar bass is the classical boogiewoogie beat.)

**1941**    British Prime Minister Winston Churchill, a guest of President and Mrs. Franklin D. Roosevelt in the White House in Washington, is introduced to the American press conference. To one reporter in the President's oval office who asked the Prime Minister how long it will take to "lick" the Axis powers, Mr. Churchill gives one of his famous answers: "If we manage it well, it will take only half as long as if we manage it badly."

**1948**    Ex-Premier Hideki Tojo of Japan and six other war leaders of that country are hanged at Sugamo Prison in Tokyo by an Allied War Crimes commission. (Tojo shouted "Banzai!" as he was led up to the gallows.)

**1953**    In a mysterious purge of top-level Communist officials, the Soviet Union executes Lavrenti P. Beria, former head of that country's dread secret police force and more recently Minister of the Interior.

**1962**    The first of 1,113 prisoners captured by Fidel Castro in the attempted 1961 invasion of Cuba start arriving in Miami, flown from Cuba in a series of air-lifts. (This was history's biggest ransom to date. In exchange for the prisoners, Castro received in excess of fifty million U.S. dollars in food and medicines, including $2,925,000 in cash for some 60 wounded prisoners. Adding it all up, Castro received about $50,000 for each prisoner he released. The money was raised by a committee of prominent Americans who appealed to private donors for funds, foodstuffs, and medicines.) (*See December 29*)

## DECEMBER 24

**1814**  A treaty of peace between the United States and Great Britain is signed at Ghent, Belgium, thus bringing to an end the War of 1812.

**1860**  Joseph Jefferson is cheered as he starts his faithful impersonation of Rip Van Winkle in the play of that name at the Winter Garden in New York. (He spent most of the rest of his life playing this role.)

**1865**  Six men, most of them veterans of the Confederate Army, organize a secret fraternal society in Pulaski, Tennessee, to be known as the Ku Klux Klan.* (While the original founders sought social camaraderie and were motivated by a desire to "protect" the white women and children of the South, within a few months the newly established chapters were concentrating on one objective: to control the newly freed Negro.)

**1871**  Verdi's spectacular opera *Aïda* has it world *première* in Cairo, Egypt. The composer was commissioned to write the opera at the request of the Khedive of Egypt as a climax to the festivities celebrating the opening of the Suez Canal.

**1912**  Christmas Eve in San Francisco is highlighted by the dramatic appearance of the Italian coloratura soprano, Luisa Tetrazzini, who has shocked everybody in New York by her statement that she would rather sing on a curbstone in San Francisco than in the finest opera house anywhere else in the world. Madama Tetrazzini, good as her word, takes her stand at a spot on Market Street, shortly before midnight, and sings an impromptu concert before a delighted audience of local residents. (The evening was balmy and the San Francisco Chamber of Commerce promptly photographed the crowd and distributed prints all over the United States to prove the superiority of the Golden Gate's weather to snowbound cities in most other parts of the country.)

**1915**  Sharp differences of opinion among the members of Henry Ford's "peace mission" to end the war in Europe causes the Detroit automobile manufacturer to drop out of the group. Mr. Ford leaves the rest of the party and sails from Norway to the

---

* The strange name was derived from the Greek word *kuklos,* meaning "circle" or "band." This word was broken up into *ku klux,* to which was added *"clan,"* but spelled with a "k" for consistency, as Ku Klux Klan.

United States. (When he returned home, a reporter asked him what satisfaction he had derived from the peace junket. Said Mr. Ford: "I didn't get much peace, but I learned that Russia is going to be a great market for tractors.")

**1941** Prime Minister Winston Churchill of Great Britain, staying at the White House over Christmas, joins President Franklin D. Roosevelt in the tree-lighting ceremonies on the White House grounds. Afterwards, the President and the Prime Minister address a crowd of 20,000 people from the South Portico of the Executive Mansion. Says Mr. Churchill: "Let the children have their night of fun. Let the gifts of Father Christmas delight their play. Let us grown-ups share to the full in their unstinted pleasures before we again turn to the stern task and the formidable years that lie before us. And so, in God's mercy, a happy Christmas to you all."

**1942** Admiral Darlan, the French administrator of North Africa, is assassinated there by a sympathizer of the French Vichy regime. (WORLD WAR II)

**1943** In a Christmas Eve broadcast, President Roosevelt announces to the American public the appointment of General Dwight D. Eisenhower as commander-in-chief of Allied forces in the projected invasion of Europe. (WORLD WAR II)

**1949** The most popular Christmas song all over America is the new and sprightly "Rudolph, the Red-Nosed Reindeer."

**1963** The House of Representatives ends its longest continuous Congressional session in twenty-one years.

# DECEMBER 25

## Christmas Day

**1776** George Washington leads his troops across the Delaware River to Trenton in New Jersey, for a surprise attack on the Hessians encamped there.

**1818** "Stille Nacht, Heilige Nacht" ("Silent Night, Holy Night"), a beautiful Christmas carol composed the day before by Franz Gruber, the village schoolmaster, is sung for the first time in the village church at Oberndorff, Austria. A fellow townsman, Josef Mohr, is the author of the lyrics.

**1827** Mrs. Frances Trollope, her friend Frances Wright, and three of the Trollope children and a manservant land at New Orleans from England. The ladies will travel to Ohio where they hope to establish a bazaar. (The bazaar came to nothing, but this trip was to provide Mrs. Trollope with source material for her biting and yet successful book, *The Domestic Manners of the Americans*.)

**1868**    President Johnson's Christmas gift to the South: Despite bitter opposition from many people in the North and West, President Johnson proclaims an unconditional pardon and amnesty to "all who directly or indirectly participated in the late rebellion."

**1875**    A group of men prominent in the theatre, music, art, and literature band together and found the Lambs Club in New York.

**1905**    Theatregoers in New York hail both Victor Herbert's operetta *Mademoiselle Modiste* and its leading lady, the vivacious Fritzi Scheff. Before the final curtain comes down, the audience clamors for repeated encores of the hit song of the show, "Kiss Me Again."

**1922**    Nikolai Lenin, Communist leader of Russia, fearful of a struggle for power in the Party after his death, dictates the so-called "Lenin Testament," presenting a characterization of several of his associates. With reference to Joseph Stalin, Lenin says: "I propose to the comrades to find a way to remove Stalin (as General Secretary) and appoint another man more loyal, more courteous and more considerate to comrades."

**1936**    Mutinous war lords in China release Chiang Kai-shek after having kidnapped him 12 days ago.

**1941**    Japanese Imperial Headquarters in Tokyo announces that the British military garrison at Hong Kong, "no longer able to withstand our continuous attacks," surrendered at 3:50 o'clock in the morning, Eastern Standard Time. (World War II)

**1942**    For 12 hours, American radio listeners are entertained by the longest one-day sponsored program in the history of broadcasting. The program is "The Victory Parade's Christmas Party of Spotlight Bands," sponsored by the Coca-Cola Company and heard over the facilities of 142 stations affiliated with the Blue Network of the National Broadcasting Company.

**1962**    As Americans celebrate Christmas Day, the census clock of the Department of Commerce in Washington records the population of the United States at 188,000,000, a gain of 2,710,000 since New Year's Day at the beginning of 1962.


## DECEMBER 26

**1776**    The Battle of Trenton: 1,000 Hessians are captured by General Washington's troops at Trenton, New Jersey, after the Continental Army inflicts a major defeat on the British position there.

**1799**    Colonel Henry ("Light-Horse Harry") Lee eulogizes George Washington who died 12 days ago: "To the memory of the Man, first in war, first in peace, and first in the hearts of his countrymen."

**1865**    James Nason of Franklin, Massachusetts, is awarded a patent for his invention of a coffee percolator, the first such device in the United States.

**1917**    By order of President Wilson, the federal government takes over the operation of all railroads in the United States for the duration of the war. (WORLD WAR I)

**1931**    An enthusiastic audience is on hand at the Music Box Theatre in New York to greet the opening of George Gershwin's musical comedy, *Of Thee I Sing*, starring William Gaxton, Victor Moore, and Lois Moran. (Besides being a smash hit, this show was the first musical to win a Pulitzer Prize for drama.)

**1941**    Winston Churchill, in Washington for conferences with President Roosevelt, addresses a crowded Joint Session of Congress, the first British Prime Minister to do so. Says Mr. Churchill: "Twice in a single generation the catastrophe of world war has fallen upon us. . . . If we had kept together after the last war, if we had taken common measures for our safety, this renewal of the curse need never have fallen upon us. . . ." (WORLD WAR II)

**1943**    A destroyer of the British Navy sinks the 26,000-ton German battleship *Scharnhorst* off the coast of Norway. (WORLD WAR II)

**1944**    As the Allies begin a counteroffensive against the Germans in the Ardennes sector, troops of the U.S. Third Army relieve the hard-pressed 101st Airborne Division at Bastogne, Belgium. (WORLD WAR II)

**1947**    The northeastern part of the United States is blanketed by a snowfall of almost 26 inches, the heaviest experienced in New York City since the Blizzard of 1888.

**1963**    The Gallup Poll reports that the living man "most admired" by residents of the United States in 1963 was President Lyndon B. Johnson. Former President Dwight D. Eisenhower ranks second in the poll and Sir Winston Churchill is third. Similarly, Mrs. John F. Kennedy is the woman most admired by Americans, followed by Mrs. Lyndon B. Johnson and Queen Elizabeth II.

## DECEMBER 27

**1900**    Carrie Nation, violently opposed to alcoholic beverages, stages her first big "raid" as she marches on the saloon in the basement of the Carey Hotel in Wichita, Kansas, and smashes all the liquor bottles within reach. (She also showed her contempt for a nude painting of Cleopatra over the bar by throwing a handful of rocks at the canvas.)

**1903**    "Sweet Adeline," composed by Henry Armstrong to words written by Richard Gerard, is sung for the first time in New York City. (The title of the song was suggested to the composers when they observed Adelina Patti's name spelled out on a theatre marquee.)

**1927**    Theatre history is made in New York when *Show Boat,* a musical adaptation of Edna Ferber's novel, by Jerome Kern and Oscar Hammerstein II, opens at the Ziegfeld Theatre. The show is an immediate hit and a personal triumph for the actress Helen Morgan.

**1932**    The Radio City Music Hall, the largest indoor theatre in the world, is opened to the public in New York.

**1938**    Brenda Diana Duff Frazier, the highly publicized debutante of the season, makes her bow to society at a coming-out party in New York's Ritz-Carlton Hotel. The party, staged at a cost of $50,000, is attended by 1,500 guests. (In the parlance of café society, Miss Frazier achieved the distinction of becoming the first of all the so-called "glamour girls," a term used widely in the late 1930's.)

**1940**    Word comes out of Germany that P. G. Wodehouse, the noted British writer and humorist, held by the Nazis in an East German internment camp, is writing a novel about American swindlers.

**1941**    Japanese airplanes bomb Manila in the Philippine Islands despite the fact that it has been declared an open city. (World War II)

**1945**    The Big Three—the United States, Great Britain, and the Soviet Union—announce that they will govern Korea as joint trustees for the next 5 years and then grant that nation its independence.

**1962**    The American Telephone and Telegraph Company reports that the United States has 52 percent of the telephones throughout the world. According to the most recent statistics, there are 41.8 telephones for every hundred residents of the United States.

## DECEMBER 28

**1832**    Vice President John C. Calhoun, at odds with President Jackson, resigns from his office, the only Vice President in the history of the United States to do so. The former Vice President will fill a vacancy in the Senate caused by the resignation of Senator Robert Y. Hayne of South Carolina.

**1846**    Iowa, the 29th state, is admitted into the Union.

**1856**    Woodrow Wilson, the 28th President of the United States, is born in Staunton, Virginia.

**1869**    Members of the Knights of Labor observe this day as the first Labor Day in American history.

**1869**    Chewing gum, soon to be an American favorite, is patented by William F. Semple of Mount Vernon, Ohio.

**1871**    Congressman James A. Garfield of Ohio, speaking before the alumni of Williams College, pays tribute to one of the great educators of America, Mark Hopkins, the president of Williams: "Give me a log hut, with only a simple bench, Mark Hopkins on one end and I on the other, and you may have all the buildings, apparatus and libraries without him."

**1895**    Golf has become so popular in the United States that the number of golf clubs has increased throughout the nation in the past year from forty to about one hundred.

**1937**    The Irish Free State changes its name to the "State of Eire."

**1941**    President Roosevelt broadcasts a pledge to the Philippines: "I give to the people of the Philippines my solemn pledge that their freedom will be redeemed and their independence established and protected. The entire resources, in men and material, of the United States stand behind that pledge." (WORLD WAR II)

**1945**    Congress officially recognizes the patriotic "Pledge of Allegiance" to the flag of the United States.

## DECEMBER 29

**1777**    Thanks to the ingenuity of an army chef, George Washington's troops at Valley Forge are saved from mutiny. Faced with starvation, with little equipment and few clothes, the general begs his camp chef to concoct a warming dish to raise his men's morale against the bitter cold. The chef manages to secure a large quantity of tripe, some peppercorns, and a few vegetables and invents what he calls "Philadelphia Pepper Pot," thereby both nourishing the weary soldiers and preventing an incipient revolt within the ranks.

**1808**    Birthday of Andrew Johnson, 17th President of the United States.

**1845**    Texas, the 28th state, is admitted into the Union.

**1848**    An air of excitement sweeps over the White House as President Polk and the entire household staff of the Executive Mansion witness the installation of the first gas lights there.

**1851**    The first Young Men's Christian Association to be established in the United States opens its door in Boston.

**1913**    Moving-picture fans will be able to enjoy the exciting episodes of a motion-picture "serial," the first in film history, as *The Adventures of Kathlyn* is released in Chicago. The pictures will be shown in 13 weekly installments.

**1934**    Japan formally renounces the Washington Naval Treaty of 1922 and the London Naval Treaty of 1930 stating, however, that "the Japanese government has no intention whatever to proceed to naval aggrandizement or to disturb international peace."

(The treaties had provided for a naval ratio of 5–5–3 for the United States, Great Britain, and Japan.)

**1940** Adolf Hitler's airmen stage the biggest and most violent air raid ever attempted to date on the city of London. Thousands of explosive and incendiary bombs are dropped on the city, leaving many sections in flames. Historians point out that London has experienced nothing like this since the Great Fire of 1666. (WORLD WAR II)

**1940** Speaking to the nation in a "Fireside Chat," President Franklin D. Roosevelt says the United States must extend full industrial aid to the British war effort. "We must," says the President, "be the great arsenal of democracy." (WORLD WAR II)

**1947** Henry Wallace, former Vice President and Cabinet officer, announces he will accept the Presidential nomination in 1948 on a third-party ticket.

**1962** President Kennedy goes to Miami, Florida, to greet the Cuban prisoners just released by Fidel Castro in exchange for an American ransom. At a rally attended by 40,000 Cuban exiles, the President says: ". . . On behalf of my government and my country, I welcome you to the United States. I bring you my nation's respect for your courage and for your cause . . ."

## DECEMBER 30

**1799** The first "blackface" act in theatrical history is staged at the Federal Street Theatre in Boston when a musical performer named Johann Christian Graupner blackens his face and sings a chorus of "The Gay Negro Boy."

**1851** Louis Kossuth, the Hungarian patriot, receives an official welcome in Washington, D.C., including a testimonial speech by Daniel Webster.

**1853** As the result of negotiations between Mexico and the United States minister to that nation, James Gadsden, the United States acquires some 45,000 square miles of land south of the Gila River for a purchase price of $10,000,000. (The acreage included in this so-called Gadsden Purchase is incorporated in what is now the southern portions of Arizona and New Mexico.)

**1879** A troupe of actors, singers, and musicians are putting the finishing touches on Gilbert and Sullivan's operetta *The Pirates* of *Penzance* at the Fifth Avenue Theatre in New York. The musical show will have its world *première* at the theatre on New Year's Eve, the score to be conducted by the composer, Arthur Sullivan. (The operetta swept New York off its feet the next evening.)

**1903** During a performance of *Mr. Bluebeard,* starring Eddie Foy, at the Iroquois Theatre in Chicago, a fire of unknown origin breaks out and leaves in its wake 588 dead men, women, and children. (There were at least 2,000 people in the theatre. When flames and smoke started pouring into the auditorium, a terrible stampede developed, despite the pleas of Mr. Foy, the band leader, and the ushers for an orderly withdrawal.)

**1911**   Dr. Sun Yat-sen is elected the first president of the Republic of China by the revolutionary provisional Assembly.

**1927**   Taking a cue from the United States, Japan dedicates the first subway in the Orient. The underground transportation line is in Tokyo and covers a route of not quite 2 miles.

**1936**   Members of the United Automobile Workers Union stage a "sit-down" strike at the Fisher Body Plant Number One, part of the General Motors empire, in Flint, Michigan. The union is campaigning for recognition by the nation's automotive industry. (While this was not the first "sit-down" strike in labor history— the first had occurred at the Hormel Packing Company in Minnesota in 1933—it was the beginning of one of the most bitter labor-management quarrels of all time. For 44 days, the strike went on, involving 40,000 workers directly and 110,000 indirectly. Finally, on February 11, 1937, General Motors agreed to recognize the UAW as the sole bargaining agency for all employees in its plants, a clear-cut victory for both the union and the CIO.)

**1947**   King Michael of Rumania agrees to abdicate, charging that he is being forced off the throne by local Communists aided and abetted by the Soviet Union.

**1963**   During a year-end interview with American correspondent Henry Shapiro of the United Press, Soviet Premier Nikita Khrushchev calls for better U.S.-Russian relations in 1964 and states that "peaceful coexistence is the only possible way of living in peace on our planet, given the existence of . . . capitalism and socialism. With the present correlation of forces, there can be no question of eliminating one of them by war. . . ."

## DECEMBER 31

### New Year's Eve

**1776**   To curb the threat of runaway inflation, the legislature of Rhode Island fixes ceilings on some wages and commodity prices. The daily wages of carpenters are not to exceed 70 cents and those of tailors are set at 42 cents. Barbers are prohibited from charging more than 3½ cents for a shave. Ceiling prices on turkeys are established at 9 cents a pound, on milk at 9 cents a gallon, on rum at 63 cents a gallon. Taverns are forbidden to charge travelers more than 5 cents for a night's lodging.

**1877**   President and Mrs. Rutherford B. Hayes reenact their marriage ceremony on the occasion of their silver wedding anniversary. (Mrs. Hayes wore her original wedding gown and the ceremony was performed by the clergyman who officiated in 1852.)

**1879** A gay New Year's Eve crowd assembles at Menlo Park, New Jersey, to witness Thomas Edison's first public demonstration of lighting through the medium of his incandescent lamp.

**1890** Ellis Island in New York harbor becomes the receiving station of all immigrants entering the United States on the Atlantic Coast. (The immigration station was closed in 1954 and on May 11, 1965, President Johnson proclaimed the island a national shrine, noting that from 1892 through 1954, 16,000,000 immigrants had entered the United States there. Said the President: "These steerage immigrants entered into the very fiber of American life. . . . They made us not merely a nation, but a nation of nations. . . .")

**1923** Eddie Cantor opens in *Kid Boots,* a "smash" musical hit at the Earl Carroll Theatre in New York.

**1940** Adolf Hitler seeks to spur on his soldiers by issuing a New Year's proclamation to the Army, Navy, and Air Force: "The year 1941 will bring consummation of the greatest victory in our history." (WORLD WAR II)

**1943** Frank Sinatra, recently a soloist with the Tommy Dorsey dance band, starts a singing engagement at New York's Paramount Theatre and promptly becomes the idol of the nation's "bobby-soxers." (As a matter of fact, the young singer's debut at the Paramount almost set off a first-class riot. His "fans" turned out in such numbers that more than 400 policemen were called out to calm them down.)

**1946** The end of World War II is proclaimed officially by President Harry S. Truman. (WORLD WAR II)

**1962** Governor Edmund G. Brown of California proclaims New Year's Eve as "California First Day" as he announces that his state has passed New York as the most populous state of the Union. To honor the occasion, the Governor has open house at the state capitol building in Sacramento and his staff serves coffee and cake to jubilant Californians. (But back in Albany, New York's Governor Nelson A. Rockefeller refused to concede that California had overtaken his own state in population.)

# Index

424

**435**

441